Strategic Financial Management

Strategic Financial Management

Edited by **Terry Ness**

Willford Press
New York

Published by Willford Press,
118-35 Queens Blvd., Suite 400,
Forest Hills, NY 11375, USA
www.willfordpress.com

Strategic Financial Management
Edited by Terry Ness

International Standard Book Number: 978-1-68285-211-8 (Hardback)

Printed in China.

Contents

Preface

The purpose of the book is to provide a glimpse into the dynamics and to present opinions and studies of some of the scientists engaged in the development of new ideas in the field from very different standpoints. This book will prove useful to students and researchers owing to its high content quality.

Strategic financial management is a significant field in understanding of finances, revenues and organizational assets with a long term perspective. It aims at managing and allocating financial resources of a corporate enterprise. This book provides comprehensive information of this discipline to help develop a good understanding of financial theories, strategic cost management and other related fields. Different approaches, evaluations and methodologies on strategic financial management have been included in this book. It is an extensive source of knowledge on the present status of this important field.

At the end, I would like to appreciate all the efforts made by the authors in completing their chapters professionally. I express my deepest gratitude to all of them for contributing to this book by sharing their valuable works. A special thanks to my family and friends for their constant support in this journey.

Editor

Value relevance of accounting information: A case of Karachi stock exchange listed companies in Pakistan

Faisal Shahzad[1], Babar Zaheer[1] and Muhammad Anees[2]

[1]Department of Management Sciences, Iqra University, Islamabad, Pakistan.
[2]Department of Management Sciences, COMSATS Institute of Information Technology, Attock Campus Punjab, Pakistan.

As one of the basic components of economic growth and development in every country, the capital market is responsible for optimal allocation of capital. For the correct guidance of the decisions along the optimal allocation of capital, information has a main role and financial reports are of the most important information resources. So, in the present study, effort is on studying the effect of competition in the company's product market on the quality of financial reporting. Thus, the cash operational flow expected for evaluating the financial reporting quality is used. In this regard, 125 companies have been studied by applying the conditions (elimination method) in Tehran Stock Exchange during 2001 to 2008. For the hypothesis test, the correlation coefficient and the linear regression test methods have been used with the help of SPSS. Results show that there is an inverse relation between the competition in the company's product market and the quality of the financial reporting.

Key words: Financial reporting quality, competition in the market, sales, cash flows.

INTRODUCTION

The paper stumbles on the value-relevance of accounting information in the Karachi stock marketpioneering the exploration in context of Pakistan-based companies. Financial information plays a vital role for different kind of users of financial reports as indicated by Chen et al. (2001). Information is considered value relevant if it truly represent the value of company (Francis and Schipper, 1999), help an investor to make investment decision and to enable s financial manager to monitor performance of a company (Young and Bryne, 2001).

Examination of portfolio decisions by Hong and Kim (1998) suggests improvements while using the Ohlson (1995) model for Japans' firms. Various attempts have been made to explore the issue of value relevance (Lin and Chen, 2005). Kothari and Zimmerman (1995) find that company fundamental value is absolutely link with the share price of the company. Researchers have used two different perspectives while studying the value relevance of accounting information. The techniques include relative and incremental approaches. One of such techniques is selected on the basis of the statistic in the empirical results. Incremental approach is used to measure the incremental impact of some variables as compared to other variables. The relative approach relates comparison of measures providing better information as compared to others as suggested by Holthausen (2000).

Residual income valuation model is an originator of Ohlson model stating that investor's price securities is the expected present value of future dividends. Ohlson (1995) model is used to measure the value relevance of accounting information. The approach takes share price as the dependent variable affected by the book value per share and earnings per share. Two different estimation strategies are found being followed in the literature to estimate the value relevance using accounting information. First approach is called the price and the second is known as the return model. The paper follows the price model as Kothari and Zimmerman's (1995) argue that earnings coefficient is less biased in price model as compared to return model.

LITERATURE REVIEW

Most of the research in the area is based on the data on US companies' to measure the value relevance (Lev, 1989; Bernard and Stober, 1989) presented a good review of various studies asserting the relationship of accounting information with security prices in the America. Kothari and Zimmerman's (1995) examined that various studies have been conducted using different period of time under different accounting standard.

Ely and Waymire (1999) asserted that when they examined the relationship for two different accounting standard which include *APB* era (1960-1973) to the *FASB* era (1974-1993) using two different models, they find out that relationship of share price with book value per share and earnings per share is increasing when they apply price model and relationship is deteriorating when return model is used. Francis and Schipper (1999) found the same result when they use price and return model. In addition, they concluded that value relevance deteriorated due to high fluctuation in the market when they use return model.

Gjerde et al. (2011) found that if changes in economic value relevance are controlled then trend of overall value relevance has increased. Alex et al. (2004) found through empirical investigation that non information based trading is the main factor which deteriorated the relationship of share price and accounting information. Chen et al. (2001) asserted that even perception of inadequate financial reporting and young age of Chinese market can not affect the value relevance of accounting information to investor.

Collins et al. (1997) found that incremental value of earning decrease with the passage of time but there is an improvement in the accounting measure of book value per share. Further, he found that if we combine the regression coefficient of the book value per share and earnings per share with share price of the company, the beta value is positive for book value per share and earnings per share and it would increase with the passage of time. The result is also significant.

Bao and Bao (2001) examined that earning are more value relevant for large size firm while book value is more relevant for small size firm. Ely and Waymire (1999) also found the positive beta values for the period of sixty six years from 1927 to 1993. However, Lev and Zarowin (1999) show that beta value of earning per share, book value per share and cash flow declining over the period of 1997 to 1996 using the data of American based company.

Wallace (2000) found that the value relevance which is used to find out the financial position and other financial aspect are decrease with the passage of time. Barth et al. (2001) concluded that these studies are fruitful for investor to evaluate the equity. Hand (2003) found that balance sheet, income statement and cash flow are value relevant when their accounts are in line with the share price of the company. Lev (1989) claimed that quality of information present in the annual reports of the company is the main determinate of value relevance. He used earning response coefficient as a proxy of quality of accounting information when he regress the company earning with the share price of the company. Lev and Zarowin (1999) asserted that there is a weak association between share price and earning. Ou and Sepe (2002) found that accuracy of future earning can be improve through enhancing the information contents of balance sheet when they examined the relationship between financial ratios (fundamental analysis), stock prices, and future earnings.

Research hypothesis

H_a: There is a positive relationship between share price and earnings.
H_b: There is a positive relationship between share price and book value.

RESEARCH DESIGN

The data

In this study, the companies listed in Karachi stock exchange for the period of 2006 to 2010 were used as a sample. We use the variable stock price, earnings per share, and book value per share. We use the data stream of banker Thompson. The sample size is 850 which is panel data.

Econometric strategy

OLS regression model for the pooled data is as:

$$P_{it} = \beta_0 + \beta_1 V_{it} + \beta_2 E_{it} + \mu_{it} \quad (3)$$

Where the estimates from such pooled regressions for panel type datasets are found to be biased so it is required to estimate either random effects or fixed effects regression models. The two models depend on the nature of the regressors to be included into the estimation. If the regressors are variable over time, fixed effects model is best representative and if there are regressors which are constant over time, random effects model is the best. Fixed effects model is given as:

$$P_{it} = \beta_0 + \beta_1 V_{it} + \beta_2 E_{it} + v_{it} + \varepsilon_{it} \quad (4)$$

And the time demeaned model from the above regression is

$$P_{it} - \bar{P}_i = \beta_1 (V_{it} - \bar{V}_i) + \beta_2 (E_{it} - \bar{E}_i) + \varepsilon_{it} + \bar{\varepsilon}_i \quad (5)$$

On the other hand random effects mode is given as:

$$P_{it} = \beta_0 + \beta_1 V_{it} + \beta_2 E_{it} + v_{it} + \varepsilon_{it} \quad (6)$$

Where v_{it} is assumed as random variable or i.i.d. random effects and $Cov(x_{it}, v_{it}) = 0$ and the estimates are consistent and can be

Table 1. Summary statistics.

Variable	Results	Mean	S.D.	Min.	Max.	Obs.
P	Overall	1.752141	4.680222	0.01	46.65	850
	Between		4.438255	0.03	35.662	170
	Within		1.5163	-14.1419	14.99814	5
E	Overall	0.150412	0.459815	-2.74	5.46	850
	Between		0.330543	-0.19	2.31	170
	Within		0.320447	-2.96559	4.350412	5
B	Overall	0.732788	1.411292	-1.47	16.11	850
	Between		1.356773	-1.176	11.496	170
	Within		0.399479	-2.75121	5.346788	5

Table 2. Estimation results.

Dep. Var. P	Pooled	Fixed effects	Random effects
E	0.888***	0.777***	1.113***
	(4.63)	(3.95)	(5.34)
B	1.231***	0.865***	1.394***
	(9.65)	(5.49)	(11.65)
Intercept	0.717**	1.001***	0.563**
	(2.66)	(8.51)	(2.72)
N	850.000	850.000	850.000

*, ** and *** indicates significance at 10, 5 and 1% respectively. Students't-statistic is in parenthesis.

estimated from Equation (3) using the pooled regression but it is to be given in account that serially correlated error terms v_{it} and the standard errors are biased.

The following transformation is required to estimate the random effects model from the pooled regression:

$$(P_{it} - \theta\overline{P_i}) = \beta_0(1-\theta) + \beta_1(V_{it} - \theta\bar{V_i}) + \beta_2(E_{it} - \theta\overline{E_i}) + \{(1-\theta)v_{it} + (\varepsilon_{it} + \overline{\theta\varepsilon_i})\} \quad (7)$$

where $\theta = 1 - \sqrt{\frac{\sigma_\varepsilon^2}{T\sigma_v^2 + \sigma_\varepsilon^2}}$. If $\theta$is equal to 1, RE estimation is similar to FE, but if it is equal to 0, the RE estimation is similar to pooled regression. Normally, θ is assumed to have value between 0 and 1. If $Cov(x_{it}, v_{it}) = 0$, it is appropriate and the results are efficient and in case where it is not 0, the RE estimator turns to be biased and the degree of bias depends on value to θ. If $\sigma_v^2 \gg \sigma_\varepsilon^2$, then θ is expected to be close to 1, and the bias in results to be low.

Data description

The study is based on the financial and accounting information derived from the Thomson One Banker and 170 companies were selected from Pakistan, for which the relevant data was available for 2006 to 2010, thus resulting in 850 firm-year observation for the panel. Details of the summary results are given in Table 1. The table indicates that mean of price per share is 1.7 and with range from 0.01 to 16.65. Similarly, earnings per share have mean 0.15 and range -2.74 to 5.56 and book value per share has mean 0.73 and range -1.47 to 16.11.

REGRESSION RESULTS

The model has been estimated using Stata 10.1 and user written commands for panel data regressions. The results for fixed effects model, random effects model and pooled regression have been reported in Table 2. The table shows that there is positive relationship between price and earnings per share. It is statistically significant at the 1% in the entire model but as the econometric theory suggests one cannot use the results from such models equivalently therefore we have to select one model from the available options.

The Hausman test statistic has been used to choose a first a model between pooled and panel regression and then between the fixed effects and random effects. We have used Sargan-Hansen statistic which has the advantage of overcoming the over identification restrict-tions in panel data estimation using fixed and random effects models.

The test statistic has a significant Chi-sq value of

Table 3. Year regression results.

Dep. Var. P	2006	2007	2008	2009	2010
E	10.353*** (13.62)	10.385*** (11.07)	1.802** (3.04)	3.749*** (7.18)	4.809*** (6.67)
B	-0.134 (-0.63)	0.256 (1.16)	1.959*** (7.92)	1.582*** (8.68)	0.361 (1.38)
Intercept	0.011 (0.06)	0.317 (1.15)	0.021 (0.06)	0.178 (0.77)	0.214 (0.69)
AIC	727.483	881.944	933.675	812.018	909.809
BIC	736.891	891.351	943.082	821.426	919.217
R-squared	0.793	0.668	0.429	0.556	0.380
F	319.465	168.371	62.768	104.422	51.154
p-value	0.000	0.000	0.000	0.000	0.000
n	170.000	170.000	170.000	170.000	170.000

*, ** and *** indicates significance at 10, 5 and 1% respectively. Student's-statistic is in parenthesis.

212.947 with degrees of freedoms equal to 2 which indicates to use preferably the results from the fixed effects. It is similar to the traditional Hausman test but Sargan-Hansen statistic approach has its advantages over Hausman. Furthermore, we have used yearly regressions and the results have been reported in Table 3. The results also indicate that there is positive relation between the price per share and earnings per share and book value per share for most of the year except a few.

Table 3 summarizes the result of yearly as well as pooled regression of stock price against earnings and book value per share. The adjusted R^2 for the yearly and pooled regression indicates that earnings and book value per share explain the variation in stock prices about 79.3 (2006), 66.8 (2007), 42.9 (2008), 55.6 (2009), 38.0 (2010), and 79.2% (pooled). The results show that the regression coefficients of earnings per share and book value per share are significantly positive at $p < 0.001$ level in year 2006, 2007, 2008, 2009, 2010 and pooled. Thus, the results support hypothesis a and b that earnings and book value are value relevant because co-efficent are positive.

Conclusion

The objective of this study is to assess the value relevance of earnings and book value by using Ohlson's model, which expresses stock price as a linear function of earnings, book value of equity and various accounting numbers for the purpose of assessing those numbers' usefulness in equity valuation. The results of this study support the hypothesis that earnings and book value are value relevant. Result also show that value relevance are deteriorate with the passage of time but value relevance of book value per share increases with the passage of time. Future research need to investigate which factor deteriorates the value relevance of earning per share.

REFERENCES

Bao BH, Bao DH (2001). Characteristics of earnings versus book value firms in the Taiwan stock exchange. Adv. Int. Acc. 14:101-114.
Barth ME, Beaver WH, Landsman WR (2001). The relevance of the value relevance literature for financial accounting standard setting: another view. J. Acc. Econ. 31(1/3):77 -104.
Bernard VL, Stober TL (1989). The nature and amount of information in cash flows and accruals. Acc. Rev. 64(4):624-652.
Chen SC, Charles JP, Sua X (2001). Is accounting information value-relevant in the emerging Chinese stock market? J. Int. Acc. Aud. Tax. 10:1-22.
Collins DW, Maydew EL, Weiss IS (1997). Changes in the value-relevance of earnings and book values over the past forty years. J. Acc. Econ. 24(1):39-67.
Alex D, Radhakrishnan S, Ronen J (2004). The Declining Value-relevance of Accounting Information and Non-Information-based Trading: An Empirical Analysis. Cont. Acc. Res. 21(4):795-812.
Ely K, Waymire G (1999). Accounting standard-setting organizations and earnings relevance: longitudinal evidence from NYSE common stocks, 1927-93. J. Acc. Res. 37(2):293-317.
Francis J, Schipper K (1999). Have financial statements lost their relevance? J. Acc. Res. 37(2):319-352.
Gjerde O, Knivsflaa K, Saettem F (2011). The value relevance of financial reporting in Norway. Scan. J. Manag. 27:113-128.
Hand JRM (2003). The value relevance of financial statements in private equity markets. Univ. N. Carol. Chap. Hill WP.
Holthausen RW (2000). The relevance of the value relevance literature for financial accounting standard setting. Univ. Roch.
Hong BK, Kim JB (1998). The usefulness of earnings versus book value for predicting stock returns and cross corporate ownership in Japan. Jpn. World Econ. 10(4):467-485.
Kothari SP, Zimmerman JL (1995). Price and return models. J. Acc. Econ. 20(2):155-192.
Lev B (1989). On the usefulness of earnings and earnings research: Lessons and directions from two decades of empirical research. J. Acc. Res. 27:153-192.

Lev B, Zarowin P (1999).The boundaries of financial reporting and how to extend them. J. Acc. Res. 37(2):353-385.

Lin LZ, Chen F (2005). Value relevance of international accounting standards harmonization: Evidence from A-and B-share markets in China. J. Int. Acc. Aud. Tax. 14(2):79-103.

Ohlson JA (1995). Earnings, Book Values, and Dividends in Equity Valuation. Cont. Acc. Res. 11(2):661-687.

Ou JA, Sepe JF (2002). Analysts earnings forecasts and the roles of earnings and book value in equity valuation. J. Bus. Financ. Acc. 29(3/4):287-316.

Wallace W (2000). The value relevance of accounting: The rest of the story. Eur. Manag. J. 18(6):675-682.

Young SD, O'Byrne SF (2001). EVA and value based management: a practical guide to implementation. McGraw-Hill.

2

Eco-management and audit scheme (EMAS) and its implementation in Serbia

Marija Kostic , Goranka Knezevic and Vule Mizdrakovic

Singidunum University, Faculty of Business Belgrade, Serbia.

The way people are doing business are changing fast under pressures such as growing number of environmental concerns, public pressure, regulatory measures, demands of consumers and shareholders for environmentally friendly products and services, so it is becoming more and more important for organizations/companies to demonstrate sustainability of their investment strategies and operations. A management tool for companies and other organizations to evaluate, report and improve their environmental performance is eco-management and audit scheme (EMAS), regulated by Regulation (EC) No 1221/2009. Having in mind intentions of Serbia to join European Union (EU), as well as a fact that Regulation 1221/2009 allows participation in EMAS also for organizations in non EU member countries, it is quite obvious that EMAS implementation will create necessary conditions for more intensive participation of our country in all European processes. In this article, we present Serbian companies included in calculation of stock market index Belgrade Stock Exchange Index (Belex 15) and their stage in EMAS implementation. Research results shows at what stage of EMAS implementation are Serbian "blue chip" companies and future activities needed for them to apply this important EU regulation.

Key words: Eco-management and Audit Scheme (EMAS), Regulation (EC) No.1221/2009, environmental accounting, environmental reports.

INTRODUCTION

ESTABLISHMENT AND VOLUNTARY PARTICIPATION IN ECO-MANAGEMENT AND AUDIT SCHEME (EMAS)

Notion and development

The eco-audit system has developed from classical auditing system, which on the other hand was created as industrial management inventory in corporations that had to make and submit the report on their activities at the end of each year to their auctioneers (Lechelt, 1998). At the end of 70's in the United States of America (USA) shown up different kind of auditing system, which did not include exclusively industrial-management data, but also environmental data. The first eco-audit systems were check of respect of the environmental regulations during manufacturing activities, because in case of disturbing public (their environment), very strict USA penal system, has predicted significant sums for the agreement and compensation (Lechelt, 1998). Meantime, along with this system of control of the activities of the firm together with the environmental regulations, developed system which controlled functioning of eco-management system in the enterprise, so-called "performance audits" (Lindlar, 1999; Feldhaus, 1994).

Eco-audit systems can have internal or external audit function. Internal eco-auditing is an independent appraisal activity established within a company for the review of operations as a service to management (Lechelt, 1998). The objective of internal eco-auditing is to assist company's management in discovering lacks of environmental management system, technical installat-ions and plans, operations, functions and processes of a company. External eco-auditing serves for informing the public or other institutions about company's environmental performance, comprising information about results achieved in relation to defined environmental objectives, as well as about steps for further improvement of company's environmental performance in the future. Impartiality of this system is ensured by the fact that external eco-auditors are independent (both in fact and in appearance) of the company, which is a subject of auditing.

VOLUNTARY PARTICIPATION IN ECO-MANAGEMENT AND AUDIT SCHEME (EMAS)

The new approach to environmental policy is perhaps the most evident in the 1993 EMAS (Waskow 1994, p. 5-9). EMAS does not replace existing community or national environmental regulations or technical standards (Lechelt, 1998), but rather, facilitates voluntary participation by companies in a standardized and auditable community scheme for environmental management (Köck, 1997). Its aim is to promote continuous environmental performance improvements of industrial activities by committing sites to evaluate and improve their own environmental performance and to report to the public on that performance.

In accordance with Council Regulation 1836/93/EEC 281, Environmental Management and Audit Scheme (EMAS I) has been available for participation by companies in industrial sectors since 1995 (Council Regulation, 1993). Since 2001, in accordance with Regulation 761/2001/EC allowing voluntary participation by organizations in a community eco-management and audit scheme (EMAS II), EMAS has been open to all economic sectors, including public and private services, operating in EU and European Economic Area (EEA). The main objective of EMAS II was "to promote continual improvements in the environmental performance of the organizations". Enterprises that have accepted voluntary to participate into EMAS scheme and on the basis of its criteria have established and implemented environmental management system are obliged to inform the public in the form of environmental statement, about their activities and all questions in relation with those activities which have significant impact on the environment (emissions, waste, use of row materials, etc). From 2008 to 2010 the number of EMAS registered organizations in Europe increased for 28%.

ECO-MANAGEMENT AND AUDIT SCHEME (EMAS III) AND ITS SIGNIFICANCE FOR SERBIA

Eco-management and audit scheme (EMAS II) – a step further from eco-management and audit scheme (EMAS II)

Entering into force of Regulation (EC) No 1221/2009 on the voluntary participation by organizations in a community EMAS on 11 January 2010, initial EMAS I and later on EMAS II Regulation have been revised and modified to so call EMAS III.

Beside amendments and modifications made to increase (even more) quality of the environmental management scheme, regulation also includes new measures for reducing administrative burdens for EMAS registered organizations and creating incentives for raising the attractiveness of the scheme, particularly for smaller organizations.

Certainly the most important innovation of EMAS III regulation for Serbia is the fact that the scope of the scheme has been extended to allow organizations outside of the EU to gain EMAS registration within EMAS verifiers within EU. In relation to that, Article 3 of Regulation (EC) No 1221/2009 states "applications for registration from organizations outside the community, including corporate registration consisting only of sites located outside the community, shall be made to any competent body in those member states that provide for the registration of organizations from outside the community in accordance with the second subparagraph of Article 11(1)".

LEGAL FRAMEWORK IN SERBIA

Even before Regulation (EC) No 1221/2009 entered into force Serbian legislator has shown an intention to follow-up with European environmental trends. Thus, it has adopted a new version of Serbian Law on Environmental Protection (Official Gazette of RS; 2009) which includes a few provisions on EMAS (Law on Environmental Protection, articles 44 to 50). Although, this is the only Serbian regulation promotion and mentioning EMAS, it should be recognized as a positive example of national law-maker. In benefit to this statement, let us remind you that at the time when law on environmental protection entered into force, European Union was still regulating EMAS on a basis of Regulation 761/2001/EC allowing voluntary participation by organizations in a community EMAS II, which has allowed applications for registrations only for organizations in a EU Member states.

After adoption of Regulation (EC) No 1221/ 2009 provisions on EMAS in Serbian Law on Environmental Protection need to be revised and harmonized with EMAS III. Ministry of Environmental Protection is familiar with this request and it is only the question of time when harmonization process shall begin.

According to- still current version of the Law- EMAS procedure in Serbia is voluntary and allowed to all "natural and legal persons ......". Competent body is Ministry for Protection of the Environment, which is also the one to keep and maintain the register of all EMAS participants. Information in Register is public and everyone has a right to access it. Unfortunately, even though possibility for EMAS participation exists in Serbian since 2004, EMAS register has never been created and Ministry for Protection of the Environment has no data on any request for registration submitted.

ADVANTAGES OF ECO-MANAGEMENT AND AUDIT SCHEME (EMAS) IMPLEMENTATION

European organizations, unlike Serbian ones, know very well that the environmental management system in accordance with EMAS represents not only a company's active approach to the monitoring, management and gradual decrease of its environmental impact, but also increases their credit and the competitiveness, brings cost savings, credibility and order in operating document-tation. EMAS implementation and maintenance also improve the communication and awareness of staff and partner companies, enhancing emergency preparedness. Using EMAS, an excellence level, exceeding legislative requirements, may be achieved.

Based on the latest study that has been conducted by European Commission in 2009, the most common reason for EMAS implementation is resource/production efficiency and most common reasons for re-registration are costumer requirements. On the other hand, the highest number of respondents as greatest barrier recognizes unclear/unjustified benefits of EMAS implementation. As it can be expected, the highest costs of maintaining and implementing EMAS are in the first year (€40.000 to €65.000 - depending on the size of the company), but later on they decrease significantly (€18.000 to €38.000). Estimated average registration cost, based on previous study of European Commission, goes from €40.000 to €50.000 which is especially important information for our research.

Knowing all those EMAS advantages, we are quite confused what is the real reason for almost zero interest of Serbian organizations for participation in EMAS? We could only guess, but we certainly hope for recent changes. We hope that intensive preparations for European integrations will also affect field of the environment and bring good changes not only in legal framework, but also in awareness of widest public and entire society.

IMPLEMENTATION OF ECO-MANAGEMENT AND AUDIT SCHEME (EMAS) IN SERBIAN "BELEX 15" COMPANIES

Belex 15 Index is one of the most popular and leading index that measures and describes movement of prices of the most liquid Serbian shares and is calculated in real time. Belex 15 is composed of 15 most liquid shares of the following companies: Messer Tehnogas, Soja protein, Energoprojekt holding, Metals bank, AIK bank, Komercijalna banka, Agrobanka, Univerzal banka, Imlek, Metalac, Privredna banka, Tigar, Alfa plam, Telefonija and Veterinarski zavod Subotica.

Belex 15 companies are synonym for "blue chip" Serbian companies meaning big companies, with huge annual turnover, good financial results and good prospects in the future. Implementation of EMAS is costly and voluntary and this was one of the reasons why we compose our sample of those companies having financial flexibility and strong corporate culture and responsibility needed for EMAS implementation. Companies from the sample were sent an e-mail message regarding EMAS implementation (stage of implementation, future outlook for the imple-mentation, describing reasons why it is not implemented yet and so on). The second part of our research consists of fact findings regarding EMAS on companies' web sites. Our findings are presented in the Table 2 and 3.

As we may conclude from the Table 3, findings are more than disappointing. Only two companies responded on e-mail message out of 15 companies who were sent an e-mail regarding EMAS. One company that responded to our e-mail, and was very willing to cooperate and share its views on this important topic, was Messer Tehnogas, a.d., Belgrade, Serbia. We conducted a personal phone interview with an experienced professional who told us that EMAS probably would be implemented in this company in the year 2011 and told us about problems regarding EMAS implementation. One of the problems mentioned was waste disposal problems. Companies, like Messer, having solid disposal, are much more interesting in EMAS implementation, but one of the problems emerging are situation of having no register of companies certified for solid waste destruction. Because of that, our companies do not know where to bring their waste for destruction, and even if they recognize names of some of these waste recipients, the majority are located in EU and costs of having waste destructed (transportation charges, handling etc.) outweight incentives for doing it. The second company that replies our e-mail was Metals bank, a.d. from Novi Sad, Serbia. We performed a personal phone interview and found that Metals bank has no EMAS certification and it prepares environmental impact reports only as a part of compliance with European Bank for Reconstruction and Development (EBRD's) environmental and social procedures for corporate lending. In this case, Metals bank prepares environmental reports about environmental procedures applied in the bank and educates its employees on environmental and social risk management. This is due to the fact that when EBRD is exposed to financial intermediaries (Metals bank) in loan transactions, than that financial intermediare should provide reports on environmental and social matters. EBRD demands from financial intermediaries certain reports and other information regarding compliance with environmental standards and EBRD has mechanism to force them to apply those standards.

Second part of our research consists of web site fact findings regarding EMAS. The same sample of companies was used and results show zero reporting on EMAS matters. Information is presented neither on the group level nor on company level. Sometimes other members of the group has EMAS certification and no information regarding this fact can be found on the web site on other companies in the group (for example, Messer company in Austria has been certified, and Messer, Serbia has no information on web site about EMAS at all). We expected that some of these matters would have been cascaded from the group level to the company level, but obviously this is not the case.

Some of companies from the sample (Energoprojekt, Messer, Metalac, Tigar, Telefonija) provide a link to the environmental part of the web site with only one page providing an overview of company's dedication to environmental and social responsibility issues, usually in the form of Environmental Protection Policy Declaration as a part of ISO 14001 compliance. It seems that this part of web site for companies from the sample does not serve as a communication device; it serves only for cosmetical purposes.

Many of companies mentioned in the sample have ISO 14001 certification (Sojaprotein, Metalac, Messer, Tigar and Telefonija) as a first step towards EMAS. Alignment with ISO 14001 is completely voluntary, as well as EMAS compliance, and that is why we expect that compliance with ISO 14001 is a first step towards EMAS III implementation. This fact also tells us that 5 out of 15 companies mentioned in the research have made that first step toward environmental consciousness and responsibility.

For the purposes of this research we would like to point out some important differences between EMAS and ISO 14001 (Table 4). Companies ISO 14001 certified need some minor modifications in order to comply with EMAS and those modifications are the following (European Commission, 2008)

- Environmental policy – organization must strengthen its statement of commitment included in its environmental policy to make provisions for regulatory compliance.
- Planning – in planning stage required by ISO 14001 companies should make sure that all items are addressed, specifically items listed in Anex VI which is applicable for EMAS. In initial environmental review companies should make sure that all items from Anex VII of EMAS have been considered and incorporated.
- Implementation – EMAS requires active participation of employees in the environmental improvement program (suggestion book, environmental committee etc.).
- Checking and corrective actions – companies should check the frequency of the audit cycle in compliance with Anex II of the EMAS regulation and should take place at intervals no longer than 3 years
- Certification of ISO 14001– In order to comply with the requirements of EMAS, the ISO 14001 certificate must be issued under one of the accreditation procedures recognized by the European Union.

From the above mentioned, we strongly believe that 5 companies from the sample with ISO 14001 certification would be the first companies applying for EMAS registration in Serbia. Our believes are based on the following facts;

- Companies are financially viable to support EMAS registration,
- Companies already have environmental policies and they need to adjust them to comply with EMAS procedures which is neither costly nor hard to do,
- Many of these companies are privatized by foreign parent companies and many of their group companies have already apply for EMAS in other EU countries, so historical evidence about EMAS implementation already exits in other group companies and could be used for EMAS implementation in Serbian subsidiaries
- Companies may ask for professional support in EMAS implementation from their foreign group companies,
- Employees included in ISO 14001 certification procedures in Serbian “blue chip” companies could be used for EMAS registration as well, because they already have environmental procedure knowledge and they could share that knowledge with other employees.

What we consider as negative signal is the fact that implementation of EMAS means more public participation in these matters, and it seems that many of “blue chip” Serbian companies are not aware of that. This is based on the fact that only two companies from the sample were willing to answer our questionnaire and to provide us some environmental facts. What surprise us is that all companies from the sample and even those responded to our e-mail messages; treat their environmental reports as confidential. Based on the previous results shown in the Table 1 we may conclude that companies in Serbia lack of corporate responsibility to the general public regarding environmental information transparency, as a necessary condition for EMAS implementation.

Also, we have contacted Accreditation Board of Serbia (ABS) in order to get more information of EMAS implementation in Serbia, since they had conducted many presentations and seminars on EMAS advantages and implementation. Its public relations manager was rather willing to help us in our research. So far, there is no EMAS verifier in Serbia accredited by ABS. ABS, for several years (from the date of enactment of the Act) in its plans enters new accreditation scheme for EMAS verifiers, but it has not been realized so far, since no one signed up. This leads to conclusion that EMAS is not implemented in any organization in Serbia. The only exception could be the possibility that one organization could register abroad, but obviously this is not the case, because no information regarding EMAS is found to support this fact in Serbian companies.

Table 1. Number of EMAS registered organizations in Europe.

Country	Number of organizations
Austria	255
Belgium	49
Bulgaria	0
Cyprus	5
Czech republic	26
Denmark	92
Estonia	2
Finland	24
France	17
Germany	1372
Greece	67
Hungary	21
Ireland	8
Italy	1035
Latvia	5
Lithuania	0
Luxemburg	2
Malta	1
Netherlands	7
Poland	20
Portugal	76
Romania	4
Slovakia	4
Slovenia	3
Spain	1217
Sweden	75
United kingdom	62
Norway	21
Total	4470

Source: http://www.emas-register.eu/statistic.php?view=all_sites, accessed 06.05.2010.

Table 2. Belex 15 companies by sectors.

Sectors	Listed companies Belex 15
Construction	1
Processing industry	3
Automobile tires industry	1
Food and beverage	2
Banking and finance	6
Telecommunication	1
Medicine	1
Total	15

CONCLUSIONS AND RECOMMENDATIONS

Implementation of EMAS have some shaded future in Serbia, meaning that some of the most important issues have not been resolved yet, neither on governmental nor on companies level. Ministry of Environmental Protection in Serbia has a primary responsibility for providing procedures and conditions required by companies to comply with EMAS III. All countries are expected to organize their institutions and procedures in order to

Table 3. EMAS facts from Serbian “Belex 15” companies.

Companies	Email request results	Web site facts about EMAS	Environmental protection declaration or ISO 14001 certification
AIK banka, a.d. Niš	N/R (no response)	N/F (no facts)	N/F
Komercijalna banka, a.d., Beograd	N/R	N/F	“Report on progress of the UN global compact 2008”, principles 7,8,9- protection of environment
Energoprojekt Holding a.d., Beograd	N/R	N/F	Link to UN global compact, social responsibility section and declaration to these matters
Agrobanka, a.d. Beograd	N/R	N/F	N/F
Univerzal banka, a.d. Beograd	N/R	N/F	N/F
Soja protein a.d., Becej	N/R	N/F	ISO 14001- environmental protection policy declaration
Imlek a.d, Beograd	N/R	N/F	N/F
Metalac, a.d Gornji Milanovac	N/R	N/F	Environmental protection policy declaration
Metals banka, a.d., Novi Sad	responded	N/F	N/F
Privredna banka, a.d. Beograd	N/R	N/F	N/F
Messer Tehnogas, a.d. Beograd	responded	N/F	ISO 14001 environmental protection policy declaration
Tigar, a.d. , Pirot	N/R	N/F	ISO 14001 environmental protection policy declaration
Alfa plam, a.d., Vranje	N/R	N/F	N/F
Telefonija, a.d. Beograd	N/R	N/F	ISO 14001 environmental protection policy declaration
Veterinarski zavod, a.d. Subotica	N/R	N/F	N/F
Total number of responses	2	0	

Table 4. Differences between EMAS and ISO 14001.

	ISO 14001	EMAS
Status	It is a internationally adopted standard	It is an EU regulation
Organization	Does not go toward entities or sites	The entity to be registered shall exceed EU boundaries and go beyond candidate countries for EU
Environmental review	Initial review is recommended but not required	Obligatory preliminary review when it is the first time the organization sets its status
Environmental policy	Does not include a commitment to continual improvement of environmental performance	Commitment to continual improvement of environmental performance
Environmental aspects	Procedure able to identify environmental aspects	Identification and evaluation of the environmental aspects, direct and indirect. Establishment of the criteria for assessing the significance of the environmental aspects
External communication	No open dialogue to the public. Control by public is not possible	Open dialogue with the public. Public Environmental statement (validated for verifiers)
Employees involvement	No involvement of employees	Active involvement of employees
Continual improvement	Required periodical improvement without a defined frequency	Required annual improvement
Internal environmental auditing	Include audit against the requirements of the standard	Includes system audit, a performance audit and environmental compliance audit

Source: European Commission. “EMAS Factsheet“, May 2008, p.1.

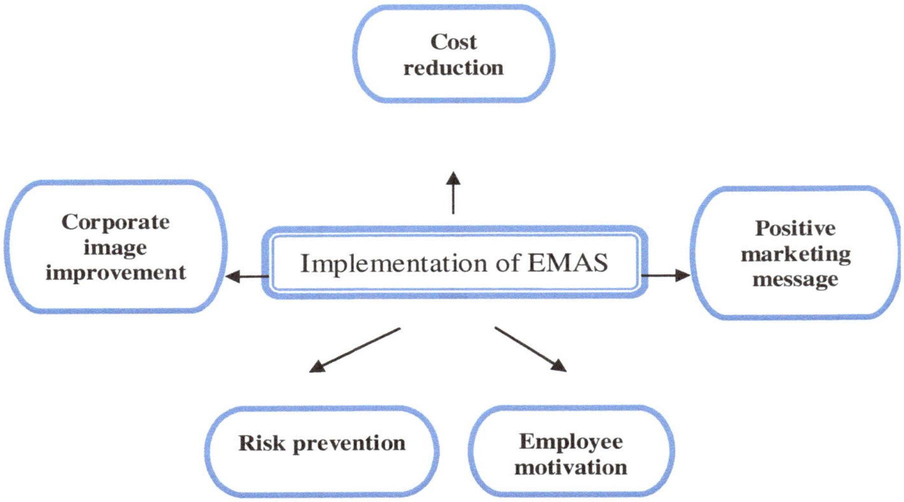

Figure 1. Advantages of EMAS implementation.

enable implementation of EMAS. Ministry of Environmental Protection in Serbia is currently creating national program and action plan for EMAS implementation, also this Ministry should establish EMAS council and EMAS secretariat. We are hoping that these measures will aid in better implementation of EMAS in Serbia. Also, we consider that education and promotion are key factors in greater EMAS implementation in Serbia. Ministry of Environmental Protection and Accreditation board of Serbia can contribute greatly in education of managers and employees by conducting seminars, promotions on fair trades and exhibitions and conferences on this topic. Especially important is the possibility that organizations that do not belong to EU can be EMAS registered, since Serbia is not EU country. Registration costs could be very important Figure 1 for EMAS implementation in companies in Serbia. They can be quite significant for our companies, and maybe that is the real reason for poor implementation in Serbia. Knowing this, Serbian government and Ministry of Environmental Protection could demand EMAS amongst environmental non-governmental organizations (NGO) at the start, and later on organize financial support for EMAS registration for business organizations. Demanded EMAS application could be desirable as well for greatest environmental pollutants.

Implementation of environmental management system in one company is more than a matter of image, it has multiple benefits. EMAS helps in controlling environmental protection processes and continuous improvement of the environmental management system. By implementing EMAS companies can save resources and reduce environmental impacts. Costs like energy, water and disposal-waste can be reduced. Also, sum of these measures enhances employee motivation and increases performance quality, making the competitiveness of company even stronger. Whole range of organizations to which EMAS is applicable can benefit from its implementation, and not only industrial sector. We strongly recommend to all managers, especially in Serbia, to implement this regulation because of its numerous advantages.

ABBREVIATIONS

EMAS, Environmental management audit scheme; **Belex 15,** Belgrade Stock Exchange Index; **EEA,** European economic area; **EU,** European Union; **EBRD,** European Bank for Reconstruction and Development; **ABS,** Accreditation Board of Serbia; **NGO,** non-governmental organizations.

REFERENCES

Council Regulation (1993). No. 1836/93/EEC of 29 June 1993 on the Community scheme enabling the voluntary participation by companies in the industrial sector in the ecomanagement and audit scheme. (168): 1.

European Commission (2008). EMAS Factsheet.

European Parliament (2001). Regulation 761/2001/EC of the European Parliament and of the Council of 19 March 2001 allowing voluntary participation by organisations in a Community ecomanagement and audit scheme (EMAS II). OJ. No. L 114 p. 1 on 24 April 2001; on 4 December 2002 a corrigendum to the EMAS Regulation was published OJ. (327):10

Fldhaus G (1994). Eco-audit and Business Organization in Environmental Law (Umwelt-Audit und Betriebsorganisation im Umweltrecht). Kormann, Joachim (Edit.): Environmental Liability and Environmental Management (Umwelthaftung und Umweltmanagement). 5: 9-36.

Köck W (1997). Eco-audit Regulation; Conception - Regulatory Philosophy - Influences on the administrative law (Die Öko- Audit-Verordnung; Konzeption – Regulative Philosophie – Einflüsse auf das Ordnungsrecht). Epiney, Astrid (Edit.): „ Eco- audit and Switzerland" („Öko- Audit und die Schweiz"). University Publishing Freiburg: 15-17.

Law on Environmental Protection (2009). Official Gazette of the

Republic of Serbia. 135(04).
Lechelt R (1998). Environmental Audit System- History (System des Umweltaudits- Entstehungsgeschichte). in: Ewer; Lechelt; Theuer (Edit.): „Guide to Environmental Audit“ (“Handbuch Umweltaudit”); C.H. Beck's Publishing: 18.
Lindlar A (1999). Eco-audit. Economica: 2.
Waskow S (1994). Business Eco-management: EC Eco-audit Regulation Requirements. A guide to EC Regulation on Eco-management and Eco-audit (Betribliches Umweltmanagement: Anforderungen nach der Audit- Verordnung der EG. Ein Leitfaden über die EG- Verordnung zum Umweltmanagement und zur Umweltbetriebsprüfung). in Feldhaus, Grhard: „ Eco-audit and Business Organization in Environmental Law“ („Umwelt-Audit und Betriebsorganisation im Umweltrecht“), in Kormann, Joachim (Edit.): „Environmental Liability and Environmental Management“ („Umwelthaftung und Umweltmanagement“). 5: 41

Electronic sources

http://ec.europa.eu/environment/emas/pdf/news/costs_and_benefits_of_emas.pdf, “Study on the costs and benefits analysis on EMAS to registered organizations”
http://www.emas-register.eu/statistic.php?view=all_sites, listed number of organisations that have implemented EMAS, accessed on date 06.05.2010
http://www.tmsconsultancy.com/index

Audit firm size and quality: Does audit firm size influence audit quality in the Libyan oil industry?

Nedal Sawan* and Ihab Alsaqqa

Liverpool Business School, United Kingdom.

This study examines the relation between size of audit firm and audit quality, and the choice of accrual measures for a large sample of firms. In relation to the impact of different sizes of audit firms on audit quality, a clear majority of oil companies and audit firms agreed that Big Four firms are superior to their non-Big Four counterparts in all of the reputation issues presented to them, and that the size of the audit firm is positively associated with audit quality. Such superiority is seen in terms of resources and audit technology, and the consequent motivation to perform as professionally as possible. A questionnaire was used to collect data. To confirm and support the questionnaire findings, semi-structured interviews were conducted. The data used for this study were collected from two sources: the demand side (Libyan oil companies) and the supply side (audit firms working in Libya). The data for the Libyan oil companies were gathered from three different types of respondents: internal auditors, financial managers and accounts managers. For the audit firms, data were gathered from employees at all levels in the firm: managing partners, audit supervisors and auditors.

Key words: Libya, audit quality, audit firm size, oil company, audit firms.

INTRODUCTION

The literature indicates that satisfactory levels of audit quality are usually more evident in large audit firms than in small ones, one reason being that the larger the firm, the higher the number of clients, and the greater the probability that the range of services provided is bigger. This minimises dependency on particular clients (Makarem, 2011). And despite the high-profile lawsuits that some big auditing firms have faced in recent years, it is argued by Francis (2004) that these firms do, nonetheless, provide audits of a higher quality than their smaller counterparts. Additionally, large firms have more resources and are able to take steps to publicise their services and develop a reputation. As a result of this, they are usually considered as providing a high quality service, and the size of the audit firm has, therefore, been used as a surrogate for audit quality (DeAngelo, 1981a; Dehkordi and Makarem, 2011; Francis, 2004; Jeong and Rho, 2004; Krishnan, 2005). Large audit firms (the Big Four for example) can devote much investment to the provision of training courses and other resources necessary to ensure their staff are competent, able to audit to a high standard, and are less likely to be compromised by actions of clients (Francis and Yu, 2009; Dopuch, 1984; Gul, 1991; Behn et al. 2008; Wilson and Grimlund, 1990; Rusmin, 2010; Lawrence et al, 2011).

LITERATURE REVIEW

Although there are short studies recently dealing with the relationship between sizes of firms and audit quality in Libya, the topic still raises interest and calls for further and more in-depth research. The following provides an overview of the key literature in order to gain a deeper understanding of the topic under consideration.

A number of reasons exist to explain the importance of

*Corresponding author. E-mail: ne2000dal@hotmail.com.

the relationship between firm size and audit quality. One of these is the fact that audit firm size is immediately observable and can, therefore, be readily used as an indicator of audit quality; and another justification is that if a positive relationship can indeed be demonstrated between size of audit firm and audit quality, then a rationale is provided for the demand for continuing professional education in all audit firms, irrespective of their size. Thirdly, if audit quality and size are shown to be related, the structure of liability insurance premiums could also be affected (Colbert and Murray, 1998). Nevertheless, despite these arguments for the importance of audit firm size in producing a quality outcome, it is nonetheless suggested that audit quality is independent of firm size (Arnett and Danos, 1979; Francis, 2004; Jeong and Rho, 2004; Krishnan, 2005; Chandler, 1991; Lee et al., 2007; Ferguson and Stokes, 2003; Francis and Yu, 2009).

However, audit firms do provide differing quality audits, increasing with the size of firms, in response to varying demands for quality amongst clients because different companies have different levels of agency costs (Arrunada, 1999). The extent of the debate on this particular issue suggests a difficulty in reaching a policy decision on it, and it is argued (Arnett and Danos, 1979; Behn et al, 2008) that it is unfair to distinguish between large and small audit firms if professional standards and qualifications are maintained throughout the sector. In this respect, Arnett and Danos (1979) comment: "If we assume that the quality of the auditing is the same regardless of the size of the firm performing it, the banker would be supplied with the same information on which to base his decision; in this way the size of the firm should not necessarily be a consideration".

Within the auditing literature, it is firm size that has attracted the greatest attention, with the assertion being that bigger firms deliver a higher quality audit than their smaller counterparts. And many studies have found evidence to support the notion that firm size has an impact on audit quality, with quality improving as the size of the firm increases (DeAngelo, 1981b; Rusmin, 2010; Lawrence et al, 2011; Davidson and Neu, 1993; Becker et al., 1998; Abu Bakar et al., 2005; Ferguson and Stokes 2003; Francis and Yu 2009; Choi et al, 2010).

There is reason to believe that one explanation for this phenomenon is that bigger firms have more and better resources than smaller firms, that they have greater research facilities, that they can undertake the strongest tests, and that their technological capacity is such that they can generally do much more than their smaller counterparts (Reisch, 2000). More recently, analyst forecast accuracy has been included as a proxy for audit quality, by Behn et al (2008), who assert that in the case where one category of auditor increases the reporting reliability of earnings in comparison to the other type, analysts of the superior type clients should be able to make more accurate forecasts of future earnings than those analysts of the non-superior type clients. Accepting this line of argument, it was found by Behn et al. (2008) that analysts of Big 4 clients have higher forecast accuracy than analysts of non-Big 4 clients.

Moreover, as noted by DeAngelo (1981b), the larger audit firms are not concerned in the same way as are smaller firms, with the loss of a client, and hence they produce higher audit quality because they are not afraid to be objective. Additionally, it is confirmed by Krishnan and Schauer (2000), that the degree of compliance observed is directly correlated to audit firm size, this increasing on a continuum moving from the small non-Big Six to the large non-Big Six to the Big Six.

However, there are many critics of this view and it has been argued that high quality corporate reporting is, in fact, an outcome of the audit firm's status (Naser and Al-Khatib (2000). The large international firms have a reputation for disclosing information of a high quality, so any audit firm with an affiliation to one of the international firms, is automatically elevated in the reputation stakes. Clearly, once a reputation has been earned, it must be protected, and in the case of audit firms, this is done by delivering credible audits on a consistent basis. In a recent study by Michael (2007), it was confirmed that the clients of large audit firms tend to have lower abnormal accruals, and to satisfy the benchmark earnings objectives of small profits and small earnings increases, than do clients of small audit firms; moreover, large firms were found to be more likely to issue going-concern reports.

Such behaviour on the part of large firms testifies to their independence, which has been reported in the literature, it being noted that Big Four auditors are less likely than smaller auditors to provide a personalized services approach (McLennan and Park, 2004). The fact that larger audit firms have several clients and are not reliant upon the revenue from simply one or two leads to increased auditor independence, which is a recognized principal component of audit quality (Arrunada, 1999; Niemi, 2004; Alleyne et al., 2006). Francis and Yu (2009) document a systematic association between Big 4 office size and audit outcomes consistent with larger offices producing higher quality audits.

Indeed, in their research into forecasted and reported earnings, Davidson and Neu (1993) found that firms with a reputation for delivering higher audit quality reported more forecast errors than audit firms without such prestige. Becker et al. (1998) found non-Big Six auditors had more discretionary accruals for increasing income than Big-Six auditors. Francis et al. (1999) also found that aggressive earnings management was much more likely to be contained by Big Six auditors than non-Big Six firms; and in confirmation of this phenomenon, Davidson et al. (2006) reported that the receipt of modified audit reports from Big Six auditors often induces companies to appoint non-Big Six auditors, and that thereafter, they report increased levels of earnings management.

This suggests overwhelmingly, that Big Six auditors are much stricter, and provide audits that are much more accurate, much more conservative and less optimistic than non-Big Six auditors (Lennox, 1999; Gaeremynck and Willekens, 2003; Lee and Taylor, 2001). And for investors, companies that are audited by the Big Six audit firms would seem to be more attractive since there are likely to be less unwelcome surprises. Indeed, Hussainey (2009) found that the ability of investors to forecast future earnings is improved in such a circumstance since any going concerns are readily identified.

Mutchler et al. (1997) confirm that Big Six auditors are more likely than their non-Big Six counterparts to issue going-concern opinions, suggesting that larger firms are prepared to take an aggressive stance in issuing an appropriate opinion, that they have better technical ability to detect the going-concern issue, or have more clients with such issues. Additionally, auditors are less likely to issue going-concern modifications to larger companies which later go bankrupt, possibly because they are more confident that larger companies can sit out their financial difficulties, or maybe because they fear that issuing the going-concern modification will itself precipitate failure. Similarly, Morris and Strawser (1999) assert that banks receiving modified audit reports from Big Six audit firms were more likely to continue, and not face closure by the regulators than those receiving modified audit reports from non-Big Six audit firms. In contrast, banks with non-modified audit reports from non-Big Six audit firms were more likely to be closed than those receiving non-modified audit reports from Big Six audit firms. Hence, banks audited by the Big Six are more likely to be allowed to continue, consistent with regulators' perceptions that economic reporting incentives may result in Big Six audit firms being more likely to modify their opinions to reflect going-concern uncertainties.

O'Keefe and Westort (1992) considered the reasons why a positive relationship has been found to exist between large firm size and the probability of error detection. They identified these as being: firstly, personnel in large firms become more specialized, and secondly, CPAs in larger firms are involved in significantly more continuing professional education than CPAs in small firms. Hence, audit teams in big firms are expected to have greater technological knowledge than those in small firms, and to be more skilled in the detection and correction of errors. Indeed, it has been argued for some time (see Deis and Giroux, 1992) that larger firms have less deficient paperwork than smaller firms.

That said, there has been a line of argument against the idea that accounting quality is a product of audit firm size, with Imhoff (1988) asserting that no such difference occurs, and Chandler (1991) arguing that quality is produced by individual auditors rather than the firms for which they work. And Lee et al. (2007) go so far as to say that there is no quality advantage in big audit firms because they face less of a litigation risk than smaller firms, and because they are involved in the provision of non-audit services as well, which often creates very special relationships with particular clients.

Offering a different viewpoint on the relationship between firm size and audit quality, Dopuch and Simunic (1980) argue that product-differentiation theory can explain many of the apparent monopolistic characteristics of the industry. They suggest that different auditing firms are perceived by investors to offer auditing services that are qualitatively different, and specifically the former Big Eight are considered to be more credible than other auditing companies. Dopuch and Simunic (1980) consider audit quality to result from the number and extent of audit procedures performed by the auditor, and this in turn relates to the resources available to audit firms, since these may allow for more powerful tests to be performed. In order to test this hypothesis, Nichols and Smith (1983), using a market model methodology on event studies, examined whether positive abnormal returns accrue to organizations that move from being audited by non-Big Eight to Big Eight auditors, and also whether negative abnormal returns accrue to firms which move in the opposite direction. They found an apparent positive, but not statistically significant, reaction from the market, and consequently did not offer strong support for the Dopuch and Simunic (1980)'s argument. In fact, it has not been determined whether this disagreement comes from a weakness in the model, or its application by Nichols and Smith (1983).

Choi et al (2010) show that office size has significantly positive relations with both audit quality and fees, after analyzing national-level audit firm size and office-level industry expertise. These positive relations support the view that large local offices provide higher-quality audits compared to small local offices, and that such quality differences are priced in the market for audit services.

In contrast, Knapp (1991), investigating the effect of key audit variables on the assessments of audit quality of a sample of audit committee members, found no significant effect of audit size on the discovery assessments, although there was more probability of disclosure among the Big Eight.

Research by Krishnan and Schauer (2000) found a relationship between a firm's participation in a peer-review process, and financial disclosures, which were more likely to be made when such a review was in place. The reason is that large audit firms are often in partnership with others and each partner is liable for the firm's debt, so peer-review monitoring is required to protect all parties' reputations and financial standing (Watts and Zimmerma,, 1986), and according to Beattie et al. (2001), to stand as an additional guarantee of auditor independence. Some large audit firms also establish their own internal quality review. In the UK, independent units, such as the Joint Monitoring Unit (JMU) and the ACCA monitoring unit are responsible for reviewing the audit quality of audit professionals.

Colbert and Murray (1998) contribute to the literature, which concentrates mainly on the larger audit firms, by conducting research with a nationwide sample of 422 small firms selected from the Private Companies Practice Section (PCPS), the Peer Review Programme (PRP), and the American Institute of Certified Public Accountants (AICPA 1992, 2002), which provides comprehensive measures of audit firm quality. They found a positive association between firm size and audit quality in firms that perform audits, reviews, and compilations (but not in firms that perform reviews and compilations, without audits). Hence, audit firm size is only a useful quality surrogate for firms that conduct audits.

On a similar theme, Krishnan and Schauer (2000) examined the relationship between firm size and audit quality in a sample of 164 Voluntary Health and Welfare Organizations (VHWOs), using their compliance with eight Generally Accepted Accounting Principles (GAAPs) disclosure requirements as the audit quality measure. Investments, valuation of fixed assets, form of audit report, cash donations and pledges, donated materials and services, presentation of statement of functional expenses, presentation of balance sheet and other statements were the principles. The auditors were considered as three groups: the Big Six, large non-Big Six, and small non-Big Six. It was found that the extent of compliance increased as organizations moved from small non-Big Six to large non-Big Six and from large non-Big Six to the Big Six. Furthermore, other influential factors in respect of audit quality were identified, these being client size and financial health, which had a positive relationship, and client wealth which had a negative impact on audit quality. Geiger et al. (2006b) observe that when compared with non-Big Four firms, Big Four firms significantly reduce their issuance of going-concern modifications to bankruptcy clients after the Private Securities Litigation Reform Act, suggesting lower quality reporting for Big Four firms.

In a more recent study, Chung and Kallapur (2003) found that incentives offered to auditors definitely compromised their independence. This issue was related to client importance and was based on the economic theory of auditor's independence. They used ratios of client fees and NAS fees divided by audit firms' US revenues as surrogates for audit practice, business revenues and measure of client importance, and examined the association with abnormal accruals in the Jones Model using a sample of 1,871 clients of Big Five audit firms. No statistical association was reported between client importance ratios and abnormal accruals in part of the sample based on size, and client opportunities, as proxies by business and geographical segment diversification. In another study in a similar context, Krishnan (2003) explored the relationship between audit quality and pricing of discretionary accruals, finding that Big Six clients report lower amounts of discretionary accruals than non-Big Six clients, and the relationship between stock returns and discretionary accruals is greater for firms audited by Big Six auditors than for those audited by non-Big Six auditors. Furthermore, the discretionary accruals of Big Six auditors' clients have a greater association with future profitability than those of non-Big Six auditors. And finally, the stock market acknowledges the superiority of Big Six auditors to non-Big Six auditors only for discretionary accruals. Overall, the outcomes of Krishnan's (2003) study are consistent with the idea that higher audit quality is associated with Big Six auditors, and this is reflected in the security returns of the clients of Big Six auditors.

In recent research, Choi et al. (2008) indicated that a fee premium is charged by large audit firms because they face higher legal liability costs, and hence, have more incentive to make a better effort than smaller firms. These researchers suggest that the fee premium decreases as the legal regime becomes stronger because small auditors have a higher audit failure rate than Big Four auditors, and increase audit fees significantly more to compensate for their increase in legal liability costs.

The literature on firm size has clearly highlighted that whilst different samples and methods have been used by different researchers, there is a positive relationship between firm size and audit quality. Specifically, large audit firms have more resources which they can direct to the recruitment and training process, thereby providing them with the human capability to detect and correct errors in financial statements. Moreover, as larger audit firms have reputations to preserve, they are careful to report deficiencies. That said, many of the differences between large and small firms should be eliminated by the maintenance of professional standards and qualifications, and a more efficient regulatory framework.

Nonetheless, the literature does show that some studies have not found a relationship between audit firm size and measures of quality. In 1988, Imhoff surveyed financial analysts, finding that they saw no difference in quality between Big Eight and other audit firms. Likewise, the American Institute of Certified Public Accountants (AICPA 1992, 2002) argued that audit quality is independent of firm size. Additionally, Chandler (1991) found audit quality to be a feature of particular auditors, and not firms. All Certified Public Accountants (CPAs) meet the same exacting standards for admission to the profession and participate in professional education annually (AICPA, 2002). Moreover, all AICPA members are subject to three-yearly external review of their auditing practice (AICPA. 1992). And, the collapse of Arthur Andersen and the opposition to peer review in large audit firms, as found by Fearnley et al. (2005), would seem to indicate that it is individuals who are responsible for providing audit quality rather than audit firms.

In addition, the Sarbanes-Oxley Act (2002) introduced the Public Company Accounting Oversight Board (PCAOB) as a monitor for auditor professionalism, and as a replacement for the peer review system because of anxieties concerning the potential for compromising quality control among peers. Krishnan (2005) has consistently argued that audit quality differs between and within audit firms. Hence, it is wrong to attribute audit quality to firms on the basis of their size, irrespective of the fact that larger firms have more resources. Given the stage in Libya's development, no consensus has yet been reached on this issue.

METHODS AND THE SAMPLING UNIT

A mixed methods approach was utilised in this study to gather a range of views from all the professional groups involved in Libyan auditing. Questionnaires were used to collect data concerning the perceptions of two sources: the demand side (Libyan oil companies) and the supply side (audit firms working in Libya). The data for the Libyan oil companies were gathered from three different types of respondents: internal auditors, financial managers and accounts managers. The reason for choosing these three groups of respondents, rather than other employees in the company, was the fact that the literature of auditing indicates that the external auditor usually has more contact with these groups than any others. For the audit firms, data were gathered from employees at all levels in the audit firm: managing partners, audit supervisors and auditors.

The rationale for choosing oil companies was because of their high level of organisation and the fact that most of these companies employ personnel who hold degrees from the United States or Britain – these two facts enabled the researcher to access the right people and obtain the appropriate data.

The magnitude of the activities of the oil companies, and hence the scale of the accounting systems, represent an attraction for large numbers of qualified accountants, who hold qualifications and different accounting backgrounds, a fact that allowed the researcher to have access to a large community of accountants, with diverse careers and work experience.

In order to refute and support the questionnaire findings, semi-structured interviews were conducted. The sample for the interviews was broadly similar to the sample for the questionnaire, which involved representatives from Libyan oil companies, namely, internal auditors, financial managers, accounts managers, and representatives from audit firms working in Libya, namely, managing partners, auditors and audit supervisors. Regulators working in the LAAA were also included in the interviewee sample, partly due to the fact that, after analysing the questionnaire survey, the researcher found it necessary to interview regulators to clarify some grey areas found in the analysis, and more importantly, to triangulate the sample of the study and to obtain different opinions from different dimensions. The total number of interviews conducted with the oil companies was ten (three with internal auditors, four with financial managers, and three with accounts managers), and the total number of interviews conducted with the audit firms working in Libya was thirteen (four with managing partners, six with audit supervisors, and three with auditors). Lastly, two interviews were conducted with regulators working for the LAAA. This process aimed to enhance and supplement the questionnaire findings providing an in-depth clarification and understanding of the effects that the selected factors have on evidence obtained by Libyan auditors. Content analysis was used to analyse the data collected in the interviews.

The first part of the questionnaire was designed to obtain the views of external, internal, state and taxation auditors relating to the effects of the professional and academic qualifications of the auditor on quality of evidence. The second section aimed to gather the participant's opinions regarding the effects of the consistency of evidence on audit evidence. The final section asked the participants about the effects of the amount of evidence on quality of evidence.

A 5-point Likert-scale ranging from *strongly undermines evidence* to *strongly enhances evidence* was utilised to measure perceptions regarding quality of audit evidence (Saunders et al., 2007).

For the purpose of this study, 147 questionnaires were distributed to the oil companies. Of these, 52 went to internal auditors, 50 to financial managers, and 45 to accounts managers. Additionally, 300 questionnaires were sent to the audit firms working in Libya, 100 to managing partners, 100 to audit supervisors, and 100 to auditors. The samples from the demand side (internal auditors, financial managers and accounts managers) represent the agent of the principal, and conduct business on behalf of the principal. Hence, a monitoring mechanism is needed to assess their performance (Jensen and Meckling, 1976). The samples from the supply side (managing partners, audit supervisors and auditors) represent the main subjects of the issue of interest that provide certification and/or information credibility assessment to the stakeholders (Humphrey, 1997). Hasan (2000) points out that audit firms and their clients evaluate audit quality in different ways, and it was, therefore important to receive responses from both sections of the research population.

Considerable effort was made in order to avoid problems of non-response and to ensure the completeness of the questionnaire that was designed using mainly closed questions which are easy for respondents to answer. The questionnaire sample consisted of all listed oil companies in the NOC and 100 audit firms working in Libya. The wording of the questionnaire was clear and straightforward, the instrument was of a reasonable length, and there were no complaints about layout. Most of the questionnaires were personally administered (Managing Partner - 52 questionnaires; Audit Supervisor - 52 questionnaires; Auditor - 56 questionnaires; Internal Auditor - 45 questionnaires; Financial Manager - 47 questionnaires; and Accounts Manager - 35 questionnaires), and some questionnaires were delivered personally by the researcher and returned by mail.

The overall response rate to the questionnaire was extremely encouraging at 64% (Table 1). Remenyi et al. (2002) suggest that a response rate above 60% is considered to be exemplary. The response rates for internal auditors and financial managers were 86.5 and 94% respectively, higher than those of accounts managers, managing partners, and audit supervisors, which were 77.7, 52 and 52%, respectively. Some were unable to complete the questionnaires, and the researcher was unable to contact respondents outside Tripoli because of poor communication facilities, including the official postal system.

RESULTS AND DISCUSSION

Quantitative findings

In order to elicit their perceptions of the relationship between audit firm size and audit quality, respondents from oil companies and audit firms were asked to indicate on a scale ranging from 1 - strongly disagree, to 5 -

strongly agree, their disagreement or agreement with the five statements given in Table 2.

The statement *The Big Four firms are more risk averse in respect of damage to their reputation from public scandals and/or audit failures* had the highest mean score (3.93), resulting from 70.1% of oil company respondents agreeing or strongly agreeing with it. The statement *The local audit firms achieve a lower level of audit quality* had the second highest mean score (3.91) with as many as 71.6% of oil company respondents agreeing or strongly agreeing with it.

The statement *The companies audited by the Big Four firms are more attractive to investors and creditors* had the third highest mean score (3.77) based on the responses from oil company participants. As many as 63.8% either agreed or strongly agreed with this statement. The statement *The Big Four Firms achieve a high level of audit quality* had the fourth highest mean score (3.75), with 70.9% of respondents agreeing or strongly agreeing with it. The statements *The Big Four firms perform more powerful, effective tests and are more credible than others* and *the size of the audit firm is positively associated with audit quality* had the fifth highest mean scores (3.65 and 3.63), with 69.3 and 64.6% of respondents agreeing or strongly agreeing with them, respectively.

As many as 66.1 and 63.8% of respondents either agreed or strongly agreed with the statements *The Big Four firms can plan the audit process more effectively and can obtain a greater variety of clients* and *the Big Four firms are more independent and more likely to issue qualified reports*. These statements achieved nearly the same mean scores (3.58 and 3.57). The Statement *The Big Four firms can report the real financial situation of the clients more readily than other firms* had the lowest mean score (3.49).

In the responses from audit firm representatives, the statement *The local audit firms achieve a lower level of audit quality* had the highest mean score (3.96), with 70.7% of audit firm respondents supporting it. The statements that *The size of the audit firm is positively associated with audit quality, The Big Four firms achieve a high level of audit quality* and *The companies audited by the Big Four firms are more attractive to investors and creditors* had the second highest and same mean score (3.78), with as many as 66.9, 63.8 and 68.1% of respondents either agreeing or strongly agreeing with them, respectively. The statement that *The Big Four firms perform more powerful, effective tests and are more credible than others* had the third highest mean score (3.71), with 61.9% of respondents either agreeing or strongly agreeing with it. The statement that *The Big Four firms are more risk averse in respect of damage to their reputation from public scandals and/or audit failures* had the fourth highest mean score (3.70), with 63.2% of respondents either agreeing or strongly agreeing with it. The statement that *The Big Four firms can plan the audit process more effectively and can obtain a greater variety of clients* had the fifth highest mean score (3.66) with as many as 62.8% of respondents either agreeing or strongly agreeing with it.

The statement that *The Big Four firms can report the real financial situation of the clients more readily than other firms* had the second lowest mean score (3.61), with as many as 57.8% of respondents either agreeing or strongly agreeing with it.

The statement that *The Big Four firms are more independent and more likely to issue qualified reports* had the lowest mean score (3.11), with 48.8% of respondents either agreeing or strongly agreeing with it.

Once again, because the overall responses of oil companies and audit firms' respondents were not completely homogeneous, an attempt was made to isolate the determinants of responses.

The analysis of differences between oil companies' and audit firms' responses is reported in Table 2, which reveals one significant difference at the 1% level and one at the 5%, as measured by the Mann Whitney U test.

An inspection of each sample group's distribution of responses (which is reflected in the mean scores) shows a significant difference at the 1% level of significance between oil companies' and audit firms' respondents for one of the nine statements, and a significant difference at the 5% level for another one of the nine statements, using the Mann Whitney U test. These findings suggest that oil companies' respondents perceived the Big Four as producing a higher level of audit quality than non-Big Four audit firms. The Big Four firms are more risk averse in respect of damage to their reputation from public scandals and/or audit failures, and that the Big Four firms are more independent and more likely to issue qualified reports, which is consistent with the findings of Michael (2007) who determined that clients audited by large audit firms tend to have lower unusual accruals, and are more likely to meet the benchmark earnings targets of small earnings increases. He also found that large audit firms are more likely to issue going-concern reports. These results show that there is a significant variation in audit quality across different sizes of auditor practice offices, with larger offices providing higher quality audits. They are consistent with the conclusions drawn by Beatty (1989) and Titman and Trueman (1986) that since large audit firms (Big Four) have greater resources and possess identical technological capabilities, they are capable of performing more powerful tests. As a result, larger audit firms are more likely to be associated with more precise information than smaller audit firms.

The perceptions of size of audit firms based on position

Table 3 presents the analysis by position. Distributions of

Table 1. Questionnaire survey response rate.

Group	Distributed questionnaires	Useable questionnaires	Response rate
Managing partner	100	52	52
Audit supervisor	100	52	52
Auditor	100	56	56
Internal auditor	52	45	86.5
Financial manager	50	47	94
Accounts manager	45	35	77.7
Total	447	287	64

the responses from oil company staff and audit firm staff were significantly different at the 1% and 5% level, as measured by the Kruskal-Wallis statistic.

Overall perceptions of respondents showed one significant difference in the distribution of responses at the 1% level of significance as measured by the Kruskal Wallis test. Auditors had a significantly lower mean score (2.5) and accounts managers and financial managers had the highest mean score (4.26 and 3.49) for the statement *The Big Four firms are more independent and more likely to issue qualified reports*. This difference in the responses perhaps indicates that the oil company's respondents believe large firms are wealthier than small firms and would potentially be required to give in to larger claims in the event that they were to be sued. Hence, they might be more concerned about maintaining audit quality and their reputation in the audit market than smaller firms. The result might also explain why the Big Four have been reported as providing higher quality auditing and being more independent than non-Big Four firms in the literature (Michael, 2007; Becker et al., 1998; Francis et al., 1999; Francis and Krishnan, 1999; Dehkordi and Makarem, 2011; Francis, 2004; Jeong and Rho, 2004; Krishnan, 2005).

The perceptions of size of audit firm based on type of audit firm

The analysis by type of audit firm, as reported in Table 4, shows five significant differences between local audit firms, Arab or international firms, and local firms affiliated to one of the Big Four audit firms (non-Big Four and Big Four) at the 1 and 5% levels of significance, respectively, as measured by the Kruskal-Wallis test. The level of agreement with the statements *The companies audited by the Big firms are more attractive to investors and creditors* and *The Big Four firms are more independent and more likely to issue qualified reports* at the level of1% of significance was significantly higher for Big Four respondents (4.33 and 3.86, mean score, respectively) than for local, Arab, and international audit firm's (non-Big Four) respondents (3.83, 2.9 and 3.37, 3.21, respectively). This outcome is consistent with the study conducted by Michael (2007) who found that clients audited by large audit firms tend to have lower unusual accruals, and are more likely to meet the benchmark earnings targets of small earnings increases.

In addition, the analysis by type of audit firm in Table 4 shows three significant differences between local audit firms, local firms affiliated to an Arab or international audit firm, and local firms affiliated to one of the Big Four audit firms, (non-Big Four and Big Four) at the 5% level of significance, as measured by the Kruskal-Wallis test. The level of agreement with these three statements by Big Four audit firms' respondents was significantly higher than it was by non-Big Four audit firms' respondents. This disagreement in the responses from the Big Four audit firms' respondents perhaps indicates the main reasons why, in their view, the Big Four are perceived as producing a higher level of audit quality than the non-Big Four. The reasons may be summarised as follows:

1. The Big Four firms are more independent and more likely to issue qualified reports.
2. The Big Four firms can report the real financial situation of the clients more readily than other firms.
3. The Big Four firms perform more powerful, effective tests and are more credible than others. The Big Four firms can plan the audit process more effectively and can obtain a greater variety of clients.

It is worth mentioning here that these results strongly support previous studies, such as the one undertaken by De Angelo (1981a) who argued that audit quality is directly related to the size of auditing firm, that conducted by Dopuch and Simunic (1980) who reported that the Big Four are perceived as providing a higher level of audit quality than non-Big Four auditors because they are viewed as being more credible and have more resources, and the research by Morris and Strawser (1999) that found that banks receiving modified audit reports from Big Six audit firms were more likely to continue, and not be closed by the regulators, than those receiving

Table 2. Distribution of the evaluations given by the different statements regarding the size of audit firm and audit quality.

Statement	Audit firms							Oil companies							Sig
	SD %	D %	NV %	A %	SA %	Mean	Median	SD %	D %	NV %	A %	SA %	Mean	Median	
The size of the audit firm is positively associated with audit quality.	5.6	7.5	20	37.5	29.4	3.78	4.00	10.2	13.4	11.8	32.3	32.3	3.63	4.00	
The Big Four firms can report the real financial situation of the clients more readily than other firms.	6.3	10.6	25.6	30.6	26.9	3.61	4.00	10.2	12.6	22.8	26.8	27.6	3.49	4.00	
The Big Four firms are more risk averse in respect of damage to their reputation from public scandals and/or audit failures.	2.5	11.9	22.5	39.4	23.8	3.70	4.00	3.1	9.4	17.3	31.5	38.6	3.93	4.00	**
The Big Four firms perform more powerful, effective tests and are more credible than others	8.1	10	20	26.3	35.6	3.71	4.00	15	11.8	3.9	32.3	37	3.65	4.00	
The Big Four Firms achieve a high level of audit quality	5.6	11.3	19.4	27.5	36.3	3.78	4.00	10.2	7.9	11	38.6	32.3	3.75	4.00	
The local audit firms achieve a lower level of audit quality	3.8	6.9	18.8	31.3	39.4	3.96	4.00	3.9	9.4	15	35.4	36.2	3.91	4.00	
The companies audited by the Big firms are more attractive to investors and creditors.	6.3	8.1	17.5	38.1	30	3.78	4.00	3.9	7.9	26	33.1	30.7	3.77	4.00	
The Big Four firms can plan the audit process more effectively and can obtain a greater variety of clients.	5.6	13.8	18.1	33.8	28.8	3.66	4.00	7.9	11	21	34.6	25.2	3.58	4.00	
The Big Four firms are more independent and more likely to issue qualified reports	18.1	15.2	21.3	27.5	17.5	3.11	3.00	9.4	11	18.9	34.6	26	3.57	4.00	*

*,** indicates distribution of responses is significantly different at the 1%, 5% levels, respectively using the Mann Whitney U test.

modified audit reports from non-Big Six audit firms. In contrast,banks receiving non-modified audit reports from non-Big Six (as the Big Four were then) audit firms were more likely to be closed than those receiving non-modified audit reports from Big Six audit firms. Overall, respondents' perceptions of the relationship between firm size and level of audit quality are consistent with the notion that higher audit quality is associated with the Big Four audit firms.

Qualitative findings

Audit firm size has been used as a surrogate for audit quality in prior literature (DeAngelo, 1981a). Moreover, prior research (Becker et al., 1998; Francis et al., 1999) has reported that Big Four audit clients present lower discretionary accruals than those of non-Big Four firms because Big Four auditors may have more expertise, resistance to clients' discretion, and awareness of financial and reputation loss, than non-Big Four auditors. Therefore, this section aims to demonstrate whether the size of the audit firm affects audit quality in Libya, and to identify reasons for possible quality difference by firm size.

The majority of interviewees (88% of oil companies and audit firms) agreed that the size of audit firms does indicate different levels of audit quality, and that they believe the Big Four audit firms to be more powerful, effective and

Table 3. Distribution of different statements regarding the size of audit firm based on position.

Statement	Audit firm staff						Oil company staff						
	Managing partner		Audit supervisor		Auditor		Internal auditor		Financial manager		Accounts manager		
	Mean	Median	Mean	Median	Mean	Median	Mean	Median	Mean	Median	Mean	Median	Sig
The size of the audit firm is positively associated with audit quality.	3.88	4.00	3.62	4.00	3.82	4.00	3.58	4.00	3.64	4.00	3.69	4.00	
The Big Four firms can report the real financial situation of the clients more readily than other firms.	3.67	4.00	3.44	400	3.71	4.00	3.58	4.00	3.30	3.00	3.63	4.00	
The Big Four firms are more risk averse in respect of damage to their reputation from public scandals and/or audit failures.	3.90	4.00	3.67	4.00	3.45	4.00	3.91	4.00	3.77	4.00	4.17	4.00	
The Big Four firms perform more powerful, effective tests and are more credible than others	3.63	4.00	4.10	4.00	3.43	3.00	3.42	3.00	3.62	4.00	3.97	4.00	
The Big Four Firms achieve a high level of audit quality.	3.92	4.00	3.71	4.00	3.70	4.00	3.84	4.00	3.51	4.00	3.94	4.00	
The local audit firms achieve a lower level of audit quality.	4.08	4.00	3.63	4.00	4.14	4.00	3.73	3.00	3.83	4.00	4.23	3.00	
The companies audited by the Big firms are more attractive to investors and creditors.	3.73	4.00	3.65	4.00	3.93	4.00	3.62	4.00	3.91	4.00	3.77	4.00	
The Big Four firms can plan the audit process more effectively and can obtain a greater variety of clients.	3.58	4.00	3.62	4.00	3.79	4.00	3.78	4.00	3.53	4.00	3.40	3.00	
The Big Four firms are more independent and more likely to issue qualified reports	3.40	4.00	3.42	4.00	2.54	2.50	3.11	3.00	3.49	4.00	4.26	4.00	*

*,** indicates distribution of responses is significantly different at the 1%, 5% levels, respectively using the Kruskal-Wallis test.

independent than the non-Big Four firms. This finding confirms the questionnaire responses which showed that 69.3% of oil companies, and 61.9% of audit firms agreed that the Big Four firms perform more powerful and effective tests, and are consequently, more credible than other firms.

More than three-quarters of the interviewees (76%) believed that the level of audit quality in Libya depends upon the status of the audit firm, example, local audit firm affiliated to a foreign audit firm, and again, this confirmed the question-

Table 4. Distribution of different statements regarding the size of audit firm based on type of audit firm.

Statement	Local audit firm		International audit firm		Big Four audit firm		Sig
	Mean	Median	Mean	Median	Mean	Median	
The size of the audit firm is positively associated with audit quality.	3.71	4.00	3.72	4.00	4.19	5.00	
The Big Four firms can report the real financial situation of the clients more readily than other firms.	3.67	4.00	3.35	4.00	3.90	4.00	
The Big Four firms are more risk averse in respect of damage to their reputation from public scandals and/or audit failures.	3.71	4.00	3.44	4.00	4.19	4.00	**
The Big Four firms perform more powerful, effective tests and are more credible than others.	3.73	4.00	3.42	4.00	4.24	5.00	**
The Big Four Firms achieve a high level of audit quality	3.79	4.00	3.44	4.00	4.38	5.00	**
The local audit firms achieve a lower level of audit quality	3.89	4.00	4.00	4.00	4.19	4.00	
The companies audited by the Big firms are more attractive to investors and creditors.	3.83	4.00	3.37	4.00	4.33	4.00	*
The Big Four firms can plan the audit process more effectively and can obtain a greater variety of clients.	3.71	4.00	3.58	4.00	3.62	4.00	
The Big Four firms are more independent and more likely to issue qualified reports	2.90	3.00	3.21	3.00	3.86	4.00	*

*,** indicates distribution of responses is significantly different at the 1%, 5% levels, respectively using the Kruskal-Wallis test.

naire survey results, which showed that more than half of the oil company and audit firms' respondents (66.9 and 59.4%, respectively) similarly agreed this was the case.

The interviews indicated that Big Four firms are more structured in terms of staff training, technical support, and have wider resources than their counterparts in smaller audit firms. This is consistent with GAO (2003a), Mautz and Sharaf (1961) and Niemi (2004). It was pointed out that because of the greater availability of resources, the Big Four firms are able to employ more upright indivi-duals who have better qualifications and background. The quality of people is clearly influential on the quality of the service they provide, and well-qualified personnel have a positive impact on the audit process, since their professionalism motivates them to comply with accounting standards and codes of ethics and not to concur with irregularities in clients' accounts. This result confirms the questionnaire that 66.1% of oil companies and 62.8% of audit firms believed that the Big Four firms are more likely to issue qualified reports and to plan the audit process more effectively, thereby obtaining a greater variety of clients, and in consequence, being able to provide their audit staff with greater experience.

In addition, the interviews indicated that the Big Four firms are also in a position to offer job security, which makes their staff more confident in their work and in reporting their results. Therefore, they are better able to fight against management pressure.

On this issue, an auditor in one of Big Four audit firms remarked:

If it is a Big Four firm, I would have more confidence. There is a greater spread of expertise and there is less likely to be an independence problem whereas with a smaller audit firm, they may be more dependent on one audit.

This result confirms the questionnaire finding in respect of the statement The companies audited by the Big Four are more attractive to investors and creditors which had a high mean score (3.77 and 3.78), resulting from 63.8 and 68.1% of oil companies' and audit firms' respondents agreeing or strongly agreeing with it. This result might also explain why Big Four auditors have been reported as providing higher quality auditing than non-Big Four auditors in prior literature (Dehkordi and Makarem, 2011; Francis, 2004; Becker et al., 1998; Francis et al., 1999; Francis and Krishnan, 1999; Teoh and Wong, 1993; Niemi, 2004; Francis and Yu, 2009).
On this issue of the external perception of audit firm size, a financial manager in an oil company remarked:

There is a greater opportunity to influence a smaller practice than a larger practice because the latter is very well organised and has its own structures in place. A small firm won't have the same resources and will depend on individuals within the practice to try and bring the same checks and balances which a large firm, by having the structures in place, can automatically impose.

As Big Four audit firms have many audit clients, they might not be economically dependent on just a few of them. In addition, large firms have more wealth to pay larger potential claims if sued, than smaller firms (Simunic and Stein, 1996) and so, might be more concerned about maintaining audit quality and their reputation in the audit market than smaller firms. In addition, large size companies with good accounting systems and less earnings manipulation might possibly hire Big Four auditors because they might be concerned about the quality of their financial statement quality and the reputation of their companies. Therefore, they might select Big Four audit firms to signal a positive company image to the public (Chung and Kallapur, 2003).
An accounts manager in an oil company remarked:

I wouldn't necessarily be comfortable that the smaller audit firms would have the procedures or methodologies that the Big Four would have.

In addition, the interviewees disclosed that the Big Four firms have adequate resources and the financial ability to train their staff in related areas. Indeed, all of the Big Four firms encourage their staff to pursue professional qualifications by giving the appropriate support, such as study leave under the 'article-ship' scheme. Over the study period, personnel are given flexibility to attend classes and examinations, whereas many of the small and medium firms are unable to offer similar schemes. Thus, the interviewees indicated that staff from the Big Four firms are more loyal to, and honest with, their employers, and more able to resist clients' pressure than their counterparts from local audit firms. Furthermore, the knowledge gained from the training given makes the Big Four staff members more skilful and effective in terms of diagnosing activities that are inconsistent with clients' going-concern status.
An internal auditor in one of the oil companies raised the issue of greater objectivity, saying:

The Big Four are part of international groups which are obliged to satisfy international standards. The smaller firms don't have such ties, reporting structures or quality standards. The Big Four are less likely to give a personalised approach to their clients.

The majority of the interviewees (84% overall) believed that the foreign audit firms' claim that they provide a higher level of audit quality is due to their good international reputation, and their well-known brand names. It was pointed out that a large majority of the oil companies still prefer to engage the Big Four firms as their auditors, a preference which portrays that their financial reporting is consistent with global standards. Indeed, some companies that operate internationally associate themselves with reputable auditors to ease their dealing with foreign investors and companies. The interviews revealed that their foreign associates would always assess the credibility of their financial statements by reference to the auditor's name.

The importance of the auditor being known to be credible was raised by a managing partner in one of the Big Four audit firms who commented:

In the bigger audit firms you would find a huge diversity of clients whereas in the smaller audit firms, you may find that the auditor is a close friend of the company.

According to a Big Four managing partner:

The Big Four firms' auditors are able to maintain a higher level of audit quality, possibly due to their organisational structure, technology and competency.

Also, the interviewees commented on the fact that the Big Four firms have larger customer portfolios as compared to their counterparts in small firms, which means that they do not have to rely on any single customer. Thus, they are better placed to resist management pressure in situations of conflict and more able to report any negative findings. Small audit firms, on the other hand, have limited customer portfolios as pointed out by Pearson (1980a), and the termination of any audit job could affect their financial position. Interviewees did reveal that small audit firms might easily compromise with clients in order to retain them. In relation to the size of customer portfolio, one audit supervisor from a Big Four firm noted:

The Big Four can afford to lose customers, are more flexible and more powerful than small firms, and they want to keep the major companies such as oil companies.

On the other hand, a small minority of the interviewees disagreed that audit quality differs according to the size of audit firms. These participants believed this to be a misconception that comes from the clients' management, as a result of clients attempting to boost their reporting image by associating with audit firms that have a good reputation. It may be the case that the management does not have confidence in the company's reporting practices, and tries to find an easy way to divert the audience's attention by employing an international audit firm. It was pointed out that the differentiation is only to meet the consumers' requirements. The small firms' ability is in question simply because they are not being tested. Commenting on the difference between the Big Four and non-Big Four firms, an auditor of a local audit firm believed that the quality of Big Four and non-Big Four auditors in Libya did not significantly differ because it depended on individual competence and attitude rather than firm size. He said:

In my opinion, the quality of Big Four and non-Big Four auditors in Libya does not differ since I believe that their quality depends on individual competence and attitude Size does not matter. However, auditors in Big Four firms have advantages from international working systems and quality control, so people may have stereotyped image of Big Four quality without considering individual competency.

However, a chief internal auditor from a large oil company disagreed with this view, arguing that:

The quality of Big Four and non-Big Four auditors differs because Big Four firms have more hi-tech resources. They hire competent staff and provide them with good training courses in order to render good services to their clients. Moreover, audit clients come from different groups. Big Four clients are large listed companies with higher audit fee whereas non-Big Four clients are small or medium size companies with lower fee. These differences contribute to differences in audit quality.

Considering all the responses from the interviewees, it seems obvious that the Big Four audit firms have more resources at their disposal, and are able to offer better on-going training to their staff. This appears to be understood in the marketplace and associated with a better quality service, as also is the non-reliance on clients to the same extent that smaller firms who have less of a reputation are compelled to do. Hence, audit quality might well differ by size of audit firm.

SUMMARY AND REVIEW OF FINDINGS

In relation to the impact of different sizes of audit firms on audit quality, a clear majority of oil companies and audit firms agreed that Big Four firms are superior to their non-Big Four counterparts in all of the reputation issues presented to them, and that the size of the audit firm is positively associated with audit quality.

Firstly, the questionnaire respondents concluded that Big Four audit firms are more attractive to investors and creditors because they are seen to provide reliable information that enables investors to properly assess risk and return profiles. Investors usually trust audit firms with a professional approach to auditing and a high level of audit quality. In the same manner, oil companies usually engage audit firms with a good reputation because they wish to enhance their own attractiveness to investors and creditors, and Big Four audit firms are considered to be better able to resist management pressure in conflict situations, thereby bringing enhanced credibility to any company that uses their auditing services. The Big Four auditors have greater resources, technical knowledge and global reach, which allows them to deal with clients more efficiently, and they are thus able to freely express their opinions without fear of their engagement being terminated by the client. In fact, Big Four audit firms may also exhibit higher levels of ethical reasoning and attract a greater variety of clients because of their appeal on quality grounds, and the associated benefits their reputation brings. Indeed, as the Big Four audit firms have greater resources and possess technological capabilities, they can plan the audit process more effectively, perform more powerful tests, and be more likely to publish more precise information.

Secondly, the majority of oil companies and audit firms agreed that Big Four audit firms are more risk averse and consequently, more disinclined to be associated with public scandals and/or audit failures than non-Big Four audit firms. These opinions might be an indication of the faith that the respondents still have in the ability and competence of the Big Four to undertake their duties effecttively and professionally, despite the well-publicised audit failures involving large firms that have occurred in different economic, political, geographical and cultural settings, which may not be applicable to the Libyan audit market. It is possible that the invention of communication technology that allows business to be done in real-time has made the Big Four auditors more careful in conducting their business and more risk averse, with the result that their reluctance to be associated with any wrongdoings is enhanced, since the availability of such technology would result in faster spread of negative news.

Finally, the majority of the respondents to the questionnaire recorded their belief that Big Four audit firms are more independent than non-Big Four auditors. Indeed, the Big Four auditors are likely to become the subject of interest to the public and regulators, especially when they are suspected of exhibiting negative behaviour. Therefore, Big Four audit firms have more incentive to behave independently than non-Big Four audit firms.

The results of the interview survey revealed that the perceived relationship between firm size and level of audit quality is consistent with the notion that higher audit quality is associated with foreign audit firms, in general.

In this connection, the interviewees were of the opinion that the Big Four firms were more independent than their counterpart non-Big Four firms, and this was seen as a direct result of their size, since this provided them with more resources that in turn filtered through to organisational practices, such as the provision of more training that ensures staff are skilled and effective in diagnosing activities that are inconsistent with a client's going-concern status. Such elements of organisational culture allow for the recruitment of more professionally-minded people, who subsequently provide a higher quality of service. It was felt by the interviewees that such high quality staff would naturally comply with international professional standards and work ethically, thereby being predisposed to resist management pressure. Overall, the Big Four firms were reported to be more powerful, effective and independent than the non-Big four firms, not least because after various accounting scandals and litigation concerning fraud and irregularities, they have more incentive to protect their reputation and continue with their high earnings.

REFERENCES

Abu BN, Rahman A, Rashid H (2005). Factors Influencing Auditor Independence: Malaysian Loan Officers' Perceptions. Managerial Audit. J. 20(8):804-822.

Alleyne PA, Devonish D, Alleyne P (2006). Perceptions of auditor independence in Barbados. Managerial audit. J. 21(6):621-635.

American Institute of Certified Public Accountants (AICPA) (1992). SEC Practice Section. Statement of Position Regarding Mandatory Rotation of Audit Firms of Publicly Held Companies. New York: AICPA.

American Institute of Certified Public Accountants (AICPA) (2002) International Education Standards for Professional Accountants. New York: AICPA.

Arnett H, Danos P (1979). Michigan Researchers Cite Excessive Regulation of Accounting Profession. C.P.A. J. (49):6.

Arrunada B (1999). The Economics of Audit Quality: Private Incentives and The Regulation of Audit and Non-Audit Services, Dordrecht, The Netherlands: Kluwer Academics Publishers.

Beattie V, Fearnley S, Brandt R (2001). Behind Closed Doors: What Company Audit is Really About. New York: Palgrave.

Beatty RP (1989). Auditor Reputation and the Pricing of Initial Public Offerings. Account. Rev. 64(4):693-709.

Becker C, Defond M, Jiambalvo J, Subramanyam K (1998) The Effect of Audit Quality on Earnings Management. Contemp. Account. Res. 15:1-24.

Behn BJ, Choi H, Kang T (2008). Audit quality and properties of analyst earnings forecasts. Account. Rev. 83(2):327-359.

Chandler RA (1991). "Guardians of Knowledge and Public Interest": A Reply. Account. Audit. Account. J. 4(4):5-13.

Choi J, Kim C, Kim J, Zang Y (2010). Audit Office Size, Audit Quality, and Audit Pricing. J. Pract. Theory Am. Account. Assoc. 29(1)73-97.

Choi J, Kim J, Liu X, Simunic D (2008). Audit Pricing, Legal Liability Regimes, and Big 4 Premiums: Theory and Cross-country Evidence. Contemp. Account. Res. 25(1):55-99.

Chung H, Kallapur S (2003). Client Importance, Non-Audit Services, and Abnormal Accruals. Account. Rev. 78(4):931-955.

Colbert G, Murray D (1998). The Association between Auditor Quality and Auditor Size: An Analysis of Small CPA Firms. J. Account. Audit. Financ. 13(2):135-150.

Davidson WN, Jiraporn P, DaDalt P (2006). Causes and Consequences of Audit Shopping: An Analysis of Auditor Opinions, Earnings Management, and Auditor Changes. Q. J. Bus. Econ. 45(1/2):69-87.

Davidson R, Neu AD (1993). A Note on the Association between Audit Firm Size and Audit Quality. Contemp. Account. Res. 9(2):479-488.

DeAngelo LE (1981a). Auditor Size and Audit Quality. J. Account. Econ. (3):183-199.

DeAngelo LE (1981b). The Auditor-Client Contractual Relationship: An Economic Analysis. USA: UMI Research Press.

Dehkordi DF, Makarem N (2011). The Effect of Size and Type of Auditor on Audit Quality. Int. Res. J. Financ. Econ. 80(2011):122-137.

Deis DR, Giroux GA (1992). Determinants of Audit Quality in the Public Sector. Account. Rev. 67(3):462-479.

Dopuch N, Simunic D (1980). The Nature of Competition in the Auditing Profession: A Descriptive and Normative View. Ed. Buckley J and Weston F, In Regulation and the Accounting Profession. Lifetime Learn. Publications, Belmont, CA. 34(2):283–289.

Dopuch N (1984). The Demand for Quality-Differentiated Audit Services in an Agency-Cost Setting: An Empirical Investigation: Discussion, in Abdel-Khalik, A. and Solomon. Auditing Research Symposium, University of Illinois at Urbana/Champaign. pp. 253-263.

Fearnley S, Brandt R, Beattie V (2005). Auditor Independence and Audit Risk: A Reconceptualisation. J. Int. Account. Res. (4):39-71.

Ferguson D, Stokes J (2003). The effects of firm-wide and office-level industry expertise on audit pricing. Account. Rev. 78 (2):429-449.

Francis J, Krishnan J (1999). Accounting Accruals and Auditor Reporting Conservatism. Contemp. Account. Res. (16):135-165.

Francis JR, Maydew EL, Sparks HC (1999). The Role of Big 6 Auditors in the Credible Reporting of Accruals. Auditing 18(2):17.

Francis J (2004). What do we know about audit quality? Br. Account. Rev. 36(4):345-368.

Francis J, Yu M (2009). Big 4 Office Size and Audit Quality. Account. Rev. 84(5):1521-1552.

Gaeremynck A, Willekens M (2003). The endogenous relationship between audit-report type and business termination: evidence on private firms in a non-litigious environment. Account. Bus. Res. 33(1):65-79.

GAO (2003a). General Accounting Office. Public Accounting Firms: Mandated Study on Consolidation and Competition. GAO Report No. GAO-03-864,[www]<URL :http://www.gao.gov/>[accessed 15 March 2012].

Geiger MA, Raghunandan K, Rama DV (2006b). Auditor decision-making in different litigation environments: The Private Securities Litigation Reform Act, audit reports and audit firm size. J. Account. Public Policy 25:332-353.

Gul FA (1991). Size of Audit Fees and Perceptions of Auditors' Ability to Resist Management Pressure in Audit Conflict Situations. Abacus 27(2):162-173.

Hasan SA (2000). Indications to Audit Quality. J. Econ. Bus. 35(2):203.

Humphrey C (1997). Debating Audit Expectations, Second ed. London: Paul Chapman, pp. 3-30.

Hussainey K (2009). The impact of audit quality on earnings predictability. Managerial Audit. J. 24(4):340-351.

Imhoff EA Jr (1988). A Comparison of Analysts' Accounting Quality Judgments Among CPA Firms' clients. Auditing 7(2):182.

Jeong S, Rho WJ (2004). Big Six auditors and audit quality: the Korean evidence. Int. J. Account. 39(2):175-196.

Jensen MC, Meckling WH (1976). Theory of the Finn: Managerial Behaviour, Agency Costs and Ownership Structure. J. Financ. Econ. 3(4):305-360.
Knapp MC (1991). Factors that Audit Committee Members Use as Surrogates for Audit Quality, Auditing. J. Practice Theory 10(1):35-52.
Krishnan GV (2003). Audit Quality and the Pricing of Discretionary Accruals, Auditing: J. Practice Theory 22(1):109-126.
Krishnan GV (2005). Did Houston clients of Arthur Andersen Recognize Publicly Available Bad News in a timely Fashion? Contemp. Account. Res. 22(1):165-193.
Krishnan J, Schauer PC (2000). The Differentiation of Quality among Auditors: Evidence from the Non-For-Profit Sector, Auditing: J. Practice Theory 19(2):9-25.
Lawrence A, Minutti-Meza M, Zhang P (2011). Can Big 4 versus Non-Big 4 Differences in Audit-Quality Proxies Be Attributed to Client Characteristics? Account. Rev. 86(1):259-286.
Lee B, Cox BS, Roden D (2007). Have the Big Accounting Firms Lost Their Audit Quality Advantage? Evidence from the Returns-Earnings Relation. J. Forensic Account. 8:271-286.
Lee P, Taylor S (2001). Auditor Conservatism and Audit Quality: Evidence from Australian IPO Earning Forecasts, Working Paper, University of Technology, Sydney.
Lennox C (1999). Are large auditors more accurate than small auditors? Account. Bus. Res. 29(3):217-227.
Mautz RK, Sharaf HA (1961). The Philosophy of Auditing, American Accountants Association, USA. Sarasota Springs, 4th ed, pp. 111-112.
McLennan A, Park IU (2004). The Market for Liars: Reputation and Auditor Honesty. ISER Discussion, p. 587.
Michael YD (2007). The Effect of Big Four Office Size on Audit Quality. PhD thesis, University of Missouri – Columbia.
Morris RE, Strawser JR (1999). An Examination of the Effect of CPA Firm Type on Bank Regulators' Closure Decisions, Auditing: J. Pract. Theory 18(2):143-158.
Mutchler JF, Hopwood W, Mckeown JM (1997). The Influence of Contrary Information and Mitigating Factors on Audit Opinion Decisions on Bankrupt Companies. J. Account. Res. 35(2):295-310.
Naser K, Al-Khatib K (2000). Determinants of the Depth of Voluntary Disclosure in the Board of Directors Statement in a Sample of Jordanian Listed Companies, Advances. Int. Accounting (13):99-118.
Nichols DR, Smith DB (1983). Auditor Credibility and Auditor Changes. J. Account. Res. 21(2):534-544.
Niemi L (2004). Auditor size and audit pricing: evidence from small audit firms. Eur. Account. Rev. 13(3)541-560.
O'Keefe T, Westort P (1992). Conformance to GAAPs Reporting Standards in Municipal Audits and the Economics of Auditing: The Effects of Audit Finn Size, CPA examination performance and competition, Issues in Accounting Regulation, pp. 27-32.
Pearson MA (1980a). A Profile of the "Big Eight" Independence Position. Baylor Bus. Stud. (11):7-27.
Reisch JT (2000). Ideas for Future Research on Audit Quality The Auditor's Report 24(1).
Remenyi D, Williams B, Money A, Swartz E (2002). Doing Research in Business and Management, London, SAGE Publications.
Rusmin R (2010). Auditor quality and earnings management: Singaporean evidence. Managerial Audit. J. 25(7):618-638.
Saunders M, Lewis P, Thornhill A (2007). Research Methods for Business Students, Fourth Edition, Prentice Hall.
Simunic DA, Stein MT (1996). The Impact of Litigation Risk on Audit Pricing: A Review of the Economics and the Evidence, Auditing: J. Pract. Theory 15 (Supplement):119-134.
Sarbanes-Oxley Act (2002). 117th Congress of United States of America. H.R. 3763.
Teoh SH, Wong TJ (1993). Perceived Auditor Quality and the Earnings Response Coefficient. Account. Rev. 68(April):346-366.
Titman S, Trueman B (1986). Information Quality and the Valuation of New Issues. J.Account. Econ. 8(2):159-173.
Watts RL, Zimmerman JL (1986). Positive Accounting Theory. New Jersey: Prentice Hall.
Wilson T, Grimlund R (1990). An Examination of the Importance of an Auditor's Reputation, Auditing: J. Pract. Theory 9(2):43-59.

4

Accounting reforms in the Middle East: A portfolio - returns approach

Jamal Barzegari Khanagha

Faculty of Economics, Management and Accounting, Yazd University, Iran.

This paper examines the value relevance of accounting information in selected Middle Eastern countries (Bahrain, Saudi Arabia and UAE) for the per-period and post-period of accounting reforms, which could describe the effect of accounting standards reform in these countries. The result obtained from portfolio approach shows accounting information is value relevant to investor in all selected stock exchanges. A comparison of the results for the periods before and after reforms shows an improvement in value relevance of accounting information after the reform in accounting standards in Bahrain and Saudi Arabia stock markets, while the results for UAE stock market shows a decline in value relevance of accounting information after the reform in accounting standards. It could be interpreted that following IFRS in UAE did not improve value relevancy of accounting information.

Key word: Value relevance, IFRS, accounting information, Bahrain, UAE, Saudi Arabia.

INTRODUCTION

Middle East countries have begun to implement economic reforms to stimulate private investment, promote economic growth and support the transition to market economy. Although, it is difficult to define the direct impact of the accounting system reform on economic transformation, as there are many other conditions that have influence on the transition process. However, with the central position of financial reporting and control in the economic system based on market economy, it is reasonable to assume that countries that are more effective in reforming the accounting system would move faster toward economic transformation (McGee, 2008). In this way, Middle East accounting bodies have experienced some major changes during the past several years. Prior to 1980, as a result of absence of accounting organizations there were no national accounting standards for countries in this region. Underdevelopment of accounting and auditing standards was one of the main problems for auditors' confirmative job and for investors in making investment decisions. For example, this was one of the main reasons for Kuwait's stock market crash in 1982 (Wagdy, 2001). Therefore, Middle East countries had to use accounting standards of other countries to start the process of making value relevant information. Development of accounting during this period was essentially a result of the influence of several economic factors: multinational enterprises moved in, international accounting firms entered, international financial institutions were licensed, expatriate accountants and foreign technology made a presence (Yapa and Wijewardena, 1995). After 1980 a number of important international forces created significant changes in the Middle East markets and accounting bodies. International economic/political interdependence, foreign direct investment and multinational corporate strategy, new technology, international financial markets, the growth of business services and activities of international regulatory organizations started to flourish. The core of these reforms was in the financial sectors, which enabled most of the Middle East countries to establish or resurrect their stock markets and improve the security market regulations. As a result of these steps, stock markets indicators such as market capitalization and foreign direct investment (FDI) to Middle East gradually increased. Khan (2006) indicates that criteria such as reliability, comparability and usefulness may be used to assess the quality of information for attracting FDI.

Wagdy (2001) asserts that investors' need for reliable and relevant financial information have been the key factors of accounting reform in the Middle East. These two factors protect domestic and foreign investors from any fraud or misleading financial data. However, value relevance approach measures both relevance and reliability because accounting information is reflected in the price (Barth et al., 2001).

Despite all efforts to develop financial markets, accounting and economic growth, a crucial gap in the literature still remains. To the best of our knowledge, there is no empirical research on identifying the effect of accounting standards reforms on value relevance of accounting information in this region. Consequently, this study aims to investigate the value relevance of accounting information in selected countries (Bahrain, Saudi Arabia and UAE). In particular, it measures whether the quality of accounting information in these countries has improved or whether it has not yet become relevant despite all efforts.

The remainder of this paper is organized as follows. The next section describes background and literature review. The third section discusses the methodology issues. Data and sample selection are presented in the fourth section. The fifth section sets out the findings of the research. Conclusions and suggestions for future research are discussed in the final section.

BACKGROUND AND LITERATURE REVIEW

A value relevance study is an evaluation of the relationship between accounting information and capital market values (market values). Beaver (2002) indicated that the theoretical groundwork of value relevance studies adopting a measurement approach is a combination of valuation theory plus contextual accounting and financial reporting arguments (accounting theory) that allow the researcher to predict how accounting variables and other information relating to market value will behave. Holthausen and Watts (2001) suggest that value relevance studies use two different theories of accounting and standard setting to draw inferences: (i) "direct valuation" theory and (ii) "inputs-to equity-valuation" theory. Direct valuation theory proposes a link between accounting earnings and stock market value. In direct valuation theory, accounting earning is intended to be either measured or be combined with the equity market value changes or levels. However, Zaleha et al. (2008) point out that the conclusion usefulness paradigm proposes that accounting information is useful if utilized by users of financial statements, or significantly associated with their decision making (Riahi, 2000) even though the information might not be stated at their best current value (Scott, 2000). Within this conception, the main users are those who make decisions having an impact on firms' value, specifically decision-making by capital market participants (Beaver, 2002; Belkaoui, 2000). Studies seeking to demonstrate a link between accounting numbers and equity values were first published over 40 years ago. The first of such article was by Miller and Modigliani (1966), who used data from the electricity industry to demonstrate that capitalized earnings from assets make the largest contribution to marketplace value. Ball and Brown (1968) and Beaver (1968) are generally recognized as the fundamental studies on the information value of accounting numbers. Ball and Brown showed that the information content of the earnings figure is related to stock prices, and Beaver observed both price and volume reactions to earnings reports.

Numerous value relevance studies have been established; one stream of literature focuses on whether the value relevance of accounting information has declined/increased over time. Prior research provides conflicting views. On the one hand, several prior literatures have found that the value relevance of accounting information has declined in recent years (Core et al., 2003; Ely and Waymire, 1999; Francis and Schipper, 1999; Graham and King, 2000; Ho et al,, 2001; Lev and Zarowin, 1999; Marquardt and Wiedman., 2004; Thinggaarda and Damkierb, 2008). On the other hand, A number of studies also have been carried out in recent years that showed value relevance of accounting information has increased (Qystein and Frode, 2007; Dung, 2010; Filip, 2010).

Among the literature documented for the Middle East region, there is some empirical evidence on Tunisian stock market (Ben Naceur and Goaied, 2004), Kuwait stock market (El Shamy and Kayed, 2005), Tehran stock exchange (Pourheydari et al., 2008), Saudi Arabia stock exchange (Alsalman, 2003), Egypt stock market (Ragab and Omran, 2006) and in some selected countries in MENA (Anandarajan and Hasan, 2010). The findings of these studies showed selected accounting factors have influenced the perception of investors, even though the effect of these factors was not the same in different markets.

In all research studies done, none was on the reform of the accounting standards in this reign. For example, Saudi Arabia reviewed and developed accounting standards over 1996 and 1999 (Saudi Organization for Certified Public Accountants). Bahrain Commercial Companies Law 2001 requires all companies to prepare their financial statements in accordance with the International Financial Reporting Standards, IFRs (Marat and Shoult, 2005). Moreover, all companies listed on the Abu Dhabi Securities Markets (ADSM) are required to publish IFRS financial statements since 2003 (Aljifri, 2008; Deloitte, 2007). And also to the best of our knowledge, there is no empirical research that uses regression-variations and the portfolio-returns approaches to test value relevance. Therefore, an evaluation of the value relevance of accounting information, especially after changes in the economic and accounting environment in recent years is an important area to research.

METHODOLOGY

In this study, the portfolio-returns approach was used to investigate and to operationalize the value relevance of accounting information. It was because they provide different perspectives on the issue of value relevance of accounting information. Portfolio-returns approach shows a portion of total returns that could be earned from financial statement information which control changes in the volatility of market returns over time.

The portfolio-returns approach defines the value relevance of accounting measures as the proportion of information in security returns captured by the accounting measures (Alford et al., 1993; Barzegari, et al., 2011; Chang, 1998; Francis and Schipper, 1999; Hung, 2001). Thinggaarda and Damkierb (2008) further defined value relevance as the difference between the return on the long position and the return on the short position; that is, the market-adjusted return that can be earned on the long position and the market-adjusted return that can be lost on the short position. This approach measures value relevance as the total return that could be earned from a portfolio based on perfect foresight of earnings. This study used two portfolios a) a portfolio selection based on sign (SIGN-ΔEARN, SIGN-ΔROE, SIGN-ΔCF) and b) a portfolio section based on sign and magnitude (ΔEARN, ΔROE and ΔCF).

Portfolio selection based on sign (SIGN-ΔEARN)

The Portfolio-Returns Approach is based on Alford et al. (1993), Francis and Schipper (1999), Hellstrom (2006) and Thinggaarda and Damkierb (2008). As an example, the following is the procedure for selecting a portfolio based on sign of changes in EARN. First, an earnings-based hedge portfolio is created. The primary Firm-specific return $(P_{it}-P_{it-1}+d)/P_{it-1}$ is calculated for all firms over a 15 month period. The market-adjusted return on security j, $R_{,t}$, is defined as the compound (with dividend) return minus the return on the value-weighted market portfolio for each year sample (The study uses all share index return). All companies in the total sample are ranked according to the change in accounting earnings. The change in accounting earnings is calculated on a yearly basis. A hedge portfolio is formed by going long in shares with positive earning changes and short in shares with the negative earning changes. The market-adjusted return is later calculated for both the long position and short position as an average of returns for all companies included in the long short positions, respectively:

$$R_L = \sum_{j=1}^{N_L} \frac{R_j}{N_L} \qquad R_S = \sum_{j=1}^{N_S} \frac{R_j}{N_S}$$

Where Rj is a market-adjusted return for an individual company and NL and NS are the number of companies in the long position and in the short position, respectively. Note that NL and NS are equal. The hedge portfolio return (value relevance) is defined as the difference between the return on the long position and the return on the short position: that is, the market-adjusted return that can be earned on the long position and the market-adjusted return that can be lost on the short position:

$$R_H = R_L - R_S$$

Second, for each accounting-based hedge portfolio and year, the market-adjusted returns on a portfolio formed on the basis of perfect foreknowledge of future stock returns are calculated. This portfolio takes long (short) positions in the stocks in each accounting-based hedge portfolio with positive (negative) 15-month market-adjusted returns. The market-adjusted return on this returns-based hedge portfolio in year t is denoted R_t^H where H is the type of accounting hedge portfolio. The accounting-based hedge portfolio returns are expressed as a percentage of R_t^H. This controls time-series differences in the variation in market-adjusted returns (Francis and Schipper, 1999), and the resulting ratio (denoted mkt%) describes the proportion of all information impounded in stock prices that is captured by accounting information in a given period (Thinggaarda and Damkierb, 2008).

Portfolio Selection based on sign and magnitude

As mentioned above, portfolio selection based on sign and magnitude applies to ΔEARN, ΔROE and ΔCF. The following is a description for calculating the value relevance of earning with this method. The method for calculating other factors with the same ROE and cash flow is similar. The primary calculations of market-adjusted returns are similar, based on the sign of accounting information. For example, for the ΔEARNjt portfolio, we take long positions in the stocks with the highest 40% of $\Delta EARN_{j,t}$ and short positions in the stocks with the lowest 40% of $\Delta EARN_{j,t}$; thereby, disregarding the middle 20%. Thus, both the sign and the strength of the change in earnings are extracted from the total available information in financial statements. The market-adjusted return is afterwards calculated for both the long position and short position as an average of returns for all companies included in the long short positions, respectively.

Data and sample selection

Selected countries (iBahrain, Saudi and UAE) qualify from many respects to be a good location for investment and doing business. In recent years, these countries have initiated reforms, especially in financial sectors, accounting and particularly in capital markets. Therefore, the study selected these countries because market participants in capital market need to know whether the value relevance of current accounting number is increasing or not.

Data for selected countries obtained from Gulfbase database, the stock exchange website of these countries and other database such as Bloomberg and DataStream. Observations were compared across data sources for data accuracy. The UAE sample is selected from Abu Dhabi stock market (ADSM) for the period 2001 through 2008; Saudi Arabia for the period 1993 through 2008; and Bahrain from the period 1996 through 2008. The number of companies selected was based on several criteria. First, since this study investigates the effects of accounting reform on value relevance of accounting information. It was necessary to have companies in existence both before and after the reform in order to examine the effect of the reform on the value relevance of accounting information. Therefore, companies that were listed just before or just after the reform were excluded. Second, for most companies in selected countries, the fiscal year ends in December. Since it was necessary to have a common period for the calculation of stock return accumulation across all the sample companies, whose fiscal years ended at some time other than December were excluded from the sample. Third, overseas companies listed in Bahrain stock exchange were excluded due to their different accounting standards and regulatory. Fourth, banks and insurance companies in Saudi are excluded due to their different accounting standards. In pursuant of the application of these selection criteria, the final samples for UAE consisted of 119 firm-year observations (17 companies for 7 years). The final samples for Bahrain consisted of 216 firm-year observations (18 companies for 12 years). The final sample for Saudi Arabia consisted of 640 firm-year observations (40 companies for 15years).

EMPIRICAL RESULTS

Table 1 presents the results of portfolio approach based on the sign of accounting numbers. The results obtained from the preliminary analysis of the value relevance of accounting information based on sign and yearly are presented in panel A of Table 1. The empirical results reveal the investigated period; the highest relevancy of accounting number belongs to ΔROE (74%) at 2004 in UAE. Lower relevancy (lack) belongs to ΔCFP (-75.9%) at 2002 in Bahrain. The results in Panel B of the Table 1 based on the sign clearly demonstrate that foreknowledge of information in the financial statements is relevant for investors in all selected countries. Investment strategies based on a preview of the sign of the change in ROE would earn a higher average market-adjusted return throughout the sample period in UAE (38.7%), Saudi Arabia (18%) and Bahrain (25.68%) than other accounting numbers. On the hand, investor based on a preview of the sign of the change in CFP would earn a lower average market-adjusted return throughout the sample period in selected countries. It means that investments based on accrual-based information are more profitable than cash based information.

The results in second and third column of panel B reveal that accounting information is value-relevant in both periods before and after reform in selected countries. In first period relevancy of ΔEARN information is more than others while in second period (after reform) relevancy of ΔROE information is more than others. A comparison of results shows value relevance of ΔCASH increased after reform in all selected countries, while value relevance of ΔROE and ΔEARN increased after reform but just in Saudi Arabia.

Table 2 presents results of portfolio approach based on the sign and magnitude of accounting numbers. The empirical results reveal the investigated period; the highest relevancy of accounting number belongs to ΔROE (76%) at 2005 in Bahrain. A lower relevancy (lack) belongs to ΔCFP (-49.4%) at 2007 in UAE. The results in Panel B of the Table 2 based on the sign and magnitude show that foreknowledge of information in the financial statements are relevant for investors in all selected countries. Investment strategies based on a preview of the sign of the change in ROE would earn a higher average market-adjusted return throughout the sample period in all selected countries. On the other hand, investor based on a preview of the sign of the change in CFP would earn lower average market-adjusted return throughout the sample period in selected countries. It means that investments based on accrual-based information are more profitable than cash based information. This conclusion is same as results of portfolio approach based on the sign.

The results in second and third column of panel B reveal that accounting information is value-relevant in both periods before and after reform in selected countries. In first period relevancy of ΔEARN information is more than others in Saudi Arabia and UAE while in second period (after reform) relevancy of ΔROE information is more than any other accounting number in all selected countries. A comparison of results shows value relevance of ΔCASH increased after reform in all selected countries, and value relevance of ΔROE and ΔEARN increased after reform in Saudi Arabia and UAE.

A comparison of the result based on two portfolio method shows that although the details of the results are not same, there are similar in conclusion and main results. Both of them show accounting numbers have value relevance in selected countries and reforms in accounting standards have effect on value relevancy of accounting information in these countries.

Conclusion

This paper has examined the impact of reforms in Selected Middle East countries on the value-relevance of accounting information in these countries. The value-relevance of accounting information is clearly supported by the current findings from portfolio approaches in the selected stock exchange. A comparison of the results for the periods before and after adoption, based on both regression and portfolio approaches, shows an improvement in value relevance of accounting information after the reform in accounting standards in Bahrain and Saudi Arabia stock exchanges, while the results for UAE stock market show a decline in value relevance of accounting information after the reform in accounting standards. It could be interpreted to mean that following IFRS in UAE did not improve value relevancy of accounting information. This may be due to the availability of only one year of data for model in the period before reform. This also may be because of economic conditions in country and world crisis in recent years.

Findings from this study are relevant to standard setters and regulators for future directions in developing accounting standards. The results may be helpful to investors for understanding capital markets of selected countries, and may also provide insights for accounting standard setters and regulators. Investors tend to be more tolerant of overvaluation when the economy and

Table 1. Portfolio-returns approach based on sign.

Year	Saudi Arabia						UAE						Bahrain					
	ΔEARN		ΔROE		ΔCFP		ΔEARN		ΔROE		ΔCFP		ΔEARN		ΔROE		ΔCFP	
	%	mkt%	%	mkt%	%	mkt%	%	mkt%	%	mkt%	%	mkt%	%	mkt%	%	mkt%	%	mkt%
1994	-1.4	-3.3	-2.9	-6.9	3.6	8.4												
1995	28.3	65.4	20.2	46.8	13.3	30.7												
1996	-1.2	-2.1	-6.8	-12.3	-6.4	-11.4												
1997	-2.8	-5.2	-3.1	-5.8	16.6	30.5							9.1	18.5	4.1	8.3	-12.8	-26.0
1998	-2.3	-2.6	-13.1	-14.6	15.3	17.0							16.0	43.6	14.5	39.3	-8.5	-23.0
1999	12.5	19.0	2.6	4.0	0.4	0.7							4.6	21.9	6.9	32.8	4.8	22.7
2000	19.7	32.0	19.8	32.3	23.0	37.5							12.5	25.7	11.7	24.1	-0.3	-0.6
2001	29.9	39.1	42.5	55.5	30.2	39.5							19.5	60.2	12.5	38.6	10.1	31.2
2002	1.6	3.2	8.2	15.8	23.9	46.2	19.4	58.1	15.1	45.1	-4.4	-13.3	-12.7	-25.0	-2.7	-5.2	-38.8	-75.9
2003	15.9	9.2	53.7	30.8	34.6	19.9	21.5	64.1	21.5	64.1	-7.3	-21.7	3.4	11.7	11.7	40.8	7.1	24.7
2004	64.6	57.5	36.9	32.8	-32.6	-29.0	-34.8	-22.6	114.	74.0	-11.1	-7.2	21.3	41.2	3.9	7.4	21.7	41.8
2005	30.2	27.9	10.2	9.4	-10.6	-9.8	30.5	42.4	-10.7	-14.8	-3.2	-4.5	17.3	32.4	15.3	28.7	-14.3	-26.9
2006	33.7	19.5	37.5	21.7	1.7	1.0	0.8	2.4	12.6	37.9	2.2	6.7	11.7	51.6	10.8	47.6	-3.5	-15.3
2007	-16.5	-26.8	-0.4	-0.7	-11.2	-18.2	49.4	49.2	46.5	46.3	-45.9	-45.8	-30.3	-89.5	-9.8	-28.9	-21.1	-62.4
2008	11.9	20.3	12.6	21.6	-2.3	-3.9	-3.3	-9.5	1.2	3.5	25.0	72.2	-1.6	-4.4	15.1	40.5	10.9	29.2

Year	Saudi Arabia						UAE						Bahrain					
	ΔEARN		ΔROE		ΔCFP		ΔEARN		ΔROE		ΔCFP		ΔEARN		ΔROE		ΔCFP	
	%	mkt%	%	mkt%	%	mkt%	%	mkt%	%	mkt%	%	mkt%	%	mkt%	%	mkt%	%	mkt%
T.Per	16.6	19.5	16.3	18.0	10.8	15.4	17.4	30.9	30.1	38.7	3.9	11.3	9.62	25.56	8.87	25.68	4.54	12.47
B.Re	6.8	14.1	3.8	8.5	8.2	14.5	19.4	58.1	15.1	45.1	0.0	0.0	10.6	27.40	9.30	26.11	1.20	5.68
A.Re	23.1	23.2	24.6	24.4	12.6	16.0	17.0	26.4	32.6	37.6	4.5	13.2	9.15	24.64	8.66	25.47	6.21	15.86

Panel A: Mean market-adjusted returns (MAR)on accounting hedge portfolio (%) and proportion of the total hedge portfolio MAR can be earned by the per-knowledge of accounting information(%mkt) based on Sign in selected countries. Panel B: Mean MAR on accounting hedge portfolio (%) and proportion of the total hedge portfolio MAR can be earned by the per-knowledge of accounting information based on Sign in selected countries. EARN= Earnings Per Share; ROE= Return On Equity Per Share; CFP= Cash Flow Per Share; T.per= total period; B.Re= Before Reform; A.Re= After Reform.

Table 2. Portfolio-returns approach based on sign and magnitude.

Year	Saudi Arabia						UAE						Bahrain					
	ΔEARN		ΔROE		ΔCFP		ΔEARN		ΔROE		ΔCFP		ΔEARN		ΔROE		ΔCFP	
	%	mkt%	%	mkt%	%	mkt%	%	mkt%	%	mkt%	%	mkt%	%	mkt%	%	mkt%	%	mkt%
1994	-7.0	-17.4	-7.0	-17.4	1.7	4.2												

Table 2. Contd.

1995	29.6	63.4	24.9	53.3	14.4	30.7												
1996	8.9	13.9	1.4	2.1	-5.0	-7.9												
1997	13.8	21.8	4.4	6.9	14.7	23.1							0.0	-0.1	-3.3	-6.4	-1.5	-2.9
1998	2.4	2.9	8.0	9.7	4.3	5.2							16.9	41.2	12.8	31.3	-8.5	-20.7
1999	21.0	26.6	10.6	13.4	-7.1	-9.0							-0.6	-2.7	-0.1	-0.6	-3.6	-15.7
2000	27.8	38.3	23.7	32.7	25.7	35.3							12.1	46.2	17.5	67.0	2.4	9.1
2001	48.0	50.6	45.4	47.8	36.1	38.0							25.4	68.1	16.6	44.5	12.4	33.3
2002	5.7	8.6	17.4	26.2	26.2	39.3	33.5	62.1	21.8	52.3	-2.2	-5.4	-9.9	-14.7	-16.1	-23.9	-1.4	-2.1
2003	-18.7	-7.6	54.9	22.4	-34.6	-14.1	10.9	27.7	24.7	62.9	-4.2	-10.7	4.3	12.3	8.2	23.9	5.0	14.4
2004	14.2	9.7	48.1	32.7	-14.2	-9.6	127.3	67.0	126.1	66.4	-18.4	-9.7	13.5	26.2	5.9	11.4	2.0	3.9
2005	39.3	35.7	29.0	26.3	-14.2	-12.9	19.5	22.4	31.0	35.7	11.1	12.8	10.4	32.8	24.1	76.0	-10.6	-33.2
2006	22.0	27.3	46.9	58.3	23.6	29.3	2.3	5.8	-4.6	-11.4	5.4	13.3	9.6	37.4	12.2	47.5	3.3	12.6
2007	-7.4	-9.2	-1.5	-1.9	0.2	0.3	-16.8	-15.4	8.7	7.9	-53.9	-49.4	-7.5	-18.3	-5.7	-13.8	-16.5	-40.4
2008	9.4	11.7	11.5	14.4	1.0	1.2	-5.3	-12.6	14.4	34.0	25.6	60.7	2.2	6.7	12.0	36.3	6.3	19.0

Year	Saudi Arabia						UAE						Bahrain					
	ΔEARN		ΔROE		ΔCFP		ΔEARN		ΔROE		ΔCFP		ΔEARN		ΔROE		ΔCFP	
	%	mkt%	%	mkt%	%	mkt%	%	mkt%	%	mkt%	%	mkt%	%	mkt%	%	mkt%	%	mkt%
T.Per	16.1	20.7	25.5	23.1	9.8	13.8	27.6	30.7	31.9	35.9	3.9	11.4	7.86	22.57	9.12	28.16	2.61	7.69
B.Re	12.6	21.4	8.2	14.2	5.8	10.5	33.5	62.1	18.4	44.2	0.3	0.9	7.23	21.84	7.58	24.58	0.59	2.26
A.Re	18.5	20.2	37.1	29	12.5	15.9	26.7	20.5	34.1	34.5	4.5	13.2	8.18	22.94	9.89	29.94	3.62	10.41

Panel A: Mean market-adjusted returns (MAR)on accounting hedge portfolio (%) and proportion of the total hedge portfolio MAR can be earned by the per-knowledge of accounting information(%mkt) based on Sign and magnitude for selected countries. Panel B: Mean MAR on accounting hedge portfolio (%) and proportion of the total hedge portfolio MAR can be earned by the per-knowledge of accounting information (%mkt) based on Sign and magnitude for selected countries. EARN= Earnings Per Share; ROE= Return On Equity Per Share; CFP= Cash Flow Per Share; T.per= total period; B.Re= Before Reform; A.Re= After Reform.

financial markets are doing well, and less accepting during bear market and economic slowdowns (Al-Hogail, 2004). Future research might consider the relationship between this measure and other macroeconomic measures, such as overall growth in the economy or total market performance, which might influence investors' behavior.

REFERENCE

Alford A, Jones J, Leftwich R, Zmijewski M (1993). The relative informativeness of accounting disclosures in different countries. J Account Res. 31:183-223.

Al-Hogail A A (2004). The Valuation Effect of Investor Behavior on the Relevance of Financial Information. Case Western Reserve University.

Aljifri K (2008). Annual report disclosure in a developing country: the case of the UAE. Adv. Int. Account. p.21.

Alsalman Ahmad M (2003). The Value Relevance of Accounting Numbers And The Implications For International Accounting Standards Harmonization: Evidence From Saudi Arabia And Kuwait. Florida Atlantic University, Florida.

Anandarajan A, Hasan Iftekhar (2010). Value relevance of earnings: Evidence from Middle Eastern and North African Countries. Adv. Account. 26(2):270.

Ball R, Brown P (1968). An empirical evaluation of accounting income numbers. J. Account. Res. (6):159-178.

Barth ME, Beaver WH, Landsman WR (2001). The relevance of the value relevance literature for financial accounting standard setting: another view. J Account. Econ. 31(1-3):77-104.

Barzegari kJ, Shamsher M, Taufiq H, Zulkarnain M (2011). The impact of reforms on the value relevance of accounting information: Evidence from Iran. Afr. J. Bus. Manag. 5(1):96-107.

Beaver WH (2002). Perspectives on Recent Capital Market Research. Account. Rev. (77):453-474.

Beaver WH (1968). The information content of eamings. J Account. Res. (6 (Supplement):).

Ben Naceur S, Goaied M (2004). The value relevance of accounting and financial information: panel data evidence. Appl Financ Econ, 14.
Chang J (1998). The Decline in Value Relevance of Earnings and Book Values: Wharton School University of Pennsylvania.
Core J, Guay W, Van Buskirk A (2003). Market valuations in the new economy: An investigation of what has changed. J. Account. Econ. 34:43-67.
Deloitte (2007). IAS Plus, 31 December 2007: New page for United Arab Emirates from http://www.iasplus.com/country/uae.htm.
Dung NV (2010). Value-Relevance of Financial Statement Information: A Flexible Application of Modern Theories to the Vietnamese Stock Market. Paper presented at the Development and Policies Research Center, Vietnam.
El Shamy, Kayed, Metwally A (2005). The Value Relevance of Earnings And Book Values In Equity Valuation: An International Perspective -- The Case Of Kuwait. Int J Commerce Manag, 15(1):68-79.
Ely K, Waymire G (1999). Accounting standard-setting organizations and earnings-relevance: Longitudinal evidence from NYSE common stocks, 1927–1993. J. Account. Res. 37:293-317.
Filip A (2010). IFRS and the value relevance of earnings: evidence from the emerging market of Romania. Int J Account Audit Perform Eval. 6(6):191-223.
Francis J, Schipper K (1999). Have Financial Statements Lost Their Relevance? J. Account. Res. 37:319-352.
Graham RC, King RD (2000). Accounting practices and the market valuation of accounting numbers: Evidence from Indonesia, Korea, Malaysia, the Philippines, Taiwan, and Thailand. Int. J. Account. 35(4):445-470.
Hellstrom K (2006). The Value Relevance of Financial Accounting Information in a Transitional Economy: The Case of the Czech Republic. Eur Account Rev, 15(3), 325-349.
Holthausen RW, Watts RL (2001). The relevance of the value-relevance literature for financial accounting standard setting. J. Account. Econ. 31(1-3):3-75.
Ho LC, Liu C-S, Sohn P (2001). The value relevance of accounting information around the 1997 Asian financial crisis-The case of South Korea. Working paper, University of Texas at Arlington.
Hung M (2001). Accounting standards and value relevance of financial statements: An international analysis. J. Account Econ. 30:401-420.
Khan M (2006). Statement provided by the Ambassador and Permanent Representative of the Islamic Republic of Pakistan on behalf of the Group of 77 and China. 10th Session of the ommission on Investment.
McGee RW (2008). Accounting Reform in Transition and Developing Economies. Springer Science , Business Media, LLC.
Marquardt CA, Wiedman CI (2004). The effect of earnings management on the value relevance of accounting information. J. Bus. Financ. Account. 31(3&4) :297-332.
Marat T, Shoult A (2005). Doing Business with Bahrain: A Guide to Investment Opportunities and Business Practice (Capter five, Accounting, Auditing and Taxation in Bahrain. by Doug Tait, KPMG).
Miller MH, Modigliani E(1966). Some estimates of the cost of capital to the electric utility industry, 1954-57. Am. Econ. Rev. (56):333-391.
Pourheydari O, Aflatooni A, Nikbakhat Z (2008). The Pricing of Dividends and Book Value in Equity Valuation: The Case of Iran. Int. J. Financ. Econ. (13):1450-2887.
Qystein G, Kjell K, Frode Sættem (2007). The Value-Relevance of Financial Reporting in Norway 1965-2004. Norwegian School of Economics and Business Administration, Norway.
Riahi BA (2000). Accounting theory (4th ed.). London: Thomson Learning.
Ragab.Aiman A, Omran.Mohammad M (2006). Accounting information, value relevance, and investors' behavior in the Egyptian equity market. Rev. Account. Financ. 5:279-297.
Scott WR (2000). Financial accounting theory (2nd ed.). Ontario: Prentice-Hall Canada Inc.
Thinggaarda F, Damkierb J (2008). Has financial statement information become less relevant? Longitudinal evidence from Denmark. Scand.J. Manage, in press.
Wagdy M, Abdallah (2001). Managing multinationals in the Middle East : accounting and tax issues: Quontm Books, 88 Post Road West, Westport, An imprint of Greenwood hblishing Group, Inc. Printed in the United States of America.
Yapa S, Wijewardena H (1995). The Development of Accounting Systems And Accounting Education in High Income Oil Exporting Countries: An Overview. Paper presented at the The University of Wollongong.
Zaleha AS, Muhd-Kamil I, Jagjit K, Hamezah MN (2008). The Value Relevance of Intangibles Non-Current Assets in Different Economic Conditions. Int. Rev. Bus. Res. Pap. 4 (2):316-337.

5

The challenges of innovations in Brazilian accounting: A study applied to the public sector

Rosaly Machado[1] , Dálcio Roberto dos Reis[2] and Antonio Carlos Francisco[3]

[1]Accounting Department, State University of Paraná, Brazil.
[2]Graduate Department of Production Engineering, Federal Technological University of Paraná, Brazil.
[3]Federal Technological University of Paraná (UTFPR), Brazil.

This study presented the challenges of the new approach, registration design and measurement and accounting control of the property of the public sector using the Brazilian Accounting Standards. These were applied to the public sector (NBCASP) 16.9 (2008), arising from the innovations of International Financial Reporting Standards (IFRS). The sample consisted of two institutions of public administration, one at federal level and the other at state level. The study revealed that there is a challenge that instigates the continuous innovation of activities. The research reveals that before these changes, there was no depreciation of fixed assets in public goods. Furthermore, the study shows that to lead this process of change and to implement the procedures, it will require a well structured system of physical control, using the register controls that already exist and innovating them according to requirements proposed by NBCASP 16.9. The survey also revealed that there are difficulties in interpreting the law of IFRS, due to lack of guidance on how to deal with the new accounting practices in public institutions.

Key words: Public accounting, International Financial Reporting Standards, innovation, standards, permanent assets.

INTRODUCTION

For many decades, corporate accounting in Brazil was ruled by Law No. 6.404/76 (Law of Societies, by accounting actions that lead the corporations in Brazil), which is currently going through a new stage, breaking paradigms conducted by accounting norms. This is made possible through the approval of Law No. 11.638/2007 (amending and repealing provisions of Law No. 6.404/64) that brought relevance to the financial statements after its enactment. This led to numerous changes caused by the adoption of International Accounting Standards, commonly known as IFRS (Iudícibus et al., 2010; Lima, 2011). Accounting is the language of business, expressed in monetary terms, an essential information for making decisions in domestic and foreign markets.

Recently, the trend of innovations also reached public account, which had its starting point with the publication of Microfinance Ordinance No. 184 of August 25, 2008 done by the Federal Government regarding changing devices applied to the public sector accounting. The ordinance leads to the observation of the guidelines by the public sector in relation to procedures, practices, preparation and dissemination of financial statements. This makes them convergent standardization of IFRS (International Financial Reporting Standards) to the Brazilian Accounting Standards applied to Public Sector (NBCASP), which was issued by the Federal Accounting Council (CFC). IFRS of public sector entities should present information that responds to the needs and knowledge base of users. For example, explanations of financial and non-financial information and commentary on service delivery and other achievements during the reporting period and expectations for future periods should be written in plain language, and presented in a manner that is understandable by users. Under-standability is enhanced when information is classified, characterized and presented clearly and concisely. Comparability can also enhance understandability (IPSASB, 2013).

The guidelines of convergence to international standards of Public Accounting were required from the Management of 2012, with the determinations of the International Accounting Standards Board (IASB) and International Standards on auditing and assurance issued by the International Federation of Accountants (IFAC).

Thus, the accounting applied to the public sector adhered to IFRS, and went through a unique moment, since this requirement has been granted by the interrelationship of business, and also by its users. Feijó (2011) reported that the standardization will allow the society to compare the financial statements of all entities (federal, states and municipalities). Along with the process of transparency of public accounts, it will enable societies and organizations (trade unions, NGOs, agencies) to better assess the management of rulers.

However, Coutinho (2010) describes in CRC MG Journal, "with the adoption of International Public Accounting in federal and state governments, accounting will provide a series of innovative rulers' information about financial position".

The model known as IFRS is present in over 110 countries; and in Brazil, the convergence is still in the process of adoption and adaptation. IPSASB (2013) reported that users of IFRS are assumed to have a reasonable knowledge of the entity's activities and the environment in which it operates; be prepared to read IFFRs, and to review and analyze the information presented with reasonable diligence. Some economic and other phenomena are complex and particularly difficult to represent in IFRS; and some users may need to seek the aid of an advisor to assist in their under-standing of them. All efforts should be undertaken to represent economic and other phenomena included in IFRS in a manner that is understandable to a wide range of users. However, information should not be excluded from IFRS solely because it may be too complex or difficult for some users to understand without assistance.

The identification of the criteria of IFRS to be satisfied for inclusion in the group reporting entity consistent with these principles will then be developed and fully explored at the standard level (IPSASB, 2013). Through this process, the need for change arises on the NBCASP 16.9 Depreciation, Amortization and Depletion, published on 21/11/2008, by the Federal Accounting Council through resolution of CFC No. 1.136/08.

According to the Manual of Patrimonial Procedures – MPP (2011), the public entity will have autonomy in adopting the annual depreciation rates, which will depend on the estimated useful life of each asset, which in turn is directly linked to the policy adopted by the entity in use of that part.

Research problem

According to Lima (2011), "Brazil presents salient features of low relevance as their accounting information, but is migrating to an accounting regime that is asso-ciated with a higher quality and transparency of information".

This report provides confirmation of the need for changes in accounting in public institutions. Before the adoption of 16.9, NBCSP did not practice procedures for preserving proper value of the assets, so that they remain with historical values (outdated), not a necessary feature for configuring the application of depreciation.

Severo and Oliveira (2012) said: "The accounting procedures of this sector, based on NBCASP and accounting principles, came as an essential guidance for the recognition of equity in government's accounting phenomena".

This leads to the problem of the search. There are the first procedures to be performed on the adoption of NBCASP 16.9, because adjusting the values of the fixed assets has certain complexity, mainly in the acquisitions made in previous years.

Justification of the study

This study is justified by the adoption of NBCASP 16.9 guidelines, which foster innovation in records of internal controls to protect public property, besides having greater transparency to the application of resources in society.

Severo and Oliveira (2012) reported that: "the adoption of the new accounting model for the public sector does not disqualify the budgetary regime provided by law, but surely represents a potentiality in terms of financial control, budgeting, and especially equity. Here, public managers, accounting professionals and society as a whole cannot see a way more abstract, but consistently and definitely, they see increasing standardization and harmonization of accounting globally".

There is the need for more discussion of issues related to public accounting, primarily with respect to recent changes, since there are few studies in this field for there to be a recent theme in Brazil. This hampers the development of techniques and improvement practices of public accounts.

Research objectives

The overall goal of this research is to check how the procedures of innovations requested by NBCASP 16.9 are being inserted into the Brazilian Public Accounting. And for the achievement of the overall goal, other specific points are :

a) Identify the difficult changes relating to the proposed NBCASP 16.9;
b) Analyze the criteria for determining the depreciation record of the property by monitoring the inventory of assets in comparison with the record of depreciation;
c) Check which financial statements will be changed due to the depreciation calculated.

The objectives of this research are intended to elucidate possible challenges in this new phase of transition of Public Accounting in Brazil.

Structure of research

This research begins with the introduction that covers the research problem, its justification and objectives. The next section is the research methodology and limitation of the study. Furthermore, there is literature review on changes in Public Sector Accounting, and after that, the results and conclusion of the study.

METHODOLOGY

This research is classified as an exploratory, qualitative and quantitative literature having a notorious contribution reviewed from various sources such as books, laws, manuals and internet. Triviños (1987) and Gil (1991)'s research purpose was to find out the procedures for the adoption of depreciation of NBCASP 16.9.

Samples of two government agencies were used; one at federal and the other at state level. From the samples studied, this work does not only aim to learn the routines of accounting entries themselves, but how these institutions are adapting to the deployment of depreciation on fixed assets.

The sample was defined by eleven professionals working in public institutions: State and Federal, located in the State of Paraná. The selection of respondents was based on the titration (Accountant, Bachelor of Science in Accounting, Accounting Technician), and also took into consideration if the role they play is somehow connected with the accounts.

In order to adapt to the new scenario of public accounting and meeting the new requirements, institutions formed in mid-2011, through internal control, a team called "Commission for valuation of assets and reassessment of their property values," formed by members of its staff. This committee started the objectives of gathering documents for the situation in the records of the property; checking the irregular records in regulatory agencies, conducting a survey of all assets; making necessary adjustments in accounting matters involving equity; reassessing values goods that are outdated, and finally accounting for depreciation.

Thus, data collection began with a probing documentary, based on materials collected and provided by the committee of two public institutions who worked on this research (Gil, 1991).

Shortly thereafter, in order to capture more data on certain aspects of the reality studied, open interviews were held, with free response questions (Oliveira, 2003), by the eleven professionals working in the accounting section of public institutions.

Following the collection of information, a questionnaire was designed with semi-open questions and open questions, which facilitated the interpretation of the information quickly (Gil, 1991). However, before the questionnaire was exposed, pilot test was done to see if there were understanding and clarity in the questions (Oliveira, 2003).

After the application of pilot questionnaire, the data obtained were then tabulated.

Limitation of survey

The limitation is that the work is theoretical. Because the subject of this work is being studied recently, there are few authors that deal with it, and it is restricted to law and accounting manuals applied to the public sector.

THEORETICAL

Regarding the Guidelines for Convergence to International Financial Reporting Standards applied to the Public Sector - IPSAS, Bergmann (2010) declares in the newspaper CRC MG, that its adoption "is realistic and achievable, but it is not fast. Transparency in public demonstrations is essential for governments that use or intend to use resources efficiently and effectively".

In Brazil, the initial approval of NBCASP, in view of Severo and Oliveira (2012), represents: "The appearances of new social demands that include demanding a new standard of information generated by the public accounts, and that its statements - essential part of the checks and balances of public managers - should be provided to its users and the whole society: a proper interpretation of equal changes in the public sector; monitor the budget process and the analysis of financial results and cash flow".

The issue of CFC Resolution No. 1.136/08, which approved the NBC T 16.9 - Depreciation, Amortization and Depletion, "became mandatory from the accounting year, 2012, which is the record of accumulated depreciation on fixed asset items" (MANUAL SIAFI, 2011).

Regarding the public registry of property assets, the T NBCASP 16.9 states that value depreciation, depletion or amortization shall be calculated monthly, with proper registration in the accounts of the income statement. And this should be recognized until the carrying amount of the asset is equal to the residual value. The residual value and useful life of an asset should be reviewed at least at the end of each financial year (Daros and Pereira, 2009).

Analyzing this, Silva (2011) points out that the financial statements of the public sector will have changes from the time the depreciation of fixed assets is included in their reports.

Above all, to meet the principle of competence, public entity must take ownership costs (depreciation) by using this vehicle monthly (Severo and Oliveira, 2012, p. 13).

According to MPP (2011), public entity will have autonomy in adopting annual depreciation rates, which depend on the estimated useful life of each asset, which in turn is directly linked to the policy adopted by the entity in the use of that right.

With the completion of the calculation of depreciation, and the effective registration of its launching in Public Accounting, changes will certainly occur in the Chart of Accounts, Balance Sheet,

Statement of Income in the Budget (DRE), the Statement of Changes in Equity (DVP) and Statement in the Indirect Cash Flow (Silva, 2011).

According to the Handbook of Applied Public Sector Accounting (MCASP, 2010), "the depreciation starts from the time the asset item becomes available for use". Therefore, it is necessary to form a basis for initial calculation. Thus, "the value of acquisition, production or construction includes an additional or complementary spending to the asset in place and operational conditions intended by management" (MOTA, 2009).

The residual value, in turn, was based on the percentage value, as quoted in SIAFI Manual (2011), where the property included in each ledger account has a useful life and residual value standard. But as for real estate, the depreciation shall be calculated solely based on the cost of construction, minus the value of the land.

Item 6 of the NBC T 16.09.08 provides that, "the impairment should be recognized until the net book value is equal to the residual value. So, even if the well is temporarily withdrawn from operation or becomes obsolete, depreciation does not cease" (MOTA, 2009).

However, not all assets are depreciated. According to Darós and Pereira (2009), NBCASP 16.9 enrolls assets that are not subject to depreciation regime as follows: Material products of cultural nature, such as works of art, antiques, documents, assets with historical interest, assets integrated into collections, among others; products of common use which absorb or absorb public funds, considered technically, with indefinite useful life; animals intended for exhibition and preservation; rural and urban lands.

According to the information of item 14 of NBC T 16.9 (2008), the following methods can be used to calculate depreciation charges: the straight-line method; method of sums of digits and the units of production method. This means that the accounting practices of the public sector need to direct a new way to fixed assets that need to be depreciated.

Feijó (2011) cites that the importance of NBCASP 9.16 is within the context of scare resources to social needs, managing public assets based on existing best practice processes for comparability between different managements.

IFRS providing innovations in public accounting practices

The adoption of an accounting standard implies a higher quality information; the informational asymmetries between investors and companies can be minimized and accounting will be contributing to resource allocation in the economy (Lima, 2011).

Innovative basic practices (essential) are simply responsible for all the waves of progress of the modern system. Sawhney[1] (2011), while participating in the HSM Innovation and Growth Forum, said, "it is necessary to enjoy the benefits of innovation, and that it makes institutions to have open mind and change their culture, be protective of their intellectual property, overcome internal barriers that can arise and try to set new mechanisms for innovation. In Brazil Accounting will adopt the International Accounting Standards, commonly known as International Financial Reporting Standards (IFRS) from 2008, with the enactment of Law No. 11,638 of December 28, 2007. The factors that are likely to signal the existence of users of IFRS either in a public sector entity or group of entities include: an entity that has the responsibility or capacity to raise or deploy resources, acquires or manages public assets, incurs liabilities or undertakes activities to achieve service delivery objectives. The greater the resources that a public sector entity raises, manages and/or has the capacity to deploy, the greater the liabilities it incurs and the greater the economic or social impact of its activities; the more likely there will exist service recipients or resource providers who are dependent on IFRS for information accountability and decision-making purposes.

In this context, Antunes et al. (2012) note: "The main innovation brought by this process of convergence to international standards is that the Brazilian accounting practices shall be much more based on interpretation of the pronouncements of the Accounting Pronouncements Committee (CPC) than the mere application of national rules, as in the recent past".

The convergence to International Financial Reporting Standards was applied in the public sector. According to Troiano [2](2011)'s report in the Journal HSM, management innovation is already the goal of most Brazilian managers, but the practice of creating a culture of innovation is still lacking in companies. Continuing, Troiano (2011) cites some essential tips for institutions to use to modify their internal environment for innovation:

1) Do not punish them for wrong decisions. Many companies lose their innovativeness by being afraid of taking risk; instead, create a work environment where working "outside the box" is something that is valued and desired.
2) Anticipate errors. Today's innovation is closely linked to the market rate; so the sooner you can face the possibility of error risks, the faster you can replenish them and come out on top.
3) Set goals for new ideas, products and services included in the business plan and let them represent a significant part of the operations of the institution.
4) Do not confuse innovation with technology. It is a very common error to think that only digital innovations are able to bring innovation to a company or brand.
5) Be innovative leaders. To be part of the routine of the teams, it is essential that innovation is, first of all, a goal for all executives of the institution.
6) Communicate. Being able to offer their products and services is the best way to demonstrate the innovative capacity of companies to the public. However, remember that aggregate marketing and communication by itself does not create an innovative company.

As seen, some tips help innovation strategies to be achieved in all governmental levels, for a greater focus on transparency of financial reporting sheet, which was put in second plan in public administration; prevailing only in the budget of accounting practice.

In this context, Jochen (2011) notes, "IFRS gave Brazil a greater volume of investment in international capitals, since convergence has brought greater confidence in the financial statements".

Thus, the scenario of management strategies is defined by the ability to recognize the goals to be achieved, as well as methods, concepts, principles and laws; after all, organizational guidelines arise from the need to innovate a set of priorities or factors that need changes.

In Reis' thoughts (2004), innovation does not mean having a great idea, but to identify the needs and problems of the market and transform them into a process operating in industry, commerce and service delivery.

According to Antunes et al. (2012), "The changes seek to improve the quality of accounting information, focusing mainly on its usefulness to the user; improvements to enhance understandability, relevance, reliability and comparability of disclosures, which are the qualitative and useful characteristics of accounting information".

For the innovation process to be successful in any type of

[1] Mohanbir Sawhney, Director and Professor of the Center for Research in Technology and Innovation at Kellogg School of Management will, of Northwestern University.

[2] Jaime Troiano. Innovation Specialist, President of Troiano Group in Branding.

organization, it is necessary to establish clearly where the change will occur, and what we must change.

However, Coutinho (2010) says that with the adoption of NBCASP, the public accounts under federal and state will focus more on equity and will provide a series of rulers' innovative information about the assets, revenues and expenses, focusing on the accrual basis. This important information is relevant to public managers.

Under the accrual basis of accounting, transactions and other events in financial statements are recognized when they occur, not only when cash or its equivalent is received or paid. Therefore, transactions and events are recorded in the accounting records and recognized in the financial statements of the periods in which they report (IPSASB, 2012).

Thus, by adopting the IFRS Accounting, the Brazilian public will submit a standard language in their reports; and is being used in several countries for reporting of financial statements and financial management.

DATA PRESENTATION AND ANALYSIS OF RESULTS

The research question is: What are the first procedures to be performed on the adoption of NBCASP 16.9? This is because the adjustment of the fixed assets values has certain complexity primarily to the acquisitions made in previous years. Accomplishing this task was entrusted to the commission created by the institutions, mainly for the acquisitions made in previous years. This is because the control sheet is done individually, and it takes time and resources.

The results showed that the pubic shareholders of both institutions were being treated in the background, only allowing the practice of accounting and financial budget to prevail.

Through the questionnaires and interviews, we were able to know how innovations requested by NBCASP 16.9 were inserted in public accounting.

The research identified that only three of the respondents attended courses/trainings, conducted in the Regional Accounting Council in Curitiba, in 2009 and 2011, which was conducted by auditors of the Court of the State of Paraná (TCE / PR). They aimed to standardize the actions to be developed in the state and federal agencies.

However, almost one third of the research participants said they did not participate in the courses for various reasons: lack of opportunity and information on courses conducted in this area in the region. This result demonstrates that it is necessary to seek assertions about the challenges presented by public managers.

When the NBC T 16.9 regulation was quoted (CFC Resolution No. 1.136/08), one of the respondents says it is properly instructed in relation to its content, but seven of the eleven respondents that have knowledge about the norm asked questions about its application and three did not have knowledge about the norm. Figure 1 presents the data in percentages.

The lack of information and internal controls in public administration are clear. The absence of these two prerequisites entails major management and material difficulties for closure of adjustments in order to start the calculation and recording of accounting for depreciation of public assets. Therefore, it was pertinent to illustrate an example of how to calculate the depreciation of fixed assets of the institutions under analysis, as directed by SIAFI Manual (2011) (Table 1).

Considering the releasing date of these vehicles and the starting date of their use to be equal, they can be impaired because of conditions placed in use from January 2010, thus representing a reliable monetary base.

According to the Manual SIAFI (2011), the period of useful life and residual value percentage for such property is fifteen years old (10%), although each of these goods has specific data values provided in the manual, leading to the standardization of criteria of organs.

Using the straight line method and in adherence to the principle of competence, depreciation is calculated based on the formula, and the data are arranged as follows (Table 2):

(1) Share of monthly depreciation = R $ 45,000.00 -R$ 4,500.00 = R $ 225.00 / month 180 months
(2) Share of monthly depreciation = R $ 30,099.00 - R$ 3,009.90 = R $ 150.50 / month 180 months
(3) Share of monthly depreciation = R $ 32,390.00 - $ 3,239.00 R = R $ 161.95 / month 180 months
(4) Share of monthly depreciation = R $ 21,988.00 - $ 2,198.80 R = R $ 109.94 / month 180 months
(5) Share of monthly depreciation = R $ 32,390.00 - $ 3,239.00 R = R $ 161.95 / month 180 months
(6) Share of monthly depreciation = R $ 66,142.50 - $ 6,614.25 R = R $ 330.71 / month 180 months

Splitting the difference between the acquisition cost and the residual value of the estimated useful life, we get the depreciation quota that will be recorded monthly. This quota is multiplied by the months that have not got depreciation yet (from the acquisition date to the end of 2011). This results in accumulated depreciation of previous years, and the year 2012 corresponds to multiplying the monthly amount of depreciation for the twelve months of the year. The sum of these two totals equals the total accumulated depreciation. Finally, the net book value corresponds to the value of the property recorded in the accounting, less accumulated depreciation.

ANALYSIS OF THE INFLUENCE OF DEPRECIATION IN RELATION TO THE FINANCIAL STATEMENTS

The influence of calculating depreciation modifies the

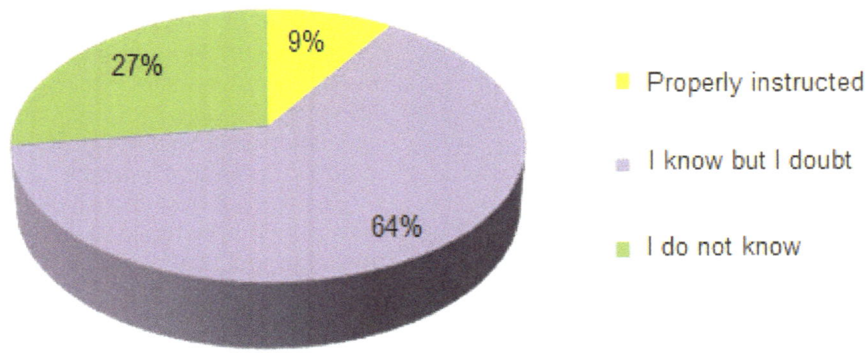

Figure 1. Knowledge on NBC 16.9 T.
Source: Data compiled by the authors.

Table 1. List of vehicles to be depreciated from 2012.

Item	Description	Nº Pat.	Launching date	Value (R$)
1	Truck, brand: Mercedes Benz/ model: 914, Year: 1997, Color: Red	41778	13/07/2011	45,000.00
2	Car, brand: Ford, model: Fiesta, 1.6 flex, 4 door, color: White	36226	05/03/2010	30,099.00
3	Car, brand: Ford, model: Fiesta/Sedan, Year: 2010, 1.6 flex, color: White, 0 km	39396	07/12/2010	32,390.00
4	Car, brand: Renault, model: Logan, 1.6- 16v, 4 door, Year 2008	42921	05/10/2011	21,988.00
5	Car, brand: Ford, model: Fiesta/Sedan, 1.6 flex, color: white	39484	27/12/2010	32,390.00
6	Van/Minibus, brand: Renault, model: Master 16v, 0 km	42923	05/10/2011	66,142.50
			Total	228,009.50

Source: Compiled by the authors, according to documents supplied by the institution.

Table 2. Calculation of monthly depreciation (items 1-6).

Item	Monthly depreciation (R$)	Accumulated depreciation (previous year) (R$)	Accumulated depreciation (2012) (R$)	Total accumulated depreciation (R$)	Net book value (R$)
1	225.00	1,350.00 (6 meses)	2,700.00	4,050.00	40,950.00
2	150.50	3,311.00 (22 meses)	1,806.00	5,117.00	24,982.00
3	161.95	2,105.35 (13 meses)	1,943.40	4,048.75	28,341.25
4	109.94	329.82 (3 meses)	1,319.28	1,649.10	20,338.90
5	161.95	1,943.40 (12 meses)	1,943.40	3,886.80	28,503.20
6	330.71	992.13 (3 meses)	3,968.52	4,960.65	61,181.85
	Total	10,031.70	13,680.60	23,712.30	204,297.20

Source: The authors.

chart of accounts. Through a cast of standardized accounts, it will facilitate the inclusion of new releases.

In the balance sheet, accumulated depreciation will be presented in a reductive account of non-current assets, in the subgroup of fixed assets, re-adjusting the value of the property in order to highlight its real value.

In DRE, operating expenses are registered through depreciation expense account, computing the monthly depreciation expense.

The depreciation in the DVP will be treated as a quantitative variation in item such as uses of products, services and consumption of fixed capital. Because the calculation of depreciation directly affects equity of public entities, it is considered as diminutive variation in equity DVP.

In the statement of cash flows, the depreciation will

only appear in the indirect method, and the cash flow from operating activities, because this method has cash flow to net income from operations (from the DRE). It adds up the values that do not represent cash disbursement, but that affect the outcome; better saying, depreciation is one of the adjustments that will be added.

Thus it is clear that depreciation will hit the financial statements of the institution in many ways, and should also disclose, for each class of asset, notes containing detailed information about the components of relevant depreciation, as determined by the NBC T 16.9.

Conclusion

The innovations that are happening at the research institutions of the public sector have a great impact in accounting, and providers, who will have to revise their concepts, need to be updated given the current context. The followings are fundamental: a wide transmission of knowledge and its standard application, through courses, seminars, orientations, the availability of consulting material, and the ability to show the real value of their assets, which are the object of accounting.

With the incorporation of patrimonial dimensions from the new accounting rules, society will be able to visualize, in the financial statements, the depreciation of fixed assets of the public sector.

The survey reveals some challenges in public institutions surveyed that must be overcome. Among them is the traditionalism that may possibly hinder large-scale innovative capacity of Brazilian institutions.

However, the main challenge found in this research is to converge public accounting to international standards. The lack of qualified professionals contributes to the delay of the actualization of this transition. The difficulties to be overcome for implementation must be recognized.

Other relevant factors found in this research is that public institutions are being challenged to move through the study of NBCASP 16.9, along with the process of raising equity, and later checking the accounting for depreciation in order for it to conform to current legislation. It is felt that the challenge is not only to understand the rule, but also to have information on public property, making strategic managers have confidence in making innovation to their teams.

REFERENCES

Antunes MTP, Grecco MCP, Formigoni H, Mendonça N, Otavio R (2012). The adoption in Brazil of international accounting standards IFRS: the process and its impact on the quality of accounting information. J. Econ. Int. Relat. São Paulo 10(20):5-19.

BRAZIL. Law No. 4320 of March 17, 1964. Stipulates general rules of law for financial preparation and control of budgets and balance sheets of the Union, the States, the Municipalities and the Federal District. Available at: <http://www.planalto.gov.br/ccivil_03/leis/L4320.htm> Accessed: 09 September 2012.

Bergmann A (2012). Report of the Regional Accounting Council of Minas Gerais. Journal of CRC MG. [online], Minas Gerais, Belo Horizonte. Year XVII. N.145. Sep/Oct 2010. http://www.crcmg.org Accessed

Brazil. Manual accounting applied to the public sector: applied to the Union, the States, the Federal District and Municipalities (2010). Valid for the year 2011. STN No. 664, of November 30, 2010. Part II - Accounting Procedures Sheets - 3. ed. - Brasília.

Coutinho WR (2010). Report of the Regional Accounting Council of Minas Gerais. J. CRC MG. http://www.crcmg.org Accessed.

Manual SIAFI (2011). Ministry of Finance. National Treasury. Manual SIAFI - Revaluation, Reduction to Recoverable Value, Depreciation, Amortization and Depletion in the direct administration of the Union Councils and Foundations. Brasília-DF, Oct 07. 2011. Available at: <http://manualsiafi.tesouro.fazenda.gov.br>. Accessed on: 18 Sep 2012.

CFC Resolution No. 1136 of November 21, 2008. NBC Approves T 16.9 - Depreciation, Depletion and Amortization. Available at: <http://www.cfc.org.br>. Accessed on: 27 Aug. 2012.

Federal Board of Accountancy (CFC) (2008). Principles and Brazilian Accounting Standards. Brasilia

Federal Council of Accounting (2012). CFC Resolution No. 1128 of November 21, 2008. NBC Approves T 16.1 - Concept, Purpose and Application Field. http://www.cfc.org.br.

Darós LL, Pereira AS (2009). Analysis of the Brazilian Accounting Standards Applied to the Public Sector - NBCASP: Changes and Challenges for Public Accounting. In 9th Congress Usp Controller And Accountant, 9. 2009, São Paulo. Anais ... São Paulo. USP.

Feijó PH (2011). Public sector prepares for Convergence. Transparency Magazine - IBRACON. São Paulo 1(1):42-45.

Gil AC (1991). How to design research projects. Sao Paulo: Atlas.

Iudícibus SD, Martins E, Gelbcke ER, Santos A (2010). Handbook of Corporate Accounting: applicable to all societies in accordance with international standards and the CCP. Sao Paulo: Atlas.

Jochen L (2011). Accounting for small and medium businesses - in accordance with international standards (IFRS) and the CPC. Curitiba: Ed Editorial Focus.

Internacional Public Sector Accounting Standart Board (IPSASB) The Conceptual Framework for General Purpose Financial Reporting by Public Sector Entities. January, 2013. New York. IFAC.

Lima JBN (2011). The relevance of accounting information and the process of convergence to IFRS in Brazil. Thesis (PhD in Accounting Sciences) - Graduate Program in Accounting, Department of Accounting and Actuarial Science, Faculty of Economics and Administration Accounting from the University of São Paulo.

Mota FGL (2009). Applied to the Public Sector Accounting. 1st edition . Brasilia: Public Management.

Oliveira ABS (2003). Methods and techniques of accounting research. Sao Paulo: Saraiva.

Reis DR (2004). Management of technological innovation. Sao Paulo: Manole.

Sawhney M (2011). Demystifying collaborative innovation. In: Forum HSM. Innovation and Growth. July/2011. São Paulo. Brazil. www.hsm.com.br / articles / demystifying-collaborative-innovation.

Severo RP, Oliveira SM (2012). Public Sector Accounting: A Focus on Measurement and Evaluation Heritage. In: XV SEMEAD. FEA - USP. Anais ... October 2012.

Silva LM (2011). Government accounting: a focus of the new administrative public accounting. 9th. Sao Paulo: Atlas.

Triviños ASN (1987). Introduction to social science research: qualitative research in education. Sao Paulo: Atlas.

Troiano J (2011). Innovation: competitive from start to finish. HSM Management. 14/02/2012 Access <http://www.hsm.com.br/editorias/inovacao/inovacao-competitividade-do-inicio-ao-fim>.

6

The role of accounting in public governance process

Lívia Maria de Pádua Ribeiro , José Roberto Pereira and Gideon Carvalho de Benedicto

Department of Administration and Economy, Federal University of Lavras, Brazil.

The intensification of the relations between government and society, whether by means of public-private interaction or of the participation of civil society, contributes to the appreciation of accounting in the scope of public administration. Accounting gains a new feature with this configuration. In addition to its basic capacities of registering and interpreting all phenomena, among which are public budgets, accounting may also provide citizens power and perform an active role in the socio-economic development of a country or a community. The main objective of this article is to analyze literature on accounting from the public governance context. Specific objectives are: to comprehend the role of accounting in the process of public governance, present the experiences in Brazil and present challenges of the accounting reform in Brazil. This investigation is characterized as a qualitative, descriptive bibliographic and documental research. In the documental research we analyzed normative instruction, law and the Federal Accounting Council in Brazil, all related to the functionality of accounting in Brazil and its accounting reform. This study demonstrates that accounting presents a potential to perform the role of strengthening democracy, social control, accountability, creating a social power in the dynamic process of public governance.

Key words: Public accounting, public governance, accounting reform.

INTRODUCTION

In previous years, the development of the financial and accounting information of the governments in countries such as Australia, Canada, France, Spain, United Kingdom and New Zealand has grown due to the influence of a culture based on a more transparent management, with larger control and emphasis on citizen (Pérez et al., 2005). A New Public Management (NPM) and public governance contributed so that the countries would implement changes in accounting, budget and accountability. Many studies reveal the influence of NPM in the academy, education and research in accounting area (Lawrence and Sharma, 2002; Parker, 2002; Roberts, 2004). After a series of administrative reforms, Brazil progresses to the implementation of an accounting reform aiming at a larger transparency and disclosure of governmental transactions. The need of the governments to provide reliable accounting information to all users is growing in Brazil. Administrative and accounting reforms, in addition to strengthening public accountability, incorporate a series of incentives to encourage a better management and provide better allocation of economic resources (Vicente et al., 2012).

This article's main objective is to analyze literature on accounting based on public governance context. Its specific objectives are to: 1) comprehend the role of accounting in the process of public governance; 2) present the experiences in Brazil; 3) present the challenges of the accounting reform in Brazil. A few questions orient this investigation: what is the role of accounting in the process of public governance? Public accounting for what and for whom? What are the main changes brought by the accounting reform in the

Brazilian public sector?

In order to perform the discussion proposed on this research, we studied national and international articles, in addition to investigating documents regarding Brazilian legislation on the matter.

We may verify that the accounting reform in Brazil has an arduous path to follow. However, larger transparency, responsibility, efficiency, effectiveness and economy are indispensable, especially in order to have better control of the public accounts, for the general benefit of all. In addition to transmitting information, accounting presents various utilities which contribute to strengthening the development of public governance. Brown (2009) and Chan (2010) state that accounting is capable of providing power to the citizens and perform an active role in the socio-economic development of a country or a community.

LITERATURE REVIEW

Accounting in the context of the new public management and public governance

Public governance has become a key concept in the public sector modernization (Kisser and Heidemann, 2006). However, the complexity of the "public governance" construct ensures that many use the expression without knowing exactly what it means. A widely usual and respected concept, derived from the Organization for European Co-operation and Development (OECD) (2001), refers to governance as development politics which are oriented by assumptions of: management, responsibility, transparency and legality of the public sector.

Bovaird and Löffler (2003) believe that public governance represents a new generation of administrative reforms of the State. For these authors, governance refers to the values and ideas of the New Public Management or Public Management Administration, characterizing an evolution of the term. New Public Management (NPM) propelled the administrative reform in various countries and has gained force, which made it known worldwide. According to Rhodes (1997), the debate of public governance is a consequence of the NPM movement. In Brazil, the influence of the NPM was preponderant for the administrative reform which created the Master Plan for Reforming the State (PDRAE), stimulating a management with less government and more governance. The PDRAE was the inductor to the growth of non-governmental organizations, executive regulative agencies in the Brazilian scenario. The non-governmental dimension is relevant to governance debate. There are no doubts that the emergence of these non-governmental players contributes to the development of public governance. According to Kooiman (1993), with this dynamic in society, governance is needed, providing interaction between public organizations, non-governmental organizations, citizens, public politics networks and private organizations, seeking solutions for collective problems.

Watkins and Arrington (2005) explained that the practices from NPM may be found all over the world. The authors acknowledge the importance of accounting and its expansion in the NPM process and American politics. They also mention that the NPM provided the development of various initiatives such as the reform program denominated National Performance Review (NPR), created in the 90s in the administration of Clinton and Al Gore. The NPR was oriented by the ideas from NPM which aimed at an administration with smaller cost, based on performance indicators financial goals and resource allocation rules. In the NPR, Vice-president Al Gore organized teams with the objective of identifying problems and offering solutions and ideas, implementing new practices which would diminish the costs and increase the profits of governmental activities (Watkins and Arrington, 2005). In order to achieve these objectives, it was necessary to examine the federal organs, such as the budget politics, its acquisitions and personnel contingencies. In this sense, the accounting practices were crucial in performing the objectives of the NPR. The report from NPR showed that it was necessary to issue a set of accounting norms in order to provide standards and methods for identifying, for example, the actual unit cost of government activities (Watkins and Arrington, 2005). In addition to the NPM, the new governance concept, emphasizing the financial responsibility of the governments, contributed to the changes in accountability, budget and accounting reforms in various countries, especially developed countries such as the USA and Europe. These reforms embody a series of incentives to encourage a better management and provide a larger economic resource allocation. In this context, accounting becomes an important tool for the constitution of responsible institutions (Pina et al., 2006). Even in less industrialized countries and those with low alphabetization rates, it is possible to find initiatives of citizen group capacitation by means of education on fiscal politics. Rahaman (2010) mentions the African governments in this challenging task and explains that accounting and technology have contributed to the democratic process.

The public governance approach defends deliberative democracy, the participative tools and the arrangements in which citizens may discuss public politic matters. Under this approach, different from the NPM, citizens are not only clients of the public administration, but are actively involved in various phases of the public politics cycle: elaboration, implementation, control and evaluation.

Public governance implies collaboration between government and citizens in all phases of the political cycle (Snijkers, 2005). In this context, Pina et al. (2006) explain that citizens are not subordinate to the government; citizens and government are in a relationship of equality, since they are seen as partners. In this sense, the government needs to have larger transparency and responsibility in the accountability dimension, promoting information disclosure and improvement in engaging citizens in public matters.

Public accounting for what and for whom?

Public accounting is a branch of accounting sciences with objective of registering, controlling, interpreting and informing the phenomenon which affects budget, financial and patrimonial situations of direct and indirect administration of the public entities, be them of the union, states, municipalities and federal district (Matias-Pereira, 2009). Public accounting is as important as the accounting applied to organizations of the private sector. However, in the past, public accounting was limited to accounting of public organs and it set aside using its information and controls in order to better conduct public negotiations. The information generated by accounting, according to Santos and Reis (2005), must be an instrument in the planning, budget (elaboration, approval study, execution and result evaluation), control and disclosure processes of the management performed in all societies, that is, accounting information does not concern only public organs.

In fact, accounting must fulfill its finality which, according to Iudicibus (2000), is "providing relevant economic information so that each user may make his own decisions and perform judgment securely". In this sense, this study raises a few reflections: "what is public accounting for and who does the public accounting information interest". The information provided by accounting does not have value if one does not know what it represents, if there is no interested user and if there is no use or credibility. The changes in paradigms, administrative reform and alterations in the legislation have revealed a new conscience, that in which public things concern all of the citizens. Public accounts are of interest to citizens, for they finance public entities by means of paying tributes and duties. According to Governmental Accounting Standards Boards (GASP) (1987), the three groups of users of accounting information in the public sector are: citizens; government and representatives; investors and creditors. In the works developed by GASP, citizen is evidenced as a part of the group of users of accounting information in the public sector.

If public accounting does not generate information, it will not be achieving its objective. Accounting, according to Iudicibus (2000), must generate information in lead time and be useful to its users. When the information is useful but not timely, it has only the effect of a "photograph" which informs a situation of the past, for it loses its validity in time. And when the information is timely but not useful, it is generating cost and rework for the public sector. Therefore, with the evolution of public accounting and of the acknowledgment of these users, emphasizing the citizen group, it is primordial to debate on the quality of the accounting information, which is also responsible for promoting public governance.

METHODOLOGY

In this section are presented the methodological procedures used in this study. This investigation is characterized as a qualitative research. The qualitative research may be defined as that which is based on analysis which, at first, does not use statistical tools in the interpretation of the data. The qualitative approach, that is, the qualitative investigation is most prone to guide this research, since the focus of this article is in comprehending facts more than in its measurements (Lazzarini, 1997). We highlight that the main objective of this article is to analyze the literature on accounting from the public governance context.

This research may also be characterized as descriptive, since it describes the role of accounting in the public governance process and the challenges of the accounting reform in the Brazilian public sector. In regard to the logic of the research, we used the inductive, that is, the theory will be formed from the empirical observation of reality. In this study, the theory will be formed from the observation of aspects of the Brazilian public governance process and the public accounting reform.

In addition to qualitative and descriptive, this research is considered bibliographical. Koche (2009) states that, in this type of research, the investigator makes a survey of the knowledge available on the area, identifying the produced theories, analyzing them and evaluating its contribution to aid in comprehending the object of the investigation. For the collection of the theoretical texts, we sought: the identification and selection of the pertinent bibliographical material; reading and annotations of the material with the purpose of identifying the central ideas; elaboration of a list of keywords to facilitate locating the themes at the time of writing; and analysis of the content of the noted material in order to elaborate the final considerations (Ferrarezi, 2011).

In order to perform the bibliographical research, we consulted the following bases of periodic portal of the Coordination of Improvement of Higher Education Personnel (CAPES): Web of Science (Thomson Scientific / ISI Web Services), Sage Journals Online, Science Direct (Elsevier) and Scientific Electronic Library Online (Scielo). A few of the periodic mentioned in this study did not use this selection criteria but were chosen for discussing a subject of interest of this investigation, that is, presented proximity to the theme and objective of the research. The main keywords of this investigation were: public accounting; public governance; and accounting reforms.

In this research, the data were collected by means of a bibliographical research and documental research. For Richardson (2008), "documental analysis consists of a series of operations which address studies and analysis in one or many documents in order to discover the social and economic circumstances with which they may be related." Thus, we analyzed the following documents in this research: normative instruction, law and resolutions of the federal accounting council in Brazil. All of the documents are related to the functioning of accounting in Brazil and its accounting reform.

RESULTS AND DISCUSSION

The results and discussion of this study are divided into two parts. The first presented the role of accounting in the governance process, presenting experiences in Brazil, such as the implementation of the Fiscal Responsibility Law (LRF) of the Computerized System for municipal accounts (SICOM), and of the by the Brazilian Accounting Standards Applied to the Public Sector (NBCASP), among others. The second part approached the challenges of the accounting reform in the Brazilian context.

The use of accounting in the Public Governance process

In previous decades, governments have tried to improve their accounting information systems in a manner to make them more useful, reliable, efficient and transparent. As a result, it is possible to verify important accounting reforms in different countries around the world (Christiaens, 2004; Darós and Pereira, 2009; Nasi and Steccolini, 2008; Pérez and López-Hernández, 2009; Ramadhan, 2009; Vicente et al., 2012). Carlin (2003) explains that public accounting is going through a period of changes. Seeking to provide public governance leads the international organisms to question the quality of the information and review the accounting practices.

Many studies such as the work of Daniels and Daniels (1991) and Pallot (1992) have highlighted the importance of accounting in the public sector with the needs to promoting public governance. Pallot recognized the paramount importance of accountability, of the democratic control over public resources, since the scenery needs to offer visibility to the citizen and emphasize the socio-political nature of accounting. Public governance paradigm announces that the public sector needs to strengthen its transparency; stimulate the participation of the citizens; reinforce its managerial capacity; orient and accompany contracts, partnerships and relations with the private sector and among the public sector, encouraging the formation of public networks for public interest. Along previous years, accounting has been assuming importance in other disciplines such as in problems regarding public politics and a simpler wider manner of management. Thus, we present a model noting the potential contributions of accounting for the development of public governance and its possible results in this process (Figure 1).

Performing registry, classifying and controlling patrimony which concerns the citizens;

For Silva and Felix (2012), accounting aims at fulfilling control capacity performance planning, registry and classification. Silva and Félix (2012) explain that for an effective accounting control, accounting must perform registry faithful to all operations and point out irregularities, seeking to preserve the patrimony of the entity (be them city halls, public organs) which concerns the citizens. The accounting survey in the public sector refers to the following premises: “a) all operations must be accounted for; b) the operations must be related to the entities’ purpose; c) the accounting documentation must be filed; d) all accounting release must be done after the exam or control of the proof or document” (Félix, 2012). According to the authors, the accounting survey includes: bookkeeping, accounting verification, inspection and information.

Bookkeeping is the permanent registry of the public entity which allows the monitoring of the modification which reaches the patrimony and in chronological order of events. Accounting verification corresponds to inventory, determination of the results and balances. Inventory consists of verifying the characteristics of goods, rights and obligations. In this sense, it is important to highlight the classifying capacity of the active, passive and patrimony accounts, aiming at better control and management. Inventory constitutes physical and accounting survey. The balance permits the user to know the patrimony under a static point of view and the demonstration of the result shows the composition of the receipts, costs and expenditures within a dynamic conception. The inspection is directly related to the auditing and aims at inspecting if all the operations were correctly accounted, if all the releases are accompanied by bona-fide documents, if all the operations are in accordance to the law (Silva and Félix, 2012). Information, according to Silva and Félix (2012), is the central point of accounting. For these authors, knowing and studying types of users is an obligation of all governmental institutions and those responsible for the accounting system in the scope of the public sector. Information is directly related with transparency, a basic premise of a responsible management and which seeks a better interaction between the State and the citizen.

Displaying (disclosure) the accounting information in an accessible and transparent manner providing the citizens with a better vision of the *res publica* management

Many studies such as Christiaens (2004) and Ramadhan (2009) have pointed out that the emphasis in patrimony

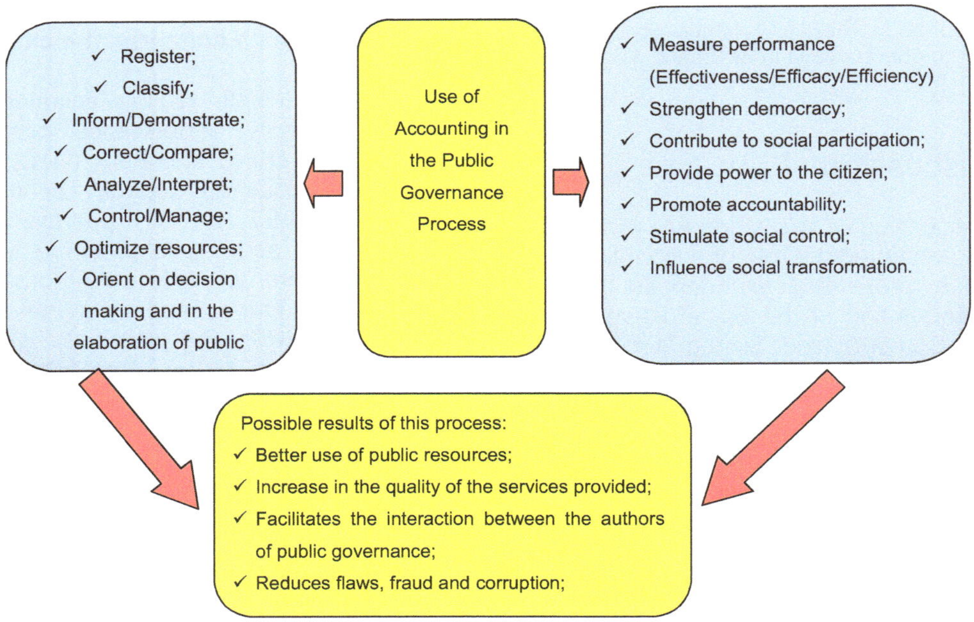

Figure 1. The potential contributions of accounting in the development of public governance and its possible results in this process. Source: Elaborated by the authors.

by public accounting is a preponderant factor for perfecting the accounting disclosures in the public sector. The emphasis in patrimony presents information more compatible to reality. In this sense, the adoption of depreciation, amortization, exhaustion accounting; the registry of intangible goods and those of common use; the evaluation and measuring of goods at market value and the acknowledgment of passive contingents provide the users of accounting information a better view of public management.

In democratic regimes, citizens' access to information is guaranteed by law. In Brazil, this right is assured by law no. 12,527 of 2011. The internet is a tool which facilitates the disclosure of public accounting information to the citizens. The use of Information and Communication Technologies in public administration has strengthened with the New Public Management movement and also with the pursuit for a good governance, emphasizing the importance of transparency in accountability (Lee et al., 2011).

Accounting presents an important role, since it can demonstrate the results in values and qualitative gains. People are not interested only in the monetary values; they also want to know the result which affects the life of citizens. For example, if a city fore sought the spending of US$ 100,000 in a year in school transportation and actually invested US$ 100,000 during the year, this information is not enough for the population. Citizens want to know the result. Therefore, did this US$ 100,000 meet the established goal for school transportation, which was 100% of the students enrolled in public schools? If of the established goal, only 80% of the students enrolled were assisted because the other 20% of the students live in rural areas with difficult access, demanding more investment in order to fulfill the goal, then there is deficiency; that is, the goal in monetary value was met, but in the qualitative scope, it was found wanting. This information may be generated by accounting and in a manner which provides larger transparency to the citizens and a better view of the *res publica* management.

Correcting deviations capable of affecting the equilibrium of the public accounts by means of developing efficacy, that is, seeking to fulfill the objectives fixated in the action programs and performing a comparison of the results actually obtained with those foreseen

Public accounting exercises an important role in controlling public accounts. In Brazil, the publication of the Fiscal Responsibility Law (LRF) impacts public accounting. The alterations in public finances induced by the LRF directly reach public accounting, suggesting the need for adaptation. The LRF adds the Fiscal Management Report (RGF) and the rendering of accounts, reinforcing the demand for the Summary Report of Budget Execution (RREO) which is elaborated with information produced by public accounting (Complementary Law no. 101/2000).

The Computerized System for municipal accounts (SICOM), tool conceived by a few audit offices of the Brazilian states, contribute so that the monitoring of the municipalities' accounting be monthly. Previously, accounting was presented every two months, four months or annually. With the implementation of the SICOM, many municipalities came to perform the monthly monitoring of the budgetary execution. Presenting the information almost at real-time strengthens accounting, reinforcing its preventive action, identifying flaws which may be corrected in time (Normative Instruction n. 10, 2011).

Silva and Félix (2012) highlight the importance of comparing the accounting data of same entities and between entities of the same sector, showing the financial economic situation of the entity along time. Machado and Holanda (2012) explain that comparative analysis is relevant to the public sector since it "facilitates the identification of inefficiencies and opportunities of cost reduction; the evaluation of results and performance, as well as benchmarking and low added value activities".

Evaluating the results under the aegis of the efficiency and economy of public expenditures, operationalizing at the minimum cost possible

Matheson (2002) states that accounting reform is one of the most current subjects in the world of public management. The new paradigm highlights the importance of accounting costs in the public sector. In the Brazilian context, the LRF and NBCASP establish that a cost system which allows the evaluation and monitoring of budgetary, financial and patrimonial management be implemented.

Most of the Brazilian public entities do not allow the identification of the precise costs of each activity and project. In reality, what occurs is the definition of costs based on a value referent to previous budgets. The new era of public accounting values the verification of costs in an accurate manner, seeking efficiency and economy (Baracho, 2000; Machado and Holanda, 2012). Population gains with the optimization of public expenditures. In addition to the benefit of the better use of public resources, the verification of costs contributes for the citizens to have larger knowledge of the actual expenditures of public administration.

Orienting public politics

To Machado and Holanda (2012), there is a direct relationship between public politics, resources, activities and cost objects. The authors mention that the "definition of public politics is the main determinant of cost in the public sector, from which derive the programs and actions, as well as the identification of the resources necessary to execute them". Graham (2010) states that accounting has contributed for the construction of public politics, such as the investigation performed in retirement politics in the Canadian system. Graham's study contributed to the debate and comprehension of the role of accounting in the definition of public politics over age and the preparation of the citizens to old age.

Many studies (Miller, 1990; Neu, 2006; Rose, 1991) have demonstrated that the relation between numbers and politics is mutually constitutive. According to Rose (1991), the exercise of politics depends on numbers. In addition, the image of the political life is molded by the reality which numbers seem to reveal. Rose (1991) explains that economy is evaluated by means of numbers. Poverty may also be demonstrated by numbers and, consequently, the claims for social benefits may also be transformed in numbers. Rose (1991) investigates accounting, noting it to be an instrument which makes modern government possible. However, there is a paradox in this context. At the same time in which numbers reach a privileged status in public politics, they may lead to the depoliticisation of politics and public spaces. Depoliticisation may occur with the use of specialized and technical knowledge and compromises the efficiency of the participation of civil society. A research performed by Fonseca et al. (2012) reveals that, though the presence of specialized and technical knowledge may constitute an obstacle for participation, there is no way to empty or reduce the space of the knowledge. Emptying the specialized and technical element may generate loss in regard to the quality of acts and deliberations emanated from a political process. Therefore, the path is to democratize accounting, develop the theory and promote the practice which aid accounting changes and transformation in the socio-political context in a more just society (Brown and Dillard, 2012).

Strengthening democracy and promoting empowerment of the citizen

Dellaportas and Davenport (2008) explain that in the 1930s, accounting was an obscured term and unknown to the public. Almost half a century later, little had changed. In 1970, accounting still did not have a direct influence over human relations. In the 1990s, accounting became of public interest, emphasizing social obligations, welfare and norms which reinforce the importance of public service. According to Dellaportas and Davenport (2008), in this context accounting aims at protecting the economic interests of third parties, facilitating an efficient and effective decision and guaranteeing collective happiness and welfare. Miller (1990), Neu (2006) and Rose (1991) illustrate how accounting data are presented in the public spaces and in democratic processes, and how these data have the potential of changing public spaces and empowering citizens.

Cosenza et al. (2012) discuss the power of accounting and the power over accounting. In the first situation, the authors explain that accounting "becomes an instrument capable of providing power to individuals who understand the issue it contemplates, since accounting provides visibility over what happens in various organizational scopes. The criticism done in regard to the power accounting may provide to its users is exactly in the scope of democratization. However, accounting in organizations and society, while bringing ideas which are difficult to understand and strange to the language and common epistemology, may restrict this power (González, 1999). In the second situation, Cosenza et al. (2012) express the power over accounting. For these authors, there is also "the accounting dependence to decisions emanated from the dominant economic and social structures and those historically established, such as State politics, capitalist spirit, ethnical and social cultures and traditions". The influence of the International Financial Reporting Standards (IFRS) or Generally Accepted Accounting Principles (USGAAP) in the accounting practices applied worldwide is an example of the dependency of accounting to the structures.

Promoting responsibility (accountability) of the auditing activity of public managers to the society

To Nakagawa et al. (2007), accountability is the reason accounting exists. The authors mention the case of a merchant in the year of 3250 b.C., who traveled to make business and left merchandise and money (silver) with his agent. When returning, he would ask for an audit in a just and legitimate manner. This responsibility in auditing is related to the concept of accountability. Thus, accountability may be interpreted as a purpose of accounting (Leemans, 1950; Nakagawa et al., 2007).

In the public sector, accountability refers to the obligation of the public agents (servers, managers and politicians) of auditing their acts, informing society on the use of public resources. In addition to the duty of auditing (answerability), accountability includes the power to impose sanctions to those who violate their obligations (Bovens, 2007).

In Brazil, the code of the best corporative governance practices published by the Brazilian Institute of Corporate Governance (IBGC) presents basic principles such as transparency, equity, auditing, corporative responsibility that, according to Slomski (2005), are also applicable to organs and entities of public administration. This code may reinforce the potential of accounting which is promoting responsibility of auditing to society.

Providing information and guarantee procedures for the instrumentation of social control, encouraging the supervision of public expenditures by society and stimulating social participation in budgetary planning and execution processes

One of the instruments that public administration relies on to perform the capacity of control is accounting. Be in internal or external control, accounting may exercise this capacity enabling useful, consistent and quality information. Accounting uses managerial or operational control, book and documental, becoming the best and most efficient instrument in the control of Brazilian public administration (Silva, 2004).

Mendes et al. (2008) explain that the initial mark of public accounts in Brazil occurred in 1988, with the creation of the homepage entitled "public accounts" (www.contaspublicas.gov.br) on the internet. After almost a decade, in 2005, it evolved into the "Transparência Pública" homepages (public transparency), obligating the organs and entities of federal public administration to transmit detailed information on the budgetary and financial execution, in order to feed the data base in this portal. This action guarantees disclosure of accounting information from the federal organs.

According to studies performed by Coelho et al. (2011), "accounting information assures popular participation, in order to achieve a responsible fiscal management politic". According to these authors, accounting is an important tool for exercising social control. Rocha (2011) states that "social control is the means by which citizens know where public resources are being allocated to". For Rocha (2011), the control and surveillance of public resources are indispensable instruments for the construction of a more equal and just society. Also according to Rocha, Brazil needs to overcome the myths of social control, such as that which says the population has no interest or capacity in supervising. It is necessary to change the Brazilian scenery which is among the most unequal societies in the world, not for lack of richness, but for lack of justice. The corruption and passivity of the Brazilian people are strongly present in the reality of the country. This shows that accounting still has a large challenge ahead to contribute to the construction of social control.

The Office of the Comptroller General (CGU), which is a Brazilian organ and aids the presidency in regard to public patrimony and management transparency, has adopted measures which encourage the use of accounting as an instrument in various acts and programs. Among the measures adopted, we may mention: a) the construction of websites of public transparency; b) the implementation of the "Olho Vivo no Dinheiro Publico" program (Keeping an Eye on Public Money Program); c) the program of surveillance by raffle of the cities; d) the creation of magazines and the celebration of agreements with universities; e) the creation of a public transparency council and battle against corruption (Office of the Comptroller General, 2013). All these measures use information generated by accounting in order to stimulate social control.

Performing an active role in social transformation

A research developed by Bryer (2011), in cooperatives located in Buenos Aires, Argentina, by means of analyzing material from ethnographic documentation, demonstrates an involvement of accounting practices in worker collaboration dynamics. The accountability regarding the cooperatives manifests identity and collectiveness in these organizations. The information contained in the accounting reports unleashes a change in the workers' attitude and behavior. After verifying the accounting reports, the workers comment in meetings that they need to be more socially responsible, improve their efforts, and accompany their competitors in order to obtain better results. Bryer's research shows that accounting practices incorporate and express many objectives and values. His study highlights that accounting does not serve to identify the result but it may also contribute to planning other activities. In the cooperatives studied by Bryer, instead of reflecting only an economic reality, accounting represents organizational meanings, leading the workers to question their needs, propose projects that may benefit the community inside and outside of the organization. Accounting is not only a technique; there is an interaction between accounting and the individuals. In the same manner in which accounting interferes in social relations, social structures also affect accounting (Ahrens and Mollona, 2007). While analyzing documents and social interactions, Bryer (2011) identifies that accounting practices may distort communication but also stimulate people to clarifying their concerns by means of constituting a social consensus.

The studies performed by Sargiacomo and Gomes (2011) acknowledge accounting as a technical and social practice, with implications of the organizational and social operation. While investigating local government accounting, the authors verified that is causes an impact in the planning and control process of local community activities. Accounting is relevant in social transformation and socio-economic development process. In addition, accounting also presents potentialities which may promote human development (Molisa, 2011).

The challenges of accounting reform in Brazil

The modifications brought on by the Brazilian Accounting Standards Applied to the Public Sector (NBCASP) in Brazil, in 2008, aim to adapt to the international standards of the International Public Sector Accounting Standards (IPSAS) of the International Accounting Standards Board (IASB) and of the International Federation of Accountants (IFAC). NBCASP aims at providing uniformity to the reports, so that these may be interpreted by various professionals in different countries (Ferreira and Marchesini, 2011). In addition, the new changes make accounting demonstrations more transparent and bring larger responsibility to public management, elevating its efficiency and efficacy (Xavier et al., 2010).

The main changes brought by these new rules regard patrimony disclosures. A criticism to public accounting is the emphasis it attributes to budgetary execution to the detriment of patrimonial disclosure. With public accounting new reality, patrimony gains relevance, adopting: accounting of depreciations, amortizations, exhaustion; registry of intangible goods and those of common use; implementation of the cost system; evaluation and measurement of goods at market value; evaluation of management risks; new demonstrations such as cash flow, economic result and patrimony mutations; consolidation of the demonstrations; among others (Brazilian Resolution of the Federal Accounting Council n. 1.121, n. 1.128, n. 1.129; 2008). The results of the research performed by Vicente et al. (2012) show that public accounting in Brazil has sought to better disclose their actives and passives, including the contingents. The Brazilian accounting reform opens possibilities for acknowledgement, evaluation and presentation of State activities, resources which values did previously not match reality; such is the case of real estate, infrastructure and common used goods.

The studies performed by Xavier et al. (2010) show that NBCASP affects the informational capacity of the accounting reports elaborated by a public entity, allowing a larger understanding of the demonstrations and transparency of expenditures, also allowing the obtaining of information of how much is raised and spent in Brazil. Ferreira and Marchesini (2011), while analyzing the alterations and innovations inserted by the NBCASP, highlight that "these changes will bring institutional strength of the public entity, offering the citizen a management of transparent resources, with relevant information of the application of money raised by tax and rate collecting". These studies highlight the importance of the role of public accounting in this new reality which requires the participation of the citizens in the implementation of public politics and social control.

The discussion of the harmonization of the accounting

norms has the purpose of improving and perfecting public accounting, aiming at a larger transparency, accountability and control, that is, it seeks to promote public governance. The next by the Brazilian Accounting Standards Applied to the Public Sector (NBCASP) in the Brazilian Resolution of the Federal Accounting Council n. 1121/2008, highlights the importance of public accounting in providing the users with information, aiding the process of decision making, adapting to accountability in order to support the orchestration of social control. In addition to the financial bias, in this new rule, public accounting is also responsible for informing physical and qualitative aspects of the patrimony of the entity in the public sector (Carvalho, 2010). Darós and Pereira (2009) explain that these new changes range aspects of patrimonial accounting, devices referent to cost implementation, amplification of accounting control, elevation of law efficiency and effectiveness (LRF and Law n. 4320 of 1964) regarding the objectives of promoting planning, transparency and responsibility of fiscal management. The new norms have the purpose of bringing public accounting to the new reality of the world, which requires larger transparency and social control. This reality also demands that the professionals acting in the area of public accounting participate in the decisions in the entities' strategic scope. NBCASP's larger concern is performing the convergence of the norms, seeking information quality. NBCASPs are legal instruments to promote public accounting reform in Brazil. Vicente et al. (2012,) state that with the new reality and the new public administration models, the proposals for reform in the accounting applied to the public sector seek to point solutions which correct this structural problem and accompany the evolution of the theories which deal with the State's performance over the administration of resources originated from citizens' contribution.

NBCASP adopts the regime of competence for public patrimony accounting; promotes the distinction of public budget and accounting; alters accounting demonstrations, expanding government fiscal transparency; institutes the cost system, uses depreciation, recognition of intangible actives, contingent passive and the evaluation of non-financial actives such as real estate and infrastructure (Vicente et al., 2012).

The theme of public accounting reform is current in the world of public administration in many countries of the Organization for Economic Cooperation and Development (OECD). According to Dees and Neelssem (2004), countries such as the United States of America, New Zealand, Australia, United Kingdom and Sweden were pioneers in adopting the regime of government budgetary competence and in public accounting. Brazil is in the process of accounting reform. After the NBCASP edition in 2008, the public entities are adapting to the new reality. A first sight, accounting reform seems to restrict itself in technical discussions. However, Matheson (2002) argues that accounting practices have deep implications for the growth of a nation and are key elements to obtain good governance.

Conclusion

In Brazil, after the influence of the NPM and public governance, a few initiatives of the accounting reform are already visible, even if not consolidated. Such changes are capable of providing comparisons of the results achieved by the governments in expanding the quality of accounting disclosure. The expectancy after adopting the norms is that accounting may report the financial economic situation of public entities and governments in a more precise and transparent manner.

The theme of public accounting reform is current in the world of public administration in many countries. Many countries have already adopted the regime of competency in government budgets and public accounting. Brazil is in the process of an accounting reform. This study shows that the accounting practices have deep implications for the growth of a nation and are key elements to obtain good governance. On the other hand, we criticize that the accounting practices and mechanisms not always seem to be capable of promoting governance. With accounting not meeting reality (without depreciations, amortizations, exhaustion, etc.) and lack of accounting information to make decisions and supervision, how will it be possible to promote public governance? This is the new challenge to public accounting: to becoming more transparent and useful, giving more responsibility to public management, aggregating larger value and stimulating all groups in society. It is possible to verify that many countries, including Brazil, are already performing accounting reforms, seeking better quality of accounting information and, consequently, good public governance.

The current context of the world demands higher quality of accounting information, which has unleashed accounting reforms. Accounting has been criticized for not presenting information in quantity and quality according to its users' desire, especially in regard to citizens' user group. On the other hand, this study performs a reflection on the potentialities of accounting in perspective of public governance, demonstrating the use of accounting in this process. The accounting systems are adapting to the new demands of public governance, which might be seen with the standardization of accounting aiming at transparency, credibility and accountability.

This research presents a contribution for the field of accounting, in the sense that the increasing citizen conscience requires that the professionals of the area use the accounting practice aiming at a better disclosure of its use and employment of public resources. The new context discussed in this study shows that public accounting may perform a relevant political and social work, from the moment in which updated demonstratives be elaborated, which would disclose with quality, efficacy, efficiency and economy the public expenditures in favor of society. In addition, the research may contribute to awaken discussions and reflections on the importance of accounting information for society, which has been shown, in this new time, intolerant to bad management, fraud and waste. In Brazil, this intolerance may be proven with innumerous population manifestations, which take the streets in many states of the country in 2013. The legislation and awareness of the population has been stimulating the disclosure of accounting information of public resources in order to provide more transparency, governance and involvement of the entities, associations, non-governmental organs and the citizen in social control. This study reinforces the relevance of accounting in public and democratic spaces, stimulating a reflection on its influence in empowering the citizen, promoting social control and the transformation of society. With the needs in this scenery, we realize that accounting is important, since when imagining how these contexts would be without accounting, we would certainly find social disorder, absence of control and confusion in the decisions regarding public politics. This is what may be seen when the immense potential of this science is not used or using inadequately. It resides in the hands of professionals and academics of the accounting area, to contribute to the improvement and expansion of accounting capability in the socio-economic development of a Nation.

The present study points to the need of performing empirical research on public accounting practices, which contribute to promoting public governance. Investigation in this domain is still scarce. We suggest that future investigations perform empirical studies using the model presented in this study, by testing accounting potentials and identifying the results.

REFFERENCES

Ahrens T, Mollona M (2007). Organizational control as cultural practice: a shop floor ethnography of a Sheffield steel mill. Accounting, Organizations and Society, 32: 305-331.

Baracho MAP (2000). A importância da gestão de contas públicas municipais sob as premissas da governance e accountability. Revista do Tribunal de Contas de Minas Gerais, 34 (1): 129-161.

Bovaird T, Löffler E (2003, september). Evaluating the quality of public governance: indicators, models and methodologies. International Review of Administrative Sciences, 69 (3): 313-328.

Bovens M (2007). Analysing and assessing accountability: a conceptual framework. European Law Journal, 1 (4): 447-468.

Bryer AR (2011). Conscious practices and purposive action: A qualitative study of accounting and social change. Critical Perspectives on Accounting, in press, available online 5 december.

Brown J, Dillard J (2012). Critical accounting and communicative action: on the limits of consensual deliberation. Critical Perspectives on Accounting, in press, available online 2 october.

Carlin TM (2003). Accrual Accounting & Financial Reporting in the Public Sector: Reframing the Debate. MGSM Working papers in management, http://papers.ssrn.com/sol3/papers.cfm?abstract_id=473643. Retrieved 12/20/2013.

Carvalho D (2010). Orçamento e Contabilidade Pública (5a ed.). Rio de Janeiro: Elsevier.

Chan JL (2004). As NICSPS e a contabilidade governamental de países em desenvolvimento. Revista de Educação e Pesquisa em Contabilidade, 4 (1): 1-17.

Christiaens J (2004). Capital assets in governmental accounting reforms: comparing Flemish Technical Issues with International Standards. European Accounting Review, 13 (4): 743–770.

Coelho MC, Cruz F, Platt AO Neto. (2011). A informação contábil como ferramenta de auxílio no exercício do controle social. Contabilidade Vista & Revista, 22 (3): 163-184.

Controladoria Geral da União, http://www.cgu.gov.br. Retrieved 12/20/2013.

Cosenza JP, Teixeira AC Filho, Lopes RSS (2012). Reflexões sobre relações entre poder e contabilidade. Contabilidade, Gestão e Governança, 15 (2): 78-94.

Daniels JD, Daniels CE (1991). Municipal financial reports: what user´s want. Journal of Accounting and Public Policy, 10 (1): 15-38.

Darós LL, Pereira AS (2009, julho). Análise das normas brasileiras de contabilidade aplicadas ao setor público – NBCASP: mudanças e desafios para a contabilidade pública. Congresso de Controladoria e Contabilidade da USP, São Paulo, SP, Brasil, 9.

Dees M, Neelissem P (2004). Five countries pioneering accrual budgeting and accounting in central government. Int. J. Audit. 31 (1): 11-15.

Dellaportas S, Davenport L (2008). Reflections on the public interest in accounting. Critical Perspectives on Accounting, 19, 1080-1098.

Ferrarezi CJ (2011). Guia do trabalho científico: do projeto à redação final: monografia, dissertação e tese. São Paulo: Contexto.

Ferreira AB, Marchesini CF (2011). A contabilidade pública em face da padronização contábil. Revista Científica Semana Acadêmica, 1 (5): 1-14.

Fonseca IF, Bursztyn M, Moura AMM (2012). Conhecimentos técnicos, políticas públicas e participação: o caso do Conselho Nacional do Meio Ambiente. Revista de Sociologia e Política, 20 (42): 183-198.

González CL (1999, enero-junio). Perspectivas alternativas de investigación em Contabilidad: una revisión. Revista de Contabilidad, 2 (3): 103-131.

Governmental Accounting Standards Board (1987). Objectives of Financial Reporting, http://www.gasb.org/cs/ContentServer?site=GASB&c=Document_C&pagename=GASB%2FDocument_C%2FGASBDocumentPage&cid=1176160039864. Retrieved 01/10/2013.

Graham C (2010). Accounting and the construction of the retired person. Accounting, Organizations and Society, 35: 23-46.

Instrução Normativa n. 10, 16 de dezembro de 2011. Dispõe sobre a remessa, pelos Municípios, dos instrumentos de planejamento e das informações relativas à execução orçamentária e financeira por meio do Sistema Informatizado de Contas dos Municípios – SICOM, http://www.tce.mg.gov.br/IMG/Legislacao/legiscont/Instrucoes%20Normativas /IN_2011/IN-10-11.pdf. Retrieved 01/10/2013.

Iudícibus S (2000). Teoria da Contabilidade (6a ed.). São Paulo: Atlas.

Kisser L, Heidemann FG (2006). Governança pública: novo modelo regulatório para as relações entre Estado, mercado e sociedade? Revista de Administração Pública, 40 (3): 479-499.

Koche JC (2009). Fundamentos de Metodologia Científica: teoria da ciência e iniciação à pesquisa. Petrópolis: Vozes.

Kooiman J (1993). Modern governance: new government-society interactions. Newbury Park, Calif.: Sage.

Lazzarini SG (1997). Estudo de caso para fins de pesquisa: aplicabili-

dade e limitações do método. In: Farina E. et. al. (Coord.) Estudo de caso em agribusiness. São Paulo: Pioneira.
Lawrence S, Sharma U (2002). Commodification of education and academic labour using the balanced scorecard in a university setting. Critical Perspectives on Accounting. 13: 661–677.
Lee C, Chang K, Berry FS (2011). Testing the development and diffusion of e-government and e-democracy: a global perspective. Public Administration Review. 71 (3): 444-454.
Lei complementar n. 101, de 04 de maio de 2000. Estabelece normas de finanças públicas voltadas para a responsabilidade na gestão fiscal, http://www.planalto.gov.br/ccivil_03/leis/LCP/Lcp101.htm. Retrieved 01/10/2013.
Machado N, Holanda VB (2012). Custos no setor público: Diretrizes, modelo conceitual e processo de implantação (a partir da experiência do Governo Federal). In N. Machado, V. B. Holanda, J. F. Ribeiro Filho, J. Lopes & M. Pederneiras (Org.). Gestão Baseada em Resultado no Setor Público: uma abordagem didática para implementação em prefeituras, câmaras municipais, autarquias, fundações e unidades organizacionais. São Paulo: Editora Atlas.
Matheson A (2002). Better public sector governance: the rationale for budgeting and accounting reform in western nations by. In: Organisation for Economic Co-operation and Development – OECD (Org.). Models of public budgeting and accounting reform (pp. 37-46).
Matias-Pereira J (2009). Finanças públicas: a política orçamentária no Brasil (4a ed.). São Paulo: Atlas.
Mendes RC, Oleiro WN, Quintana AC (2008). A contribuição da contabilidade e auditoria governamental para uma melhor transparência na gestão pública em busca de combate contra a corrupção. Sinergia, 12 (2): 37-48.
Miller P (1990). On the interrelations between accounting and the state. Accounting, Organizations and Society, 15 (4): 315–338.
Molisa P (2011). A spiritual reflection on emancipation and accounting. Critical Perspectives on Accounting, 22: 453-484.
Nakagawa MM, Relvas TRS, Dias JM Filho. (2007). Accountability: a razão de ser da contabilidade. Revista de Educação e Pesquisa em Contabilidade, 1 (3): 83-100.
Nasi G, Steccolini I (2008). Implementation of accounting reforms: an empirical investigation into Italian local governments. Public Management Review, 10 (2): 175-196.
Neu D (2006). Accounting for public space. Accounting, Organizations and Society. 31: 391-414.
Organisation for economic co-operation and development (2001). Local partnership for better governance, http://www.caravanafs.ccina.ro/PDF/DFS/dfs41.pdf. Retrieved 01/10/2013.
Pallot J (1992). Elements of a theoretical framework for public sector accounting. Accounting, Audit. Accountability J. 5 (1): 38-59.
Parker L (2002). It's been a pleasure doing business with you: a strategic analysis and critique of university change management. Crit Perspect Acc. 13: 603–619.
Pérez CC, López-Hernández, AM (2009). Governmental financial transparency in MERCOSUR member countries. International Review of Administrative Sciences, 75 (1): 169-181.
Pérez CC, López-Hernández AM, Bolívar MPR (2005) Citizens´ Access to on-line governmental financial information: practices in the European Union countries. Government Information Quarterly, 22: 258-276.
Pina V, Torres L, Acerete B. (2007). Are ICTs promoting government accountability?: A comparative analysis of e-governance developments in 19 OECD countries. Critical Perspectives on Accounting, 18 (5): 583-602.
Ramadhan S (2009). Budgetary accounting and reporting practices in Bahraine governmental units: An empirical study. Internacional Bus. Rev. 18 (2): 168-183.
Resolução do Conselho Federal de Contabilidade n. 1.121, 28 de março de 2008. Aprova a NBC T 1- Estrutura conceitual para elaboração e apresentação das demonstrações contábeis, http://www.cfc.org.br/. Retrieved 01/10/2013.
Resolução do Conselho Federal de Contabilidade n. 1.128, 21 de novembro de 2008. Aprova a NBC T 16.1- Conceituação, objeto e campo de aplicação, http://www.cfc.org.br/. Retrieved 01/10/2013.
Resolução do Conselho Federal de Contabilidade n. 1.129, 21 de novembro de 2008. Aprova a NBC T 16.2- Patrimônio e sistemas contábeis, http://www.cfc.org.br/. Retrieved 01/10/2013.
Rhodes RAW (1997). Understanding governance: policy networks, governance, reflexivity and accountability. Buckingham: Open University Press.
Richardson RJ (2008). Pesquisa social: métodos e técnicas. São Paulo: Atlas.
Roberts R (2004). Managerialism in US universities: implications for the academic accounting profession. Crit Perspect Acc. 15(4/5): 461–467.
Rocha Z (2011). Os Tribunais de Contas e os desafios para a promoção do controle social. Revista Tribunal de Contas do Município do Rio de Janeiro. 46: 4-11.
Rose N (1991). Governing by numers: figuring out democracy. Accounting, Organizations and Society, 16 (7): 673–692.
Sargiacomo M, Gomes D (2011, august). Accounting and accountability in local government: contributions from accounting history research. Accounting History. 16: 253-290.
Santos AR, Reis JAG (2005, outubro). A importância da contabilidade pública. Encontro Latino Americano de Iniciação Científica e Encontro Latino Americano de Pós-graduação, Universidade Vale do Paraíba, PB, Brasil, 9 e 5.
Silva LM (2004). Contabilidade governamental: um enfoque administrativo (7a ed.). São Paulo: Atlas.
Silva LM, Félix CL (2012). Contabilidade aplicada ao setor público: a base do controle. In N. Machado, V. B. Holanda, J. Ribeiro Filho F, J Lopes, Pederneiras M (Org.). Gestão Baseada em Resultado no Setor Público: uma abordagem didática para implementação em prefeituras, câmaras municipais, autarquias, fundações e unidades organizacionais. São Paulo: Editora Atlas.
Slomski V (2005). Controladoria e Governança na Gestão Pública. São Paulo: Atlas.
Snijkers K (2005). E-Government, intergovernmental relations and the citizen. European Group of Public Administration, 1–2.
Vicente EFR, Morais LM, Platt AO Neto (2012). A reforma na contabilidade pública brasileira e o processo de convergência: implicações e perspectivas. Revista de Informação Contábil- RIC, 6 (2): 01-20.
Watkins AL, Arrington CE (2007). Accounting, New Public Management and American Politics: theoretical insights into the National Performance Review. Critical Perspectives on Accounting, 18 (1): 33-58.
Xavier AE Jr, Paulo E, Silva JDG (2010, junho). Estudo sobre a capacidade informacional das novas estruturas das demonstrações contábeis aplicadas ao setor público. Congresso da Associação Nacional dos Programas de Pós-Graduação em Ciências Contábeis – ANPCONT, Natal, RN, Brasil. 4.

7

Consideration about global finance crisis and solution offers

Ece Demiray Erol

Faculty of Economics and Administrative Sciences, Celal Bayar University, Turkey. E-mail: ecehan.erol@hotmail.com.

Global financial crisis that started from financial markets of the United States of America, has affected many countries and refreshed the old macroeconomic ideas. At the endpoint of crisis, reorganization of national financial markets will not be enough, while at the same time, strong economic policy implementations will come into the forefront. The coordination between developed countries regarding the monetary policy for the solution of global problems is necessary. Constraints on international capital fluences and decrease of debt rates in Euro zone are also necessary. Solution for economical problems is possible with just common operations. In a lot of countries, deficiency in balance of payment occured, taxes for households was placed and saving policies came into the forefront. In spite of increase in assistance from the ınternational monetary fund (IMF), effects of global crisis could not be eliminated.

Key words: Global financial crisis, monetary policy, treasury policy, global market, finance market, debt rate, global liquidity.

INTRODUCTİON

Japan's crisis of 1989, Asia's crisis of 1997, Turkey's crisis in 2001 , global financial crisis which started from the USA in 2009 and the financial tragedy of Greece, are all indicators of a continuation of international crisis.

These crises, which started in the middle of the 1980's, were based on the expansion of monetary and financial policies (Schratzenstaller, 2011). The quest for a cure for the outbreak of crisis has caused a drop in the short term interest rates of developed countries to 0 point and an increase in global debt rates to a record level. Rescue plans about monetary and treasury policies, as seen with the last global crisis, necessitated the consolidation process, because the wealth of liquidity in global markets will create new economic crises, the amount of debts of countries will enlarge and this situation will lead to the instability of Central Banks. The end of lax monetary and treasury polices have 4 important points (Borio and Disyatat, 2009):

i. Governments must retract guarantees to the banks and leave civilization policies. Public budget balance should be provided with these steps.

ii. In accordance with the foresight of ECB (European Central Bank) and European Governments, retraction of governments from finance and asset markets should be done with the coordination of countries.

iii. The new attempts about crisis induced monetary policy require international studies and specially a co-ordination with America. Otherwise, the success of monetary and treasury policies of European countries is dependent on timing and common implementation ability.

iv. And the last point is European Central Bank's buying operation of public bonds for stability of EU (European Union). In the year 2009, European Central Bank left nontraditional monetary policy and allowed the bonds, which lost their value due to the Euro crisis, to be reflected in ECB's balance.

GLOBAL COORDINATION OF MONETARY POLICY

In the presence of global monetary expansion, monetary policy coordination between countries is important, because devaluation of national currencies is inetivable with expansion due to the introduction of speculative capital. In many countries in this situation, exchange markets have been regulated and the exchange demand and supply rate being monitore to achieve a balance. Imported inflation induced deformation can be experienced in local financial or asset markets.

Different monetary policies in developed economies complicate the exit from global crisis. Undervalued monetary policies lead to inflation expectations or deflation. Effects of idle infleunces on global liquidity expansion will affect the finacial and asset markets inside countries (Roth, 2009). Eventually, deformations in local fiscal and asset markets may occur.

GLOBAL LIQUIDITY EXPANSION AND UNCERTAINTY

Effects of idle influences on global liquidity expansion is seen mostly in national treasure and asset prices. Belke and Rees (2009) studied the effects of global shocks on national economical policies or world economy with VAR Analysis. Between 1984 and 2007, global liquidity shocks in G7 countries affected the power of national and global economic development (Belke and Rees, 2009; Belke and Schnabl, 2010).

In accordance to structural refraction test analysis, global liquidity shock increased estate prices, but became more important as a function of national and global development. Global liquidity gives information about monetary values, like monetary policies of Central Bank or risk factors that does not depend on interest rates.

Belke and Rees (2009) proved complication in national monetary policy implementation due to globalization. Idle fluencing global liquidity reduces the effectivity of national monetary policies on real or nominal variables. For example, the negative effects of global surplus of liquidity on national interest rates (Belke and Rees, 2011).

The important question is “how can the monetary policies in coutries, which depend on each other, be coordinated”. Chicago doctrine starts from the variable exchange rate stage, and so, can eliminate the imported problems about macro economy. As a result of this, there is no need for internationally coordinated monetary policies. İncreasing liquidity surplus requires international coordination. For example; if FED implements lax monetary policy, foreign Central Banks will carry some parts of cost because of liquidity fluence or surplus. The main problem is how to coordinate the unlogical monetary policies of Central Banks in the international arena and how to eliminate the liquidity surplus which can occur in the future.

Success in the coordination of economical policies or an attempt at applying foresight can asist the global financial solution. Consequently, the foundation of World Central Bank is has researched the idea and believes that the independent monetary policies of this bank can minimize the global problems. through this medium, the effects of global crises on countries can also be minimized.

GLOBAL DEBT POLİCİES

After the international financial crisis, the biggest debt was incurred by the United States of America. From 2007 to the end of 2009, the financial obligation of USA rose from $ 3916 billion to 12867. In approximately 5 years, the financial obligation of USA will rise to about $ 5.000 billion (Schmid, 2011).

For this reason, America is one of the major partners of the international coordination of financial problems. Otherwise, global liquidity surplus is due to the monetary policy of America. Price stability in Euro zone and possible crisis in Asia will be due to financial fluences in middle term. consequently, many countries started to control capital fluences in order to balance the international financial fluences (Belke and Schnabl, 2010).

So far, FED has raised discount limitations symbolically and with this, it has shown that it did not leave its traditional monetary policies. Central Banks of many countries did not consciously take the monetary and treasure policies against inflation seriously. consequently, devaluation in these countries damaged the economic stability (Spahn, 2007).

Aizman and Marion (2009) proposed the seperation of inflation from public debts (Belke and Schnabl, 2010). If the economy of the USA does not rise again, inflation and public debts seperation will manifest itself. After the 2nd World War, public debts of America was 122% of its GNP in the year 1946. After 10 years, public debts decreased to 50% by devaluation. Repeat of this policy is inevitable for USA, because too much debts have been borrowed from abroad. 44% of public debt bonds of USA is held by foreigners. Most of this bonds are held by China and Japan, and would lose its worth because of inflation.

INTERNATIONAL DEBT CRISIS AND CHINA

In the year 2010, rescue operations were implemented in Euro zone with billions of dollars. Inflation rates of Euro zone will increase in comparsion to USA. If European Central Bank would take international capital fluences seriously, ECB can allow the inflation rate increase in order to protect the image of its trusted monetary policy. Investors will prefer dollar to Euro because of this debt crisis in European countries, and this progress will push up the Euro exchange rate. Global acceptance of the dollar will cripple the Euro in days to come.

On the other hand, China criticizes the lax monetary policy of USA. Lax monetary policy renders speculative investments desirable, like estate market and stock markets. This situation prevents global development. FED creates weak dollar with low interest rates, this results in cost decrease on the debt of other countries, especially China. China, the biggest payee of USA, worries about depreciation of US dollar due to enlargement in debt stock. Imported credit enlargement, due to dollar, prevents Chinese Public Bank's credit supply reduction policy in order to stabilize the estate and stock exchange markets. Monetary policy of Chinese Public Bank became dependent on American monetary policies (Schmidt, 2009).

If China allows the yuan to increase in value, the export of China will decrease and at the same time, large amount of US dollar deposits on Chinese Public Sector will loose their value. In this case, Chinese Government will be led into a political dilemma. On the other hand, economic development of China depends on the presence of additional speculative investments.

Europaen Central Bank implemented the monetary policy of FED and kept track of this policies. However, there is disbelief in East Asia, Russia, OPEC countries and other countries. As a result of the presence of this disbelief, FED will perhaps abandon the lax monetary policy and give power to US dollar with the aim of empowering it to become world currency.

The power balance of the Euro, injured by European Countries in debt paradox, and dollar, which will be crippled in future, will make its presence felt. In spite of all negations in Euro zone, European Central Bank's intent of protecting its stabilization oriented monetary policy will contribute to the provision of monetary stabilization for both euro zone and countries in the hinterland of the dollar region. Existing debt crisis of Greece, Portugal and Spain in euro zone, injured Euro in contrast with the dollar. Inflation expectations in the euro zone increased the uncertainty that heralds, its presence in every area and featured common finance and monetary policies.

MONETARY POLICIES AND INSTITUTIONAL STRUCTURE

The study of Belke and Rees in 2009 demonstrated that, global liquidity surplus would lead to an increase in prices of raw materials and estate market. The increase of raw material prices is perceived as front indicator of prospective increase in inflation rates (Belke and Rees, 2011; Belke and Schnabl, 2010).

If the governments in euro zone supply bonds consistently and the banks rediscount this bonds again with European Central Bank, this case indicates a liquidity surplus in market conditions. Unless the expander monetary policy gets abandoned, it is not possible to avoid expansion in finance markets and monetary policies (Spahn, 2007).

Figure 1 clearly shows outrageous indebtedness of euro countries in global finance crisis duration. Excluding Germany, the debt stock of all euro zone countries has gone beyond 60% (one of Maasticht criterias) of gross domestic product (GDP). As seen in the figure, an increase in stock of European zone countries' debts is expected in year 2014. Unless additional saving maneuvers are performed, the debt rate of America, with loans taken in the year 2006 taking over 61% of its GDP and will likely increase by 100% from now till year 2014. Despite the fact that the debt rate of Japan was 191% of its GDP in year 2006, this rate will reach a point of 247% in year 2014.

The debt rates of countries like Brazil, India, China, Russia and Turkey are under 60% of GDP, Maastricht limitation, and are expected to decrease further till year 2014 (Figure 2).

In a short term, public debts in euro zone will increase the pressure on low interest rate policy that the European Central Bank has implemented so far, but radical processes of control mechanisms of monetary policies will be postponed to following terms. There is The need for serious decisions in monetary policies area, tpbe taken, because there are no convincing debt consolidation policies in many European countries.

Especially in the euro zone, there is no coordination between monetary policies and national treasury policies. Monetary policy and national policy is contained in the European Agreement just to facilitate the process of currency union and to assist the fluence of functions properly. In the instituonal frame of European system, political influencing continues its existance. European Central Bank considers stability of general prices level a superordinate goal. Foundations in public organization are responsible for the establishment of a just treasury policies and public financing.

The European Central Bank has dealings with orther Eurpoean Foundations with its clear and positive policies. To achieve the common treasury policies in European countries would be a very desirable improvement. But in fact, this target is far away from possibility; because conditions of microeconomic frames of many countries in Europe, and treasury policy targets of these countries are in contradiction with each other. consequently, there is no foundaiton in Europe to implement and coordinate this treasury policy.

Generally, there are two economic structures in the euro zone. The first group is the Anglo-Saxon: countries like England, Ireland and Spain. In these countries, economic development is intended to finance markets, estate markets and domestic consumption. The element that triggers economic development is mainly credit disposals. In economic development periods, rising public indebtedness rates are observed. In these countries, average public deficit rates are over 10% of GDP (Eder et al., 2010).

In the countries of the second group, borrowing rate of household is less than in the countries of the first group. Excluding Spain, there is no need for consolidation in these countries and budget deficits are 50% of first group countries.

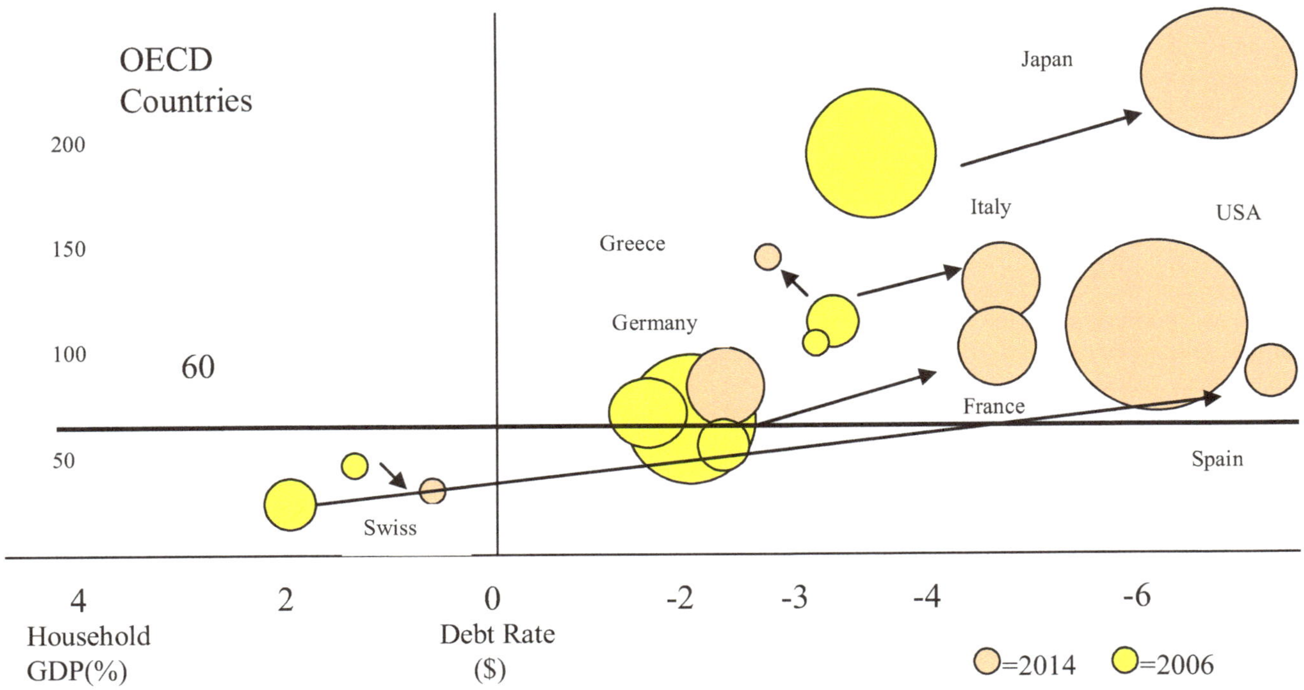

Figure 1. New debt club (Maastricht criteria = 60% of GDP).

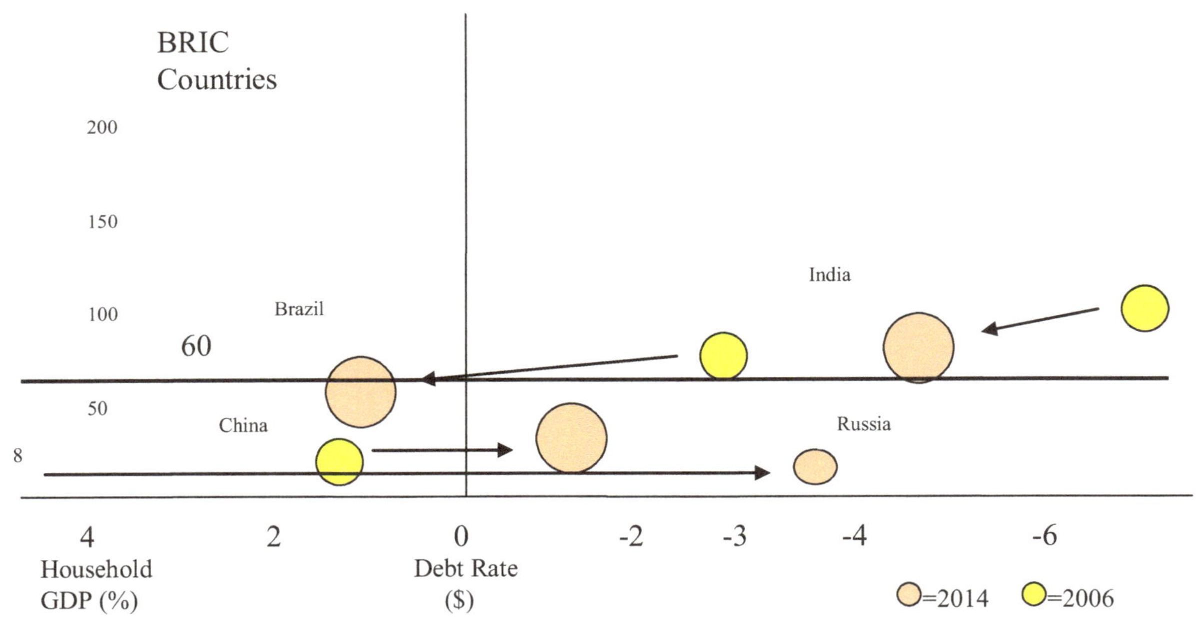

Figure 2. New debt club (source: Fluckiger and Schwab (2010)

REFORM OF INTERNATIONAL FINANCE SYSTEM

Because of global financial crisis in the year 2008, the United Nations created an international commission that consists of selected economists, presided over by Joseph Stiglitz. This commision with 18 members, contains economists selected from 16 different countries.

The commission attributed the cause of global financial crisis to the outrageous liberalization of capital markets and accentuated that global fluencing liquidity suprlus, that resulted in the financial and economy systems, becoming more intense about crisis.

The causes include: inadequacy in control mechanisms of financial systems, distortions in tax systems, inadequacy in unemployment insurances and disorgani-sation of retirement programs, played major roles in the outbreak of economic instability.

Inadequacy in financial markets featured structural discretions, and necessitated the global financial reform. In the global world, it is seen as inevitable to determine the frames of financial system, to eliminate the market paralogism, to reduce public paralogism and to constitute efficient control mechanisms with stronger rules.

National rescue programs should cost less to public budget and macroeconomic stability should be provided again. These following precautions should be taken for the reorganisation of the financial system (Hanfstangl, 2010):

i. Provision of credit fluence between creditors and borrowers and forwarding of credit fluence to small and medium sized enterprises should be guaranteed.
ii. The stronger reorganisation of credit types and SWAP operations in international bond markets is inevitable.
iii. Large and jeopardizing financial foundations should be divided and the amount of this kind of foundations should be delimited.
iv. Credit score determinator foundations should be re-evaluated and reformed, in order to prevent conflict between creditor foundations, creditor enterprises and governments. These foundations should be monitored more efficiently. So far, observations show that credit score determinator foundations acted unilateral.
v. All credit score determinator foundations sould be more clear and prove their own analyses honestly.

Stiglitz Commision recommended the following to generate secondary regulator institutions (Hanfstangl, 2010):

- New Central Bank (NCB) should be founded and be specialized in macroeconomic subjects.
- Financial Regulatory Authority (FRA) should be founded. The profession of this authority should be micro frame. FRA must specialize in consumer protection and be responsible for financial products. This authority must organise its own subcommittees, and determine professions about bond trade, insurance, financial stability and consolidation of financial products.

Commission observed that the power distrubiton in current International Finance Foundation is problematic. moreover, the voting distribution in International Monetary Fund should be reorganised and developing countries should take larger parts. On the other side, enhancement of World Bank is also inevitable. Both of these foundations should become clearer and their functions should be revised.

The commission considered the effects of crisis in underdeveloped countries. One of the biggest problems in devepoling countries is credit taken from abroad. In crisis periods, higher interest rates are applied for these credits or capital is demanded back.

Many developing countries signed agreement with other countries or signed World Trade Organisation (WTO) Agreement due to WTO rules. These signed agreements delimit these countries in foreign trade area and prevent these countries from taking decisions about their own trade organization policies.

In crisis periods, developed countries put in place rescue programs like (investment encouragements, tax reductions and direct financial assists) on the agenda, but developing countries try to manage crisis by increasing taxes and decreasing budget. This kind of strategy leads to a decrease in consumption of developing countries and make effects of crisis larger.

Commission welcomes the additional 250 billion USD in special borrowing rights of G-20 industrialised countries from the International Monetary Fund, in accordance with their decision in year 2009. Besides this, commission considers functional enlargement of World Bank and International Development Organisation and credit stock enlargements as inevitable (G20 Kommission, 2010).

Stiglitz Commission recommends progressive tax systems, unemployment insurance and retirement programs in order to provide economic stabilisation. The specialized fund to handle this case must be founded. Foundations, like United Nations and World Bank, and developed countries must take part in this fund.

Independence with International Monetary Fund, new credit options must be improved fast. This credits must be used for the stabilisation of developing countries' budget deficits and structural accordance programs. This fund (automatic stabiliser) must be financed by United Nations, Developed Countries or World Bank (Hanfstangl, 2010).

Developed countries should spare 0,7% of their GDP for underdeveloped countries. Commission demands CO2 tax, new finance taxes or equal other taxes in order to eliminate undevelopment and negations of global climate conditions.

One of the most important opinions of this commission is functionalise the global economic policy through improvement of new methods.

In the long term, Global Economic Policy Commission must be generated in the United Nations structure. The function of this foundation to search for solutions about global economic,social, ecological problems, and political improvement of this commission.

The most important subject, this commission recommended, is the global currency. The connection of national currencies to USD causes incremental costs and fluctuations on Exchange rates. Fluctuations on Dollar affects the foreign exchange reserves and import options of other countries negatively. consequently, the commission discussed about a new exchange rate system. For example; by generating a new foundation, like International Monetary Fund, this foundation can act as new World Central Bank. Or a new currency, like Special Drawing Rights in International Monetary Fund , can be constituted.

There plans underway to form a new Global Reserve Bank and to give larger positions to developing countries in this structure.

CONCLUSION

Immoderate monetary, treasury and financial policies, inadequate arrengements in financial markets and inadequate inspection of finance markets caused global crisis. Developed Countries prepared large rescue programs and prioritised saving policies. But the increasing debt rates in many countries in the EURO zone became a threat for European Unions.

In developed countries, finance crisis led to increases in the monetary demand and public debt demand, this situation supports enlargement oriented treasury policies. however financial crisis did not create any effect on Balance of Payments or Balance of Capital.

On the other hand, in the presence of global liquidity surplus, international capital fluences will accelerate and cause instability in national exchange markets.

The effects of global financial crisis in developing countries are more complicated, because restriction of credits causes decrease in demand and productivity gets harmed, this causes increase in unemployment.

In developing countries, the effects of financial crisis has been managed with tax increases and saving policies on households. In most underdeveloped countries, capital inflow decreased because of financial crisis and this countries had to quit their programs. In accordance to the projection of the World Bank, additional 55 million people will experience hunger (Hanfstangl, 2010).

One of the biggest threats is the decrease in international trade. Unless the necessary reforms will be performed, prosperity of world will decrease and underdeveloped countries will sustain the biggest blow from this condition.

REFERENCES

Belke A, Rees A (2009). The importance of Global Shocks for National Policy-Makers- Rising Challanges for Central Banks, DİW Discussion Paper, Deutsches İnstitut for Wirtschaftsforschung 922:1-38.

Belke A, Rees A (2011). İnternationale Geldpolitik im Zeichen von QEZ 13:99-101.

Belke AE, Schnabl G (2010). Finanskrise, Globale Liquidität und Makro-Ekonomische Exit,in: Wirtschaftspolitische Konsequenzen der Finanz Und Wirtschaftskrise, HRG. Von Theresia Theurl, Berlin pp.1-13.

Borio C, Disyatat P (2009). Unconventional Monetary Policies: An Appraisal,BİS Working Paper, Bank for İnternational Settlements, Basle, November Eurostat, Pressemitteilungen, Euroindikatoren, 292:1-37.

Eder G, Meyer CA, Petersen AK, Schneider R (2010). Staats-verschuldung in Europa –Analyse und Handlungsoptionen, workingspaper, 135(4):1-21.

Fluckiger S, Schwab M (2010). Globalization: The second wave, look at Switzerland offers two commentaries by Konrad Hummler & Rudolf H. Strahmbuch 0.2 to 3 Verlag Neue Zürcher Zeitung: 89.

G20 Kommission (2010). Erstes Massnahmen Paket nach G20: Kommission legt Strategie zur unterstützung der Entwicklungsländer vor. http:De.welcomeeurope.com/.../erstes-ma-nahme... pp.1-2.

Hanfstangl EM (2010). Wie lasst sich eine weitere Finanskrise vermeiden? Vorschläge der UN-Expertenkommission zur Reform des internationalen finanssystem: http:www.dgun.der.../Hanfstaengl_stiglitz_kom... pp.1-7.

Roth JP (2009). Globale Krise: Wie ist die Schweiz betroffen? Schweizerische Natio-nalbank, Frankfurt, Montag pp.1-8.

Schmid F (2011). Schulden-Supermacht USA, İnstitut für social-ökologische Wirtschafts-Forschung pp.10-20

Schmidt D (2009). China und İnternationale Finanskrise, Bundeszentrale für politische bildung: http: www. Bpb.de/.../80N33L,0,china_und_die_.. pp. 1-2 .

Spahn HP (2007). Realzins, intertemporale Preise und makroökonomische Stabilisierung, Hohenheimer Diskussionsbeiträge, Nr. 292, Stuttgart pp.1-24.

Cost analysis of a discrete-time queue with a single vacation and randomized activation

Tsung-Yin Wang[1], Jau-Chuan Ke[2], Chuen-Horng Lin[3] and Fu-Min Chang[4]

[1]Department of Accounting Information, National Taichung Institute of Technology, Taichung 404, Taiwan, ROC.
[2]Department of Applied Statistics, National Taichung Institute of Technology, Taichung 404, Taiwan, ROC.
[3]Graduate School of Computer Science and Information Technology, National Taichung Institute of Technology, Taichung 404, Taiwan, ROC.
[4]Department of Finance, Chaoyang University of Technology, Taichung 404, Taiwan, ROC.

This paper considers a discrete-time Geo/G/1 queue, in which the server operates a single vacation at end of each consecutive service period. After all the messages are served in the queue exhaustively, the server immediately leaves for a vacation. Upon returning from the vacation, the server inspects the queue length. If there are some messages waiting in the queue, the server either resumes serving the waiting messages (with probability p) or remains idle in the system (with probability $1-p$) until the next message arrives; and if no message presents in the queue, the server stays dormancy in the system until at least one message arrives. Using the generating functions technique, the system state evolution is analyzed. The probability generating functions of the system size distributions in various states are obtained. Some system characteristics of interest are also derived. With the vacation of fixed length time (say T), the long run average cost function per unit time is analytically developed to determine the joint optimal values of T and p at a minimum cost.

Key words: Cost, busy period, discrete time queue, markov chain, randomized vacation.

INTRODUCTION

Starting from Levy and Yechiali (1975), the modelling analysis for the queueing systems with vacations has been done by a considerable amount of work in the past. A comprehensive and excellent study on the vacation models, including some applications such as production/ inventory system and communication/ computer systems, can be found in Doshi (1986), Takagi (1991), and Tian and Zhang (2006).

On the other hand, along with the advent of computer and communication technologies, the analysis of discrete-time queueing systems has received more attention in the scientific literatures over the past years (Meisling, 1958; Hunter, 1983; Bruneel and Kim, 1993; Takagi, 1993; Woodward, 1994). The reason for this is that discrete-time systems are more appropriate than their continuous-time counterparts in their applicability for the study of many computer and communication systems applications in which time is divided into fixed-length time intervals ('slots'). The applications to communication and computer systems include asynchronous transfer mode multiplexers in the broadband integrated services digital network, slotted carrier-sense multiple access protocols, and time-division multiple access schemes. An excellent and complete study on discrete-time queueing systems with vacations has been presented by Takagi (1993). Zhang and Tian (2001) investigated a Geo/G/1 queue with multiple adaptive vacations. Tian and Zhang (2002) analyzed a GI/Geo/1 queueing system with multiple vacations by matrix-geometric solution method and Li and Tian (2007) used the same method to study a GI/Geo/1 queueing system with working vacation and vacation interruption.

Zhang and Tian (2001), and Li and Tian (2002), they gave the stochastic results for the queue length and waiting time. We should note that in Zhang and Tian (2001), and Li and Tian (2002), no optimal vacation policies for sensitivity analysis are obtained.

In this paper, a discrete-time Geo/G/1 system with a single vacation policy with randomized activation (namely <*V*, *p*> policy) was considered. The <*V*, *p*> policy is performed under the following conditions: (i) the server leaves for a single vacation when the system is empty, (ii) if the server returns from the vacation and at least one message is waiting in the queue, the server may either activates with probability p or stays dormancy in the system with probability $q(=1-p)$,and (iii) when the server is dormant in the system, he activates to serve the waiting messages as the next message arrives.

To the best of our knowledge, the discrete-time Geo/G/1 queue with <*V*, *p*> policy has not been studied. Such a model has a potential application in wireless local area networks (WLANs). Access Points (APs) are specially configured nodes on WLANs and act as a central transmitter and receiver of WLAN radio signals. To keep the APs functioning well, some maintenance activities are needed. For example, virus scan is an important maintenance activity for the APs. It can be performed when the AP is idle and be programmed to perform on a regular basis. After finishing the maintenance activity, AP can enter the sleep mode when there is no radio signal to be transmitted for power saving. It can also enter the sleep mode after finishing the some kinds of maintenance activities such as refreshing AP current status. AP will awake from sleep mode and begin to serve when the new radio signal arrives.

In this study, we first investigate the Markov chain, the probability generating functions and probability distributions of queue length in various server states, including their main expectation. Next, we derive the turned-off period, turned-on (busy) period of the server and the waiting time distribution in the queue. Finally, we develop a cost model with a fixed positive integer V (say T), and the joint optimal threshold values (T^*, p^*) are determined which minimize the cost.

MODEL DESCRIPTION

The study considers a discrete-time queue with a single-server where the time is divided into constant length intervals (called slots). It is well-known that the probability of an arrival and a departure occurring simultaneously is not zero in discrete time. This probability is positive in the discrete-time setting. That is why the order of the arrivals and departures must be stated. There are two different laws: if the arrivals precede the departures (late arrival system (LAS)) and if the departures precede the arrivals (early arrival system (EAS)). These concepts and other related ones can be found in Takagi (1993). We adopt the LAS policy in the present model (Figure 1).

Messages arrive according to a Bernoulli process with rate λ, that is, λ (respectively, $\bar{\lambda}=1-\lambda$) is the probability that a message arrives (respectively, does not arrive) in each slot. The service times of the messages are independent and identically distributed according to a general probability mass function $\{b_i\}_{i=1}^{\infty}$ with probability generating function (pgf) $B(u)=\sum_{i=1}^{\infty} b_i u^i$ and jth factorial moments B_j. After all the messages are served in the queue exhaustively, the server operates a <*V*, *p*> policy. As soon as the system becomes empty, the server immediately takes a single vacation, where the vacation time is a discrete random variable, denoted by V, with probability mass function $\{v_i\}_{i=1}^{\infty}$ having pgf $V(u)=\sum_{i=1}^{\infty} v_i u^i$ and jth factorial moments V_j. At the vacation completion instant, the server checks the system to see if there is any waiting message and decides the action to take one of the following two cases according to the state of the system:

Case 1: If there is any message waiting in the queue, the server will resume serving the queue with probability p or to stay dormancy in the system with probability $q\ (=1-p)$ until at least one message arrives.

Case 2: If there is no message waiting in the queue, the server remains idle in the system until the next message arriving.

Arriving messages form a single waiting line based on the order of their arrivals; that is, they are queued according to the first-come, first-served (FCFS) discipline. The server can serve only one message at a time. If the server is busy, arriving message has to wait in the queue until the server is available. All messages arriving to the system are assumed to be eventually served, that is, $\lambda B_1 < 1$. Furthermore, various stochastic processes involved in the system are independent of each other.

THE ANALYSIS: MARKOV CHAIN AND PROBABILITY GENERATING FUNCTION

At time n^+, the state of the system is described by the process $(\Phi^{(n)}, L^{(n)}, \xi^{(n)})$. $\Phi^{(n)}$ denotes the state of the server, where it can be 0, 1, or 2 representing the server on vacation, idle, or busy, respectively. As Takagi (1993), $L^{(n)}$ is the number of messages in the system. If $\Phi^{(n)}=0$, then $\xi^{(n)}$ denotes the remaining vacation time. If $\Phi^{(n)}=2$, then $\xi^{(n)}$ represents the remaining service time. The sequence of triplets

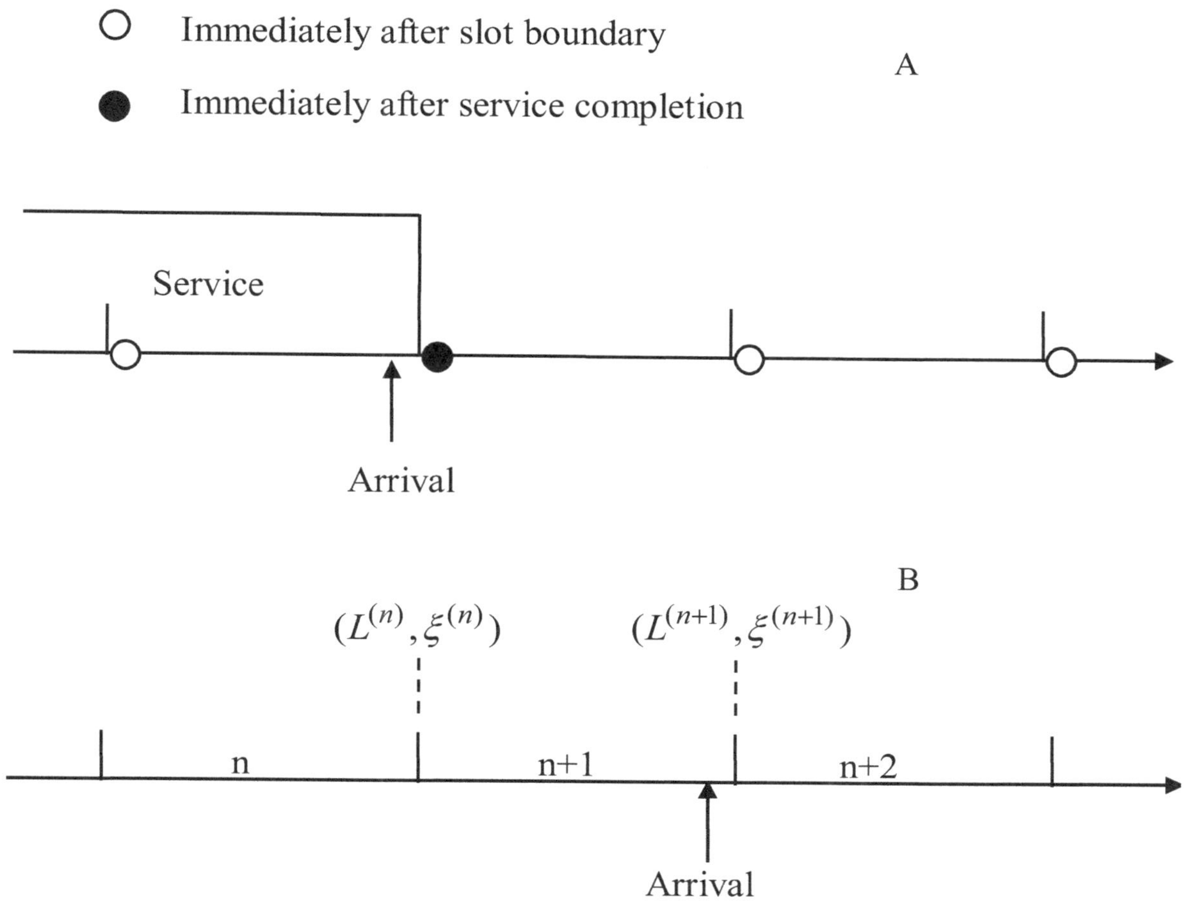

Figure 1. A: Late arrival model. B: Queue size and remaining service time observed immediately after slot boundaries.

$\{(\Phi^{(n)},L^{(n)},\xi^{(n)});n=0,\ 1,\ 2,\cdots\}$ is a Markov chain whose state space is as $\{(j,k,i):j=0,2,k\geq 0,i\geq 1;(1,k):k\geq 0\}$.

Let us define the following limiting probabilities:

$\tilde{\pi}_{k,i}=\lim_{n\to\infty}\Pr[\Phi^{(n)}=0,L^{(n)}=k,\ \xi^{(n)}=i]$, $k\geq 0,\ i\geq 1$, $\Omega_k=\lim_{n\to\infty}\Pr[\Phi^{(n)}=1,\ L^{(n)}=k]$, $k\geq 0$, $\pi_{k,i}=\lim_{n\to\infty}\Pr[\Phi^{(n)}=2,L^{(n)}=k,\xi^{(n)}=i]$, $k\geq 1,\ i\geq 1$.

The Kolmogorov equations for the stationary distribution are given by

$$\widetilde{\pi}_{0,i}=\pi_{1,1}\bar{\lambda}v_i+\widetilde{\pi}_{0,i+1}\bar{\lambda},\ i\geq 1 \tag{1}$$

$$\widetilde{\pi}_{k,i}=\widetilde{\pi}_{k,i+1}\bar{\lambda}+\widetilde{\pi}_{k-1,i+1}\lambda,\ k\geq 1,\ i\geq 1 \tag{2}$$

$$\Omega_0=\widetilde{\pi}_{0,1}\bar{\lambda}+\Omega_0\bar{\lambda} \tag{3}$$

$$\Omega_k=q\widetilde{\pi}_{k,1}\bar{\lambda}+q\widetilde{\pi}_{k-1,1}\lambda+\Omega_k\bar{\lambda},\ k\geq 1 \tag{4}$$

$$\pi_{1,i}=\Omega_0\lambda b_i+p\widetilde{\pi}_{0,1}\lambda b_i+p\widetilde{\pi}_{1,1}\bar{\lambda}b_i+\pi_{1,i+1}\bar{\lambda}+\pi_{2,1}\bar{\lambda}b_i+\pi_{1,1}\lambda b_i,\ i\geq 1 \tag{5}$$

$$\pi_{k,i}=\Omega_{k-1}\lambda b_i+p\tilde{\pi}_{k-1,1}\lambda b_i+p\tilde{\pi}_{k,1}\bar{\lambda}b_i+\pi_{k,i+1}\bar{\lambda}+\pi_{k+1,1}\bar{\lambda}b_i+\pi_{k-1,i+1}\lambda+\pi_{k,1}\lambda b_i,\ k\geq 2,\ i\geq 1. \tag{6}$$

To resolve (1) to (8), we use the following generating functions:

$$G_V(u,z)=\sum_{k=0}^{\infty}\sum_{i=1}^{\infty}z^k u^i\widetilde{\pi}_{k,i},\ G_I(z)=\sum_{k=0}^{\infty}z^k\Omega_k,\ V(u)=\sum_{i=1}^{\infty}u^i v_i,$$

$$B(u)=\sum_{i=1}^{\infty}u^i b_i,\ G_B(u,z)=\sum_{k=1}^{\infty}\sum_{i=1}^{\infty}z^k u^i\pi_{k,i},\ \varphi_V(z)=\sum_{k=0}^{\infty}z^k\widetilde{\pi}_{k,1},$$

$$\varphi_B(z)=\sum_{k=1}^{\infty} z^k \pi_{k,1} \; (|z|\le 1 \text{ and } |u|\le 1),$$

And the normalization condition

$$G_V(1,1)+G_I(1)+G_B(1,1)=1.$$

Multiplying (1) and (2) by z^k and summing over k after multiplying (1) and (2) by u^i and summing over i, it finally yields:

$$\frac{u-(\bar{\lambda}+\lambda z)}{u} G_V(u,z)=\bar{\lambda}\pi_{1,1}V(u)-(\bar{\lambda}+\lambda z)\varphi_V(z). \quad (7)$$

Inserting $u=(\bar{\lambda}+\lambda z)$ in (7), we obtain

$$\varphi_V(z)=\frac{\bar{\lambda}V(\bar{\lambda}+\lambda z)}{(\bar{\lambda}+\lambda z)}\pi_{1,1}. \quad (8)$$

Substituting (8) into (7), we get

$$G_V(u,z)=\frac{\bar{\lambda}u\left[V(u)-V(\bar{\lambda}+\lambda z)\right]}{u-(\bar{\lambda}+\lambda z)}\pi_{1,1}. \quad (9)$$

Multiplying (3) and (4) by z^k and summing over k, we obtain

$$\lambda G_I(z)=p\bar{\lambda}\tilde{\pi}_{0,1}+q(\bar{\lambda}+\lambda z)\varphi_V(z). \quad (10)$$

Substituting (8) into (10), it gives

$$G_I(z)=\frac{\bar{\lambda}}{\lambda}\left(p\tilde{\pi}_{0,1}+qV(\bar{\lambda}+\lambda z)\pi_{1,1}\right). \quad (11)$$

Multiplying (5) and (6) by z^k and summing over k after multiplying (5) and (6) by u^i and summing over i, we have

$$\frac{u-(\bar{\lambda}+\lambda z)}{u} G_B(u,z)=\lambda z B(u)G_I(z)+p(\bar{\lambda}+\lambda z)B(u)\varphi_V(z)-p\bar{\lambda}B(u)\tilde{\pi}_{0,1}$$

$$+\left[\frac{B(u)-z}{z}\right](\bar{\lambda}+\lambda z)\varphi_B(z)-\bar{\lambda}B(u)\pi_{1,1}. \quad (12)$$

Letting $u=(\bar{\lambda}+\lambda z)$ in (12), it gives

$$\varphi_B(z)=\frac{\bar{\lambda}zB(\bar{\lambda}+\lambda z)\left\{p(1-z)\tilde{\pi}_{0,1}+\left[1-(p+qz)V(\bar{\lambda}+\lambda z)\right]\pi_{1,1}\right\}}{(\bar{\lambda}+\lambda z)\left[B(\bar{\lambda}+\lambda z)-z\right]} \quad (13)$$

Substituting (8), (11), (13) into (12), we obtain

$$G_B(u,z)=\frac{\bar{\lambda}uz\left[B(u)-B(\bar{\lambda}+\lambda z)\right]\left\{p(1-z)\tilde{\pi}_{0,1}+\left[1-(p+qz)V(\bar{\lambda}+\lambda z)\right]\pi_{1,1}\right\}}{\left[u-(\bar{\lambda}+\lambda z)\right]\cdot\left[B(\bar{\lambda}+\lambda z)-z\right]} \quad (14)$$

Letting u = 1 in (9) and (14) respectively, it yields

$$G_V(1,z)=\frac{\bar{\lambda}\left[1-V(\bar{\lambda}+\lambda z)\right]}{1-(\bar{\lambda}+\lambda z)}\pi_{1,1}, \quad (15)$$

and

$$G_B(1,z)=\frac{\bar{\lambda}z\left[1-B(\bar{\lambda}+\lambda z)\right]\left\{p(1-z)\tilde{\pi}_{0,1}+\left[1-(p+qz)V(\bar{\lambda}+\lambda z)\right]\pi_{1,1}\right\}}{\left[1-(\bar{\lambda}+\lambda z)\right]\cdot\left[B(\bar{\lambda}+\lambda z)-z\right]} \quad (16)$$

Let S(z) be the probability generating function of the number of messages in the system. Since $S(z)=G_V(1,z)+G_I(z)+G_B(1,z)$, it follows from (11), (15) and (16) that

$$S(z)=\frac{\bar{\lambda}B(\bar{\lambda}+\lambda z)\left\{p(1-z)\tilde{\pi}_{0,1}+\left[1-(p+qz)V(\bar{\lambda}+\lambda z)\right]\pi_{1,1}\right\}}{\lambda\left[B(\bar{\lambda}+\lambda z)-z\right]} \quad (17)$$

The derivation of $\tilde{\pi}_{0,1}$ and $\pi_{1,1}$

Differentiating $G_V(u,z)=\sum_{k=0}^{\infty}\sum_{i=1}^{\infty} z^k u^i \tilde{\pi}_{k,i}$ with respect to u and then setting $u=z=0$, we obtain

$$\left.\frac{\partial}{\partial u}G_V(u,z)\right|_{u=z=0}=\left.\sum_{k=0}^{\infty}\sum_{i=1}^{\infty} i z^k u^{i-1}\tilde{\pi}_{k,i}\right|_{u=z=0}=\tilde{\pi}_{0,1}. \quad (18)$$

By proceeding similar manner with Equation (9) yields

$$\left.\frac{\partial}{\partial u}G_V(u,z)\right|_{z=u=0}=V(\bar{\lambda})\pi_{1,1}. \quad (19)$$

It follows from (18) and (19) that

$$\pi_{1,1}=\frac{\tilde{\pi}_{0,1}}{V(\bar{\lambda})}. \quad (20)$$

Using the normalization condition $S(1)=1$ and Equation (20), it yields

$$\tilde{\pi}_{0,1}=\frac{\lambda(1-\rho)V(\bar{\lambda})}{\bar{\lambda}\left[q+\lambda V_1+pV(\bar{\lambda})\right]}, \tag{21}$$

and

$$\pi_{1,1}=\frac{\tilde{\pi}_{0,1}}{V(\bar{\lambda})}=\frac{\lambda(1-\rho)}{\bar{\lambda}\left[q+\lambda V_1+pV(\bar{\lambda})\right]}. \tag{22}$$

Substitution $\tilde{\pi}_{0,1}$ and $\pi_{1,1}$ to Equation (17) gives

$$S(z)=S_0(z)\cdot\frac{\left\{p(1-z)V(\bar{\lambda})+\left[1-(p+qz)V(\bar{\lambda}+\lambda z)\right]\right\}}{(1-z)\left[q+\lambda V_1+pV(\bar{\lambda})\right]}, \tag{23}$$

Where $S_0(z)$ is the pgf for the classical Geo/G/1 queue without vacation and

$$S_0(z)=\frac{(1-z)(1-\rho)B(\bar{\lambda}+\lambda z)}{\left[B(\bar{\lambda}+\lambda z)-z\right]}.$$

Remark: As p = 1, $S(z)$ can be simplified into

$$S(z)=S_0(z)\cdot\frac{\left\{(1-z)V(\bar{\lambda})+\left[1-V(\bar{\lambda}+\lambda z)\right]\right\}}{(1-z)\left[V(\bar{\lambda})+\lambda V_1\right]},$$

This is referred to the Geo/G/1 queue with a single vacation.

Stationary distribution of the server state

Let us define the following probabilities

$P_V \equiv$ The probability that the server is on vacation;

$P_I \equiv$ The probability that the server is idle;

$P_{on} \equiv$ The probability that the server is turned on (working);

$P_{off} \equiv$ The probability that the server is turned off (vacation or idle).

Substituting (21) and (22) into (11), (15) and (16) and then setting z = 1, it yields

$$P_V=\lim_{z\to 1}G_V(1,z)=\frac{\lambda(1-\rho)V_1}{\left[q+\lambda V_1+pV(\bar{\lambda})\right]}. \tag{24}$$

By proceeding similar manner with $G_I(z)$ and $G_B(1,z)$, it finally yields

$$P_I=G_I(1)=\frac{(1-\rho)\left[q+pV(\bar{\lambda})\right]}{\left[q+\lambda V_1+pV(\bar{\lambda})\right]}, \tag{25}$$

and

$$P_{on}=\rho. \tag{26}$$

From (24) and (25), the study obtains

$$P_{off}=P_V+P_I=1-\rho. \tag{27}$$

The probability of system empty

Now, we want to find that the probability of system empty. Inserting u = 1 and z = 0 in (9) and using (22), we obtain:

$$\sum_{i=1}^{\infty}\tilde{\pi}_{0,i}=\frac{(1-\rho)\left[1-V(\bar{\lambda})\right]}{\left[q+\lambda V_1+pV(\bar{\lambda})\right]}. \tag{28}$$

It follows from (3) and (21) that we have

$$\Omega_0=\frac{(1-\rho)V(\bar{\lambda})}{\left[q+\lambda V_1+pV(\bar{\lambda})\right]}. \tag{29}$$

Thus the probability of system empty is as

$$P_0=\sum_{i=1}^{\infty}\tilde{\pi}_{0,i}+\Omega_0=\frac{(1-\rho)}{\left[q+\lambda V_1+pV(\bar{\lambda})\right]}. \tag{30}$$

The expected number of messages in the system

Differentiating $S(z)$ in (23), we note that the numerator and denominator are both 0. The study applies L'Hospital's rule twice and finally find the expected number of messages in the system given by,

$$L_{V,p}=L+\frac{2q\lambda V_1+\lambda^2 V_2}{2\left[q+\lambda V_1+pV(\bar{\lambda})\right]}, \tag{31}$$

Where $L=\rho+\dfrac{\lambda^2 B_2}{2(1-\rho)}$ is the expected number of messages in the system for the classical Geo/G/1 queue without vacations (Takagi, 1993: 6).

THE TURNED-OFF PERIOD AND TURNED-ON PERIOD

This section studies the turned-off period (which is comprised of vacation period and idle period) and turned-on period (busy period). Let us define the following terminology: A vacation period starts at the departure instant of a message which leaves the system empty and terminates at returning instant from a vacation.

An idle period starts the end of a vacation and terminates at the end of the next succeeding slot during which an arrival occurs. A busy period starts at the beginning of a service and terminates when a service is completed and the system is empty.

The turned-off period

According to the definition, we have

1. The joint pgf for the length of a vacation and the probability that no message arrives during that vacation is given by $\sum_{i=1}^{\infty} u^i v_i \bar{\lambda}^i = V(\bar{\lambda} u)$.
2. The joint pgf for the length of a vacation and the probability that at least one message arrives during that vacation is given by $V(u) - V(\bar{\lambda} u)$.
3. The pgf for the length of an idle period is given by $I(u) = \lambda u / (1 - \bar{\lambda} u)$.

From the results listed previously, the pgf of the server turned-off period is given by

$$I_V(u) = p[V(u) - V(\bar{\lambda} u)] + V(\bar{\lambda} u) I(u) + q[V(u) - V(\bar{\lambda} u)] I(u),$$
(32)

Which leads to the expected length of the turned-off period as

$$E[S_{off}] = I_V'(1) = V_1 + \frac{pV(\bar{\lambda}) + q}{\lambda}. \tag{33}$$

The turned-on (busy) period

Let Ψ be the pgf of busy period of classical Geo/G/1 with late arrive delay access. From Takagi (1993), we have

$$\Psi(z) = B(\lambda z \Psi(z) + \bar{\lambda} z) \tag{34}$$

The busy period begins as one of the following three cases:

Case 1: j messages arrive during the vacation period which vacation time is k slots. After the vacation completion instant, the server begins service with probability p. Such event occurs with probability $pv_k^{(j)} = pC_j^k \lambda^j \bar{\lambda}^{k-j} v_k$, $(k = 1,2\cdots, j = 1,2,\cdots k)$.

Case 2: j messages arrive during the vacation period which vacation time is k slots. At the end of the vacation, the server remains idle in the system with probability q. In this case, the server begins providing service as next message arrives. Such event occurs with probability

$$qv_k^{(j)} \sum_{m=1}^{\infty} \bar{\lambda}^{m-1} \lambda = qC_j^k \lambda^j \bar{\lambda}^{k-j} v_k,$$

$(k = 1,2\cdots, j = 1,2,\cdots k)$.

Case 3: No message arrives during the vacation period which vacation time is k slots. In this case, the server starts providing service as a message arrives. Such event occurs,

$$\bar{\lambda}^k v_k \sum_{m=1}^{\infty} \bar{\lambda}^{m-1} \lambda = \bar{\lambda}^k v_k, k = 1,2\cdots.$$

According to the definition, the pgf of the sub-busy period is extended by case 1 as

$$\sum_{k=1}^{\infty} \sum_{j=1}^{k} pv_k^{(j)} \sum_{n=1}^{\infty} b_n z^n \sum_{l=0}^{n} C_l^n \lambda^l \bar{\lambda}^{n-l} (\Psi(z))^{l+j-1}.$$

The pgf of the sub-busy period extended by case 2 is given by

$$\sum_{k=1}^{\infty} \sum_{j=1}^{k} qv_k^{(j)} \sum_{n=1}^{\infty} b_n z^n \sum_{l=0}^{n} C_l^n \lambda^l \bar{\lambda}^{n-l} (\Psi(z))^{l+j}.$$

The pgf of the sub-busy period extended by case 3 is given by

$$\sum_{k=1}^{\infty} \bar{\lambda}^k v_k \sum_{n=1}^{\infty} b_n z^n \sum_{l=0}^{n} C_l^n \lambda^l \bar{\lambda}^{n-l} (\Psi(z))^l$$

.

From the results listed previously, the pgf of the busy period for the <V, p> policy Geo/G/1 queueing system is given by

$$\overline{\Psi}(z) = \sum_{k=1}^{\infty} \sum_{j=1}^{k} pv_k^{(j)} \sum_{n=1}^{\infty} b_n z^n \sum_{l=0}^{n} C_l^n \lambda^l \bar{\lambda}^{n-l} (\Psi(z))^{l+j-1} + \sum_{k=1}^{\infty} \sum_{j=1}^{k} qv_k^{(j)} \sum_{n=1}^{\infty} b_n z^n \sum_{l=0}^{n} C_l^n \lambda^l \bar{\lambda}^{n-l} (\Psi(z$$

$$+ \sum_{k=1}^{\infty} \bar{\lambda}^k v_k \sum_{n=1}^{\infty} b_n z^n \sum_{l=0}^{n} C_l^n \lambda^l \bar{\lambda}^{n-l} (\Psi(z))^l$$

$$= B(\bar{\lambda} z + \lambda z \Psi(z)) \left\{ \left(\frac{p}{\Psi(z)} + q \right) [V(\bar{\lambda} + \lambda \Psi(z)) - V(\bar{\lambda})] + V(\bar{\lambda}) \right\}, \tag{35}$$

Which implies the expected length of the turned-on period (busy period) is given by

$$E[S_{on}] = \overline{\Psi}'(1) = \frac{\rho\left[q + \lambda V_1 + pV(\bar{\lambda})\right]}{\lambda(1-\rho)}. \quad (36)$$

From (33) and (36), we obtain the expected length of busy cycle

$$E[C_V] = E[S_{off}] + E[S_{on}] = \frac{\left[q + \lambda V_1 + pV(\bar{\lambda})\right]}{\lambda(1-\rho)}. \quad (37)$$

WAITING TIME IN THE QUEUE

The waiting time in the queue (measured in slots) in the slot n +1 as the time that a message would wait in the corresponding system if it arrived in the slot n +1 (Takagi, 1993). Thus, the waiting time in the system (measured in slots) in the slot n +1 is the sum of the waiting time in the queue in the slot n +1 plus the service time. Let us define the following pgfs:

$W_V(z) \equiv$ The pgf of the waiting time in the queue of a test message (that arrives in the slot n +1) when server is on vacation.
$W_I(z) \equiv$ The pgf of the waiting time in the queue of a test message (that arrives in the slot n +1) when server is in idle period.
$W_B(z) \equiv$ The pgf of the waiting time in the queue of a test message (that arrives in the slot n +1) when server is busy.

$W_Q(z) \equiv$ The pgf of waiting time in the queue of a test message that arrives in the slot n +1.

For the Geo/G/1 system with <*V*, *p*> policy, an arrival may occurs as one of the following three cases:

Case 1: The test message that arrives while the server is on vacation and find k message($k \geq 0$) in the system: (i) while the vacation is just end, the server is switched to busy period with probability p, the test message must wait the service time of the preceding k messages; and (ii) while the vacation is just end, the server is switched to idle period with probability q until the next message arrives, the test message must wait the next message arriving plus the service time of the preceding k messages.
Case 2: There are exactly k messages in the queue and the server is idle in the system when the message arrives.
Case 3: The test message that arrives while the server is busy and finds k messages in the system. In this case, the waiting time in the queue of the message consists of:

(i) The remaining service time of the message being served at time n^+; and
(ii) The service time of the k-1 messages in the queue at time n^+.

From Case 1 yields,

$$W_V(z) = \frac{1}{(1-\rho-P_I)}\left[p\sum_{k=0}^{\infty}\sum_{i=1}^{\infty}\tilde{\pi}_{k,i}z^{i-1}\left[B(z)\right]^k + q\sum_{k=0}^{\infty}\sum_{i=1}^{\infty}\tilde{\pi}_{k,i}z^{i-1}[B(z)]^k\left(\frac{\lambda z}{1-\bar{\lambda}z}\right)\right]$$
$$= \frac{1}{(1-\rho-P_I)}\left[\frac{p}{z}G_V(z,B(z)) + \frac{q}{z}G_V(z,B(z))\left(\frac{\lambda z}{1-\bar{\lambda}z}\right)\right]$$

Inserting (9) in the previous equation, it yields:

$$W_V(z) = \frac{\bar{\lambda}\left[p(1-\bar{\lambda}z) + q\lambda z\right]\left[V(z) - V(\bar{\lambda} + \lambda B(z))\right]}{(1-\rho-P_I)(1-\bar{\lambda}z)\left[z - (\bar{\lambda} + \lambda B(z))\right]}\pi_{1,1}. \quad (38)$$

Which $\pi_{1,1}$ is given by (22). Following Case 2, it gives,

$$W_I(z) \equiv \frac{1}{P_I}\left[\sum_{k=0}^{\infty}\Omega_k\left[B(z)\right]^k\right] = \frac{1}{P_I}G_I(B(z)) = \frac{1}{P_I}\frac{\bar{\lambda}}{\lambda}\left(p\tilde{\pi}_{0,1} + qV(\bar{\lambda} + \lambda B(z))\pi_{1,1}\right). \quad (39)$$

From Case 3, we have

$$W_B(z) = \frac{1}{\rho}\sum_{k=1}^{\infty}\sum_{i=1}^{\infty}\pi_{k,i}z^{i-1}\left[B(z)\right]^{k-1} == \frac{\bar{\lambda}\left\{p(1-B(z))\tilde{\pi}_{0,1} + \left[1-(p+qB(z))V(\bar{\lambda}+\lambda B(z))\right]\pi_{1,1}\right\}}{\rho\left[\left(\bar{\lambda}+\lambda B(z)\right)-z\right]}. \tag{40}$$

The pgf of waiting time in the queue of a test message when server is on vacation or in idle period is as $W_{OFF}(z) = \frac{1}{(1-\rho)}\left[(1-\rho-P_I)W_V(z) + P_I W_I(z)\right]$. From (38) and (39), we obtain

$$W_{OFF}(z) = \frac{1}{(1-\rho)}\left\{\frac{\bar{\lambda}\left[p(1-\bar{\lambda}z)+q\lambda z\right]\left[V(z)-V(\bar{\lambda}+\lambda B(z))\right]}{(1-\bar{\lambda}z)\left[z-(\bar{\lambda}+\lambda B(z))\right]}\pi_{1,1} + \frac{\bar{\lambda}\left(p\tilde{\pi}_{0,1}+qV(\bar{\lambda}+\lambda B(z))\pi_{1,1}\right)}{\lambda}\right\}. \tag{41}$$

Finally, the pgf of the waiting time in the queue of a test message is given by

$$W_Q(z) = (1-\rho)W_{OFF}(z) + \rho W_B(z)$$

Which implies

$$W_q = \frac{2qV_1 + \lambda V_2}{2\left[q + \lambda V_1 + pV(\bar{\lambda})\right]} + \frac{\lambda B_2}{2(1-\rho)}. \tag{42}$$

Which is in accordance with $L_{V,p}/\lambda - B_1$ which confirms the result of Little's formula.

OPTIMIZATION ANALYSIS

As a particular case, the Geo/G/1 queueing system with <*T*, *p*> policy, in which the server takes a vacation of fixed length *T* at the ending of the busy period and the server begins service with probability *p* if messages present in the queue at vacation completion instant. We construct the total expected cost function per unit time for the <*T*, *p*> policy system. The main objective of this study is to determine the discrete time T, say T^*, and the probability p, say p^*, simultaneously so that the expected cost function is minimized. To do this, we define the following cost elements:

$C_h \equiv$ Cost per unit time per message present in the system,

$C_s \equiv$ Cost per unit time for a cycle,

$C_r \equiv$ Profit per unit time due to vacation.

Using these cost elements listed in the foregoing and the corresponding system characteristics, the expected cost function $F(T,p)$ per message per unit time is given by

$$F(T,p) = \frac{\lambda}{\left[q+\lambda T+p\bar{\lambda}^T\right]}\left\{C_h\frac{\left[2qT+\lambda T(T-1)\right]}{2} + C_s(1-\rho)\right\} - C_r\frac{\lambda(1-\rho)T}{q+\lambda T+p\bar{\lambda}^T}. \tag{43}$$

The cost function in (43) would have been a hard task to develop analytic results for the optimum value (T^*, p^*) because one is discrete variable *T* and one is continuous variable *p*. We first use direct search method to find the discrete variable, say T^* when p is fixed. Next, we fix T^* and derive the continuous value of p, say p^*.

Direct search method

In practical use, the discrete variable T is bounded by a positive integer T_U. Under a given *p*, we successively use direct substitution of ascendant values of $T = 1,2,\ldots,T_U$ into the cost function. The optimum value T^* could be determined by the following:

$$F(T^*|p) = \underset{\rho<1}{Minimize}\, F(T|p),\ T \in \{1,2,\ldots,T_U\} \tag{44}$$

Some numerical examples are presented to demonstrate that the cost function is really convex in T and the solution gives a minimum. For convenience, the numerical experiments are performed by considering $B_1 = 1.0$ and the following three cases with cost parameter elements: C_h = \$20/message/unit time, C_s = \$1000/unit time, and C_r = \$50/unit time.

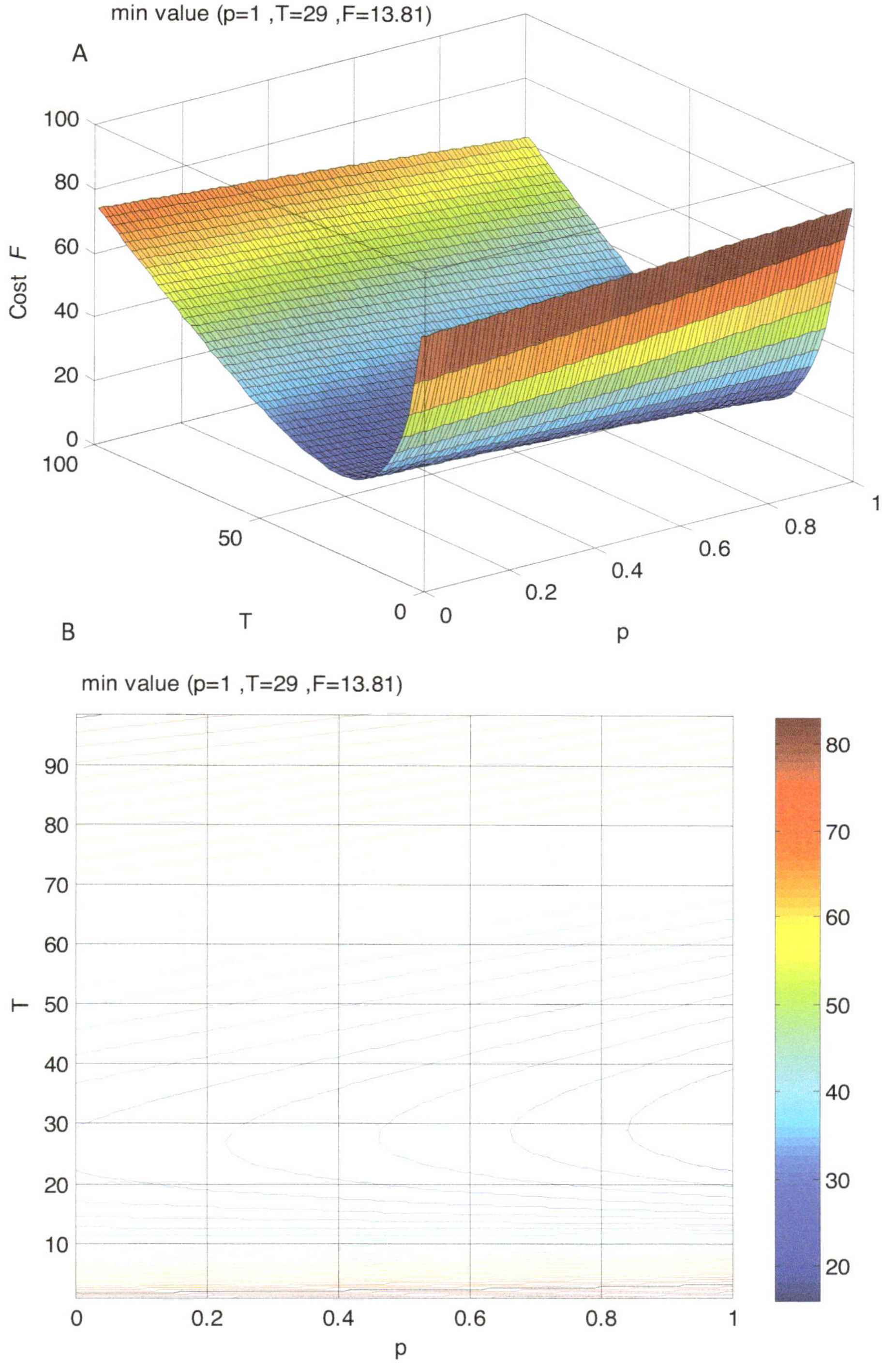

Figure 2. A: Cost with different values of T and p (λ = 0.1, B_1 = 0.1, C_h = \$20, C_s = \$1000, and C_r =\$50). B: Cost contour with different values of T and p (The contour of Figure 2A).

Case 1: λ = 0.1 and vary the values of p and T.
Case 2: λ = 0.5 and vary the values of p and T.
Case 3: λ = 0.9 and vary the values of p and T.

The numerical results are displayed in Figures 2 to 4

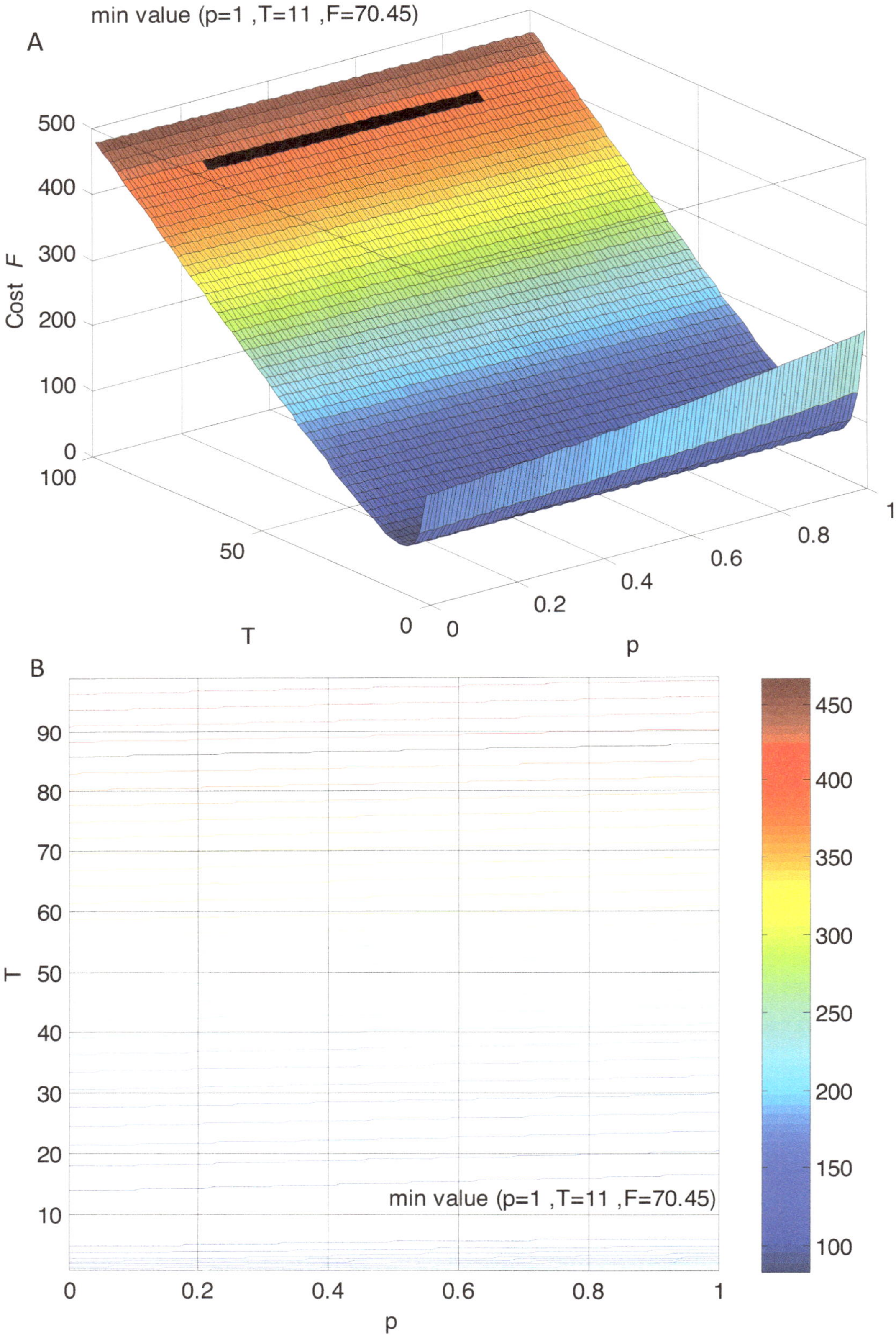

Figure 3. A: Cost with different values of T and p (λ = 0.5, B_1 = 0.1, C_h = \$20, C_s = \$1000, and C_r = \$50). B: Cost contour with different values of T and p (The contour of Figure 3A).

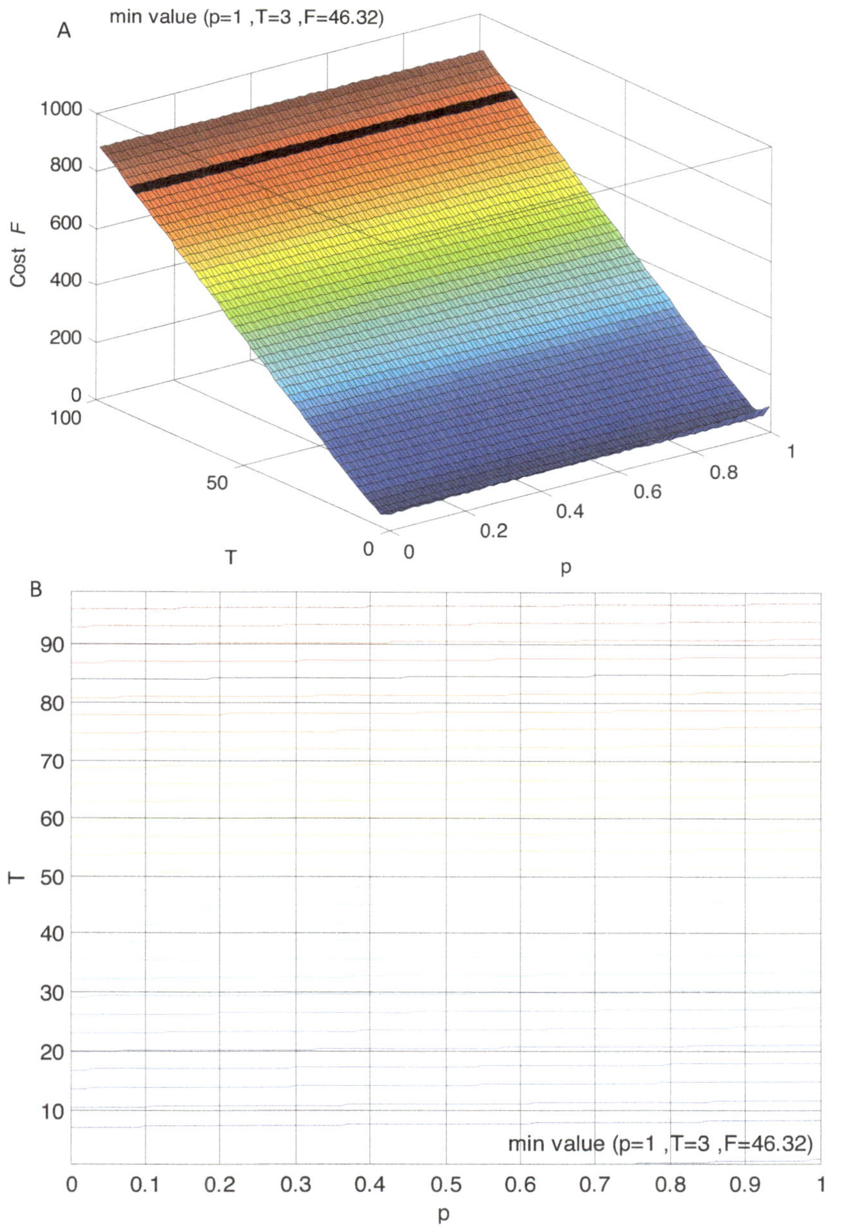

Figure 4. A: Cost with different values of T and p (λ = 0.9, B_1 = 0.1, C_h = \$20, C_s = \$1000, and C_r =\$50). B: Cost contour with different values of T and p (The contour of Figure 4A).

for the three cases, respectively. Figures 2 to 4 (both 3-D and cost contours graphs) show the global optimal values can be obtained.

Optimize p

After we find T^*, we will find p such that the minimum value of $F(T^*, p)$ is achieved, say $F(T^*, p^*)$. The cost minimization problem can be illustrated mathematically as

$$F(T^*, p^*) = \underset{\rho<1}{Minimize}\, F(T^*, p) \tag{45}$$

The study notes that the derivative of the cost function F with respect to p indicates the direction which cost function increases.

Table 1. The illustration of the implement process of p^*.

(λ, B_1)	(0.1, 0.2)	(0.1, 0.5)	(0.1, 0.8)	(0.1, 1.0)	(0.5, 1.0)	(0.9, 1.0)
T^*	31	30	30	30	10	3
p^*	1	1	1	1	1	1
$F^*(T^*, p^*)$	12.46	12.98	13.48	13.8	69.99	46.32
$\frac{dF(p)}{dp}$ in (0,1)	-15.94	-15.63	-15.48	-15.38	-6.02	-2.86
	<0	<0	<0	<0	<0	<0

$$\frac{dF(p)}{dp} = \frac{\lambda}{(q+\lambda T^* + p\bar{\lambda}^{T^*})^2}\left\{-\frac{1}{2}C_h T^*\left[\lambda T^* + \lambda + 2\bar{\lambda}^{T^*} + \lambda\bar{\lambda}^{T^*}(T^*-1)\right] + (1-\bar{\lambda}^{T^*})(1-\rho)(C_s - C_r T^*)\right\} \quad (46)$$

The first derivative test supposes that *p* is a critical number on the interval [0, 1] of the continuous cost function F with respect to p. From Equation (46), $\frac{dF(p)}{dp}$ does not change sign at *p*, then F has no local maximum or minimum at *p*.

If

$$C_s < C_r T^* + \frac{1}{2(1-\bar{\lambda}^{T^*})(1-\rho)} C_h T^*\left[\lambda T^* + \lambda + \bar{\lambda}^{T^*} + \lambda\bar{\lambda}^{T^*}(T^*-1)\right]$$

then the derivative $\frac{dF(p)}{dp}$ of equation (46) is negative, and shows that F cost function is decreases on the interval [0, 1] of p. Thus, the cost function F has an absolute minimum (or global minimum) at $p = 1$.

If

$$C_s > C_r T^* + \frac{1}{2(1-\bar{\lambda}^{T^*})(1-\rho)} C_h T^*\left[\lambda T^* + \lambda + \bar{\lambda}^{T^*} + \lambda\bar{\lambda}^{T^*}(T^*-1)\right],$$

then the derivative $\frac{dF(p)}{dp}$ of equation (46) is positive on the interval [0, 1] of p, and shows that F cost function increases. Thus, the cost function F has an absolute minimum (or global minimum) at $p = 0$.

A numerical illustration is provided by consider the cases:

Case 4: C_h = \$20, C_s = \$1000, C_r = \$50, and vary the values of λ and B_1.

Case 5: λ = 0.5, B_1 = 1.0, C_s = \$1000, C_r = \$20, and vary the values of C_h = 1, 10, 100, 1000 and \$10000.

Case 6: λ = 0.5, B_1 = 1.0, C_h = \$20, C_r = \$20, and vary the values of C_s = 1, 10, 100, 1000 and \$10000.

Case 7: λ = 0.5, B_1 = 1.0, C_h = \$20, C_s = \$1000, and vary the values of C_r = 1, 10, 100, 1000 and \$10000.

For illustrative purpose, we present the four cases listed previously to illustrate the optimization procedure shown in Tables 1 to 4, respectively. The results are in accordance with the analysis listed previously. From Tables 1 to 4, it is seen that (i) T^* increases as λ or B_1 decreases; (ii) T^* increases as C_h decreases or C_s (C_r) increases.

CONCLUSIONS

The study introduces the <*V*, *p*> policy for a discrete-time Geo/G/1 queueing system, in which a single server randomly reactivates when some messages present in the queue at ending of vacation completion instant. Some important system characteristics are derived, including the system length distribution, the turned-off period, the busy period distribution and waiting time distribution.

The study finally develops efficient methods to find the optimal <*T*, *p*> policy that minimizes the expected cost function.

Table 2. The illustration of the implement process of p^*.

C_h	**1**	**10**	**100**	**1000**	**10000**
T^*	45	14	4	1	1
p^*	1	1	1	1	1
$F^*(T^*, p^*)$	12.11	58.21	184.24	245	245
$\frac{dF(p)}{dp}$ in (0,1)	-0.46	-1.68	-13.22	-377.5	-4877.5
	<0	<0	<0	<0	<0

Table 3. The illustration of the implement process of p^*.

C_s	**1**	**10**	**100**	**1000**	**10000**
T^*	1	1	3	10	32
p^*	1	1	1	1	1
$F^*(T^*, p^*)$	-4.75	-2.5	15.38	84.98	301.25
$\frac{dF(p)}{dp}$ in (0,1)	-12.38	-11.25	-10.18	-3.02	-1.17
	<0	<0	<0	<0	<0

Table 4. The illustration of the implement process of p^*.

C_r	**1**	**10**	**100**	**1000**	**10000**
T^*	8	8	9	10	10
p	0	0	0	1	1
$F^*(T^*, p^*)$	543.6	540	462.73	44.99	-4454.13
$\frac{dF(p)}{dp}$ in (0,1)	92.3	91.58	67.6	-11.01	-909.78
	>0	>0	>0	<0	<0

REFERENCES

Bruneel H, Kim BG (1993). Discrete-time models for communication systems including ATM. Kluwer Academic Publishers, Boston.

Doshi BT (1986). Queueing systems with vacations – a survey. Queueing Syst. 1(1):29-66.

Hunter JJ (1983). Mathematical Techniques of Applied Probability, Discrete Time Models: Techniques and Applications, vol. 2. Academic, New York.

Levy Y, Yechiali U (1975). Utilization of idle time in an M/G/1 queueing system. Manage. Sci. 22(2):202-211.

Li J, Tian N (2007).The discrete-time GI/Geo/1 queue with working vacations and vacation interruption. Appl. Math. Comput. 185(1):1-10.

Meisling T (1958). Discrete time queueing theory. Oper. Res. 6(1):96–105.

Takagi H (1991). Queueing Analysis: A Foundation of Performance Evaluation, Vacation and Priority Systems, Part 1, vol. 1. North-

Holland Elsevier, Amsterdam.
Takagi H (1993). Queueing analysis: A foundation of performance evaluation, Discrete-Time Systems, Vol. 3. North-Holland, Amsterdam.
Tian N, Zhang ZG (2002). The discrete-time GI/Geo/1 queue with multiple vacations. Queueing Syst. 40(3):283-294.
Tian N, Zhang ZG (2006). Vacation Queueing Models: Theory and Applications. Springer-Verlag, New York.
Woodward ME (1994). Communication and computer networks: modelling with discrete-time queues. IEEE Computer Society Press, Los Alamitos, CA.
Zhang ZG, Tian N (2001). Geo/G/1 queue with multiple adaptive vacations. Queueing Syst. 38(4):419-429.

The impact of corporate governance on dividend decision of firms: Evidence from Pakistan

Shahid Iqbal

Institute of Management Sciences, Peshawar, Pakistan. E-mail:shahid_ims@yahoo.com.

This study has been conducted to investigate the impact of corporate governance attributes especially board attributes on the decision of dividend payment of firms in developing economy of Pakistan. Board attributes are measured by three variables: Board Size, Board Independence, and CEO duality while dividend payment decision is measured by a dummy variable DIVID. A total of 77 non financial firms listed on Karachi Stock Exchange (KSE) are used to determine the relationship of the board attributes and decision of dividend payment of firms for the period 2007 to 2011. Descriptive statistics, Correlation Matrix, Logistic Regression, and Probit regression are used for the analysis of data. A significant positive relationship is found between the Board Size and dummy variable DIVID. It has also been found that presence of Independent Board leads to no declaration of dividend payment. The study also found insignificant positive relationship between the CEO duality and DIVID of the firms.

Key words: Corporate governance, dividend decision, board composition, logistic regression, probit regression.

INTRODUCTION

The board composition is mainly controlled by the corporate governance mechanism. The corporate governance greatly attracted the attention of people after the occurrence of big scandals like Enron and WorldCom in USA and Crescent Investment bank in Pakistan (Shah and Khan 2009). If these financial scandals are examined closely, one would recognize that all these scandals have one thing in common: the role of board of directors that affected the financial results of these companies (Bajwa et al. 2011). These scandals increased the demand to conduct research on the impact of board attributes on the dividend policy of the firms and to avoid such problems in future because of few reasons. The first one is that the occurrence of such big scandals badly hit the trust of investors on corporate governance system. The second one is that Pakistan is a growing economy in Asia with limited laws about the board composition; therefore there is a great research potential about the impact of board composition on dividend payment of firms in Pakistan (Bajwa et al. 2011).

Corporate governance contains some regulatory bodies such as board of directors, management, shareholders, and auditors of the firm who protect the shareholders rights and have significant impact on dividend payment of the firms (Kowalewski et al., 2007; Bebczuk, 2005). Corporate governance is defined by Shleifer and Vishny (1997) as: "corporate governance deals with the ways in which suppliers of finance to corporations assure themselves of getting a return on their investment." However, Organization for Economic Cooperation and Development (OECD), in 1999, defined corporate governance as "a set of relationship between board of a firm, its shareholders and stake holders."

Investors invest in corporations for the purpose of return on their investments. The decision to pay dividends is the basic part of the corporate policy that is taken by the board of directors of a firm.

According to Berkley and Myers (2005) the decision of dividend payment is one of the top ten unsolved issues in corporate finance. However, it becomes more important in case of corporate gover-nance because Dittmar et al. (2003) argue that agency problem is more serious in weak corporate governance system. In weak corporate governance system, agency problem arises in which the internal shareholders take personal benefits on the part of external shareholders. Due to this reason, external shareholders prefer to pay dividends (Jensen, 1986; Mayers and Frank, 2004).

Dividend payment gives information about the financial position of a firm (Afza and Mirza, 2011). Financial researchers agreed with the view that no single factor affects the dividend policy of a firm. The problem of dividend policy becomes more complicated because of this inconclusiveness of determinants of dividend policy. Dividend policy acts as a control mechanism in reducing the conflict in the interests of shareholders and managers because shareholders want to get dividends while managers want to retain the firm resources under their control by not declaring dividends. Jensen (1986) and Rozeff (1982) argue that firms use dividend payment for the reduction of agency problem.

Besides dividend payment, corporate governance is also assumed as an effective control mechanism to reduce the agency cost. Gugler and Yurtuglo (2002) carried out a study on the relationship of corporate governance and dividend payment of firms in Germany. They used ownership concentration and ownership structure as proxy variable to measure the corporate governance and analyzed the six years dividend announcements of the firms. They found a significant negative relationship between corporate governance variables and dividend payment of firms. Mitton and Todd (2004) conducted a study on the relationship of corporate governance and dividend payout ratio of firm. He used a sample of 19 emerging economies and found that strong corporate governance significantly and positively affects the dividend payment of the firms.

D'Souza and Saxena (1999) argues that agency cost is negatively related with dividend payment of firms. Dittmar et al. (2003) argue that agency problem is more serious in large boards. Hellman and Puri (2000) argue that large board of director leads to weak corporate governance system due to the involvement of more people in decision making process. This study shows that BSIZE is positively related with dividend decision of firms. This finding is opposite to the findings of D'Souza and Saxena (1999) in agency theory who argues that agency cost is negatively related with dividend payment of firms.

The objective of this study is to determine the relationship of board attributes on dividend decision of non financial firms in Pakistan. Board attributes are measured by three variables such as CEOD, BIND, and BSIZE while dividend decision is measured by a dummy variable DIVD which is equal to 1 if a firm pays dividend in the respective fiscal year and equal to 0 if the firm does not pay the dividends in the respective fiscal year. This study contributes to the literature on several grounds.

Afza and Sehrish (2011) conducted a study on the relationship of board mechanism with dividend policy with a sample of 42 firms. This study gives a new dimension to it by adding a new variable of CEO duality to measure the governance system of board and increasing the sample size to 77 non financial firms. Shah et al. (2011) also conducted a study on the relationship of board attributes with dividend policy in Pakistan. They used only the dividend payout ratio to measure the dividend policy. However, the current study adds a dummy variable DIV to measure the dividend policy of the firms that includes the dividend paying and non paying firms. The study applies Logit Regression, Probit Regression, Descriptive statistics and correlation.

LITERATURE REVIEW

The decision of dividend payment is the hot and unresolved problem of the corporate fiancé sector. Many studies have been carried out for this purpose. Mayers (2000) and Jensen (1986) argue that according to agency theory the conflict between the external shareholders and managers of the organization can be reduced by paying dividends to shareholders and thus the managers cannot expropriate the retained earnings. Rozeff (1982) argued that dividend payment decreases due to the presence of inside shareholders. He used dividend payout ratio as a measure of dividend policy for a sample of 1000 US firms and found negative relationship between dividend payout ratio and the presence of inside shareholders. Belden et al. (2005) argue that the presence of outside directors in the board increases dividend payment. They used a sample of 524 largest American companies and found negative relationship between the outside directors in the board and dividend payment of the companies.

Mitton and Todd (2004) conducted a study on the relationship of corporate governance and dividend payout ratio of firm. He used a sample of 19 emerging economies and found that strong corporate governance significantly and positively affects the dividend payment of the firms.

Agency theory

In agency theory, Jensen and Meckling (1976) argue that the agency relationship is created between agent and principal when the principal hires the agent to carry out his duties on his behalf. D'Souza and Saxena (1999) argues that agency cost is negatively related with dividend payment of the firms. Similarly, Rozeff (1982) argues that dividend is a tool for reducing agency cost. Jensen (1986) suggested that dividend payment reduces the conflict between managers and shareholders of the firm. Managers want to retain the resources of the firm instead of dividends. They follow the growth opportunities of the firm because in this case more resources of the firm will come under their control. On the other hand, share-holders of the organization want dividends instead of retaining earnings. Therefore, if dividends are not paid, the managers may use these resources for their personal benefits or they may invest these resource in unprofitable projects.

Theory of irrelevance

Miller and Modigliani (1961) gave theory of irrelevance that is also known as MM theory. They argue that dividend is not important for shareholders in perfect capital market, because in perfect capital market dividend payment does not have any impact on the value of the firm. It does not make a difference for shareholders whether to get the cash in the form of dividend, or in the form of share prices, or in the form of capital gains.

The bird in hand theory

Gordon (1963) gave a theory known as "The bird in hand Theory". This theory suggests that investors prefer the payment of cash instead of future return on capital because they want to reduce future risk. Bhattacharya (1980) and John and Williams (1985) gave Signaling Theory which states that asymmetry is created between managers and shareholders by the presence of insider information. Therefore dividend must be paid to shareholders according to the stock prices.

Signaling theory

Signaling theory assumes that dividend is a tool through which a firm delivers information to the market (Miller and Rock, 1985; Bali, 2003). This theory has set an idea that managers send information to the shareholders in order to create a relation of trust. As managers are involved in day to day operations of the firm, therefore, they have more information as compared to the shareholders of the firm. However, managers do not reveal all information to the shareholders. Therefore, dividend policy can be used to reduce information asymmetries between principle and agents by delivering internal information about the future prospects of the firm.

Literature from Pakistan

Shah et al. (2011) carried out a research study on the impact of ownership structure on dividend policy of firms in Pakistan. Using Common Effect Model, they found a positive relationship between ownership structure of board of directors and dividend payout of the firms listed on KSE.

Afzal and Sehrish (2011) conducted a study on the relationship between ownership structure, board composition and dividend of policy of firms listed on KSE. Using OLS model they found that board size, firm size, individual ownership, and investment opportunities are significantly positively related with dividend payout of the firms. They also found a positive relationship between board independence and dividend payout of the firms but the result was not significant.

Ullah et al. (2012) determined the impact of institutional ownership on dividend policy of firms listed on KSE-100 index for a period of eight years, that is from 2003 to 2010. Using stepwise multiple regression models they pointed out that managerial share ownership is negatively related with dividend policy of the firms in Pakistan. While institutional and foreign share ownership were negatively related with dividend policy of the firms.

Board independence and dividend policy

D'Souza and Saxena (1999) argues that agency cost is negatively related with dividend payment of the firms. Similarly, De Angelo et al. (2004) conducted a study on the relationship between agency cost and dividend payments of the firms to their shareholders. He found that agency problems can be prevented by dividend payments. Therefore, a positive relation is expected between non-executive directors and dividend payment.

H1: *There is positive relationship between non-executive directors (board independence) and dividend payments of the firm.*

Board size and dividend Policy

Yermack (1996) argues that large boards are less effective control mechanism. Jensen (1993) argues that a board having large number of directors is less effective because of the inclusion of more people, the decision making process becomes slower. In less effective control mechanism the agency cost increases. Therefore, a negative relation is expected between large boards and dividend payments. However, Klein (2002) argues that large boards play effective control mechanism. In this case a positive relation is expected between board size and dividend payments. Therefore, mixed results are expected.

H2: *There is negative relationship between board size and dividend payments.*

CEO duality and dividend policy

Baliga et al. (1996) found that firms where chief executive officer is not the chairman of the board of directors, corporate governance mechanism is more effective there. Therefore, CEO duality (where CEO is also the chairman) is negatively related with effective corporate governance system. When corporate governance mechanism is weak, agency cost will be higher (Dittmar et al., 2003). D'Souza

Table 1. Variables explanation.

Variable		Explanation
Dependent		
DIVID	Dividend decision	Dummy variable equal to 1 if a decides to pay dividend in the current fiscal year and equal to 0 if it does not the dividend
Independent		
BIND	Board independence	The ratio of non executive directors to total number of directors
CEOD	CEO duality	A dummy variable is equal to 1 when chairman and CEO is the same person
BSIZE	Board size	Total number of directors in the board
Size	Size of firm	Log of total assets
LEV	Leverage	Total debt/total assets
SGRT	Sales growth	Percentage change in annual sales
FV	Firm's volatility	Variations in Net income before taxes

and Saxena (1999) argues that agency cost is negatively related with dividend payment of the firms. Therefore, negative relation is expected between CEO duality and dividend payments of the firm.

H3: *There is negative relationship between CEO duality and dividend payments.*

DATA AND METHODOLOGICAL FRAME WORK

Population of this study includes all the non financial firms in Pakistan listed on KSE. The sample of this study contains 77 non-financial firms from Pakistan listed on KSE. These firms are conveniently selected from all the major sectors of Pakistani economy. The data are collected for five years (from 2007 to 2011). The data are collected from the annual reports of the concerned companies. The data regarding the financial variables have been collected from the "balance sheet analysis of non-financial companies", a publication of state bank of Pakistan. Certain constraints reduced the sample size. Financial firms are not included in the sample because the financial structure of these companies is different from that of non-financial firms. Only those firms were included who provided their annual reports for five years (2007 to 2011).

Variables of the study

Dividend is taken as a dependent variable while board attributes are taken as independent variables. Table 1 shows the variables explanations. Dividend payment is measured by a dummy variable equal to 1 if a firm pays the dividend and 0 if the firm does not pay the dividend in the respective fiscal year. Corporate governance is measured by three variables, BSIZE, BIND, and CEOD. BSIZE is the total number of directors sitting in the board following Yermack (1996) and Klein (2002). CEO duality is measured by a dummy variable CEOD equal to 1 if the CEO is also the chairman of the board, according to Baliga et al. (1996) and Kusnadi (2011). Board independence is represented by BIND and measured by taking a ratio of number of non- executive directors in the board to total number of directors in the board. Size of the firm (Size), Leverage (LEV), Firm volatility (Fv) and sales growth (SGRT) are used as control variables in the study. Size of the firm is measured by taking log of total assets.

Table 2 shows descriptive statistics that has been applied to determine the nature of the data. Among the independent variables, the board size has highest mean value which shows the greater impact of firm's size for determination of dividend payment of firms. The second highest value occurs for BIND which shows its importance for dividend payment of firms.

Table 3 shows the correlation between the dividend payment of firms and corporate governance variables. Board size and dummy variable DIVID have significant positive correlation. Board independence and dividend have significant negative correlation. CEOD has negative correlation with dividend payment of the firms. Size of the firm and sales growth have positive correlation with dividend payment of the firms while firm's volatility and leverage have negative correlation with dividend payment of the firms.

Logistic regression

Logistic model is used in those cases where the dependent variable is a binary outcome variable which takes a value of 1 and 0. It is a nonlinear regression model which predicts the dependent variable to be either 0 or 1. This study seeks to investigate the impact of board composition on dividend policy of firms in Pakistan. The dependent variable dividend payment is measured by a dummy variable DIVID which is a binary outcome variable. Logistic model assumes cumulative logistic distribution.

Probit regression

Probit model is also used in those cases where the dependent variable is a binary outcome variable which takes a value of 1 and 0. Probit model gives the same results like the Logit model. However, the main difference between the Probit and Logit models is in the distribution function. Probit model assumes cumulative normal distribution while Logit model assumes cumulative standard logistic distribution.

There are certain limitations of these models as well. These models are simple but often not appropriate. These models assume that probabilities will fall between 0 and 1 for sufficiently large or small values of independent variables. The models may be less appropriate for several independent variables.

Table 2. Descriptive statistics.

Variable	Observation	Mean	Std Div	Max	Min
DIVID	385	0.6736292	0.469498	1	0
BSIZE	385	0.9211591	0.090968	1.17609	0.69897
BIND	385	0.5975406	0.251596	0.92857	0
CEOD	385	0.1948052	0.396566	1	0
SIZE	385	6.800108	0.606211	8.41793	5.46375
LEV	385	0.559073	0.193131	1.17133	0.01968
SGRT	385	0.4879052	3.378031	56.4145	-1
FV	385	0.0810098	0.117085	.868074	0.00603

Table 3. Correlation matrix.

	DIVID	BSIZE	BIND	CEOD	SIZE	LEV	SGRT	FV
DIVID	1.00							
BSIZE	0.147*	1.00						
BIND	-0.153*	0.131*	1.00					
CEOD	-0.012	-0.146*	-0.024	1.00				
SIZE	0.112*	0.405*	-0.0006	-0.001	1.00			
LEV	-0.332*	0.053	-0.066	0.051	-0.021	1.00		
SGRT	0.012	0.028	0.071	-0.013	-0.043	-0.047	1.00	
FV	-0.213*	-0.001	0.134*	0.208*	0.159*	-0.005	0.0371	1.00

$DIVD_{(i,t)} = \alpha + \beta 1(CEOD) + \beta 2(BSIZE) + \beta 3(BIND) + \beta 4(Size) + \beta 5(LEV) + \beta 7(SGRT) + \beta 8(FV) + \dot{\varepsilon} i$

Where
i = i^{th} firm in the sample
t = time period (from 2007 to 2011)
α = is the intercept
β = (β1....β7), slope coefficients
ἑ = error term

RESULTS AND DISCUSSION

Table 4 shows the results of Logistic and Probit models used for analysis of the data. The interpretation of odds ratio is different from simple coefficients of OLS model. If the odds ratio is greater than 1 then the probability of Dividend=1(company pays dividend) increases. The logit coefficient of BSIZE is 219.8813 which represents the probability of Dividend =1 when BSIZE increases by 1 unit. The z value of BSIZE is 3.22 which is greater than 1.96 which shows that BSIZE has significant positive impact on dividend policy of the firms. This finding supports the findings of Afzal and Sehrish (2010) who also found a positive relationship between BSIZE and the decision to pay dividends. One possible explanation for it is that large board includes more diversified portfolio of directors and in the presence of large number of directors, dividend announcement gains more importance. It also means that large boards in Pakistan are effective tool of monitoring. To keep the management under their control and to avoid misuse of cash, high dividend payment is made. However, this finding is opposite to the finding of Hellman and Puri (2000), who found that large boards result in weakness of corporate governance.

The odds ratio of BIND is 0.154 which is less than 1. Its z value is -3.43 and p value is 0.001 which shows that BIND has significant impact on dividend policy of the firms. As the odds ratio is less than 1 therefore, the probability of dividend=1 (company pays dividend) decreases. Therefore BIND has significant negative impact on dividend policy of the firms. The odds ratio, 0.154 represents the probability of dividend=1 when BIND decreases by 1 unit. This finding does not support the findings of Belden et al. (2005), who found a positive relationship between BIND and dividend decision of the firms. The negative relationship between BIND and dividend decision shows that due to the lack of clearly defined roles of non executive directors in code of corporate governance of Pakistan, boards of directors in Pakistani firms may include incapable non-executive directors who are not effective tool of monitoring or strong corporate governance and the chances of the decision to pay dividends decrease. Table 4 shows that the odds ratio of CEOD is 1.651083 which is greater than 1. Its z value is 1.51 while p value, 0.132 clearly shows that

Table 4. Logistic and probit models.

Variables	Logistic model			Probit model		
	Odds ratio	**Z values**	**P values**	**Odds Ratio**	**Z vale**	**P value**
BSIZE (board size)	219.8813	3.22	0.001	3.132181	3.21	0.001
BIND (Board Independence)	0.154338	-3.43	0.001	-1.1137	-3.56	0
CEOD (CEO duality)	1.651083	1.51	0.132	0.319781	1.61	0.107
SIZE (size of the company)	1.440574	1.53	0.126	0.213824	1.53	0.126
LEV (leverage)	0.004248	-6.51	0.000	-3.21632	-6.84	0
FV (Firm volatility)	0.006760	-3.38	0.001	-2.73468	-3.73	0
SGRT (sales growth of the company)	1.006505	0.15	0.882	0.003026	0.13	0.898
No of observations	385			385		
Number of firms	77			77		
LR chi2 (7)	96.52			96.7		
Prob > chi2	0.000			0.000		
Pseudo R2	0.2004			0.2004		

CEOD has insignificant positive impact on dividend policy of the non financial firms listed on KSE. This positive relationship shows that in the firms where CEO and chairman hold the same post, the chance of the decision to pay dividends increases. Baliga et al. (1996) and Tsui et al. (2001) argue that the board where the CEO is not the chairman the board is a more effective control mechanism than when CEO is also the chairman of the board. Here one person is the chairman as well as the CEO of the board who strongly monitors the board and to avoid the misuse of cash balances, he declares the dividend payment. This can be also explained from the view that most of the firms in Pakistan are family owned and run by one powerful person (Cheema, 2003). Both models show that size of the firm and sales are positively related with dividend decision of the firm while LEV and FV are significantly negatively related with dividend decision of the firms.

Conclusion

This study empirically investigates the impact of board composition on the decision of dividend payment in non financial firm listed on KSE. The data have been collected for 77 non financial firms for five years (from 2007 to 2011). Descriptive statistics, correlation matrix and Logistic regression are used for analysis of the data. Logistic regression is used because the dependent variable DIVID is a binary outcome variable.

A significant positive relationship is found between board size and the decision of dividend payment. Firms with large boards will likely decide to declare dividends to shareholders. One possible explanation for it is that large board includes more diversified portfolio of directors and in the presence of large number of directors, dividend announcement gains more importance. It also means that large boards in Pakistan are the effective tool of monitoring. To keep the management under their control and to avoid misuse of cash, high dividend payment is made. However, this finding is opposite to the finding of Hellman and Puri (2000) who found that large boards result in weakness of corporate governance.

BIND has significant negative impact on dividend policy of the firms. This finding does not support the findings of Belden et al. (2005) who found a positive relationship between BIND and dividend decision of the firms. The negative relationship between BIND and dividend decision shows that due to the lack of clearly defined roles of non executive directors in code of corporate governance of Pakistan, boards of directors in Pakistani firms may include incapable non-executive directors who are not effective tool of monitoring or strong corporate governance, and the chance of the decision to pay dividends decreases.

CEOD has insignificant positive impact on dividend policy of the non financial firms listed on KSE. This positive relationship shows that the firms where CEO and chairman hold the same post, the chance of dividend payment increases. Size of the firm and sales are insignificantly positively related with dividend decision of the firm while LEV and FV are significantly negatively related with dividend decision of the firms. This finding supports the Agency Theory. In agency theory D'Souza and Saxena (1999) argues that agency cost is negatively related with dividend payment of the firms. Similarly, Rozeff (1982) argues that dividend is a tool for reducing agency cost. Jensen (1986) suggested that dividend payment reduces the conflict between managers and shareholders of the firm. Baliga et al. (1996) argue that CEOD is a more effective type of control. Therefore, when corporate governance is strong, the chance of the decision to pay dividends increases which supports the agency theory.

RECOMMENDATIONS

Board size is a vital part of corporate governance. Therefore, for good governance board size should be kept small. There should be more Independent Non Executive Directors in the board for effective governance. There is no clear distinction between Independent Non Executive Directors and Non Executive Directors. Therefore, in code of corporate governance there should be clear distinction between these two terms.

FUTURE RESEARCH DIRECTION

A deep investigation can find more interesting facts regarding the impact of board attributes on dividend payment of firms in Pakistan. Besides using annual reports, other sources of data collection such as interviews with chief financial officers, managers, and investors can also be used to see the impact of corporate governance on dividend payment of firms. Practitioner based corporate governance index can be used to check corporate governance utility.

REFERENCES

Afzal M, Sehrish S (2011). Ownership Structure, Board Composition and Dividend Policy inPakistan.

Bajwa AS, Bashir A, Lions C (2011). The impact of ownership and board composition on financial performance of the firm. Empirical Evidence pp.1-126.

Bali R (2003). "An Empirical Analysis of Stock Returns around Dividend Changes", Appl. Econ. 35:51-61.

Baliga B, Moyer R, Ramesh P (1996). CEO duality and firm performance: What's the fuss? Strateg. Manage. J. 17:41-53.

Bhattacharya S (1979). "Imperfect Information, Dividend Policy and "the Bird in the Hand"Fallacy", Bell J. Econ. 10(1):259-270.

Bebczuk RN (2005). "Corporate Governance and Ownership: Measurement and Impact on Corporate Performance and Dividend Policies in Argentina", Research Network Working Papers, R-516, Center for Financial Stability and Universidad Nacional De La Plata.

Belden S, Fister T, Knapp B (2005). "Dividends and Directors: Do Outsiders Reduce Agency Costs?" Bus. Soc. Rev. 110(2):171-180.

Berkley R, Myers S (2005). "Principles of corporate finance. 8th ed, London: McGraw- Hill. Black F, 1976 'The Dividend Puzzle', J. Port. Manage. 2:5-8.

Cheema A (2003). "Corporate governance in Pakistan: issues and concerns" The NIPA J. 8:2.

De Angelo H, De Angelo L, Douglas JS (2004). "Are dividends disappearing? Dividend concentration and the consolidation of earnings", J. Financ. Econ. 72:425-456.

Dittmar A, Mahrt-Smith J, Servaes H (2003). International corporate governance and corporate cash holdings, J. Financ. Quantit. Anal. 38:111-134.

D'Souza J, Saxena AK (1999). "Agency cost, market risk, investment opportunities and dividend policy - an international perspective." Manag. Finan. 25:35-44.

Gordon MJ (1963). "Optimal Investment and Financing Policy" J. Finan.18 (2):264-72.

Gugler K, Yurtoglu BB (2002). "Corporate Governance and Dividend Pay-out Policy in Germany", Eur. Econ. Rev. 47:731-758.

Harford J, Li K, (2007). Decoupling CEO wealth and firm performance: the case of acquiring CEOs. J. Finan. 62:917-949.

Hellman T, Puri M (2000). The interaction between product market and financing strategy: the role of venture capital. Rev Financ. Stud.13:959-984.

Himmelberg C, Hubbard RG, Palia D (1999). Understanding the determinants of managerial ownership and the link between ownership and performance. J. Financ. Econ. 53:353-384.

Jensen MC (1993). The modern industrial revolution, exit and the failure of internal control Systems, J. Finan. 48:831-880.

Jensen M, (1986). Agency costs of free cash flow, corporate finance and takeovers. Am. Econ. Rev. 76:323-329.

Jensen M, Meckling W (1976). Theory of the firm: Managerial behavior, agency costs and ownership structure. J. Financ. Econ. 3:305-360.

John K, Williams J, (1985). "Dividends, dilution, and taxes: A signaling equilibrium", J. Finan. 40:1053-1070.

Kim CS, Mauer DC, Sherman AE (1998). The Determinants of Corporate Liquidity: Theory and Evidence. J. Financ. Quant. Anal. 33(3):335-359.

Klein A (2002). "Audit Committee, Board of Director Characteristics, And Earning Management", J. Account. Econ. 33:375-400.

Kowalewski O, Stetsyuk I, Talavera O (2007). "Corporate Governance and DividendPolicy in Poland", Discussion Papers 702, DIW Berlin, German Institute for Economic Research.

Kusnadi Y (2011). Do corporate governance mechanisms matter for cash holdings and firm value ? Pacific-Basin Financ. J. 19(5):554-570. doi:10.1016/j.pacfin.2011.04.002.

Miller MH, Rock K (1985). "Dividend Policy under Asymmetric Information", The J. Financ. 40(4):1031-1051.

Miller MH, Modigliani F (1961). "Dividend Policy, Growth and the Valuation of Shares", J. Bus. 34(4):411-433.

Myers M, Frank B (2004). The Determinants of Corporate Dividend Policy. Acad. Accout. Financ. Stud. J. 8(3):17-28.

Mitton Todd (2004). "Corporate Governance and dividend Policy in emerging markets", Emerging Market Rev. 5:409-426.

Pettit RR (1977), "Taxes, Transactions Costs and the Clientele Effect of Dividends", J. Finan. Econ. 5(3):419-436.

Rozeff MS (1982). "Growth, Beta and Agency Costs as Determinants of Dividend Payout Ratios", J. Finan. Res. 5(3):249-259.

Shah A, Khan SA (2009). Empirical Investigation of Debt-Maturity Structure: Evidence from Pakistan, Pakistan Dev. Rev. 48(4):565-578

Shah U, Hasnain (2011). Impact of ownership sturcture on dividend policy of firm. 3: 22–26.

Shleifer A, Vishny R (1997). A survey of corporate governance. J. Financ. 52:737-783.

Tsui J, Jaggi B, Gull F (2001). CEO domination, growth opportunities, and their impact on audit fees. J. Account. Audit. Financ 16:189–208.

Ullah H, Fida A, Khan S (2012). The Impact of Ownership Structure on Dividend Policy Evidence from Emerging Markets KSE-100 Index Pakistan. Int. J. Bus. Soc. Sci.3(9):298-307.

Yermack D (1996). "Higher Market Valuation of Companies with a Small Board of Directors", J. Finan. Econ. 40(2):185-211.

Microfinancing in Pakistan: Growth prospects and poverty reduction strategy

Rizwana Bashir[1], Shafiq-ur-Rehman[2] and Atif Hassan[3]

[1]Bahria University, Karachi, Pakistan.
[2]Department of Economics, University of Karachi, Pakistan.
[3]Defence Housing Authority (DHA) Suffa University, Karachi, Pakistan.

Microfinance institutions (MFIs) are globally considered as a distinctly effective way to make the living standard of the people better. The purpose of conducting this research study is to investigate the growth prospects of microfinance programs in Pakistan to eradicate poverty. The microfinance program has been operative in Pakistan since October 1972 in one form or the other. It was first launched by the then government to attack poverty. But the current development took place in the 1990s in Pakistan, when most of the MFPs were established in the form of Microfinance Banks (MFBs), Rural Support Programs (RSPs), Microfinance Institutions (MFIs) or others. The responses of MFPs were quite encouraging. Most of them have demonstrated the expansion in terms of number of branches as well as the borrowers. The outreach is also expanding during the time period studied (2006 to 2008). Though the rate of growth is very slow and currently MFPs could serve only 11% of prospective clients. Large number of MFPs also reported a repayment rate of 90 to 100% which witnesses the positive changes in the lives of their clients.

Key words: Microfinance outreach, empowerment of poor, poverty eradication, growth.

INTRODUCTION

Microfinance seems to provide a permanent source of income for the clients making them independent of any further financial aid. Since microcredit finance capital expenditures of micro enterprise help increase the regular income of the enterprise making the enterprise economically independent and self-reliant. It provides the financial capital for a smallest enterprise and let it increase the size of its operation and capable of permanently generating the finances for its operation in contrast to one time help (financial aid) to finance consumption expenditure of clients.

Usually formal banking sector excludes low income households, because of non availability of any collateral to cover their borrowings, increasing the risk for the banker. Clients of microfinance are low income people excluded by formal financial sector, that is, self-employed small entrepreneurs (household based), self-employed women, small farmers, artisan, small shopkeepers and small service providers etc. Microfinance institutions provided the enduring solution for the poor. It enables clients maintaining self-reliance and dignity discover their own solutions with the external financial assistance (by a microfinance provider) to come out of deprivation state.

According to World Bank's Global poverty report (Joanna 2000), internationally, the percentage of poor people reduced from 29% in the year 1987 to 26% in 1998 but the number of poor people remained almost same at around 1.2 billion witnessing an increase in population effected the results achieved through various efforts to reduce poverty. Some of the countries in East

Asian region made notable progress to combat poverty like China and endorsed reduction in global poverty. South Asia, Latin America and Africa could not demonstrate any achievements to reduce poverty during this time period.

In these regions there was either little or no decline in poverty levels. Some regions like Latin America even reported an increase in poverty level, the figure for poverty in this region increased by 12 million taking it up to 78 million. These figures will further amplify if a poverty line of $2 per day (World Bank 2000) is used, which is said to be more suitable for these regions. The most noteworthy conclusion of the said report was, "approximately 75% of the world's poor people live in the Asian and Pacific region" out of total 2.8 billion poor people of the world. Amongst these 75% poor people the largest proportion of poor live in South Asia. According to an estimate 522 million people are living in poverty in South Asian Region. The occurrence of poverty also rose to 5 from 3% in countries of Eastern Europe and Central Asia. These regions are expected to host the largest amount of poor people surviving under "poverty line".

Well-designed micro-lending schemes are capable to push people above poverty line by augmenting their sources of income. The microfinance institutions can be at advantageous position to continue providing loans to their old clients that are not poorer now. If MFPs continue their relationship with old clients, they can provide enormous financial source to the microfinance institutions in the form of savings. Furthermore, the mechanism of delivering microfinance to only middle and upper poor creates a gap amongst the poor. Not serving core poor by MFIs can increase the number of poorest people, being too risky to do business with due to very high transaction costs involved. If we consider the fact, microfinance only prefer the clients who are already running micro enterprises and need external assistance to augment their incomes. Therefore, they can make negligible or no effect on the income of extreme poor. It is comparatively easier to move middle upper poor above poverty line through microfinance programs thus indeed reducing the number of poor people living below poverty line. Another reason for exclusion of poorest could be the "Group Lending Schemes" offered by most of MFPs globally, since most of the borrowers would have a preference to combine other no risk members (excluding poorest). To aid the extreme poor in Pakistan, other financial assistance programs can be more helpful; like rural support programs, income support programs, subsidies, donations and other schemes of Pakistan Poverty Alleviation Fund.

Apart from their core function of financing micro enterprises for income generation, MFPs also lend for micro-enterprise development purpose. Though, micro enterprise development has nothing to do with poverty alleviation objective but it promotes economic growth which leads to poverty reduction as proven through various studies (Adams 2003). In a broader context microfinance can be helpful in reducing unemployment by promoting self-employment. High interest rate of micro loans is also seen by critics as a hindrance in its success as a poverty targeting tool. This issue is also addressed in the current research in relation to its impact on repayment rate.

Incidence of poverty in Pakistan

Pakistan ranks 141st on the 182 countries "UNDP (2009) Human Development Index" (HDI) based on 2007 data. It is a comprehensive indicator of well being of people. Various poverty bands of Pakistan's poverty profile show different poverty levels for different provinces. A study conducted by Social Policy Development Center in 1996 to 1997, suggests that the highest incidence of both rural and urban poverty was recorded in Balochistan, 54 and 35% respectively, followed by Punjab, 29 and 33%, Sindh, 53 and 20%, and NWFP, 24 and 18%.

When poverty is not addressed promptly, it may cause serious impression on socio-economic structure of the society. Increase in the degree of poverty together with illiteracy, propensity of crime also increases resulting in socio-economic unrest in the country. Efforts have been made by government and non-government institutions to combat poverty in terms of one time financial aid, donation programs, financial subsidies, income support programs. In pursuit of such effort Pakistan Poverty Alleviation Fund was also established and many rural support programs were initiated. All these efforts played their role in poverty reduction but these efforts require continuous financial support and could not provide permanent solution for poor people. Microfinance with global success stories was also adopted by government and non-government organization as a strategy to fight against poverty. Microfinance alleviates poverty by offering micro-credit to low-income households to kick-start a small income generating venture. Various research studies have shown positive impacts of micro-finance on lives of poor throughout the world in provision of fundamentals of life as well as vulnerability in life.

Microfinance in Pakistan

The microfinance program is not new in Pakistan. It has been in operation since October 1972 in one form or the other. It was first launched by the then government to curb poverty. The latest economic survey of Pakistan indicates that as in June 1999, the government had disbursed over rupee 4.2 billion to alleviate the poverty level in Pakistan. The current growth of MFPs is observed in late 1990s.

Microfinance as an anti-poverty strategy

Anti-poverty strategies floated by poor countries achieved

less success due to many reasons. However, the breakthrough came when the new Bottom-Up (BP) approach introduced a few years back. It was felt that empowering people and allowing them to create their own jobs and revenues were recognized as ways through which poverty could be alleviated permanently. The new BP approach gave new life to anti-poverty strategies and a special role to credit in the overall poverty eradication process.

LITERATURE REVIEW

Pitt and Khandker (1998) the World Bank economist, conducted a survey. Their study was recognized as "mother of all studies" by David Hulme. They acknowledged the microfinance industry with their immense words in their study, for demonstrating the encouraging impacts on their clients. They concluded for their surveyed MFIs that their lending offered an almost 18% return on investment for their funded micro enterprises. That is for each taka lend to a woman borrower increased their annual household expenditure by an extra 0.18 taka. This survey was conducted from 1,798 sampled households in total. These households were clients of either BRAC, Grameen Bank, or RD-12 (Bangladesh Rural Development Board, a government agency). This survey was also compared with non-member households. Particularly, male borrowers could not get similar return; the returns they could get were only 11%. The research reports range of positive impacts, for instance:

a) A one percent rise in credit to Grameen women increased the probability of girls' school enrollment by 1.86 % points.
b) A 10% rise in credit provided to women increased the arm perimeter of girls by 6%.
c) A one percent rise in credit to women increased the height-for-age of both boys by 1.42% and girls by 1.16%.

Otero (1991) defined microfinance as "the provision of financial services to low-income poor and the core poor self-employed community". According to Otero the objective of microfinance is much more than provision of financial capital to the individual poor. Microfinance has its impact at a broader level. It urges to establish such institutions which contribute to well being of the poor as well as bring a change at global level. Otero further demonstrate the microfinance mechanism to combat poverty.

Dichter (1999) refer to the 1990s as "the microfinance decade". He recognized 1990s as the era of accelerated growth in the number of microfinance service providers. This time period is recognized for microfinance turning into an industry.

Ledgerwood (2000) stresses on provision of expanded financial services like insurance and payment services. He emphasized on making microfinance more than it generally include such as savings and credit.

Schreiner and Colombet (2001) described microfinance as it involves the provision of loans, savings services, insurance and other financial services to the poor households. Due to lack of collateral, they could not qualify to receive any type of financial services from the conventional banking sector. Whether they live in rural and urban locales they remain incapable. Schreiner and Colombet identify microfinance as an endeavor to develop an access to financial services for under-privileged individuals on small scale ignored in formal financial sector.

UNCDF (Garson, 2004) found that the outreach of microfinance service providers is alarmingly low. Approximately 10,000 MFIs could reach about 30 million people of the world which has made them to achieve an outreach of four percent of potential clients. Through its research studies UNCDF identified three very important functions performed by microfinance in development of any country. First, it promotes gender equity by empowering women and making them economically practical component of economy. Second, it is very helpful in promoting economic welfare of the households. Thirdly, it also helps attain the very basic needs of the poor and guard against risks in life.

PPAF (2002) states that the conventional micro credit programs generally exclude extreme poor (the poorest). PPAF identifies two reasons for the exclusion of very poor clients from the network of conventional micro-credit programs. One reason is, poorest keep themselves away from such activities, not considering themselves "credit worthy" either, or may be lack of awareness about micro credit programs lead to their exclusion. Another important reason is that some of the flourishing micro-credit institutions remain cautious to exclude out potentially risky customers from their programs. Most MFIs reported the poorest as most risky to work with.

Khan (2001) commented that Pakistan is clearly on the right course, though significant gains in the fight against poverty are not so far visible. Ultimately, Pakistan's growth and development will depend on the governments' ability to remain persistent with strong fiscal and monetary policies and to continue the momentum of advancing broad-based structural reforms to promote private sector development. Intensifying implementation capacity will be crucial to improving public service delivery to the poor as well as sufficient resources being provided to key social sectors.

Musharaf (2002) says that inequalities between the richest and the poorest communities are widening. Pakistanis are well cognizant of the challenges poverty poses to humanity. Action is required on a number of fronts, as only a multi-pronged strategy can deal with the dilemma of poverty. Women are worst hit by poverty, and with them the family unit gets entangled in a vicious cycle of poverty, ignorance, diseases and even more poverty.

Table 1. Year of establishment of MFPs.

MFP category	MFPs	Year of establishment
RSP	SRSP	1991
	NRSP	1991
MFI	KASHAF	1997
	ASASAH	2003
MFB	FMFBL	2001
	KHUSHALI	2000
Others	ORIX	1992
	JWS	1990
	TF	1994

Source: Computed.

Littlefield et al. (2003) referred to a number of researches performed in Bangladesh, Uganda, Zimbabwe, India and Indonesia on various microfinance projects and found that all those projects demonstrate achievements in poverty reduction and brining positive changes. They state that "various studies document increase in income and assets, and decreases in vulnerability of micro-finance clients". They for example, mentioned a report on India's 'SHARE project', demonstrating three-quarters of customers witnessed "significant improvements in their economic well-being and that half of the clients graduated out of poverty"

RESEARCH METHODOLOGY

In this research, methodology includes primary as well as secondary data analysis. For collection of primary data research tool used is questionnaire and it covers the data collection period of 2006 to 2008. Equal importance is given to qualitative and quantitative data both. A variety of sources were helpful for gathering secondary data including various international reports issued by United Nations, Economic Surveys of Pakistan and various periodic publication of Pakistan Microfinance Network. Secondary data analysis was helpful in connecting what has been done earlier and findings of the current research. The selected sampling procedure is quota Sampling. The sample is collected from all four types of MFPs operating in Pakistan as classified by PMN 2007, so that participation of all categories of MFPs could be ensured to make the scope of the research comprehensive. We know that Microfinance Banks (MFBs), Microfinance Institutes (MFIs), Rural Support Programs (RSPs) and others all have different scope, different clientele, and different objectives. In this view it was important to have representation of all of these four categories in the sample extracted from them.

FACTS AND ANALYSIS

Growth in microfinance providers

As reported by MFPs, it is revealed that microfinance sector experienced growth during 1990s in Pakistan. Around 70% MFPs established from 1990 to 2000.

It further revealed that the microfinance in Pakistan is not very aged. Therefore in our analysis of microfinance achievements we have to take into account this fact that microfinance sector is very young in Pakistan in comparison with international success stories. In such small time it can not be compared with achievements of microfinance worldwide. It requires time and resources to expand and achieve desired objectives. The sampled MFPs established and started their operations during 1990 to 2003 as mentioned in Table 1. In the current research study growth of microfinance is measured in terms of branch offices as well as number of borrowers (clients).

Growth in number of branches

The objective of analyzing the success of MFPs in reaching the core poor can be witnessed through growth in their branch office. The scope of this research is country wide therefore it was considered appropriate to analyze the outreach of microfinance from 2006 to 2008 in terms of growth in number of branches.

Table 2 summarizes the growth in number of branches of sampled MFPs from 2006 to 2008. Figure 2 depicts the overall growth in number of branches based on data received from MFPs and summarized in Table 2. The 30% sample studied from all four categories; that is, RSPs, MFIs, MFBs and others show overall growth in number of branches during the period. From 2006 to 2007 MFPs represented around 12% growth and from 2007 to 2008 the overall number of branches increased by 15%.

Therefore, looking at Figure 1 it can be concluded that microfinance outreach is increasing year after year in Pakistan though the pace of growth is slow due to industry constraints. To reveal growth prospects of microfinance sector an in-depth analysis of the data received from MFPs has shown growth in number of branches from 2006 to 2008 in all categories except RSPs. RSPs experienced an initial decline in number of branches from 2006 to 2007 which slightly recovered in 2008.

Figure 2 represent growth in outreach of MFPs all over Pakistan in last three years. RSPs experienced around 15% decline in number of branches from 2006 to 2007 but it recovered by 5% in 2008. MFIs grew in terms of number of branches by 189% from 2006 to 2008 whereas MFBs also reported positive signs and grew by 88% during the same period. Others, which include NGOs and Commercial Financial Institutions (CFIs), also show growth of 117% in terms of branches.

Growth in number of borrowers

Growth in terms of number of borrowers is going to reveal

Table 2. Growth in number of branches of MFPs.

MFI category	MFPs	Year		
		2006	2007	2008
RSP	SRSP	11	14	11
	NRSP	581	499	537
Total		592	513	548
MFI	KASHAF	41	145	159
	ASASAH	22	27	23
Total		63	172	182
MFB	FMFBL	44	92	159
	KHUSHALI	112	120	135
Total		156	212	294
Others	ORIX	6	9	9
	JWS	4	5	6
	TF	13	21	35
Total		23	35	50
Total number of branches		834	932	1074

Source: Computed.

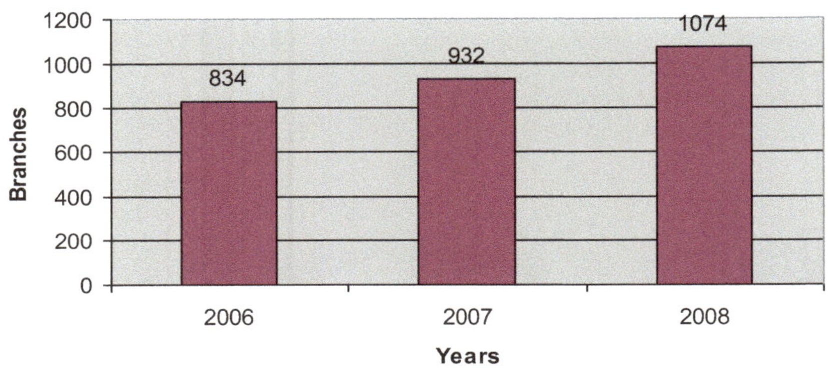

Figure 1. Growth in number of branches. Source: Computed.

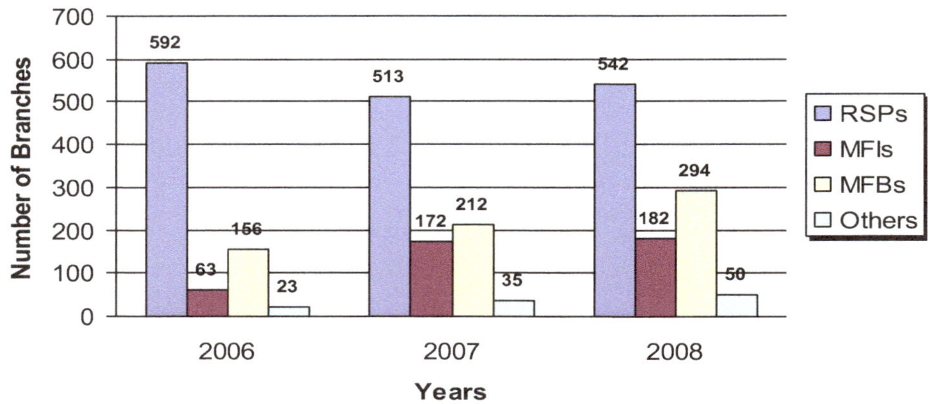

Figure 2. Categorical growth in number of branches. Source: Computed.

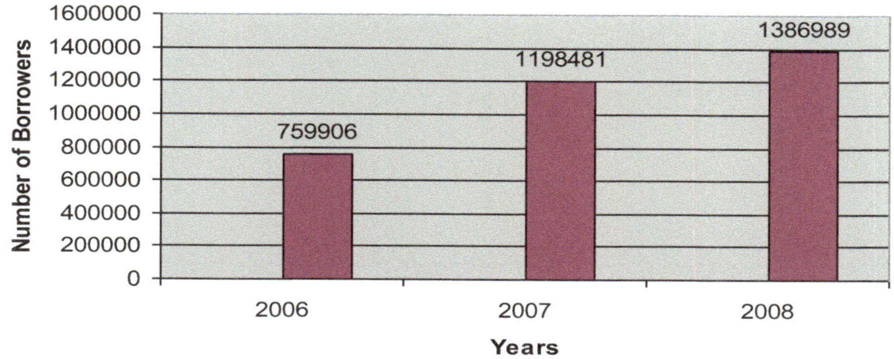

Figure 3. Growth in number of borrowers. Source: Computed.

Table 3. Categorical growth in number of borrowers.

MFP category	Type	Year		
		2006	2007	2008
RSP	SRSP	5081	9082	8991
	NRSP	236329	407641	463383
Total		241410	416723	472374
MFI	KASHAF	136012	295275	319652
	ASASAH	28424	24692	25192
Total		164436	319967	344844
MFB	FMFBL	52679	102604	171795
	KHUSHALI	280526	330952	366714
Total		333205	433556	538509
Others	ORIX	6114	12173	15445
	JWS	3487	5152	5262
	TF	11254	10910	10555
Total		20855	28235	31262

Source: Computed.

the success or failure of MFPs in reaching poor. Figure 3 indicate growth in terms of number of borrowers during the period 2006 to 2008 based on Table 4. The sample reveals an overall growth of around 57% in number of borrowers from 2006 to 2007 and a further increase of 16% in 2008. This fact strongly highlights "the success of microfinance in reaching the core poor".

We can additionally analyze the growth prospects of microfinance industry category wise. Amongst all categories MFIs and RSPs experienced maximum growth in number of borrowers which is above 100% during 2006 to 2008. Whereas MFBs also grew in terms of number of borrowers by around 70% during the same period. Others category too reported a growth of around 44% during this period. These findings undoubtedly indicate "the success of microfinance in reaching the core poor". Table 3 outlines the categorical growth in terms of number of borrowers of sampled MFPs which is also illustrated graphically in Figure 4. It additionally witnesses the achievement of microfinance programs in reaching the poor. We can observe an increase for all four categories (MFIs, MFBs, RSPs and others) in terms of borrowers during 2006 to 2008.

An in depth analysis of the sample MFPs taken for the current study in all four categories can be done to evaluate their respective contribution towards growth of microfinance. Therefore, after having a glance at the growth prospects of MFPs it enables us conclude that regardless of not being too established industry in Pakistan microfinance remain successful in reaching the core poor with financial services and growing at a reasonable pace.

Effectiveness of microfinance can also be judged through some more significant indicators extracted from "MicroWatch (2006; 2008)", a quarterly publication of Pakistan Microfinance Network (Table 5).

Table 4. Growth in number of borrowers of MFPs.

MFP category	Year		
	2006	2007	2008
RSPs	241410	416723	472374
MFIs	164436	319967	344844
MFBs	333205	433556	538509
Others	20855	28235	31262
	759906	1198481	1386989

Source: Computed.

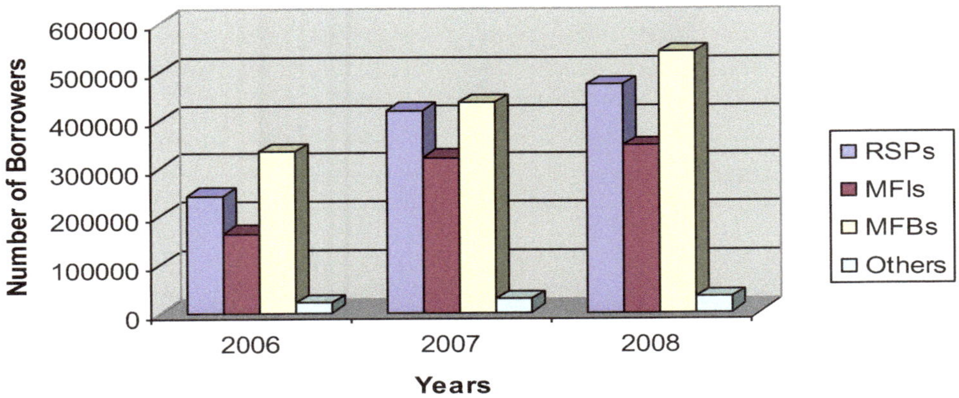

Figure 4. Categorical growth in number of borrowers. Source: Computed.

Table 5. Growth in loan and savings profiles of MFPs.

Indicator	June'06	December'08	Percentage (↑,↓)
Gross loan portfolio (PKR Million)	7,197	18,752	160 Increase
Average loan balance (PKR)	9,846	10,821	9.9 Increase
No. of loans disbursed	291,899	576,943	97.6 Increase
Disbursement (PKR Million)	3,683	8,358	126.9 Increase
Average loan size (PKR)	12,620	14,487	14.79 Increase
No. of savers	1,052,368	1,743,609	65.68 Increase
Value of saving (PKR Million)	1,659	5,384	224.5 Increase
Average saving balance (PKR)	1,577	3,088	95.8 Increase

Source: MicroWatch (quarterly publication) of Pakistan Microfinance Network.

Gross loan portfolio increased by 160% during the time period being observed witnessing the expanded outreach by microfinance providers. Average loan balance to a client also increased by 9.9%. Numbers of loans disbursed during the same time period rose by 97.6% enabling more microfinance clients to overcome financial constraints. Total disbursement of micro loans through microfinance providers also augmented by 126.9%.

Average loan size to a single client increased by 14.79%. A very strong indicator of a self-sustained enterprise is its savings. Number of savers and value of saving both witnessed an increasing trend during the same time period. Number of savers increased by 65.68% with extraordinary intensifying the value of saving with microfinance providers of 224.5%. Average saving balance per saver also displays an increasing trend by 95.8%. Therefore, noticeably augmented loan and saving is indicating that through microfinance people can be self-reliant and make them come out of deprivation state.

Conclusion

In the current research study it is revealed that microfinance sector experienced growth during 1990s in Pakistan. In such small time MFPs have achieved very little and it can not be compared with achievements of microfinance worldwide. It requires time and resources to expand and achieve desired results. The 30% sample studied from all four categories; that is, RSPs, MFIs, MFBs and others show overall growth in number of branches during the period 2006 to 2008. In the years 2007 and 2008 MFPs demonstrated around 12 and 15% growth respectively. Therefore it can be concluded that microfinance outreach is increasing year after year in Pakistan however the pace of growth is slow due to industry constraints. The sample study further reveals an overall growth of around 57% in number of borrowers in 2007 and an additional increase of 16% in 2008. This fact strongly highlights the success of microfinance in reaching the core poor by existing MFPs. On average currently MFPs are serving only 11% of prospective clients leaving 89% unaddressed. There is a strong need to fill this massive gap. Existing MFPs are serving very little fraction of the huge pie. The poverty profile of Pakistan indicates that the core poor live in more remote or hard to reach areas where it is very difficult to reach with such service like microfinance. Because to reach them and provide them with microfinance service require human resource but very few microfinance experts show their willingness to work in these areas and charge high remunerations. Therefore providing microfinance to them becomes not only operationally difficult but the cost of operating there also amplifies. Outreach in hard to reach areas is further diminutive as compare to their total outreach. MFPs at the moment are capable to reach only 4% core poor clients in hard to reach areas. If more microfinance providers are introduced in Pakistan their outreach could be expanded further. As seen in many researches that microfinance clients were able to achieve self-reliance for their micro enterprises as well as it helped them in coming out of poverty situation. Therefore it can be concluded that expansion in microfinance outreach connote poverty reduction.

RECOMMENDATIONS

Before allocating the resources (like microfinance) under poverty alleviation objective it is vital to identify the target. Ineffective poverty targeting will lead to wastage of poverty resources from the task of poverty alleviation leaving the efforts unsuccessful. To avoid corruption and misuse of resources microfinance industry should be regulated and supervised. Generally, in international practices participatory methods ensure transparency, make possible to expand outreach, and facilitate in the choice of priorities that reveal the needs, capabilities and ambitions of poor households. More MFPs with diverse services should come and take it as an opportunity, not only to earn but to provide microfinance service to the poor so that poor people could improve their living standard by empowering and making them capable of benefiting from better nutrition, health and education facilities. To make use of microfinance as more effective instrument of poverty alleviation MFPs should be established not only in the public sector but private sector and to be be motivated or wherever necessary public-private partnership should be encouraged with variety of services and broad financing options. Internationally successful MFPs may also be given incentives to open their offices in Pakistan to get benefit from their experiences since the major limitation observed in the current study was the undersized industry for such a big market and less experienced MFPs in Pakistan. To overcome the problem of funding MFPs should also encourage micro savings in Pakistan. The outcomes may be more favorable and thriving if conventional commercial banks' set up 'microfinance' division and operates in the hard to reach areas making use of their existing branch network.

REFERENCES

Adams R (2003). Economic Growth, Inequality and Poverty: Findings from a New Dataset. World Bank's Poverty Reduction Network. (Please cite in work body) http://info.worldbank.org/etools/BSPAN/PresentationView.asp?EID=399&PID=783

Dichter TM (1999). Non-governmental Organizations in Microfinance: Past, Present and Future – An Essay, Case studies in Microfinance. World Bank, Washington, DC, p. 12.

Garson J (2004). Microfinance and Anti-Poverty Strategies. A Donor Perspective UNCDF. Available at, http://www.undp.org/uncdf/pubs/mf/mf-chap1.html.

Joanna L (2000). Microfinance Handbook: An Institutional and Financial Perspective. Washington, DC: The World Bank Publications, pp. 97-100.

Littlefield E, Jonathan M, Syed H (2003). Is Microfinance an Effective Strategy to Reach the Millennium Development Goals? CGAP Focus Note 24.

MicroWATCH (2006). A Quarterly Update of Pakistan Microfinance Network. Seen at http://www.microfinanceconnect.info/ user_articles_display.php?sno=32.

MicroWATCH (2008). A Quarterly Update of Pakistan Microfinance Network. Seen at http://www.microfinanceconnect.info/user_articles_display.php?sno=41.

Musharaf S (2002). Pakistan Support Micro-credit Campaign. Tuesday November 12, 2002, THE NEWS, Pakistan.

Otero M (1991). Savings Mobilization And Microfinance Programmes. Evolution, Achievements and Challenges. ITDG Publishing and Samskriti, New Delhi pp.25-36.

Pitt M, Khandker S (1998). The Impact of Group-Based Credit Programs on Poor Households in Bangladesh: Does the Gender of Participants Matter? J. Polit. Econom. 106(5):958-996.

Pakistan Microfinance Network (PMN) (2007). Available at http://www.microfinanceconnect.info/in_mfb%20.php, Microfinance Connect. Pakistan Microfinance Network Islamabad, Pakistan.

PPAF (2002). Pakistan Poverty Alleviation Fund, Micro-finance and Social Safety, quarterly newsletter 1(1) Autumn 2002, Islamabad.

Schreiner M, Colombet H (2001). From Urban to Rural: Lessons for Microfinance from Argentina. Dev. Policy Rev. 19(3):339-354.

UNDP (2009). Human Development Index. Human Development Report 2009. UNDP available at; http://hdrstats.undp.org/en/countries/country_fact_sheets/cty_fs_PAK.html.

Capital adequacy, management and performance in the Nigerian commercial bank (1986 - 2006)

Ikpefan Ochei A.

Department of Banking and Finance, Covenant University, Ota, Ogun State, Nigeria.

This study investigates the impact of bank capital adequacy ratios, management and performance in the Nigerian commercial bank (1986 - 2006). The objectives of this paper are: to determine to what extent bank capital adequacy ratios impact on bank performance and also to investigate the extent to which operation expenses has impacted on the return on capital. The study captured their performance indicators and employed cross sectional and time series of bank data obtained from Central Bank of Nigeria (CBN) and Annual Report and Financial statements of the sampled banks. The formulated models were estimated using ordinary least square regression method. The overall capital adequacy ratios of the study shows that Shareholders Fund/Total Assets (SHF/TA) which measures capital adequacy of banks (risk of default) have negative impact on ROA. The efficiency of management measured by operating expenses indice is negatively related to return on capital. The implication of this study, among others, is that adequate shareholders fund can serve as a veritable stimulant in strengthening the performance of Nigerian commercial banks and also heighten the confidence of customers especially in this era of global economic meltdown that has taken its toll in the Nigerian financial system.

Key words: Buffer capital theory of capital adequacy, expense theory, capital adequacy ratios.

INTRODUCTION

Bank capital can be seen in two ways. Narrowly, it can be seen as the amount contributed by the owners of a bank (paid-up share capital) that gives them the right to enjoy all the future earnings of the bank. More comprehensively, it can be seen as the amount of owners' funds available to support a bank's business (Athanasoglou et al., 2005). The latter definition includes reserves, and is also termed shareholders' funds (Anyanwaokoro, 1996). Adewumi (1997) gives two connotations of capital in banking. He opines that at the outset, capital in the form of issues and paid-up share is money with which the business of banking is started. Overtime, the capital funds of the bank reflect the accumulated (addition or depletion) capital. The question of adequate capital of a bank is more crucial especially in the light of the global financial meltdown where bail out measures is now being employed by the regulatory authorities to keep the financial system afloat. In fact, question as to whether existing levels of capital are considered adequate for the increasing levels of risk has been an issue of debate between bankers and the supervisory authorities. Universally, Basle Committee's specified minimum capital adequacy ratio of eight percent relating to banks' credit is taken as the benchmark of measuring the capital adequacy of a bank. This implies that for every Naira given as credit a bank needs eight kobo capital. A bank that has lesser ratio is said to be undercapitalized. No empirical method has been used to determine banks' capital adequacy in Nigeria.

This study is an attempt to investigate the relationship between bank capitalization (dependent or explained variable) management and performance in Nigerian banking industry (independent variables) on the other hand. The following variables are used as indicators for gauging bank capitalization: return on assets (ROA) and return on capital (ROC).

The following indicators are used as internal determinants of bank management and performance. They are: (BL/BD) ratio of bank loans and advances to total deposit (B DEPOSIT), (LA/BD) ratio of liquid assets to bank deposits (LAD), (OE/TA) ratio of operating expenses to total assets (EOM that is, Efficiency of Management), (SHF/TA) ratio of Shareholders Fund to total assets, (CAP) and (BL/BA) ratio of bank loans to Bank assets (B LOAN). On the other side, capital cannot perform without good management from those at the top echelon of the organization. Capitalization in this study refers to a number of variables of interest which are produced from the existence of funds for use in the process of intermediation. From these funds, obviously concepts such as Return on Capital (ROC) and Return on assets (ROA) are derivatives from the use of funds.

Management need to employ the assets and capital of the bank judiciously for positive results. Absence of corporate governance has been attributed to the distress experienced in the banking industry in the past. The CBN Governor noted that the vision or prospect of the CBN and the Federal Government of Nigeria is a banking system that is part of the global change, and which is strong and reliable. It is a banking system which must be efficient, depositors can trust and investors can rely upon. Capital adequacy is important for banks to absorb risks till banks are able to generate profit. However, banks that are able to exceed the capital requirement stand a better chance of luring customers and instilling confidence in the system. Like other sectors, this sub-sector is also faced with poor infrastructural facilities and poor performance of regulatory authorities. According to Ajekigbe (2009), from the classical and historical perspective, "several factors led to the failure of banks between 1977 and earlier 2000. Some of the reasons advanced are poor asset quality, under capitalization, inexperienced personnel, illiquidity, inconsistent regulatory policies and supervision".

The issue of bank capitalization in most economies today has been how to resolve the problem of unsound bank, enhance efficient management of the banking system, provide better funding for banks lending activities, reduce non-performing loans and advances, increase profitability, reduce risk, to ensure quality asset management and to put banks in a strong liquid position to meet customers obligation at all times (Soludo, 2004). For instance, the distress that was pervasive in the Nigerian banking system in the mid-1990's and early 2000 was due to amongst others, illiquidity in the banking system which led to the lost of customers confidence in the banking industry. The move by the CBN to raise the minimum paid up capital of banks to N25 billion was aimed at strengthening the Nigerian banking industry. It is imperative for banks to meet up the required level of capital for sound and safe banking.

The evolving competition in the banking industry as a result of globalization has made it difficult for Nigerian banks to play their major role of financing economic activities arising from inadequate capital. Inadequate bank capital has led to a crisis of confidence in the banks to the extent that the original functions which is to support the volume, type and character of a bank's business, to provide for the possibilities of losses that may arise there from and to enable the bank to meet a reasonable credit need of the community have been eroded. Losses suffered by banks led to bank failure especially in the areas of lending. The soundness, safety and profitability of a bank affect the quality of its loan portfolio. The last few years have both been traumatic and revolutionary for the Nigerian banking system. According to Eke (1999): "Since the introduction of structural adjustment programme (SAP) in 1986 and the deregulation of the nation's financial system, banking business has raised a variety of performance questions. Although, insured banks had recorded an appreciable increase in the volume of assets and deposits, their overall financial condition had deteriorated tremendously".

According to the Governor of Central Bank of Nigeria cited in Egene (2009), of the ten banks audited so far as at August 2009, the banks' balance sheets of five banks (Union bank, Finbank, Oceanic bank, Afrique bank and Intercontinental bank) had shrunken, shareholders' funds impaired and they now have liquidity problems. Their huge exposure to non-performing loans (margin loans) has affected the banks. These banks had spent length of time at the expanded discount window (EDW) introduced in September, 2008 by the apex bank. These five banks accounted for 90% of transactions at the EDW. The remaining banks accounted for 10%. According to the apex banks, these banks took money from the inter-bank to repay their exposure to the discount window. It is an indication that their balance sheets had shrunk. The management teams had acted in a manner that was detrimental to the interest of their depositors and creditors. According to the apex bank, the temporary capital injection of N420 billion into the banks in the form of Convertible Tier 11 Debt, is expected to be repaid to the CBN once the banks are recapitalized. Considering the fact that ownership of banks has moved from family to private, existing shareholders have not been informed how these funds would be converted when the bailout fund is fully repaid. The measure adopted by CBN to bail out the banks is adjudged as misuse of taxpayers' money and may eventually displace existing shareholders.

While there have been several studies on bank capitalization and performance very few of them have focused on bank capitalization and performance of the Nigerian banking industry. Several studies about bank capitalization exist in United Kingdom (UK), United States (US) and Asia, Africa, South Africa and Tunisia. However, the extent to which such research findings can be applied to Nigerian banking industry should be studied. Therefore, this study hopes to establish the relationship that exists between bank capital adequacy ratios, management and performance. The empirical study that will be carried out on this study will fill the gap in the existing literature especially as it relates to variables that affects bank performance. The following dependent variables are used as indicators for gauging bank capitalization: return on capital (ROC) return on assets (ROA). The questions being asked are: does capitalization reduce the operational expenses of the banks? Increase capitalization reduces the operational risk and bank failure? To what extent do bank capital adequacy ratios affect bank performance? The objectives of this study are:

(i) To determine to what extent bank capital adequacy ratios impact on bank performance.
(ii) The extent to which operation expenses has impacted on the return on capital.

Section 1 above discusses the introduction; Section 2 examines the conceptual framework and literature while Section 3 discusses the method of analysis. Section 4 dwells on the estimation, model specification and discussion of results. Section 5 ends the paper with summary, findings and recommendations. We shall now proceed to examine some conceptual framework and literature review underpinning of this paper.

CONCEPTUAL FRAMEWORK AND LITERATURE REVIEW

Buffer theory of capital adequacy

As a consequence, banks may prefer to hold a 'buffer' of excess capital to reduce the probability of falling under the legal capital requirements, especially if their capital adequacy ratio is very volatile. Capital requirements constitute the main banking supervisory instrument in Nigeria. The Central Bank of Nigeria intervenes little in banks' activities but does directly conduct on-site examination and at times delegating this task to external auditors. By contrast, a breach of the capital requirements is considered a major infringement of banking legislation and is not tolerated by the Central Bank of Nigeria. Banks remaining undercapitalized for prolonged periods are closed. The withdrawal of some banking license at the expiration of the recent capitalization of banks in Nigeria in 2005 is a pointer to this fact. Banks will require more capital if deposits are not fully mobilize from the public.

Capital is more reliable, dependable and can be used for long term planning. Ability of banks to mobilize enough deposits obviates the capital base from being eroded. The buffer theory of Calem and Rob (1996) predicts that a bank approaching the regulatory minimum capital ratio may have an incentive to boost capital and reduce risk in order to avoid the regulatory costs triggered by a breach of the capital requirements. However, poorly capitalized banks may also be tempted to take more risk in the hope that higher expected returns will help them to increase their capital. This is one of the ways risks relating to lower capital adequacy affects banking operations. In the event of bankruptcy of a bank, the risks are absorbed by the bank, customers and Nigeria Deposit Insurance Corporation (NDIC). At present NDIC pays a maximum of N200,000 to a customer in the event of bank failure. Hence, customers are concerned about capital position of banks at all time. Banks are expected to insure and pay 15/16 of customers deposit liabilities multiplied by 1% to NDIC to enable their customers benefit from the scheme. The above practice of NDIC in Nigeria is applicable to other countries but varies in amount.

In model 1 of this study, capital our dependent which is represented return on assets (ROA) and explained by our buffer theory of capital adequacy helps us to test the propositions in hypothesis one. The higher the return on assets the better is bank liquidity and capital adequacy. The Deposit insurance scheme, which is compulsory in Nigeria, also exerts regulatory pressure on banks. In his study, Vojta (1980) opined that adequate capital provision against excess loss permits the bank to continue operations in periods of difficulty until a normal level of earning is restored. The benchmark set by regulators of bank capital sometimes differs from those of the bankers. These capital standards have led to questions on whether or not regulators have been able to bring about changes in bank capital when their standards of capital adequacy differed from those of bankers. Aggressive banks may try to extend the frontiers of "imprudent management policy" by operating with less capital base, often in violation of the regulatory guidelines. But the supervisory agencies usually stand their ground by resisting decline of capital to avoid bank failure with the concomitant high cost to the society.

Portfolio regulation theory

The study also uses the theory of portfolio regulation to gauge the performance of banking firms. The theory opined that the regulation of banks is necessary to maintain safety and soundness of the banking system, to the extent, which put them in a position to meet its liabilities without difficulty. This made it imperative for the regulatory authorities to compel greater solvency and liquidity on individual banks than making it optional. This theory is represented in model 1 of this paper. It captures LAD that is Liquid Assets (LA)/ Bank Deposit (BD) and depicts the liquidity position of the banks. The higher this ratio, the better liquidity and solvency of the individual banks. According to Peltzman (1970), if the asset portfolio is deemed too risky or capital inadequate, the relevant supervisory agency will attempt to compel a change in the bank's balance sheet.

Expense theory

According to the expense theory of Williamson (1963) cited in Nyong (2001) otherwise called the theory of managerial discretion, managers have the option in pursuing policies, which maximize their own utility rather than profit maximization for shareholders. Such utility include the satisfaction which mangers derive from certain types of expenditure. Managers' prestige, power and status are to some extent reflected in the amount of slack they receive in the form of expense account, luxurious offices and building, company cars and other perquisites of office. Operating efficiency attempts to capture this aspect of bank behaviour. Operating expenses captured by (EOM) is represented in model 1 and 2 as one of the control variables to explain the dependent/regressand that is return on assets and return on capital (ROA and ROC). Operating expenses is derived from the use of resources and can have positive or negative implication on the dependent variable.

Literature review

Furlong (1992), Haubrich and Wachtel (1993), and Berger and Udell (1994) investigated whether the 8% capital backing for loans to private enterprises required by the 1988 Basle Accord encouraged banks to reallocate their assets from such loans to government securities. With the exception of Berger and Udell, these authors find evidence that the risk-based capital requirement set by the Basle Accord significantly contributed to the credit crunch. No matter the definition adopted, a bank's capital is widely used to analyze the status of its financial strength (Bobakova, 2003). Positive correlation between returns and capital has been demonstrated by Furlong and Keeley (1989), Keeley and Furlong (1990), Berger (1994), Berger (1995b), Demirguc-Kunt and Huizinga (1999), Naceur (2003) and Eisenbeis and Kwan (2005). Investigating the determinants of Tunisia banks' performances during the period 1980 to 1995, Naceur and Goaied (2001) indicated that the best performing banks are those who have struggled to improve labour and capital productivity and those who have been able to reinforce equity. Bourke (1989), Abreu and Mendes (2002) and Naceur (2003) agree that well capitalized banks face lower need to external funding and lower bankruptcy and funding costs; and this advantages translates into profitability.

Therefore, researches widely posit that the more capital a bank has, the more resistant it will be to failure for example, Uche (1998). Capital regulation is motivated principally by the concern that a bank may hold less capital than is socially optimal relative to its riskiness as negative externalities resulting from bank default are not reflected in market requirements. In this framework, an unregulated bank will take excessive portfolio and leverage risks in order to maximize its shareholder value at the expense of the deposit insurance (Benson et al., 1986, Furlong and Keeley 1989; Keeley and Furlong, 1990). Capital requirements can reduce these moral hazard incentives by forcing bank shareholders to absorb a larger part of the losses, thereby reducing the value of the deposit insurance put option. With more capital and less risk taking, the effect is clearly a decrease in the bank's default probability.

The results obtained by the literature for the relationship between size and profits are diverse. Using market data (stock prices) instead of accounting measures of profitability, Boyd and Runkle (1993) find a significant inverse relationship between size and rate of return on assets in U.S banks from 1971 to 1990, and a positive relationship between financial leverage and size. They do not provide, however, any theoretical model to rationalize this evidence. Goddard et al. (2004) use panel and cross-sectional regressions to estimate growth and profit equations for a sample of banks for five European countries over the 1990s. The growth regressions suggest that, as banks become larger in relative terms; their growth performance tends to increase further, with little or no sign of mean aversion in growth.

Al-Hashimi (2007) finds that operating inefficiencies appear to be the main determinants of high bank spreads in Sub-Saharan Africa (SSA) economies. Heggestad (1977) studied the interaction of market structure, profitability and risk, and argues that banks with monopoly power systematically reduce the risk they take at the expense of greater profitability. Given the importance of bank credit as factor of production for almost all firms, this effect may plausibly affect market concentration in other sectors of the economy by making the expansion of smaller firms more difficult. The extent to which inflation affects bank profitability depends on whether future movements in inflation are fully anticipated, which, in turn, depends on the ability of firms to accurately forecast movements in the relevant control variables. An inflation rate that is fully anticipated raises profits as banks can appropriately adjust interest rates in order to increases revenues, while an unexpected change could raise costs due to imperfect interest rate adjustment. Other studies, for example, Bourke (1989), Molyneux and Thorton (1992), Demirguc-Kunt and Huizinga (1998), have found a positive relation between inflation and long term interest rates with bank capital and performance. Adewunmi (1997), Oyetan (1997) and Obadan (2004) agreed that there are other critical factors, which combined with capital adequacy, would guarantee a healthy banking sector. Oyetan (1997) argues that indicators or measures of a bank financial condition and performance are based on capital adequacy, asset quality, managerial capability, profitability and liquidity. According to CBN report (2005), the following should be considered along with capital ratios as conditions influencing capital adequacy: the quality of management influences outsider' perception of capital adequacy because, if management is good the bank will be profitably, and efficiently operated and there will be no need to rely unduly on capital to cushion disaster; a bank carrying good quality and adequate liquid assets will not be in danger of prolonged and damaging illiquidity. Consequently, the need for capital will be minimized; the history of earnings and retention thereof: good earnings and write-back policy will continually enhance the capital adequacy of a bank.

A bank that allows itself to be politicized and which put ethnic consideration before business prudence can only contribute to the failure of the bank and increase its need for capital; the potential volatility of deposit structure will affect the liquidity of a bank which will in turn affect the profitability and need for capital; the quality of management will impact on the efficiency of operation and consequently the need for capital; the restrictions placed on the maintenance between capital funds and loans and advances, the higher a bank's capacity to meet the potential credit needs of its environment. With Central Bank of Nigeria (CBN) and Nigeria Deposit Insurance Corporation (NDIC), technical and financial support traditionally given to banks in Nigeria, it is easy to tolerate temporary and relative inadequacy of bank capital in our banking system.

According to Ebhodaghe (1994), reported in Oluitan (2004), "Capital inadequacy has affected the financial health of banks. He explained that an analysis of bank capitalization revealed that as at the end of 1992, almost all banks (120) operating in Nigeria required additional capital totaling N0.6billion to support their volume of trading. This amount was the variance between the amount stipulated by the monetary authorities for prudential minimum capital and the aggregate capital outlay. By 1993, this variance further deteriorated to N9.1 billion".

Ojo (1992) and Oluyemi (1995), cited in Eke (1999) opined that the financial condition of banks can be assessed using some basic indicators and trend analysis such Capital Adequacy, Asset Quality, Earnings and Liquidity. Apart from quantitative factors, qualitative factors such as quality of management, the degree of compliance by banks with applicable banking laws and regulations (for example, Monetary and Credit policy Guidelines), as well as banking services to the local economy are relevant. In the literature of finance, CAMEL parameter that is Capital Adequacy, Asset Quality, Management, Earnings is to gauge financial performance of bank. The measures of ascertaining a bank's financial condition and Performance by the regulatory authority are encapsulated in the acronym CAMEL, which stands for: Capital Adequacy (Owners fund to total risk-weighted assets), a quantitative factor is one of the important indicators of the strength and performance of a bank. The best management cannot turn around an ailing bank if it does not have adequate capital. Assets Quality (Non-performing assets to total loan and advances portfolio); the incidence of large amounts of non-performing loans (bad debts) can put bank management under severe stress. Management (in terms of quality, competence and depth of experiences); the quality of management can make an important difference between sound and unsound banks. Poor management often manifests itself in the form of excessive operating expenses, inadequate administration of loan portfolio, overly aggressive policies to attract deposits. Earnings/Profitability (adequacy and sustainability of earnings over the long term); continued build-up of non-performing assets, would seriously affect banks in generating adequate income on their loan portfolio. The implementation of CBN Prudential Guide-lines in 1991 for licensed banks has reduced the paper profit formerly reported by some banks in terms of liquidity to meet maturing obligations and demand for new credits; inadequate liquidity damages banks' reputation while excess liquidity will retard their earnings.

Where a bank management fails to pay close watch to any of these indices, it could have adverse effect on bank performance. Where a bank is distress or healthy it would ultimately have recourse to new prospective investor, both local and foreign. Any attempt aimed at successfully recapitalizing any bank must focus on the bank's assets quality, management competence and experience, level of earnings, adequacy of liquidity and image/perception among other factors outside the control of the banks themselves. Healthy banks that intend to attract potential investors should start getting their overall business strategies and focus right.

According to Myers and Majluf (1984), in the absence of periodic adjustments in the capital ratio, banks would never hold more capital than required by the regulators or the market. In practice, however, adjusting the capital ratio may be costly. Equity issues may, in the case of information asymmetries, convey negative information to the market on the bank's economic value. Moreover, shareholders may be reluctant to contribute new capital if the bank is severely undercapitalized, as most of the benefits would accrue to creditors. In the absence of these capital adjustments, banks falling under the legal capital requirements will not be able to react instantaneously. They may then be subject to repeated regulatory penalties, or even worse, closed down.

METHOD OF ANALYSIS

This section tries to capture empirically the relationship between bank capitalization and performance. When we speak of bank capitalization we are referring to variables such as Return on Capital and Return on Assets. Therefore, our equations looks at the extent to which these variables are brought into light or the realization is facilitated by the existence of what we generally referred to as adequate capitalization. Thus the kernel of this paper is to examine how bank capital adequacy and performance have been enhanced by the existence of bank capitalization/ consolidation. Further, the crux of this paper is to see how bank

Table 1. Population of the study

S/N	Name of Banks	Frequency of bank capital	Bank capital 'billion	Remark
1	Access	Between 25 - 34.9 billion	28.8	
2	Bank PHB	"	28	
3	Fidelity	"	25.6	
4	FCMB	"	25.2	
5	ETB	"	28.4	N.Q.B
6	First Inland	"	29.4	
7	Standard Chartered	"	26	N.Q.B
8	Spring	"	25	
9	Afribank	"	26	
10	Wema	"	34.8	
11	Diamond	"	34.7	
12	GTB	"	36.4	
13	Sterling	Between N35 billion and above	35	
14	NIB	"	35.2	N.Q.B
15	Oceanic	"	37.1	
16	Ecobank	"	35.3	
17	Skye	"	37.7	
18	Unity	"	35	
19	Intercontinental	"	53	
20	FBN	"	58.9	
21	Zenith	"	93	
22	UBA	"	47	
23	UBN	"	95.6	
24	IBTC/Stanbic	"	60	

Source: CBN Banking Supervision Annual Report 2006 and 2007
N.O.B = Non-Quoted Banks

capitalization and consolidation in Nigeria make funds available for the realization of adequacy of capital and performance. Obviously, a number of years can be look into given the fact that bank consolidation took place only three years ago. This is what makes it impossible to make use of time series analysis because there is only two years to seriously discuss issues. This is why the use of panel data is preferred in this exercise to time series analysis. Also, we have not used cross sectional data analysis in this paper because it is not possible to complete set of data on any bank for any particular year if only because merger has taken place randomly and banks have also come into existence randomly. The panel data methodology provides a useful answer to all these, hence, the choice. This paper uses the econometric approach in estimating the effect and to be specific it uses the E-view software employing panel of data.

POPULATION AND SAMPLE SIZE

The population of this research is drawn from the Nigerian banking industry (Commercial banks) referred to as the conventional banks because they are deposit-taking institutions. This is because they dominate the financial sector in terms of number and coverage. Despite the involvement of other financial institutions such as non-bank financial institutions - insurance companies, development banks, finance houses, etc. in the intermediation process, commercial banks still control the major proportion of the nation's deposits and savings. There were 89 commercial banks in Nigeria before the 2005 bank recapitalization exercise and the number has been reduced to 25 banks after consolidation and to 24 (after merger of IBTC and Stanbic bank to Stanbic-IBTC) in 2008. Of the 24 banks, four of them that is: Unity bank, Sterling bank, Spring and Skye banks are new creation of mega banks. A sample size of 14 out of the 24 commercial banks was employed in the study. The sample (of 14 commercial banks) was drawn from both the old and new generation banks using the Stratified sampling technique based on simple random sampling supported by Judgment Sampling (Table 1). The selection process is restricted to banks quoted in the Nigerian Stock Exchange Daily official List (SEDOL).

The sample drawn from the population was grouped into categories based on the size of their capital as at the 2006. The sample size consists of both old generation and new generation banks. Banks that commenced operation before 1988 are old generation banks while those that commenced operation from 1989 are new generation banks. Amongst others new generation banks started aggressive marketing a departure from armchair banking which old generation banks were noted. New generation banks also introduced new technology for efficient service delivery change. There is a modified sample size for banks in this study. Since this study is between 1986 to 2006, banks that are not quoted are eliminated because their data are not readily available. During the field work, it was observed that these banks had no data bank for their Annual financial statements. Hence, such banks are not considered. Thus, in the sample size banks such as Nigerian International Bank, Standard Chartered Bank, Equatorial Trust bank that are not (listed) quoted were eliminated and this reduced the population of study to 21. This represents 14/21 (67%) of the quoted banks in Nigeria.

The study analyses the data as contained in the financial report of 14 commercial banks out of the 24 banks operating in Nigeria as at the end of 2006, representing about 60% of the commercial banks and about 67% of the quoted banks. The bank data were obtained from CBN Banking Supervision and Annual Reports, (2006 - 2007) and Annual financial Statements from various years of the selected banks for the years 1986 - 2006 are used for the analysis. The end of the cut-off date represent just one year after the bank consolidation mandate of 2004 by the Central Bank of Nigeria which took effect on 31st December, 2005. The study of bank capitalization and performance thus covers the period from the structural adjustment program of 1986 to 2006. The period of 1986 was the beginning of bank deregulation and liberalization (more banks were licensed) while we projected from 2005 the commencement year of the study to a cut-off date of 2006 (one year after bank consolidation) when financial statements of banks are expected to be available. Audited bank financial statements most time fall in arrears. As stated earlier, this study employed the Stratified Sampling Technique. In stratified sampling, the population is categorized into groups that are distinctly different from each other on relevant variables. Each group is called stratum (plural strata). In applying stratified sampling, we categorized the population and stratified using bank capital (Table 1).

In this study, the elements in a particular stratum are the same with respect to the relevant parameter (bank capital). The banks are grouped into stratum and were selected using simple random sampling supported by judgment sampling (non-probability) methods. The table above shows that 11 banks (9 banks excluding non-quoted banks) fall into the frequency of bank capital between N25 < N34.9. This means that 2/3 multiplied 9 gives approximately 6 which were selected from the first stratum. The name of nine banks were written on a piece of paper, wrapped and put in a tray from where they were picked. The six out of the nine banks picked are Access bank, Fidelity bank, First Inland bank, Wema bank, Spring bank and Diamond bank. However, Spring bank was dropped because the data is only for one year (that is, 2006) and would not be very useful. Using Judgment sampling an additional bank that is Afribank was selected to complete our simple random sampling of 2/3 x 9 = 6 in the first stratum of N25 < N34.9 billion frequency. The remaining 8 out of the 12 banks were also selected by writing the names of the banks on a piece of paper, wrapped and put in a tray from where they were picked. Our table above shows that of the 13 banks (12 banks excluding non-quoted banks) fall into the frequency of bank capital between N35 billion and above that is 2/3 multiplied 12 gives 8. The following banks were picked Oceanic bank, Guaranty Trust bank, Intercontinental bank, First bank of Nigeria, Union Bank of Nigeria, United Bank, Zenith and IBTC/Stanbic bank

At the of end of the selection process, 60% that is 6 out of the 9 banks fall into the frequency of between N25 < N34.9 billion while 72% that is 8 banks out of the 12 banks fall into the frequency of between N35 billion and above. The selection process picked 50% (7) of the old generation banks and 50% (7) of new generation banks (Table 1).

The panel data method

Instead of using time series data or a cross section of banks, this study looks at a panel data specification for individual banks. In cross section analysis, data are collected across units of observation at a given point in time. For cross section unit the study observe the same attribute on different people, geographical units, etc. using same year. For example, one can collect data on total deposits of banks in say 2006. Here the variation is across the units, that is different banks and not for different years, say time. In time series, data span across time a horizon usually on quarterly or yearly basis. An example is the total deposits of First Bank from 1986 to 2006 as could have been used in this study. In this case the variation is over time. Panel data or data set is a technique that combines the features of both time series and cross section methods. For example, total deposits of banks (one of the explanatory variables) in Nigeria from 1986 to 2006 as used in this study. Thus, panel data has the features of time series and cross section.

PRESENTATION OF RESULT

The results of the paper on bank capitalization, management and performance are presented below in Tables 2 and 3 precisely; are results of the models: (Portfolio Regulation theory, Expense theory and Buffer theory of capital adequacy) as generated by the computer. This paper enables the study to provide answer to questions of macroeconomic variables such as (interest rate, exchange rate and inflation); if inadequate capital affects the Nigerian banks to compete effectively in the international market and play their major role of financing economic activities. It also provides answer to the soundness, safety, profitability, quality of loan portfolio, asset, and deposit in the Nigerian banking industry. The selection of bank management has not been taken seriously and the performance is a function of the inputs.

This paper also provides answer to the impact of cost of operation on bank capital. The macroeconomic variables of interest rate, inflation and exchange rates have had no significant effect on Return on Capital (ROC).This is represented in model 2 and Table 3 (results) of this paper. Thus, it means that macro economic variables that is interest rate, inflation and exchange rates have not led to significant change on Return on Capital (ROC) one of the indicators of bank capitalization. The result shows that inflation rate, interest rate and exchange rate have negative association with return on capital. This implies that return on capital and inflation rate, interest rate and exchange rate move in opposite direction. The coefficient points to the fact a percentage increase of these macroeconomic variables will lead to about 66.2 in exchange rate, 163.0 inflation rate and 761.4 interest rate decrease in return on capital. As reported by Ige (2006) recent studies incorporating these variables indicated they could be statistically significant since they are more often than not at the mercy of the free market and not by government fiat. This does not conform to our a priori expectation that capitalization will be affected positively by interest rate, inflation and exchange rate.

Foreign exchange (forex) pricing mechanism(s) over the years has been an important macroeconomic variable in an open economy such as Nigeria. In an open economy, we expect a flourishing banking sector now awash with capital fund to affect the external sector. Borrowing for the purchase of machines and raw materials from abroad should be expected as banks make more demand for forex at the periodic bidding using the Dutch Auction

Table 2. ROA

Dependent Variable: ROA
Included observations: 225
Excluded observations: 64 after adjusting endpoints
Convergence achieved after 10 iterations

Variable	Coefficient	Std. Error	t-Statistic	Prob.
BL_BA01	0.090600	0.024388	3.714970	0.0003
BL_BD01	0.024091	0.022290	1.080807	0.2810
CAP_SF_TA01	-0.004666	0.025794	-0.180900	0.8566
EOM_OE_TA01	0.092903	0.030697	3.026444	0.0028
LAD_LA_BD01	0.9504	0.009414	2.071941	0.0395
SHF_BD01	-0.050925	0.024804	-2.053062	0.0413
SHF_BL01	0.036365	0.014697	2.474369	0.0141
C	-0.009340	0.016474	-0.566949	0.5713
AR(1)	0.595940	0.052842	11.27786	0.0000

R-squared	0.372843	Mean dependent var	0.056176
Adjusted R-squared	0.349615	S.D. dependent var	0.064093
S.E. of regression	0.051688	Akaike info criterion	-3.047988
Sum squared resid	0.577085	Schwarz criterion	-2.911344
Log likelihood	351.8987	F-statistic	16.05140
Durbin-Watson stat	2.040680	Prob(F-statistic)	0.000000
Inverted AR Roots	.60		

Source: E-View Software Package: Computer Print Out

Table 3. ROC (Profit).

Dependent Variable :PT
Included observations: 238
Excluded observations: 51 after adjusting endpoints

Variable	Coefficient	Std. Error	t-Statistic	Prob.
BA	0.023594	0.003308	7.133410	0.0000
BD	-0.023017	0.003185	-7.226430	0.0000
BL	0.032228	0.003467	9.295387	0.0000
EXCH	-66.20895	69.96019	-0.946380	0.3450
INFL	-163.0124	158.2960	-1.029795	0.3042
INTR	-761.4167	778.1650	-0.978477	0.3289
LA	0.066479	0.003096	21.47500	0.0000
OE	0.508664	0.370432	1.373165	0.1710
C	31328.88	20141.62	1.555430	0.1212

R-squared	0.997883	Mean dependent var	157309.1
Adjusted R-squared	0.997809	S.D. dependent var	916476.3
S.E. of regression	42899.94	Akaike info criterion	24.20821
Sum squared resid	4.21E+11	Schwarz criterion	24.33951
Log likelihood	-2871.777	F-statistic	13491.71
Durbin-Watson stat	1.973462	Prob(F-statistic)	0.000000

Source: E-View software package: Computer print out

System (DAS). This will only drive up the exchange rate, causing the Naira to depreciate, posing an inverse relationship, and very little or no statistical significance. Interest rate and return on capital share a negative relationship, thus as interest rate rises, return on capital decreased during the period covered by this study. However, historically, the study knows that even when prime interest rate was falling it made no significant impact on the economy. Banks have not made concerted effort to transmit to the economy the benefit of lower interest rate. In the past excess money balances will normally go for purchase of foreign exchange from the CBN auction market for a premium in the foreign exchange parallel market. In this new era of mega banks, it is expected that bank management to have another look at their interest rate policy such that it will re-engineer and stimulate the growth of the economy. Inflation rate possesses an inverse relationship to return on capital, thus as inflation rises, return on capital during the period covered by the study falls. This conforms to a priori expectation. Where the economy is resting at a sub-optimal level, it requires government's fiscal policy or perhaps any external shock, a change in expectation (output) etc to boost aggregate demand and subsequently aggregate supply. An important tool to stem the tide of rising inflation in Nigeria is massive expenditure in infrastructure development.

ESTIMATION, MODEL SPECIFICATION AND DISCUSSION OF RESULTS

The ordinary least square method and multiple regression analysis will be used in estimating the impact of shareholders funds on performance of the Nigerian Commercial banks. To test for the significance, reliability and validity of the result, F- statistic, T-statistic, and their related probabilities, Coefficient of determination (R^2), R bar, Durbin Waston (DW), Sum Square Residual (SSE), Standard Error (SE) of the explanatory variables and coefficient of determination R^2 are employed. The model will be estimated using annual data and the study will involve the use of multiple regression technique. Ordinary Least Square (OLS) using E-View package will be used in presentation of the result.

From the theoretical perspective, literature review and research questions the following hypotheses are postulated to justify our statement of problem and objectives of study.

1. H_1: Return on Assets has significant relationship with bank capital ratios (Capital adequacy, Liquidity and Efficiency/Quality of Management)
H_0: Return on Assets has no significant relationship with bank capital ratios (Capital adequacy, Liquidity and Efficiency/Quality of Management)
2. H_1: Operation expenses have significant impact on return on capital.
H_0: Operation expenses have no significant impact on return on capital.

The study postulates that the return on assets of banks will be affected positively by bank performance and management indicators. Therefore, the functional relationship in model forms can be represented as follows:

ROA = f (B Loan, B Deposit, EOM, LAD, CAP, μ) .... Equation 1

Where BLoan = the ratio of bank's loan (L) to total assets (TA) that is L/TA. Bank loan depicts Efficiency/Quality of management.
B deposit = the ratio of bank's loans and advance (LA) to bank deposit (D) that is LA/D. This depicts liquidity position of banks.
EOM = the ratio of operating expenses (OE) to total assets (TA) that is OE/TA. This depicts efficiency of management.
LAD = Liquid asset (LA) to deposit (D) that is LA/D. This depicts the liquidity position of banks.
CAP = the ratio of shareholders fund (SHF) to total assets (TA) that is SHF/TA. This depicts the capital adequacy of banks.

Restating the variables in equation 1 in explicit form, the model can be represented as follows:

ROA = a_0 + a_1 Bloan + a_2B deposit + a_3 EOM + a_4 Lad + a_5 Cap + Uit .... Equation 2

Where the a prori expectation is stated as $a_1 >_0 a_2 >_0 a_3 <_0 a_4 >_0 a_5 >_0$
$u_{it} \approx U(0,1)$

ROA measures the profit earned per naira of assets and reflect how well bank management use the bank investments resources to generate profits. We postulate that the Return on Assets (ROA) of the banks will be affected positively by the bank management and performance; captured by capital ratios, for example, the ratio of bank's loan (L) to total assets (TA) L/TA that is (B Loan), the ratio of bank's loans and advance (LA) to bank deposit (D) LA/D that is (B Deposit) depicts the liquidity position of banks, Efficiency of Management that is OE/TA (EOM), Shareholders fund (SHF)/Total Assets (TA) that is risk of default (CAP) and Liquid Assets (LA)/Bank deposit (BD) represented by (LAD).

δROA/ δBPM > 0.

All the explanatory variables with the exception of expenses are expected to have positive signs with respect to the return on assets. Model 2 is stated as:

ROC = f (Bank deposit, Bank Asset, Bank Loan, Inflation, Interest, Expean ,Exch, Liquid asset, Uit .... Equation 3

Restating the variables in equation 3 in explicit form, we can represent the model as follows:

$ROC = a_0 + a_1 BD + a_2 BA + a_3 BL + a_4 Infl + \Delta lnr_5 + a_6 Expean + a_7 Exch + a_8 LA + Uit$ .... Equation 4

Discussion of results

The result of Model 1 (Portfolio regulation theory and buffer theory of capital adequacy) was presented in Table 2 above that is:

$ROA = a_0 + a_1 B loan + a_2 B deposit + a_3 EOM + a4 Lad + a_5 Cap + Uit$ ......Equation 2

Where the a priori expectation is stated as $a_1 >_0 a_2 >_0 a_3 <_0 a_4 >_0 a_5 >_0$

Model 1 explains our hypothesis 1 and has coefficient of determination (R^2) of 0.373 and adjusted (R^2) of 0.350. This shows that the regression has low explanatory power. However, the values (that is,R^2 and adjusted R^2) indicate that over 37 percent of the variations in the dependent variables (return on assets) is attributable to the explanatory variables selected by the model and include Liquidity ratios (LAD = LA/BD), Bloan (BL/BA), Efficiency/Quality of management ratio (Operating Expenses = OE/TA), and Capital Adequacy ratio (CAP = SHF/BL). Though the R^2 and R^2 adjusted appear low, it is significant judging from the significant F-statistics, which is equally high. The implication of this is that the model is well specified and does not suffer mis-specification bias. In other words, the result from the model can be relied upon in making useful deductions with respect to return on assets. The S.E regression and Durbin-Watson statistics equally lend credence to the fact that there is no auto correlation. The financial implications of this regression will be further explained in 4.3 that is result of hypotheses.

Model 2 has coefficient of determination (R^2) of 0.9978 and adjusted (R^2) of 0.9978. This shows that the regression has high explanatory power. The values (that is, R^2 and adjusted R^2) indicate that over 99 percent of the variations in the dependent variables (return on capital) is attributable to the explanatory variables selected by the model and include Bank Deposit (BD), bank asset (BA), bank Loan (BL), Inflation (Infl), Interest (Intr), exchange rate, (Exch), Expean (OE) and Liquidity (LA). This high goodness of fit is further supported by the significant F-statistics, which is equally high. The implication of this is that the model is well specified and does not suffer mis-specification bias. In other words, the result from the model can be relied upon in making useful deductions with respect to return on assets. The S.E regression and Durbin-Watson statistics equally lend credence to the fact that there is no auto correlation. The financial implications of this regression will be further explained in 4.3 that is result of hypotheses.

Discussion of hypotheses

Hypothesis one is captured by model 1 (Buffer theory of capital adequacy and Portfolio regulation theory). Table 2 presents the return on asset as dependent variable and the indicators of bank performance and management. The result shows that the indicators of bank performance and management are significant at 10% in explaining the dependent variable. Our explanatory variables are represented by liquidity ratio: Liquid Asset/ Bank deposits (LAD = LA/BD) and Bank loan/ Bank Assets (BL/BA), Efficiency of Management represented by Operating expenses/Total Assets (EOM = OE/TA), Capital Adequacy indices represented by Shareholders Fund /Bank deposits (SHF/BD) and Shareholders fund/Bank loan (SHF/BL) are statistically significant in their influence on return on asset. However, while others are positive in their influence, the result further shows that Capital adequacy ratio represented by Shareholders fund/Total Assets (CAP = SHF/TA) and Shareholders fund/ Bank deposit (SHF/BD) have negative association with ROA.

The overall liquidity position for the banks as computed and regress by the panel data shows that bank liquidity is statistically significant. The result shows that bank performance indices (Capital adequacy ratios) such as Shareholders Fund/Total Assets (SHF/TA), Shareholders fund/bank deposits (SHF/BD) have negative association with Return on Asset (ROA). This implies that return on assets (ROA) and capital adequacy ratios move in opposite direction. The coefficient points to the fact that a percentage increase of capital adequacy ratio will lead to about 0.05 Shareholders Fund/Bank deposit (SHF/BD) and 0.0047 Shareholders Fund/ Total Assets (SHF/TA) decrease in return on asset (ROA). This could be attributed to the sterility/volatility of deposits and reserves which do not stay long in banks vault. Deposits in bank vaults can be volatile and vulnerable that is subject to withdrawer without notice, for example, saving and current account of governments, customers (individuals), corporate bodies and permanent deposits that stay with banks for some time for example, (fixed deposit). As a result capital base may be eroded and could make the return on asset susceptible to fluctuation. The reserve ratio may also affect the ability of banks to comply with regulatory directive as it has not been consistent. The efficiency and quality of management captured by Operating Expenses/Total Assets (OE/TA), Bank Loan/Bank Assets (BL/BA) shows that a percentage increase in operating expenses will lead to little increase of 0.0929 and 0.0906 increases in ROA.

Hypothesis two is explained in Table 3 in which return on capital (ROC) as reflected by profitability is stated as the dependent variable. This is represented in Model 2 of the study. The result shows that the null hypothesis of no significant relationship between managerial efficiency and return of capital cannot be rejected at 10% level of significance. This is because the probability value of 0.171 is greater than 0.10. Thus, the operating efficiency, though it is positively related to return on capital, its impact is not significant in its influence. This does not conform to a priori expectation that efficiency of bank management measured by operating expenses is expected to be negatively related to ROC.

Wrong signs and/or significance or non-significance of the parameters does not necessarily imply that violation of a priori expectations is tantamount to poor empirical result. Rather one is led to ask the ultimate question whether in posterior and a priori expectations Nigerian commercial banks can be expected to utilize bank capital to the ends required by the shareholders and the economy. The real issue in Nigeria case has been that of mismanagement of funds which is aptly explained by our expense theory. A good explanation may be found with management expertise, which presupposes that high capital requirement as stipulated by the buffer theory of capital adequacy may not curtail reckless spending by managers who may indulge in reckless spending of bank capital. In other words a bank without good management may worsen the position it was before the injection of new funds. In the Pre and Post consolidation era in Nigerian banking industry what was seen is bank management establishing more bogus bank branches everywhere rather using bank capital for worthwhile projects that will enhance shareholder wealth and the economy.

SUMMARY, FINDINGS AND RECOMMENDATIONS

Summary

This paper has attempted to find the relationship between bank capital adequacy and performance in the Nigerian banking industry specifically commercial banks. In this paper ROA and ROC represent the dependent variables whereas the controlled independent variables are: bank capital adequacy ratios, operating expenses, macroeconomic variables such interest rate, exchange rate and inflation. Availability of funds facilitates return on capital. Further, the crux of this paper is to see how bank capitalization has facilitated the realization bank performance.

Implications of findings

The analyses from Table 2 shows that shareholders fund/bank deposits and shareholders fund/total assets indices of bank management and performance have negative association to ROA. Perhaps the energy crisis in the Nigerian nation has had effect on adequacy of bank capital and consequently performance of banks. Operational expenses affected by absence of electricity, access roads has affected banking performance for example, overall profitability tough the impact is not too significant. The positive and insignificant coefficient in our operating expenses, instead, suggests that banks are able to pass on most of the high overhead costs to customers through higher spreads in order to keep profits unaffected. To the extent that banks' ability to overcharge is a function of their market power, this outcome presents evidence of market power incidence in the banking sector. Because of the rising cost of doing business the tendency is that interest rate on lending might continue to rise except it is controlled by government. The overall capital adequacy ratios of the study shows that Shareholders Fund/Total Assets (SHF/TA) which measures capital adequacy of banks (risk of default) have negative impact on ROA. The efficiency of management measured by operating expenses indice is negatively related to return on capital. Inflation rate, interest rate and exchange rate have negative association with return on capital. This implies that return on capital and inflation rate, interest rate and exchange rate move in opposite direction. Macroeconomic policies are important. Inflation reduces credit expansion by contributing to higher interest margins. Therefore, policies aimed at controlling inflation should be given priority in fostering financial intermediation. Fiscal and monetary policies designed to promote output stability and sustainable growth is good for financial intermediation.

From Table 2, the null hypothesis of no significant relationship between managerial efficiency and return on capital cannot be rejected at 10% level of significance. Thus, the operating efficiency, though it is positively related to return on capital, its impact is not significant in its influence. Perhaps the energy crisis in the Nigerian nation has had effect on adequacy of bank capital and consequently performance of banks. Operational expenses affected by absence of electricity, access roads have affected banking performance, for example, overall profitability tough the impact is not too significant. The positive and insignificant coefficient in our operating expenses, instead, suggests that banks are able to pass on most of the high overhead costs to customers through higher spreads in order to keep profits unaffected. To the extent that banks' ability to overcharge is a function of their market power, this outcome presents evidence of market power incidence in the banking sector.

Because of the rising cost of doing business the tendency is that interest rate on lending might continue to rise except it is controlled by government. The study also finds that there is significant relationship between shareholders' fund and banks' liquidity, bank deposits, and bank loans. This also conforms to a priori expectation that bank capitalization will be affected positively by bank liquidity, bank deposits and bank loans. The efficiency of management measured by operating expenses indice is negatively related to return on capital. Inflation rate, interest rate and exchange rate have negative association with return on capital. This implies that return on capital and inflation rate, interest rate and exchange rate move in opposite direction. Macroeconomic policies are important. Inflation reduces credit expansion by contributing to higher interest margins. Therefore, policies aimed at controlling inflation should be given priority in fostering financial intermediation. Fiscal and monetary policies designed to promote output stability and sustainable growth is good for financial intermediation.

Recommendations

(i) The overall capital adequacy ratios shows that Shareholders Fund/Total Assets (SHF/TA) which measures capital adequacy of banks (risk of default) have negative impact on Return on Asset (ROA). This implies that the regulatory authorities should put in place measures to raise the level of this ratio to avoid future bank collapse.

(ii) A bank without good management (input) may worsen the position it was before the injection of new funds. Where managers prefer prestige, power and status, it would be reflected in the amount they receive in form of expense account and luxurious. Management capability should be better supported, for the best of assets can be overturned in short period by management. It is a known fact that CBN plays an important role in the selection of bank executives at the directorate level. The policy for the selection of this class of bank workers should emphasize strict consideration of good track records and sequential growth phase through the ranks as some of the imperatives.

(iii) Where there exists a viable financial infrastructure, bank management should lobby governments for the provision of an enabling environment for banks to strive. This will help to minimize the operation expenses (OE) of the banks.

(iv) Bank returns are affected by macroeconomic variables, suggesting that macroeconomic policies that promote low inflation rate, stable exchange rate, low interest rate and output growth will boost credit expansion. Government should provide an enabling environment and also control interest rate on credit in the short term to enable customers such as corporate bodies, manufacturers, and industrialists obtain loans in order to stimulate economic growth.

LIMITATIONS AND FUTURE LINES OF RESEARCH

This study is limited to commercial banks in Nigeria whereas in the financial intermediation process, there is a gamut of non-bank financial institutions such as insurance companies, finance houses, investment companies, mutual trust fund/unit trust, development and specialized banks, etc. that are involved in funds mobilization. The impact of bank capitalization on performance for the entire Nigerian banking industry should be investigated to strengthen and confirm the results of the study. Secondly, in the course of the field work the study observed that many banks do not have data bank for their annual financial statements and made it cumbersome to obtain data for this study. The study also observed some inconsistency in annual financial statements of banks and that of the regulatory authority (Central Bank of Nigeria).

REFERENCES

Abreu M, Mendes V (2002). "Commercial Bank Interest Margins and Profitability: Evidence from E.U Countries", Porto Working Paper Series pp.1-10.

Adewunmi W (1997). "The N500 Million Paid-Up Capital for Bank", The Nigerian Banker, Jan-June, pp. 16-19.

Al-Hashimi A (2007). "Determinants of Bank Spreads in Sub-Saharan Africa", draft.

Ajekigbe JM (2009). "The Nigerian Banking Industry: Challenges and Prospects (1977-2008)", Being a Text Valedictory Lecture Presented at Muson Centre, Onikan, Lagos on Tuesday 13 January, 2009, Organized by the Chartered Institute of Bankers of Nigeria. Annual and Financial Reports of Banks (Various issues).

Anyanwaokoro M (1996). Banking Methods and Processes, Hosanna Publications, Enugu.

Athanasoglou PP, Brissimis SN, Delis MD (2005). Bank-Specific, Industry Specific and Macroeconomic Determinants of Bank Profitability, Bank Greece Working Paper 25:1-10.

Benson GJ, Eisenbeis R, Horvitz P, Kane EJ, Kaufman G (1986): Perspectives on Safe and Sound Banking: Past, Present, Future, MIT Press, Cambridge, MA.

Berger AN (1994). "The Relationship between Capital and Earnings in Banking," Financ. Econ. Discussion Series No. 94-92.

Berger AN, Udell GF (1994). "Did Risk-Based Capital Allocate Bank Credit and Cause a "Credit Crunch" in the United States? J. Money Credit Bank. 26:585-628.

Berger A (1995b). "The Relationship Between Capital and Earnings in Banking," J. Money Credit Bank. 27:404-431.

Bobakova IV (2003). "Raising the Profitability of Commercial Banks," BIATEC 11:21-25, Retrieved on April 8, 2005 from http://www.nbs.sk/BIATEC/BIA04_03/21_25.PDF.

Boyd JH, Runkle DE (1993). "Size and Performance of Banking Firms, Testing the Predictions of Theory", J. Monet. Econ. 31:47-67.

Bourke P (1989): Concentration and other Determinants of Bank Profitability in Europe, North America and Australia," J. Bank. Financ. 13:65-79.

Calem PS, Rob R (1996). "The Impact of Capital-Based Regulation on Bank Risk-Taking: A Dynamic Model, Board of Governors of the Federal Reserve System," Finance and Economics Discussion Series 96/12 (February), 36.

Central Bank of Nigeria "Annual Report and Statement of Accounts" (1999-2003).

Central Bank of Nigeria Supervision Annual Report 2006 and 2007.

Demirguc-Kunt A, Huizinga H (1999). "Determinants of Commercial Bank Interest Margins and Profitability: Some International Evidence", World Bank Econ. Rev. 13:379-408.

Demirguc-Kunt A, Huizinga H (1998). "Determinants of Commercial Bank Interest Margins and Profitability: Some International Evidence", World Bank Econ. Rev. 13:379-408.

Ebhodaghe JU (1994). "Boardroom/Management Practices and Distress in the Banking System", NDIC Q. 4(2):15-25.

Egene G (2009). "CBN, Sacked Banks' MDs and Stock Market", This Day 14(5232):31.

Eisenbeis RA, Kwan S (2005). "Bank Risk, Capitalization and Inefficiency," Paper Retrieved on September 8, 2005 from http: wharton.upenn.edu/fic/papers/96/9635.pdf.

Eke MS (1999). "Banking Soundness and Monetary Policy: Issues and Experiences in the Nigerian Economy" Nigerian Journal of Banking and Finance, B & F Publication, Enugu pp.1-14.

Furlong FT, Keeley MC (1989). "Capital Regulation and Bank Risk-Taking: A Note," J. Bank. Financ. 13:883-891.

Furlong FT (1992). "Capital Regulation and Bank Lending," Federal Reserve Bank of San Francisco, Econ. Rev. 3:23-33.

Goddard J, Molyneux P, Wilson JOS (2004). "Dynamics of Growth and Profitability in Banking", J. Money Credit Bank. 36:1069-1090.

Heggestad A (1977). "Market Structure, Risk and Profitability in Commercial Banking", The Journal of Finance 32:1207-1216.

Haubrich JG, Wachtel P (1993): "Capital Requirements and Shifts in Commercial Bank Portfolios," Federal Reserve Bank of Cleveland, Econ. Rev. 29:2-15.

Ige CS (2006). "Macroeconomics of Commercial Banks Recapitalization in Nigeria", Covenant University Journal of College of Business, Ota 1:5-10.

Keeley MC, Furlong FT (1990). "A Reexamination of Mean-Variance Analysis of Bank Capital Regulation," J. Bank. Financ. 14:69-84.

Molyneux P, Thornton J (1992). "Determinants of European Bank Profitability: A Note," J. Bank. Financ. 16:1173-1178.

Myers SC, Majluf NC (1984). "Corporate Financing and Investment Decisions When Firms Have Information that Investors Do Not Have," J. Financ. Econ. 13:187-221.

Naceur SB, Goaied M (2001). "The Determinants of the Tunisian Deposit Banks' Performance," Appl. Financ. Econ. 11:317-319. Evidence," Paper Retrieved on April 8, 2005 from http://www.academicdb.com/risk-management_case_study.

Naceur BS (2003). "Bank Capitalization and Performance in Tunisia", Universite. Librede Tunis, Avenue Khereddine Pacha, 1002 Tunis sbennaceur@eudoramail.com pp. 1-10.

Nyong OM (2001). "Monetary Policy and Commercial Banks' in Nigeria: Some Theoretical and Empirical Extensions", CBN Econ. Financ. Rev. 34(3):777-795.

Obadan MI (2004). "Merger Acquisition and New Minimum Capital Base: Matters Arising," The Guardian 24:24-27.

Oluitan T (2004). "Managing Liquidity and Profitability in Banking", The Nigerian Banker CIBN, Lagos, July- December pp.9-10.

Oyetan JA (1997). "Packaging Banks for Successful Recapitalization," The Nigerian Banker Jan-June, pp.21-24.

Peltzman S (1970). "Capital Investment in Commercial Banking and its Relationship to Portfolio Regulation", J. Financ 78(1):1-26.

Soludo CC (2004). Consolidation of the Nigeria Banking Industry to Meet the Development Challenges of the 21st Century", Being an Address Delivered to the Special Meeting of the Bankers' Committee held on July 6, CBN Headquarters, Abuja.

Uche CU (1998). "Bank Share Capital Regulation in Nigeria", Journal of International Banking Law 13(1):30-34.

Vojta G (1980). "Bank Capital Adequacy in Thomas Havrilesky and John Boorman (eds.), Current Perspectives in Banking: Operations, Management and Regulation", AHM Publishing Corporation, Illinois.

The effects of information asymmetry on budget slack: An experimental research

Juliano Almeida de Faria[1] and Sônia Maria Gomes da Silva[2]

[1]Mestre em Contabilidade, Universidade Estadual de Feira de Santana, Av. Transnordestina, s/n, Bairro: Novo Horizonte CEP: 44.036-900 Depto CIS, Feira de Santana, Bahia - Brasil.
[2]Dra em Engenharia da Produção, Universidade Federal da Bahia, Praça 13 de Maio, n.6- CEP: 40070-010, Salvador, Bahia-Brasil.

Budget slack has been investigated as an organizational and behavioral matter and defined as the value through which managers intentionally set additional obligation to the resource of a certain budget or consciously underestimate productive capability. Based on the principles of agency theory, this research aims to scrutinize the effects of information asymmetry on budget slack in an organizational context where agents are compensated through budget-based compensation plans. In order to do so we used a positive approach-based research in which an experiment with independent samples which comprised of 233 professionals was carried out; its instruments for data analysis were the test *t* and factorial analysis. The results confirm the hypotheses of agency theory. We identified that, regardless of the position held in a company (principal or agent), they both use information asymmetry to set budget goals with slack, that is, beyond real necessity. This action occurs *ex ante* and *ex post* the company sets out the budgeting deadline date. We also identified that budget slack is transversal to the position held and is not only a means of manipulation by the agents. Through this experiment we could prove that information asymmetry sets a favorable environment for increasing budget slack.

Key words: Budget slack, Information asymmetry theory, business budget.

INTRODUCTION

The budget slack phenomenon has aroused theorists' and researchers' as Lukka (1988), Libby (2003), Douglas and Wier (2005), Davis et al. (2006), Junqueira et al. (2010), interest due to its impact on organizational performance and, as a consequence, on the shareholders' ROI. Economy theory postulates that a subordinate knows more about his task and the environment it developed than his superior (Berle and Means, 1932; Jensen and Meckling, 1976). Participative budgeting is used to diminish this gap as well as to get information and reduce uncertainty. Therefore, based on the agency theory, budget slack causes inefficient allocation of organizational resource and underestimation of the profit on investment.

One of the mechanisms predicted by agency theory to understate interest conflicts between subordinate and superior is performance compensation and efficient and incessant monitoring of the agent's actions (Jensen and Meckling, 1976; Martinez, 1988). Performance compensation is an alternative to ease such conflicts but it is preceded by a contract. Budgeting concretizes one of these contracts and is one of the most used managerial instruments for planning, controlling and evaluating resource allocation under agent's responsibility, especially, when the principal compen-sates agents based on the outcomes shown on the budget, evaluating the difference between planned expenses and real expenses.

The opportunity for budget slack arises from this relation of interest conflicts in an environment of information asymmetry between the involved agents (Libby, 2003; Nascimento et al., 2008). The slack is used in order to provide each actor advantage over the others due to conflicts, and this aspect is increased by information asymmetry, which enables different classified information between actors (Chow et al., 1988; Dunk, 1993; Chong and Eggleton, 2007). Accordingly, information asymmetry is one of the intrinsic factors in the relation principal *versus* agent and, therefore, it can provide conditions for building slack and the consequent compensation through achieved outcomes, regardless of real losses caused to the principal (Martinez, 1988; Fisher et al., 2002; Marginson and Ogden, 2005). Thus the problem which guides this research is: what are the effects of information asymmetry on budget slack in an organizational context where agents are compensated for the results in the budget?

In this context information asymmetry appears in several sorts of relationships between the principal and the agent, such as in the relationships between shareholders and managers in which the principal wants the agent to maximize his wealth or between the community and the company in which the latter (agent) is supposed to preserve the community interests, culture, values, environment *et cetera* (Berle and Means, 1932; Martinez, 1998). This relationship is explained by the agency theory. Jensen and Meckling (1976) define the agency relationship as a contract through which a person or more people (the principal) hire another person (the agent) to carry out a job for them and provide the agent with authority for making decisions over their patrimony, is what happens in the relationship between superior and subordinate in the process of budgeting.

In this paper, we aim to scrutinise the effects of information asymmetry on budget slack in an organizational context where agents are compensated for the results in the budget. As outspreads of our main objective we have: how adverse selection may favor the actors (agents and principal) in building budget slack during elaboration of participative budgeting; to identify how the incidence of moral hazard may influence actors' (agents and principal) actions in building budget slack during the execution of participative budgeting; and to investigate whether reduction of information asymmetry causes increasing of managers' and directors' efforts to set budget goals and actions closer to reality, since they are evaluated through the results shown in the budget.

This research is to contribute to the explanation of budget slack in the context of agency theory. Besides demonstrating through empirical evidence that information asymmetry is a factor which triggers budget slack, above all, the studies of the relation between asymmetry and budget slack, comprehending the behavior of asymmetry in the budgeting process before (adverse selection) and after defining the budget (moral hazard), this investigation is especially relevant because there is no literature with similar mechanism of research yet (Faria, 2010).

Understanding the influence of information asymmetry on budget slack in Brazil is important for understanding and showing national reality to the world so that we can check whether it has the same problems we find in other countries already studied. Besides, there are companies in Brazil which use the model of business budget applied in this research, therefore our findings may assist Brazilian companies in setting up their strategic planning and assessment policy. Finally, information asymmetry is discussed here under an endogenous perspective of micro-economy, namely, it is discussed taking into account the relationships inside the companies.

THEORETICAL BASES

Budget slack

Budget slack has been investigated by theorists and researchers as an organizational and behavior matter defined as "the value through which managers intentionally set additional obligation to the resource of a certain budget or consciously underestimate productive capability" (Young 1985). For Douglas and Wier (2005), discussions on budget slack have its origin in managerial accountability literature early in the 1950s. Budget slack studies have aroused researchers' attention in the international scene due to the relevance of this phenomenon in the budgeting process of organizations and in its results.

Lukka (1998, 281) states that polarization of budget slack is still an untreatable matter in organizations since it is a complex and multi-faceted phenomenon which results from the interaction of several factors. Budget slack occurs when managers without prior consent from superiors overestimate expenses, underestimate receipts and overestimate demand of resource under their responsibility, aiming at self-satisfaction in a process of compensation for results related to the budget (Onsi, 1973; Libby, 2003; Davis et al., 2006; Junqueira et al., 2010).

Budget slack is the difference between estimated costs and real amounts needed to meet established needs, to represent the excess of resource requested to accomplish a task, namely, it is an underestimation and/or overestimation of expenses or production foreseen in a budget (Dunk and Pereira 1997; Libby, 2003; Anthony and Govindarajan, 2006; Lima, 2008). This behavior, identified in the professionals related to budgeting, badly affects the planning and budgeting processes through the bias of allocation or use of resource (Nascimento et al.,

2008). Through budget slack the actors involved in the process elaborate budgets using information different from reality, summing or subtracting from real data so that the budget becomes flexible in the results which are presented according to one's interests.

Amongst the factors which affect this phenomenon, identified in prior research, we find: the size of the company; diversity and decentralization (Merchant, 1985; Rankin et al., 2008); uncertainty of the environment (Anthony and Govindarajan, 2006); features of the task (Young, 1985); information asymmetry (Chow et al., 1988; Dunk, 1993; Chong and Eggleton, 2007; Onsi, 1973); budget goals negotiated versus goals imposed by company governance; managers who use the budget to allocate resource and/or performance evaluation (Fisher et al., 2002), using a system of incentives based on the budget, thereby prompting truth versus a bonus payment system as a way of prompting budget slack (Chow et al., 1988; Waller, 1988); management of the actions to achieve budget goals (Dunk, 1993; Merchant, 1985; Onsi 1973); aversion to individual hazard (Kim 2006; Young, 1985); and social pressure (Young, 1985) and reputation (Waller, 1988; Marginson and Ogden, 2005).

In this sense, Yuen (2004) investigated the relation between attribute of goals and managers' divisional propensity to build budget slack. He also researched managers' perceptions of communication and rewarding systems – factors which influence the relation between the features of goals and the propensity to build budget slack. He used a sample of managers from 108 hotels in Macau. Results indicated that clear communication of goals and a rewarding system can help to address the problems of the budgeting process.

On the other hand, it is worth mentioning that budget slack may not always be the villain of the conflicting relationship between directors and managers, especially if there is a reduction in information asymmetry. By using quantitative and qualitative data in four logistical units of a hard disc manufacturer during 24 months, D'Avila and Wouters's (2005) research showed empirical evidence of how a company can use budgeting as a way of allocating additional financial resource (budget slack) aiming at making the task of achieving the goals of the company easier for managers, since they are free to exceed costing budgets in order to ensure the quality of available products as well as clients' full satisfaction. However, in this research we focus on the aspect of information asymmetry used as a means of self-benefit by the actors involved in the budgeting process.

Information asymmetry

Applications and solutions proposed by the agency theory up to now have been used in several fields. Economists use the structure principal-agent predicted in agency theory to analyze the interactions of companies with their employees (Bensanko, 2006). An agent is found by a principal in order to make decisions or to take actions which affect the principal's profit. This relation can be rightly found in the position in which a director (principal) of a big industry, responsible for managing several manufacturing units, hires specialized managers of production (agents) to administer those units; they are, in turn, the director's legal responsibility. Problems arise in the agency relationships when actions taken by the agent or the information available to the agent cannot be used as the basis for a contract of incentives, that is, when a contract is incomplete (Klein, 1983; Bensanko, 2006).

On the basis of Ackerlof's (1970) assumptions and on Klann (2009) research, we can state that a direct consequence of information asymmetry is that, in a certain transaction, the party who owns more information derives greater benefits from the other. Thus information asymmetry occurs largely when there are differences in the level of information between two or more subjects of a contract (Cardoso et al., 2007; Pires, 2008). In the employee-employer relationship, for instance, there is information asymmetry when some information is available to the employee but it is not to the employer (Penno, 1984). It occurs because the employee intends to use classified information to enable self-satisfaction even when it means causing losses to the employer. In this context, agency theory is intensely related to it since it predicts interest conflicts between the principal and the agent, which are mostly promoted by the existence of information asymmetry between them (Stiglitz, 2000; Andrade and Rossetti, 2006).

Accordingly, the establishment of suitable rules and procedures under the directors' point of view to enable managers to work on budget planning is a means of enabling a secure flux of information and of making the budgeting process more transparent (Bruni and Gomes, 2010). The action of information asymmetry shows itself in two ways: adverse selection, which occurs *ex ante* the contract, and moral hazard, which occurs after the contract (Santos et al., 2007). Regarding budgeting, among some of its limitations, it can suffer from adverse selection and moral hazard since before budget closure information can be low-qualified and agents' behavior can change after it respectively (Covaleski et al., 2003). Figure 1 illustrates when these two effects show up in the trade relation as well as in the budgeting process:

Adverse selection

Within the problem of information asymmetry in trade, adverse selection appears while actors (principal-agent) have not been constituted in the trade relation yet, generally a process of purchasing and selling a product

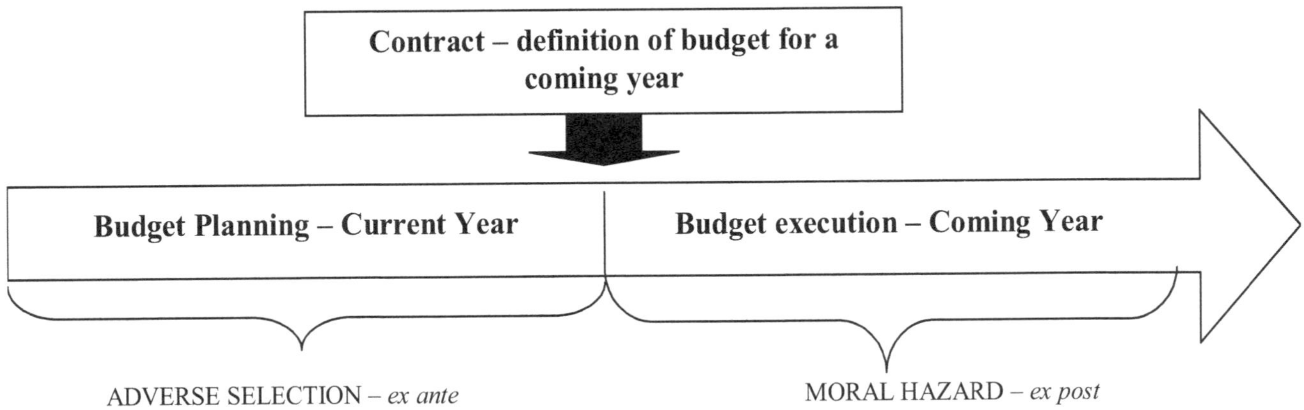

Figure 1. Occurrence of information asymmetry in budgeting.
Source: Adapted from Santos, 2007 p. 467.

or service. Martinez (1998, 5) says:

Adverse selection emerges when information is not equally allocated between principal and agent and, as a consequence, information asymmetry emerges. In other words, there is an amount of different information between agent and principal. The principal is incapable of determining whether the agent's actions are great or not. Actually in the context of adverse selection the problem of hidden information emerges.

Therefore an adverse selection consists of obtaining information which drives the other actor's satisfaction to decisions, that is, biased information turned to the perspective of maximizing results just for one party (Varian, 2006). In this sense both subjects (principal and agent) have information about the process they are part of (budgeting) but they keep it far from those who may reduce their possibilities of benefits. The agent also has classified information about his business and he keeps it hidden so that he can enjoy what his position provides him, inclusive to increase or not financial gains. Hence adverse selection can be found in the relationship between shareholders and directors, in which the first ones do not know some information about the budgets since directors have classified information. Accordingly, this phenomenon may occur in the relationship between directors and managers, for instance, the values to be negotiated as goals for the coming year's budget.

Thus managers can transfer information to directors that causes them to agree with joint decisions which may favor managers over directors. If there are not mechanisms for publicizing real information, then in extreme cases there is a hazard of eliminating market (confidence) to budget because there will not be any reliability on that information (Akerlof, 1970). Directors may not use budget due to its lack of truth in information presented in proposals by managers, which would cause bad effects in the short-term business planning.

Besides, the same way government regulation in the market does not guarantee reliability nor perfect absence of faults in delivering fuel and in carrying out a surgery, standardizing budgeting procedures in a company does not guarantee that the budget will be perfectly elaborated and executed with real information (Pindyck, 2002; Mankiw, 2005). In this case, moral hazard is eminent because individual's behavior after establishment of the contract (starting point of budget execution) may be amended, namely, as managers know the norms of the contract, they will portray different behavior in order to maximize self-interest. This aspect is worsened when the budget and contracted goals are already of low-quality information because this way the manager will have greater freedom to deal with a budget with slack so that he can perform his duties and maximize his own benefits.

Moral hazard

"Moral hazard has its origin in the impossibility of predicting which opportunistic actions agents would take after their hiring, that is, it appears after the contract has been signed by both parties" (Nascimento and Reginato, 2009, 279). The problem of moral hazard is that there is a tendency of changing behavior from one of the parties of a contract after it has been signed, causing substantial damage to the other party (Mcconnell, 2001; Pindyck, 2002). For example, after concretizing budget planning for the following year, the agent commits himself to fulfilling what was planned. Part of (or all) the manager's compensation goals are related to the efficiency in complying with the budget and therefore both parties are very interested in achieving the results. However, the director cannot entirely predict the opportunistic action that the manager can take to guarantee achievement of goals, using information asymmetry for both of them.

Figure 1 shows that moral hazard, in the budgeting process, occurs in a time perspective different from adverse selection. While adverse selection phenomenon happens before the budget planning deadline, moral hazard phenomenon occurs after the budget planning deadline; it may or may not coincide with the early implementation of the budget. Moreover, information asymmetry also acts during the implementation of the budget, especially in the relationship between directors and managers because the agent will pursue maximization of his interests and the principal will try to control the agent's actions more effectively, in this case, with the aid of the budget.

Thus, moral hazard occurs when directors are not able to observe the agent's actions after the establishment of the contract, hence there is a hidden action, in other words, the agent's action cannot be verified (Bronwing and Zupan, 2002; Santos et al., 2007). Information asymmetry comes from this system since the director is not able to perfectly control the manager's actions, whom in his turn also maintains information under his control so that he can use it for self benefit. On the other hand, the agent does not know the principal's actions perfectly either, strengthening the situation of information asymmetry between the actors in this process. Therefore, the principal can do something to test the agent, for instance, by creating a monitoring system without the agent's awareness of it.

Information asymmetry and participative budgeting

The participative budgeting process, in which the manager negotiates with the director, allows the first one to present a budget with slack, since he will use it to bargain results and ease achievement of the goals which will be set (Anthony and Govindarajan, 2006; Dechow and Shakespeare, 2009). In the participative budgeting process, a manager's situation is privileged for providing him a condition of generating opportunistic behavior, taking advantage of the information he has to bargain favorable results to his own interests, especially when the goals negotiated in the budgeting are to be the basis for variable compensation. However, just the manager's participation in the budgeting process does not explain slack, because it is necessary that this slack is not known by the director (asymmetry) so that the manager can establish a reserve and protect himself from an unsatisfactory performance evaluation, prioritizing his own interests over the ones of the organization (Libby, 2003; Dechow and Shakespeare, 2009; Junqueira et al., 2010).

In this perspective, Fischer et al. (2002) developed an experimental study with two groups of students in which the authors used two mechanisms: a) the use of budgets to allocate scarce resources; b) the use of budgets for performance evaluation. They posited that such competition not only would reduce the amounts subordinates would earn as a result of budget slack, but would also increase subordinates' effort and task performance, in contrast to compensation methods; all the results are the consequence of the presence or absence of information asymmetry, which is the independent variable of their research. On the other hand, D'avila and Wouters (2005) investigated budget management as a determinant to explain budget slack. Budget slack plays an important role in operating budgets in companies. Although this theory has negative results, as well as positive elements related to its presence, empirical literature has seen it as dysfunctional to organizations.

Chia (1995) researched the interaction effect of information asymmetry and decentralization on subunit managers' level of job satisfaction. He used a questionnaire as a technique for collecting data, which was submitted to 42 managers in Singapore. The results showed that a higher level of information asymmetry has a close relation to a higher level of job satisfaction for those managers who work under high decentralization conditions. Chong and Eggleton (2007) analyzed the effects of information asymmetry and organizational commitment on the relation between the level of confidence on compensation schemes based on incentives and management performance of 109 managers from a transversal section of Australian manufacturing companies. The results show evidence of greater management performance for managers with low organizational commitment and great dependence on compensation schemes based on incentives in high information asymmetry conditions.

When information asymmetry is used opportunely by managers in the company they can use it to hide any information, from behavioral evaluation results to low sales, not undertaking to justify such negative variations. Hence, we can relate the presence of information asymmetry to the subunit managers' low performance. They will not feel motivated to develop alternative methods of improving results because their inefficiencies can be covered by information asymmetry (Dechow and Shakespeare, 2009; Chong and Eggleton, 2007; Dunk, 1993).

METHODOLOGY

In order to achieve our objective in this research, we carried out an experimental study. For this experiment we split participants into two groups: a control group, comprised of people who have not been manipulated by the independent variable; and an experimental group, comprised of people who have been manipulated by the independent variable. The manipulation of

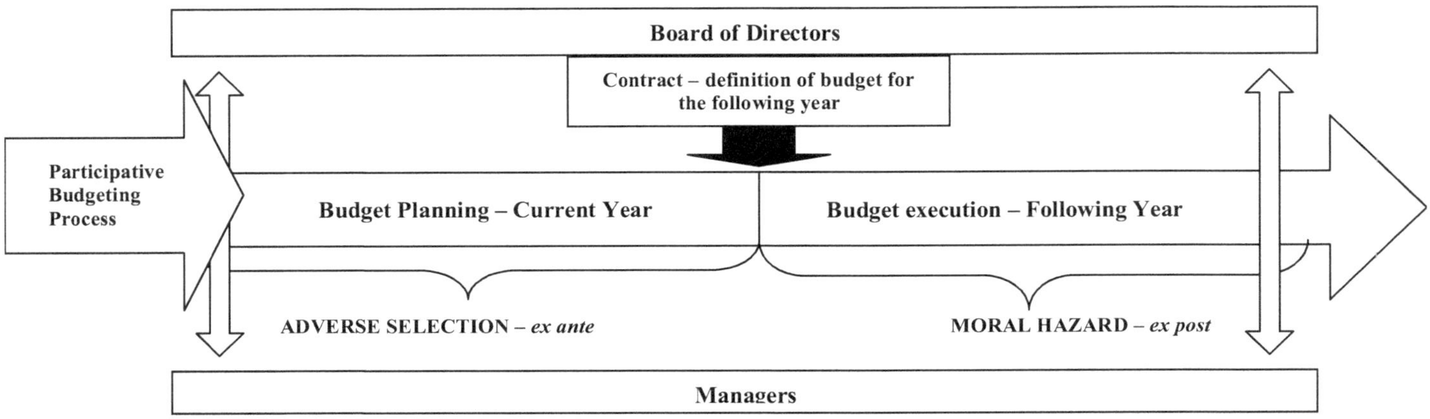

Figure 2. Research model.
Source: Designed by the authors, 2011.

variable incidence between the groups, maintaining other variables under control, allowed us to measure and to compare results, which constitute the main advantage of this method (Cooper and Schindler, 2003; Cozby, 2009).

Accordingly, this research shows that the presence of information asymmetry explains the existence of budget slack built by managers in the context of participative budgeting, which is a reference for results-based compensation; all of this was supported by Jensen and Meckling's (1976) ideas about agency theory. Information asymmetry can be found in the relationship between the unit manager and director, linked to the interest conflict between the parties and to the budgeting process, affording building of slack. In this proposed model of research (Figure 2), the relationship director/manager follows the agency theory approach, which proposes the interest conflict. Participative budgeting occurs between them; through it they set goals and resource allocation for the following year. During negotiations (*ex ante*) adverse selection works to provide information with slack from managers to directors. After establishing the budget and while carrying it out the next year, moral hazard (*ex post*) works to provide information with slack in order to feed the budget, maintaining results in accordance with the estimated goals, that is, managers' behavior is modified according to the results achieved at that time.

In this research the independent variable is information asymmetry, from which its incidence was manipulated in the questionnaires applied to the experimental groups. Both groups were subjected to situations based on real facts in which the unit manager (agent) and director (principal) made decisions. The only difference between the situations of the groups was that, in the experimental one information asymmetry was eliminated. Thus, we tried to identify the variations among the options of the experimental group participants in the dependent variable, compare them to the results of the controlling group and also collect such variations about this process among directors and managers.

The population comprised of graduate alumni of the MBA in Administration, Finance and Comptrollership. We chose this population for two reasons: firstly because in these faculties the number of people who are in the labor market and hold managerial and directorship positions is higher than the ones in under-graduate courses and graduate academic programs; the second reason is supported by the results of prior researches, such as Lima and Raimundo (2010). Moreover, Liyanarachchi and Milne's (2005) and Elliot et al. (2007) research empirically legitimate the studies carried out on the basis of collecting data with alumni (undergraduate and graduate). The research sample of this research comprised of 233 questionnaires answered completely, 112 in the controlling group and 121 in the experimental one.

The dependent variable – budget slack – is the difference between estimated costs and real value necessary to satisfy foreseen needs, and the slack represents the excess of requested resources to carry out a task. The higher the estimated value is in relation to the real value, the higher budget slack will be. The independent variable – information asymmetry – was eliminated in the experimental group. Henceforth, we gauged the effect of this elimination on the dependent variable supported by participants' answers under this new condition – absence of information asymmetry (Merchant, 1985; Moene, 1986; Waller, 1988; Dunk and Perera, 1997; Lima, 2008). Four hypothetical situations, based on real ones, were created from an operational context where participants played the roles of directors (questions 1 and 3) and of managers (questions 2 and 4), whose decisions were demands in the operational context proposed in this research. Based on this structure and on the studies approached here, it was possible to establish eight researching hypotheses.

We used the questionnaire as a tool for collecting data; they comprised of multiple-choice questions and were split as follows: the experimental questions are presented; the statements on the *Likert* scale to gauge the sample's knowledge about budgets; and data about the respondents' profile are established. Questionnaires were randomly delivered to students since this is a main feature for the experiment success, above all for splitting the groups into controlling and experimental (Field, 2009). Lastly it is about an independent sample (people from the controlling group will not afterwards answer the questionnaire of the experimental group, neither *vice-versa*), so we tried to maintain equal numbers of participants in the groups in relation to the number of questionnaires delivered in this sample, obeying the random delivery.

In order to validate the questionnaires, we previously tested them with a group of 22 Accountancy *lato-sensu* graduate students from one of the Higher Education Institutions chosen. We wrote down their comments and suggestions and, where it was possible, we inserted them in the questionnaire, that is, since they did not hinder the main objective of this research. We call attention to the fact that the students who participated in this previous test did not comprise the sample of this research so that we could avoid bias of previous knowledge of the questionnaire. To measure the effect of

Table 1. Sample experience.

Role	Experience (years)	Number of subordinate managers
Director	10.7	3
Manager	6.9	0

Source: Research data, 2011.

information asymmetry on budget slack, we compared the averages (Test *t*) between the questionnaires of the controlling group and experimental one. The independent test *t* is used in situations where there are two experimental conditions and different participants in each one (Vieira, 2006; Field, 2009). The analysis, compilation and tabulation of all data from the questionnaires were conducted by using specific software, in our case, the SPSS (Statistical Package for Social Sciences), version 15 or higher, and freeware.

To work with the data provided, we used the factorial analysis. Based on the data from the questionnaire and taking into consideration the number of questions which guides the theme, we decided to use the factorial analysis because, according to Bezerra (2007), "it is a statistical technique which tries, from evaluation of a group of variables, to identify the ordinary dimensions of variability that exist in a group of phenomena". As a requirement, Spearman's test was applied in order to check out the level of correlation among the 10 alternatives available in this section. The significance index (Sig.) was calculated and is relevant in case of results under 0.005 (Field, 2009).

PRESENTATION AND INTERPRETATION OF RESULTS

Participants' characteristics

We collected a total of 254 questionnaires, but only 233 were duly availed to this research. The others were discarded for presenting dubious answers, unanswered, lack of knowledge on budgeting or for filling in incorrectly. After classifying the sample data, we identified 112 questionnaires as the controlling group, from which 51 had a profile of director and 61 of manager. Regarding the experimental group, 57 had a profile of director and 64 of manager, a total of 121 questionnaires. Under exclusive look of roles, this research counts on 108 questionnaires of professionals who have managers (more than 1) as subordinates, holding the position of director. Furthermore, it counts 125 questionnaires answered by professionals who hold the position of managers (administrative, accounting and operational ones) experienced in business budgeting.

In the sample, the Accountancy major prevails both for the role of director (23% of total) and for the role of manager (30% of total). Secondly, the Administration major consists of 15% of directors and 18% of managers. The other majors altogether totaled 15%. This number lived up to our expectation because the focus of these majors is on administrative and controlling management. This is a positive aspect to our research since we assume that most of them have already studied the basic contents of a business budget. Finally, we show the years of professional experience of this sample, as we can see on Table 1.

This sample shows that directors have an average experience of 10.7 years and managers have 6.9 years of professional experience. This difference also lived up to another expectation of ours that more important positions are held by more experienced people in the field. The directors also have an average of 03 subordinate managers, and this is a fundamental prerequisite for classifying this group. Besides, this is a natural consequence in the market that assigns greater responsibility to more experienced professionals.

Participants' level of knowledge on budgeting

Block II affirms on the Likert scale which aims at measuring the involvement of the respondent with the budget. The data were subjected to and approved in the test of normality and in the factorial analysis which identifies the reduced factors of available variables in this research. The first result of the factorial analysis shows the creation of three groups of factors with accumulated capacity of 61.25% of explanation. It evidences that the items available in the generated factors have a close relation between data in this sample. The KMO presented the result 0.763 as an acceptable one, indicating that the identification of factors is adequate for the level of the test carried out. We also carried out Bartlett's sphericity test to check the correlation significance between the scale items. The results (chi-square 640; 470 and significance of 0.000) prove that the scale factorial analysis can be considered appropriate, suggesting the existence of significant relations between the scale items. As predicted in the literature, only the Factor 1 was approved in the test, obtaining 0.796 as a result, so it is superior to the reference rate 0.700 (Hair et al., 2009).

Accordingly, the four items pointed out by this factor are taken into consideration for gauging respondents' involvement with the budget since they have greater correlation of results. It means that respondents chose similar answers in the questionnaire to the options q1 (Business budget is used in the company I work for), q2 (Among the activities related to my position there are

Table 2. Comparing averages of the sample H1 and H3.

Item	Group	Hypothesis (R$)	Average of the sample (R$)	Slack of the sample (R$)	%
H1	Controlling Director	200,000.00	212,254.90	12,254.90	5.77
H3	Experimental Director	200,000.00	204,122.81	4,122.81	2.02

Source: Data from this research, 2011.

Table 3. Comparing averages of the sample H2 and H4.

Item	Group	Hypothesis (R$)	Average of the sample (R$)	Slack of the sample (R$)	%
H2	Controlling Manager	40,000.00	44,139.34	4,139.34	9.30
H4	Experimental Manager	40,000.00	39,921.88	-78.13	-0.20

Source: Data from this research, 2011.

activities related to annual budget), q3 (I develop activities related to budget elaboration and daily monitoring) and q5 (I work for a company that improved its financial performance by using business budget), which demonstrate involvement with business budgeting. Thus, we may infer that this sample has significant relation to the theme and so the answers we got in the experiment are reliable, after all, we got them from professionals able to contribute to this research. If we add this information and the average time of professional experience together, we can confirm the quality of this sample, giving reliability to the collected opinions and, as a consequence, to the results disposed earlier.

Analysis of information asymmetry on budget slack

We emphasize that the data from this section were also subjected to the test of normality. The test carried out in the SPSS shows that the data was validated and approved, namely, this sample has a normal distribution. Afterwardst we conducted the statistical analysis with test *t*.

In Table 2 we present the results collected regarding Question 1 of the questionnaire. We compare the averages (test *t*) between the controlling and experimental groups as foreseen in H1 and H3. Concerning the information collected in H1, we observe that the general average of the respondents (R$ 212,254.90) demonstrates that the director decided to alter the budget value building the total slack of R$ 12,254.90, namely, 5.77% in relation to the original value. Therewith, he maximized his profit supported by asymmetry since he altered it based on classified information (information asymmetry).

From this result, it was possible to achieve the first part of specific objective 1 (1.1) through the H1 test. Confirmation of H1 makes it feasible to identify that adverse selection favors the principal (director) in building budget slack during elaboration of participative budgeting because he decided to alter the budget value ($\mu_{Orç}$), building budget slack even when it was not necessary to the company aiming at maximizing his own interest. Yet based on Table 2, corresponding to H3, we can see the result of this same Question 1 that was applied to the experimental group, manipulating the independent variable – information asymmetry.

Regarding the information collected from H3, we can observe that the general average of the correspondents (R$ 204,122.81) demonstrates that the director decided to alter the budget value, building the total slack of R$ 4,122.81, that is, 2.02% in relation to the original value. This result shows that even without information asymmetry the director causes alteration in the budget value to maximize his own interest through the request of resources over real necessity of the budget. So, the value found in the experimental group – R$ 204,122.81 ($\mu_{Orç}$) – is different from zero, in other words, H3 was rejected. However, we can also observe on Table 2 that the elimination of information asymmetry in the budgeting context substantially decreased slack (from 5.77 to 2.02%). Even without total elimination of slack, this finding clearly demonstrates the influence of information asymmetry on budget slack. From the result gauged it was possible to achieve the first part of specific objective 3 (3.1) and prove that reduction of information asymmetry causes the increasing of directors' efforts in setting budget goals closer to reality, since they are evaluated through the results of this budget. After all, slack was reduced, representing a decrease of 3.75%.

In Table 3 we portray the results collected from Question 2 of the questionnaire, asked to managers. The averages (test t) are compared between the controlling and experimental groups as foreseen in H2 and H4. Concerning the information collected in H2, we observe that the general average of the respondents (R$

44,139.34) shows that the manager decided to alter the budget value, building slack into the total of R$ 4,139.34, that is, 9.38% in relation to the original value. From this he maximized his profit supported by asymmetry since he altered it based on classified information (information asymmetry) as it was proposed by the question.

From this result, it was possible to achieve the second stage of specific objective 1 (1.2) through the test of H2. Confirmation of H2 makes it feasible to identify that adverse selection favors the manager (agent) in building budget slack during the elaboration of participative budgeting because he decided to alter the budget value ($\mu_{Orç}$), which builds budget slack even when it is not really necessary to the company, aiming at maximizing his own interest.

Yet based on Table 3, corresponding to H4, we have the result of this same Question 2, which was applied to the experimental group with manipulation of the independent variable – information asymmetry. Regarding the information collected from H4, we can see that the general average of the respondents (R$ 39,921.88) demonstrates that the manager decided to alter budget value, eliminating slack with proposals of lower values in the budget. Therewith, the general average presents a negative slack total of R$ 78.13, that is, -2% in relation to the original value. This result shows that without information asymmetry the manager tries to eliminate budget slack without using adverse selection and may require resources when necessary.

Thus, the value we found in the experimental group – R$39,921.88 ($\mu_{Orç}$) – is different and lower in relation to the budget. So, H4 was confirmed. Moreover, it enables us to infer that the elimination of information asymmetry has an effect on budget slack, affording its elimination. The second part of specific objective 3 (3.2) was completed and it was proved that reduction of information asymmetry increases managers' efforts in setting budget goals closer to reality, since they are evaluated through the results presented in the budget.

Accordingly, it is possible to identify that an adverse selection favors the agent (manager) in building budget slack during the execution of participative budgeting because he decided to alter the budget value ($\mu_{Orç}$), building budget slack even when it was not necessary to the company, aiming at maximizing his own interest. However, the result demonstrates that managers, in a public information context during the budget elaboration, may not propose alterations in the budget, building budget slack to maximize their own interest. They may even set lower goals in relation to the original budget as a personal challenge in the context of performance evaluation based on budget results.

Furthermore, we can observe in Table 3 that the elimination of information asymmetry in the budget substantially reduced slack (from 9.38 to -0.20%). In this case, budget slack was completely eliminated among managers, confirming the strong influence of information asymmetry on budget slack given the amplitude of slack decreasing in the experimental context. Finally, we emphasize that there is no difference between managers' and directors' behavior in adverse selection, in other words, they choose information that facilitates self-interest accomplishment. Regardless of position, we noticed that they both used asymmetry to favor themselves and reduce slack when there is no information asymmetry during the budget elaboration.

In Table 4, concerning the information collected from H5, we observe that the general average of the respondents (R$ 300,784.31) demonstrates that the director decided to alter the budget value, building the total slack of R$ 10,784.31, that is, 3.59% in relation to the original value. Therewith he maximized his own profit supported by information asymmetry, since he altered it based on classified information (information asymmetry) even after the establishment of the budget, revealing the inherent moral hazard of this situation.

Therefore, the average found (R$ 300,784.31) confirms H5. With this result we achieved the first part of specific objective 2 (2.1) since we can see that the incidence of moral hazard may influence directors' actions, enabling building of budget slack during the elaboration of participative budgeting because they decided to alter the budget value ($\mu_{Orç}$), building budget slack even when it was not necessary aiming at maximizing their own interest. As proposed in this research, this same Question 3 was applied to the experimental group with manipulation of independent variable – information asymmetry – which corresponds to H7.

Regarding the information collected from H7, we observe that the general average of the respondents (R$ 290,087.72) demonstrates that the director decided to alter the budget value, building the total slack of R$ 87.81, that is, 0.03% in relation to the original value. This result shows that even without information asymmetry the director altered the budget value to maximize his own interest by requesting resources over the real needs estimated in the budget. So, the value found in the experimental group – R$ 204,122.81 ($\mu_{Orç}$)– is different from zero, that is, H7 was rejected. However, we also see on Table 4 that the elimination of budget slack in the budgeting context substantially decreased slack (from 3.59% to 0.03%). Even without total elimination of slack, this finding clearly demonstrates the influence of information asymmetry on budget slack given the amplitude of slack decreasing in the experimental context.

After carrying out H7 test, it was possible to achieve the third part of specific objective 3(3.3), proving that reduction of information asymmetry leads to increasing of directors' efforts in proposing actions closer to reality (a little difference of 0.03% in relation to the real value in the budget), since they are evaluated through the results

Table 4. Comparing the averages of the sample H5 and H7.

Item	Group	Hypothesis (R$)	Average of sample (R$)	Slack of sample (R$)	%
H5	Controlling Director	290,000.00	300,784.31	10,784.31	3.59
H7	Experimental Director	290,000.00	290,087.72	87.72	0.03

Source: Data from this research, 2011.

Table 5. Comparing averages of the sample H6 and H8.

Item	Group	Hypothesis (R$)	Average of the sample (R$)	Slack of the sample (R$)	%
H2	Controlling Manager	30,000.00	20,819.67	- 9,180.33	-44.09
H4	Experimental Manager	30,000.00	21,875.00	- 8,125.00	-37.14

Source: Data from this research, 2011.

presented in this budget. It is possible to infer that the absence of information asymmetry contributes to increase quality in the budget since this latter will present information really closer to reality.

In Table 5 we present the results collected from question 4 of the questionnaire applied to managers. We compared the averages (test *t*) between the controlling and experimental groups as foreseen in H6 and H8. Concerning the information collected from H6, we observe that the general average of the respondents (R$20,819.67) shows that managers decided to recognize in the task the least value in current year then to start the following year with the total budget slack of R$ 9,180.33, that is, -44.09% in relation to the original value. Therewith he maximized his own profit supported by asymmetry since he identified the then current value as strategy to guarantee leftover of resources to start the following year.

Ergo the second part of specific objective 2 (2.2) was achieved, proving that the incidence of moral hazard influences managers' actions in building budget slack during the execution of participative budgeting. So, we notice that moral hazard favors the agent (manager) in building budget slack during the execution of participative budgeting because he decided to inform a lower value to build resource slack for the following year so that he could maximize his own interest. Therefore, the average achieved (R$ 20,819.67) confirmed H6. As proposed in this research, this same Question 4 was applied to the experimental group by manipulating the independent variable – information asymmetry – which corresponds to H8.

Concerning the information collected from H8, we observe that the general average of the respondents (R$21,875.00) demonstrates that the manager decided to present part of the credit available in the then current year, having R$ 8,125.00 (37.14%) as budget slack to begin the following year with credit. So, by manipulating information asymmetry and eliminating it, the value achieved in the experimental group – R$ 21,873.00 ($\mu_{Orç}$) is different from the amount of credit received, which should be included in the current year then. Thus, H8 was rejected.

The result shows that even in a context of public information managers tend to propose alterations, building budget slack in order to maximize their own interest. In this case, by presenting just part of credit in the current year then and only presenting the other part of it in the following year so that slack is maintained in the following budget. Therewith, we observe on Table 5 that the elimination of information asymmetry in the budget reduced slack (from -44.09 to -37.14%). Thus, even not totally eliminating slack in this experimental situation, this finding clearly shows the influence of information asymmetry on reducing budget slack.

Finally, it was possible to achieve the fourth part of specific objective 3 (3.4), attesting that reduction of information asymmetry increases managers' efforts in proposing actions closer to reality since they are evaluated through the results presented in this budget. At last, we emphasize that there is no difference between managers' and directors' behavior in adverse selection, that is, when they choose information which facilitates their own interest. Regardless of position, we notice that both of them use asymmetry in order to favor themselves and reduce slack when there is no information asymmetry during the budget elaboration.

The analysis of specific objective 1 in this study is supported by H1 and H2, both of them confirmed by the collected data. From it, we could achieve the first (1.1) and second (1.2) parts of specific objective 1, which is to check out how adverse selection is able to favor the principal (director) and the agent (manager) in building budget slack when elaborating the participative budgeting. We can see that in both positions there was alteration of the budget value, building budget slack even when it was not necessary so that they could maximize their own interest and guarantee easy access to the goals set from that value.

The analysis of specific objective 2 in this study is supported by H5 and H6, both of them confirmed by the collected data. From it, we could achieve the first (2.1) and second (2.2) parts of specific objective 2, which is to check out how the incidence of moral hazard can influence principals' (directors) and agents' (managers) actions in building budget slack during the execution of participative budgeting.

After the establishment of budget (*ex post*), we observe that in both positions there was alteration of the budget value, building budget slack to maximize their own interest. In other words, even after the definition of budget rules, users, availing themselves of information asymmetry, decided to get alterations in the budget and/or in its entries to guarantee easy access to the goals and then get the variable compensation.

The analysis of specific objective 3 is supported by H5, H6, H7 and H8; all of them corresponding to the experimental group, where manipulation of information asymmetry occurred. It was also possible to fully achieve specific objective 3 (3.1, 3.2, 3.3 and 3.4), which is to investigate whether reduction of information asymmetry increases directors' efforts in setting budget goals closer to reality, since they are evaluated through the results presented in the budget. Even after rejection of H3, H7 and H8, it was possible to achieve specific objective 3 because there was reduction of budget slack in the four proposed situations (manager *ex ante*, manager *ex post*, director *ex ante* and director *ex post*), revealing that reduction of information asymmetry played an important role in the sample decisions. This rejection involved above all the impossibility of complete elimination of budget slack just with the variable information asymmetry, demonstrating that other studies must be carried out in order to identify other variables which can contribute to this matter.

In this context, models of business budget are used by a superior to obtain information and then reduce uncertainty (Shields and Shields, 1998). However, in the presence of this phenomenon – slack – business budget usefulness is compromised, organizational resources are unduly allocated and investment profit is biased to the interest of a certain group, which cannot be the shareholders', increasing transaction risk of a company (Fisher et al., 2002).

Regarding participative budgeting during building of budget slack, researches show that managers find it less necessary to build slack into their budgets when their participation in the process is reduced (*Top-down*) since budgets may have little (or no) influence from them, so their task is only to pursue goals set by the Board of Directors (Murray, 1990; Davis et al., 2006) (Table 6). Results also contrast with other researches because this sample is comprised of professionals who constantly use participative budgeting in activities related to building of slack in the controlling group, namely, using information asymmetry. So, in the sample analyzed, reduction of participation in the budgeting is not a determiner for building of budget slack.

We clearly notice this correlation when the manipulation of the variable information asymmetry occurred in specific objective 3, where we tried to check out our hypotheses (H3, H4, H7 and H8) concerning elimination of asymmetry, which facilitates direct reduction of budget slack. Supported by the results of researches which are the bases of this approach (Ramaswami et al., 1997; Denison, 2009; Kim, 2006), this research attests this understanding since results from the experimental group presented reduced budget slack (in a group it reached zero) when dealing with a situation without information asymmetry. Thus, it is clear in this sample that, when faced with such risk of favorable performance, unit managers (and the director in this research) will make use of information asymmetry in order to manage data and information which may completely, or as close as possible, achieve their objectives, confirming findings such as Chong and Eggleton's (2007), Denison's (2009) and Dechow and Shakespeare's (2009).

We also emphasize that absence of information asymmetry did not cause budget slack elimination in all hypotheses. This finding matches approaches that confirm the complexity of this phenomenon such as Lukka's (1988), Young's (1985), Shields and Shields's (1998) and Davis et al. (2006) studies. Therefore, various studies have been carried out on different sides of budget slack supported by sociological and psychological approaches and especially aesthetical studies in this context. Some results have been achieved such as improvement in communication and setting of goals in compensation schemes, which are indicated as a way of eliminating slack (Yuen, 2004). Moreover, D'avila and Wouters's (2005) studies state that budget slack plays an important role in the operation of budgets in organizations. So budget slack needs to be further studied for being a phenomenon closely related to the human being, whom makes the decisions, and so it is complex.

Conclusion

For evaluating the effects of information asymmetry on budget slack, this study lines up with the attention many authors have given to the theme such as Onsi (1973), Chow et al. (1988), Dunk (1993), Dunk and Perera (1997), Libby (2003), Fisher et al. (2002) and Lima (2008). Budget slack occurs when an individual over-estimates expenses and costs and understates receipts in order to facilitate achievement of his own goals.

Table 6. Researching hypotheses.

H1 – Directors will choose the option which will maximize their profit supported by information asymmetry on decisions made before the budget (adverse selection)
H2 – Managers will choose the option which will maximize their profit supported by information asymmetry on decisions made before the budget (adverse selection)
H3 –With public information directors will not try to maximize their profit on decisions made before the budget (adverse selection).
H4 – With public information managers will not try to maximize their profit on decisions made before the budget (adverse selection).
H5 – Directors will change their behavior and will try to maximize their profit supported by information asymmetry on decisions even after budget establishment (moral hazard).
H6 – Managers will change their behavior and will try to maximize their profit supported by information asymmetry on decisions even after budget establishment (moral hazard).
H7 – With public information directors will not change their behavior and will maintain their decisions even after budget establishment, eliminating moral hazard.
H8 – With public information managers will not change their behavior and will maintain their decisions even after budget establishment, eliminating moral hazard

Source: Elaborated by the authors, 2011.

In a context of agency relation where agents and directors are the actors, the effects of slack can be harmful to companies and in a residual level to the shareholders as well. Through budget slack the individuals involved in this process provide budgets with information different from reality. By adding and/or subtracting values from true data to make the budget flexible in the results, which disloyally guide all information demonstrated according to their own interest.

In this research we aimed to respond to what the effects of information asymmetry on budget slack are in an organizational context where agents are compensated on the basis of budget results. The final result reveals that the influence of asymmetry on budget slack is substantial and causes an increase in slack. This finding was confirmed especially through comparing data in an experimental context (without asymmetry). Thus we observed a sharp decrease, and in some cases total elimination, of budget slack when there was no information asymmetry, corroborating Yuen's (2004) studies which argues in favor of disclosing information as a preponderant factor to eliminate budget slack.

Therewith, we state that information asymmetry is one of the factors which contribute to building budget slack and is manipulated by agents in order to have budgets presenting convenient results so they can be compensated on achieved results regardless of real losses caused to the principal. This study contributes to general research for confirming that the influence of information asymmetry on budget slack is substantial. Individuals' behavior clearly shows it in the experimental group regardless of position held, manager or director; groups notably with interest conflicts in organizations. Therewith, we contribute to Hopwood's (1973), Fisher et al. (2002) and Kren's (2003) studies which identified that just managers evaluated through budget were more susceptible to dysfunctional behavior building slack only to achieve the goals set in the budget. In this research we also noticed this behavior among directors, whom tried to negotiate budgets which give them expectations of higher profit.

It is possible to confirm that, faced with interest conflicts, information asymmetry between both of them and performance evaluation somehow (or totally) linked to budget, actors' behavior suffered alterations due to these factors, resulting in budget slack which residually disfavors shareholders. Therewith, we confirmed that in Brazil (sample) the results match Chow et al.'s (1998), Young's (1985), Kren's (2003), Douglas and Wier's (2005) and Lima's (2008) studies. In this context, the use of questions-problem with different groups permitted us to identify that slack is used so that each actor may have advantage over others because of conflicts and this aspect is increased by asymmetry, which enables the existence of different information among the actors. Information asymmetry favors both sides when there are interest conflicts because both of them have access to classified information.

Direct reduction of budget slack was also noticed under adverse selection and moral hazard views, that is, in different stages of budgeting. Thus, agent or principal, if any actor has got classified information he will use it to build budget slack, raising up the budget value even when it is not necessary so that he can maximize his own interest. With these new aspects, this research aims at contributing to consolidate discussions on information asymmetry as a factor which triggers off budget slack in the attempt to explain and predict slack behavior in business budget.

Our limitations in this research were the sample and the hypothetical situations which participants were subjected to, but real situations, where several sentiments are present, may have different results. Furthermore, the field of approach was directed strictly to information asymmetry as well as focus on participative budgeting. We may also take into consideration that according to positive approach of research, we carried out this study based on a sample which represents part of a population, therefore more information may be intrinsic within all the population and not included in this sample.

For future researches, we suggest checking out whether directors will use asymmetry to bargain better results together with managers through access to information managers may not know then such as strategic goals. We also suggest broadening the study and evaluating other variables which can explain the existence of slack even without information asymmetry. Finally, it is possible to check out whether policies for investigating budget variables (*ex post*) may result in lower budget slack, since strict mangers tend to concern about uncovering asymmetry.

ACKNOWLEDGEMENT

The authors would want to thank Mr. Cliver Dias for translating this work into English.

REFERENCES

Akerlof G (1970). The market for 'Lemons': quality uncertainty and the market mechanism. Quart. J. Econ. 84:488-500.
Andrade A, Rossetti JP (2006). Governança corporativa: fundamentos, desenvolvimento e tendências . 2. ed. São Paulo : Atlas.
Anthony RN, Govindarajan V (2006). Sistemas de controle gerencial. Tradução Adalberto Ferreira das Neves. São Paulo: Atlas.
Bensanko D (2006). A economia da estratégia.Tradução Bazán Tecnologia e Lingüística. 3ed. Porto Alegre: Bookman.
Berle A, Means G (1932). The modern corporation and private property. New York: MacMillan.
Bezerra FA (2007). Análise fatorial. In: Corrar Luiz J, Paulo Edilson, Dias Filho, José Maria (Coords.). Análisemultivariada para cursos de adm, ciencias contábeis e economía. São Paulo: Atlas.
Bruni AL, Gomes, SMS (Orgs.). (2010) Controladoria: conceitos, ferramentas e desafíos. Salvador: EDUFBA.
Cardoso RL, Mário PdC, Aquino, ACB. de. (2007). Contabilidade gerencial: mensuração, monitoramento e incentivos. São Paulo: Atlas.
Chia YM (1995). The interaction effect of information asymmetry and decentralization on managers job satisfaction: a research note. Hum. Relat. 48(6):609-624.
Chong VK, Eggleton IRC (2007). The impact of reliance on incentive-based compensation schemes, information asymmetry and organisational commitment on managerial performance. Manage. Account. Res. 18:312-342.
Cooper DR, Schindler PS (2003). Métodos de pesquisa em adm.7ªPorto Alegre:Bookman.
Covaleski MA, Evans III, JH, Luft JL, Shields MD (2003). Budgeting research: three theoretical perspectives and criteria for selective integration. J. Manage. Account. Res. 15:3-49.
Cozby PC (2009). Métodos de pesquisa em ciências do comportamento. Tradução Paula Inez Cunha Gomide, Emma Otta. São Paulo: Atlas.
D'avila, T, Wouters M (2005). Managing budget emphasis through the explicit design of conditional budgetary slack. Account. Org. Soc. 30(7-8):587-608, oct./nov.
Davis S, DeZoort FT, Koop LS (2006).The effect of obedience pressure and perceived responsibility on management accountant´s creation of budget slack. Behav. Res. Account. 18:18-35.
Dechow PM, Shakespeare C. (2009). Do managers time securitization transactions to obtain accounting benefits? Account. Rev. 84(1):99-132.
Denison CA (2009). Real options and escalation of commitment: a behavioral analysis of capital investment decisions. Account. Rev. 84(1):133-155.
Douglas PC, Wier B (2005).Cultural and ethical effects in budgeting systems: a comparison of U.S. and chinese managers. J. Bus. Ethics. 60:159-174.
Dunk AS (1993). The effect of budget emphasis and information asymmetry on thhe relation between budgetary participation and slack. Account. Rev. 68(2): 400-410.
Dunk AS, Perera H (1997). The incidence of bugetary slack: a field study exploration. Account. Auditing Accountability J. 10(5):649-664.
Elliot WB, Hodge F, Kennedy J, Pronk M (2007). Are MBA students a good proxy for nonprofessional investors? Account. Rev. 82(1):139-168.
Faria de JA (2010). Information asymmetry in budgeting: an analysis of scientific production in international journals between 2005 and 2009. In: ANPCONT, 4., 2010, São Paulo.
Field A (2009). Descobrindo a estatística usando o SPSS. 2. ed. Porto Alegre: Bookman.
Fisher JG, Maines LA, Peffer S, Sprinkle GB (2002). Using budgets for performance evaluation: effects of resource allocation and horizontal information asymmetry on budget proposals, budget slack, and performance. Account. Rev. 77(4):847-865.
Hopwood AG (1973). An empirical study of the role of accounting data in performance evaluation. J. Account. Res. 10:156-182.
Jensen MC, Meckling WH (1976). Theory of the firm: managerial behavior, agency costs and ownership structure. J. Financ. Econ. 3(4):305-360.
Junqueira ER, Oyadomari José CT, Moraes RdO (2010). Reservas orçamentárias: um ensaio sobre os fatores que levam à sua constituição. In: CONGRESSO USP DE CONTROLADORIA, 10., 2010, São Paulo. Anais... São Paulo: USP.
Kim D (2006). Capital budgeting for new projects: on the role of auditing in information acquisition. J. Account. Econ. 41(3): 257-270.
Klann RC (2009). Influência do risco moral e da accountability nastomadas de decisões. In: ANPCONT, 2., 2009, São Paulo. Anais... São Paulo: ANPCONT.
Klein B (1983). 'Contracting Costs and Residual Claims: The Separation

of Ownership and Control'. J. Law Econ. 26: 367-374
Kren L (2003). The role of accounting information in organizational control: the state of the art. In: Advances in management accounting. New York: Elsevier Science.
Libby T (2003).The effect of fairness in contracting on the creation of budgetary slack. Adv. Account. Behav. Res. 6:145-169.
Lima AF (2008). Estudo da relação causal entre os níveis organizacionais de folga, o risco e o desempenho financeiro de empresas manufatureiras. 2008. Tese (Doutorado em Administração) - Universidade Presbiteriana Mackenzie , São Paulo.
Lima F, Raimundo N (2010). Quando mais faço, mais erro? um estudo sobre a associação entre prática de controladoria, cognição e heurísticas. 2010. Dissertação (Mestrado em Contabilidade) – Faculdade de Ciências Contábeis, Universidade Federal da Bahia, Salvador.
Liyanarachchi GA, Milne MJ (2005) Comparing the investment decisions of accounting practitioners and students: an empirical study on the adequacy of students surrogates . Account. Forum 29:121-135.
Lukka K (1988). Budgetary biasing in organizations: theoretical framework and empirical evidence. Account. Org. Soc. 13(3):281-301.
Mankiw NG (2005). Princípios de microeconomia. Tradução Allan Vidigal Hastings. São Paulo: Thomsom Learning.
Marginson D, Ogden S (2005). Coping with ambiguity through the budget: the positive effects of budgetary targets on managers' budget behaviours. Account. Org. Soc. 30(5): July.
Martinez AL (1998). Agency theory napesquisacontábil. In: Enanpad, 22. 1998, Foz do Iguaçú. Anais... Rio de Janeiro: ENANPAD.
Merchant KA (1985). Budgeting and the propensity to create budgetary slack. Account. Org. Soc. 10(2):201-210.
Moene KO (1986). Types of bureaucratic interaction. J. Public Econ. 29:333-345.
Murray D (1990). The performance effects of participative budgeting: an integration of intervening and moderating variables. Behav. Res. Account. 2:104-123.
Nascimento ARd; Ribeiro DC, Junqueira ER (2008). Estado da arte da abordagem comportamental da contabilidade gerencial: análise das pesquisas internacionais. In: CONGRESSO DE CONTABILIDADE E CONTROLADORIA, 8., 2008. São Paulo. Anais... São Paulo: USP.
Nascimento AM, Reginato L (2009). Controladoria: um enfoque na eficácia organizacional. 2. ed. São Paulo: Atlas.
Onsi M (1973). Factor analysis of behavioral variables affecting budgetary slack. Account. Rev. 48: 535-548.
Pindyck RS (2002). RUNBINFELD. Microeconomia.Trad.: Eleutério Prado. São Paulo: Prentice Hall.
Penno M (1984). Asymmetry of pré-decision information and managerial accounting. J. Account. Res. 22(1) Spring.
Pires RG (2008). A informação contábil e a teoria de agência: um estudo da assimetria informacional em companhias abertas listadas no novo mercado da Bovespa. Dissertação (Mestrado em Contabilidade)- Pontifícia Universidade Católica de São Paulo, São Paulo.
Ramaswami SN, Srinivasan SS, Gorton SA (1997). Information asymmetry between Salesperson and supervisor: postulates from agency and social exchange theories. J. Pers. Selling Sales Manag. 18(3):29-50.
Rankin FW, Schuartz ST, Young, RA (2008).The effect of honesty and superior authority on budget proposals. Account. Rev. 83(4):1083-1099.
Santos JL (2007). Teoria da contabilidade. São Paulo: Atlas.
Shields JF, Shields MD (1998). Antecedents of participative budgeting. Account. Org. Soc. 23(1):49-76.
Stiglitz JE (2000) The contributions of the economics of information to twentieth century economics. Q. J. Econ. 463:1441-1479.
Varian HR (2006). Microeconomia: princípiosbásicos – uma abordagem moderna. Trad.: Local: Campus.
Vieira S (2006)Análise de variância (ANOVA). São Paulo: Atlas.
Waller W (1988).Slack in participative budgeting: the joint effects of a truth-inducing pay scheme and risk preferences. Account. Org. Soc. 13(1):87-98.
Young SM (1985). Participative budgeting: the effects of risk aversion and asymmetric information on budgetary slack. Account. Rev. 23(2) autumm.
Yuen DCY (2004). Goal characteristics, communication and reward systems, and managerial propensity to create budgetary slack. Manage. Auditing J. 19(4):517-532.

13

The effects of exchange rate on the trade balance in Ghana: Evidence from co-integration analysis

Keshab R. Bhattarai[1] and Mark Armah[2]

[1]Business School, University of Hull, Cottingham Road, HU6 7RX, United Kingdom.
[2]Department of Economics, University of Cape Coast, Ghana.

This paper examines the effects of exchange rates on the trade balance of Ghana. First, by deriving the real exchange rate as a function of preferences and technology of two trading economies and then by applying small price taking economy assumption to the Ghanaian economy, using annual time series data from 1970-2000 we estimate the trade balance as a function of the real exchange rate, domestic and foreign incomes. Co-integration analyses of both single equation models and VAR-Error correction models confirm a stable long run relationship between both exports and imports and the real exchange rate. The short-run elasticities of imports and exports indicate contractionary effects of devaluation, in terms of the Marshall-Lerner-Robinson conditions, though these elasticities add up to almost 1 in the long run estimates. The overall conclusion drawn from the study is that, for improved balance of trade in Ghana, coordination between the exchange rate and demand management policies should be strengthened and be based on the long run fundamentals of the economy.

Key words: Exchange rate, trade policy, Ghana, co-integration.

INTRODUCTION

Ghana had disastrous performance on economic growth in the two decades between 1970 and 1990. Real per capita income fell by a factor of two during this period. This is reflected in a pattern of trade that continuously deteriorated from 1970 to 1990 in real terms, but started to pick up in recent years, only after it reformed and liberalised the economy and made the exchange rate regime responsive to market fundamentals. Despite these successive reforms and devaluations, the tendency for imbalances has widened even further. Why these reforms in the exchange rate system have not been effective is an interesting issue to investigate.

The exchange rate has been used as a tool for regulating flows of trade and capital by many developing economies, which tend to have persistent deficits in the balance of payments because of a structural gap between the volumes of exports and imports. These economies tend to have inelastic demand for both exports and imports. In addition, the rate of growth of imports is often higher than the rate of growth of exports resulting in rising imbalances in trade. There have been many discussions in the literature about the determinants of real and nominal exchange rates and how these affect the trade and growth in an economy. Should an economy adopt a fixed or flexible exchange rate system or should it target for the real or the nominal exchange rate?

Models of real exchange rates reflect the relative prices of one country in terms of preference of households, technology of firms and institutional arrangements as well as taxes and tariffs between two countries. The real exchange rate is, then, the outcome of general equilibrium in markets for goods and services (Singer,

1950; Meade, 1955; Johnson, 1957; Armington, 1969; Whalley, 1985). Financially, nominal exchange rates can be fixed by authorities or allowed to change according to the differences in the purchasing power parity and the differences in the interest rates (Johnson, 1954; Fleming, 1962; Dornbusch, 1976; Krugman and Miller, 1992; Taylor, 1995). Under a flexible exchange rate system both real and nominal exchange rates are aligned to each other through the market mechanism. Under the fixed exchange rate system these automatic (Buiter and Miller (1992)) adjustments are not guaranteed leaving room for appreciation or depreciation of currency, with its consequence for the relative competitive position of the economy.

Since a correct exchange rate has been (Krugman (1979)) one of the most important factors for economic growth in the economies of Southeast Asia and volatility in exchange rates has been one of the major obstacles to economic growth of many African and Latin American economies, it is interesting to investigate whether correcting the exchange rate system could solve some of the structural rigidities, imbalances in trade and slow growth of the Ghanaian economy.

The fact that Ghana experienced economic crises partly reflects the breakdown of a stable exchange rate system and more importantly reflects imprudent policies adopted by governments in the past, that rendered it less competitive in the world. One after another economies started artificially adjusting exchange rates, aiming to correct the balance in international trade. These arrangements have destabilised the international payment system and led to exchange rate crises. These global phenomena are partly responsible for the Ghanaian crises.

The Ghanaian problem illustrates how a free exchange rate system can destabilise an economy and why it is important to maintain the basic fundamentals right in order to let an economy grow over time.

Evolution of exchange rate system in Ghana

Ghana's policies on the exchange rate have been influenced by the contrasting political regimes that have been in place since independence in 1957. Exchange rate management in Ghana is summarised in Table 1.

From the table, we can see that, from independence in 1957 to 1982, Ghana adopted a fixed exchange rate regime in the management of its exchange rate. During this period, the Ghanaian cedi was pegged to the main convertible currencies, notably the British pound and the American dollar.

With the launching of the economic recovery programme (ERP), the government made a series of devaluations of the cedi between 1983 and 1986. In particular, the cedi was devalued in stages from ¢ 2.75: US$1.00 in 1983 to ¢90.00: US$1.00 by the third quarter of 1986. The new foreign exchange policy was characterised by a scheme of bonuses on exchange receipts and surcharges on exchange payments.

The foreign exchange bureaux system was established in 1988, an attempt to absorb the parallel market into the legal foreign exchange market. These "forex" bureaux are fully licensed entities operated by individuals, groups or institutions. Their operation alongside the auction meant that the foreign exchange market was characterised by two spot foreign exchange rates.

The exchange rate system, as discussed above, has had profound influence on the flows of exports and imports in Ghana. The pattern of trade has changed significantly since the trade reforms were initiated. In particular, the export to GDP ratio was higher (between 32.1 and 49.2%) in 1996 - 2000 than in 1994- 1995 where the export to GDP ratio actually fell from 25.3 to 24.5%. In the later period, however, the import to GDP ratio was higher (between 40.09 and 69.59%) than in 1994-1995 (between 32.56 and 32.93%) (Table A1 in Appendix 2).

The nominal exchange rate is known not to be the only influencing variable on the real exchange rate, and the effect of the nominal exchange rate on the real exchange rate has not been clear. Some classical economists hold the view that nominal exchange rate regimes are neutral, but that view is rejected by the neo-Keynesian group. The latter argue that the increased variability or otherwise of the real exchange rate is caused by a shift from either the fixed or flexible exchange rate regime that is adopted. The computed correlation coefficient between the nominal exchange rate and the real exchange rate in Ghana seems to confirm the neo-Keynesian view (Table A3 in Appendix 2). This result suggests that the variability of the real exchange rate is largely accounted for by the changes in the nominal exchange rate (Musila, 2002).

One of the most important problems identified in developing economies, especially in Africa, is the deficit in the government budget and balance of payments. These countries have sought aid in the form of grants and loans from the IMF, the World Bank and other financial institutions to meet these deficits. As a result, developing countries governments have been put under enormous pressure to abandon inward - oriented, export pessimism, import substitution industrialisation (ISI) development strategies and to stake the future of their people on increasingly 'unprotected' participation in the international market. The free-market adjustment programmes have advocated liberalisation of markets, allowing prices to be set through the free play of market forces, promoting export-oriented growth and ensuring that the exchange rate was set at a competitive level for exports. In most cases, developing countries have devalued their currencies to reduce the deficit in the balance of payments.

Ghana was successful in using the exchange rate as a tool for macroeconomic stability since its independence

Table 1. Exchange rate policy episodes in Ghana (1957-2011).

Episode	Period	Policy
1	1957-1966	Fixed to the British Pound.
2	1966-1982	Fixed to the American Dollar.
3	1983-1986	Multiple exchange rate system.
4	1986-1987	Dual exchange rate system-auction determined, dual retail auction rate
5	1987-1988	Dutch auction system.
6	1988-1989	Foreign exchange bureaux.
7	1990-1992	Wholesale and inter-bank auction system.
8	1992-date	Inter-bank market. The Bank of Ghana (BoG) selling and buying rates were determined by the average daily retail rates of commercial banks.

Source: Bank of Ghana, IMF.

in 1957 until the 1980s. However, since the mid 1980s trade and budget deficits have become larger and persistent (See trade balance in Table A1 and graph of trade balance ($million) and overall budget deficit (GDP%) in Figure A1 in Appendix 2), various exchange rate policies, including policies under the Economic Recovery Programme (ERP) have been pursued for stabilisation. Nonetheless, there is debate whether devaluation really does improve a country's trade balance.

This paper examines whether changes in the real exchange rate, domestic and foreign national income affect the trade balance, in both short and long run. Section two reports recent development issues and gives an overview of trade and exchange rate policies. It is followed by the theoretical justification of the study, in Section three. Section four discusses model specification and estimation methods. Section five presents the data and an econometric analysis of the short and long run impacts of exchange rates on imports and exports. Sections six and seven constitute summary, policy discussion and conclusion, respectively.

Recent development issues and an overview of exchange rate policies

Ghana adopted the fixed exchange rate system in the 1960s, immediately after independence. The Bretton Woods system supported the policy of fixed exchange rates. In particular, the Ghanaian cedi was pegged at two cedis to the British pound. Adjustments were only supposed to occur when there were fundamental balance of payments disequilibria. The choice of a fixed exchange regime in Ghana was, therefore consistent with the thinking of the time. Due to the inheritance of huge foreign exchange reserves from the colonial era, Ghana exercised practically no control over the foreign exchange markets which were in the hands of a few commercial houses and the commercial banks.

Tavlas (2003) offers a review of exchange rate issues particularly the types of exchange rate regimes, and also a critique of Goldstein (2002) and Corden (2002).

There are other analyses and reviews of the real exchange rate, such as those of Perroni and Whalley (1996) and Edwards (1999, 2002) (Real exchange rate is also known as fundamental equilibrium exchange rate or the actual real exchange rate (Mussa et al., 1994)). In particular, Mussa et al. (1994) pointed out that exchange rate misalignment issues figure prominently in the exchange rate regime literature. When fundamentals (including macroeconomic policies) change, the equilibrium real exchange rate changes and, if the nominal exchange rate remains fixed the result is misalignment between the real exchange rate and the new equilibrium rate. It follows that exchange rate misalignment can occur because of misaligned policy and because macroeconomic policies are included in the set of fundamentals.

Various articles have sought to identify effective exchange rate regimes (Rogoff and Obstfeld, 1996) in a world increasingly charac-terised by high capital mobility (See Tavlas and Ulan (2002) for detailed discussion and references). According to Goldstein and Isard (1992), policy advice from official circles (example, IMF and World Bank) proposed that countries could choose among a broad spectrum of exchange rate arrangements and that exchange rate commitments should be tailored to the characteristics and circumstances of individual countries.

Sowa and Acquaye (1998) have pointed out that the massive industrialisation and modernisation programme implemented by the government in early 1960s depleted the country's external reserves and Ghana began to see the signs of foreign exchange constraints. In September 1986, Ghana reformed its exchange rate policy with the support of the IMF and the World Bank under the ERP/SAP. Initially this was a two-tier system which aimed particularly at an official fixed rate to take care of imports and exports of selected goods and a weekly auction rate for the remaining two thirds of Ghana's external transactions. In February 1987, the two systems were unified with all transactions determined at weekly auction(Oduro and Harrigan, 2000).

In spite of the increased flexibility in the exchange rate in the years after the reforms and in recent years, the trade deficit has increased and the balance of payments has continued to show strains (See Table A1 in Appendix 2). Recent trends in the overall balance of payments and its major components are depicted in Table A1. The table also shows the sources of financing, both domestic and foreign. The overall balance was in surplus by US$ 250.8m in 1995 and in a small deficit (US$20.4m) in 1996. In 1998, it registered a surplus again but declined again in 1999. In 2000, a large deficit of US$258.5m was registered yet again. This erratic behaviour of the economy has led to many questions being asked about the wisdom of implementing the ERP/SAP and has fuelled the already intense debate on the rationale of the reforms.

Theoretical justifications of study

The standard analysis of exchange rate changes and the trade balance uses the specification of the domestic demand for imports and the foreign demand for exports derived from a postulated 2 good-2 country utility maximisation framework (Samuelson, 1949; Meade, 1955; Mundell, 1962; Fleming, 1962; Dornbusch, 1976; Miller and Spencer, 1977; Whalley, 1985; Nguyen and Whalley, 1989; Bhagwati and Srinivasan, 1992; Krugman and Miller, 1992; McKinnon, 1993; Taylor, 1995; Harrison et al., 1997; Bhattarai, 2001; Greenaway et al., 2002)). The 2 good- 2 country assumption splits the goods into those that are produced at home and those produced abroad. A simple theoretical model for the determination of the exchange rate is outlined as follows and in Appendix 1.

Real exchange rate model

Labour supply in country 1: $L_1 = L_{11} + L_{12}$

Household preference: $U_1 = X_{11}^{\alpha} X_{12}^{1-\alpha}$

$\alpha \succ 0;$

Production of good 1 by country 1: $X_{11} = a_{11} L_{11}$

Production of good 2 by country 1: $X_{12} = a_{12} L_{12}$

Production Possibility Frontier of country 1:

$$L_1 = \frac{X_{11}}{a_{11}} + \frac{X_{12}}{a_{12}}$$

Labour supply in country 2: $L_2 = L_{21} + L_{22}$

Household's preference in country 2: $U_2 = X_{21}^{\beta} X_{22}^{1-\beta}$

$\beta \succ 0;$

Production of good 1 by country 2: $X_{21} = a_{21} L_{21}$

Production of good 2 by country 2: $X_{22} = a_{22} L_{22}$

Production possibility frontier of country 2:

$$L_2 = \frac{X_{21}}{a_{21}} + \frac{X_{22}}{a_{22}}$$

Where a_{ij} denotes the productivity of labour in country *i* in producing good *j*, α and β are the consumers' preferences in countries 1 and 2 respectively.

When we solve the model taking into consideration the preferences of household and firm technology, trade equilibrium requires the real exchange rate (*RER*) in the general equilibrium setting, to be the price ratios in the two countries; these in turn reflect the ratio of labour productivity (parameters) in the two countries. The solution is given as:

$$MRS_{12}^{1} = MRS_{12}^{2} = \frac{a_{11}}{a_{12}} = \frac{P_{11}}{P_{12}} = \frac{P_{21}}{P_{22}} = \frac{a_{21}}{a_{22}} = MRT_{12}^{1} = MRT_{12}^{2} \quad ;$$

$$\frac{a_{12}}{a_{11}} P_{11} = P_{12} = P_{22} = \frac{a_{21}}{a_{22}} P_{21}.$$

Therefore, the real exchange rate will depend on relative productivity of labour in the model,

$$\frac{P_{22}}{P_{11}} = \frac{a_{12}}{a_{11}} \frac{a_{22}}{a_{21}}$$

The framework is based on the assumption that the consumer chooses a bundle of goods that maximises utility subject to a budget constraint. In the 2 good-2 country model, the sum of imported bundles over consumers in the foreign country yields aggregate demand for exports of the domestic country while the sum of imported over consumers in the domestic country yields aggregate import demand.

The present work is based on a 2 good-2 country utility maximisation framework which has a major advantage of accommodating general functional form or demand consistent with utility maximisation. The only condition imposed by utility maximisation in this model is that the compensated own price effect (elasticities with respect to the exchange rate) should be negative.

Details of the analytical solution are given in Appendix 1. For subsequent econometric analysis Ghana is assumed to be a small price taking economy in the global context.

Model specification and estimation methods

The functional forms of the exports and import models used in this paper are standard in the empirical trade literature and are used in Haque et al. (1990) (HKM hereafter) and Musila (2002) (Empirical applications of this specification are widely discussed in Goldstein and

Khan (1985)). Unit root, cointegration and stability tests following Dickey-Fuller (1976), Johansen (1995), Philips and Perron (1983) and Johansen (1988) are carried out using PcGive. A logarithmic functional form is adopted because it allows imports and exports to react proportionately to changes in their arguments. In addition, Khan (1974) pointed out that this specification avoids the problem of drastic falls in elasticities. HKM (1990) argue that to capture partial adjustment behaviour, a lagged term in both dependent variables should be included in the estimated equations. Hence, there is the inclusion of lags on exports and imports, respectively, in the model; which assumes a small open economy similar to the Ghanaian economy.

The export and import demand equations are,

$$\ln(x)_t = \delta_0 + \delta_1 \ln(re)_t + \delta_2 \ln(y)_t^* + \delta_3 \ln(x)_{t-1} + \varsigma_t \quad (1)$$

$$\ln(z)_t = \gamma_0 + \gamma_1 \ln(re)_t + \gamma_2 \ln(y)_t + \gamma_3 \ln(z)_{t-1} + \mu_t \quad (2)$$

Where,
x = real exports of goods and services;
z = real imports of goods and services;
re = $\frac{eP^*}{P}$ = real exchange rate;
y = income proxied by the real GDP of Ghana;
y^* = trading partners' income proxied by the real GDP (The author chose United States, Germany, United Kingdom and Japan for the developed countries because they constitute a greater share of Ghana's trade) of four major industrial countries.

In (.) denotes natural logarithm operator;
P^* denotes foreign price approximated by a trade weighted GDP deflator;
P denotes domestic price approximated by the GDP deflator;
and e denotes the nominal exchange rate:
δ_0, γ_0 are constant / intercept terms;
δ_1, γ_1 are the price elasticities of exports and imports respectively; and
δ_2, γ_2 are the income elasticities of exports and imports respectively,

Where,
ς, μ denotes disturbance terms and;
t is the time subscript.

Equations (1) and (2) are estimated and used to evaluate the effect of changes in the exchange rate on the trade balance.

Estimation techniques

To be meaningful a regression model should reflect the relationship among stationary variables, with constant mean and variance. If the data are non stationary, logs or differences need to be taken to make them stationary. Engle and Granger (1987) have shown that regression among non-stationary variables can be valid only when these variables are cointegrated. They also showed that an error- correction mechanism (ECM) exists for each cointegrated model. By the nature of time series data, it is important to check first for non- stationarity and thus, ascertain whether the variables have unit roots. This is necessary to avoid spurious correlation and misleading and incorrect regression results that might otherwise arise despite the absence of any correlation between the underlying series.

If a series must be differenced d times before it becomes a stationary non-deterministic AR/ARMA representation, then it contains d unit roots and is said to be integrated of order d, denoted by I(d). In general, using this definition, any linear combination of the two series will also be I(d). However, Engle and Granger (1987) argue that if there exists a vector β such that the disturbance term from the regression ($u_t = y_t - \beta x_t$) is of a lower order of integration *I*(d-b), where b is positive, then x_t and y_t are cointegrated of order *CI*(d, b). Thus, if the two series x_t and y_t are both I(1) and u_t~I(0), then the two series would be cointegrated of order CI(1, 1). The co-integration of y_t and x_t also implies the existence of a restriction on the standard vector autoregressive (VAR) model and therefore, the estimates obtained from the VAR can be misleading (Engle and Granger, 1987). They further argue that when y_t and x_t are cointegrated, the relationship between them can be expressed as an error-correction model (ECM) and estimated correctly. With this context, a more appropriate simple dynamic representation of the ECM is of the form:

$$A(L)\Delta y_t = \mu + B(L)\Delta x_t - (1-\pi)\left[y_{t-p} - \hat{\beta}_0 - \hat{\beta}_1 x_{t-p}\right] + \omega_t \quad (3)$$

where A (L) is the polynomial lag operator $1 - \alpha_1 L - \alpha_2 L^2 - ... - \alpha_p L^p$; B(L) is the lag polynomial operator $\gamma_0 + \gamma_1 L + \gamma_2 L^2 + ... + \gamma_p L^p$; $\pi = \alpha_1 + \alpha_2 + ... + \alpha_p$; Δ is the first difference operator; $\hat{\beta}$ is a vector in the co-integrating equation; μ, α, and γ are coefficients; ω is the error term and $(1-\pi)$ term provides information on the speed of adjustment of the level variables. This is the preferred representation for estimation since it incorporates both short and long run effects (Harris and Sollis 2003) have pointed out that using the dynamic modelling procedure results in a more powerful test for co-integration as well as giving generally unbiased estimates of the long run relationship and the standard t

Table 2. Unit root test of variables (level and first differenced): annual data (1970 -2000).

Variable	Lags	DF/ADF	Order of integration
lnx	2	-0.533	I(1)
Δlnx	1	-3.420*	I(0)
lnz	2	-0.4706	I(1)
Δlnz	1	-3.663*	I(0)
lnre	1	-1.289	I(1)
Δlnre	1	-3.868**	I(0)
lnrei	1	-1.289	I(1)
Δlnrei	1	-3.868**	I(0)
lny	2	-0.3890	I(1)
Δlny	1	-3.101*	I(0)
lny*	1	-1.628	I(1)
Δlny*	1	-5.978**	I(0)

Notes: DF/ADF - Dickey Fuller/Augmented Dickey Fuller; **Significant at 1%; *Significant at 5%. y* is the real GDP of Ghana's major trading partners in industrial countries.

statistics for conducting statistical hypothesis testing. He attributes it to the dynamic model not pushing the short run dynamics into the residual term of the estimated OLS regression. Indeed, in the estimation of the UK money demand, the DF test for interest rate R was based on the significant lagged and found to be important for the test of unit root. Similar results were obtained when lag length was set by the l_{12} formula).

We start by checking the order of integration of the variables. This is reported in Table 2. The Augmented Dickey-Fuller test is used for this purpose, with sufficient lags to whiten the residuals. The results indicate a unit root in the original series but stationarity in the first difference in all of the series. Thus, the level variables are integrated to order one represented as I(1) (Table 2).

The lag length (the value of p) was set by the maximum R^2 approach. This approach uses the model selection procedure that tests to see if an additional lag is significant, that is, if it increases the value of R^2. Harris (1995) argues that this procedure of selecting a lag length is consistent with the formula reported in Schwert (1989), that is, $l_{12} = \text{int}\left\{12(T/100)^{1/4}\right\}$ and the Philips-Perron (PP) tests.

Data and econometric analysis

The data used in this study were obtained from the World Bank CD-ROM (2000), IFS Yearbook (2001) and IMF Direction of Trade Statistics (DOTS). All the variables are real and in logs. The frequency of the data used is annually and runs from 1970 to 2000. The variables used as fundamentals were determined by three basic considerations, namely the availability of data, theory and the fact that the variable would fit well in the model in statistical terms.

Table 3. Export and import functions: Cointegration estimates for Ghana (Annual Data, 1970-2000).

Cointegrating equation: ECT			
Exports (x)		Imports (z)	
ln(x)	1.000	ln(z)	1.000
ln(re)	0.717(2.67)**	ln(re)	0.468(1.75)***
ln(y*)	-0.544(-0.98)	ln(y)	0.106(1.57)
D91	0.829(2.10)*	D91	0.698(1.97)***
Constant	34.83	Constant	20.64

Wald Test(χ^2) 12.7199(0.0053)**; Wald Test(χ^2) 9.9415(0.0191)*. Figures in parenthesis are t-values. ** denotes 1% level of significance;* denotes 5% level of significance and *** denotes 10% level of significance.

In most theoretical studies, the real exchange rate is defined as the ratio of the prices of tradable to non-tradable goods. The real exchange rate was constructed as re $= \frac{eP^*}{P}$, where e is the official (nominal) exchange rate, P* is proxied by the trading partners' trade weighted GDP deflator, and P is Ghana's GDP deflator. The definitions of exports and imports of goods and services are based on the national accounts and the definition as contained in the IMF Direction of Trade Statistics (DOTS) and the World Bank CD-ROM (2002).

As has been established already, the variables are integrated of order I(1) at the 5 and 1% significant levels. A dummy variable D91 was used to account for the effect of reforms, notably in exchange rates and trade (Exchange rate and trade reforms included the gradual abolition of the controlled rate regime to a somewhat managed rate regime and the abolition of extra tariffs on importable).

A cointegration analysis using the Engle and Johansen (1995) procedure to determine the long run relationship between the variables was conducted. Having confirmed the variables were cointegrated, we then applied the error correction model to estimate equations (1) and (2) as set out in section 4. We used PcGive version 10.3 econometric software package for the estimation.

Estimation results

The results of the cointegrated and the error correction model (ECM) tests are presented in Tables 3 and 4. Table 3 shows the long run cointegrating estimates.

It is clear from Table 3 that the null hypothesis of long run cointegrating vectors (a stable relationship among the endogenous variables) is accepted at 1 and 10% significant levels. In particular, the long run export and import demand functions can be written as:

$$\ln x = 0.717 \ln re - 0.544 \ln y^* + 0.829 D91 + 34.83$$
$$\ln z = 0.468 \ln re + 0.106 \ln y + 0.698 D91 + 20.64$$

Table 4. Short- run estimates: error correction model (ECM) (Annual Data 1970-2000).

Error correction model :ECT			
Dependent variable =Δln(x)		**Dependent variable=Δln(z)**	
$\Delta ln(re)_{-2}$	0.161(2.37) *	$\Delta lnre_{-2}$	0.192(2.87)**
$\Delta ln(y^*)_{-2}$	- 0.019(-0.118)	$\Delta ln(y)_{-2}$	0.007(0.04)
$\Delta ln(x)_{-2}$	-0.171(-1.09)	$\Delta ln(z)_{-2}$	-0.254(-1.51)
ECT	-0.846(-4.16)**	ECT	-0.003(0.013)
D91	0.151(2.64) *	D91	0.139(2.13)*

Notes: Figures in parenthesis are t-values; ** denotes 1% level of significance;* denotes 5% level of significance.

The estimated long run elasticities of prices of export and imports have the expected signs and are significant at the 1 and 10% levels respectively. For both equations (The estimates passed the entire diagnostic test but these are not reported here), the Wald tests decisively reject the null that the long run coefficients are zero.

This relationship indicates that a 10% devaluation in the real exchange rate increases the value of exports by only 7.2% and raises the value of imports by 4.68%. The positive elasticity of imports reflects the inelastic nature of Ghanaian imports. This is a clear manifestation of the fact that the price elasticities (greater than 1) meet the Marshall-Lerner-Robinson (MLR), the condition for a successful devaluation in the long run. The devaluation has impact on a trade balance in the longer term. Although the trade balance may improve because of the long run stable relationship among the variables, such improvement is likely to be small.

The long run relationships for income in both equations have the expected signs. However, their coefficients are not statistically significant at conventional levels. The relationship indicates that a 10% increase in the real income of the major trading partners of Ghana (industrial countries), that is foreign income would reduce the value of Ghana's exports by about 5.44 percentage points while a 10% increase in the real income of Ghana also increases the value of its imports by just 1% (0.106) in the long run. The inclusion of the dummy (D91) to reflect the impact of the reforms is effective. In particular, the coefficients have the expected signs and are significant at conventional levels (Table 3). This result shows the effect of the structural changes that have taken place in the Ghanaian economy as a result of the reforms. In a nutshell, the real exchange rate rather than real incomes are important in the determination of the export and import demand for Ghana in the long-run. It is also clear that the very high magnitude of the elasticities with respect to the exchange rate suggests that exchange rate policies have been effective but they alone would not improve the trade balance unless pursued with other policies, notably appropriate aggregate- demand policies.

The unit root tests indicate that the short- run dynamic model must be specified in the differences of the relevant variables. The results of the estimated short- run export and import demand functions are presented in Table 4.

Diagnostics

Exports

R^2 =0.582; FPE =0.0194033; SE =0.126409; F (5, 22) =6.131[0.001];
F_{ar} (2, 20) =0.34181 [0.7146]; F_{arch} (1, 20) =0.058094 [0.8120];
F_{het} (9, 12) =1.2585 [0.3477]; RESET F (1, 21) =11.584 [0.0027]; Normality (2) =3.0523 [0.2174].

Imports

R^2 =0.381; FPE =0.0253010; SE = 0.143878; F (5, 22) =2.585[0.057];
F_{ar} (2, 20) =1.7212[0.2056]; F_{arch} (1, 20) =0.088495[0.7693];
F_{het} (9, 12) = 0.22581[0.9832]; RESET F (1, 21) = 0.51991[0.4792]; Normality (2) = 7.5872[0.0225].

Diagnostic analyses reported for both the export and import functions are significant at 95 percent critical value (except the F-test that all the slope coefficients are zero), and therefore, there is nothing to suggest that the model is mis-specified.

A diagnostic check for structural breaks in the model is evidenced in the parameter non-constancy of estimates. The sequential one-step ahead Chow test and one-step ahead residuals tests were conducted. Plots of these residuals and Chow tests for both export and import equations are presented in Figures A2 and A3 respectively, for the estimated short-run ECM. The plots of the one-step ahead residual for export and import equations show that there are no problems in the observations. In addition, the Chow tests imply parameter stability for the period of study.

The results presented in Table 4 show that the elasticity of exports with respect to the real exchange rate has the expected positive sign and is statistically significant at the 5% level. The price elasticity of imports with respect to the real exchange rate also has the expected sign, but is statistically significant at the 1% level.

However, the sum of the absolute values of the two elasticities is less than unity (0.353). This suggests that the MLR condition for successful devaluation is not met in the short run (Musila (2002) found similar results for Malawi). Therefore, any nominal devaluation of the exchange rate would not improve the trade balance in the short to medium term. This situation may be attributed to the relatively low elasticity value of the export demand function which is explained by the fact that Ghana's exports are mainly basic agricultural products which command low prices in the world market. This clearly implies that Ghana need to diversify its economy away from agriculture towards the manufacturing or services sectors.

The estimated coefficients of the error correction term (ECT) in each of the two equations have the expected signs. However, the coefficient of the ECT for exports is significant at the 1% level whilst that for imports is insignificant at conventional levels. Thus, if in the long run the value of exports increased by 1%, over its equilibrium path, then its growth has to fall by about 0.846% in the short run to force exports back to its long run growth path. Similarly, the results of the import demand equation suggests that an increase of 1% in imports over its long run equilibrium growth path would require an adjustment (fall) of about 0.003% to bring imports back to their long run growth path. The greater volatility of exports compared to that of imports again reflects the structure of the Ghanaian economy.

The results indicate that foreign income, though negatively related to Ghanaian exports, is not significantly different from zero and therefore not an important determinant of export demands in the short run. The results further show that domestic income is also not an important determinant of import demand. It has the expected sign but is significantly not different from zero. One possible explanation might be that both exports and imports are inelastic relative to domestic and foreign income. These low income elasticities indicate that Ghanaian exports are inferior commodities in the global market. The growth of income in the rest of the world does not transmit to Ghana. Ghana's exports consist mostly of basic agricultural produce that is not processed and it is therefore subject to the dictates of its trading partners in the international market. Another possible explanation is that Ghana's imports might not depend on its past income and therefore does not do more to strengthen its exports with its trading partners. Again, the result shows that the real exchange rate in the short run does affect the export and import demand. This might be explained by the rapid fluctuations in the nominal exchange rate (devaluations) that have occurred with its concomitant increases in price levels.

As has been stated earlier, the dummy variable D91 is included to capture the impact of the economic reforms (exchange rate and trade policy reforms) through the implementation of the ERP/SAP. As expected, the overall impact of the reform was positive for exports, reflecting the significant structural change in the demand for exports. The implementation of the reforms also impacted positively on imports with a significant structural shift occurring in import demand as well (refer to coefficient of D91 in Table 4). Increased exports were accompanied by increased imports. Accordingly, the reforms embarked on by the government (trade and exchange rate) since 1983 did open up the economy in terms of trade (Tables A2 and A4). However, the reforms did not improve the trade balance in the short run as expected (Figure A1).

Impulse response analysis of Ghanaian trade: co-integrated VAR analysis

Due to the likelihood of simultaneity bias in the use of the single equation procedure, we employed the multiple estimation method to correct it. In employing the Johansen (1988) procedure, to determine the number of cointegrating vectors, we first estimated the unrestricted VAR with sufficient lags to whiten the residuals. We started with a lag length of three and were pared down after checking the significant levels of the coefficients. The F-test for reducing the number of lags from three to two is accepted.

We also checked the properties of the residual in the preferred VAR model. The diagnostic tests are presented in Table 5a. The table reports individual tests for export and imports and also the system wide test. The test results show that they are all insignificant at the 5% level.

Cointegrated Results

The null hypothesis of no cointegration is rejected in favour of the alternative that there are at most two cointegrating vectors at the 1 and 5% levels of significance. This is evident by the λ_{trace} and $\lambda_{\max}$ statistics, respectively. In addition, when adjusted for the degrees of freedom, the two test statistics reject the null also at 1 and 5% significant levels (Table 5b). Therefore, we proceeded with the assumption of two cointegrating vectors. This conclusion is supported by the plot of the first two vectors in the cointegration space. The two cointegrating vectors look fairly stationary, with fitted and actual series tracking each other reasonably closely (Figure A5 in Appendix).

The Johansen method for the error correction mechanism, in the case of multiple equation models, is represented by $\Pi = \alpha\beta'$, where β is the long run relationship among the variables and α denotes the adjustment toward the long-run relationships. The estimated cointegration vectors for a 3 x 3 VAR are given in Table 6.

The long run general joint restriction that the lags of the explanatory variables are the same and the hypothesis that there is no trend in the original series are strongly rejected. The static long run relationship for export and import demand functions respectively, as presented in Table 7 can be written as:

$$\ln x = 1.9875 \ln y^* + 0.0330 D91 + 0.58630 Trend + 70.31$$

$$\ln z = 2.0271 \ln y - 0.1201 D91 + 0.52139 Trend + 46.03$$

$$\ln re = 0.0347 \ln y + 3.6748 \ln y^* + 0.33908 D91 + 0.10914 Trend + 87.72$$

Table 5a. Diagnostic tests.

Variable	Equation	Test	Test distribution and statistics
lnx	VAR	Portmanteau (4)	4.3599
		Serial Correlation	F(2,14) 2.6820(0.1033)
		Normality	$X^2(2)$ 7.8310(0.0199)
		Arch 1-1 Test	F(1,14) 0.0508(0.8249)
lnz	VAR	Portmanteau (4)	3.2508
		Serial Correlation	F(2,14) 0.6198(0.5522)
		Normality	$X^2(2)$ 1.1586(0.5603)
		Arch 1-1 Test	F(1,14) 0.0109(0.9181)
lnre	VAR	Portmanteau (4)	3.99028
		Serial Correlation	F(2,14) 3.2124(0.0664)
		Normality	$X^2(2)$ 1.4263(0.4901)
		Arch 1-1 Test	F(1,14) 0.3809(0.5470)
System-wide tests		Portmanteau (4)	33.8133
		Serial Correlation	F(18,23) 1.4928(0.181)
		Normality	$X^2(4)$ 10.755(0.0963)

Table 5b. Cointegration results.

	H₀:rank=P	λ_i	λ_{trace}	*Adj. for df*	$\lambda_{\max}$	*Adj. for df*
System test	P=0	-	90.06[0.000]**	71.42[0.000]**	43.83[0.001]**	34.76[0.000]**
	P<=1	0.77937	46.23[0.000]**	36.67[0.001]**	29.35[0.001]**	23.28[0.010]**
	P<=2	0.63653	16.88[0.007]**	13.39[0.034]*	16.88[0.007]*	13.39[0.034]*

Notes: **Significant at 1 percent level;* denotes 5% level of significance; λ_i column reports the eigenvalues.

Table 6. Normalised (to diagonal) cointegrating vectors.

lnx	1.0000	-0.84632	-0.80383
lnz	-1.6080	1.0000	-0.36484
ln(re)	-0.075171	-0.36554	1.0000
$ln(y)_{-1}$	0.84993	0.93255	1.3207
$ln(y)_{-2}$	-0.0091221	-0.89787	1.3309
$L(y^*)_{-1}$	0.026187	1.3107	-0.66011
$L(y^*)_{-2}$	0.29997	0.44759	-0.95487
D91	-0.20073	0.27205	-0.35635
Trend	0.24387	-0.065084	0.77065

Impulse response functions are presented in Figure A6 in Appendix 2. A shock to the export function largely reflects similar hump- shaped response in both the exports and imports. Although exports fall immediately, imports first rise by 75% and fall gradually. The real exchange rate falls sharply and then begins to rise (hump-shaped as well). Evidently, little similar dynamics can be observed between the response in the export and import functions as a result of a shock to the system.

Indeed, an unanticipated increase in the real exchange rate shows export and imports behaved similarly (increase) while the real exchange rate decreases.

SUMMARY AND POLICY ISSUES

This paper sets out to examine the effects of the exchange rate on the trade balance of Ghana. Cointegrating and error correction modelling technique have been used to estimate the demand equations for exports and for imports. The data used are annual observations obtained from the Direction of Trade Statistics (DOTS) and the World Bank CD-ROM World Development Indicators (2002). The study explored whether the devaluation of the country's currency (cedi) would improve the trade balance. The results indicate that the price elasticities of the export demand and import demand equations in the long run are consistent with the theoretical predictions of utility maximisation based model which this study adopts. However, the elasticities of exports and imports relative to the real exchange rate in the short-run are very small suggesting supply and

Table 7. Long-run cointegrating equations in VAR (exports, imports and real exchange rate).

	Export (x)	Imports(z)	Real exchange rate(re)
lny	-	2.0271(1.8014)	0.03476(1.1586)
lny*	1.9875(1.8014)	-	3.6748(1.4035)
D91	0.0330(0.72117)	-0.1201(0.45896)	0.33908(0.56188)
Trend	0.58630(0.39232)	0.52139(0.24968)	-.10914(0.30567)
Constant	70.31	46.03	87.72

Notes: Figures in parenthesis are the standard errors.

demand side rigidities in export and import demand flows of Ghana. In the short run estimated export and import elasticities with respect to the real exchange rate do not satisfy the Marshall-Lerner-Robinson (MLR) condition for a successful devaluation. Therefore, any nominal devaluation of the cedi is bound to weaken the trade balance at least in the short to medium term. In the long run, the results show that a stable linear relationship exists among the exports, imports, and trade balance, domestic and foreign income. Ghana has no choice other than to adhere to the fundamentals of foreign exchange rate market to solve its perennial problems of deficit, by applying prudent fiscal and monetary policies and exchange rate policies based on purchasing power parity. These policy rules will also improve the confidence of consumers and investors in the economy and improve Ghana's competitiveness in the global market.

Conclusion

The results from this study show that the trade balance of Ghana will not improve in the short run unless it adopts policy rules in the foreign exchange market but it may be costly if such adjustment were to occur unaided in the long run. The standard theoretical propositions in the trade and exchange rate literature for a small open economy, such as Ghana, are tested using results from time series based single equation, VAR-cointegration models. The results obtained are very similar to the findings of earlier studies on contractionary devaluation as reported in Khan (1974), Musila (2002), the IMF and the World Bank. However, the estimates for Ghana also show that even in the long run, the MLR condition for a successful devaluation is barely met and therefore, in Ghana's case the gains would not be enough to offset the losses in the trade balance in the short run.

The results also show that in the short to medium term as well as in the long term, income levels are not important determinants either of the import demand or the export demand of Ghana. Imports are inelastic and the exports, being predominantly of primary commodities are an inferior commodity in the global market. The results show that it is the exchange rate that is the significant factor in the short term. In the long-run however, the study reveals that only the real exchange rate significantly affects the trade balance.

In short, the econometric model shows that the policies that have been adopted by Ghana have not been effective when evaluated in terms of the MLR conditions for a successful devaluation. Furthermore, the model and the associated results indicate that more effective policies may be founded on a sharper appreciation of the interaction and the interrelationships between the policy instruments (exchange rate and aggregate demand management) which have been considered here. Changes to exchange rates is in fact a part of the demand management policy; in theory external demand in Ghana could be increased by devaluation of the Ghanaian Cedi as it raises exports and checks increase in imports. However, such measure may increase the cost of living of Ghanaians and may have detrimental consequences on their welfare because of associated shrinkage in the value of Cedi in the international market. Thus manipulating exchange rates as a part of demand management policy can be unsafe and may generate unwanted outcome. On the other hand, expansionary fiscal and monetary policies may lead to achieving the objectives of exchange rate managements if used appropriately. Fiscal expansion with lower taxes, higher spending and deficit would increase demand for consumption and investment as well as for imports. Exports may increase if the increase public spending is targeted to the export oriented sectors. Expansionary monetary policy by lowering the interest rate results in increase in investment and durable consumption and may cause an expansion of export sectors. Thus, demand management policies could be considered complementary to trade rebalancing policies when exchange rate is determined to be the fundamentals of the market.

It would be interesting to see how far these low elasticities relate to the preferences of households, the technology of firms, and the policy instruments under consideration by the government, taking account of the structural realities of the Ghanaian economy, in order to establish an incentive structure for Ghana that is conducive to macroeconomic stability and a higher rate of growth. These issues will be taken up in subsequent work.

REFERENCES

Armington PS (1969). A Theory of Demand for Products Distinguished by Place of Production, IMF Staff Papers 16:159-76.

Bhagwati JN, Srinivasan TN (1992). Lectures on International Trade, MIT Press.

Bhattarai K (2001). Welfare Gains to UK from a Global Free Trade, the European Research Studies 4(3-4).

Buiter WH, Miller M (1992). Exchange rate economics. Int. Lib. Crit. Writ. Econ. 1: 233-265.

Corden WM (2002). Too Sensational: On the choice of Exchange Rate Regimes Cambridge, MA: MIT Press.

Doornik JA, Hendry DF (2001). Give Win: An Interface to Empirical Modelling, Version 2, Timberlake Consultants Ltd. London.

Dornbusch R (1976). Expectations and Exchange Rate Dynamics, J. Polit. Econ. 84(6).

Edwards S (1999). How Effective are Capital Control? J. Econ. Perspect. 13:65-84.

Edwards S (2002). Capital Mobility, Capital Controls, and Globalisation in the Twenty First Century, Ann. Am. Acad. Pol. Soc Sci. 579:261-70.

Engle RF, Granger CWJ (1987). Cointegration and error correction: Representation, estimation and testing, Econometrica 55:251-76.

Fleming JM (1962). Domestic financial policies under fixed and under floating exchange rates, IMF staff paper 9, November pp.369-379.

Goldstein M, Isard P (1992). Mechanisms For Promoting Global Monetary Stability In: Goldstein M, Isard P, Mason P and Taylor M (eds), Policy Issues in the Evolving International Monetary System, IMF Occasional Paper, 26(Washington, D.C: International Monetary Fund).

Goldstein M, Khan MS (1985). Income and Price Effects in Foreign Trade, in Handbook of International Economics, Vol. 2, ed. by Roland WJ and Kenen PB. Amsterdam: North-Holland.

Greenaway D, Morgan W, Wright P (2002). Trade Liberalisation and Growth in Developing Countries, J. Dev. Econ. 67:229-244.

Haque NU, Karjal L, Montiel P (1990). Estimation of Rational Expectations Macroeconomic Model for Developing Counties with Capital Controls (Unpublished; Washington: International Monetary Fund).

Harris R (1995). Using Cointegration Analysis in Econometric Modelling, Prentice Hall, Harlow.

Harris R, Sollis R (2003). Applied Time Series Modelling and Forecasting, John Wiley & Sons Ltd, West Sussex.

Harrison GW, Rutherford TF, Tarr DG (1997). Quantifying the Uruaguy Round, Econ. J. 107(444):1405-1430.

Hendry DF, Doornik JA (2001). Empirical Econometric Modelling Using PcGive, Volumes I and II, Timberlake Consultants Ltd. London.

IMF, Direction of Trade Statistics Reports, Various issues, Washington D.C

IMF, International Financial statistics Yearbook, various issues, Washington D.C.

Johansen S (1988). Statistical analysis of cointegration and Statistics vectors, J. Econ. Dyn. Control 12:231-254

Johansen S (1995). A Statistical analysis of I(2) variables, Econom. Theory 11:25-59.

Johnson HG (1953-54). Optimal tariffs and Retaliation, Rev. Econ. Stud. 21(2):142-43.

Khan MS (1974). Imports and Export Demands in Developing Countries, Staff Papers, International Monetary Fund (Washington) 21:678-93.

Krugman P (1979). A Model of Balance of Payment Crisis, J. Money Credit Banking 11(3):311-325.

Krugman P, Miller M (1992). Exchange Rate targets and Currency Bands, Econ. J. 102(415):1548-1550.

McKinnon RI (1993). The order of Economic Liberalization: Financial Control in the Transition to a Market Economy, JHUP, Baltimore.

Meade JE (1955). Problems of Economic Union, Am. Econ. Rev. 45(4):700-704.

Miller MH, Spencer JE (1977). The Static Economic Effects of the UK Joining the EEC: A G eneral Equilibrium Approach, Rev. Econ. Stud. 44(1):71-93.

Mundell RA (1962). Capital mobility and stabilisation policy under fixed and flexible exchange rates, Can. J. Econ. Polit. Sci. 29:475-85.

Musila JW (2002). Exchange Rate Changes and Trade Balance in Malawi, Can. J. Dev. Stud. 23(1):87-103.

Mussa M, Goldstein M, Clark PB, Mathieson D, Bayoumi T (1994). Improving the International Monetary System: Constraints and Possibilities, International Monetary Fund Occasional Paper, 116. (Washington DC: International Monetary Fund).

Nguyen TT, Whalley J (1989). General Equilibrium Analysis of Black and White Markets: A Computational Approach, J. Public Econ. 40:331-347.

Oduro AD, Harrigan J (2000). Exchange Rate Policy and the Balance of Payments 1972-96 In: Aryeetey E, Harrigan J and Nissanke M (ed.), Economic Reforms in Ghana: The Miracle and the Mirage, James Currey Ltd., Oxford.

Perroni C, Whalley J (1996). How Severe is Global Retaliation Risk under Increasing Regionalism, AER Papers and Proceedings. 86(2).

Phillips PCB, Perron P (1988). "Testing for a Unit Root in Time Series Regression," Biome. 75: 335–346.

Rogoff K, Obstfeld M (1996). Foundation of International Macroeconomics, MIT Press.

Samuelson PA (1949): International factor price equalisation, Econ. J. pp.181-197.

Schwert GW (1989) Tests for unit roots: A Monte Carlo investigation, J. Bus. Econ. Stat. 7:147-159.

Singer HW (1950). The distribution of trade between investing and borrowing countries, Am. Econ. Rev. 40:472-485.

Sowa NK, Acquaye IK (1998). Financial and Foreign Exchange Liberalisation in Ghana, Centre for Policy Analysis Research Papers. No.10 Accra: CEPA.

Tavlas GS, Ulan M (eds) (2002). Exchange Rate Regimes and Capital Flows, Special Issue of The Annals of American Academy of Political and Social Science, 579. Philadelphia.

Tavlas S (2003). The Economics of Exchange Rate Regimes: A Review Essay, Blackwell Publishing Ltd, Oxford.

Taylor M (1995). The Economics of Exchange Rates, Journal of Economic Literature, March, vol 33, No. 1, pp. 13-47.

Whalley J (1985). Trade Liberalization Among Major World Trading Areas, MIT Press, Cambridge.

World Bank CD-ROM (2002). World Development Indicators, Washington D.C.

APPENDIX 1. Determination of real exchange rate as a function of preferences, technology and endowments between two countries.

Country 1 (Ghana)

By optimising using the Lagrangian procedure, we have:

$$\angle_1 = X_{11}^{\alpha} X_{12}^{1-\alpha} + \lambda\left[L_1 - \frac{X_{11}}{a_{11}} - \frac{X_{12}}{a_{12}}\right]$$

$$\frac{\partial \angle_1}{\partial X_{11}} = \alpha X_{11}^{\alpha-1} X_{12}^{1-\alpha} - \frac{\lambda}{a_{11}} = 0 \qquad \text{(1a)}$$

$$\frac{\partial \angle_1}{\partial X_{12}} = (1-\alpha) X_{11}^{\alpha} X_{12}^{-\alpha} - \frac{\lambda}{a_{12}} = 0 \qquad \text{(1b)}$$

(1a)/(1b)

$$MRS_{12}^1 = \left(\frac{\alpha}{1-\alpha}\right)\frac{X_{12}}{X_{11}} = MRT_{12}^1 = \frac{a_{12}}{a_{11}} = \frac{P_{12}}{P_{11}}$$

$$X_{12} = \left(\frac{1-\alpha}{\alpha}\right)\frac{a_{12}}{a_{11}} X_{11} \qquad \text{(1c)}$$

but,

$$L_1 = \frac{X_{11}}{a_{11}} + \left(\frac{1-\alpha}{\alpha}\right)\frac{a_{12}}{a_{11}a_{12}} X_{11}$$

By substitution, we have

$$= X_{11}\left(\frac{1}{a_{11}} + \frac{(1-\alpha)}{\alpha}\frac{1}{a_{11}}\right) = X_{11}\left(\frac{1}{\alpha a_{11}}\right)$$

$$X_{11} = \alpha a_{11} L_1 \qquad \text{(1d)}$$

Substituting (1d) into (1c), results

$$X_{12} = \left(\frac{1-\alpha}{\alpha}\right)\frac{a_{12}}{a_{11}} \alpha a_{11} L_1$$

$$X_{12} = (1-\alpha) a_{12} L_1$$

$$\frac{X_{12}}{X_{11}} = \frac{(1-\alpha)}{\alpha}\frac{P_{12}}{P_{11}}$$

$$MRS_{12}^1 = \frac{P_{12}}{P_{11}} = \frac{a_{12}}{a_{11}}$$

Country 2 (Rest of the World)

Again, using the Lagrangian procedure, we have:

$$\angle_2 = X_{21}^{\beta} X_{22}^{1-\beta} + \lambda\left[L_2 - \frac{X_{21}}{a_{21}} - \frac{X_{22}}{a_{22}}\right]$$

$$\frac{\partial \angle_2}{\partial X_{21}} = \beta X_{21}^{\beta-1} X_{22}^{1-\beta} - \frac{\lambda}{a_{21}} = 0 \qquad \text{(2a)}$$

$$\frac{\partial \angle_2}{\partial X_{22}} = (1-\beta) X_{21}^{\beta} X_{22}^{-\beta} - \frac{\lambda}{a_{22}} = 0 \qquad \text{(2b)}$$

(2a)/(2b)

$$MRS_{12}^2 = \left(\frac{\beta}{1-\beta}\right)\frac{X_{22}}{X_{21}} = \frac{a_{22}}{a_{21}} = MRT_{12}^2 = \frac{P_{21}}{P_{22}}$$

$$X_{22} = \left(\frac{1-\beta}{\beta}\right)\frac{a_{22}}{a_{21}} X_{21} \qquad \text{(2c)}$$

but,

$$L_2 = \frac{X_{21}}{a_{21}} + \frac{X_{22}}{a_{22}}$$

By substitution, we have

$$= X_{21}\left(\frac{1}{a_{21}} + \frac{(1-\beta)}{\beta}\frac{1}{a_{21}}\right) = X_{21}\left(\frac{1}{\beta a_{21}}\right)$$

$$X_{21} = \beta a_{21} L_2 \qquad \text{(2d)}$$

Substituting (2d) into (2c), results

$$X_{22} = \left(\frac{1-\beta}{\beta}\right)\frac{a_{22}}{a_{21}} \beta a_{21} L_2$$

$$X_{22} = (1-\beta) a_{22} L_2$$

$$\frac{X_{21}}{X_{22}} = \frac{\beta}{(1-\beta)}\frac{P_{21}}{P_{22}}$$

$$MRS_{21}^2 = \frac{P_{21}}{P_{22}} = \frac{a_{21}}{a_{22}}$$

Global market clearing:

$$X_{11} + X_{21} = X_1,\ P_{11} = P_{21} \qquad MRS_{12}^1 = MRS_{12}^2 = \frac{a_{11}}{a_{12}} = \frac{P_{11}}{P_{12}} = \frac{P_{21}}{P_{22}} = \frac{a_{21}}{a_{22}} = MRT_{12}^1 = MRT_{12}^2;$$

$$X_{12} + X_{22} = X_2,\ P_{12} = P_{22} \qquad \frac{a_{12}}{a_{11}} P_{11} = P_{12} = P_{22} = \frac{a_{21}}{a_{22}} P_{21} \rightarrow \frac{P_{11}}{P_{22}} = \frac{a_{11}}{a_{12}}\frac{a_{21}}{a_{22}}$$

APPENDIX 2

Table A1. Balance of payments of Ghana, 1994-2000 (US$m).

	1994	1995	1996	1997	1998	1999	2000
Current account							
bal(incl. grant)	-254.6	-144.7	-324.7	-549.7	-443.1	-932.5	-412.6
(%GDP)	4.68	2.24	4.68	7.98	5.92	11.9	7.94
exports	1542.4	1582.7	2256	2345.5	2596.3	2910.2	2843.9
(%GDP)	25.3	24.5	32.1	32.4	33.9	31.9	49.2
of which: cocoa total	320.2	389.5	552.1	470	617.4	N/A	N/A
(% contribution)	25.9	27.2	35.1	31.6	34.1	N/A	N/A
minerals(incl. Gold)	588.2	678.8	641.4	613	717.8	N/A	N/A
(% contribution)	13.4	13.3	9.3	11.5	9.4	N/A	N/A
timber total	165.4	190.6	146.8	172	171	N/A	N/A
(% contribution)	13.4	13.3	9.3	11.5	9.4	N/A	N/A
other non traditional products	86.6	100	143.6	157.1	228	N/A	N/A
(%contribution)	6.9	6.9	9.2	10.5	12.6	N/A	N/A
Imports	2022.2	2126.2	2777.3	3823.8	4131.6	4583.8	3790.8
(% GDP)	32.56	32.93	40.09	52.99	46.74	49.21	69.59
Trade Balance	-615.5	-538.7	-666.5	-978.4	-104.1	-142.1	-935.9
*(% GDP)	9.9	8.3	9.9	13.9	1.41	1.84	11.7
Services Balance	-273.3	-282.1	-299.6	-340.1	-235	-198.1	-93
(% GDP)	4.4	4.38	4.4	4.8	3.2	2.6	1.2
Capital account bal.(incl.errors & omissions)	1	1	1	1	1	1	1
*(% GDP)	0.016	0.015	0.015	0.014	0.014	0.013	0.013
Overall Balance	172.1	250.8	-20.4	26.7	107.9	-89.6	-258.5
*(% GDP)	2.77	3.88	0.3	0.38	1.46	1.17	3.24
GDP	6209.1	6457.4	6754.6	7038.1	7368.9	7693.6	7978.3
Financing							
Domestic	-26.7	-27.7	531.1	728	672.6	N/A	N/A
Foreign	-85	-42.6	-195.7	-430.3	-376.2	N/A	N/A

Source: World Bank CD Rom (2002) University of Hull; IFS Yearbook 2001. *Percentage figures calculated by author using GDP values obtained from the World Bank CD Rom, 2002.

Table A 2. Ghana's trade analysis (1994-2000).

	1994	1995	1996	1997	1998	1999	2000
Exports (%)	**100**	**100**	**100**	**100**	**100**	**100**	**100**
Indust. countries of which:	72.5	70.3	67	63.6	64.9	62.7	58.8
United States	12.6	11.3	9.5	8.3	7.1	9.3	11.3
United Kingdom	13	14.4	15.6	11.6	11.8	11.4	7.6
Germany	14.8	11.8	8.9	9.1	6.8	5	6.2
Japan	3..9	3..9	3.8	4.4	3.3	2.9	2.5
Develop. Countries of which:	23.4	25.1	27.8	30.8	29.5	31.3	33.8
Nigeria	2.8	2.9	3	3.4	3.2	3.1	4.3
Cote d'voire	0.2	0.5	0.3	0.1	0.1	0.1	0.1
Togo	0.4	0.4	0.5	0.5	0.6	0.5	0.4
Imports (%)	**100**	**100**	**100**	**100**	**100**	**100**	**100**
Indust. Countries of which:	59.8	57.6	61.3	59.7	56.1	55.3	51.9
United States	6.7	6.8	10.2	10.5	7.2	8.2	6.6
United Kingdom	15.8	16.4	16.2	15.1	11.8	9.7	9
Germany	5.6	7.6	5.4	6	5	5.6	4.5
Japan	6.8	4	3.4	2.5	2.6	3	1.5
Develop. Countries of which:	39.1	41.3	37.7	39.3	42.8	43.5	46.6
Nigeria	17	15.3	13.4	14.3	14.2	15	19.3
Cote d'voire	3.2	4	4.3	5.1	8.1	4.7	4.8
Togo	0.4	0.4	0.4	0.4	0.5	0.5	0.6

Percentage figures calculated by author using data from Direction of Trade Statistics (DOTS), Various issues.

Table A3. Correlation matrix for the endogenous variables.

	NER	RE	EXPORT	IMPORT	GDP
NER	1				
RE	0.985652	1			
EXPORT	0.759654	0.74217	1		
IMPORT	0.72921	0.680486	0.909757	1	
GDP	0.873181	0.87579	0.758854	0.747134	1

Notes: NER, RE and GDP denote nominal exchange rate, real exchange rate and gross domestic product respectively.

Table A4. Export, imports and trade balance ($million) (1970-2000).

YEAR	NOMINAL EXCHANGE RATE	EXPORT ($mill)	IMPORT ($mill)	GDP DEFLATOR	TRADE BALANCE ($mill)
1970	1.02041	458.03	410.67	42.239	47.36
1971	1.034859	337.66	418.33	44.431	-80.67
1972	1.333392	429.52	290.5	51.303	139.02
1973	1.165	626.86	450.28	62.011	176.58
1974	1.15	729.44	818.59	77.243	-89.15
1975	1.15	807.21	790.69	100.000	16.52
1976	1.15	856.26	965.56	128.053	-109.3
1977	1.15	1010.5	1205.1	214.170	-194.6
1978	1.76358	890.6	955.6	371.159	-65
1979	2.75	1041.2	894.4	512.010	146.8
1980	2.75	1432.6	1071.3	773.781	360.9
1981	2.75	1154.2	1093.7	1359.020	60.5

Table A4. Contd.

1982	2.75	1227.8	712.7	1738.058	515.1
1983	8.829975	895.3	719	3876.933	176.3
1984	35.98619	415.9	568.7	5245.972	-152.8
1985	54.365	617	793.6	6329.182	-176.6
1986	89.20417	876.4	783.4	8968.817	93
1987	153.7333	976.5	987.9	12484.729	-11.4
1988	202.3458	1075.3	1034.8	16654.984	40.5
1989	270	1069.7	1124.2	21367.398	-54.5
1990	326.3317	1365.9	1387.6	28026.891	-21.7
1991	367.8308	617	511	33643.859	106
1992	437.0867	1237	2139	37395.172	-902
1993	649.0608	1137	2043	49273.371	-906
1994	956.7108	1482	2041	64045.773	-559
1995	1200.429	1609	2557	91714.391	-928
1996	1637.232	1692	3185	128251.328	-1493
1997	2050.167	1725	3285	153206.688	-1560
1998	2314.147	1756.1	3421.6	179326.078	-1665.5
1999	2669.299	1754.2	3251	204366.047	-1496.8
2000	5455.056	1563	3145.7	260021.703	-1582.7

Source: IMF Direction of Trade Statistics (DOTS); various issues.

Table A4b. Indicators of the Ghanaian economy.

Year	1983	1993	2002	2003
Total Debt /GDP	41.1	81	119.1	103.5
Total debt service/export	30.4	24.6	7.3	23.1
Export price index	94	76	81	88
Import price index	102	96	96	97
Terms of Trade`	92	79	85	90
current budget balance	-1.9	5.5	0.2	4.1
Overall surplus/deficit	n/a	-5.6	-5.9	-4.5

Source: World Bank Group (2003).

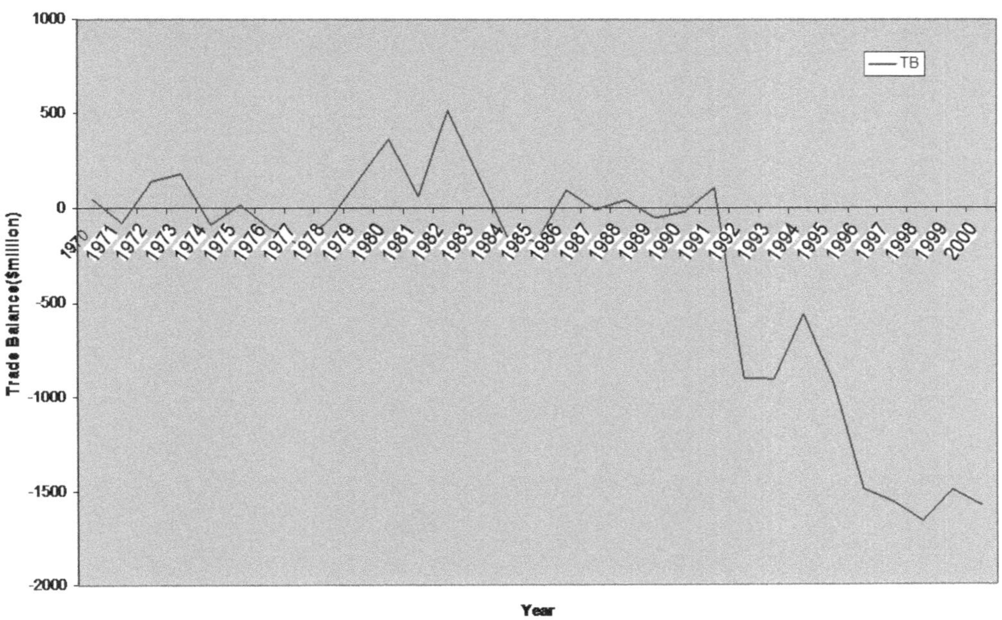

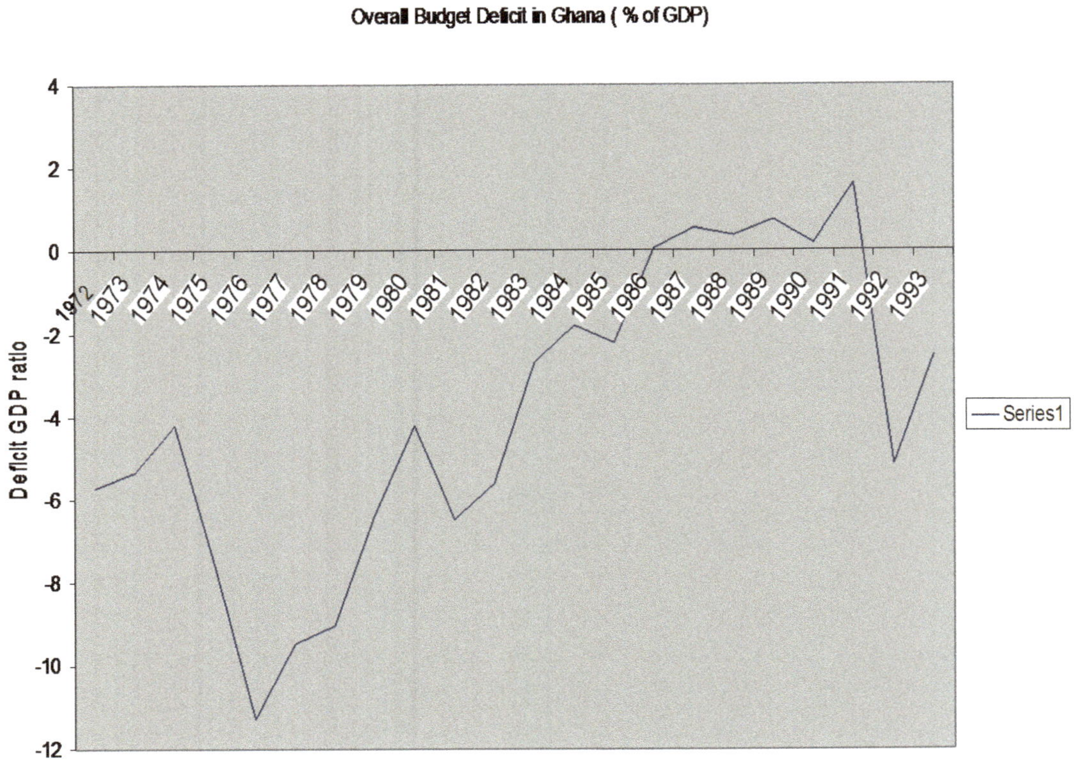

Figure A1. Graph of Trade Balance ($millions) and overall Budget Deficit (GDP%).

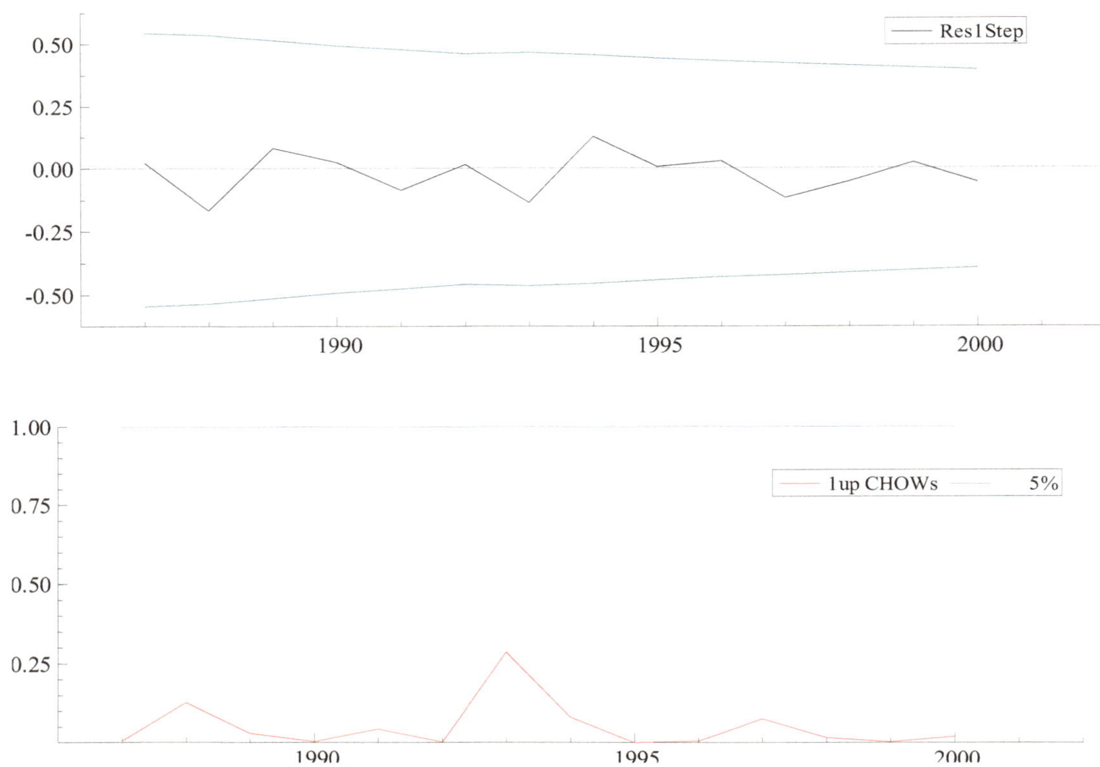

Figure A2. Diagnostic testing of the short run ECM: one step ahead residuals and Chow tests for export.

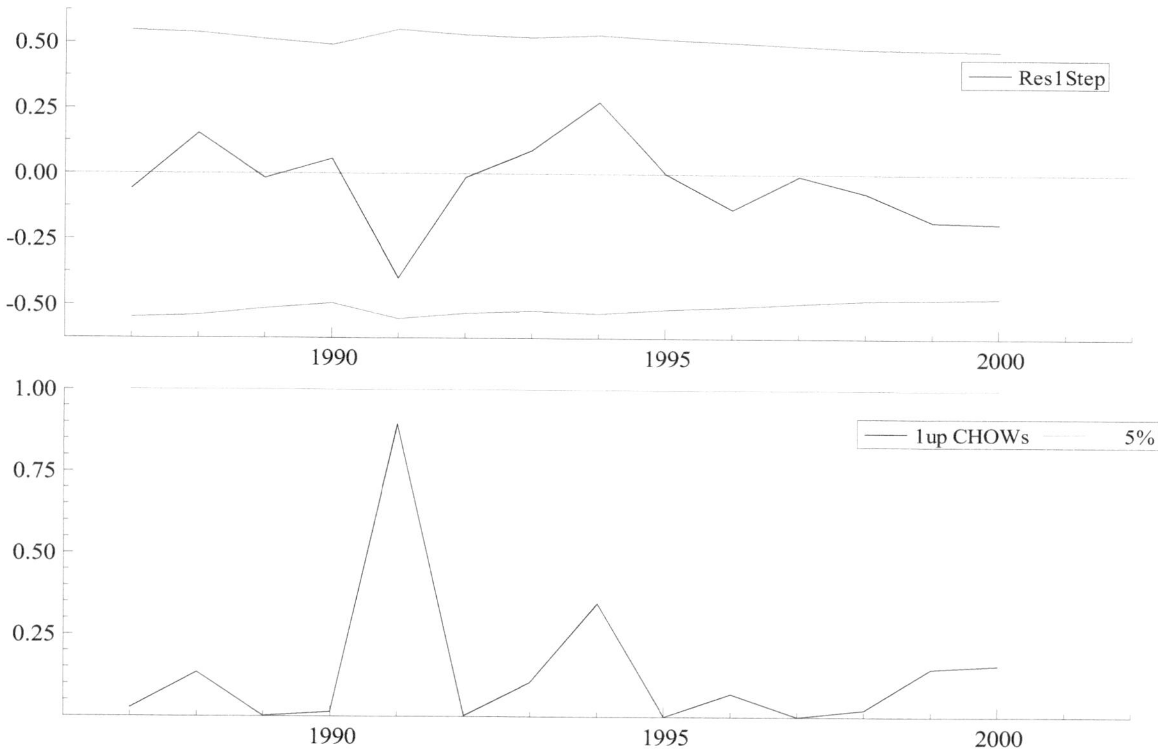

Figure A3. Diagnostic testing of the shot run ECM: one step ahead residuals and Chow tests for imports.

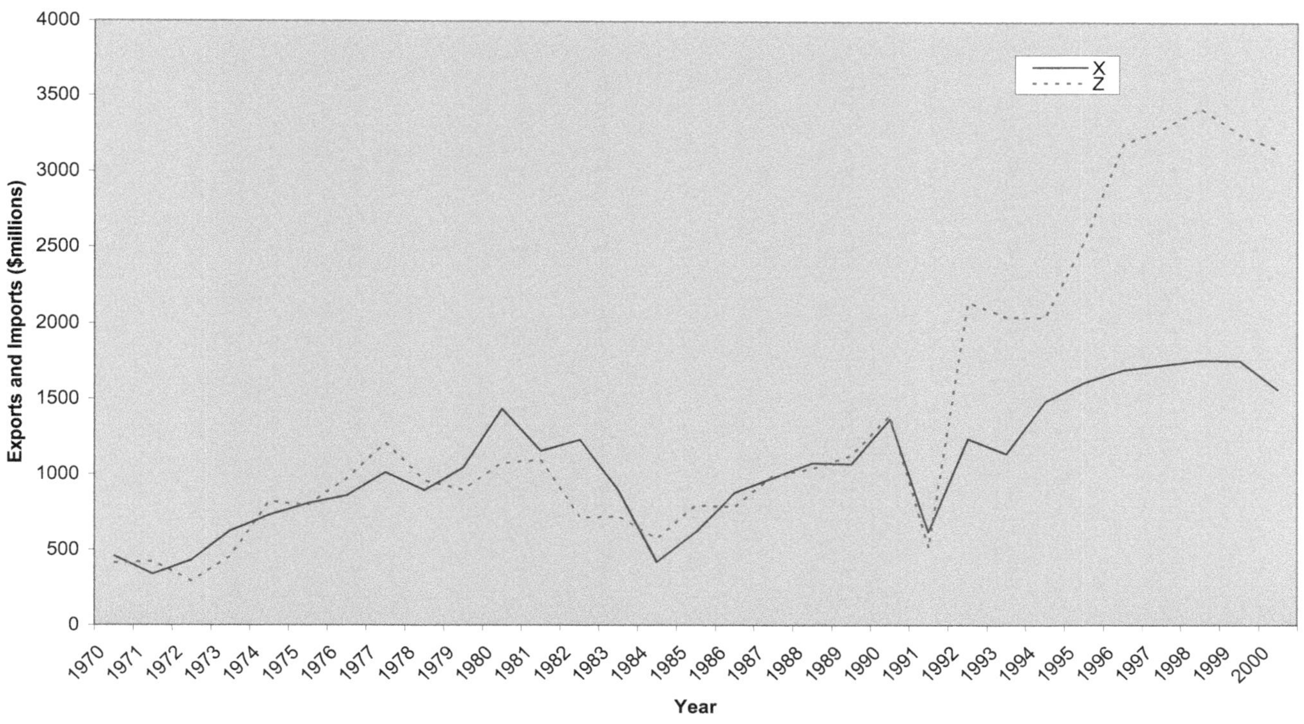

Figure A4. Graph of export and import showing the trade gap ($millions).

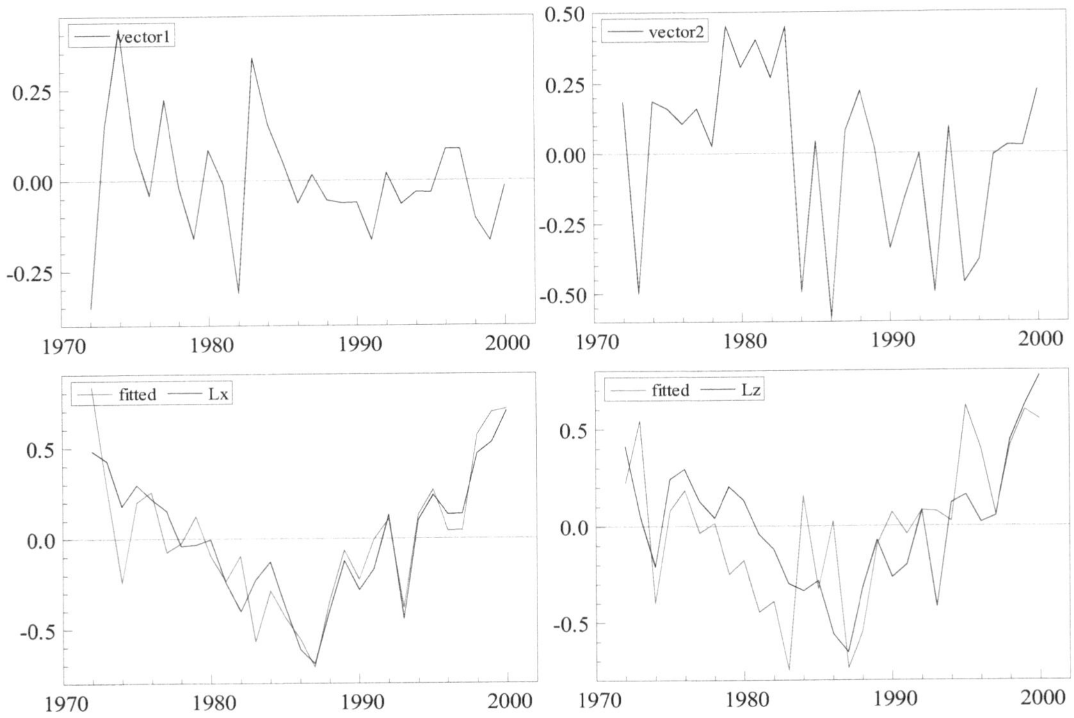

Figure A5. Graph of cointegrating vectors.

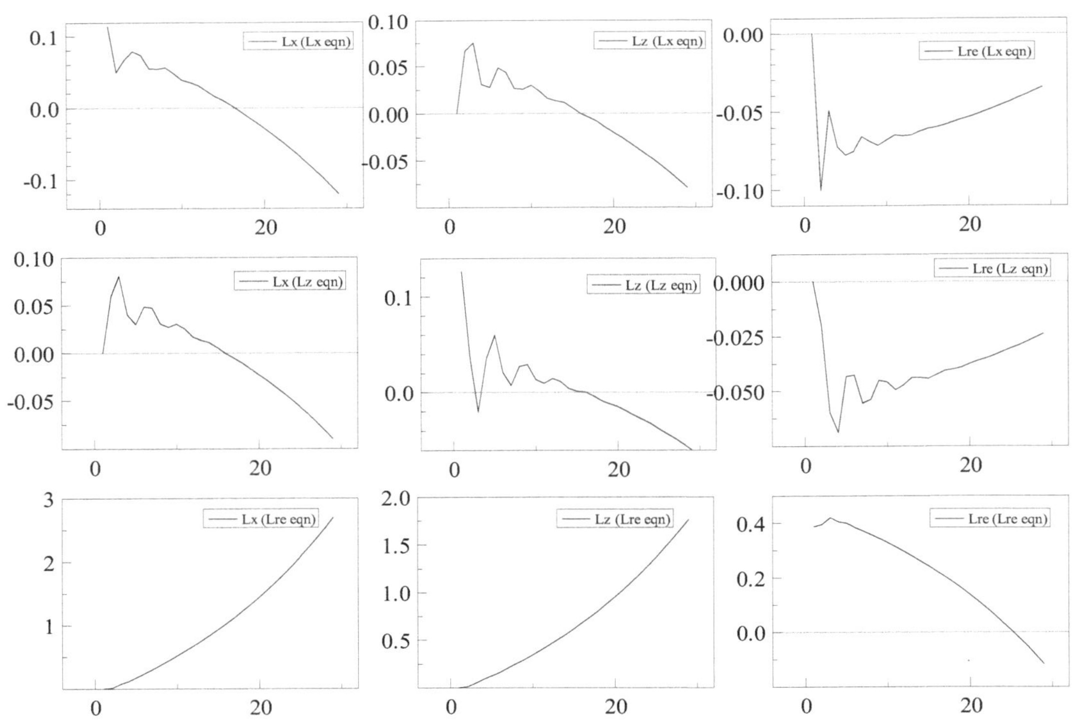

Figure A6. Impulse response analysis from the reduced form VAR model.

An investigation of the relationship between productivity indices and systematic risk based on the capital asset pricing model (among accepted companies in Tehran stock market)

Seyed Reza Hasani

Islamic Azad University, Kermanshah Branch, Theran, Iran.

Systematic risk (beta) is one of the most effective factors in predicting the appropriate required rate of returns of portfolios. By understanding the systematic risk of usual portfolios of various companies, investors will be able to consider financial investment more confidentially. The aim of this study was to examine the relationship between productivity indices (operating leverage, financial leverage, combined leverage) as independent variables and systematic risk (Beta) as dependent variables. To do so, 112 companies accepted in Tehran Stock Market were selected based on screening (systematic deletion) in a five-year- period, 2004 to 2008. The required data were gathered from basic financial statements, committee reports, and other available documents in Tehran Stock Market. Regression and Pearson correlation were applied to analyze the data. The results of the study revealed that there was no significant relationship between productivity indices and systematic risk. Some suggestions are provided regarding the topic of the research.

Key words: Operating leverage, financial leverage, combined leverage, systematic risk (beta).

INTRODUCTION

Research on the financial fields in Iran is in its initial stages. Economic conditions and traditional characteristics of investors and managers of business units have not yet provided desirable conditions to address serious and rigorous research; especially that stock price is shrouded in mystery.

The evidence suggests that investors do not use quantitative methods to determine the value of shares. Assumptions are subjective and data are not based on empirical research. To improve the conditions of expanding capital market activities and to prevent failures and measures taken to attract public participation in investment, mental imagination must be replaced by scientific results and how to use known methods should be taught to both managers and investors to select the proper methods and be able to maintain their presence in the capital markets and through which the wheels of economic activities get rolling on.

Common stock includes tools that, due to its lack of future returns, will make investors doubtful. Thus, if desirable conditions are provided to both investors and corporate managers to get necessary knowledge about capital market, and make them familiar with all the factors affecting investment, consequently, they will be assisted in decision-making and this, in turn, will be an influential factor in capital market.

The returns that an investor acquires is unpredictable, so he is forced to bear the risk, on the other hand, non-systematic risk in an intellectual investment can be eliminated or reduced with variation in investments. In fact, the rate of risk and returns should be considered in investments. Financing is the most challenging responsibility of financial managers.

Providing finance such as loans and credit requires the payment of principal and interest levels in the committed periods. Fixed financial costs such as interest have led financial managers to consider the power of the financial unit in comparison with such costs using financial leverage and computing the leverage level.

Leverage can be divided into two main categories; the first category is operational leverage in which the percentage of changes in dependent variable (operational returns) is measured on the percentage of changes in independent variable (sale). The second category is financial leverage which refers to changes in the interest of ordinary shareholders. The given change is caused by selling shares and outstanding debt. The third category is combined leverage; a combination of EBIT volatility, operating leverage and financial leverage – in which the relationship between profits of ordinary shares and sale is taken into account.

No evaluation of investing projects can be performed without knowledge of the minimum rate of returns and risk for accepting the investments. However, any decision or change that occurs within the company affects the returns and risk of company's common stock, for instance changing the capital structure and using low cost debt may reduce company's capital cost, however, it may increase financial risk.

IMPORTANCE AND NECESSITY OF RESEARCH

This study is important in this view that it examines the relationship between two concepts; one is the corporate finance and the other is capital market and investors. Of course, in the theoretical world, the positive relationship between capital structure and systematic risk of ordinary shares in the company has been proven, and we know that in the theoretical world, capital markets are efficient. If we can prove the relationship between these two, we can claim that our market is efficient at least in relation to the variables of this theory. If the relationship between these two variables in the market is observed, contrary to the relationship between these two variables in the theory, we can claim that our capital market is not efficient.

Another significance of this study is that another series of relations, information, and related variables of the corporate can be accessed by all people under different conditions so that one of the most important conditions of labor market, that is transparency of information, will be provided in the stock market.

LITERATURE REVIEW

Regarding the leverage ratio and its relation to accounting and financial issues in different economic sectors inside and outside the country, a lot of researches have been carried out and are mentioned in Table 1 as examples in the research literature. In terms of internal researches, we can refer to the studies carried out by Farhad et al. (2009). In the case of external research, we can mention Keen and Mansour (2010), Piotroski (2007) and Pirjeta and Vesa (2007).

According to studies carried out so far, there has been no research in the literature that has investigated the relationship between leverage ratio (operational, financial, and combined leverages) and systemic risk (Beta). Therefore, according to the previous research, although the present study may have similarities to the aforementioned studies in terms of methodology and procedures, its whole structure and objective are quite different (Tables 1 and 2).

THE OVERALL PURPOSE AND SPECIFIC OBJECTIVES OF THE RESEARCH

The overall goal

The overall goal of this study is to describe the relationship between leverage and systematic risk based on capital asset pricing model.

Specific objectives

The main objective of this study is to help to investors, both natural and legal investors, stock brokers, and all capital market players to identify appropriate criteria for determining the rate of returns and risk in the shares of companies listed in the Tehran Stock Exchange. Another major objective of this study is to determine how extremely important and helpful the relationship between leverage and systematic risk in investment decisions is.

Also, this study seeks to describe and assess the relationship between leverage and systematic risk based on the capital assets pricing model. In addition, the study seeks to examine whether information about a company's size is a criterion for assessing systemic risk companies in Tehran Stock Exchange. In the capital assets pricing model, the beta coefficient is the only factor used for determining the expected returns. Thus, having an understanding of the relationship between leverage and systematic risk can help investors and activists to estimate the rate of returns and risk in the shares of companies.

RESEARCH QUESTION

Being an extensive and comprehensive study, this research study seeks to answer the question: "Does a significant relationship exist between the ratio leverage and systematic risk based on the capital assets pricing model in companies listed in the Tehran Stock Exchange or not?"

Table 1. Theoretical framework for research: International studies.

The researchers named	Year	Research subject	Research Result
Farhad Shah visi	2010	Study the relationship between systematic risk and engineering analysis tools in companies listed in Tehran Stock Exchange	The results showed that there are relationship between systemic risk analysis and engineering tools
YousefJalilian	2010	Effects of firm size on systematic risk-based capital asset pricing model (Stock market value, book value , shares of the company's sales, trading volume, stock prices relative to dividends)	The results showed there is a relationship between the effects of firm size on systematic risk-based capital asset pricing model
GholamRezaEslamiBidgoli and Mohammad Ali Khojaste	2009	Three-factor model of Fama and Frnch relationship between expected return using the capital productivity For the period 1379-1386 in the manufacturing companies in Tehran stock exchange	The results showed that the four-factor model, using the efficiency factor along the three factors in Fama and Frnch model, the model in explaining boosts efficiency. Add the decisive factor determining the efficiency and moderate increases. And also with the operating efficiency of the capital asset pricing, this area is recommended to researchers and activists.
Reza Tehrani and others	2008	Consider relationship between risk and return based on CAPM comparison with CCAPM	Despite the use of beta should theoretically be a better measure of systematic risk, but the empirical performance of traditional pricing model shows more success
ZarifiFard and Ghaemi	2004	empirical tests of CAPM model and relationship between risk and return	systematic risk cannot lonely justify the corporate efficiency
Namazi and Zare	2004	Application of information theory in the determination of systemic risk	Systematic risk can be estimated using analysts and financial reports entropy of the information contained in the balance sheet and profit and loss statement reports there is a relation with systematic risk
Shahram Band Pey	2000	The relationship between systematic risk and return on common stocks in Tehran Stock Exchange during the years 77-73, with special emphasis on food industry	According to the results of these studies except one portfolio to another portfolio of four 5 indicate rejection of the hypothesis of a significant relationship between systematic risk and stock returns and according to the results of the test result was between five portfolio between systematic risk and there is no significant relationship between average stock returns
SeyedYahyaAssadullahi	2000	Investment performance of companies listed on stock exchange in terms of risk and return in five-year period, 74 to 78	The results showed that firms in this period, according to sources who were involved have been somewhat successful in the policy applied to move and act.

Table 1. Contd.

Hassan Ghalibaf	1993	The effect of capital structure (financial leverage) on the systematic risk beta of common stock 26 companies listed in Tehran Stock Exchange during the years 72-68	The results show that the average beta of un leverage is smaller than the average beta leverage

Table 2. Theoretical framework: Foreign studies.

The researchers names	Year	Research subject	Research Result
M. Christ and others	2010	Estimating systemic risk in different time scales in the Persian Gulf emerging markets using Mojak techniques	Average beta coefficients in all Persian Gulf countries with a desire to show the multiple and different that representing different time horizons for investors is the stock market
David Alen and AlberaynBojang	2009	Beta stability and systemic risk index based on research results F&FandFSS	Estimates of abnormal earnings increase for the duration of the two models differ considerably
Ben Mebrok and thers	2007	CAPM models used in different time scales in the French market	Between profits and stock market beta in the time scales there is a strong relationship and works well in predicting short-term
Pear Jeta and Putnen	2007		Higher than roiclining of the joint are more likely to move from value to growth a s a result, more efficient and economical value they provide growth factors in their research, sales, operating profit margin, profit margin, return on equity and the rock was considered the decisive was power of the roic variables that had a more dramatic and more significant in the tests
Brown and Rouye	2007	Measures the productivity of capital in America ROIC index among the Top 1000 in stock returns from 1970 to 2005	It was found that the operating efficiency of capital by ROIC index, estimators is a positive return on equity selection of companies to increase efficiency and value and growth has been the source for additional returns to which intercept model of Fama and Frnch increased sense is not meanless
Kens Lamm	2005	Comparing the three-factor model with single-factor model based on market beta America	Models to test the validity of the type used depends on Three-factor model of portfolio choice in the top 25 was the test of time series but in cross-sectional results of the test CAPM model was better
Jonathan Laven	1999	Compared CAPM with the three-factor model of Fama and Frnch	Three-factor model of risk and return has a more explanatory power than the CAPM model.

THE RESEARCH HYPOTHESES

Due to the fact that leverage ratio (operational, financial, and composite leverage) which is used as the independent variable and systematic risk (beta) which is used as the dependent variable are both defined, a main hypothesis and three sub-hypotheses are presented as follows. The three sub-hypotheses are: (1) modify the terms of the wholesale price index of goods and services (2) no adjustment (3) adjustment should be tested based on inflation indicators.

The base year is 1383 and the index number is 100.

The main hypothesis

"*The leverage ratio and systematic risk-based capital assets pricing model, there is a significant relationship*".

Sub hypothesis

H_1: Between operating leverage and systematic risk-based capital asset pricing model, there is a significant relationship.

H_2: Between financial leverage and systematic risk-based

Table 3. Conceptual and operational definitions of words and technical terms and specialized research.

Variable name	Type of variable	Defining variables	Operational definition of variables
Operational leverage	Independent	The degree of change in operating profit before interest and taxes to a percentage change in sales shows	$OL = \frac{Q(P-V)}{Q(P-V)-F}$ Q = Total Sales, P = Price per unit of goods V = Variable costs per unit of goods, F = Fixed costs.
Financial Leverage	Independent	It shows financial position of the percentage change is the percentage change in earnings per share versus a profit before interest and taxes	$FL = \frac{S-F-VC}{S-F-VC-I-\frac{E}{1-t}}$ S = Sale, F = Fixed costs, VC = Variable costs, E = Preferred dividends, I = Interest costs, T = Tax rate.
Combined Leverage	Independent	Leverage the combined rate of change in earnings per share in a percentage change in sales shows	$CL = \frac{S-VC}{S-F-VC-I-\frac{E}{1-t}}$ S= Sale F= Fixed costs, VC= Variable costs, E=Preferred dividends, I= Interest costs, T= Tax rate
Indicators of systemic risk(b)	Dependent	Systematic risk (non reduced) or a measure of the variability of portfolio investment assets, compared with the market; Systematic risk (non decreasing) the risk of an asset is that the portfolio was not available and therefore reducing the risk that investors will demand a risk	$\beta = \frac{Cov(R_i, R_m)}{VAR(R_m)}$

capital asset pricing model, there is a significant relationship.

H₃: The compound leverage and systematic risk based capital asset pricing model, there is a significant relationship. Conceptual and operational definitions of words and technical terms and specialized research are shown in Table 3.

THE RESEARCH METHODOLOGY

Research in terms of goal

This kind of research is applicable.

Methods of data type

Descriptive survey in which to describe the relationship between variables using correlation and regression deals.

Method in terms of data collection

This study includes all companies listed in Tehran Stock Exchange.

Required information from the research literature, books, specialized journals, and articles derived from Persian and Latin, has been collected (the library).

Data needed to test this hypothesis by referring to the Tehran Stock Exchange and annual financial statements and explanatory notes of the companies listed in Tehran Stock Exchange (including balance sheet, profit and loss), board reports and financial information companies such as summarizer software, the new RA and exchange sites for the period of 5 years (1387 to 1383) collected, and for the calculation of variables such as Excel is stored in a database.

Measure the presence and extent of the relationship, the variables measuring the level of correlation is used, and to assess the effect of each variable on the dependent variable separately, of inferential statistical tests, regression analysis, step by step (Step wise).

The method of least squares in the 95% level, determined coefficient (R^2), determine the adjusted coefficient ($\overline{R}^2$) and P size and if the P - Value <% 5 is supposed to confirm, otherwise be reject . In addition to the statistical tables, data analysis and statistical modeling of software, Excel, Spss and Matlab will be used.

The statistical study of all companies listed in Tehran Stock Exchange is included. Considering the following four criteria, sample size and sampling method (based on the systematic

Table 4. Test hypotheses.

Adjusted price index	Hypothesis		
	The first hypothesis (H_1)	**The second hypothesis (H_2)**	**The third hypothesis (H_3)**
Kind of relation	Linear	Linear	Linear
Error level	%5	%5	%5
The number N	112	112	112
R value	-0/044	0/014	0/065
R2 value	0/001	0/0001	0/004
value-P	0/322	0/444	0/247
Confidence level	%95	%95	%95
Hypothesis is confirmed	H_0	H_0	H_0

elimination of a screening rule) determined, based on 112 companies that have been selected as examples.

1. 5 years of financial information (2006 to 2011) is available.
2. The fiscal year end is the end of March each year.
3. 6 month intervals over the trading companies were not.
4. The companies studied here are not financial intermediaries and investment companies.

Note: Financial intermediaries and investment companies, because of the special nature of their community, were excluded from the investigated of this study.

SURVEY FINDINGS: DATA, CALCULATIONS AND TEST HYPOTHESES

1. Test the H_1: Between operating leverage and systematic risk based capital asset pricing model, there is a significant relationship.
The findings of the study indicate that: Between operating leverage and systematic risk-based capital asset pricing model and the three criteria set forth in the research; (1) Adjust the wholesale price index of goods and services (2) No adjustment (3) Adjustment for inflation, and the significance level (322 / 0 327 / 0 322 / 0) and accepted error (5%) and confidence level 95% have no meaningful relationship with each other. Hence, H0 base on no significant relationship, are accepted.
2. Test the H_2: Between financial leverage and systematic risk based capital asset pricing model, there is a significant relationship. The findings of the study indicate that: Between financial leverage and systematic risk-based capital asset pricing model and the three criteria set forth in the research (1) Adjust the wholesale price index of goods and services (2) No adjustment (3) Adjustment for inflation, and the significance level (444/0, 448/0, 469/0) and accepted error (5%) and confidence level 95% have no meaningful relationship with each other. Hence H0 base on no significant relationship, are accepted.
3. Test the H_3: Combined leverage and systematic risk based capital asset pricing model, there is a significant relationship. The findings of the study indicate that: Between combined leverage and systematic risk-based capital asset pricing model and the three criteria set forth in the research (1) Adjust the wholesale price index of goods and services (2) No adjustment (3) Adjustment for inflation, and the significance level (444/0, 448/0, 469/0) and accepted error (5%) and confidence level 95% have no meaningful relationship with each other. Hence, H0 base on no significant relationship, are accepted.

LIMITATIONS OF RESEARCH

Despite the limitations of this work, the researcher was able to control the variables and the relationship between these variables in order to provide results that will be more accurate and scientific. Therefore, it is necessary that these limitations be outlined so that further researchers can carry out researches on the negative effect of these limitations. The limitations of this study are as follows:

1. Given that many companies do not develop appropriate cost accounting system, the costs and expenses of these companies as well as their product differentiation may not be correct and precise, thus resulting in changes in the financial statements.
2. There were discrepancies between the basic financial statements of stock companies and the information obtained through summarizer software; the data collected by the researcher from the named sources were confusing and incorrect.

CONCLUSION AND SUGGESTIONS

1. Given the importance of systemic risk, can be associated with other indicators and accounting and financial variables (such as financial ratios, indicators of productivity, etc.) and industry-focused venture with systemic risk.
2. The study could be used as a case study of a particular industry or enterprise and obtained results could be compared with the results of this study.

Table 5. Test hypotheses.

No adjustment	The hypothesis		
	The first hypothesis	The second hypothesis	The third hypothesis
Kind of relation	Linear	Linear	Linear
Error level	5%	5%	5%
The number N	112	112	112
R value	043/0-	013/0	063/0
R2 value	001/0	0001/0	003/0
value-P	327/0	448/0	256/0
Confidence level	95%	95%	95%
Hypothesis is confirmed	H0	H0	H0

Table 6. Adjusting for inflation.

Adjusting for inflation	The hypothesis		
	The first hypothesis	The second hypothesis	The third hypothesis
Kind of relation	**Linear**	**Linear**	**Linear**
Error level	5%	5%	5%
The number N	112	112	112
R value	-0/042	0/007	0/061
R2 value	0/001	0/00004	0/003
value-P	0/330	0/469	0/261
Confidence level	%95	%95	%95
Hypothesis is confirmed	H_0	H_0	H_0

3. Future research can yield more reliable results if the research is conducted for longer period, say a 10-year period or more.
4. Given the importance of systemic risk in investment decisions, investors, creditors and stock market participants are recommended, when trading decisions should consider the results of this study and similar research.
5. Given the importance of systemic risk in investment decisions, investors, creditors and stock market participants are recommended, when trading decisions should consider the results of this study and similar research.
6. In the present study, the linear regression method was used to predict the variables. It is recommended that in future studies, non-linear equations, quadratic, logarithmic, etc. be used, since non-linear equations indicate that a strong relationship does not exist between variables (that is, there is a weak or no correlation between variables).
7. Due to the importance and usefulness of accounting information in determining the risk and stock returns of companies listed in the Stock Exchange, it is recommended that the financial statements of various companies be placed on their Internet sites to facilitate public access.

REFERENCES

Allen D, Bujang I (2009). Conditional Beta CAPM and duration dependence Tests, 18th world IMACS Congress cains: pp.13-17.

Bandpey S (2000). Relationship between systematic risk and return on common stocks in Tehran Stock Exchange. MS Thesis. Tehran Sci. Res. pp.21-22.

Ben M, Ben A, Rhaiem S (2007). Estimation of CAPM at different time scales Application to French stock market. 1(2):79-82.

Brown DP, Bradford JR (2007). The Productivity Premium in Equity Returns, University of Wisconsin Us: Www. Ssrn.com.

Farhad W, Saleem MF, Cheema MA, Hammad HM (2009). Effect of poultry manure levels on the productivity of spring maize (*Zea mays* L.). J. Anim. Plant Sci. 19:122-125

Keen M, Mansour M (2010). "Revenue Mobilisation in Sub-Saharan Africa: Challenges from Globalisation II; Corporate Taxation." Develop. Policy Rev. 28(5):573-596.

Lam K (2005). Is the Fama- French Three Factor Model Better than The CAPM?. http://www.ssrn.com.

Leven J (1999). The time –series relations among expected return risk and book –to –market. J. Financ. Econ. 54: 5-43.

Masih M, Alzahrani M, Al-titi O (2010). Systematic risk and time scales. Int. Rev. Financ. Anal. 19:10-18.

Namazi MZ and Zare B (2004). Application of information theory in the determination of systemic risk. J. Account Audit Financ. 35:100-179.

Piotroski JD (2007).Discussion of The Book-to-Price Effect in Stock Returns: Accounting for Leverage. J. Account. 45(2):469-479.

Pirjeta A, Vesa P (2007). Style Migration in the European Markets Helsinki School of Economics, Electronic Working Paper w-426. ISBN 9789524881456. HSE Print Finland: www.hse.fi/fms.

Tehrani R, Goudarzi M, Moradi M (2009). CAPM model CCAPM test compared with the Tehran Stock Exchange Econ. Res. 43:81-61.

Yahyazadehfar M, Shams S, Garshasebi A (2012). Comparative analysis of stocks returns' predictable factors in Tehran Stocks Exchange and New York Stocks Exchange using artificial neural network and linear regression. Afr. J. Bus. Manage., 6(2):501-513.

Zarififard A, Ghaemi MH (2004). empirical testing capital asset pricing model in the Tehran Stock Exchange. J. Soc. Sci. Hum. Shiraz. 19(20):41-53.

Internal Control and Accounting Policies and Procedures Practices: An Institutional Perspective

Muhammad H. Al-Hazmi

Department of Accounting and MIS, King Fahd University of Petroleum and Minerals, Saudi Arabia.

The present studies demonstrate the importance of organizational routines and institutions in shaping the internal control and accounting policies and procedures practices in two Saudi firms operate in the real estate sector. An attempt has been made to distinguish the control environment, which represents management's overall attitude, awareness and actions, from control policies and procedures, which are the detailed set of guidelines and procedures that management stabilities over information and transactions processing.

Key words: Internal Control, Accounting Policies and Procedures, Accounting Practices, the Institutional Economic Perspectives, Organizational routines and Institutions.

INTRODUCTION

Accounting links decision makers with economic activities and with the results of their decisions. The more important the decision is the greater the need for accurate information. Accounting information is simply the means of measuring and communicating economic events to decision makers. Organizations are expected to have certain systems, policies and procedures in place for managing and controlling business operations to reduce exposures and any negative occurrence of potential financial effect.

Exposures are inherent in the operation of any organization and may result from a variety of causes such as excessive costs, deficient revenues, and loss of assets, inaccurate accounting, business interruption, statutory sanctions, competitive disadvantage, fraud and embezzlement. Internal controls are methods and procedures used to authorize transactions and safeguard assets, encourage adherence to company policies, promote operational efficiency and ensure accurate and reliable accounting record. At a minimum, certain financial controls should be in place as part of the financial management system.

Although a large body of empirical research has been undertaken during the last five decades in the area of existing accounting policies and procedures practices of the internal control accounting system, more efforts are needed to uncover the economic, organizational and political aspects of these policies and procedures practices of the internal control. In particular, more research is needed in developing countries as the bulk of research existed to date relate to the practices in developed economies.

The Internal Control Structure and Accounting Policies and Procedures

There was a considerable agreement in the literature that the scope of internal control structure includes: (1) control environment (2) accounting information system; and (3) control policies and procedures (Felix and Niles, 1988; lea et al., 1992; Gadh et al., 1993; Felix, 1998; Kinney, 2000; O'Leary et al., 2006). The current USA auditing standards and Committee of Sponsoring Organisations (COSO) model include general statements, which suggest that the internal control structure comprises these three elements. O'Leary et al. (2006) compare these three elements of the internal control structure to the national auditing standards in USA, Australia and UK

*Corresponding author. E-mail: talha@kfupm.edu.sa.

and conclude that they are comparatively consistent.

The scope of the internal control structure can therefore, be summarized into three main elements: the control environment, the accounting information system and control policies and procedures. The control environment covers management's philosophy and operating style, organizational structure, assignment of authority and responsibility, internal audit, use of the information technology, human resources and audit committee. The accounting information system component includes database contents, data input-processing-output and inclusion in the financial report. The accounting control policies and procedures component includes segregation of duties, authorization procedures, adequate documentation, independent checks, physical controls and records (O'Leary et al., 2006).

Leary et al. (2006) found out that prior research has not studied the relative importance of the component elements of internal control structures or the consequential effects of one element on the other. They concluded that the control environment forms a critical component of the internal control structure and is considered to be the most important element mitigating the effect of other elements. Felix (1998) suggests that most of the research into the internal control evaluation has not assisted internal control evaluation. Rather, it appears to have assessed auditors and their behavior. Research that contributes to our understanding of the role of internal controls in either the management of the enterprise or external auditing has been sparse. Most research that has appeared in the last ten years with internal control content has been focused on auditor judgments rather than use of enterprise internal controls in management or auditing" (Felix, 1998: 8).

The audit profession views the internal control structure of an organization as 'management's philosophy and operating style, and all the policies and procedures adopted by management to assist in achieving the entity's objectives' (AUS 402.10). This view further suggests the internal control structure comprises various elements, as managements' philosophy and operating style is quite distinct from specific control policies and procedures. However, managements' philosophy and operating style is likely to influence the design and implementation of specific control policies and procedures (Felo, 2001).

This research contributes to this on-going empirical research by investigating and evaluating the existing accounting policies and procedures practices of the internal control accounting system and the way data and accounting information flow in two Saudi firms operate in the real estate sector. Specifically, the research stemmed from the fact that, firstly, the maintenance of accounting records in reasonable detail and accuracy, and the adequacy of the internal control structure, which includes the assessment of control environment, accounting system, and control procedures over revenue and expenditure cycles, is a management priority and responsibility. Secondly, the management choices of policies and procedures practices of the internal control is delineated in each organization to a system of clear roles and responsibilities and subjected to economic, organizational and political aspects of these policies. This study distinguishes the control environment, which represents management's overall attitude, awareness and actions, from control policies and procedures, which are the detailed set of guidelines and procedures that management establishes over information and transaction processing.

The Conceptual Framework

The theoretical framework of this paper builds on the institutional perspective. The institutional perspective literature outlined three areas of institutional economic namely: old institutional economic, new institutional economic and the socialist institutional economic.

Ahmed and Scapens (2000) distinguish three broad forms of institutionalism which have impacted, to different degrees, on accounting research: new institutional economic (NIE), new institutional sociology (NIS), and old institutional economics (OIE).

OIE approach provides a useful basis for understanding the institutionalized character of organizational routines and ruled-based behavior (Hodgson, 1988; Scapens, 1994). The OIE framework emphasizes the interplay between institutions and actions in economy and society and brings into focus both the enabling and constraining qualities of institutional (Nelson and Winter, 1982; Hodgson, 1988). In this case, whilst, existing routines and institutions may constrain individual action, by establishing more or less fixed patterns of human actions. They provide information, which enables actors in a highly complex world (Scapens, 1994).

Burns and Scapens (2000) differentiate between rules and routine. The rules are formalized statement of procedures and normally changed only at discrete intervals, where as routines are the procedures actually in use and have the potential to be a cumulative process of change as they continue to be reproduced.

Internal control policies and procedures constitute organizational rules and routines, which represent the structuring properties of institutions and the day to day actions and thoughts of organizational members. In order to understand the practices of accounting control policies and procedures, the institutional character is used to explain these practices. Although such an approach may be able to explain certain practices, it may not assist our understanding of how these practices come to be used in organizations, or the nature of resistance to their use. However, the extent to which specific routines are modified may depend on other rules and routines, including control procedures.

In this study, the rules are defined as the formal accounting control policies and procedures, as they are set out in the manual procedures. Whiles routines are the management practices actually in use. It is assumed that management practices in use may not actually replicate the system set out in the policies and procedures manual as demonstrated by Roberts and Scapens (1985).

The new institutional sociology (NIS) approach explores the process through which organizations and social agencies initiate and design structures, political and procedures in order to demonstrate conformity with institutionalized rules, value and expectations (DiMaggio, 1988; Scott, 1995; Ahmed and Scapens, 2000). NIS approach has been used to explain: (1) The role of these broader institutions in shaping organizational accounting practices (Mezias, 1990; Covaleski et al. (1993), (2) the success and survival of the firms (Ahmed and Scapens, 2000). While NIS approach explains how the institutionalized rules and values and expectations influence the firm and the design of its accounting system, it does not explore how the latter shape the institutionalized rules and values and expectations (Ahmed and Scapens, 2000).

The new institutional economics (NIE) approach focus on the analysis of market and individual rationality, and based on Williamson transaction cost approach and the two core assumptions of neoclassical economics: the rational maximizing economic agent and the general equilibrium of market forces (Scapens, 1994). While the NIE approach seeks to broaden the domain of economic analysis by examining the transactions and governance structures internal to the firm, it is used to explain the choice and use of management accounting control systems (Scapens and Arnold, 1986; Scapens, 1994; Spicer and Ballow, 1993; Colbert and Spicer, 1995).

However, NIE approach is criticized by not recognizing the impact of the broader economic, political, and social institutions, which can be important in understanding the development of accounting practices. The complex set of relationships between economic, political and social institutions is grounded in the specific context and history of the company, and this lead to limit the use of NIE model to focus on the study of accounting history and management choices within the framework of neoclassical economics approach (Ahmed and Scapens, 2000). Thus the NIS approach demonstrates the impact of external forces on the organizational norms and practices, and control and structure.

Due to the complex set of the relationship between accounting, routines and institutions, the focal point of this study is limited to OIE and NIS approaches. The NIS approach considers the external macro-focus while the OIE focus on intra-organizational behaviors. This study focuses on both approaches in order to understand: (1) the conformity with institutionalized rules and values and expectations (NIS); and the institutionalized character of organizational routines and ruled-based behavior (OIE). Subsequently, the study presents (1) the research method and data collection, (2) a description of the control environment, the accounting information system, and the control policies and procedures operating of both revenue and expenditure cycles, and (3) findings, limitations and conclusions.

RESEARCH METHOD AND DATA COLLECTION

Given the wide view in a very complex area, we were limited to exploring the internal control structure and practices and their relationship. Specifically, we describe the internal control structure and practices and how they have arisen and used over the previous years in both companies. Because of the complex set of the relationship between the variety of accounting and behavioral issues that relate to internal control structure, it is intended to use a case study method. One advantage of using this research method is that it provides the possibility of an in-depth investigation and analysis of the subject matter of research under consideration. In addition, to the rich description, the major strength is that it allows researchers to deal with a variety of evidence and internal checks including observation, interviews and documentation on its validity (Ryan et al., 2002).

The reasons for limiting the study to two cases are, firstly. It allows replication of comparative logic among individual cases. Secondly, it permits the development of rich description of budgeting practices in a wide range of circumstances, which takes into account the differences that exist between the two cases. Thirdly, it ensures that research topic itself is of a manageable size. Finally, it improves the chances of being accepted to the organization that we will be dealing with.

In this section, we provide an overview of the case study method and outline how the fieldwork was conducted. This is followed by a description of the two cases under-consideration.

The Case Study Method

Its proponents see case-based research as the salvation of accounting research from an overly normative approach to accounting theory formulation (Yin, 1984; Snow and Thomas, 1994). Many accounting researchers have shown that a case-based research strategy is particularly useful when "what, how and why" questions are being asked and when the researcher's wish is to explore new ideas (Ansari and Euske, 1987; Simons, 1990; Bakar, 1991; Berry et al., 1991; Archer and Otley, 1991). One of the major strengths of the case study is that it allows rich description of issues under considerations.

Case study research appears to have a number of potential roles to play (Scapens, 1990), but the central role seems to be that of exploration (Otley and Berry, 1994). It has been argued that the case study is more correctly a method of data collection, a point made by Scapens (1990), Llwellyn (1992) and Otley and Berry (1994). Each method of data collection has its own strengths and weaknesses. The case study allows researchers to deal with a variety of evidence and internal checks on its validity; for example, interviews, observations and documentation (Campbell and Fiske, 1959; Webb et al., 1966; Gross et al., 1971; Denzin, 1978; Yin, 1981, 1984; Hoque and Hopper, 1994; Snow and Thomas, 1994). However, the integration of such differently derived data might be confusing because of the danger of using, by accident, different epistemologies and ontological assumptions, which could lead to theoretical opportunism and incoherence (Berry et al., 1991; Hoque and Hopper, 1994). In addition, as the context of each case is particular, the findings lack generalisability (Halfpenny, 1979; Huberman and Miles, 1983; Yin, 1984; Patton, 1987; Scapens, 1990; Spicers, 1992; Otley and Berry, 1994; Snow and Thomas, 1994). Despite these criticisms, there is a prima facie case for the use of a case-based research method in a wide variety of contexts with the caveat that greater clarity concerning the initial theoretical position is needed (Scapens, 1990; Spicers, 1992; Otley and Berry, 1994). The literature on case-based research has been centered on the debate about the theoretical presuppositions of researchers. Sometimes, it was not clear whether the written case studies reflect the initial theoretical position of researchers or new positions taken up in the light of the empirical evidence available (Otley and Berry, 1994).

Some researchers (Gersick, 1988; Bettenhausen and Murnigham, 1986, Eisenhardt, 1989, 1991) switched their research focus pursuant to issues emerging during data collection. There is thus an argument that a review of theory or assumptions is an essential precursor for the case study method. "It argued that, it is incumbent upon researchers using case-based methods to be clear about their initial theoretical positions, and to interpret their results in a way, which indicates the theoretical modification the empirical observations have triggered" (Otley and Berry, 1994).

Access for Data

The data for the two case studies were collected over three-month periods. The researcher had an access to two Saudi companies operate in the real estate industry through consultation projects. Data were collected from the two companies using semi-structured questionnaires, personal interviews, written narrative, secondary data, and direct observation of group discussion and a study of archival and documentary materials.

The findings were communicated to the consulting group and participants for feedback. Personal interviews were conducted during on site-visits with the discussion group and managers at various levels of management. The time to complete an interview varied in length between ½ - 3½ h. Key personal interviews were conducted with the following key administrators and management teams in the two companies, including the managing director (CEO), the internal auditor, the chief accountant, the financial controller and accounting staff. Seven meetings were conducted during the project time. A discussion group was formed and attended by all higher management team and the consulting group. The interview techniques involved the following:

1. A semi-structured questionnaire was developed and used as a guideline during the interview to make sure that all relevant topics were covered and to help the researchers conduct the interviews in a systematic and comprehensive fashion (Berry, 1976; Otley, 1976; Patton, 1987; Murshed, 1989; Hoque, 1993).

A copy of the interview guideline was sent in advance for each company. The guideline to interview meetings served several purposes: to introduce the subject, we are interested in and the proposed method of data collection, and to stress the confidentiality of information provided the possible involvement of employees. It also emphasized the importance placed on the view of the respondents regarding their perception and attitudes towards the internal control structure and accounting policies and procedures practices, market conditions and the strategic responses of their organization.

2. Note-taking: The members of the consultant team take notes in each interview. It was found useful to take notes of selected key issues to help formulate new questions if a subject showed especial interest, to help to review the discussion when written up the manuscript text, and it makes the researcher aware of the documentary evidence deemed relevant during the interview and serve as a reminder for him to collect it.

A manuscript text was written up for each interview usually within two weeks of the day of the interview. Each manuscript text was dated, with a note where the interview took place and who was present. The texts were used together with the study of relevant documents and direct observation to formulate the empirical evidence and database for each case. In addition to the personal interview, a study of documentary materials and direct observation of the group discussion were conducted. Documents and operating statements were collected during on-site visits, including corporate plans, financial plans and budgets, progress reports, production plans and reports, internal memos, instruction for and description of internal control structure and accounting systems. There was extensive data collection of procedures manual and reports for each company.

Secondary data was collected through the consulting group and includes but not limited to organization chart, job description for key positions, user manual and accounting system documentation, which included the chart of accounts, operating and maintenance manual, forms used with the system, accounting procedures flowcharts including the Revenue and Expenditure Cycles, and the audited annual reports.

In addition, a range of documentary materials and literature relating to the real estate sector was collected. Government rules and regulations documents on the historical development and changes in the economy and international market were collected from relevant sources.

Direct observation of the group discussion during interview meeting was carried out. These firsthand observations allowed the researchers to get a close view and personal knowledge of what is happening in the company. The management at the two companies provided full support and fruitful discussion in the area under consideration. We spent a total of 9½ h of group discussion in both companies. On these meetings we were accompanied by the managing directors, divisions' coordinators and administrative areas coordinators, controllers, financial directors/managers and senior and staff accountants. Table 1 presents a summary of interviewee and interview duration. It became clear that the market pressure in both companies were similar. Tours were given at both companies to accounting divisions and departments guided by the coordinators and directors who were senior employees in the company.

A database was created for each company and was kept in separate manual files, including the manuscript text of personal interviews and the archival documentation. While the hand written notes were kept in a separate notebook for reference purposes.

At the initial stage, a report for each company was produced and continuous discussions with each company were maintained throughout this study. Such close discussion has ensured that the focus was maintained within the framework agreed at the outset. Then a first draft for each case was submitted and discussed with the relevant managers. This was used as a confirmation process to ensure that our description regarding internal control structure and control policies and procedures practices of each company were correct. No contradictory comments were made.

To further the process of confirmation, some techniques were used to validate field data. By using several sources of data including semi-structured questionnaire, personal interview, observation and documentary analysis, data from one type of source can be checked against data from another. In some cases, cross checking of the same point was carried out with different interviewees.

THE DESCRIPTION OF THE TWO CASES

This section is devoted to describe the internal control structure, which includes the study of the existing control environment, accounting information system, and control policies and procedures over revenue and expenditure cycles within the two local companies under consideration. Firstly, a brief historical background of both the company and the business sector, followed by a detailed description of the internal control structure (control environment, the accounting information system, and the control policies and procedures).

Table 1. Data Collection (Interviewee and Interview Duration).

Company name	No. of Meeting	Interviewee	Interview duration (hours)	Observation of group discussion (hours)
Case studies in real estate sector				
X	2 meetings and 1 group discussion	Managing director, chief accountant, accounting staff, Consulting group.	4	3½
Y	5 meetings and 2 group discussions	Managing director, operation coordinator, financial controller, corporate planning director, consulting group, chief accountants Accounting staff.	7	6
Total	7 meetings and 3 group discussions		11	9 ½

Company History and the Business Activities

The two cases under consideration are regional family business organizations operating in the real estate industry and located in the gulf region. The two companies have been established for long time of periods as a proprietorship and then became family partnership companies owned by family members. Both companies represent a good name in the real estate industry.

Recently, each company is conducting a project that aims to reorganize and restructure their business activities and the way they deliver their products and services in order to meet future challenges and customer expectations. In addition, they entered into franchise brokerage agreement with the international organization to support their services and develop their own portfolios and electronic platform network over the last ten years. Both companies engage in providing commercial and residential local and international real estate services, including buying, selling, leasing, marketing, management and development of real estate. Each company defines their own market segments and business lines operating in a highly competitive and innovative marketplace. They introduced various business initiatives to coop with available market opportunities. They generate their revenues from their major business lines, including the sources from Portfolio Investment, Installment Sales, Placement, and Brokerage.

A portfolio investment activity is an administrative unit responsible for the purchase and sale of raw land. Land and real estate activities include purchasing, selling, marketing and valuation of raw land and other real estate. Each company developed their own programs with owners and investors to manage financing buy and sell raw land.

The real estate placement is one of the developed programs, where the company engages in planning and development of raw land and then resells at auction to investors at higher prices. Under placement, the company is a partner in investment of at least 20 to 25% of the project and generates additional auction brokerage fees plus any additional profit and loss from sales. The company recalls unsold shares at auction and resells at installments. Another program is the real estate portfolio where the company offers its services to potential investors for predetermined fees. In addition, both companies continue their conventional business to manage real state of other owners and as a brokerage. As their main business's activities expand in terms of products, services and geographical areas, their operations become more complex, which needs to be matched with their internal control structure in order to meet competition and market changes.

The internal control structure

In this section, the three elements of the internal control structure will be described for both companies, with a view to determining strengths and weaknesses of the revenue and expenditure cycles.

The Control Environment and the Accounting Information System

Control environment is the overall attitude of management and employees about the importance of control. The control environment covers (1) management's philosophy and operating style, (2) the integrity, ethical values, and competence of an organization's employees; (3) the way the management assigns authority and responsibility (organization structure), as well as organizes and develops its business; (4) the attention and direction provided by the board of directors and audit committee. Management's philosophy about the role of internal audit, use of information technology and personnel policies and procedures of hiring, training, evaluating, compensating and promoting of employees have great effect on the control environment. The descriptions of the control environment and the accounting information system for the two companies are as follows:

The First Company: The existing organization structure of this company is relatively very simple administrative functional units and central accounting services. The family members chaired the company's main business lines, and top management emphasizes maintaining close supervision over their business activities. The company has an internal audit, which reports directly to the chief accountant in a periodic and ad-hoc basis. The company builds excellent banking relationship and network, and the company develops good knowledge of computer applications with unified and homogenous manual accounting system and reliable source of information. However, the use of computer accounting packages is limited.

It seems that the way they develop their structure is based on the existing practices rather than on the best practices available and this leads to a position where the organization structure is not well defined and updated. In addition, the description of job responsibilities for each position in the organization is not clear due to lack of formal description, especially in the accounting department where the treasurer and the controller functions combined. This of course would sometimes result into confusion in terms of assignments and duplication of efforts.

As a matter of the control environment that relates to human resources, it seems that the company hires professional employees with good background, experience planning ability and clear analysis. However, the manpower is inadequate, and the personnel policies and procedures regarding hiring process, training programs, career path, and compensation and motivation packages are not clear.

The Second Company: Over the past decade, the organization structure of this company grew in an organic manner, and followed a relatively very simple horizontal structure with minimum communication between the different administrative units and central accounting services. The recent growth and shift in the market have led the company to add more management layers, and put pressure on the company where senior executives strive to maintain its unique culture.

Currently, the organization is structured around three segments and four core business line activities. A member of the family chair the company's main business lines and top management emphasize maintaining a close relationship with investors. The company has an internal auditor who is a trusted person report directly to the group general manager in a periodic and ad-hoc basis. Under the existing organization structure, the financial controller is carrying out the dual responsibly of treasurer and controllership. This may be contributed to the lack of formal description of job responsibilities for each position in the organization which led to assignments and duplication of efforts. This of course also indicates sometimes the nature of the way family business is structured.

Due to the recent engagement with the international organization and the creation of new segments and business lines, the company is restructuring the way they conduct their business activities with emphasis on maintaining the close relationships between management and inventors.

The company has an organization structure that is currently under revision. The proposed restructuring initiatives depict the administrative arrangement within the company where organization structure gives greater power to work directly with customers and suppliers with simple reporting communication network between all levels of the organization.

The company builds excellent banking relationship and network, and develops good knowledge of computer applications and environment with a unified and homogenous manual accounting system. The computer accounting packages used by the group's entities are separate, non-integrated and not unified, and do not contain all necessary application systems with some subsidiaries and business segments using only the manual system.

It seems that the organization structure is not well defined and updated where the revisions in practice have apparently not been documented formally and reflected in the existing organization structure. This might be explained by the fact that the increasing complexity of business activities and the new restructuring will influence the internal control structure, reporting requirements and the accounting system in general and will be reflected later in their future constructs on both their business activities and the types of information needed by the management team.

The company gives a considerable attention to human resources of their organization by hiring professional well-paid employees and reasonable employment positions. However, the manpower is inadequate due to rapid market growth and shortage of qualified manpower supply. In addition, the personnel policies and procedures regarding hiring process, training programs, career path, and compensation and motivation packages are not clear.

The Revenue and Expenditure Cycles and Accounting Policies and Procedures Practices

In this section, the revenue and expenditure cycles will be described for both companies, with a view to determining strengths and weaknesses of the existing accounting policies and procedures practices. Two processing steps are considered in the revenue cycle: the sales processing system and cash receipts processing system. In addition, two processing steps are considered in the expenditure cycle: the purchase processing system and cash disbursement processing system.

The Existing Sale and Collection Model

The essential purpose of the revenue cycle is to facilitate the exchange of products and services with customers for cash. The revenue cycle composes of the sales processing system and cash receipts processing. Sales involve cash and credit sales. The control points over sales processing include receiving the sales order, checking the customer's credit, order processing and delivering, and billing the customers. The control points over cash receipts processing include the receipt of cash, the processing of the cash deposit, and the posting of cash amounts to the ledgers. This section describes the exiting accounting policies and procedures practices related to the sales processing system and cash receipts processing system for both companies.

The First Company

Company differentiates between sales of land and real estate of the company and other owners, and the services provided by the company to them. Based on the accounting manuals of the company, the sales processing system for land and real estate as a source of revenue is described as follows: the sales process (or rent) begins in sales department with a receipt of customer to the company place or through telephone call.

The company salesperson welcomes the customer and tries to define and comply with customer's specifications and record his order in a requisite lists for future follow up. Upon meeting the customer's specification, the salespersons negotiate the sale price and brokerage fees, then prepare sales order authorized by sales manager, and then send the order to ownership department. Upon receiving the sales order, the ownership department prepares the sales contract and release and sends the release document to surveying department for approving compliance with specification. Upon approval by the surveying department, the ownership department sends the three documents including sales order, sales contract and release document to the accounting department to sign the contract and release document and to make sure that the sale amount will be paid in full. Then the ownership department follows up the change of ownership legal procedures and updates its inventory accounts for records and future follow up, and then sends copies of sales contract, release documents and the check to the accounting department for record purposes.

The accounting department receives the checks and prepares check receipt voucher with two copies. One copy is kept in the department. The original and the other copy with checks are sent to the cashier. The cashier receives and signs the check receipt voucher; give the original to the payee, then prepares an original and a copy of the daily cash lists. The cashier sends the copy of the check receipt voucher and the daily cash lists to the auditing unit for verification and then send them to the accounting department for GL posting and record. In the payment day, the accountants prepare a deposit slip and a deposit lists and sends them to the cashier for deposit in the bank.

The Second Company

Based on the accounting manuals of the company, the sales processing system for their major sources of revenues is described as follows: Cash sales sign the contract and then send the contract to the chief accountant for recording the transaction. Credit sales sign temporary contract and then send the contract to chief accountant for credit approval. Upon approval, the customer signs the binding contract and the chief accountant records the transaction. Sales contract is the only document used in this company in sales processing system. Accounting department received checks, prepares remittance advice, and then sends them to cashier. The cashier prepares deposit slips and sends copies for GL posting.

The Existing Purchasing and Payment Model

The essential purpose of the expenditure cycle is to facilitate the exchange of products and services with suppliers for cash. The expenditure cycle composes of the purchasing processing system and cash disbursements processing system. The control points over purchase processing include receiving the purchase requisition, preparing the purchase order, receiving goods/services, checking invoices. The control points over cash disbursement processing include the ascertaining the validity of the payment obligation, preparing the cash disbursement, the processing of the cash disbursement, and the posting to the ledgers. This section describes the exiting accounting policies and procedures practices related to the purchase processing system and cash disbursement processing system for both companies.

The First Company

The company differentiates between land and real estate purchasing and other inventory purchasing. Based on the manual, the inventory purchasing processing system starts with filling a purchase requisition approved and authorized by the requesting department including warehouse manager. The requisition is sent to a costing department for balance verification and then to the purchasing department. The purchasing department asks for bidding, and tenders and prepares a purchase order for the winning supplier. The purchase order is then authorized, and copies (six copies) are sent to supplier, warehouse, receiving, requesting and accounting department.

Upon receiving goods, a committee of technical and financial persons headed by the warehouse manager and the presence of the custodian of the inventory prepares an inspection memorandum. The custodian of inventory including warehouse department prepares receiving reports with three copies. A copy of the receiving report is sent to the accounting department. The invoice is sent to warehouse, purchasing and trading managers for verification and comparison with the purchase order and then to the auditing unit for revision. The accounting department receives the invoice from the auditing unit, compares the invoice with the purchase order, inspection memorandum and the receiving reports, and prepares check (or cash) payment slip.

The land and real estate purchasing is similar to the sales procedures except it is requested that the general manager (MD) appoints a person from the sales department to evaluate and follow up. Sales, surveying, and ownership departments perform similar procedures to sales processing, prepare purchasing contract and the accounting department reviews the documents, and issues the check.

The Second Company

The company differentiates between purchasing national purchasing and international purchasing. Based on the manual, the national purchasing processing system starts with filling a purchase requisition approved and authorized. The requisition is sent to the purchasing department. The purchasing department asks for bidding, and tenders sand prepares a purchase order for winning supplier. The purchase order is then authorized and copies are sent to supplier, receiving, and accounting department.

Upon receiving goods, a committee of requesting department and, purchasing department prepares receiving and inspection memorandum. The receiving department prepares receiving reports. A copy of the receiving report is sent to accounting department. The accounting department receives the invoice from the supplier, compares the invoice with purchase order, inspection memorandum and the receiving reports, and prepares check payment slip.

The foreign and international purchasing is similar to the local and national purchasing except it is requested that the purchasing department prepare a line credit and overdraft order, and the accounting department authorizes it.

Observations from the Two Cases

The control environment and the Accounting Information System

This section accentuates observations related to control environment and accounting information system for both cases. These observations take into account the overall attitude of management and employees' philosophy and operating style. Factors included within the control environment and accounting information system are: internal audit, assignment of authority and responsibility (organizational structure), human resources, use of information technology, database contents, data input-processing-output and inclusion in the financial report.

In both cases, the management at all levels lacked awareness of the overall policies and procedures used to direct operations toward desired goals, ensure accurate financial reports, and ensure compliance with applicable laws and regulations with minimum attention and direction provided by the board of directors or group general manager. This partly may be contributed by the lack of compliance to policies and procedures due to the inadequacy in the internal audit function and inadequate manpower or because organizational support attention may be directed to only some of the problem areas.

The management's philosophy emphasizes maintaining close supervision over their business activities and close relationship between management, suppliers and customers. This led family members to chair the company's main business lines. The first company has a small board of directors consist of 2 to 3 family members while the second company has 5 to 6 members who consider being a moderate size.

All members of the board are heavily involved in running their businesses and their background is varied. Nevertheless, the recent engagement with a total quality philosophy put pressures on both companies to think about how they conduct their business and restructure the way they do their business activities. However, less effort was devoted to the question of where they want to be in the future and how they cope with the recent changes in a real estate market. Under the new initiatives, both companies involve in a strategic planning project through which they determine their visions, missions, objectives and goals, and then they construct their organization structure on this basis to meet competition and market changes. Of course, the new restructuring will influence the internal control structure, reporting requirements and the accounting system in general.

The two companies have an audit function unit where internal auditor reports directly to either the chief accountant or to the general manager of the company.

However, there is a lack of proper internal auditing practices were the internal auditor possibly substitutes the functions of other that may not even be appropriate for the position. This seems a bit too ambitious when considering the existing practices of the auditing unit. Even so, the private companies are not required by the law to have an internal audit unit, both companies try to establish an internal audit unit devoted to internal auditing activities including financial and operational compliance. This might be explained by the fact that they may want to meet the expectation of external institutional pressures of financial and investor sectors.

Both companies give considerable attention to the human resources factor by hiring professional well-paid employees with good background, experience planning ability and clear analysis. However, the manpower is inadequate, and the personnel policies and procedures regarding hiring process, training programs, career path, and compensation and motivation packages are not clear. This may be contributed to both the rapid market growth and the shortage of qualified manpower supply. The overwhelming volume of work, the severe shortage in the number of qualification of employees, and lack of proper training programs put pressures on the shoulders' of their employees to meet the management expectations and carry out their functional responsibilities.

The two companies implement a manual accounting system and separate non-integrated accounting packages in certain subsidiaries. The accounting packages currently used by the group's entities are not unified and limited to a general ledger, do not contain all necessary financial and accounting application systems and some subsidiaries are still using manual accounting systems. This, therefore, creates a need to use other time consuming tools to prepare the required reports including excel sheets.

Using the manual accounting systems is a time consuming process and increases the demand on human resources. Moreover, implementing manual accounting systems in certain subsidiaries and separate non-integrated accounting packages in other subsidiaries restrict the management ability to prepare accurate and timely consolidated financial statements at the group level. The generated financial reports by the existing accounting system are not adequate, for example, financial reports are currently limited to two financial statements (balance sheet and income statement) and do not include the cash flow statement. It seems that when they report they do not comply with presentation and disclosure requirements. This may be explained by the fact that it is quite understandable that the private company is not required by law to comply with GAAP presentation and disclosure requirements.

Nevertheless, clearly the company pursued good accounting practices to enhance their financial position, but the current accounting system focuses on the book keeping activities and generating financial statement.

Limited attention is paid for other internal financial reports, including accounting receivable and collection, payroll and compensation, assets utilization. Managerial reports are completely ignored where there is no evidence of preparation of any formal financial budgets at both subsidiaries and group levels.

Given the current situation of the market opportunities, considerable attention has been paid by the management at both companies to incorporate additional financial reports emerged due to business expansion (for example, placement) including customer and product profitability, and divisional and business unit performance evaluation.

Accounting Policies and Procedures Practices

This section highlights the observations related to the accounting policies and procedure, including segregation of duties, authorization procedures, adequate document-tation, independent checks, physical controls and records for both companies. Segregation of duties is overlapping functions; confusion to whom they should report to. Lack of clear duties, proper training, and function overloading creates a problem of confusion.

Clearly, at both companies, there are inadequate policies and control procedures in certain areas of operations related to cash processing and order processing system. For example, it is possible that account receivable is increasing with expansion of business, while there are no clear credit policies and procedures or the billing procedures are not clear, which may hinder financial control. Billing procedures are subjected to wide variations depending on the type of sales and industry (cash, credit or installments).

Based on the manual and leaf lets, it is clearly written that (1) in the case of delay of payments by customers, follow up may be conducted by sales, accounting department or management, (2) accounting department issues and record checks while Purchases handles LCs and decides on payment terms. Obviously, formal description of job responsibilities for each position in the organization is not clear, especially in the accounting department where the treasurer and the controller functions combined. This of course would sometimes result into confusion in terms of assignments and duplication of efforts.

The existing accounting system does not have a clear written chart of accounts and coding in the accounting policies and procedures. Furthermore, it is not clear whether the existing manual match with the existing end user manual of existing computer packages. It seems that the accounting system is a bookkeeping driven system with weaknesses and inadequate policies and control procedures in certain areas of operation. Certain subsidiaries have drafted some policies and procedures but these are not yet complete and have not been formally approved to date. The absence of formally approved financial policies and procedures covering all aspects of the business creates uncertainty and inconsistency with regards to processes, standards, responsibilities, controls and chart of accounts.

The internal control policies and procedures (the rules) of order processing for both sales and purchasing is generally reasonable. However, compliance to these procedures (the routine) is questionable. Management attention has been paid to revise the existing control policies and procedures related to sales processing in order to expand their credit sales market. Currently, sales processing starts in the sales department without any consideration to obtain verification of credit authorization from the credit department for credit sales. It could be the case that the credit sales are at a minimum. Therefore, the second company introduces a billing department because there is a limited number of internal control procedures impeded in the company practices related to sales order processing system due to the missing of a credit and billing department. This department plays an essential role in follow up and preparing the sales journal vouchers to the accounting department for GL posting.

Based in the provided accounting manuals, the purchasing processing system starts with filling a purchase requisition approved and authorized. The requisition is sent to the purchasing department. The purchasing department asks for bidding, and tenders and prepares a purchase order for winning supplier. The purchase order will be authorized, and copies will be sent to the supplier, receiving, and accounting department. Upon receiving goods, a committee of requesting department and purchasing department prepares the receiving and inspection memorandum. The receiving department prepares receiving reports. A copy of the receiving report will be sent to the accounting department for payment arrangements.

In general, the cash processing of collecting and disbursement procedures sound good in both companies. In case of collections, accounting department received checks and then sends them to cashier. The cashier prepares deposit slip and sends a copy for GL posting. The Mailroom prepares a remittance list and sends copies to cashier and accounting department. Accounting department receives remittance advice and cashier receives checks. The cashier prepares deposit slip and cash receipts listing (journal voucher), and deposits the fund in the bank and sends the listing to the accounting department. Controller reconciles receipts and verifies all documents of remittance list, journal vouchers and deposit tickets. In case of payment, the accounting department authorizes checks and then sends them to cashier. Treasurer verifies all documents before preparing check. Controller compares the amount and payee's name on returned check with check authorization.

Conclusion and Direction for Future Research

NIS approach is used to explain how external institutions influence accounting system and their associated behavior (James, 2009; Abernethy and Chua, 1996; Bealing, 1994; Berry et al., 1985; Carpenter and Feroz, 1992; Covaleski et al., 1993; Hoque and Alam, 1999). Accounting information plays an extensive role throughout the entire organization as it searches to conform to and represents itself in some form of rationality in order to gain legitimacy to its external influences (Meyer and Rowan, 1977). NIS approach suggests that reforms would prompt organizations of an affected field to change, that is, defensive responses to changing notions of what constitutes a legitimate organizational practice (James, 2009; DiMaggio and Powell, 1991).

Recently, accounting researchers have used NIS to explain the success and survival of firms in terms of the extent to which they encapsulate social values and expectations in their organizational structures and behavior. Over the last decay, real estate sector operates in a highly competitive and innovative marketplace. The market pressure and external forces of other institutional players, including funders, professionals and investors have a dynamic impact on the adoptive nature of organizational behavior and companies within this sector find themselves immersed in a certain cultural and historical context.

As part of the management's philosophy at both companies, it was found that management is proactive in the concerns of organizational competitiveness and endeavor to incorporate components into the design that enhance an organization's ability to be rational, competitive, and consistent with the needs and objects of external institutions. It is clearly that the management tries to legitimize the organization and its management's philosophy to cope with external forces.

Each company is conducting a project that aims to define their own market and to reorganize and restructure their business activities and the way they deliver their products and services in order to meet future challenges and customer expectations. The accounting information plays an extensive role throughout the entire organization as it searches for, conforms to, and presents itself in some form of rationality in order to gain legitimacy to its external influences. For example, the second company considers a strategic planning project through which they determine their visions, missions, objectives and goals, and then they construct their organization structure on these bases to meet competition and market changes. Of course, the new restructuring will influence the internal control structure, reporting requirements and the accounting system in general.

Management at both companies considers cash processing of collection and disbursement procedures critical to maintaining the excellent banking relationship. Even so, the chief accounting officer carries out the duals' responsibilities of treasurer and controllership. Cash processing procedures and documentation flow is quite good and reasonable and both companies develop a sound and reasonable control over cash inflows and outflows. It seems that because of the overwhelming volume of work under the severe shortage in number and qualification of employee, the accounting department is just performing the daily operations, and to some extent, the main financial operations. However, management responsible to make sure that the accounting system and control procedures over cash processing are functioning and consistent with banking requirements that play the essential part in their businesses.

The observations and evidence from the two cases show that: (1) the process of institutionalization involves the creation of new structures, processes and roles that later become routines, formalized and embedded in the organizational constitution, (2) the accounting information plays an extensive role throughout the entire organization as it searches for, conforms to, and presents itself in some form of rationality in order to gain legitimacy to its external influences, and (3) the NIS approach explains how external institutions influence accounting systems and their associated behavior (Norhayati and Siti-Nabila, 2009; James, 2009; Hoque and Alam, 1999; Abernethy and Chua, 1996; Bealing, 1994; Berry et al., 1985; Carpenter and Feroz, 1992; Covaleski et al., 1993; Zucker, 1987; Meyer and Rowan, 1977).

Clearly, the NIS explained the institutionalizing process at the macro level and suggests that the impact of the competitive and innovative market and reforms prompt organizations of an affected field to change and attempt to model structures to appear legitimate. The adoptive nature of organizational behavior is defensive responses to changing notions of what constitutes a legitimate organizational practice (James, 2009; DiMaggio and Powell, 1991; Norhayati and Siti-Nabila, 2009). It seems that the NIS fairly explained how the institutional pressures motivate management to cope with external forces but does not explain the institutionalizing process at the micro level which involved social actions and interactions in individual organizations. OIE, on the other hand, helps to explain the change in the habits and routines of organizational members. The OIE approach explores the complex and ongoing relationship between actions and institutions, and demonstrates the importance of organizational rules and routines and institutions in shaping exiting accounting practices (Norhayati and Siti-Nabila, 2009).

OIE approach is used to explore the existing accounting practices as institutionalized routines, which enable organizations to function, reproduce and legitimate behavior, and achieve organizational cohesion (Scapens, 1994; Burns and Scapens, 2000). It argued that accounting as institutionalized routines creates understanding of activities according to particular sets of accounting rules and procedures, which enable decisions to be made and activities to be undertaken in a complex and uncertain world.

The OIE provides a useful basis for understanding the institutional characteristics and implementation of accounting policies and procedures. According to Burns and Scapens (2000), the new rules and routines might be institutionalized if the new system challenges the prevailing institutions. However, organizational members who champion the new system may use power to enable the change. Although it could lead to the enactment of the new rules and routines, it stayed at the level of ceremonial implementation. It means the rules and routines could be implemented but not translated into the daily of the organization (Norhayati and Siti-Nabiha, 2009).

Based on the observation from the first company, it seems that the way they develop their internal control structure is based on the existing practices rather than on the best practices available and this leads to a position where the organization structure is shaped within existing routines and institutions. It is clear that organizational member's position recognizes that the formal rules and informal routines can be changed and if the change is consistent with the existing routines and institutions it is easier to be achieved than change, which challenges those rules and institutions. However, the recent growth and shift in the market have led the company to add more management layers, and put pressure on the company where senior executives strive to maintain its unique culture. Even so, both companies develop a sound and reasonable control over cash inflows and outflows. The existing reporting system does not generate cash flow statement. This may be explained by the fact that it is quite understandable that the private company is not required by law to comply with GAAP presentation and disclosure requirements.

The internal control policies and procedures (the rules) of order processing for both sales and purchasing is generally reasonable. However, compliance to these procedures (the routine) is questionable in both companies. For example, sales processing starts in the sales department without any consideration to obtain verification of credit authorization from the credit department for credit sales. It could be the case that the credit sales are at a minimum. Lately, management attention has been paid to revise the existing control policies and procedures related to sales processing in order to expand their credit sales market. The market pressure and external forces of the institutional players, including legal and regularity system seem to exert pressure on the management of both companies in multiple and complex ways resulting in a response aiming at legitimacy rather than efficiency.

As such, although the selection of the 'new' accounting system may be based on efficiency criteria, it may not necessarily be optimal in the neo-classical economic sense, but is likely to represent a 'satisfactory' solution in a rational sense. Neo-classical economic theory is more concerned with predicting the rational or 'optimal' outcomes, rather than explaining the unfolding processes in moving from one equilibrium state to another. However, it will be path- dependent, in that the existing routines and institutions will shape the selection and implementation process. If, over time, the emerging routines become widely accepted in the organization such that they become the unquestionable form of management control, then they can be said to be institutionalized. As such, they are more than a set of routine procedures required by senior management and implemented by accountants; they are an inherent feature of the management control process, and represent the expected form of behavior and define the relations between the various groups (Burn ad Scapens, 2000).

Accounting control policies and procedures at both companies seems to be mainly driven by external institutional pressures rather than technical pressures. The routines which emerge in the two companies may be difficult to predict. However, they are not arbitrary, they can be explained where the selection of the new accounting system may be quite intentional and rational, and in a business organization will probably reflect a concern for economic efficiency while they construct normative models of organizational legitimacy. As changes occur in the institutional rules that define legitimacy, organizations respond by voluntarily adopting recommended changes or by giving the appearance of having adopted changes in order to appear legitimate (DiMaggio and Powell, 1991; Meyer and Rowan, 1977).

In conclusion, firstly, it was found that the accounting control policies and procedures practices at the two companies are closely similar while the control environment and accounting information system differs. Secondly, this study demonstrates the importance of organizational routines and institutions in shaping the internal control and accounting policies and procedures practices. Thirdly, it was found that at the macro level the NIS approach explains how external institutions influence both the control environment and the accounting information system, while the OIE approach provides a useful basis for understanding the institutional characteristic of the existing accounting policies and procedures practices at the micro level.

An interpretation of the results is that the control environment forms a critical component of the internal control structure and is considered the most important element mitigating the effect of the accounting control policies and procedures practices. This is in conformance of auditing practices and the audit profession views, which suggests that the internal control structure comprises various elements and represents the management's philosophy and operating style, which is distinct from the control policies and procedures adopted by management to assist in achieving the organization's objectives. This study provides useful insights for understanding the rules of internal control policies and procedures and the routine of compliance to these procedures.

ACKNOWLEDGEMENTS

The author would like to gratefully acknowledge the excellent research facilities and other support provided by King Fahd University of Petroleum and Minerals, Dhahran, Saudi Arabia, to carry out this work.

REFERENCES

Abernethy MA, Chua WF (1996). A field study of control systems redesign: the impact of institutional processes on strategic choice. Contemporary Account. Res. 13:569-606.

Ahmed MN, Scapens W (2000). Cost Allocation in Britain: Towards an Institutional Analysis. Eur. Account. Rev. 9(2):159-204.

Ansari SL, Euske KJ (1987). Rational, Rationalising and Reifying Uses of Accounting Data In Organisations. Account. Organ. Soc. 12(6):549-570.

Archer S, Otley DT (1991). Strategy, Structure, Planning and Control Systems and Performance Evaluation: Rumenco Ltd. Manag. Account. Res. 2(4):263-303.

Bakar M (1991). The Study of Budgets and the Processes of budgeting in an Organisation Context. Unpublished PhD Thesis. University of Manchester.

Bealing, Jr. W (1994).'Actions speak louder than words: An institutional perspective on the Securities and Exchange Commission', Account. Organ. Soc. pp.555-567.

Berry AJ (1976). Control of capital investment.Unpublished Ph.D. Thesis. Victoria University of Manchester.

Berry AJ, Capps T, Cooper D, Ferguson P, Hopper T, Lowe EA (1985). Management control in an area of the NCB: rationales of accounting practices in a public enterprise. Account. Organ. Soc. 10(3):3-28.

Berry AJ, Laughton E, Otley DT (1991). Control in a Financial Service Company (RIF): A Case Study. Manag. Account. Res. 2(2):109-139.

Burns J, Scapens RW (2000). Conceptualizing Management Accounting Change: an Institutional Framework. Manage. Account. Res. 11:3-25.

Campbell DT, Fiske DW (1959). Convergent and Discriminant Validation by the Multitrait Multimethod Matrix. Psychol. Bullet. 56:81-105.

Carpenter VL, Feroz EH (1992). GAAP as a symbol of legitimacy: New York state's decision to adopt generally accepted accounting principles. Account. Organ. Soc. 17:613-43.

Colbert GJ, Spicer BH (1995). Multi-case Investigation of a Theory of the Transfer Pricing Process. Account. Organ. Soc. 29:423-456.

Covaleski M, Dirsmith M, Michelman J (1993). An institutional theory perspective on the DRG framework, case-mix accounting systems and health care organizations. Account. Organ. Soc. 18(1):65-80.

Denzin NK (1978). The Research Act. New York: McGraw-Hill.

DiMaggio PJ (1988). Interest and Agency in Institutional Theory, In: Zucker LG (Ed.), Institutional Patterns and Organizations: Culture and Environment. Cambridge. MA. Ballinger.

DiMaggio PJ, Powell WW (1991). Introduction, In: Powell WW, DiMaggio PJ (Eds), The New Institutionalism in Organizational Analysis. The University of Chicago Press.

Eisenhardt KM (1989). Building Theories from Case Study Research. Acad. Mamage. J. 14(4):532-550.

Eisenhardt KM (1991). Better Stories and Better Constructs: The Case for Rigor and Comparative Logic. Acad. Manag. Rev. 16(3):620-627.

Felix Jr. WL (1998). Internal Control: The Ten Years Since Treadway. University of Kansas. Auditing Symposium.

Felix Jr, WL, Niles MS (1988). Research in Internal Control Evaluation. Audit. J. Pract. Theory 7(2):43-60.

Felo AJ (2001). Ethics Programs, Board Involvement, and Potential Conflicts of Interest in Corporate Governance. J. Bus. Ethics 32(3):205-218.

Gadh VM, Krishnan R, Peters JM (1993). Modeling Internal Controls and Their Evaluation. Audit. J. Pract. Theory (12 Supplement):113-129.

Gersick C (1988). Time and Transition in Work Teams: Toward a New Model of Group Development. Acad. Manag. J. 31:9-41.
Gross N, Giacquinta JB, Bernatein M (1971). Implementing Organisational Innovation. New York: Basic Book.
Halfpenny P (1979). The Analysis of Qualitative Data. Soc. Rev. 27(4):799-825.
Hodgson G (1988). Economics and institutions: a manifesto for a modern institutional economics. Cambridge: Polity Press.
Hoque Z (1993). Management Control in Public Sector Enterprises: A Case Study of Budgeting in the Jute Industry of Bangladesh. Unpublished PhD Thesis. University of Manchester.
Hoque Z, Hopper TM (1994). Rationality, Accounting and Politics: A Case Study of Management Control in a Bangladeshi Jute Mill. Manage. Account. Res. 5(1):5-30.
Hoque Z, Alam M (1999). TQM adoption, institutionalism and changes in management accounting systems: a case study. Account. Bus. Res. 29(3):199-210.
Huberman A, Miles MB (1983). Drawing Valid Meaning from Qualitative Data: Some Techniques of Data Reduction and Display. Qual. Quant. 17:281-339.
Llewellyn S (1992). The Role of Case Study Methods in Management Accounting and Research: A comment. Br. Account. Rev. 24:17-32.
James W (2009). Rationality, institutionalism and accounting change: Understanding a performance management system within an Australian public sector entity. J. Account. Organ. Change 5(3):362-389.
Kinney Jr. WR (2000). Research Opportunities in Internal Control, Quality and Quality Assurance. Audit. A J. Pract. Theory 19Supplement:83-90.
Lea RB, Adams SJ, Boykin RF (1992). Modeling of the Audit Risk Assessment Process at the Assertion Level Within an Account Balance. Audit. A J. Pract. Theory. 11Supplement: 152-179.
Meyer JW, Rowan B (1977). Institutionalized organisations: formal structure as myth and ceremony, in Powell WW and DiMaggio PJ (Eds), The New Institutionalism in Organizational Analysis. The University of Chicago Press. Chicago. IL.
Murshed AJ (1989). The Role of Financial Information in Collective Bargaining in a Developing Country: The Case of Bangladesh. Unpublished PhD Thesis. University of Manchester.
Nelson RR, Winter SG (1982). *An Evolutionary Theory of Economic Change*, Bolston, MA: Harvard University Press.
Norhayati MA, Siti-Nabiha AK (2009). A case study of the performance management system in a Malaysian government linked company. J. Account. Organ. Change 5(2):243-276
O'Leary C, Iselin E, Sharma D (2006). The Relative Effects of Elements of Internal Control on Auditors' Evaluations of Internal Control. Pac. Account. Rev. 18(2):69-96.
Otley D (1976). Budgetary Control and Managerial Behaviour. Unpublished Ph.D. Thesis. University of Manchester. Manchester Business School.
Otley DT, Berry AJ (1994). Case Study Research in Management Accounting and Control. Manage. Account. Res. 5:5-65
Patton MQ (1987). How to Use Qualitative Methods in Evaluation. Beverly Hills. CA: Sage Publications.
Scapens RW (1990). Researching management accounting practice: the role of case study methods. Br. Account.Rev. 22:259-281.
Scapens RW (1994). Never mind the gap: towards an institutional perspective of management accounting practices. Manage. Account. Res. 5(3/4):301-321.
Scapens RW, Arnold J (1986). Economics and Management Accounting Research, In: Scapens RW, Burns J (1996). The Institutionalization of Accounting Routines: Ferac International, published in the Annual Collection of Wards Trnst Seminar Papers. Glasgow University.
Scott WR (1995). Institutions and Organizations. London. Sage Publications.
Simons R (1990). The Role of Management Control Systems in Creation of Competitive Advantage. Account. Organ. Soc. 15(1/2):127-143.
Snow CC, Thomas JB (1994). Field Research Methods in Strategic Management: Contributions to Theory Building and Testing. J. Manag. Stud. 31:457-480.
Spicers HB (1992). The Resurgence of Cost and Management Accounting: A Review of Some Recent Developments in Practice Theories and Case research Methods. Manag. Account. Res. 3:1-37.
Webb EJ, Campbell DT, Schwartz RD, Schresr L (1966). Unobrusive Measures: Non-reactive Research in the Social Science. Chicago: Rand McNally.
Yin R (1981). The Case Study Research: Some Answers. Admin. Sci. Quart. 1(26):58-65.
Yin R (1984). Case Study Research: Design and Methods, Beverly Hills. Cal: Sage Publications.
Zucker LG (1987). Institutional theories of organization. Ann. Rev. Sociol. 13:443-464.

Comparing the relationship between interest rate changes in Shariah banking system of Iran and informal USA, Britain, Australia and Japan exchange rates in the Iranian economy according to the international Fisher theory

Mohamadreza Abdoli and Hassan Valiyan

Department of Accounting, Shahrood Branch, Islamic Azad University, Shahrood, Iran.

This study has dealt with the relationship between the informal United States dollar rate and the Islamic system based interest rate of Iran and it also has compared with the informal exchange rates of Britain, Australia and Japan. The relevant data during 1991 to 2009 have been employed to compare the results. The unit root test, Dickey-Fuller, Durbin-Watson, White tests and the least-square estimate model have been used along with software Eviews7 and SPSS17 in this study. Our results unveiled a meaningful relationship between the interest rate in Iran, relying on the shariah system, and informal USD[1], GBP[2], and AUD[3] rates. However, no meaningful relationship was found between the interest rate and informal JPY[4] rate. Similarly, the results of such comparisons imply a stronger relationship between the interest rate and informal USD rate to other mentioned informal exchange rates. The coefficients of determination between interest rate in Iran and informal exchange rates of USD, GBP and AUD are 23, 20 and 16%, respectively. Accordingly, relying on the interest rate changes, changes of the informal USD rate enjoys more explanatory power than changes of the informal GBP and AUD rates.

Key words: Exchange rate, interest rate in Shariah system, Islamic finance, theory of international Fisher effect.

INTRODUCTION

During the recent decades numerous efforts have been exerted to regulate the interest rate. In fact, the remarkable effect of such variable on solving or making economic problems and turmoil in some societies has provoked the mentioned efforts. The exchange rate is defined as a key and important variable for policy making and its importance is so high that it is referred to as nominal anchor by a group of experts, particularly across the developing countries. Exchange transactions rate is drastically influenced by the financial factors particularly interest rate. Many authors believe in direct effect of interest rate on the exchange rate. The exchange rate specifies business process, capital flows, foreign direct investment, inflation, international storage and payments in a certain economy (Aziz, 2008; Serven, 2002).

When stock market investors assail the currency

of a certain country, then controlling the exchange rate, even under governmental supports, can become very costly and even futile policy. High interest rate impedes return of capital and hence scratches the economy (Solnik, 2000; Gould and Nelson, 1979).

Several factors can change the exchange rate: Foreign demand and supply changes, problems on repaying dues, inflation growth, interest rate, national incomes, financial supervisions and changes of predictions and stock market (Fisher, 1930; Johnson, 1976; Khalwaty, 2000).

Zaher and Kabir (2001) and Tarek and Kabirhassan (2001) review on the Comparative Literature of Islamic Finance and Western Banking system have dealt with analysis of the mentioned systems and their differences. These systems have substantial differences; of course the common tools used in the Islamic banking system suffer some problems and challenges related to depositors; however, they can progress quickly along with capitalism-based western banking system.

Iran is an Islamic country and takes advantage of Islamic principles, known as Islamic contact, to govern its banking system. Islamic contracts allow banks to grant loans to people and to invest indirectly. In this system, depositors will share in the banks investments which are conducted using their funds; hence, they are shared in profit/loss due to the contract. But depositors in the western banking system expect fixed and predetermined interests for their deposits in banks, so apart from banks status (loss/profit), they will receive the firm profits during the contract period (Schreiner, 2010; Sargent, 2010; Hedayati, 2000).

The 11 constituting Islamic contracts which form the Islamic economy are (Law of Bank Islamic, 1979; Hedayati, 2000; Zarrokh, 2010):

Garzolhasaneh: Is a kind of contract in which a party transfers a certain amount of his/her assets to another in the present time. In return, the debtor is bound to return the same asset or its value during a certain period without any interest; such funds are spent on charity and welfare works. Bank would be a party and another party would be its customer.

Mozarebe: Is a kind of contract in which bank supplies the capital as a party and the other party begins to trade using the capital and finally the obtained profits will be divided between both parties.

Mosharekat Madani: Is a business contract by which two or more real or legal entities including bank combine their cash or non-cash capitals in a common mode in order to make profit.

Mosharekat Hogogi: is a kind of contract by which a bank supplies a part of required capital for new stock companies or it buys a part of shares of the current stock companies and will participate in their profits.

Installment sales: According to their customers' written requirement, banks will purchase machineries and facilities whose useful life is more than 1 year and then sell them to their customers in installment.

Salaf: Bank will purchase the upcoming products of enterprises such as factories in forward; such enterprises sell their products in the framework of this contract to bank and take facilities in return.

Capital lease: Is another facilities granted by banks in which it is provided that the tenant (mainly housing constructors) must be the owner of the property at the end of rental term (in the case of fulfilling all terms of contract). Such contracts usually are concluded in the housing field and are paid by banks to housing constructors.

Joaleh: According to this contract the employer is bound to pay a certain commission to the agent in return of his/her certain act.

Mozareaeh: Under terms of this contract bank lends a land for a certain period to another party for cultivation. Finally, the obtained interests are divided between both parties.

Mosagat: A contract between the owner of an orchard/garden with another party in which the latter safeguards the garden and harvests its products in return of a part of the products.

According to the International Fisher effect, the foreign exchanges with the relatively high interest rates will be depreciated over time, because high nominal interest rate reflects the expected inflation rate (Madura, 2000). The theory also specifies that point exchange rate changes between two countries will try to homogenize nominal interest rate changes (Demirag and Goddard, 1994).

In this study, we try to answer these questions that firstly, whether there is a relation between interest rate and informal exchange rate in the Iranian economy and secondly, which one of the mentioned informal exchange rates have more explanatory power in the Iranian economy.

LITERATURE AND DEVELOPMENT HYPOTHESIS

Aziz (2008) has analyzed the role of the exchange in trade balance in Bangladesh. His results indicated that the real exchange rate positively affects both short and long-term trades in Bangladesh and he concluded that high instability of exchange rate, for any reason, will bring about macroeconomic variables such as inflation, high interest rate and/or restrictions on money supply. Ogaki and Santaella (2005) examined experimentally the effects of interest rate on exchange rate in Mexico and they have come to the conclusion that 1-month and 3-month interest rate fluctuations in Mexico have exerted an inverse effect on exchange rate of the country.

Bhati and Bhati (2011) have embarked on analysis of the Islamic shariah-based corporate governance system and they presented a relevant model. Their model is relied on the Koranic instructions, more and more transparency and revelation, loyalty in the accounting and economic professional demeanor and reporting truth.

Zettelmeyer (2003) has analyzed the relation between exchange rate and interest rate in Chile and studied the domestic money policy and its impacts on exchange rate in Chile since September 1999 and he found an inverse relation between exchange rate and interest rate.

Zhonzia (2003), in China during 1980 to 2002 has examined the relation between interest rate and exchange rate. For China's economy, he concludes that during unprecedented and oriented reforms of the market during two past decades both the real exchange rate as well as balance of payments have exerted considerable impact on each other.

Kandil (2000), studied on relation of fluctuations of exchange rate and interest rate and has found that exchange rate fluctuations in dramatically depend on the daily interest rate. MacDonald and Nagayasu (1999) have embarked on analyzing the relationship between the long-term interest rate and real exchange rate and they used the panel data of 14 industrial countries to conduct this study. Their studies on long-term panel data of different countries deny any relationship between long-term interest rate and real exchange rate in the equilibrium mode, even when the real exchange rate is constant.

Bidabadi and Rabiee (2010), in the relation between interest rate and exchange rate in the Iranian economy have analyzed these variables in the Iranian economy. The results point out to the fact that if currency exchange rate enhances in the economy, then the monetary officials must allow the interest rate to be decreased.

Bidabadi (2004) has taken advantage of macro econometric models of Iran, as the broadest econometric model, to evaluate effects of decreased interest rate on other economic variables of Iran. Using this model he succeeded to decline banking loans interest rate along different scenarios and then has begun to simulate the model.

The results show that decreased banking loans interest rate will lead to decrease import and export supply in economy of Iran and to improve trade balance of the country. Similarly, decreased interest rate will increase liquidity volume and will affect positively the economic growth through increasing non-oil GDP growth and also popularize the private investment in the economy.

METHODOLOGY

In this study, annual time series data were used for an 18-year course, that is, from 1991 to 2009. Given the economic statistics of Central Bank of Iran (CBI) the necessary information have been collected. In order to test hypotheses, the unit root test was used for reliability of variables of the study, Dickey Fuller test was used to test time series and Durbin-Watson statistic (D.W) was used in this paper.

White test was used to discern the difference of variance and eventually the Least Square Estimate Model and econometric models, particularly Fisher Model, using Eviews7 and SPSS17 were employed to estimate the questioned functional parameters. The estimative function between 1-year interest rate changes and informal exchange rates of the selected countries:

H_1: There is a meaningful relationship between 1-year interest rate changes and informal USD rate in Iran (Table 1).

In the estimative model, the correlation strength between the independent variable (1-year interest rate) and the dependent variable (exchange rate) is -0.48; on the other hand the coefficient of determination indicates that 0.23% of changes are caused by the dependent variable exchange rate due to independent variable changes (1-year interest rate) which is acceptable.

Likewise, the regression value (sig.) has been measured as 0.03, thus the research hypothesis is verified. It means that there is a meaningful relationship between exchange rate and 1-year interest rate in the Iranian economy.

H_2: There is a meaningful relationship between 1-year interest rate changes and informal GBP rate in Iran (Table 2).

In the estimative model, the correlation strength between the independent variable (1-year interest rate) and the dependent variable (the British informal exchange rate) is -0.44; on the other hand, the coefficient of determination indicates that 0.20% of changes are caused by the dependent variable , Britain exchange rate due to independent variable changes (1-year interest rate) which is acceptable. Likewise, the regression value (sig.) has been measured as 0.019, thus the research hypothesis is verified. It means that there is a meaningful relationship between exchange rate (GBP) and 1-year interest rate in the Iranian economy.

H_3: There is a meaningful relationship between 1-year interest rate changes and informal AUD rate in Iran (Table 3).

In the estimative model, the correlation strength between the independent variable (1-year interest rate) and the dependent variable (the Australian informal exchange rate) is -0.40; on the other hand, the coefficient of determination indicates that 0.16% of changes are caused by the dependent variable that is. Australia exchange rate due to independent variable changes (1-year interest rate) which is acceptable. Likewise, the regression value (sig) has been measured as 0.05, thus the research hypothesis is verified. It means that there is a meaningful relationship between exchange rate (AUD) and 1-year interest rate in the Iranian economy.

H_4: There is a meaningful relationship between 1-year interest rate changes and informal JPY rate in Iran (Table 4).

Either regression value or F = 0.30 are known, therefore the regression hypothesis is not meaningful: H_1 is verified reliably, hence the extracted regression is denied. Meaningfulness coefficient (T) and meaningfulness level/reliance level show coefficients of model parameters. As a result, according to t_1 = -0.55, sig = 0.59, it can be stated that there is not any relation between informal JPY and 1-year interest rate in the Iranian economy (CI = 95%).

Comparing the results of the relation between interest rate and informal exchange rates of 4 countries

In this section we have compared the results of interest rate and

Table 1. Results linear regression evaluation first hypothesis.

Probability	Probability of multiplier	Variable	Variable name
012.0	66.58	β1	α
036.0	107.0 - 15	R	Interest rate–per year
T2 = -2.28	T1 = 3.04	F-Statistic	21.15
R = 0.48	R2 = 0.23	Durbin-Watson	14.2

Y = F(X), Y = β0 + β1x + vi, UE2 = 58.66 – 15.107 R.

Table 2. Results linear regression evaluation second hypothesis.

Probability	Probability of multiplier	variable	Variable name
0.09	45.62	β1	α
0.019	-2.556	R	Interest rate –per year
T2 = -3.41	T1=5.90	F-Statistic	22.00
R = 0.44	R2=0.20	Durbin-Watson	2.15

Y = F(X), Y = β0 + β1x + vi; UE = 45.62 – 2.556 R.

Table 3. Results linear regression evaluation third hypothesis.

Probability	Probability of multiplier	Variable	Variable name
0.02	18.98	β1	α
0.05	-5.61	R	Interest rate – per year
T2 = -2.24	T1 = 2.70	F-Statistic	11.53
R = 0.40	R2 = 0.16	Durbin-Watson	2.09

Y = F(X), Y = β0 + β1x + vi, UE = 18.98 – 5.61.

Table 4. Results linear regression evaluation fourth hypothesis.

Variable	R	R^2	Sign	F	T_1	R_1	Std. error
R1	0.193	0.037	0.594	0.309	-0.556	-5.184	9.147

Informal USD rate with interest rate and informal GBP, AUD and JPY rate. The obtained results are summarized as follows: The correlation strength between interest rate and informal USD rate is 48%; on the other hand, the correlation strength between interest rate and informal GBP rate and informal AUD rate are 44% and 40%, respectively.

Accordingly, it can be concluded that the relation between interest rate and exchange rate (USD) enjoys more explanatory power. This task is designed to determine the exchange rate which gains the highest influence from 1-year interest rate in the Iranian economy.

1. The coefficient of determination between interest rate and informal USD rate is 23%, it means that 23% of informal USD rate changes caused by interest rate changes in the Iranian economy. The coefficients of determination between interest rate and informal GBP and AUD are 20% and 16%, respectively. Accordingly, it can be concluded that changes of the explainable variable, informal USD rate, enjoy more explanatory power rather than informal GBP and AUD rates changes.
2. One percent increasing in the Iranian economy will decrease the informal USD, GBP and AUD rates as large as 15.10, 2.55 and 5.61%, respectively. Accordingly, effect of interest rate changes on the exchange rate (USD) is more than effect of interest rate on GBP rate.

DISCUSSION AND CONCLUSION

The main objective of the study is analyzing the relationship between 1-year exchange rate changes and informal USD, AUD, GBP and JPY rate changes in Iran using the International Fisher Model. Regarding the economic relation of countries to each other and fluency of exchange rate changes of various countries in economies of other countries and also dependency of the Iranian economy, in export and import field, on foreign exchanges, it is expected that changes of exchange rate of other countries affect meaningfully the interest rate of Iran.

Our findings imply that: The effect of one-year interest rate changes on informal USD rate enjoys more explanatory power rather than informal GBP and AUD rates. Also, according to the obtained results, it can be stated that the USD currency exchange rate must be considered in the Iranian economic trades still. Because the estimative function is between interest rate and JPY rate is indicative of lack of a meaningful relation between them.

Another result of the paper is the inverse relationship between interest rate and informal exchange rate. It means that the more the interest is, the less the exchange rate will be. Thus, it is evident that higher interest rates strengthen and support exchange currency rate, so increasing interest rate makes more attractive depositing and investment in the country. Therefore, the demand for national exchange rate will be increased which is called hot cash flow.

Finally, it must be stated that the interest rate can be considered as a tool to control exchange rate in the Iranian economy. Whenever CBI begins to increase money supply, the interest rate falls, it quickly will results in decreasing exchange trade rate. So if the general level of prices is escalated because of increased money supply, it can be expected that the interest rate will be decreased very slowly in the long term.

RECOMMENDATIONS

1. The government uses the currency policy to control the exchange rate, but using currency policies always results in adjustment of the exchange rate in short term and creates the multi-exchange system in long term. We recommend to government to emphasize the floating exchange rate instead of exchange multi-rate policy. It must be kept in mind that dwindling exchange policy indicator indicates floating exchange rate.
2. With regard to the Iranian economic condition, the ability to control monetary authorities in terms of interest rate of banks has introduced it as one of the most important economic tools to provoke the main aspect of the economy. The efficiency of this political tool can be restricted by two following factors:
3. Inattention to competition in this kind o control may result in fact that interest rate suffer a lower efficiency to provoke investment, hence imperative change of banking interest rate will be devoid from the sufficient efficiency to provoke the real part of the economy.
4. Determination of the banking interest rate without considering the inflation rate changes fails to justify why funds are not deposited in banks. Hence, a great deal of savings of citizens is not available for banks which it decreases capacity of banking system to affect the real part of the economy through changing banking interest rate in turn.

Therefore, providing the necessary tools for CBI in order to provoke the real part of economy entails statesmen to authorize the CBI to rationalize banking interest rate along with to reduce the economic risk. As a result, CBI will be able to employ the banking interest rate as a helpful tool to manage cash flow and convert it into investment and production trend.

REFERENCES

Aziz N (2008). The role of exchange rate in trade balance: Empirics from Bangladesh. University of Birmangham. UK.

Bhatti M, Bhatti I M (2011). Toward understanding islamic corporate governance issue in islamic finance . J. Asian Polit. Policy 2(1):25-38.

Bidabadi B (2004). Models of econometric in Iran . Fifths edition. Monetary research center of Iran.

Bidabadi B, Rabiee M (2010). The relation of interest rate and exchange rate in Iran .J. Econ. Res. 6(2):67-99.

Demirag I, Goddard S (1994). Financial management for international business. McGraw-Hill Book Company. Berkshire. Europe.

Fisher I (1930). The theory of interest. New York. Macmillan.

Gould JD, Nelson CR (1979). The stochastic structure of the velocity of money. Am. Econ. Rev. 64(3):405-428.

Hedayati R (2000). Research center of Melli Bank of Iran, Practical procedure of transaction and loan payment in Shariah law, Law of bank procedure on Shariah in Iran. Parliament of Iran.

Johnson HG (1976). The monetary approach to the balance of payment theory. Jacoba Frenkel & Johnson HG. Eds. George Allen and Unwin Ltd. NY.

Kandil M (2000). The asymmetric effect of exchange rate fluctuation: Theory and evidence from developing countries. IMF Working Paper.

KhalwatyT (2000). Inflation and solutions. 1st Edition. gramedia pustaka utama. Indonesia.

MacDonald R, Nagayasu J (1999). The long-run relationship between real exchange rates and real interest differentials: A panel study. IMF Working Paper 99:37.

Madura J (2000). International financial management . 6th Edition. South-Western College publishing.

Ogaki M, Santaella JA (2005). The exchange rate and the term structure of interest rates in Mexico. Ohio State University. Department of Economics. Working Paper 99:21.

Sargent C (2010). Islam and new kinship: reproductive technology and the shariah in Lebanon. Cont Islam. Oxford: Berghahn Books, 8: 249.

Schreiner M (2010). Islamic finance. J. Econ. 100:91-93.

Serven L (2002). Real exchange rate uncertainty and private investment in developing countries. The World Bank Published.

Solnik B (2000). International investment . Addison Wesley Longman inc. New York.

Tarek SZ, Kabirhassan M (2001). A Comparative literature survey of islamic finance and banking. J. Financ. Markets Institutions Instr. 10:4.

Zaher TS, Kabir HM (2001). Acomparative literature survey of Islamic Finance and banking .Finacial market, institutions and Instrument. Vol. 10. New York University. Salomon Center. Blackwell Publisher USA.

Zarrokh E (2010). Iranian Islamic banking. Euro. J. Law Econ. 29:177-190.

Zettelmeyer J (2003) .The impact of monetary policy on the bilateral exchange rate: Chile versus the United States. IMF Working Paper. IMF WP/03/71.

Stock return and market risk: A comparison between conventional insurance and takaful

Zaidi bin Isa[1] and Rubayah binti Yakob[2]

[1]Centre for Modelling and Data Analysis (DELTA), Faculty of Science and Technology, National University of Malaysia, 43600 UKM, Bangi, Selangor, Malaysia.
[2]School of Business Administration, Faculty of Economics and Management, National University of Malaysia, 43600 UKM, Bangi, Selangor, Malaysia.

The focus of this study was to examine the relationship between market risk and stock return of different markets of insurance, namely, conventional insurance and takaful. In order to estimate the market better with care, the variance of the stock return was examined as well. Earlier studies in determining the relationship between risk and return of insurer stock return employed the assumption that variance is constant over time. However, empirical evidence rejected the notion of a constant better and pointed to changing risk premium and returns variability over time. As a consequence, this study employed CAPM-GARCH (1,1) in order to estimate the market return coefficient and took the time varying volatility into consideration. Data for monthly stock return for Syarikat Takaful Malaysia as representative of the Takaful market, Hong Leong Finance Group as representative of the conventional insurance market and Kuala Lumpur Composite Index as market return were obtained from Bursa Malaysia. The time period of study was from February 1997 to February 2008. The results showed that there are clusters of volatile movements in both companies stock return with intervening periods of relative stability. This implied that GARCH is the appropriate model for insurance stock return. The results also proved that for market movements, the effect varies across these two firms. These results were expected since each company will have a different exposure towards the fluctuation of market movements.

Key words: risk, return, CAPM-GARCH, conventional insurance, takaful

INTRODUCTION

The traditional concept of risk and return relationship applies to life insurers the same as it does to other investors. The market movement is considered very crucial to the insurance companies due to the fact that the investment function is a critically important subset of the overall financial management of life insurance companies. According to Black and Skipper (2000), investment risk is generally defined as the potential variability of returns and comprises the insurance pricing risk and the asset-liability risk. In general, the total investment portfolio of insurance company consists of two categories. First, assets which are invested for providing guaranteed and fixed benefit payment. Second, other invested assets used to support the liabilities associated with investment risk through the products or lines of business. Any changes in the market can simultaneously affect the value of a company's assets and liabilities and the behaviour of its customers. Because of their unique operations and balance sheet structure, and also the special risk profile that results, fixed income investments make up the significant majority of life insurer's assets.

*Corresponding author. E-mail: zaidiisa@ukm.my

Abbreviations: ARCH, auto regressive conditional heteroscedasticity; **ADF,** Augmented Dickey Fuller.

Table 1. Assets of Life Insurance Fund and Family Takaful (% of total assets).

Year	Fixed Asset	Investment Property	Financing	Investment	Foreign Asset	Cash and Deposit	Other Asset	Total
Takaful								
2003	0.2	1.7	2.2	57.6	0.2	2.6	35.5	100
2004	0.1	1.6	0.9	63.1	0.2	0.8	33.3	100
2005	0.1	3.6	1.1	65.0	0.3	2.9	27.0	100
2006	0.0	3.1	0.9	60.5	0.9	1.7	32.8	100
2007	0.1	2.7	0.6	57.9	0.8	1.9	36.1	100
Conventional Insurance								
2003	0.7	4.4	12.7	65.6	0.5	13.7	2.4	100
2004	0.5	4.3	12.1	67.9	0.2	12.8	2.2	100
2005	0.5	3.8	12.4	70.2	0.3	10.5	2.2	100
2006	0.6	3.3	12.0	69.3	1.2	11.5	2.1	100
2007	0.5	2.9	11.2	70.4	1.6	11.4	2.0	100

Source: Annual Insurance Report and Takaful Annual Report 2007.

In the Malaysian context, the insurance market is divided into conventional insurance and takaful. There were eight players in both markets in 2007. The takaful market only began in 1984 when the first takaful company, namely, Takaful Malaysia Bhd. was established, whereas, conventional insurance was established back in 1967 or earlier. Table 1 shows the allocation of assets of conventional insurance and Family Takaful for 2007. In general, the allocation of assets in each component for conventional life insurance is higher than Family Takaful except for the other assets component. This is because of the addition of investment accounts and the Islamic money market to the other assets component for takaful and none for conventional life insurance. The different allocation of these assets between insurance companies that focus on life insurance versus property and casualty insurance or health insurance do matter in creating different exposure towards a specific source of systematic risk (Johnston and Madura, 2002).

Instead of the importance of systematic risk in determining stock returns, the variance of stock returns must be taken into account. This is because economic agents make decisions based on their perception of the distribution of a random variable in the future, and so the measurement of variance usually has a strong influence on the cause of action that is taken (Nicholls and Tonuri, 1995). Earlier studies assumed this variance to be constant over time but a lot of previous studies have shown that the variance of stock return is time varying. The GARCH model provides a method of estimating the variance of such returns as it changes through time, thereby improving the information available to investors. As a consequence, the GARCH model is expected to avoid the problem of mispricing, especially during times of substantial instability in the financial markets when the assumption of constant variance is an inadequate approximation.

The relationship between risk and return in finance literature is a never ending story. In Gentry and Pike (1970), Markovitz (1952) defined risk as the variance of the rate of return of a portfolio. Sharpe (1964) hypothesized a positive linear relationship between expected rate of return on an asset and the risk premium associated with that asset. Moreover, the evidence in his study implies that larger average returns are associated with a larger amount of risk. Harrington (1983), in a study of life-health insurance stocks from 1961 through 1976 found evidence of a significant relationship between mean returns and both systematic and unsystematic risks. However, his study found no abnormal return for that study period. Pritchett and Wilder (1986), Hoyt and Trieschmann (1991) used mean-variance and CAPM as well as accounting rate of return data in examining the relationship of risk-return of life health insurers. Their results indicated that life health insurers had higher returns and greater volatility from 1950 through 1963 than during the period from 1963 through 1980. Cummins and Harrington (1988) concluded that their results were inconsistent with CAPM between 1970 through 1980 but were consistent between 1980 through 1983. They analyzed the risk/return relationship of property-liability insurance companies during the period of 1970 through 1983. In a study performed by Hoyt and Trieschmann (1991) they concluded different results on the risk/return relationship between life-health, property-liability and diversified insurer. All three insurer segments provided positive excess returns relative to the market during their study period (1973-1987). Their analysis used the mean-variance and CAPM approaches. Risk/return relationship is also examined by Hatfield (1997) and his study claimed that insurance stock returns outperform the market on a risk-adjusted basis for the period 1973-1994.

In determining the risk/return relationship, the above study used the traditional CAPM. Harrington (1983) quoted findings by Sharpe (1964), Lintner (1965), and Black (1972) that CAPM implies that the proper measure of risk for an asset is its market risk as measured by beta and that diversified risk will not affect required rates of return. CAPM is based on a set of assumptions that includes the ability of all investors to diversify perfectly and that all the market participants' share identical subjective expectations of mean and variance of return distributions, namely, normal distributions. However, a study by Chong, et al. (1999) stated that many empirical studies on the return on investment in the stock market have shown evidence that the distribution is significantly non-normal. They found three important criteria: the time series of stock returns are leptokurtic, the distribution of stock returns is skewed and the variance of stock returns is observed to be non-constant and also appears to evolve in a predictable manner determined by the immediate history of the process. In other words, stock returns exhibit the so-called volatility clustering, which means large changes in these series tend to be followed by large changes and small changes by small changes. The technical term given to this behaviour is auto regressive conditional heteroscedasticity (ARCH). A model of time-varying conditional variance with the ARCH process that uses past disturbances to model the variances of the series and allow the variance of the error term to vary over time was proposed by Engle (1982). Bollerslev (1986) generalized the ARCH process by allowing the conditional variance to be a function of prior period's squared errors as well as its past conditional variances. Based on these reasons, the traditional CAPM is unable to satisfactorily describe the stock returns generating process (Mohammad et al., 2007). Many researchers suggested modification to the traditional CAPM model and came out with CAPM-GARCH, which allows risk and return to vary over time. The study by Jagannathan and Wang (1996) shows that CAPM-GARCH has the explanatory power far better than the traditional CAPM by the ratio of 30%:1%. This finding is supported by Durack et al. (2004), who reported the same conclusion with a better ratio of explanatory power 65.31%:7.25%.

Based on these previous studies that provide a significant relationship between risk and stock returns and given the importance of risk and return in the environment of insurance company's operations and also the importance of estimating an accurate distribution of stock return variance, this paper will apply CAPM-GARCH to life insurance stock returns in examining the interaction between market risk and stock returns of conventional insurance and takaful.

MATERIALS AND METHODS

The sample data used here comprises the monthly stock returns of two life insurance companies, namely, Hong Leong Financial Group Bhd. (which holds 100% of Hong Leong Assurance) as representative of the conventional insurance market and Syarikat Takaful Malaysia Bhd. as representative of the Takaful market, and the Kuala Lumpur Composite Index as the measure of market index/risk. The time period for this data set is from February 1997 to February 2008. Thus there are 132 observations for this study. Data was obtained from Bursa Malaysia. The stock return is gained by taking a first difference of stock price as below:

$$R_t = \ln\left(\frac{P_t}{P_{t-1}}\right)$$

where R_t is monthly stock return at time t and P_t and P_{t-1} are monthly price of an asset at two successive days t and $t-1$, respectively. Based on the fact that asset returns exhibit volatility clustering, and the approach that can take into account these distributional properties of asset returns is ARCH and GARCH, this project paper will employ the GARCH model to estimate the conditional volatility for insurance stock returns.

Specifically, the GARCH (1,1) model will be employed here as from the literature it is found to be excellent model for a wide range of financial data (Bollerslev et al., 1992). The following model of CAPM-GARCH is utilized:

$$R_t = \alpha_0 + \alpha_1 R_{mt} + \varepsilon_t \qquad (1)$$

$$\varepsilon_t \sim N(0, h_t)$$

$$h_t = \omega + \beta_1 \varepsilon_{t-1}^2 + \beta_2 h_{t-1} \qquad (2)$$

Equation (1) is CAPM equation where R_t is the rate of return of the insurance company's stock (Hong Leong and Takaful) at time t; R_{mt} is market return at time t and ε_t is a random error term. α_1 is market coefficient and α_0 is constant. If α_0 is positive, the insurance stocks outperform the market and α_1 is expected to be positive, which is parallel to the theory that rates of return will be positively related to risk.

On the other hand, equation (2) is GARCH (1,1) model where $\omega > 0, \beta_1 \geq 0, \beta_2 \geq 0$ to make sure that h_t is non-negative. The stationary condition for GARCH (1,1) is $\beta_1 + \beta_2 < 1$. The sizes of the parameters β_1 and β_2 determine the short-run dynamics of the resulting volatility time series. A large GARCH lag coefficient β_2 indicates that shocks to conditional variance take a long time to die out, so it is said that the volatility is persistent. A large error coefficient β_1 means that volatility reacts intensely to market movement resulting in spike volatility. In addition, if $\beta_1 + \beta_2$ is close to one, then a shock at time t will persist for many time periods, while if $\beta_1 + \beta_2$ is equal to one, any shock will lead to a permanent change in all future values of h_t.

Table 2. Descriptive statistics on monthly return of Hong Leong and Takaful.

Statistic	Takaful	Hong Leong
Mean	-0.0056	-0.0033
Standard deviation	0.1454	0.1202
Skewness	-2.7717	-0.1462
Kurtosis	26.7987	4.9702
Maximum	0.4943	0.3704
Minimum	-1.0986	-0.4538
Jarque-Bera test	3284.0790*	21.8198*
ARCH Test	43.7967*	26.5740*
ADF	-10.8696*	-10.3923*

***significance level,** 1%; **ADF,** augmented Dickey-Fuller Test for unit root.

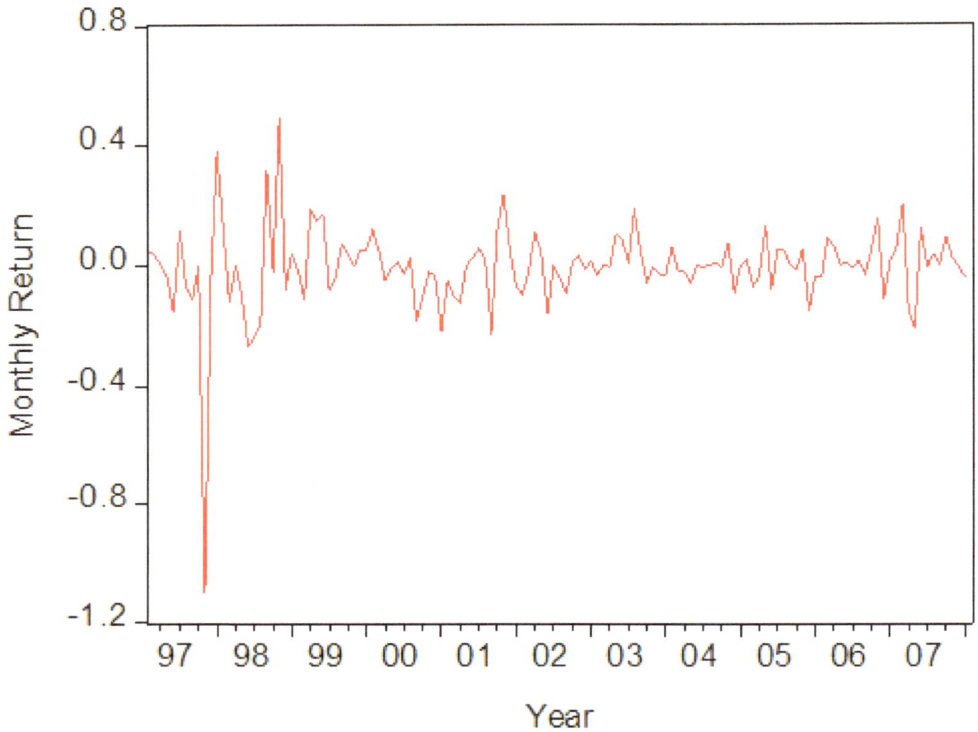

Figure 1. Volatility clustering of monthly return of Takaful.

RESULTS

Summary statistics of R_t for Hong Leong and Takaful were shown in Table 2. The average returns of both companies were negative, implying that the price series decreased over the period. The skewness gave negative values that were, the return distributions of the shares traded have the probability of a negative return. The value of the kurtosis was greater than 3, meaning that they have a heavier tail than the standard normal distribution. This showed leptokurtosis. Thus, the monthly stock returns of both companies were not normally distributed and this was confirmed by the Jarque-Bera test. The null hypothesis of normality was rejected at the 1% significance level.

Figures 1 and 2 exhibited the return series for Takaful and Hong Leong, respectively. From the Figures, it was clear that there were stretches of time where the volatility was relatively high and relatively low, which suggested an apparent volatility clustering in some period. Further evidence on volatility clustering in the series could be ascertained from the ARCH test (from Table 2) where the

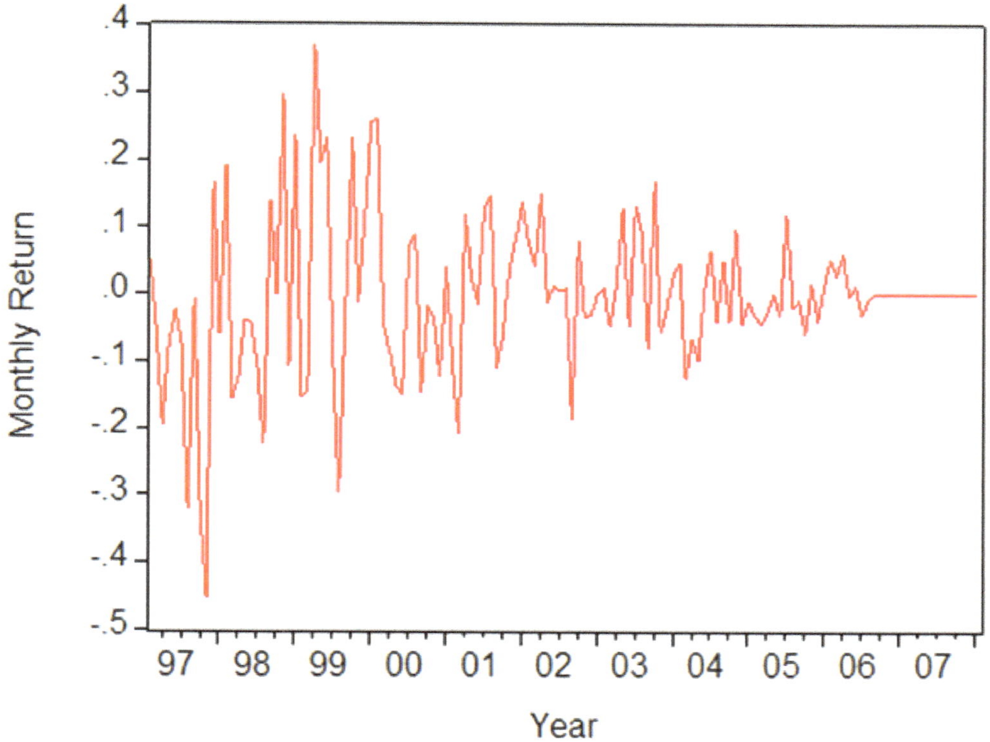

Figure 2. Volatility clustering of monthly return of Hong Leong.

null hypothesis was rejected at the 1% level of significance. Thus, the conditional variance was auto correlated. Accordingly, the GARCH specification was more appropriate for modelling insurance stock returns. Lastly, the augmented dickey fuller (ADF) unit root test indicated stationarity for the Takaful and Hong Leong return series.

Table 3 presented the results for the CAPM-GARCH model for both insurance companies' stock returns. From Table 3 (Panel A), it was shown that β_1 and β_2 were both statistically significant for Hong Leong but only β_1 was statistically significant for Takaful at 1%. These results indicated that the constant variance model could be rejected for both Hong Leong and Takaful. The relatively small value of error coefficient β_1 implied that large market surprised induce relatively small revisions in future volatility. However Takaful was more reactive in volatility compared to Hong Leong. The value of lag coefficient β_2 for Takaful was statistically not significant at any conventional level, thus the volatility in future was not affected by volatility in the past. On the contrary, the value of lag coefficient β_2 for Hong Leong was relatively large, meaning that GARCH volatilities were persistent. In other words, if there was a new shock, it will have implications on the price for a larger period. The market will take some time to digest the information fully into the price (Karmakar, 2005).

It is appropriate to examine how well the GARCH (1,1) model fits the data. The Ljung-Box Pierce Statistics at lag 25 (Q Statistics) for the standardized residuals and squared standardized residuals suggest no serial correlations and additional ARCH effect. The Lagrange Multiplier tests (ARCH Test) up to 6 lags as proposed by Engle (1982) to ascertain these results. The results indicate that the ARCH test is not statistically significant at the 1% level. However, there is still excess kurtosis in the return series of Takaful. As a result, this suggests that the GARCH (1,1) model is an adequate description of the volatility process and no higher lags are needed to capture autocorrelation.

As mentioned earlier, CAPM-GARCH is a better model to determine the relationship between market risk and stock return. From Table 3 (Panel A), for both Takaful and Hong Leong, the value of α_0 (measure of abnormal return) are negative and statistically not significant. This result is not consistent with Lown et al. (2000) in Najand et al. (2007), which claims that life insurance companies are among those companies that can be more profitable if they offer both bank and insurance products (in the case of Hong Leong). However, the measure of market risk, α_1 is positive and highly significant at the 1% level for both Takaful and Hong Leong. In terms of magnitude, the

Table 2. Descriptive statistics on monthly return of Hong Leong and Takaful.

Statistic	Takaful	Hong Leong
Mean	-0.0056	-0.0033
Standard deviation	0.1454	0.1202
Skewness	-2.7717	-0.1462
Kurtosis	26.7987	4.9702
Maximum	0.4943	0.3704
Minimum	-1.0986	-0.4538
Jarque-Bera test	3284.0790*	21.8198*
ARCH Test	43.7967*	26.5740*
ADF	-10.8696*	-10.3923*

* **significance level,** 1%; **ADF,** augmented Dickey-Fuller Test for unit root.

Table 3. Estimates of Monthly return GARCH (1,1) Model (February 1997-February 2008).

Panel A: Coefficient	Takaful	Hong Leong
α_0	-0.0047	-0.0066
	(0.3309)	(0.1895)
α_1	0.9199	0.8076
	(0.0000)	(0.0000)
ω	0.0034	-2.00E-06
	(0.0004)	(0.9811)
β_1	1.1125	0.1171
	(0.0000)	(0.0111)
β_2	0.0781	0.8796
	(0.5167)	(0.0000)
R^2	0.2613	0.5043
Panel B: Diagnostic statistic		
Q(25)	28.302	25.966
$Q^2(25)$	13.447	14.340
ARCH test	1.1170	1.7535
	(0.9807)	(0.9409)
Skewness	-0.8378	-0.2435
Kurtosis	7.1655	2.9344

$p-value$ is in parentheses; $R_t = \alpha_0 + \alpha_1 R_{mt} + \varepsilon_t$; $h_t = \omega + \beta_1 \varepsilon_{t-1}^2 + \beta_2 h_{t-1}$

market return coefficient (α_1) are all below unity with Takaful having a higher α_1 (0.919945) compared to Hong Leong (0.807611). Using this α_1 as a measure of market risk, the insurers in the sample, considered collectively, are less risky than the average market portfolio.

DISCUSSION AND CONCLUSION

The main objective of this project paper is to investigate the risk/return relationship for Syarikat Takaful Malaysia Bhd. and Hong Leong Finance Group Bhd. First of all, the distribution of the monthly return is examined. The distribution of the data suggests a non-normal distribution and the conditional variance exhibit volatility clustering. Previous studies, such as Jagannathan and Wang (1996), Durack et al. (2004) and Mohammad et al. (2007), show that the CAPM-GARCH model is more appropriate because of the time-varying volatility of monthly return for both companies.

For this study, the results also indicate that the constant variance model (CAPM) can be rejected for both

Hong Leong and Takaful. From the context of stability and volatility, Takaful is more reactive in volatility compared to Hong Leong, however, the value of the lag coefficient β_2 for Takaful is statistically not significant, and, thus, the volatility in future is not affected by volatility in the past. On the contrary, the monthly stock return of Hong Leong is persistent. According to Nicholls and Tonuri (1995), high levels of volatility can lead to a general erosion of investor confidence and a flow of capital away from equity markets.

The results prove that for market movements, the effect varies across these two firms and these results are expected as each company will have different exposure towards the fluctuation of market movements. This is related to the composition of the product offered and the investment policy (asset-liability management) practiced by the insurers. A greater investment link and variable products offered by the companies will lead to greater sensitivity towards market movements. This is due to the investment policy towards the separate accounts portfolio that might comprise only common stock, only bonds, any mortgages, or any combination of these or other investments. However, due to *syari'ah* compliance, Takaful is quite careful in offering the guaranteed and fixed benefit payments to the consumer as compared to Hong Leong.

In conclusion, our results shared some light on the risk/return relationship on the insurance stock return after considering the time varying volatility of a particular stock return of both insurance markets in Malaysia namely conventional insurance and takaful.

REFERENCE

Black F (1972). Capital market equilibrium with restricted borrowing. J. Bus. 45(3):444-455.

Black Jr. K, Skipper Jr. H (2000). Life and health insurance.13th Edition. Prentice Hall Inc, New Jersey.

Bollerslev T (1986). Generalized autoregressive conditional heteroscedasticity. J. Econom. 31(3):307-327.

Bollerslev T, Chou R, Kroner K (1992). ARCH modelling in finance. J. Econom. 52(1/2):5-59.

Chong CW, Muhammad ID, Mat Yusoff A (1999). Performance of GARCH model in forecasting stock market volatility. J. Forecast. 18(5):333-343.

Cummins JD, Harrington SE (1988). The relationship between risk and return: Evidence for property-liability insurance stocks. J. Risk Insur. 55(1):15-31.

Durack N, Durand RB, Maller RA (2004). A best choice among Assets Pricing Model? The conditional Capital Asset Pricing Model in Australia. J. Account. Finan. 44(2):139-162.

Engle RE (1982). Autoregressive conditional heteroscedasticity with estimates of the variance of United Kingdom inflation. Econometrica: J. Econom. Soc. 50(4):987-1007.

Gentry J, Pike J (1970). An empirical study of the risk-return hypothesis using common stock portfolios of life insurance companies. J. Financ. Quant. Anal. 5(2):179-185.

Harrington SE (1983). The relationship between risk and return: Evidence for life insurance stocks. J. Risk Insur. 50(4):587-610.

Hatfield GB (1997). Risk and portfolio returns for life insurance stocks in bull and bear markets. J. Insur. Issues 20(1):67-83.

Hoyt RE, Trieschmann JS (1991). Risk/return relationships for life-health, property-liability, and diversified insurers. J. Risk Insur. 58(2):322-330.

Insurance Annual Report (2007). Bank Negara Malaysia. KualaLumpur.

Jagannathan R, Wang Z (1996). The conditional CAPM and the cross-section of expected returns. J. Finan. 51(1):3-53.

Johnston J, Madura J (2002). The relevance of a real estate factor in modelling insurance company returns. J. Real Estate Portfolio Manage. 8(2): 97-106.

Karmakar M (2005). Modelling conditional volatility of Indian stock markets. Vikalpa 30(3):21-37.

Lintner J (1965). The valuation of risk assets and the selection of risky investments in stock portfolios and capital budgets. Rev. Econ. Statis.,. 47(1): 13 – 37.

Lown CS, Osler CL, Strahan PE, Sufi A (2000). The changing landscape of the financial services industry: What lies ahead?. Federal Reserve Bank New York Econ. Policy Rev. 6(4):39-55.

Markowitz H (1952). Portfolio selection. J. Finan. 7(1):77-91.

Mohammad N, John G, David CM (2007). Do life insurance stocks provide superior returns? J. Asset Manage. 8: 52-57

Najand M, Griffith J, Marlett DC (2006). Do life insurance stocks provide superior returns? J. Asset Manage. 8(1):52-57.

Nicholls D, Tonuri D (1995). Modelling stock market volatility in Australia. J. Bus. Account. 22(3):377-396.

Pritchett ST, Wilder RP (1986). Stock life insurance company profitability and workable competition. Wharton School, University of Pennsylvania.

Sharpe WF (1964). Capital assets prices: A theory of market equilibrium under conditions of risk. J. Finan. 19(3):425-442.

Takaful Annual Report (2007). Bank Negara Malaysia. Kuala Lumpur.

Estimating Private Investment Functions for the Brazilian's capital formation industries: Evidence from the panel data and fixed effects models

Hugo Ferreira Braga Tadeu*, Jersone Tasso Moreira Silva and Carlos Alberto Arruda de Oliveira

Dom Cabral Foundation, FDC. Rua Bernardo Guimarães, 3071 – Santo Agostinho – Belo Horizonte, MG. 30140-083, Brazil.

This article examines the determinants of private investment in Brazil from sectorial industry data of 1996 to 2010. The series of gross fixed capital ormation, commonly used in empirical studies of aggregate investment eliminates irregular adjustments of individual production units due to the aggregation process. Using the industry's sectorial data it is possible to avoid smoothing in this aggregate series and it may help to understand aggregated investment dynamics. The results reveal the importance of the volume of available funds for investment with the complementarity between public and private investment. The results also indicate that the real high interest rates prevailing in the market did not affect the private sector's investment negatively during the considered period. The investment financing alternative from own resources and subsidized credit seems to be more important. As expected, economic instability adversely affected private investment during this period.

Key words: Panel data, private investment, fixed effects, capital formation.

INTRODUCTION

Almost all economists lay emphasis on capital formation as the major determinant of economic growth. Capital formation means that society does not apply all of its current productive activity to the needs and desires of immediate consumption, but directs a part of it for the making of capital goods, such as tools and instruments, machines and transport facilities, plant and equipment, and all the various forms of real capital that can so greatly increase the efficacy of productive effort.

This consists of adding the producer's assets with tangible reproducible goods, which have an expected lifetime use of one year or more. The producers in question can be industries, government services producers and private household non-profitable service producers. The capital formation is responsible for the machinery and equipment production that are used to produce other goods, always keeping a direct relationship with the production of other industrial segments, besides playing an important role in the creation and diffusion of new technology.

The machinery and equipment industry comprises many other industrial segments, such as machinery and equipment manufacturing; automotive vehicles, trailers and vehicular bodies; electrical machines, devices and materials; information technology equipment and peripherals and communication equipment.

The investment in equipment does not only increase production but also increases opportunities. Capital formation leads to technical progress, which helps to use the economies of large-scale production and increases specialization. It provides machines, tools and equipment for the growing labor force. Thus, capital formation also benefits labor.

The most important capital formation industry segment in the Brazilian economy is the machinery and the equipment-manufacturing sector, which is concentrated in the State of São Paulo. In 2010, according to the IBGE Census Bureau, São Paulo accounted for 57% of ITV –

*Corresponding author. E-mail: hugofbraga@gmail.com.

Industrial Transformation Value, or $8.7 billion, and for 53% of all employed labor (198,000 employees) by this industry in the country. It ranks among the five first major activities in the São Paulo industrial structure.

According to De Oliveira et al. (2012b), Brazil needs to improve its investments in infrastructure, given the limited usage capacity by the national industry. The authors demonstrate that an increase in the credit supply through an increase of credit operations for the private sector has as result an increase of private investment in subsequent periods. Another relevant fact is that, due to the effects of the high interest rates over the financial fundings for the private investment, the Brazilian businesses end up having to use their own resources to finance their investments, as also the scarce availability of resources. This study indicates the need of investments in industries such as the machinery and equipment manufacturing industry, the automobile, trailers and body work manufacturing and assembly sectors, and other transportation equipment.

Seeking to encourage economic growth, the Federal Government announced its PAC – Growth Acceleration Program for Equipment. The purpose is to make available R$8.4 billion to streamline government procurement, giving preference to products of the national industry. This is another series of measures with the objective of avoiding the reduction of the Gross Domestic Product (GDP), the sum of all the possessions and services produced in the country, due to the international crisis initiated in 2008.

In order to implement this program, the National Economic and Social Development Bank – BNDES created specific financing investment programs to modernize the industry, such as the BNDES PSI program – Producers' Goods, for the production and pacquisition of new machinery and equipment; as well as, the Industrial Production Capacity Program, which is focused on the implementation, modernization and expansion of the industries that produce machinery and equipment, among others.

According to De Oliveira et al. (2012a), the determinants of private investments in Brazil are not only associated with the economic performance, but also depend on the behavior of all sectors. In this perspective, it is necessary to develop new studies, in order to better understand the most representative segments of the country's economy.

Thus, the objective of this study is to estimate private investment functions in the Brazilian capital formation industrial sectors using the panel econometric model with fixed effects of 1996 to 2010.

LITERATURE REVIEW

The literature review identified very few articles that contribute to the econometric studies that analyze sector's performance, especially the financial sector and insertion of products or services. As a result of these analysis, it is essential that data surveys should be conducted to simulate the impacts of macroeconomic variables on private investments by the productive sectors in Brazil (De Oliveira et al., 2012a).

According to De Oliveira et al. (2012b), there is a great need of improvements in the electric power segments, tele communications, road, rail and air transportation, harbours, waterways and sewage systems, as also in a model where private investment offers substantial returns, becoming in this manner more attractive than the public investment. Capital formation industry sectors, such as, machinery and equipment manufacturing industries, themotor vehicles, trailers and body works manufacturing and assembly sectors, and other transport equipment sectors are essential sectors related to these needs.

The capital formation industry is directly related to the production of the remaining industrial sectors, and plays a prevalent role in the diffusion of new technologies. This industry can be characterized by its heterogeneity, given the substantial variability of product types, applications and purposes and by its competitive market conditions.

Besides being directly related to the production chains of other industries, the capital formation industry is also a consumer of the goods it makes. Therefore, the industry plays a prevalent role as an economic growth driving industry. It comprises a set of products for different applications, which can be grouped as follows.

Mechanical capital goods – mechanics, mechanical equipment, industrial equipment, farm machinery and implements, mining machines and highway machines;
Transportation equipment – buses and trucks, shipbuilding, aeronautic industry;
Electrical capital goods – electrical equipment.

According to the data from the Brazilian Association of Machinery and Equipment, the sector is setup as indicated in Table 1. The data indicate that the Brazilian mechanical capital goods ended the year 2011 having an actual gross turnover of R$ 81.2 billion, which represents a growth of 9.2% above the results of 2010. The sales from January through December of 2009 were of R$ 64.05 billion.

Table 1 shows that farm machinery and wood working machines are the most important segments with a sales increase of 30.1 and 48.2%, respectively. On the other hand, textile machinery, plastic-working machines and valves – which already had a small share in the capital goods industry – continue to face challenging conditions and ended the year 2011 with turnovers smaller than those of 2010.

In the first half of 2012, the Trade Balance recorded a

Table 1. Mechanical capital goods actual gross sales by segment in 2011.

Segment	Percentage	Actual gross sales in R$ billion
Other machines	57.5	8.1
Made-to-order goods	16.6	6.2
Farm machinery	12.4	30.1
Pumps and motor pumps	5.9	6
Hydraulics and pneumatics	2.0	14.7
Machine tools	1.9	1.7
Valves	1.3	- 18.1
Plastic-working machines	1.2	- 14.3
Woodworking machines	1.0	48.2
Textile machines	0.2	- 45.5

Source: ABIMAQ (2012).

larger deficit of 5.2% than that of last year's, which is same period for the machinery and equipment manufacturing industry. Altogether, the capital goods industry reported an R$ 9,244 billion deficit, compared to the R$ 8,784 billion recorded between January and June of 2011 (BACEN, 2012). Exports alone accrued an 11.6% increase in the year, and amounted to R$ 5,987 billion in the period. Conversely, imports reported R$ 15,231 billion, for a 7.6% growth compared to the first half of 2011. Exports presented a good performance in the first quarter alone, which grew by 29.4% if compared to March 2011, while imports dropped by 1.5% in the same period.

The Latin American region, notably, represents the main destination of Brazilian capital goods exports; however, the share of this destination in the exported volumes has lost its momentum, including the results from Mercosul, which dropped from 41% in the first quarter of 2011 to 33% in 2012 (ABIMAQ, 2012).

Imports keep increasing, with the exception of the machinery group for consumer goods that recorded a result below the numbers of the first quarter of previous year. The groups with the most significant growth were the farm machinery, machines for logistics and construction engineering and for the manufacturing industry. The United States, China and Germany are the main origins of machinery and equipment imports.

In sales terms, the machinery and equipment manufacturing industry ended the first half of 2012 with the gross sales amount of R$39,932 billion, which represents a growth of 2.1% increase over the equal period of 2011.

De Oliveira et al. (2012b) suggested investments in the infrastructure, logistics areas and some segments of the transformation industry, as confirmed by the Brazilian Growth Acceleration Program (PAC).

MATERIALS AND METHODS

The quantitative research used explains the theoretical regression model and also tests the existence of stationarity and the co-integration between the used time series data. The used econometric method used is the panel data with fixed effects.

Panel data or longitudinal data are characterized by observations with two dimensionswhich are often time and space. These data contain information enabling a better research about the dynamics variables change, making it possible to consider the effect of unobserved variables. Another important aspect is the improvement in the parameter inference that was studied, since it provides more degrees of freedom and a greater variability in the sample, when compared with the data in cross-section or time series, which refines the efficiency of econometric estimators. Hsiao (1986, 2006) presents a more detailed analysis of the advantages in using thePanel Data.

Generally, the panel data cover a small period of time, due to the high cost of obtaining new information or information unavailability in the past. As the estimated parameters are asymptotically consistent, it is desirable to have a large number of observations. Accordingly, when the covered time period is small, the property of consistency will be satisfied if the number of subjects is large. The following section presents the general model for panel data and fixed effects model used in this study.

General model for panel data and fixed effects model

$$y_{it} = \beta_{oit} X_{1it} + \cdots + \beta_{kit} X_{kit} + \varepsilon_{it} \qquad (1)$$

In this notation, the subscript i denotes the different individuals and the subscript t the time period being analyzed. The β_0 refers to the intercept parameter and β_k refers to the angular slope coefficient correspondent to the kth explanatory variable of the model.

In this general model, the intercept and response parameters are different for each individual and for each time. There are, therefore, more unknown parameters than observations, not being possible, in this case, to estimate their parameters.

Thus, it is necessary to specify assumptions about the general model in order to make it operational. Among the models that combine time series data and cross-section, three are the most used: Seemingly Unrelated Regressions Models (SUR), Random Effects Models and Fixed EffectsModels, being the latter applied in this research.

The fixed effects model aims to control the effect of omitted variables that vary between individuals and remain constant over time. For this, it is assumed that the intercept varies from individual to individual, but is constant over time, whereas the response parameters are constant for all subjects and for all time periods.

According toHill et al. (1999), the model assumptions are:

$$\beta_{0it} = \beta_{0i}\beta_{1it} = \beta_1 \cdots \beta_{kit} = \beta_k \quad (2)$$

The fixed effects model is therefore given by:

$$y_{it} = \alpha_i + \beta_1 X_{1it} + \cdots + \beta_k X_{kit} + \varepsilon_{it} \quad (3)$$

In this model, the intercept is a fixed and unknown parameter that captures the differences between individuals that are in the sample. Thus, the inferences made about the model are only about individuals, which provide the data.

It is possible to make a specification of the fixed effects model using dummy variables to represent the intercepts for each specific individual. In this case, the general equation is defined as:

$$y_{it} = \beta_0 + \beta_1 X_{1it} + \cdots + \beta_k X_{kit} + \gamma_1 D_{1i} + \gamma_2 D_{2i} + \cdots + \gamma_n D_{ni} + \varepsilon_{it} \quad (4)$$

Where, D_{ni} represents a binary variable for each individual and is equivalent to one when *i=n* and zero, otherwise. However, this equation shows a binary variable for each individual, resultingin the problem of perfect multicollinearity. To clear up multicollinearity we should omit a binary variable. Thus, the model proposed byStock and Watson (2004) will bewritten as:

$$y_{it} = \beta_0 + \beta_1 X_{1it} + \cdots + \beta_k X_{kit} + \gamma_2 D_{2i} + \cdots + \gamma_n D_{ni} + \varepsilon_{it} \quad (5)$$

Thefixed effects model is the best option to model the panel data when the intercept α_i is correlated with the explanatory variables in anytime period. In addition, as the intercept of this model is treated as a fixed parameter, it is also desirable to use fixed effects when the observations are obtained from the entire population and you want to make inferences for individuals that have the data.

The applied econometric model is intended to test the hypothesis that the series of private sector investment, the gross value of industrial production sector, public administration's investment, interest rate, among others are co-integrated, which allows the modeling of the long-term private investment behavior. Through anempirical study, we will seekto identify whether there is a role in inhibiting private investment played by macro economic instability and by government's investment, during the proposed period.

To explain the sectorial private investment, the following data were chosen to integrate the functional form: the Gross Sectorial Industrial Production Value, Sectorial Industrial Capacity Use, Government Investment, and Actual Interest Rates, a proxy for Credit Availability, External Restrictions and Foreign Exchange.

Due to the above-exposed, the following generic theoretical model is proposed:

Invest_priv = f(VBPI, UCAP, R, Cred, FBKF, E, EE) (6)

Where, Invest_priv = a proxy for sectoral investment spending; data refer to Fixed Assets Acquisitions (machinery and equipment) by industrial segments (the transformation Industry), in thousands of Reals, at 1995 prices; VBPI = a proxy for the economic activity level; data refer to the Gross Industrial Production Value per industrial segment, in thousands of Reals, at 1995 prices; UCAP = Capacity Utilization rate (%) – time series data for installed capacity utilization by industrial segment are available at Fundação Getúlio Vargas (FGV) and were made compatible for the CNAE according to information provided by the IBGE Census Bureau; R = Actual Interest Rate (%), representing the nominal interest rate on Bank Certificates of Deposit (BCD) as deflated by the General Price Index (IGP-DI) and annualized, provided by the Brazilian Central Bank (BCB); Emprest_BNDES = Credit Indicator – represented by Credit disbursements made by the National Bank for Social and Economic Development (BNDES), available for each segment of the transformation industry, in millions of Reals, at 1995 prices; FBKF = Government Investment – represented by the Fixed Capital – Gross Formation – Public Administration series, in millions of 1995 Reals, applying the GDP deflator as computed by the data available from the IBGE Census Bureau/ National Accounts System; EE = External Restriction – the proxy used is the annual Debt Service/GDP (%) series provided by DEPEC-BCB, Central Bank of Brazil (BCB); E = Actual Foreign Exchange Rate; D1 = Dummy control variable for international crises periods.

From the previous expression, the following general econometric model was estimated for the period between 1996 and 2010, with the variables expressed in natural logarithms (except for actual interest rates) such as to directly derive variable elasticities:

$$LogInvest\_priv_t = \beta_0 + \beta_1 LogVBPI_{it-1} + \beta_2 LogUCAP_{it} + \beta_3 R_{it} + \beta_4 LogCred_{it-1} + \beta_5 LogFBKF_{it-1} + \beta_6 LogE_{it-1} + \beta_7 LogEE_{it-1} + \beta_8 LogEE_{it-1} + \beta_9 D1 + \varepsilon_t \quad (7)$$

In which ε_t is a random disturbance.

The period under analysis is justified by the fact that sectoral data are limited due to changes in CNAE nomenclature and by the unavailability of more recent data.

For the estimates, the data used were from the Brazilian Institute of Geography and Statistics (IBGE, 2012), which are available in the Annual Industrial Survey and are broken down by sector, according to the national classification of economic activities (CNAE) for the period of 1996 to 2010. This periodization is due to data availability of PIA, which, since 1996, has changed the classification in terms of the division of activities and sampling methodology.

Table 2 presents three sectors of the Brazilian manufacturing industry, according to the division of activities, and their CNAE classification, which identifies the industrial sectors.

RESULTS

For the econometric analysis, all variables, except the real interest rate, were log-linearized using natural logarithm. The usual estimation methods and inference assume that these variables are stationary. The non-stationarity of a stochastic process is due to the existence of a unit root or stochastic trend in autoregressive process (AR) that generates the variable, and tests on the unit root hypothesis, in order to help to evaluate the presence (or absence) of stationarity in the variables used in these estimations.

As in the study of time series, the existence of a unit root in panel data may cause estimated econometric relations to become spurious. To avoid this problem, variables were tested for the Levin unit root: Lin and Chu (LLC), Im, Pesaran and Smith (IPS), FisherADF and FisherPP. The test LLC assumes the existence of a common root unit, such that ρ_i is the same for all cross-sections, or all industrial sectors (where the auto-correlation coefficientis $\alpha = \rho - 1$). The tests IPS, Fisher-ADF and Fisher-PP assume that the coefficient ρ_i may

Table 2. Brazilian capital formation industrial sectors.

CNAE	Transformation industry
29	Manufacture of machinery and equipment
34	Manufacture and assembly of motor vehicles, trailers and bodies
35	Manufacture of other transport equipment

Table 3. Level stationarity tests results for variables in the private investment model.

Commo unitary root		Individual unitary root			
	LLC	IPS	Fisher ADF	Fisher PP	Integration order
LnInv_Priv	-3.0204	-2.0946	15.4443	15.5092	I(0)
LnVBPI	-2.4586	-0.3463	7.4197	19.8849	I(0) ou I(1)
LnUCAP	-1.2232	-1.2507	3.0069	7.0761	I(0)
R	-6.1459	-2.4812	20.9721	18.4267	I(0)
LnFBKF	-15.0851	-6.1227	66.2767	72.6854	I(0)
LnCred	-9.4456	-4.7382	45.6314	50.9166	I(0)
LnE	-1.9957	-0.0058	33.8701	36.5349	I(0)
LnEE	-10.346	-4.5487	90.4013	100.5060	I(0) ou I(1)

Source: Research results.

vary according to the industrial sectorin question, characterized by the combination of individual unit root tests, by deriving a panel specific result. The number of lags in each case was determined by Schwarz's information criterion (SC).

The analysis, presented in Table 3, indicates that most of the series are stationary; in other words, do not present a unit root. For some variables, however, such as exchange rate and industrial production, the tests confirm the absence of a unitary common root, but do not eliminate the possibility of an individual unit root, which means that the average of each panel *t*-statisticsindicates that the series can be non-stationary.

In the case of the VBPI variable, a possible explanation for this is the heterogeneity between the industrial sectors, which naturally have quantitative and qualitative distinct data. It also suggests the existence of an individual unit root. However, as industrial production exhibits temporal tendency, based on tests LL andFisherPP, we choose to use the variable in levels.

Regarding the macro economic variables (R, FBKF, E, EE), the results for the considered period (1996 -2010) indicate that these are stationary, not showing neither common unit root nor individual. The only exception made is with relation to the exchange rate series (E), which needs to be differentiated to become stationary.

Initially, to identify the feasibility of using the panel data methodology, the models are estimated by Ordinary Least Squares (OLS), with all the pooled units (pool cross-section or pooling); in other words, without taking into account the possible specific sector's effects.

The existence of specific factors in each sector can be tested by the hypothesis that there are significant individual effects in the regression through a joint restrictions F test. If the value of the F's statistic exceeds the critical value, there are evidences that specific sectoral effects are present in the estimated model (Greene, 1999).

The F test (Ho:fixed effects =0) results suggest that using the panel data methodology provides relevant information gain, and in this case, the OLS estimation (pooling) may generate biased results. As the panel data methodology is the most appropriate, the issue now is to choose the estimation method for fixed effects (FE) o rrandom effects (RE).

In this case, in which the used data are not random extractions from a larger sample, the fixed effects model is the most appropriate estimation method. Furthermore, in the fixed effects model, the estimator is robust to the omission of relevant explanatory variables that do not vary over time, and even when the random effects approach is valid, the estimator of fixed effects is consistent, but less efficient. Therefore, the estimation by fixed effects appears to be the most appropriate for sector's investment models.

The investment equations are estimated by fixed effects and are robust to the presence of multicollinearity between variables, estimated by the Generalized Least Squares method (GLS) with weighting for individuals (industry sectors), which makes the model also robust to the heteroscedasticity between the individual error terms. Moreover, standard deviations were calculated by the

Table 4. Investment sectorial equations.

Estimation by Fixed Effects - Dependent Vabriable: Private Investiment 1996-2010							
Explanatory variables (1)	**EQ1**	**EQ2**	**EQ3**	**EQ4**	**EQ5**	**EQ6**	**EQ7**
C	-2.2574	-1.9176	-1.4650	-3.0611	-6.4315	-11.0640	-13.9077
	[-0.3120]	[-0.2579]	[-0.1788]	[-0.4179]	[-0.8675]	[-0.9718]	[-1.1724]
	(0.7570)	(0.7981)	(0.8592)	(0.6788)	(0.3921)	(0.3392)	(0.2509)
LnVBPI(-1)	0.6134	0.8560	0.6171	0.6108	0.6900	0.9317	0.8993
	[3.0732]	[3.5707]	[3.0361]	[3.0476]	[3.4756]	[3.8041]	[3.6193]
	(0.0042)	(0.0011)	0.0047	0.0046	(0.0015)	(0.0007)	(0.0012)
LnUCAP	1.1611	0.2673	1.1255	1.2991	1.7204	1.1576	1.6455
	[0.6921]	[0.1461]	[0.6581]	[0.7677]	[1.0372]	[0.5824]	[0.7956]
	(0.4937)	(0.8847)	(0.5152)	(0.4482)	(0.3074)	(0.5647)	(0.4329)
R	0.0197	0.0215	0.0192	0.0219	0.0209	0.0256	0.0322
	[1.5618]	[1.7484]	[1.4729]	[1.6920]	[1.7061]	[1.9003]	[2.0886]
	(0.1279)	(0.090)		(0.1004)	(0.0977)	(0.0674)	(0.0460)
LnCred(-1)		0.2900				0.2393	0.2663
		[1.7212]				[1.3930]	[1.5217]
		0.0949				(0.1742)	(0.1393)
LnFBKF (-1)			0.0710			0.4529	0.6076
			[0.2179]			0.9280	[1.1694]
			(0.8289)			0.3610	(0.2521)
LnE(-1)				-0.2242		-0.1241	-0.3793
				[-0.8581]		[-0.2893]	[-0.7336]
				(0.3972)		(0.7744)	0.4693
LnEE(-1)					-0.2346	-0.4298	-0.5134
					[-1.7488]	[-1.8332]	[-2.0269]
					0.0899	(0.0770)	(0.0523)
Dummy							-0.1906
							[-0.8914]
							(0.3803)
R-squared	0.9204	0.9272	0.9206	0.9222	0,9274	0.9370	0.9387
Adjusted R-squared	0.9084	0.9135	0.9057	0.9077	0.9138	0.9174	0.9768
S.E. of Regression	0.3382	0.3286	0.3432	0.3396	0.3281	0.3211	0.3222
SSR	3.7757	3.4557	3.7701	3.6907	3.4463	2.9909	2.9084
Log Likelihood	-9.8066	-8.0800	-9.7776	-9.3629	-8.0265	-5.2633	-4.7175
DW stat	1.2576	1.4946	1.2753	1.2955	1.2964	1.6326	1.5897
Prob (F-statiscs)	0.0000	0.0000	0.0000	0.0000	0.0000	0.0000	0.0000

Source: Research findings. (1) t-statistics in brackets, followed by p-values in parentheses.

White matrix (period) making them robust to the serial correlation and heteroscedasticity in the model´s time dimension. The results are presented in Table 4. The results in the table indicate that the quantitative variables, Gross Value of Industrial Production (LogVBPI) and utilization of industrial capacity (LogUCAP) were relevant in explaining private investment. The signs found for the estimated coefficients were positive.

The coefficient for real interest rate (R) is positive which is contrary to the theory of investment. However, the magnitude of the coefficient is close to zero, indicating that changes in the levels of real interest rates for the period 1996 to 2010 do not affect the decision making of private sector investment.

Despite the theoretical importance of the investment opportunity cost, the difficulty of finding negative and significant coefficient for this variable is abundantly reported in the literature (Chirinko, 1993). In the Brazilian case, the result found for the interest rates effect upon private investment can be explained by the common practice of Brazilian companies resorting to their own retained earnings to fund their investments. Another possible explanation for the result is that the interest rate may be related to the low availability of funds.

The importance of credit availability on the private investment is confirmed in Equation 2 (EQ2). The results show that increases in credit supply through the increases of BNDES's credit disbursements system intended for industrial sectors increase the investment in subsequent periods, unveiling the importance of offering long-term financing lines funded with stable amounts, and designed to finance the private sector's investment projects.

The impact of public investment on the private sector's investment is tested in Equation 3 (EQ3). The variable public investment coefficient (FBKF) is significantand has a positive sign, indicating that public investment tends to complement private investment.

The estimated coefficient for the exchange rate is negative (see EQ4 in Table 4), suggesting that a more depreciated exchange rated encourages the import of capital goods, at least in the short term, and increases the financial commitments of companies' external indebtedness.

In relation to external debt, the Equation 5 (EQ5) indicates the existence of a negative relationship between investment and external debtservices. In recent years, the existence of external constraints may have limited private sector's investment. This can be explained by the increase of the private sector's external debt in the 1990s and the decrease of thepublic sector's participation in the fund raising and financing investment programs.

Equation 6 (EQ6) tests all the variables together, but without the dummy variable control. The signs are coherent with the theory and they were the same if compared with the equations that were tested with each variable separately.

Finally, a variable control was included in the estimated Equation 7 for periods of economic instability, represented by a Dummy (D1), which assumes unit values for 1997 (Asian Crisis), 1998 (Russian crisis), 1999 (Argentina Crisis and Brazilian Exchange Rate Devaluation) and 2008 (World Crisis) and zero for periods without crisis. It is observed from the results, a negative coefficient which indicates a negative effect on private investment variable.

Coefficients with fixed effects

To evaluate the specificities of each sector, we estimated the magnitude of sectoral fixed effects. Each estimated sector coefficient corresponds to the pure effect of each sector, that is, the difference in the average investment of a particular sector, compared to the annual average for the sector, which is not due to the variations in the dependent variables (Greene, 1999). Thus, the co-efficient represents the actual investment related to the specific factors of each industry sector, regardless the included variables in the model.

Table 5 shows the estimated coefficients sectors. It is noted that the coefficients signs vary according to the sectors, and also show the distinctive magnitudes among the sectors and models. The sectors with positive co-efficients have invested relatively higher than other sectors during the period in question, regardless of the changes in the explanatory variables that were considered in the model. On the other hand, sectors that exhibit negative coefficients are those who, without taking into account variations in the explanatory variables, had a level of investment below the annual average per sector. The results presented in Table 5 indicate that sector 29 (Manufacture of machinery and equipment) and sector 34 (Manufacture and assembly of motor vehicles, trailers and bodies) showed positive signs. It is observed that the intensity varies with the inclusion of the tested variables along the equations. The Brazilian industry sectors that have reduced coefficients, close to zero, invest relatively more according to changes in the explanatory variables; in other words, have few specific effects and are fairly well represented by the estimated models.

The case of sector 29 (Machinery and Equipment) is symbolic in this aspect. Thus, it can infer that the credit variable (EQ2), pointed out by the economic theory, as an indicator to determine investment in developing countries, is also included in the models that most explain investment in the Brazilian economy.

As for the sectors that have more specificity, they tend to have higher sectorial coefficients, indicating that they invest according to other factors, other than those identified in empirical models. This situation can be observed by the sector 35 in the Equations1, 3, 4 and 5. Sector 35 (Manufacture of other transport equipment) showed a negative sign, which means that it had an investment below the annual average level per sector. The negative sign can be explained byseveral reasons: international policies effects (trade liberalization and exchange arte), international crises or also because of its low technological intensity.

Finally, a comparative analysis suggests that Equation 2, which tests the hypothesis of credit constraints, presents lower sectorial magnitude coefficients for the three analyzed sectors, followed by Equations 6 and 7. This means that these two last models are perhaps the best ones to reflect the investment sector of the manufacturing goods industries that were analyzed in this study.

Conclusion

This study analyzed preliminarily the main determinants of private investments for a few segments of the Brazilian capital goods industry, as of a panel analysis of the period between 1996 and 2010.

Table 5. Coefficientswith fixed effects.

Sectors	EQ1	EQ2	EQ3	EQ4	EQ5	EQ6	EQ7
29(1)	0.1891	0.1320	0.1865	0.1970	0.2063	0.0322	0.0190
34(2)	0.5926	0.5323	0.5918	0.5864	0.4999	0.3801	0.3807
35(3)	-0.7817	-0.4003	-0.7783	-0.7835	-0.7054	-0.3478	-0.3617

Source: Research findings.(1) Manufacture of machineryand equipment; (2) Manufacture and assembly of motor vehicles, trailers and bodies; (3) Manufacture of other transport equipment.

The estimated investment models have confirmed the relevance of the quantitative Gross Industrial Production Value and Capacity Utilization variables to explain private investment. The relationship found between the interest rate and private investment were positive and significant in the sectoral models, but the coefficient found is close to zero, suggesting that the actual interest rate increase between 1996 and 2010, dooes not exert a negative impact over the private investment.

This empirical evidence, apparently contradicting the economic theory, may be related to this country's private investment financing conditions, which, because of the low volume of available resources, limits the businesses investments to the use of retained earnings and bank credit.

Sectoral results also indicated that increases in the credit supply through the increases of BNDES credit system disbursement increased private investment in subsequent periods, confirming the hypothesis that Brazilian companies depend upon long-term funds offered by official development agencies.

The presence of instability may also be a harmful factor for investment financing, since instability creates uncertainty and hinders long-term funds sources. The negative relationship between differentiated interest rates and investment also reflects the entrepreneurs' aversion to uncertainty and instability, since the result suggests that highly volatile foreign exchange periods exert a negative effect upon the private investment. A devaluated foreign exchange rate also discourages capital goods imports and raises the financial liabilities of foreign-indebted companies, which decreases investment in the economy.

The industry-estimated coefficients (individual sectors effects of the processing industry) suggest that certain sectors, such as the industry responsible for manufacturing of other transport equipment showed a negative sign, meaning that they had a level of investment below the annual average per sector. On the other hand, the other two sectors analyzed indicate that the manufacturing machinery and equipment sector and the manufacturing and assembly of motor vehicles, trailers and bodies sectors showed positive signs. These sectors had invested relatively more in accordance with the changes in the explanatory variables.

ACKNOWLEDGMENT

We are indebted to an anonymous reviewer for constructive comments. The authors are thankful to Dom Cabral Foundation and to Prof. David Macintyre for his English review.

REFERENCES

ABIMAQ (2012). Department of Competitiveness, Economics and Statistics. [Web:] http://www.abimaq.org.br/site.aspx/pginicial_DCEE. [Date of Access: 06/07/2012].

BACEN (2012). Economia e Finanças. Séries Temporais. [Web:] http://www.bcb.gov.br[Date of Access: 03/06/2012].

Chirinko RS (1993). Business fixed investment spending: modeling strategies, empirical results, and policy implications. J. Econ. Lit. (31):1875-1911.

De Oliveira CA, Tadeu HFB, Silva JTM (2012a). Determinants of Private Investment in Brazil: An Empirical Analysis of the Period 1996-2011. Int. Bus. Manag. (6):471-475.

De Oliveira CA, Tadeu HFB, Silva JTM, Berger D (2012b). Infrastructure, Competitiveness and Determinants of Private Investment in the Brazilian. Fundação Dom Cabral. Working papers, CI12141: 1-12. [Web:] http://acervo.ci.fdc.org.br/AcervoDigital/Cadernos%20de%20Idéias/2012/CI1214Inglês.pdf[Date of Access: 03/9/2012].

Greene WH (1999). Econometric Analysis. Prentice-Hall, New Jersey. 3rd Edition.

Hill RC, Griffiths WE, andJudge GG (1999). Econometria. São Paulo: Saraiva.

Hsiao C (1986). Analysis of panel data. Econometric Society Monographs. Cambridge: Cambridge University Press. No. 11.

Hsiao C (2006). Panel Data Analysis: Advantages and Challenges. University of Southern California. Wise Working Paper Series 0602: pp.1-35.

IBGE (2012). Sistema de Contas Nacionais Consolidadas. [Web:] http://www.ibge.gov.br[Date of Access: 03/06/2012].

Stock JH, Watson MW (2004). Econometria. Sao Paulo: Addison Wesley Bra. p.486.

The role of internal audit function in the public sector context in Saudi Arabia

Abdulaziz Alzeban[1] and Nedal Sawan[2]

[1]King Abdulaziz University, Saudi Arabia
[2]Liverpool Business School, United Kingdom.

This paper contributes to the debate on the role of internal auditing in the public sector by focusing on the nature and practice of internal auditing in organisations that are subject to audit by the General Audit Bureau. Archival and documentary analysis, supported by 29 semi-structured interviews revealed that the underpinnings of the Saudi Internal Audit Regulation did not tie in directly with perceived international best practice - the International Standards for the Professional Practice of Internal Auditing. Institutional factors are also likely to play a part in terms of the existence of the state-required 'Follow-up department' in all organizations, tasked with performing investigation and inspection, the 'auditing department' (which monitors the propriety of transactions and accounting), and the work of the mandatory 'Financial Representative (Controller)'.

Key words: Saudi Arabia, internal audit, public sector, competence, audit regulation.

INTRODUCTION

In the broader context of governance and control, increasing importance has been attached to the internal auditing function (Prawitt et al., 2008), and questions as to its effectiveness in discharging its responsibilities are being asked with greater frequency. Indeed, the various corporate scandals, coupled with the recent worldwide financial crisis have fuelled debate on whether internal auditing is being performed appropriately, not only in terms of ensuring compliance with the range of controls to which organizations are subject, but also in respect of its role in risk management, much more recently assumed by the function. In consequence, the regulatory framework has demanded greater disclosure of governance information, and internal audit function (IAF) has risen to this challenge, adopting an enhanced focus on corporate governance processes generally. Without doubt, IAF is inextricably linked with governance, given its role within the organization, and should therefore, be capable of responding to all regulatory requirements effectively.

However, the IAF is not developed to the same extent in all organizations. For example, in Australia, a large number of listed firms either do not operate any IAF at all, or employ only one or two staff for this activity (Goodwin and Kent, 2006; Carey et al., 2000). And in the United States, Nagy and Cenker (2002) found that where the IAF is in evidence, its character differs substantially, appearing in its traditional role in some organizations, whilst assuming risk management and consultancy operations in others, and taking a middle road elsewhere. Moreover, there is evidence (Maher and Akers, 2003) that CEOs in America do not generally want internal audit involvement in the development of organizational systems. Clearly, the influence of senior management is a determining force in the scope of the IAF, as noted by Sarens and De Beelde (2006b), reporting on Belgian firms.

In the Saudi Arabian context, internal audit has traditionally concentrated on the propriety of transactions and accounting, and indeed until 2004, there was no legal requirement for such a function to exist. However, with the issue of Resolution No 235 (2004), all organizations that are subject to audit by the General Audit Bureau (GAB) are required to establish an IAF. Nonetheless, currently, there are still many large organizations that have not complied with that directive, and are operating

*Corresponding author. E-mail: ne2000dal@hotmail.com.

without IAF (Alzeban and Gwilliam, 2012).

Against this background, this paper explores current practice of IAF in Saudi Arabia's public sector organisations, with the intention of determining the present state of internal auditing in the public sector, and how its performance is influenced. This involves a consideration of the development of internal auditing in Saudi Arabia, concentrating on the competence of the internal audit, independence and objectivity of internal audit, management support for internal audit, internal audit activities, and interaction between audited organisations and external auditors (as performed by the GAB). The paper contributes to the understanding of the nature and characteristics of the IAF by empirically exploring these aspects of the function in the Saudi Arabian context. Previous studies into the role of audit and internal audit in Saudi Arabia have largely been focused toward the private sector (Al-Shetwi et al., 2011; Al-Twaijry et al., 2004; Woodworth and Said, 1996; Asairy, 1993) and to date there has been few systematic academic enquiry into the role of internal audit in the public sector (Alzeban and Gwilliam, 2012). Given the dominance of the public sector within the Saudi State and economy this research seeks to make a contribution to redressing this imbalance.

The paper is structured as follows: the next section presents the development, in general, of internal audit in Saudi Arabia, and the manner in which it was established in the public sector. A summary of the related literature appears in the section thereafter, and the paper then proceeds to describe the nature of the research work conducted, including the rationale underlying the semi-structured interview methodology utilised in the study. The main results of the interviews are subsequently described, and the final section provides an overview and conclusion.

Saudi Arabia: internal audit background

The development of internal audit in Saudi Arabia

The Kingdom of Saudi Arabia has a relatively recent development trajectory. Since oil was discovered in the 1930s, its economy has gradually prospered, reaching the stage where it is now the largest oil supplier worldwide. Indeed, the world's largest oil company, ARAMCO (Arabian American Oil Company) is wholly owned by the state, and despite a slight drop in oil revenues over recent years, they continue to account for over 75% of the state's income (Ministry of Economy and Planning, 2009). Accompanying this rapid economic growth has been a large and dominating public sector (characteristic of most developing countries), which operates according to a set of strong and deeply-rooted cultural beliefs underpinned by Islamic values and tribal relationships. It can be understood, therefore, that ideas regarding accountability and audit that have emerged in western economies are somewhat alien in the Saudi environment, but nonetheless, in the last few decades they have been introduced incrementally, and have spread since they first appeared in the banking sector and in very large companies (Al-Twaijry et al., 2003).

The first IIA Chapter was formed in 1982 in Saudi Arabia, being in ARAMCO, with the purpose of increasing the number of IIA members, and supervising CIA examinations to allow internal auditors within the region to gain the CIA qualification (Al-Twaijry et al., 2003). Additionally, it aimed at encouraging good practice and disseminating information through such media as newsletters. The Chapter gained in size and operation, developing links with King Fahad University in Dhahran, and at the time of Al-Twaijry's study, there were approximately 75 members, a quarter of these being Saudi nationals. During its operation, the Chapter has suffered from resource shortages and legal limitations on the scope of its activities – but that said, it has been innovative in facilitating the uniform CIA examination in the Kingdom (Al-Twaijry et al., 2003). Now, as a result of the various efforts over the last 30 years to professionalise the IAF, the Council of Ministers has passed a resolution to establish the Saudi Institute of Internal Auditors (SOCPA, 2011).

This came in the aftermath of Resolution No 235 (2004), requiring all organizations to establish an IAF to be monitored by the GAB, and the subsequent Resolution No 129 (2007) containing additional guidance and addressing issues such as: the requirements and objectives of internal audit, recruitment of the head of internal audit and audit staff, responsibilities of the head of internal audit, scope of work, internal audit reports, relationship with other parties, and adherence to professional auditing standards.

Not surprisingly, given the gradual acceptance of the IAF in Saudi Arabia, there has been some interest in this respect by scholars (Al-Shetwi et al., 2011; Al-Twaijry et al., 2004; Woodworth and Said, 1996; Asairy, 1993) but they have concentrated on the private sector, and very few researchers (Alzeban and Gwilliam, 2012) have considered the IAF in public sector organizations. Clearly, this situation reflects a serious omission that should be rectified considering the fact that the Kingdom is dominated by the public sector. This study attempts to remedy that imbalance in literature.

The resolution of 2004

As already indicated, over the last quarter of a century, Saudi Arabia has developed considerably in all aspects, such that significant economic expansion has been witnessed. This is characterised by the increased involvement of the private sector, much diversification of activity, significant business activity both within and outside of the Kingdom, and an increased concentration and expenditure on development projects. Naturally, these levels of development have raised the appreciation of financial monitoring and reporting as crucial in all organisations since ultimately the country prospers or suffers according to the way in which its financial resources are employed. The GAB, with responsibility for financial oversight, recommended the establishment of IAF in all organisations that are subject to its audit, and as a logical outcome to that recommendation, Resolution No 235 issued in 2004 mandated all such organisations to establish an IAF.

Commenting on the motivation for that resolution, Al-Rahaily and Al-Zahrany (2007) highlighted several reasons for its issuance. An important one was the need to eliminate the corruption existing in public sector organisations and to reduce the number of errors, irregularities and fraud. Associated with this was the need to identify and remove weak internal control systems, and replace them with robust systems. Furthermore, the increased number and size of government organisations had led to additional government expenditures and greater complexity of transactions, all of which were too many for the GAB to monitor efficiently and effectively, given the Bureau's lack of qualified staff. Moreover, it was clear that some organisations did not take the IAF seriously, not being prepared to improve their financial errors and irregularities from one year to the next. Additionally, was the need to respond to the request from the International Organisation of Supreme Audit Institutions (INTOSAI) to establish IAF in all public sector organisations, and the growing awareness within the GAB of the importance of the need to provide a means to safeguard assets and public resources.

The resolution of 2007 for the internal audit regulation

In 2007, Resolution No 129 was issued in respect of the Internal Audit Regulation (IAR). According to Al-Rahaily and Al-Zahrany (2007), several steps were involved in drafting the regulation before its final approval and release by the Council of Ministers in 2007. The first was the formation of a committee by the GAB President after the Resolution in 2004, to issue an IAR in collaboration with the Institute of Public Administration. The first draft of the draft of the regulation was issued in May 2005. This was followed in October (2005), when the King requested the GAB to re-consider the regulation in co-operation with four other bodies - the Institute of Public Administration, the Ministry of Finance (MoF), the Ministry of Civil Service (MCS), and the Investigation and Control Board (ICB). The next year (March 2006), the second draft was released and submitted to the King who in turn, referred it to the Bureau of Experts at the Council of Ministers. Finally, in 2007, the Regulation was released as Resolution No 129.

LITERATURE REVIEW

Within the literature, there are different approaches to the exploration of IAF. In this study, the focus is on competence of internal audit, independence and objectivity of internal audit, management support for internal audit, internal audit activities and interaction between audited organisations and external auditors.

Competence of internal audit

The competence of all staff involved in the IAF is crucial, being clarified as a prime component of effective internal audit activity (IIA, 2006). Internal auditors must be sufficiently qualified, and in possession of all the requisite knowledge and skill to discharge the responsibilities associated with audit duties *International Standards for the Professional Practice of Internal Auditing* (ISPPIA).

Previous academic studies have focused on the need for personnel to be appropriately qualified if a high level of IAF is to be achieved (Alzeban and Gwilliam, 2012; Vijayakumar and Nagaraja, 2012; Unegbu and Kida, 2011; Ahmad et al., 2009). Internal audit quality is very much identified as reliant upon the competence, as demonstrated by qualifications and experience, of the auditors involved (Gramling and Hermanson, 2009; Zain et al., 2006). Moreover, two types of skill are suggested by Seol and Sarkis (2005) as being relevant, these being cognitive skills and behavioural skills. In the case of the former, the auditor is required to demonstrate technical, analytic, and appreciative skills, whereas in behavioural terms, it is essential that s/he has good interpersonal and organizational skills. These ideas are echoed by other scholars. For example, Harrington (2004) concentrates on paper qualifications, experience and IT skills, whilst Picket (2004) highlights the value of abilities in the cognitive domain (that is being focused, helpful, decisive and balanced). Not surprisingly, superior communication skills are pinpointed as crucial (Smith, 2005; Sawyer et al., 2003; Loss, 2000).

Independence and objectivity

The independence and objectivity of the IAF is also paramount. The ISPPIA and IIA Practice Advisory indicated that this can be achieved by: ensuring appropriate reporting mechanisms such that the internal audit department has direct access to the Board and senior management, by giving it the authority to access any records it deems fit, by allowing full access to all employees and departments, by placing strict conditions on the appointment and removal of the head of internal audit, and by not undertaking non-audit work. Internal audit independence is challenged by the function being used as a stepping stone to other positions, by empowering the CEO or CFO to approve the IAF's budget and interfere with the internal plan, and implicitly, in the relationship between the internal audit manager and the audit committee (Christopher et al., 2009). The audit committee must be invested with the authority to appoint, dismiss and assess the performance of the internal audit manager. IAF should be treated and therefore, seen, as credible. In this respect, it was shown by Sarens and De Beelde (2006b) in their examination of the expectations and perceptions of senior management and internal auditors in Belgium, that objectivity is absent when the IAF operates mainly to support management, and when it has a weak relationship with the audit committee. Three factors have been suggested by Peursem (2005) as impacting upon internal auditors' ability to be independent from management, these being: their professional status, the presence of a formal and informal communication network, and the internal auditors' reporting position.

Ahlawat and Lowe (2004) argue that internal auditors are highly influenced by their reporting position, and hence, a reporting hierarchy that includes senior management is inappropriate. That said, Leung et al. (2004) observe that despite best practice suggesting chief internal auditors report to the audit committee, in Australia, more than 22% of a sample of such individuals were found to report to the CEO or CFO. This is clearly a poor national situation, since when reporting is to senior management rather than the audit committee, internal auditors are not able to protect the organization against fraudulent activities (James, 2003). In this circumstance, the close relationships between management and the IAF render the assurance of objectivity and independence extremely difficult (Glascock, 2002). Additionally, where internal auditors are in receipt of incentives-based compensation, which include reported earnings as one measure of performance, their objectivity and independence may well be hampered (DeZoort et al., 2000).

Management Support for Internal Audit

Irrespective of the need for internal auditors to have access to the audit committee, the IAF must nonetheless, interact with senior management on a close and regular basis since, the character of the function is determined completely by senior management's resource allocated to it, and the support and credence it gives to the role of organization-wide. Additionally, the involvement of senior management in formulating the work plan is both necessary and unavoidable (a requirement of the ISPPIA), since it is through top managers that internal auditors are empowered to secure access to the various functional departments. Hence, the ease with which internal auditors perform their duties is a reflection of senior management's sponsorship. Having access facilitated, internal auditors must keep senior managers informed of all activities it performs, and of the conclusions reached (Badara and Saidin, 2012). Reporting in the Malaysian public sector, Ahmad et al. (2009) observe management support to be the second highest contributor to internal audit effectiveness, and that with such support, sufficient resources are usually allocated for the function, and its recommendations implemented; whereas without it, a lack of commitment to independence on the part of internal auditors is likely. Further, it is also reported in studies conducted in the public sector that management support has a strong impact upon the effectiveness of the internal audit function, and management support is important as a construct in its own right but also via its links to issues of resourcing, competence and qualification, and independence (Alzeban and Gwilliam, 2012; Cohen and Sayag, 2010; Mihret and Yismaw, 2007).

Internal audit activities

Internal audit activities are also explored in the literature, specifically those included in the new IIA definition of the function. In this respect, several studies have considered the task of risk management now formally assigned to internal audit (Vijayakumar and Nagaraja, 2012; Mihret, 2010), obtaining differing outcomes. In the USA, the new requirements of the Sarbanes Oxley Act relating to internal control and review, and disclosure, emphasize the need for internal auditors to step up to the challenge of doing more than the traditional duties of assurance. Yet, Gramling and Myers (2006) report that a half of all their sample of chief internal audit executives in the USA stated that they only spent up to 10% of their time and budget on risk management activities, whereas in their comparison of the situation in Belgian and US firms, Sarens and De Beelde (2006a) reveal a much greater impact on the part of internal auditors in risk management and control awareness. Furthermore, in large Italian companies it is seen that the IAF makes a sound contribution to the risk management process (Allegrini and D'Onza, 2003), as do a large majority of internal auditors in Australian firms (Leung et al., 2003).

Alongside risk management activities are those concerned with control, in which respect, Abbott et al. (2010) found a strongly positive link between oversight of the IAF by the audit committee and the amount of the budget devoted to internal controls-based activities; and in terms of consulting activities, it is seen that these have risen significantly in UK, Irish, and Italian internal audit departments (Selim et al., 2009). Within these consulting activities, the most common in the UK and Ireland are risk management, project management, governance, contingency planning and disaster recovery, whilst in Italy, they are legislative compliance, governance and risk management. Examining this issue across 15 European countries, Paape et al. (2003) found that 64% of chief internal audit executives were involved in consultancy and management support activities. That said, the IAF appears to have little involvement in mergers, acquisitions, and divestitures (MAD) in USA and European firms (Selim et al., 2003).

Interaction between audited organisations and external auditors

Co-ordination and co-operation are essential between internal and external auditors to facilitate the overall process of audit and to raise the professional profile of the function (Messier et al., 2011). Activities such as joint planning, information exchange, reporting to each other, all prevent duplication of effort and develop mutual trust, ultimately accelerating the audit process. The internal/external auditor relationship is a prime concern within the professional standards. The ISPPIA, *Coordination Standard*, for example considers that there should be at least information exchange and co-ordination in respect of the activities undertaken by each party. Building upon such a fundamental relationship, internal and external auditors should develop a professional and mutually trusting relationship, resulting in a more effective and quality-oriented audit. Trusted and comprehensive information provided by the internal auditor helps the external auditor to work quicker as s/he is spared the need to delve deeply and has faith in the material provided. This in turn brings savings to the company concerned. In the absence of such fruitful interaction between the internal and external auditors, effectiveness of both the internal and external audit function is damaged, at least in the public sector (Alzeban and Gwilliam, 2012; Gwilliam and El-Nafabi, 2002; Brierley et al., 2001). In the Saudi Arabian public sector context, it is found (Al-Garni, 2008; Almohaimeed, 2000) that the absence of co-operation between audited organisations and the GAB impairs the ability of external auditors to discharge their responsibilities effectively, especially in respect of agreeing and implementing the GAB's recommendations. Furthermore, it is reported (Summary Reports of GAB, 2008, 2010) that the lack of such co-operation is directly responsible for repeated financial errors and irregularities.

Whilst, these five dimensions of the IAF have been well researched, it is clear from the literature that most of the effort has been in the developed country context, and that a need exists for the body of knowledge to be supplemented with information concerning these internal audit aspects in developing countries. This study assists in satisfying that need.

METHODS AND SAMPLING

A qualitative approach was used to gain in-depth understanding of the nature and characteristics of the IAF in the Saudi public sector, and consequently, interviews were conducted. Questions were built upon the general objectives of the study, and covered the main aspects including competence of the internal audit, independence of internal audit, management support for internal audit, internal audit activities and interaction between audited organisations and external auditors (who work for the GAB). A total of 29 face-to-face semi-structured interviews were undertaken with three groups: 9 internal auditors, 10 general and senior managers in Saudi public sector organisations, and 10 external auditors working in the GAB. Different sets of interview questions relating to the principal variables under investigation were prepared for these groups, but within those sets there were a number of questions that were almost identical for each group.

The duration of the interviews was between 15 and 90 min, although all the interviews were conducted, as far as possible, in the same way. This not only meant that the same questions were asked, but also sought to ensure that each interviewee would understand the questions in the same way. Moreover, interviewees were encouraged to expand on any issues that were of particular interest to them. With the help of tape recording the interview was explained to interviewees, and then interviewees were asked if they would allow this process. Almost all interviews were recorded but few interviewees (only two) were not prepared to agree to this, perhaps worried about having their responses formalized in this way. For those interviews that were not recorded, notes were taken during the interviews, and a full text was immediately written in Arabic after the interviews.

Acknowledging the investment in time made by interviewees to the interview process was an important step in ensuring the success of the interviews. An appointment was made either on the phone or face-to-face with each interviewee before conducting the interview. This step was taken to 1) consider the time commitments of the interviewee; and 2) to ensure that the interviewee was not involved in any other task during the interview time and would thus be ready for the meeting.

The interviews were restricted to two cities, Riyadh and Jeddah, where large public sector organisations, independent and quasi-independent organisations are located. These organisations are subject to audit by the GAB and are responsible for the formulation and implementation of national economic plans, administering and managing all the national service organisations, and constructing the national projects and schemes. Moreover, they are subject to investigation by the GAB auditors, and are considered large in terms of the budget received and the number of employees. Hence, they make a contribution to the country's economy, strategic plans and education.

RESULTS AND DISCUSSION

Competence of internal audit

It was unanimously confirmed that the lack of qualified staff stands represents one of the most important problems facing internal audit in the Saudi public sector. Several reasons were offered for this situation, including staff recruitment, educational qualifications, professional qualifications, work experience and continuous development.

Staff recruitment

Twenty six interviewees indicated poor recruitment

procedures and criteria in respect of internal audit staff. The selection process for such staff is performed randomly based on the choice of either the general manager of financial management or the head of internal audit. As examples, one interviewee stated: *"there are no adequate rules for recruitment"* (M9), and another (M4) said that the head of the department responsible for recruitment uses his own procedures of favouritism through which *"he chooses his friends".* Moreover, analysis of the interviews showed that the selection process in respect of internal audit staff was based on reputation and relationship with top management, for example:

The criterion used in the selection process of internal auditors does not relate to education or work experience, but [...] to friendship and having a good relationship with the top management team including the head of the internal audit department in order to be an internal auditor (M3).

This absence of recruitment procedures and criteria is addressed in the IAR (2007), Articles 4 and 5 which highlight the important criteria to be met when appointing a head of internal audit, and internal audit staff. Article 4 does specify the number of years of work experience required of the head of internal audit, but Article 5 relating to internal audit staff, refers only to the need for relevant work experience (without specification of the required length), and it permits organisations to appoint diploma holders without any reference to a minimum length of work experience. Moreover, this Article pays no attention to the knowledge, skills, and other competencies required by internal auditors to effectively perform their responsibilities. Nor does it consider the outcome of the appointment of individuals who are not qualified to discharge the duties assigned to them. This deficiency in the IAR may be one reason for the different views among organizations in their selection of internal audit staff, and the fact that some organizations choose these personnel haphazardly, merely to comply with the resolution. Another reason for inappropriate selection of internal audit staff is the simple fact that there may be insufficient qualified people available, so even if suitable selection criteria were in operation, the problem of the lack of expertise and appointments made on the wrong basis remains.

Educational qualifications

The educational qualifications possessed by internal audit staff are generally of a low calibre. A total of 21 interviewees confirmed this, and identified several reasons. One interviewee (M10) indicated that the practice of transferring staff from other departments to the internal audit department provided the opportunity to *"get rid of the worst staff"* as *"heads of other departments would not release good staff"*; and. M18, who majored in a field not related to auditing work, noted that he was transferred to the internal audit department "*under a request from general financial manager*" and that he "*cannot reject the manager's request*". He added that the acceptance of the transfer was "*part of the co-operation with management*". Another interviewee raised a separate issue relating to the fact that a transfer might be the only way to obtain promotion even though the individual concerned had no relevant auditing qualification. Seven interviewees linked this to the lack of support from the MoF as it "*is not supporting organisations by providing new posts*".

Professional qualifications

Professional certification (example CIA, CPA) is considered an important indicator of technical proficiency (Tarr, 2002; Lewington, 1996; Myers and Gramling, 1997; Felts, 1994), but sadly, interviewees revealed that internal auditors did not possess any such qualification. Indeed, they indicated that such professional qualifications are not fully recognised in the public sector, for example M2 stated "*the MCS does not co-operate in recognising the professional qualifications, and it does not give the professional qualifications the appropriate classification".* Furthermore, interview responses from members of both the MoF and the MCS suggested a lack of understanding of the importance of having qualified staff to perform the internal audit function as "*it is all simple daily transactions*" and there is no need for holders of "*professional qualifications*".

Another issue may be that the level of educational qualification creates ineligibility to sit for such examinations (to qualify as a Saudi CPA it is necessary to hold an accounting degree – but this is not the case for the CIA qualification). However it is possibly that to date, the importance of professional qualification has not yet been fully appreciated in the Saudi work environment.

A more specific consideration is that there is no separate national internal audit qualification. The Saudi Organisation for Certified Public Accountants (SOCPA) has developed the CPA, but it has not established an internal audit qualification for either the private or public sector. One reason might be that the SOCPA and Saudi Accounting Association (SAA) emphasize accounting and public accountants rather than the internal audit function (Al-Twaijry, 2000).

Work experience

Twenty four interviewees commented on the absence of sufficient experience irrespective of qualifications held; for example, "*Currently, there are no members of staff qualified to carry out internal audit duties and staff experience is not related to internal audit work"* (M22). Four interviewees believed that work experience would naturally be gained while performing the internal audit work, one in particular saying: *"a university degree is the most important thing as experience is of minor importance because the staff will obtain the experience when undertaking the work"* (M17).

Another explanatory factor might be that internal audit in the Saudi public sector is a relatively new phenomenon, and therefore, it is not surprising that many individuals performing internal audit work are relatively inexperienced. In many countries with a longer history and experience of internal audit, internal audit is not necessarily seen as a lifelong career by those working in the field (in the same way that external audit is only a lifelong career for a relative small percentage of those working as external auditors). However, it may be that the practice of rotating employees around departments contributes to a relatively high level of staff turnover – and also the absence of specific criteria in the IAR regarding the extent of experience necessary to fulfil internal audit roles below that of departmental head.

Continuous development

Continuing development and training of internal audit staff is addressed in Article 9 of the IAR, which states that the head of the internal audit department should prepare a training plan for staff and that this plan should be approved by the first official of the organisation. The plan should contain details of the location and timing of the training and the content should be designed according to the training need. At the international level, the IIA recommends that internal auditors should complete 80 h of acceptable continuous professional education (CPE) every two years (IIA, 2000),that is, an average of 40 h each year. However, analysis of the interview data revealed that there is a shortage of development and training programmes and too few opportunities to attend such training that did exist. To take an example, one interviewee said:

The quality of the staff is very low. Since most of them just have high school qualification, they need training to become sufficiently competent to carry out their duties efficiently. Internal auditors don't have the chance to attend either training programmes or conferences abroad to develop their skills (M5).

Interviewees identified several reasons for the lack of training, including financial issues (example, the amount allocated for training staff), shortage of internal audit-related programmes available to internal auditors, and a small number of internal audit staff such that the head of department might not allow staff to attend such training because of the department's inability to continue operating during their absence. Another explanatory factor might be that to date, there is no specific training centre for either internal auditors or accountants in public sector organisations as a whole.

Given the relative paucity of professional qualifications (and that internal auditors possessed either only high school educational qualifications or a non-relevant degree), and the low levels of work experience, there does appear to be scope for a greater focus on the need to upgrade the skills of internal audit personnel via continuing professional training and development. Organisations should pay more attention to developing the skills of those without adequate educational or work experience in the field of internal auditing.

This lack of qualified staff was seen as one of the reasons for the absence of an audit plan. Eight interviewees indicated that the low level of educational qualifications and lack of training influenced the preparation of such plan, one saying: "*Internal auditors need more training to improve their skills in order to be able to prepare plans (M21)"*. Another interviewee stated that *"internal auditors have high school qualifications and cannot design any such plan because they do not know how to do this"* (M23).

Independence and objectivity of internal audit

Interviewees explained that it is difficult for internal auditors in the Saudi public sector to achieve independence as they are employees of the organisation they audit, and essentially the IAF has no real organisational status. There are issues around the reporting level, freedom of enquiry, the provision of non-audit activity, and the relationships with auditees. It was confirmed by all interviewees that whilst internal auditors have their own separate departments in the organisational structure, these departments, nonetheless, operate under the administrative leadership of lower level managers. Additionally, the interviewees identified a diversity of practice concerning the location of the department within the organisation. In one instance, internal audit was located under the General Manager of Financial Management, as reported by M3, who said: *"Internal audit is working under the General Manager of Financial Management. If internal audit marginalises the general manager, the internal auditors would be in trouble"*.

It was revealed that internal audit report to the same level in which they are placed in the organisational structure. This is a situation required by the Saudi culture which operates norms concerning organisational status and reporting levels, these being that staff are not allowed to marginalise their managers. Indeed, if an employee bypasses his/her immediate manager, problems can occur because high power distance forbids any staff, whether internal auditors or otherwise, from reporting directly to top level management when there is a chain of command below that level. M4 explained this situation, saying: *"Internal audit cannot jump over the deputy since it works under him in the organisational structure. If one of my staff ignores me and goes to a higher manager, I will transfer him to another department. Each staff member must respect his direct manager".*

Almost all interviewees indicated a significant gap between the theoretical and the actual reporting structures, with M5 pointing out that *"theoretically, the internal audit department is placed under the President of the organisation, but in reality, it works under the Vice-President".*

According to the IAR, the internal audit should be placed at the highest point of the organisational hierarchy reporting to the first official of the organisation, but the interview data showed a lack of adherence to the IAR. Reasons for the differences in the organisational structure and reporting level as indicated by the interviewees included the possibility of the marginalisation of the manager responsible for financial matters if the internal auditor reports to someone other than to him. Also, there is the question of delegation and assignment of authority from the highest level of management which may be too busy to deal with the auditors. Clearly, though, there is a misunderstanding of the role of internal audit and its main duties, since the requirements for the effective performance of internal audit are not met by the prevailing structural obstacles in Saudi Arabia.

In addition to the above reasons, twenty one interviewees indicated two other main causes of the restricted access faced by internal auditors in respect of their ability to meet with personnel and to obtain the relevant information needed to fulfil their duties. These reasons are: 1) auditees who are involved in confidential work are unwilling to share this with the internal audit team, as shown by the comment *"there are some confidential documents. We cannot easily allow anybody to see these"* (M10), and 2) employees at certain levels of authority had immunity and were thus not subject to any type of audit, as noted by M7 who said, *"internal auditors cannot investigate and raise queries with some staff in special positions … who have immunity".* Moreover, it was observed that even when the internal audit was located at a relatively senior managerial level, it might still be subject to pressure from more highly placed management. For instance, internal auditors could be prevented from exploring a particular issue simply by higher management directing them to examine a different one. Simultaneously, top level managers control organisational resources which they may withhold to prevent an in-depth investigation by internal auditors of a matter which they do not want to be probed. In any situation where the internal audit is prevented from examining an item of business that falls within its jurisdiction, there is likely to be an element of interference from some parties, whether this be the actual auditees or a higher level of management that does not wish certain particulars to be uncovered. Consequently, where it is not possible to hide misdemeanours, enhanced effectiveness can be achieved, but this is dependent upon top management support in ensuring that access to all information and personnel is made available for the internal audit team.

Some other reasons for the challenge to the independence of internal audit emerged as being the relationship between auditees and auditors. For example, personal biases and expectations brought the potential to destroy independence, in particular in respect to the audit of the personnel department, where an inherent tension existed because of the power of personnel staff to approve the promotion of internal auditors. Moreover, the strong social networking characteristic of Saudi Arabian society promotes relationships within the workplace which destroy objectivity on the part of internal auditors who are unable, through mistaken loyalty, to give a truthful opinion.

Management support for internal audit

Interviewees reported that internal audit suffers from a lack of support from top management. Resistance to the establishment of internal audit has created a negative attitude towards internal audit and consequently, low levels of support. Several reasons were offered for the perceived absence of management support. These included: ignorance on the part of top level management regarding the importance of the internal audit role and lack of attention paid thereto; the organisational status of internal audit which consequently affected its independence; and general organisational resistance to the idea of establishing an internal audit function. Moreover, external auditors also agreed that internal audit did not receive sufficient support from the highest officials of the organisations. M20 pointed out that "*there is not sufficient support for internal audit*", and he considered this as one of the reasons for the lack of independence. In addition, M21 and M27 indicated that internal audit might not be effective since the highest official did not adopt the concept of internal audit, not being *"enthusiastic to support internal audit"* (M27). Further, M25 believed that lack of support affected the competence of the department, saying "*internal audit will not have qualified staff as long as it does not receive sufficient support from top management*".

Other findings emerging from the interview responses (and these were not only confined to the perceptions of internal auditor interviewees) were that internal audit was affected by problems with regard to budget constraints, limited number of internal audit staff and lack of necessary equipment (that is computers, photocopying machines and faxes). The interview results suggested that these problems could be attributed to insufficient support from management, and a more general belief on behalf of managers that the level of resources possessed by the internal audit was satisfactory.

Certainly, the absence of support from top management affected the budget allocated to the internal auditand the number of staff available to conduct internal audit work. However, the interviewees considered that the limited budget and the insufficient staff members were general problems affecting all departments and not only internal audit. Such problems were attributed to the lack of co-operation from the MoF as the body controlling government financial matters and posts.

Since lack of posts and staff are general problems facing organisations, transferring staff from one department to the internal audit department creates a shortage in that department and consequently staff may be returned to their original departments whenever they are needed. Finally, the IAR does not specify the importance of allocating sufficient resources to ensure the effective discharge of internal audit duties.

The interview responses suggested that internal audit reporting to a lower level than appropriate and a general lack of management support for internal audit were the main reasons for internal audit recommendations not being implemented. M18 described much of the work of internal audit as a waste of time as it does not receive sufficient support from the first official and consequently many internal audit recommendations are not implemented. He said: *"the main problem that our department (internal audit) faces is complete ignorance from the highest official. It is a waste of time since we receive no attention and our recommendations are in vain".*

Internal audit activities

The interviewees were unanimous that the internal audit activities had not expanded beyond the traditional audit of financial regularity and compliance; and that the primary work of internal audit continues to focus on the traditional roles of internal audit in terms of concentrating on the reliability of financial records and compliance with procedures and regulations. M3, for example, said *"[i]t (internal audit) is focusing on the extent of compliance with regulations and policies as well as reviewing the accuracy and reliability of the financial accounts".*

In fact, staff shortages were blamed for restrictions on the type of activities that internal audit might perform, as noted by M17, who said *"I am the only one who works in the department and I cannot carry out all the required works. It is frustrating to be the only one in the department and perform the entire work".* In fact, 12 interviewees complained that the absence of qualified staff prevented expansion of internal audit activities. That said, 16 interviewees pointed to a misunderstanding of the role of internal audit as one reason for narrowing the focus of its activities merely to checking the reliability of financial records and compliance with procedures and regulations. Examples of comments in this respect were offered as follows:

To date, some organisations are not aware of the internal audit function. There is still a misunderstanding between the duties of internal audit and those of the Follow-up department. They cannot differentiate between the two departments (M23).

There is a misunderstanding of the role of internal audit and the regulation issued by the GAB; some organisations still see internal audit as a pure financial audit (M20).

In those instances where non-audit activities were performed, and this was indicated by 9 interviewees, such activities took different forms, including conducting financial tasks, participating in budget work, working in other departments where there are staff shortages, and being involved with committees that perform work at a distance to internal audit. M11, for example, stated that internal auditors *"carry out financial activities when there is shortage of staff in the other financial departments".*

Non-audit work may also be requested by top management or occur because internal audit work is placed directly under the supervision of financial management, and in such situations, internal auditors might be assigned to any financial work whether related to auditing or not. A refusal by an internal auditor to perform such work might result in transfer to another department and a low grade in the annual performance evaluation. Hence, internal auditors seek to please top management by complying with their wishes.

The interaction between external auditors and audited organisations

A weak relationship was seen to exist between external auditors and audited organisations, and in particular such a relationship does not exist with internal auditors. Interviewees indicated several influences in this respect, the first and perhaps the most important being the ingrained mutually negative attitude towards each other. One interviewee described external auditors as policemen since *"they look only for mistakes; they act as police investigators".* Another interviewee described their work as looking for "*thieves*". Strong negative attitudes of this kind seem to have resulted in inflexible behaviour, consequently depressing any willingness to respond appropriately to audit recommendations. Moreover, the presence of such attitudes can easily become infectious within organisations such that others who are not actually involved with internal audit adopt the same position, or that senior managers themselves prevent others within the organisation from co-operating with the GAB.

A second factor with potential to weaken the relationship is the limited implementation of recommendations made by the external auditor. Interviewees revealed their opinions that GAB recommendations are not implemented, for several reasons, these being: 1) mutual negative attitude; 2) out-dated recommendations "*They send a report about something that happened two or three years ago … how come I remember something that happened three years ago?*" (M10); 3) absence of discussion of the findings and recommendations of the external auditors, for example, one interviewee said "*the GAB sends its report and requests implementation of everything in the report without listening to our opinions*" (M6). Here it might be suggested that allowing the audited organisations, particularly internal audit staff, to add comments and opinions on the content of the audit findings and recommendations might minimise the amount of resistance and consequently improve the extent of implementations of audit recommendations; 4) absence of periodic meetings – and here again more frequent meetings might also open the channels to discuss the mutual interests and audit findings. This was pointed out by six interviewees, for example: "*we do not have official meetings with the external auditor. It is only a relationship on paper; we send him the papers and records that he requests, that is it*" (M4); 5) complex procedures, outdated regulations and instruction - which might affect organisations' performance and consequently result in them repeating the same errors and irregularities every year, thus ignoring audit findings as they are the same as previous years, for example "*we receive the same findings and the same recommendations every year; there is nothing to discuss. It all happened because of the complexity of the system. Regulations and in instructions have never been updated. Nothing new; every year we do the same thing, and they (external auditors) report the same findings*"(M9); 6) absence of support from top management in the audited organisations and absence of accountability "*the most important reason is the absence of accountability*" (M23) - which would create a climate in which it might be seen as possible to ignore external audit recommendations with impunity; and 7) having immunity such that no repercussions befall auditees who do not implement the recommendations, for example "*Employees are guaranteed that nothing will happen to them if they do not implement the recommendations*" (M24).

Thirdly, the lack of qualified staff working within audited organisations might be a relevant factor. Five interviewees attributed the weak relationship to the lack of qualified staff, for example, M24 raised this issue, saying "*staff are not sufficiently competent to co-operate*".

A final factor might be related to the standards and regulations issued by the GAB. Worldwide professional auditing standards highlight the importance of this relationship, but the latest version of the *Government Auditing Standards* (GAS) issued by the GAB in 2008 makes no reference thereto. Although this version was released after the issuance of the IAR (2007), it pays no attention to a number of related aspects including: 1) the new regulation of internal audit; 2) the relationship between internal and external auditors, in terms of coordination, reliance on internal audit work by external auditor, sharing working papers, and the need for frequent meetings; and 3) evaluating the objectivity of the internal audit function, the expertise of the internal auditors, quality and effectiveness of internal audit work, and the scope of work. The absence of consideration of these issues is likely to weaken the relationship between the two audit parties given that external auditors are required to comply with the GAS when performing audit work. The GAB (2008) indicated that several considerations were borne in mind when updating the latest version of its standards, one of these being the IAR. However, internal audit is mentioned only in one place in these standards (page 38) where there is a reference to internal audit as one of the five components of internal control.

The GAB (2008) indicated adherence in their content with the INTOSAI standards, but these (1998) highlight the importance of the relationship between internal and external auditors, whereas the GAS do not. With regard to the auditor's working papers, the GAS emphasized the importance of keeping these confidential, stipulating that the "GAB is the official owner of all working papers with all its contents" (GAB, 2008). Article 14 states that the "GAB must take all the required procedures to keep all organisations' information confidential". In the current study, the interviewees indicated that the reason for not sharing the external audit working papers was confidentiality.

Summary and review of findings

This study provides evidence on the current practice of internal audit in public sector organisations in Saudi Arabia that is subject to audit by the GAB. From this evidence it is seen that institutional factors are likely to play a part in the failure of internal audit to develop in the Saudi public sector. The existence of the state-required 'Follow-up department', 'auditing department', and 'Financial Representative (Controller)' have been seen, rightly or wrongly, as functioning to undertake the ascribed role of internal audit in the public sector and thereby to make internal audit as a separate function, redundant. Additionally, the perception exists that powerful government bodies, in particular the Ministry of Finance (MoF) and the Ministry of Civil Service (MCS) fail to appreciate the value of internal audit as a mechanism to improve efficiency and probity within the public sector, and therefore have not sought to enforce the requirements universally. The failure of internal audit to develop and flourish in the Saudi public sector, to a level of activity and importance which theoretically, holds in other countries, may be seen as a reflection of the historical background against which accountability, monitoring and control of public finances has developed in Saudi Arabia. Beyond this, and in common with other societies emerging from a long history of close families or 'clan' relationships (and also perhaps an overarching religious structure), the basic perception within employment is the maintenance of harmony with friends and colleagues, and this might be seen as militating against the effective discharge of an internal audit function (and also has implications for the role of external audit and audit committees) which is intended to impose control and expose those responsible for financial misdemeanours. The fear of repercussions within a clearly structured and hierarchical environment, which, it might be argued, is also a mark of Saudi society, may impair internal auditor independence beyond the more straightforward conventional concerns as to employment by the 'auditee' body and enhance the wider behavioural, psychological and behavioural issues common to almost all forms of audit, as discussed by Marnet (2008). All these cultural predispositions combine to produce a situation where internal audit is neither effective nor given sufficient credence and importance - issues identified by other researchers (Alzeban and Gwilliam, 2012; Haniffa and Hudaib, 2007; Al-Twaijry, 2000).

Against this background, a number of recommenddations are made as to the manner in which internal audit and the regulatory framework underpinning internal audit might develop if the function is to more adequately fulfil its ascribed role within the Saudi public sector. Wider transparency, in terms of making public external audit findings of the GAB, is also advocated together with the provision of more resources to support education and training of both management and internal audit staff at all stages including higher education and professional qualifications. The relative lack of progress of internal audit in the Saudi public sector to date may be attributed to a 'catching up' process with a much shorter tradition of public sector control and audit than many others. Here facilitation of education, training etc. may act to reduce miscommunication between the various stakeholders, misperceptions as to the nature of the internal audit role and perhaps influence management to provide more support and encouragement for the active pursuit of that role. It is also suggested that if the Saudi public sector moves toward a model with a greater influence of markets and more direct input from stakeholders, as has been the case in the great majority of developed industrial nations over the last thirty years, then this too is likely to create forces which will act to move audit more toward the current model in such developed countries.

REFERENCES

Abbott L, Parker S, Peters G (2010). Serving two masters: the association between audit committee internal audit oversight and internal audit activities. Account. Horizons 24(1):1-24.

Ahlawat S, Lowe D (2004). An examination of internal auditor objectivity: in-house versus outsourcing. Auditing: A J. Pract. Theory 23(2):147-158.

Ahmad H, Othman R, Jusoff K (2009). The Effectiveness of internal audit in Malaysian public sector. J. Modern Account. Auditing 5(9):53-62.

Allegrini M, D'Onza G (2003). Internal auditing and risk assessment in large Italian companies: an empirical survey. Int. J. Auditing 7(3):191-208.

Almohaimeed A (2000). Performance auditing in the Saudi public sector: its nature and effectiveness. Ph.D. Thesis. University of Kent at Canterbury, the UK.

Asairy S (1993). Evaluating the extent of effectiveness of internal auditing: an applied study on the Saudi joint stock companies. Masters Dissertation. King Abdulaziz University, Saudi Arabia.

Alzeban A, Gwilliam D (2012). Perceptions of managers and internal auditors as to factors affecting the effectiveness of internal audit in the public sector context. Paper presented at the 10th European Academic Conference on Internal Audit and Corporate Governance. University of Verona: Italy. Retrieved from http://www.iacmaster.it/iacgconference2012/.

Al-Garni A (2008). Government auditing in Saudi Arabia: auditors' opinion in the General Audit Bureau. Institute Public Admin. 48(1):39-79.

Al-Rahaily M, Al-Zahrany M (2007). Application of the regulation of internal audit in ministries and public institutions. Paper presented at the first symposium on ways to enhance co-operation to achieve the overall objectives of the audit and control performance. Institute of Public Administration: Al-Riyadh.

Al-Shetwi M, Ramadili S, Chowdury T, Sori Z (2011). Impact of internal audit function (IAF) on financial reporting quality (FRQ): evidence from Saudi Arabia. Afr. J. Bus. Manage. 5(27):11189-11198.

Al-Twaijry A (2000). The role, practice and value-added of the internal audit function in the corporate sector of Saudi Arabia: an empirical investigation. Ph.D. Thesis. University of Wales Aberystwyth, the UK.

Al-Twaijry A, Brierley J, Gwilliam D (2003). The development of internal audit in Saudi Arabia: an institutional theory perspective. Crit. Perspect. Account. 14(5):507-531.

Al-Twaijry A, Brierley J, Gwilliam D (2004). An examination of the relationship between internal and external audit in the Saudi Arabian corporate sector. Managerial Auditing J. 19(7):929-944.

Badara M, Saidin S (2012). Improving the existing functions of internal audit at organizational level. Int. J. Arts Commerce 1(6):38-46.

Brierley J, El-Nafabi H, Gwilliam D (2001). The problems of establishing internal audit in the Sudanese public sector. Int. J. Auditing 5(1):73-87.

Carey P, Craswell A, Simnett R (2000). The association between the external audit fee and external auditors' reliance on the work of internal audit. Paper presented at AAANZ Conference. Hamilton Island.

Christopher J, Sarens G, Leung P (2009). A critical analysis of the independence of internal audit function: evidence from Australia. Account. Auditing Account. J. 22(2):200-223.

Cohen A, Sayag G (2010). The Effectiveness of Internal Auditing: An Empirical Examination of its Determinants in Israeli Organisations. Aust. Account. Rev. 20(3):296-307.

DeZoort F, Houston R, Reisch J (2000). Incentive compensation for internal auditors. Internal Auditor 57(3):42-46.

Felts L (1994). Before you blame firms, ask the internal auditors. Account. Today 15(March):14-16.

General Audit Bureau (GAB) (2008). Government auditing standards. Al-Riyadh, GAB.

Glascock K (2002). Auditees or clients?. The Internal Auditor 59(4):84-85.

Goodwin J, Kent P (2006). The use of internal audit by Australian companies. Managerial Auditing J. 21(1/2):81-101.

Gramling A, Hermanson D (2009). Internal audit quality: would we know it if we saw it? Internal Auditing 24(1):36-39.

Gramling A, Myers P (2006). Internal auditing's role in ERM. The Internal Auditor 63(2):52-58.

Gwilliam D, El-Nafabi H (2002). The possibility of transition to public sector modern auditing techniques and procedures found in

developing countries; the case of Sudan. Accounting Research, the Saudi Accounting Association 6(2):161-196.
Haniffa R, Hudaib M (2007). Locating audit expectations gap within a cultural context: the case of Saudi Arabia. J. Int. Account., Auditing Taxation 16(2):179-206.
Harrington C (2004). Internal audit's new role. J. Accountancy 198(3):65-70.
Institute of Internal Auditors (IIA) (2000). Administrative directive No. 4: 2000: continuing professional education (CPE) requirements. Florida: the IIA. Retrieved from http://www.theiia.org/theiia/about-the-institute/mission/ [Accessed 7 April 2012].
Institute of Internal Auditors (IIA) (2006). The role of auditing in public sector governance. Florida: the IIA. Retrieved from www.theiia.org/download.cfm?file=3512 [Accessed 10 January 2012].
Internal Audit Regulation (IAR) (2007). Issued by Cabinet Decree No 129. Al-Riyadh: Cabinet.
International Organization of Supreme Audit Institutions (INTOSAI) (1998). Code of ethics and auditing standards. Sweden: INTOSAI. Retrieved from http://www.intosai.org/documents/intosai.html [Accessed 3 February 2012].
James K (2003). The Effect of internal audit structure on perceived financial statements fraud prevention. Account. Horizons 17(4):315-327.
Leung P, Cooper B, Robertson P (2003). The role of internal audit in corporate governance. The Institute of Internal Auditors Research Foundation, RMIT University, Melbourne.
Leung P, Cooper B, Robertson P (2004). Role of internal audit in corporate governance and management. RMIT University, Melbourne.
Lewington D (1996). 2020 Vision. Managerial Auditing J. 11(7):3-11.
Loss J (2000). The communication contract. The Internal Auditor 57(6):88.
Maher M, Akers M (2003). Internal audit's role in system development: the CEO's Perspective. Internal Auditing 18(1):35-39.
Marnet O (2008). Behaviour and rationality in corporate governance. Routledge, London andNew York.
Messier W, Reynolds J, Simon C, Wood D (2011). The effect of using the internal audit function as a management training ground on the external auditor's reliance decision. Account. Rev. 86(6):2131-2154.
Mihret D (2010). Factors associated with attributes of internal audit departments: a canonical analysis. Afr. J. Account. Econ., Financ. Bank. Res. 7(6):42-61.
Mihret D, Yismaw A (2007). Internal audit effectiveness: an Ethiopian public sector case Study. Managerial Auditing J. 22(5):470-484.
Ministry of Economy and Planning (2009). The Saudi development march. Retrieved from www.mep.gov.sa [Accessed 11 December 2011].
Myers M, Gramling A (1997). The perceived benefits of certified internal auditor designation. Managerial Auditing J. 12(2):70-79.
Nagy A, Cenker W (2002). An assessment of the newly defined internal audit function. Managerial Auditing J. 17(3):130-137.
Paape L, Scheffe J, Snoep P (2003). The Relationship between the internal audit function and corporate governance in the EU–a survey. Int. J. Auditing 7(3):247-62.
Peursem K (2005). Conversations with internal auditors: the power of ambiguity. Managerial Auditing J. 20(5):489-512.
Picket K (2004). How to spot and use the new internal auditors. J. Corporate Account. Financ. 15(4):29-39.
Prawitt D, Smith J, Wood D (2008). Internal audit quality and earnings management. Accounting Rev. 84(4):1255-1280.
Sarens G, De Beelde I (2006a). Internal auditors' perception about their role in risk management: a comparison between US and Belgian companies. Managerial Auditing J. 21(1):63-80.
Sarens G, De Beelde I (2006b). The relationship between internal audit and senior management: a qualitative analysis of expectations and perceptions. Int. J. Auditing 10(3):219-241.
Saudi Organization for Certified Public Accountants (SOCPA) (2011). Council of ministers approved the establishment of Saudi Institute of Internal Auditors. SOCPA, 68 (June).
Sawyer L, Dittenhofer M, Scheiner J (2003). The practice of modern internal auditing (5th ed). Florida: The Institute of Internal Auditors.
Selim G, Sundarsanam S, Lavine M (2003). The role of internal auditors in mergers, acquisitions and divestitures: an international study. Int. J. Auditing 7(3):223-246.
Selim G, Woodward S, Allegrini M (2009). Internal auditing and consulting practice: a comparison between UK/Ireland and Italy. Int. J. Auditing, 13(1):9-25.
Seol I, Sarkis J (2005). A multi-attribute model for internal auditor selection. Managerial Auditing J. 20(8/9):876-92.
Smith G (2005). Communication skills are critical for internal auditors. Managerial Auditing J. 20(5):513-39.
Summary Report of GAB (2008, February 4). Okaz Newspaper. Retrieved from http://www.okaz.com.sa/okaz/osf/20080204/Con20080204170563.htm [Accessed 31 January 2012].
Summary Report of GAB. (2010, January 11). Alriyadh Newspaper. Retrieved from http://www.alriyadh.com/2010/01/11/article488849.html [Accessed 31 January 2012].
Tarr R (2002). Built to Last. Internal Auditor pp.28-33.
Unegbu A, Kida M (2011). Effectiveness of internal audit as instrument of improving public sector management. J. Emerging Trends Econ. Manage. Sci. 2(4):304-309. Retrieved from EBSCO database.
Vijayakumar A, Nagaraja N (2012). Internal control systems: effectiveness of internal audit in risk management at public sector enterprises. BVIMR Manage. Edge 5(1):1-8. Retrieved from EBSCO database.
Woodworth B, Said K (1996). Internal auditing in a multicultural environment: the Saudi Arabia experience. Managerial Auditing J. 11(2):20-27.
Zain M, Subramaniam N, Stewart J (2006). Internal auditors' assessment of their contribution to financial statement audits: the relation with audit committee and internal audit function characteristics. Int. J. Auditing 10(1):1-18.

Credit risk management of commercial banks in Iran; Using logistic model

Hamid Sepehrdoust* **and Adel Berjisian**

Department of Economics, Bu-Ali-Sina University, Hamedan, Hamedan Province, Iran.

The observed crisis and profitability decreases in banking system are mainly because of the inefficiency in credit risk control and that's why, utilization of customers' ranking system is the most important tool that is required for managing and controlling the risk. The goal of the study was to present an applied model for credit scoring of real entity customers of banks with reliance on statistical information of credit customers of Parsian Bank in Iran. For this purpose the logistic regression model is used to analyze credit ranking and financial scoring of bank's customers based on their previous and current data record like; job stability, collaterals, income and some other main indicators for estimating non-default probability of facilities offered to each customer. The results of the model estimation showed that non-default probability of facilities have positive relation with variables amount of collaterals received from customer, monthly income amount of the customer, the status of applicant for taking facilities such as place of residence (be owner or tenant of the applicant), the age of applicant for taking facilities, occupational status of the applicant as stability and educational level of the applicant for taking facilities and have negative relation with amount of paid facilities to the customer and payback duration of granted facilities to the applicant.

Key words: Risk management, credit risk, commercial bank, logistic regression.

INTRODUCTION

Financial sector is the backbone of economy of a country. It works as a facilitator for achieving sustained economic growth through providing efficient monetary intermediation. A strong financial system promotes investment by financing productive business opportunities, mobilizing savings, efficiently allocating resources and makes easy the trade of goods and services (Jah and Xiaofeng, 2012). Banks as institutions that are looking for maximum profitability have responsibility for increasing the value of shareholders' equities on one side and attracting the customer satisfaction in the other side. The role of the banking industry is crucial in the pattern and pace of economic growth and development (Mogboyin et al., 2012). As it is well articulated and established in the literature (Demirguc-Kunt and Huizinga, 1997), banks occupy a position in the financial system that supplies the credits need of the economy. Both theoretical and empirical evidence suggests a positive correlation between real economic growth and banks assets-especially credits (Alashi, 1991). On the other hand since a considerable part of banks' income are resulted from absorbing resources of investors and granting facilities from the credits, therefore, they are always encountering with an important and challengeable issue of credit risk at the time of granting facilities. Many studies show that, evaluation of banking system customers risk in Iranian banks relies on expert's judgment and fingertip rule. This type of evaluation resulted in high rate of postponed claims (Salehi and Mansoury, 2011).

Risk is a concept that denotes a potential negative impact to some characteristic of value that may arise from a future event (Mojtahedi et al., 2009), or one can say that exposure to the consequences of uncertainty constitutes a risk. In everyday usage, risk is often used synonymously with the probability of a known loss. Risk communication and risk perception are essential factors

*Corresponding author. E-mail: hamidbasu1340@gmail.com.

foe all human decision making (Cooper et al., 2005). The meaning of credit risk is non-receiving cash flows of granting facilities by banks that exact timely evaluation and examination thereof, especially for average and small facilities and this requires a systematic method. Credit risk management from the primary stages of granting facilities up to the examination time of application for receiving facilities are performed by credit experts and also supervision process over granting credit. In contemporary organizations, risk management has become established as a particular method and practice of viewing and attending to such risks. As a social and cultural phenomenon, in itself, it assumes and prescribes particular views of the nature, forms, degrees and methods of dealing with risky businesses (Giddens, 1999; Power, 2008). In fact, it is required that banks examine the applicant's ability in payback of obligations and estimating the probability amount of non-fulfillment of obligations in future (non-default of facilities paid) before any payments to them through credit risk management, customers' ranking and scoring instruments toward decreasing credit facilities risk. According to Basel committee, credit risk is most simply defined as the potential that causes a borrower or counter party not to meet its obligations in accordance with the agreed terms (Gumparthi et al., 2011). The reason behind it is that when the facilities are not recovered, the loss resulted from non-default created and therefore, bank must consider the proper coverage due to loss existence probability.

Credit scoring is an instrument used to manage the risk that takes action toward ranking of customers by using quantitative statistics and information of facilities applicants and also statistical techniques (Mester, 1997). With the right credit scoring model, the bank can evaluate any new or existing profiles of customers accurately, enabling them to minimize potential risks that might be looming. Credit rating systems is used to categorize the risk's worthiness of a person as high, medium or low. This allows for decision support by accepting, extending or rejecting any credit request (Sheng and Ying, 2011).

Credit scoring models divides the credit applicants into two: good and bad credit groups. Good credit group is a group that payback their dues timely and bad credit group is a group that will probably not pay their dues (Lee et al., 2002). The Basel committee has defined credit rating as a 'summary indicator' of the risk inherent in individual credit, embodying an assessment of the risk of loss due to the default of a counter party by considering relevant quantitative and qualitative information. Credit rating, through the use of symbols, can be defined as an expression of the opinion about credit quality of the issuer of securities with reference to a particular instrument. Rating is a measure of credit risk and is only one element in investment decision making (Gumparthi et al., 2011).

Some of the benefits of credit scoring system are shortening the granting facilities process, more quick performance and reduction of credit risk toward responding increase in demand for credit products of bank. Credit scoring has obvious benefits in relation to decreasing the required time for approving facilities that causes increase in its usage in evaluating facilities. This method decreases the required time in facilities approving process. Commercial banking union found that traditional process on facilities approving on the average is 12.5 h for each small commercial facility (Allen, 1995), while in past the facility takers spend more than two weeks in this regard. Credit scoring can decrease this time to less than one hour. Therefore, Barnet Bank in its annual report confessed that the time spending on approving facilities for real entity customers or small commercial firms that was three or four weeks in the past, could be decreased to less than three hours by using the above-mentioned system (Lawson, 1995). Leonard (1995) in his study on a Canadian Bank found that after using this system for 18 months, facilities approving time that was nine days before stating the use of credit scoring system decreases to three days. Of course, scoring is vastly using in mortgage issues since the Federal National Mortgage Company encourages mortgage facilities grantors to use credit scoring system (Dezube, 1996). The goal of this study is presenting an applied model for credit scoring of real entity customers of banks with reliance on statistical information of credit customers of Parsian Bank.

LITERATURE REVIEW

The economic literature of 1950s, defines the word risk and non-assurance as knowledge related to occurrence and/or non-occurrence of event. From years relevant to 1980s henceforth, risk and non-assurance get separated and risk is applied to the condition that there was more than one event for each decision making and the occurrence probability for each event not to be distinct and definite (Greuning and Brajovice, 2003). Risk in banking defines as fluctuation or standard deviation of cash flows of a bank and its goal is augmenting shareholders' equities through acquiring ability toward achieving commercial and financial goals and maximizing the output after considering the risk. A systematic process of risk management is divided into risk identification, risk analysis and risk response (Li and Liao, 2007; Duijne et al., 2008). Risk identification requires recognizing and documenting the associated risk. Risk analysis examines each identified risk issue, refines the description of the risk and assesses the associated impact. Finally, risk response identifies, evaluates, selects and implements strategies in order to reduce the likelihood of occurrence or impact of risk events (Mojtahedi et al., 2009). In banking industry, risk is classified into four main groups including operational risk, commercial risk, event risk and financial risk. Financial risks are divided into two different risk groups: first group includes risks relevant to fluctuation in interest rate, currency and market rate, and second group includes pure risks as liquidity risk and credit risk and in the case of mismanagement, these two groups directly causes bank's loss (Joel, 2009).

Credit risk means a risk resulted from inability of facility receiver in payment of the obligations to bank and/or risk of non-returning of original and profit amount of investment which caused decrease in current value of bank's assets (Altman, 1998). Basel Committee working under the supervision of international settlement bank of Swiss for assimilating banking rules, defines credit risk as potential probability in which facility receiver get incapable toward fulfillment of its obligations against bank within certain duration (BCBS, 2000).The origin of creation the credit risk may be observed in compilation of three risks that are respectively include: default risk, recover risk and exposure risk (Joel, 2009). Default risk or non-default probability of debts by the loaner is a loss if occurred, threatens the bank. Therefore, credit risk rooted in probability in default or non-default of facilities by facility receiver and its occurrence probability fluctuate in the range of zero and one. Payment default informed by a bank institution when scheduled installments not to be paid within a certain duration after due date. Default may be economic and occurred when economic value of assets or the current value of expected future cash flows become less than the value of non-deposited debts. Loss resulted from default is pending on default definition and default definition is pending on estimating default probability (resulted from past data). Ranking agencies consider the default event after passing three months from due date of a scheduled payment and no payment performs during this period, therefore, theoretical models of credit risk which propounded after Merton model (Merton, 1974), apply economic default definition for measuring of losses amount. It is noteworthy that, different default events necessarily not to create immediate loss but increase the probability of permanent default or bankruptcy. Default risk measures through the probability of occurring default within certain duration. Of course, default probability may not be measured directly, but must be used from statistics collected from default in the past that credited from system interior.

Usually, previous statistics of default and ranking of agencies are proper and accepted standards of default which uses as a symbol of default risk. In the case of non-accessing of agencies' ranking, we can use estimation about default probability based on specifications of some applicants (real or legal). Followed by John Murray in 1909 and ranking of credit risk on bonds, some researchers realized approximation between bonds and paid facilities and examined the measurement of non-default risk of original and interest of facilities (Kiss, 2003). In this regard one may point out to the Fisher's study (Fisher, 1936) focused on the fundamentals of credit scoring method as the first evaluation system of credit demand. Dunham (1938) engaged in his studies for designing a credit risk system, used five important standards including existing condition, revenue conditions, financial conditions, guarantors or Collaterals and facilities payback information of other banks. Considering these factors, the objective of credit scoring models is to assign credit applicants to either a "good credit" group that is likely to repay financial obligation or a "bad credit" group with high possibility of defaulting. Therefore, credit scoring problems are basically a classification problem (Johnson and Wichern, 2002). Accurate credit quality estimation systems will substantially improve the profitability of the banking institutions (Thomas et al., 2002).

Many studies have been conducted in this regard as follows. Durand (1941) in his studies examined which variable has been important from facility providers' point of view and which specifications are statistically considerable for credit risk management. The most important variables examined included: applicant's job, job stability, residing years at the current place, bank accounts, saving and life insurance policies, sex and monthly installments amount that the applicant must be paid. Most experts know Durand as founder of current credit scoring system. Isaac – Fair Institute (1996) found the necessity for application and development of credit scoring systems of credit facilities' customers that needs continuous collecting and updating of data. Bogess (1967) for the first time in an article suggested using computer for developing scoring models, evaluation of mass facilities products and increasing algorithm-writing skills which caused possibility for examination and studying a bog data collection from different point of views. He examined complicated tools of multiple criteria statistical methods which lead to creating much clearer models. Jah and Xiaofeng (2012), compared the financial performance of different ownership structured commercial banks in Nepal based on their financial characteristics and identify the determinants of performance exposed by the financial ratios for the period 2005 to 2010. The results show that public sector banks are significantly less efficient than their counterpart are; however domestic private banks are equally efficient to foreign-owned (joint venture) banks. Owojori et al. (2011), managed to provide an overview of risk management practices in insured banks in Nigeria. The employed trend analysis of variables to derive its results and concluded by pointing to some steps that would help to preserve the banking system and sustain its impact on our fragile economy. Sheng and Ying (2011) studied the use of batch and incremental classifiers such as logistic regression, neural networks and C5 to obtain the best classifier to be used for improving the predictive accuracy of consumer's credit card risk of a bank in Malaysia.

Results showed that C5 emerged consistently as the technique that have generated the best models with an average predictive accuracy as high as 94.68%. Huang and Wu (2011), studied the customer credit quality assessment for banking industries, by using boosting and genetic algorithms (GA). The empirical results indicated that GA substantially improves the performance of underlying classifiers. Considering robustness and reliability, combining GA with ensemble classifiers is better than traditional models. Zribi and Boujelbene (2011), aimed to examine the determinants of bank credit risk in ten commercial banks, taking into account both macroeconomic factors and microeconomic variables that are likely to influence credit risk. Overall, the results show that the main determinants of bank credit risk in Tunisia is: ownership structure, prudential regulation of capital, profitability and macroeconomic indicators. The empirical results show that the public ownership increases the bank credit risk. Other authors that have written in the field of designing a risk measurement model include Beaver (1966), Altman (1968) and Morgan (1994).

The importance of increasing the degree of credit risk in Iran also has led to studies in this area. Zekavat (2003) in a research inspired by Altman model, examined credit risk models of customers of Tosea Saderat Bank. Mansouri (2003) in his study used regression and neural networks models for evaluating customer's credit risk of Mellat Bank. Arabmazar and Roueintan (2006), made an attempt to evaluate the credit risk of legal customers of Keshavarzi Bank Iran and examined qualitative and financial information of a 200-member random sample of companies which received credit facilities from Bank. Safari et al. (2010) took action toward presenting a model for credit ranking of legal customers of Tejarat Bank in Iran. Salehi and Mansoury (2011), have studied Iranian banking credit risk and formulated an intelligent model by neural network and logistic regression to evaluate individual customers' credit risk without prejudice and discrimination. The result revealed that neural network and logistic regression have the same ability in predicting customer credit risk. The main objective of the present study is to present a comprehensive model for credit scoring of real entity customers of banks with reliance on statistical information of credit customers of Parsian Bank in Iran.

MATERIALS AND METHODS

Data required for credit scoring of real customers have been collected from statistical information of Parsian Bank in Iran during the period of 2008 to 2010. Informative data are usually provided from data relevant to good pay and poor pay applicants. For example; in a similar study and through 5-year data of small commercial facilities less than 5 million dollar, a sample consist of data relevant to more than 5000 facility applicants related to 17 USA banks for creating a scoring model were examined (Asch, 1995) and variables used in this study are derived from five C (Character, Capacity, Capital, Collateral and Condition) model and based on five major standards for evaluating and granting regulated facilities. According to the five C model, facility providers for evaluating facility granting to its credit customers, for scoring and decision making makes use of a data bank of previous records of customer (Dunham, 1938). Type of used information in this model is pending on different conditions. This model used five major standards for evaluating facility granting to the customers. These include:

1- Character: is a standard for recognizing commitment rate of applicant for payback of credit facilities. Attended items include what was the credit background of customer and if he has ever been bankrupt? Whether previous creditors have been referred to the court?
2- Income capacity: is a standard for estimating income authority of the applicant. This standard evaluates financial authority of real or legal entity and answers to this important question that if the applicant has authority for payback of installments relevant to the applied facilities?
3- Capital: is a standard for analyzing capital and assets of the applicant which indicates customer's authority in payback of facilities.
4- Collateral: is a standard for recognizing type of free assets able to putting collateral including property and bank collaterals and any other collateral assure the creditor for compensating non-default loss.
5- Condition: is a standard for more recognizing of external environmental conditions which have effect on payback authority of credit commitments of creditors. Main axis of external environmental conditions is job security and/or job stability of the applicant.

Normally, the financial performance of commercial banks and other financial institutions has been measured using a combination of financial ratios analysis, benchmarking, measuring performance against budget or a mix of these methodologies (Avkiran, 1995). Depending on the commercial uses of credit scoring, the methodology to construct credit scoring models varies from bank to bank. It may involve firstly, a sample of historical records classified as "good" and "bad" depending on their repayment performance over a given period. Next, data could be obtained from internal or other external sources, namely, from credit bureau reports. Finally, statistical or other quantitative analysis is performed on the data to derive a credit scoring model (Koh et al., 2006). In this study the logistic regression model is used to estimate the model. Logistic regression is a type of regression analysis used for predicting the outcome of a categorical criterion variable based on one or more predictor variables. Referred to the target group, the criterion is coded as "0" to a "non-case" and "1" to a "case" in binary logistic regression as it leads to the most straightforward interpretation (Lemeshow and Hosmer, 2000). However, estimation of coefficients in this method is similar to ordinary regression model, but estimation method thereof is completely different. Because of nonlinear nature of logistic regression, coefficients of logistic model evaluate through general maximum likelihood (MLE) method. In logistic regression, dependent variables are a two-mode variable of (0 and 1) which allocated itself the amount of zero and one. If we suppose that Y is a random variable that can give up amounts of zero and one, therefore, probability of Y may be considered equations (2) and (3).

$$P(Y=1)=P=\frac{e^{\beta' X}}{1+e^{\beta' X}} \quad (2)$$

$$P(Y=0)=(1-P)=\frac{1}{1-e^{\beta' X}} \quad (3)$$

The symbol (β') stands for vector of coefficients and the symbol(x) is column vector of independent variables. The above motioned equations may be considered equation (4).

$$\ln\left[\frac{P}{1-P}\right] = \beta' X \quad (4)$$

Equation (4) is an indicator of linear relation between independent variables and neoprene logarithm chance ratio. Whereas, chance ratio and logarithm thereof is not calculated directly, therefore, mentioned coefficient is estimated by maximum likelihood ratio. Considering each observation as a Bernoulli probability distribution, the equation (5) must be established for any observation.

$$P(Y = y_i) = Pi^{Y_i}(1-P_i)^{1-y_i}$$
$$(y_i = 0,1) \quad (5)$$

The variable P_i is event probability in i^{th} observing and y_i is amount of random variable which can be zero and/or one (one for occurrence and zero for non-occurrence of event), while supposing that (n) is independent observation, therefore, likelihood equation will be according to equation (6) and with substituting Pi relevant to equation (2) in equation (6), we can reach equation (7).

$$L = \prod_{i=1}^{n} Pi^{y_i}(1-Pi)^{1-y_i} \quad (6)$$

$$L = \prod_{i=1}^{n}\left(\frac{e^{\beta' X}}{1+e^{\beta' X}}\right)^{y_i}\left(\frac{1}{1+e^{\beta' X}}\right)^{1-y_i} \quad (7)$$

By taking the natural logarithm of equation (7), we will have:

$$\ln L = l = \sum_{i=1}^{n} y_i \ln\left(\frac{e^{\beta' X}}{1+e^{\beta' X}}\right) + \sum_{i=1}^{n}(1-y_i)\ln\left(\frac{1}{1+e^{\beta' X}}\right) \quad (8)$$

Therefore, estimation of independent coefficients (β_i vector) is achieved through maximizing the above-mentioned equation which is calculated through derivation against each independent variable and when each of these derivatives is fixed, it is equal to zero. Of course, the above-mentioned equations have no analytical answer and solving the system of equations through Newton-Raphson method is possible (Ypma, 1995). Finally, on the basis of presented theoretical basics, research model is defined as description of equation (9).

$$Y = \beta_0 + \beta_1 AM + \beta_2 CO + \beta_3 I + \beta_4 O + \beta_5 S + \beta_6 T + \beta_7 DE + \beta_8 AG \quad (9)$$

Where;

(Y): is a binary variable with the values of zero and one that indicate default and nonpayment of facilities.
(AM): is the approved amount of facilities requested by the customer and examination of customer's conditions from character, collateral, income capacity, capital and external conditions in facilities committee for payment to the customer.
(CO): is the amount of collateral which is given to the customer against granting the facilities such as title deed, cheque, draft, participation bonds and long-term deposit certificate. Toward quantifying the above-mentioned variable and using thereof in the model of collaterals respectively improved liquidity and being ensure by encoded and used as virtual variables. Participation bonds and long-term deposit certificate with code No. 2, title deed with code No. 1 and cheque and draft with code No. 0 were defined.
(I): indicates the monthly income of facility applicant that is entered directly into the model.
(O): indicates the ownership status of the customer regarding his /her residence place as owner or tenant. In order to quantify this variable, the code No. 0 is assigned to the applicant being a tenant and code No. 1 will be assigned to the applicant being an owner in the model.
(S): shows job stability of the applicant for facilities or duration that the customer employed at his/her current job, and in the case of employment at the current job for more than five years, his/her status from job point of view consider as stable. In this model, if the customer has stable status with code No. 1 and otherwise, with code No. 0 was identified.
(T): shows payback duration of facilities or duration within which the customer must pay back the facilities through predetermined installments. This model insert at the model monthly.
(AG): is the age of facility applicant, inserts directly in the model and
(DE): indicates the educational degree of the applicant which toward quantifying and using them as virtual, secondary school diploma and lower code: 0, associate's degree and bachelor's degree code: one and master's degree and higher code: two, were allocated.

A comprehensive model is constructed after attaching the weights. Each client will be rated on each of the parameters based on the scorecard provided. Each score of the client will be multiplied by the corresponding weights and a weighted score will be calculated for each parameter. The weighted scores of all the parameters will be summed to arrive at the final score of each client. Based on the final score, the client is given a rating by referring to the rating scale of the model. This final score decides the risk involved in operating with each client (Gumparthi et al., 2011).
In logistic regression estimation model, independent variable have binary status, it is required to use from minimum sample of 1000-observation (Whitehead, 2004). Therefore, for estimating suggested model of credit scoring, 1500 selected files of real entity customers of Parsian Bank which received credit facilities from bank were used. Parsian Bank is the biggest private bank of Iran with more than 4000000 customers and more than 10 years record has the most granted resources and facilities among private banks. It is noteworthy that, in the examined level and performing of this research, Parsian Bank has 279 branches. Due to the fact that default files need to be recognized after the period (date) of granting of facilities, and with reference to 150 older branches of Parsian Bank in Tehran which have more considerable credit files and based on cluster sampling, ten files from each branch including five files relevant to good pay customers and five file relevant to poor pay customers, whose facilities have been defaulted, were selected randomly.

RESULTS

In this study, in order to assess the designed optimum model, at the first, the relevant data of the above-mentioned variables for 1500 real entity customers of Parsian Bank were interred into the model through trial and error method by Eviews7 software. Then, in the

Table 1. Goodness of fit criterions.

McFadden R-squared	0.447687	Mean dependent var	0.500000
S.D. dependent var.	0.500167	S.E. of regression	0.346677
Akaike info criterion	0.777668	Sum squared resid.	179.1957
Schwarz criterion	0.809548	Log likelihood	-574.2513
Hannan-Quinn criter.	0.789545	Restr. log likelihood	-1039.721
LR statistic	930.9389	Avg. log likelihood	-0.382834
Prob (LR statistic)	0.000000		
* Obs. with Dep.=0	750	Total observations	1500
** Obs. with Dep.=1	750		

*Observations with zero value of dependant variable **Observations with unit value of dependant variable.

Table 2. Estimation results of logistic regression model.

Parameter	Estimated value	P-value
C	-4/182198	0/0000
AM	-0/001231*	0/0000
CO	3/803806	0/0000
I	0/011367	0/0000
O	0/698442	0/0032
S	0/307626	0/0479
T	0	0/0000
DE	0/731247	0/0000
AG	0/021451	0/0010

*Negative sign with the values indicates an indirect relation between the relevant variables.

estimated model, meaningfulness of coefficients through Wald statistics, meaningfulness of whole regression through LR statistics in confidence level of 95% and nonexistence of co-linearity between the variables and nonexistence of specified errors in the model were examined and result thereof are inserted in Table 1.

The test of LR statistics is similar to F statistics in linear regression model having chi-square distribution with k=8 degree of freedom (k is the number of independent variables of model) and is calculated by using formula $\left[-2(\bar{l}-l)\right]$ and achieved in 930.99389 as indicated in Table 1. The probability of LR statistics that is valued less than 0.05 and near zero indicates that within the confidence level of 0.95, the null hypothesis (Ho) is rejected, that is the regression result is meaningful. Mc. Fadden R-square statistics that is similar to R^2 statistics in linear regression derived equal to 0.447687 as shown in Table 1, which is acceptable considering similar studies for logistic model. Wald statistics is used for evaluating the meaningfulness of logistic regression variables coefficients. As considered in third column of Table 2, meaningfulness level of Wald statistics for all achieved coefficients is less than 0.05 which means that considering zero for all above-mentioned coefficients were rejected. Therefore, the above-mentioned coefficients are meaningful.

In addition, Lemeshow-Hosmer test is used to examine the best fit of the model (Whitehead, 2004). Statistics of this test examines fit goodness of the model through grouping. In this examination, all observations of the sample were divided into 15 equal groups (100 observations each group). Statistics value of this test has chi-square distribution with k=8 degree of freedom and achieved in 19.9019 and its probability is 0.0977. Therefore, the null hypothesis based on equation (10) was approved and concluded that examined variables have much good proponent authority.

$$(H_0 : E[y] = \frac{e^{X'\beta}}{1+e^{X'\beta}}) \tag{10}$$

Therefore and finally the general figure of logistic equation is estimated as equation (11).

$$Y = \ln\left(\frac{p}{1-p}\right) = -4/182198 - 0/001231AM + 3/803806CO + 0/011367I + 0/698442O + 0/307626S - 0/012471T + 0/731247DE + 0/021451AG \tag{11}$$

In this study, Logistic model has been proposed for credit scoring of Bank's individual customers in order to approve or reject their requests for credit facilities. Considering the achieved coefficients from applying logistic regression model and estimating the equation as general form (11), that is required to obtain $\hat{Y}_i$ amount while putting relevant data of each facility applicants inside the introduced model and then put this obtained quantity in equation (12) in order to calculate value indicators of $\hat{P}_i$ for the mentioned customer.

$$\hat{Y}_i = \ln\left(\frac{\hat{p}_i}{1-\hat{p}_i}\right) \tag{12}$$

Indicators amount of $\hat{P}_i$ with a range of values from zero to one (0 - 1) for each facility applicants will be demonstrative of non-default probability of facilities by the

Table 3. Ranking sample of customers using Credit scoring model.

Rank	Customer code	Non-default probability	Rank	Customer code	Non-default probability
1	700	0.999999994	1491	518	0.0000001122
2	297	0.999999990	1492	176	0.0000001028
3	1167	0.999999970	1493	24	0.0000000849
4	1165	0.999999960	1494	726	0.0000000657
5	70	0.999999900	1495	344	0.0000000567
6	389	0.999999850	1496	411	0.0000000194
7	293	0.999999800	1497	406	0.0000000048
8	1164	0.999999690	1498	408	0.0000000035
9	1038	0.999999680	1499	1476	0.0000000028
10	783	0.999999620	1500	407	0.0000000010

customer. Evidently, through determining threshold limitations, if achieved probability is being more than the above determined limit, the possibility of bank facilities non-default is considered positive, otherwise, default of customer's facility is recognized to be possible. Of course, such probabilities achieved by the model can be classified into two types of classification expenses. First type error: when a bad customer is placed wrongly at good customer's group and the second type error: when a good customer is placed wrongly at bad customer's group.

As a result of the study, 1500-member of real entity sample customers of Parsian bank for facility granting, were ranked as shown in Table 3, using $\hat{P}_i$ indicator. For example; in Table 3, ten superior customers with highest non-default probability and last 10 customers with highest default probability were indexed. After calculating the non-default probability of customer's facilities and finally ranking them, it was observed that 700th customer while obtaining non-default probability in 0.999999994 has higher priority against other applicants of the facility. In addition, non-default probability of 407th customer achieved equal to 0.0000000010 and has lowest rank among applicants for facilities.

Conclusions

The results of the study indicate that for a sustainable growth in Iran, the banking sector of the country has to be effective and efficient to respond favorably to the needs of the productive sectors of the economy. Commercial banks as institutions aiming at maximum profitability are required to examine credit status of customers before any payment to the applicants for the purpose of control, decrease of credit risk and increase in efficiency level of facility granting process. On the other hand, risks are events or conditions that may occur and has a harmful effect, which requires to be effectively adopted for minimizing its undesirable results.

On the basis of discussions made, it has become clear that, credit risk management in banks and financial institutions propound in two levels of dealing with individual customers and also portfolio level in which credit scoring system is a plan to measure and control the risk, while dealing at customer's level. Performing this examination and results thereof has importance for a bank from different aspects such as shortening facility granting process, more quick performance, and decrease default risk of facilities and most important is acquiring indicators for credit risk measurement even individually or portfolio.

Nowadays, commercial banks in Iran are interested in execution of credit scoring system due to confronting more applicants of facilities and time-consuming of exact evaluation of applicant's status and preserving customers' satisfaction. On the basis of model estimation and acquired meaningful coefficients, the study comes to the conclusion that, safer received collateral, higher monthly income, more stable ownership and occupational status, higher educational degree and older age of the client on one hand and lower credit payback duration and amount of the value of the facilities on the other hand would eventually lead to increase in the non-default probability of credit facilities. That means, non-default probability of facilities have positive relation with variables amount of collaterals received from customer, monthly income amount of the customer, the status of applicant for taking facilities such as place of residence (be owner or tenant of the applicant), the age of applicant for taking facilities, occupational status of the applicant as stability and educational level of the applicant for taking facilities and have negative relation with amount of paid facilities to the customer and payback duration of granted facilities to the applicant.

ACKNOWLEDGEMENTS

Authors want to thank and appreciate comprehensive supports of Bu Ali Sina University and Parsian Bank towards their cooperation in performing this research.

REFERENCES

Alashi SO (1991). The implications of current monetary policies on safe and sound banking practice to ensure stability in the industry. NDIC Q. 1:25-35.

Allen JC (1995). A promise of approvals in minutes; not hours.J. Am. Banker 28:23.

Altman E, Saunders A (1998). Credit risk measurement: developments over the Last 20 Years. J. Bank. Financ. 21:1721-1742.

Altman EL (1968). Financial ratios; discriminate analysis and the prediction of corporate bankruptcy. J. Financ. 23:589-609.

Arabmazar A, Roueintan P (2006). Effective factors of customer's credit risk; an empirical study of Iran Keshavarzi Bank. J. Jostarhaye Eghtesadi 6:45.

Asch L (1995). How the RMA/Fair, Isaac Credit-Scoring model was built. J. Commun. Lending 78:10-16.

Avkiran NK (1995). Developing an instrument to measure customer service quality in branch banking. Int. J. Banks Mark. 12(6):10-18.

Basel Committee on Banking Supervision (2000). Principles for the management of credit risk. www.bis.org/publ/bcbs75.pdf.

Beaver WH (1966). Financial ratios and predictors of failure. J. Empirical Res. Account.: Selected Stud. pp.71-111.

Bogess WB (1967). Screen-test your credit risk. J. Harvard Bus. Rev. 45:21-113.

Cooper DF, Grey S, Raymond G, Walker P (2005). Project risk management guidelines: managing risk in large projects and complex procurements. 1st Edn., John Wiley and Sons Ltd., Chichester, England ISBN: 0-470-02281-7.

Demirguc-Kunt A, Huizinga H (1997). Financial structure and bank profitability: a cross-country comparison of banks, markets and development, Demirguc-Kunt A and Levine R (Eds.). MIT Press, Cambridge, MA pp.243-262.

Dezube D (1996). Mortgage scoring: rules of thumb. Mortgage Bank. 56:51-57.

Duijne FHV, Aken DV, Schouten EG (2008). Considerations in developing complete and quantified methods for risk assessment. Saf. Sci. 46:245-254.

Dunham HL (1938). A simple credit rating for small loans. Bankers Monthly 55:332-361.

Durand D (1941). Risk element in consumer installment lending.Studies in consumer installment financing. No8, National Bureau of Economic Research Inc., New York.

Fair Institute (1996). Low to moderate income and high minority area case studies, Fair-Isaac and company inc. Discussion Paper. Volume 4.

Fisher RA (1936). The use of multiple measurements in taxonomic problem. Ann. Eugen. 7:179-188.

Giddens A (1999). Risk and responsibility. Modern Law Rev. 62:1-10.

Gumparthi S, Khatri S, Manickavasagam V (2011). Design and development of credit rating model for public sector banks in India: Special reference to small and medium enterprises. J. Account. Taxation 3(5):105-124.

Huang SC, Wu CF (2011). Customer credit quality assessments using data mining methods for banking industries. Afr. J. Bus. Manag. 5(11):4438-4445.

Jah S, Xiaofeng H (2012). A comparison of financial performance of commercial banks: A case study of Nepal. Afr. J. Bus. Manag. 6(25):7601-7611.

Joel B (2009). Risk Management in Banking. John Willey and Son's publications.

Johnson RA, Wichern DW (2002). Applied multivariate statistical analysis (fifth edition).Prentice-Hall, Upper Saddle River, NJ.

Greuning HV, Brajovice S (2003). Analyzing and managing banking risk: a framework for assessing corporate governance and financial risk. 2nd edition. The World Bank Publications.

Kiss F (2003). Credit scoring process from a knowledge management perspective. Budapest University of Technology and Economics. www.itm.bme.hu.

Koh HC, Tan WC, Goh CP (2006). A two-step method to construct credit scoring models with data mining techniques. Int. J. Bus. Inform. 1(1):966-118.

Lawson JC (1995). Knowing the score. US., Banker Mag. November, pp. 61-65.

Lee TS, Chiu CC, Lu CJ, Chen IF (2002). Credit scoring using the hybrid neural discriminate technique. J. Expert Syst. Appl. 23:245-254.

Lemeshow DW, Hosmer S (2000). Applied logistic regression (2nd ed. ed.). New York: Wiley. ISBN 0-471-35632-8.

Leonard KJ (1995). The development of credit scoring quality measures for consumer credit applications. International J. Qual. Reliab. Manag. 95:79-85.

Li Y, Liao X (2007). Decision support for risk analysis on dynamic alliance. Decis. Support Syst. 42:2043-2059.

Mansouri A (2003). Designing and explaining bank facilities allocation mathematical model (classic and neural networks model approach).Doctorate dissertation. Tarbiat Modares University (Teacher Training University). [in Persian].

Mester LJ (1997). What is the point of credit scoring? Federal Reserve Bank of Philadelphia Business Review.

Merton RC (1974). On the pricing of corporate debt: the risk structure of interest rates. J. Financ. 29:449-470.

Mogboyin O, Asaolu TO, Ajilore OT (2012). Bank consolidation program and lending performance in nigerian banking system: an empirical analysis with panel data. Int. J. Appl. Econ. Financ. 6:100-108.

Mojtahedi SM, Mousavi SM, Aminian A (2009). A non-parametric statistical approach for analyzing risk factor data in risk management process. J. Appl. Sci. 9:113-120.

Morgan DP (1994). Bank credit commitments, credit rationing and monetary policy. J. Money Credit Bank. 26:87-101.

Owojori A, Akintoye R, Adidu A (2011). The challenge of risk management in Nigerian banks in the post consolidation era. J. Account. Taxation 3(2):23-31.

Power M (2008). Organized uncertainty: designing a world of risk management. Oxford University Press, Oxford, UK., ISBN-10: 0199253943, p.275.

Safari S, Shaghaghi ME, Sheikh MJ (2010). Credit risk management of legal entity customers in commercial banks; using data envelopment analysis.Human Sciences Instructor (Modares Oloume Ensani) Journal. No. 69:137-164. [in Persian].

Salehi M, Mansoury A (2011). An evaluation of Iranian banking system credit risk: Neural network and logistic regression approach. Int. J. Phys. Sci. 6(25):6082-6090.

Sheng KL, Ying WT (2011). A comparative study of data mining techniques in predicting consumers' credit card risk in banks. Afr. J. Bus. Manag. 5(20):8307-8312.

Thomas LC, Edelman DB, Crook LN (2002). Credit scoring and its applications. Society for Industrial and Applied Mathematics Philadelphia, PA, USA.

Whitehead J (2004). An introduction to logistic regression. Department of economics. East Carolina University. p. 10.

Ypma TJ (1995). Historical development of newton-raphson method. SIAM Rev. 37:531-551.

Zekavat SM (2003). Credit risk models of Iran Bank-e-Tosea Saderat customers. Master's Program Thesis. Banking Higher Institute, Tehran. [in Persian].

Zribi N, Boujelbène Y (2011). The factors influencing bank credit risk: The case of Tunisia. J. Account. Taxation 3(4):70-78.

Comparison of financial instruments in Islamic versus conventional banking system and liquidity management

Hafiz Mahmood Ul Hassan , Sadaf Razzaque and M. Sohail Tahir

Shaheed Zulfikar Ali Bhutto Institute of Science and Technology, Islamabad, Pakistan.

The aim of this paper is to study the financial instruments which are used for liquidity management in Islamic and conventional financial systems. For day to day operations banks need liquidity and banks must have to manage their liquidity according to the operations. Liquidity risk management is very important for banks as well as for financial institutions. Both types of financial systems have their own different types of financial instruments for liquidity management. These instruments are used and have different applications depending upon the basic idea of their construction. From the discussion it is clear that Islamic financial system has more equity based instruments than conventional system and promotes equity based instruments rather than debt base instruments. Islamic financial system is criticized by the Muslim scholars due to lack of Shariah complaint of products because most Islamic financial institutions do not follow the basic principles of Islamic financial system. Islamic instruments are more in quantity but the problem of Islamic financial products is that they are not more developed as compared to conventional financial system products. Especially, the absence of Islamic capital and money markets in most countries. Due to lack of Islamic markets Islamic products are not more compatible as conventional. If we will develop Islamic financial markets for the trade of Islamic financial instruments then products or instruments of Islamic finance will become automatically compatible.

Key words: Financial instruments, conventional banking system, Islamic banking system, liquidity management.

INTRODUCTION

Banking system is considered as very important for the development of an economy. After the introduction of Islamic banking system in the economy of Pakistan many issue were raised and discussed by the scholar in this regards. Whether this system really follow the sharpie or not? If not then why? Is interest free banking system better than the interest based banking system? What are the differences in two systems? And what are the similarities in both systems? There are lots of issues regarding interest free banking system which are under the considerations of researchers and scholars. Islamic financial sector is developed and got strength due to the development of financial institutions. Now it is not limited to only banking industry but also it is becoming a very strong competitor of conventional financial system.

Islamic financial system also has products and services of capital market based. Islamic capital markets main motive is to offer liquidity for financial instruments. Dusuki (2010) states that Islamic capital markets' most appreciable achievement is to provide the growth of Islamic sukuks in all over the world. Liquidity management of financial instruments is a very technical issue. It is not easy to manage liquidity risk. It is a science and requires special skills to diversify the liquidity risk of financial instruments.

In current economic situation of Pakistan the issue of

liquidity management gets attention of the researchers. What is liquidity? Liquidity is the firm ability to pay its short term liabilities. It also means availability of cash or liquid assets for paying firm's short term liabilities. In current economic scenario Islamic as well as conventional banks are facing the liquidity risk. It also decreases the competitiveness of the Islamic banks as compared to conventional banks because it is a very serious business risk.

There must be a reasonable availability of liquid assets. Either much higher or too low are the problems of liquidity. Too much excess of cash must be invested in profitable projects and deficiency of cash must be funded at reasonable cost otherwise it will show the operational deficiency of the bank.

Liquidity is very essential and play very important role in banking sector. Bank's basic functions are performed on the basis of liquidity. Banks having inadequate liquidity will have to face problems to perform their basic functions. Liquidity excess or deficiency for conventional banks has an effect on future implementation of monetary policy. In conventional banks too much liquidity shows that the interest rates will fall in future and too less liquidity create the expectation of high interest rates. On the other hand, Islamic banking system in which interest is prohibited and allows profit-loss sharing trade having their own modes of financing and investing in these situations. They will have to broader their functions and businesses in case of excess liquidity and will have to be financed in case of deficiency. Excess of liquidity indicates the no return or low return generating by liquid assets.

Many countries have both conventional banking systems as well as Islamic banking systems in their economies. The pioneer country of Islamic banking or interest free banking system is United Arab Emirates. In 1973, with the paid up capital of 14 million dollars Dubai Islamic bank was established in UAE. After the introduction of Dubai Islamic banking many countries followed it and started many interest free banks in their country. Now more than 396 Islamic interest free banks are performing their role in 53 different countries of the world and the total estimated amount invested in Islamic banking sector is 442 US billion dollars. (Nasser: Islamic Banking in Numbers, 2008).

Pakistan's economy faces many phases during 63 years. Pakistani banking sector also faced many major changes from 1947 to present. The act 1956 of state bank of Pakistan attracts the private banks and financial institutions in country. Privatization development in 1992 motivated the local investors as well as foreign banks to establish their structure (Ahmad et al., 2010). Now in Pakistan 5 Islamic, 5 public sectors, 4 specialized, 18 conventional and 6 foreign banks are operating their functions.

Islamic banks also face same risk in liquidity as conventional banks. However, this risk is classified into two types. First type is similar to conventional banks and also according to the laws and principles of Islamic finance. But the other type of risk which is new or modified and is supposed to meet the Islamic laws and principles. Murabaha agreement termination is one possible issue that creates liquidity risk (Anas and Mounira, 2008).

Islamic banks and conventional banks operate in different conditions but have to face similar risk and market conditions. The aim of this study is to compare the liquidity management process and financial instruments available in both banking systems and to find out best possible structure of liquidity management for Islamic banking system in Pakistan.

LITERATURE REVIEW

The issue of liquidity management is concerned with all financial institutions either Islamic or conventional. Liquidity management is a critical but complex issue in Islamic financial system as well as conventional financial system. Lack of attention on this issue leads to many serious consequences such as collapse of financial institutions and the stability of financial systems. Most banks fail due to their liquidity problems. Regulatory authorities are very much concerned with liquidity position of banks and financial institutions. Currently authorities are thinking how to strengthen the liquidity management (Majid, 2003). Both financial systems have their own instruments for liquidity management. Separate discussion about liquidity management instruments for both systems is given.

In his study Dinger (2009) suggested that in emerging economies global banks also work with national banks. So due to transactional banks the liquidity risk can be reduced. Because of normal conditions in the economy these global banks holds low liquidity assets. But when the whole economy of that country is in crisis they hold higher liquid assets as compared to the single market banks. Siddiqi (2008) also stated that the global financial crisis from 2008 t0 2009 had impact on the capability of third (liquidity risk). In current financial market managing liquidity risk is more challenging. Hassan, (2009) studied on risk mangement pratices in islamic banking in Burnei. During the study the questionaire was developed to evaluate risk mangagement practices. The results show that liquidity risk is prevail highly in Islamic banks of Burnei. But the other evidences indicates that excess liquidity were avaibale to the Islamic banks of other countries and also in Brunei. Liquidity ratio was 76% in 2005 according to his calculations. He suggested that through adopting risk management practices, which include risk assement and analysis and the other one is risk identification. Haron and Wan Azmi (2008) studied and find out that Islamic financing is related to interest-rate risk, profitability risk, credit risk and liquidity risk. The findings of the study show that commercial banks in Malaysia that are also practicing Islamic financing services have significantly lower credit and liquidity risk. The study results show that liquidity risks in those who are practicing in both types are low significant but highly significant with the conventional banks. Khan and Ahmad (2001) conducted a research on Islamic banks and finds that liquidity risk is harmful faced by the Islamic banks. When we compared liquidity risk with operational risk and rate of return risk and see the effect on banks. The results show that liquidity risk affects more than the other type of risks.

Gabbi (2004) in his research classifies risk in Islamic terminology. According to him risk means uncertainty and uncertainty makes a contract invalid in Islamic law of banks. So, according to the study of Gharar, he states that uncertainty is the physical appearance of things, as such, he implies that date and method of delivery is uncertain, contract is uncertain, subject matter, duration and price of contract are also uncertain. How et al. 2005, studied Islamic banks and the risks that the banks are faced with. In his study he argues that if the bank has increase the capital it will enhance the confidence of the customer. With the increase in the capital the other benefit is our loan portfolio will also decline. And our loan to deposit ratio will increase. But on the other hand some depositors are insured the deposit. So the change in capital level wills no effect on them. But it affects the loan portfolio this will dominate side of it.

Financial instruments available in Islamic finance

The Islamic financial instruments are classified into two groups, which have effect on both sides of balance sheet (Zaher and Hassan, 2001; Siddiqui, 2008). Liquidity management in Islamic banking system is very unique because in conventional banking system all instruments are interest based but in Islamic financial system interest is prohibited. Islamic financial institutions issue only equity finance instruments but conventional banks issue equity finance as well as debt finance instruments Liquidity management is very important because of existence of risk. Due to risk involvement Islamic and conventional systems have to manage it properly. There is absence of shariah compatible instruments in markets because of limited development in interbank money market (Majid, 2003). For liquidity management structure the money market is a vital element as the money market is the first opportunity to borrow short term finances. This issue gives more insight to understand the considerations of researchers and scholars of liquidity management due to shariah concerns and the operations of Islamic banks. Some major instruments would be discussed.

The most common instrument is Murabaha financing for short-term investment and can also be used for long term investment. Murabaha is like a mark up instrument available in Islamic finance (Warde, 2000). It is cost plus profit financing for asset acquisition. It is a sale contract through which bank sells goods to its customer on profit revealing the original cost and profit charged in the contract. In this contract a customer generate a request for the purchase of assets to financial institutions at declared cost and profit. Basic idea of Murabaha has differently applied like Bay Maujjal, Bay Salam and Istasna. Ismal (2010) said that as the contract is agreed among the parties ownership of an asset transfer from one party to other. Although it is a traditional instrument for short- term investment but banks have an inefficient use of funds due to its low rate of return (Majid, 2003). It is very sensitive mode of financing because of its deferred payments (Ismal, 2010). Murabaha has some clashes among Islamic scholars regarding its acceptability and applications in Shariha (Ayub, 2007). The clash among the scholar is due to the selling of commodity which is not yet owned by the seller and charge an obligation on the buyer. However, it is suitable and acceptable in money market and most favorite instruments among all Islamic banks. In 2008, Malaysia's national exchange – started the Bursa Suq Al-Sila', which is totally shariah-compliant commodity instrument on Murabaha's principle. Suq Al-Sila' is an Islamic money market financial tool that can be bought and sold with palm oil as a fundamental commodity. For managing short term liquidity such as palm oil commodity can be used (Gavin, 2010).

The other instrument is Sukuk al-Salam (asset back security) which is used for liquidity management in Islamic banking system. It is an Islamic investment certificate or note which is parallel to yield bond of conventional banks and have the main motive of liquidity and tradability. Islamic investment sukuk is defined by Accounting and Auditing Organization for Islamic Financial Institutions (2008b) as a certificate of investment of same value of shares representing the ownership of tangible assets of the firm. Kamil (2008) states that there are many types of sukuks which is based on Shariah compliments such as bay` bithamin Ajil, Musharkah, Ijara, Mudarba, Istisna, Murabaha, Salam and Wakalah. These can also be further categorized into three different catagories such as lease based, equity based and sale based. It is bond which is similar to conventional bond but the difference is that it is asset backed and represents ownership of sukuk holders in tangible assets that are being financed. Equity based sukuks are very important and can be issued against any tangible asset. Equity based sukuks do not mean the certificates or notes of receivables but it represents the ownership. All sukusks have different features and on the basis of their features they are treated differently. The return of sukuk is the consequent of yield which is generated by asset user and distributed among the sukukholders at the end. All central banks of Islamic countries established sukuks in 2000 for Islamic banks to invest their extra funds (Awan, 2009). Anas and Mounira (2008) wrote that Almost 14 various types of sukuks securities are known and are operated in scripless securities trading system (SSTS) in Malaysia. The certificates of sukuks have right computable rate of return as a profit sharing being the owner. Ismal (2010) said that the amount of private and government sukuks that are available in Islamic money market and capital market is limited. Recently Islamic financial scholars developed the sukuk short term certificates known as short term sukuk (Ismail, 2010). Akhtar et al. (2011) said that bank can used sukuks as a medium of risk hedging. "in the same way cash, bank balance and placements, which was more than 25% during 2004 to 2006 was reduced to around 17% in 2008 due to launching of Islamic Sukuks by State Bank of Pakistan and private companies" (Awan, 2009).

Wakalah is another important instrument used for liquidity management in Islamic financial system. Ismal (2010) said that wakalah is an agency contract in which one party appoints the other party as an agent (wakeel) by paying certain service charges against the task performed by the agent on the behalf of the investor (muwakil). It is service provision contract. In this contract investor (muwakil) pay fixed fee to bank (wakeel) for his investment in pre-agreed assets. There are many types of wakalah like Wakalah in Purchase, Wakalah in Sale, Absolute agency also called unrestricted wakalah, restricted wakalah, General Wakalah and special wakalah. But two major types of wakalah are restricted and unrestricted wakalah. Unrestricted wakalah is the pools of funds in which funds are invested in any type of assets without imposing any restriction (Greuning and Iqbal, 2009). In unrestricted wakalah Islamic banks charge only service fee rather than becoming partner in profit sharing. Greuning and Iqbal (2009) said that Islamic fee based instruments require more developments for their recognition. Hawala contract is also used for liquidity management in Islamic banking. It is also the type of agency contract. In hawala contract the bank pays the liabilities of the customer and charge a fee on this activity from the customer and customer will payback to bank after the maturity of the liability.

Ijara financing is also a very important tool for financing in Islamic banking system. Islamic bank allows the customer to use the asset against fixed charges which is paid by the customer to bank. Ownership of an asset may remain with bank or transfer to customer gradually. All terms and conditions are written in the contract. To ensure its liquidity financial institutes issue its securities in the market to get instant liquidity.

Islamic financial institutions are more concerned with the acceptability of shariah. So they have to follow the shariah principles. Due to the fast growth of Islamic financial industry and the desire of shariah compatible instruments by the investors the Islamic securitization is necessary. After the introduction of Islamic financial institutions they issue their securities against their assets. Securitization means issuing securities of equal amount against shares. It is the process of distributing firm's shares. Issuance of certificates against the ownership of the business's assets is the process of Islamic securitization. All necessary and basic guidelines are also mention to trade these certificates in secondary markets. No issue of debt certificates in Islamic financial system is permissible. In Islamic finance only ownership securities are issued of assets. These are also like sukuks but due to the difference in features we call them securities. Sukuks are fixed income certificates but securities are not fixed income securities. Security certificates are more risky to sukuks. In Islamic finance there are two classes of assets against securities that are issued. First is inventory and trade finance and second is machinery or equipment. The following types of securitization exists in Islamic financial systems which basically relates to the aforementioned classes Musharakah, securitization of diminishing Musharakah, securitization of Salam, securitization of Ijarah, hybrid securitization and Istisna securitization. Different Islamic banks issued security certificates against their assets in different countries across the world. After the introduction of Islamic banking system in the world securitization has significant business growth. Scholars also argued that securitization process has generated benefits for community. In 1999 in Indonesia Ministry of Finance issued musharka based certificates called Government Musharkah Certificates through which ownership of some profitable projects is given to general public (Majid, 2003).

All the aforementioned instruments are commonly used for liquidity management in Islamic financial institutions in all over the world. Some special instruments are also used in some countries but not all over the world. In this way Islamic banks use their idle cash and also generate cash through fee which is charged against the provision of services. Now we describe the important instruments of conventional banking system which are used.

Financial instruments available in conventional banking

In conventional banking system there are many types of financial instruments used for liquidity management. There is no issue of interest. In conventional banking system there are three main elements which are interest rate, cash settlement and liquidity transactions with government. Conventional banking system has both type of financing that is, equity and debt financing, and both type of financial instruments in market for trading.

Bills of exchange and other commercial papers are financial instruments which are used in conventional banking for liquidity management as an instrument of debt financing. Both exports and imports are financed by means of bill of exchange. As the bill of exchange accepted it becomes the marketable security and can be trade in market, and its market value depends on interest rate and maturity life (Wilson, 1991). Although, no interest exists in bill of exchange but its value is depends on interest. But in Islamic banking its value does not depend on interest. Both systems have similar process but the difference is on the market value of bill of exchange and principles of transactions. Bills of exchange and other commercial papers such as banker's acceptance and repurchase agreements are also called money market instruments because their maturity is less than one year. Conventional banks also used receivables either accounts receivables or notes receivables for liquidity management. Liquidity is managed better by enhancing the efficiency of collection departments.

Customer deposits are the other source of liquidity management in banking system. Customer deposits his savings in banks and earns interest. When central bank increases the interest rate to tight the monetary policy customers more deposit their money in the bank. Interest rate is used as a tool of monetary policy. Banks use these funds for investments as well as for their liquidity management. There are different types of deposits in conventional banking system. Deposits of the bank depend upon the public preferences. In case of high interest rate the bank's deposits increase automatically and if customer needs to withdraw some cash through ATM the bank's deposits decrease. On the other hand, there are no deposits in Islamic banking but customer acts a partner through Musharkah, Mudarbah and Murabaha, etc with bank. Actually deposits are the loan which is given to commercial bank by customers but in Islamic banking customer acts as a business partner with bank. Deposits are the liabilities of the bank and increase the banks liquidity risk because it is up to the customers to retain or withdraw their deposits.

Long term and intermediate term bonds are also used as financial instruments for debt financing. Bonds are very simple classical financial instruments but interest on the bond is little complex because of direct return and the calculation of market value (Wilson, 1991). They have less risk as compared to shares or equity securities because bond's risk is transferred to equity holders. In case of bankruptcy bondholders have priority on equity holders for repayment. As equity holders are the owners of the business and the debt induction in business is on their behalf, so in case of loss or any serious trouble they must have to pay to bondholders because equity holders are the owners of any profit and loss due to ownership. Financial institutions issue bonds either long term or intermediate term for debt financing depends on the needs of the institutions. These securities are fixed income securities. Interest must be paid to bondholders otherwise they have the right to go court against the equity holders for repayment. Sukuks have identical properties to bonds except sukuks are not loan certificates but equity certificates. Sukuks have more risk as compared to bonds because of the ownership of the assets not given loan to business. Does an Islamic bond exist? No, but zero coupon bond can be used as an Islamic bond under certain conditions as Government of Saudi Arabia issued (Wilson, 1991). Market value of conventional bonds depends upon the interest rate. As the interest rate raises market value declines and vice versa. If banks issue zero coupon bonds to those persons who dislike interest, the bond return is related to Islamic financial instruments not with interest rate, sale of bonds should be to specific persons and the bonds compliance the shariah's law.

Another and most important financial instrument is ordinary share or equity share. Every share shows the ownership of the shareholders in the firm's assets. When financial institutions need funds they can issue more shares to attain funds. It is a very common mode of financing.

A firm can also raise money through issuing preferred or common shares to the general public. The main difference of preferred and common share is the risk related with them. Common stock is more risky then preferred stock. Although both stocks are traded in the market but preferred stockholders have superior claim on the assets because of their preference and that is why this stock is less risky. Preferred stocks are like both common stocks and bonds. Basically these are stocks but also work like bonds because they guarantee the fix dividends for a fix time period. Distribution of dividend on common stock is not necessary but on preferred it is essential and in case of any missing of dividend it is essential to pay it before paying next dividend. Due to less risk related to preferred stocks their prices are less volatile as compared to common stocks and less chance of capital gains on preferred stocks. Common stocks have more risk but not more than the initial investments. In Islamic finance there are many types of shares that financial institutions issue like share of Musharakah, share of diminishing Musharakah, share of Salam, share of Ijarah, hybrid securitization and Istisna securitization. The main difference between securitization in Islamic and the conventional finance is that until the assets are not purchased by the firm the shares trade is not permitted in secondary market. In Islamic finance securitization correspond to asset's property rights instead of financial certificates. Islamic financial institutions can issue the shares only against the assets to attain funds. But in conventional financial system there is no need of existence of assets against the shares.

CONCLUSION

On the basis of aforementioned discussion it is cleared that Islamic finance has very much potential to compete with the conventional around the globe. For day to day operations banks need liquidity and banks must have to manage their liquidity according to the operations. Liquidity risk management is very important for banks as well as for financial institutions. Both types of financial systems have their own different types of financial instruments for liquidity management. These instruments are used and have different applications depending upon the basic idea of their construction. From the discussion it is clear that Islamic financial system has more equity based instruments than conventional system and promotes equity based instruments rather than debt base instruments. Islamic financial system is criticized by the Muslim scholars due to the lack of shariah complaint of products. Because most Islamic financial institutions do not follow the basic principles of Islamic financial system.

As earlier discussed, Islamic instruments are more in quantity but the problem of Islamic financial products is that they are not more developed as compared to conventional financial system products. Especially, the absence of Islamic capital and money markets in most countries. Due to lack of Islamic markets Islamic products are not more compatible as conventional. If we will develop Islamic financial markets for the trade of Islamic financial instruments then products or instruments of Islamic finance will become automatically compatible. And Islamic financial institutions will give more tough time to conventional financial institutions in terms of competition around the world. It may takes more time for development but it will be a more beneficial system for the society around the globe.

REFERENCES

Accounting and Auditing Organization for Islamic Financial Institutions. (2008b). AAOIFI Sharia Standards. Bahrain, Saudi Arabia: AAOIFI.

Ahmad A, Rehman K, Saif MI (2010). "Islamic Banking Experience of Pakistan: Comparison of Islamic and Conventional Banks",international j.Bus. Manag., 5(2):137-144.

Akhtar MF, Ali K, Sadaqat S (2011). Liquidity Risk Management: A comparative study betweenConventional and Islamic Banks of Pakistan. Interdiscip. J. Res. Bus. 1(1):35-44.

Anas E, Mounira BA (2008). Managing Risks and Liquidity in an Interest Free Banking Framework: The Case of the Islamic Banks. Int. J. Bus. Manag. pp. 80-95.

Awan GA (2009). Comparison Of Islamic And Conventional Banking In Pakistan" Proceedings 2nd CBRC, Lahore, Pakistan November 14, 2009.

Ayub M (2007). Understanding Islamic Finance. England: John Wiley and Sons, West Sussex. Case of Malaysia. Thunderbird Int. Bus. Rev. 47(1):75-94.

Dinger V (2009). Do foreign-owned banks affect banking system liquidity risk? J. Comp. Econ. pp. 647-657.

Dusuki WA (2010). Do equity-based Sukuk structures in Islamic capital Mark. Manifest Financ. 30:44-58.

Gabbi G (2004). Measuring Liquidity Risk in a Banking Management Framework. Manage. Finan., 30(5):44-58

Gavin J (2010). Islamic liquidity management finds a new cross-border focus http://www.mifc.com/index.php?ch=151&pg=734&ac=701&bb=931

Greuning VH, Iqbal Z (2009). Risk Analysis for Islamic Banks J. KAU: Islamic Econ. 22(1):197-204.

Haron S, Wan Azmi WS (2008). Determinants of islamic and conventional deposits in the Malaysian banking system. Manag. Financ. 34(9):618-643.

How JCY, Karim MA, Verhoeven P (2005). Islamic Financing and Bank Risks: The Case of Malaysia. Thunderbird Int. Bus. Rev. 47(1):75-94.

Ismal R (2010). Strengthening and improving the liquidity management in Islamic banking. Humanomics pp. 18-35.

Hassan A (2009). Risk management practices of Islamic banks of Brunei Darussalam. J. Risk Financ. pp. 23-37.

Kamil WAR (2008). Introduction to Sukuk (ed.). Kuala Lumpur, Malaysia: RAM Rating Services Berhad.

Khan T, Ahmed H (2001). Risk Management: An Analysis of Issues in Islamic Financial Industry, Occasional Paper No. 5, Islamic Research and Training Institute (IRTI), Islamic Development Bank, Jeddah.

Majid ARA (2003). Development of Liquidity Management Instruments: Challenges and Opportunities. International Conference on Islamic Banking: Risk Management, Regulation and Supervision.

Naseer L (2008). Islamic Banking in Numbers. http://www.asharq-e.com/news.asp?section=6&id=13560. Objectives of Shariah?" J. Financ. Serv. Mark. 15(3):203-214.

Siddiqui A (2008). Financial contracts, risk and performance of Islamic banking". Manag. Financ. 34(10):680-694.

Warde I (2000). "Islamic Finance in the Global Economy" Edinburgh University Press. pp. 1-201.

Wilson R (1991). Islamicf Inanciali Nstruments. Arab Law Quart. 6(2):205-214.

Zaher TS, Hassan MK (2001). A comparative literature survey of Islamic finance and banking Financial Markets, Inst. Instrum. 10(4):155-199.

Recovery period, inventories, sales growth cycles and companies' profitability: Empirical evidence of Iran

Mahdi Salehi[1] and Sohila Torgeh[2]

[1]Accounting Department, Ferdowsi University of Mashhad, Iran.
[2]Takestan Branch, Islamic Azad University, Takestan, Iran.

The current study reviews the effects of recovery period demands and inventories going through periods of circulation of profitability of companies listed in Tehran Stock Exchange from 2005 to 2010. In this research, an efficiency asset synonymous with profitability is considered. The findings of the study show that between these two variables related to corporate profitability there is reversed relation. The study also focuses on impact of sales growth on corporate profits, because increasing sale affects receivable accounts and inventory.

Key words: Recovery period demands (AR), inventories turnover (INV), sales growth (SGROW), return of assets (ROA).

INTRODUCTION

Success in of any society is a prerequisite for economic success and prosperity in the management of large community pool. At least it is expected that the manufacturing community should be active and effective in the economic. Lack of profitability is a patent sign of the so-called economic broadcasting (Solano and Teruel, 2004). Modern financial management theory is based on the assumption that the primary purpose of company is to maximize the common stock price or shareholders' wealth. To maximize profits or an annual goal at the end, a short-term goal is to maximize profit and introduce a specific period. But to maximize shareholders' wealth is primarily a long-term goal (Salehi, 2008). Most long-term financial issues and decisions of companies such as investment, capital structure, profit sharing or assessment companies are focus and short-term investments in companies current assets or sources of their financing with less than a year maturity that the main of the balancesheet items to devote less attention have been (Solano and Teruel, 2004). The most involved in organization are current assets and liabilities whose capital management is part of the capital budgeting considered and is in the short-term financial planning of companies.

In fact, capital management includes determining of size, composition of resources and capital expenditure, for the shareholders' wealth to increase (Salehi, 2009). Payments are capital assets that are invested; if the current debts of the company assets are deducted, net capital is obtained and the liquidity criterion means short-term cash requirements for the estimated liabilities of the company. Capital management in the form of effective short-term planning is needed to respond to changes in conditions and forecasts (Smith, 1980). Current assets major items include cash, funds, inventory, and accounts receivables, which are the efficient response to the ongoing operational environmental changes in the company. Capital management, operational range - financial assets and the adequacy of current risk and liability involve appropriate policies for managing assets and liabilities in order to increase the benefits of current capital management.

Accounts balance, which is about operating capital, is very sensitive; all accounts are influenced by any change in environment factors of organizations. Capital management operation should predict the possible balance in changes in environment factors by interim planning. Other things which can influence profitability of companies are: making decision about the amount of required inventory, granting credit to buyers, or receiving credit from raw material suppliers (Deloof, 2003).

Research problem

Presently, one of the basic problems of financial management is managing types of assets and current liabilities. Most people who are involved in industries know it, but they often want external organization solution to solve it. In other words, they believe that the solution is granting loan as well cheap and enough facilities to companies (Namazi and Salehi, 2010).

In fact, important reason for cash shortage is the distance and gap between input and output flow in companies. Companies do not usually have this shortage in a whole year, but they only experience it in given period of time; and these periods are not the same in different companies. So bank facility is not a unique recourse of liquidation shortage and there are other solutions too (Salehi and Bashirimanesh, 2011). Resolving this problem is required to optimize operating capital of companies. It is required to eliminate money market defects (Deloof, 2003).

Research objective

An overview of financial statement of small and medium companies showed that they have less steady assets than large companies. This is because they lack enough financial power for investing and prefer that most of their assets are current.

As current assets send debt from important part of normal and small companies' balance sheets (Salehi and Ghorbani, 2011), this research checks the effects of capital management operation on profitability of companies listed on Tehran Stock Exchange (TSE). The major purpose is to present solution to the managers of companies, which involves increasing companies' value by investing in their receivable accounts and inventory or increasing companies' profitability by controlling change in cash period. This research surveys the effect of sales improvement on companies' profitability, because increasing sale affects debtors' accounts and inventory. If the operating capital management performance of these companies is false, these companies would be unable to pay their debts and obligations on time.

THEORETICAL ISSUES

The theoretical issues of the study are as follows.

Accounts receivable nature

Accounts receivable are open accounts which companies can present to other companies or people. So, account receivable is one of the current asset accounts which show the company's demands, and is obtained from selling goods or presenting services in normal flow of business activities. Account receivable plays important role in business activities of most companies.

Most large companies present a particular credit period to suitable and old customers. Most credit sales are maintained by using account receivable. This means that any credit evidence is not exchanged for distinguishing debt with customer (Brennan et al., 1988). The only evidences shown in the sales include buying order paper, goods transportation factor and probably customer statement. Open accounts utilization causes a rapid transaction in credit sales.

Account receivable utilization goals

Any utilization of financial resource of companies should be used to maximize the present value. Utilization of cash in accounts receivable parts is not exceptional to this rule. To prove this theory, the basic goals of receivable accounts utilization can be identified as:

1. Having more sales: Companies which sell their goods on credit usually have large-scale sales than the companies which deal on cash conditions. Most customers do not prepare to pay cash when they purchase; rather they prefer their bills be sent to their accountancy unit, where the financial matters are centralized and investigated, until action is taken to write raw check. This is done for them to have check batch.
2. Increase benefits: The main goals of increasing benefits are to earn more sales in order to gain more benefits; this will become true when contribution margin or grass profits gained by credit sales politics are not more than costs. If a company could not earn more money by selling on credit, it will be better that it sells on cash.
3. Combating rival companies: To avoid combating issue, most companies plan their credit sales by the action of their rival companies. This is a normal way in marketing. It is to be mentioned that credit policy in different industries is completely different.

Management of receivables accounts

The best way to have a good managing receivables

account is to investigate credit policy, getting the companies' demand. In this field, facts have tight relations. Credit policy, on one hand, involves with choosing benefits gained by more sales due to credit sales and on the other hand, is involved with the cost of keeping account of receivables accounts and the lost gained by burned demands.

The beginning of receivables account management is an end to inventory management. When the receivables management mission is finished, cash management will begin. By transferring goods to the costumers, receivables account starts, and by getting money from costumers, receivables account management finishes.

Account receivables management is planning, guiding and supervising all facts that affect level, amount and quality of receivables accounts (Deloof, 2003). When a company sells goods, it can get its payment by cash or account. The start of receivables accounts is when company gives on credits to its costumers, so they can pay money after some times. Companies affect quality and quantity of receivables accounts into two ways:

A. Decisions the companies make about credit sales conditions.
B. Decisions companies make about credit sales to actual and juristically persons.

When companies make decision, they plan the level of receivables accounts, which is the first decision (A); but what happens and the quality of receivables accounts are related to the second decision (B).

Factors affecting receivables accounts

Three main factors determine the level of receivables accounts:

1. Credit sales level: The first main factor affecting the amount of receivables accounts is the level of credit sales of the company. Since trading conditions in most industries are similar, normally a company with a higher level of sales has more amounts of receivables accounts.
2. Credit policy: Credit policy of a company will determine the amount of risks that the company will take. A company with a flexible credit policy will have a higher recycling compared to a company with restricted policy.
3. Credit duration: Level of receivables accounts in a company has relation with credit period. If a company doubles its credit period it can have a 100% increase in its receivables accounts (Brennan et al., 1988).

Inventories

Goods inventories can be defined as the amount of goods kept for sales. Thus inventory is an important factor for earning a particular level of sales. The goods may be durable, not cheap or expensive.

The work inventory flow during the construction increases by reducing production time. A way to improve this period is improving engineering techniques in order to accelerate production flow. The other way is initial buying instead of producing when the work inventory is reduced during the construction.

Amount of inventory made is related to coordination of production and sales. The financial manager can support sales with more risk by changing the sales conditions or selling on credit to customers. Therefore, products will be recorded in offices as inventory or receivable accounts. In some cases, many institutions prefer to sale their goods and make them nearer to cash (Blinder and Manccini, 1991).

Advantages of inventory maintenance

A company will be able to separate the steps of buying, producing and selling by inventory maintenance. If the company does not want to maintain raw material or produce enough goods, purchase is made only when production is predicted based on immediate sales. In case of being out of stock, when the contract is signed by the customer, the company cannot deliver the goods immediately. Inventory can be used to create suitable conditions for production and to do sales activities well.

Number of inventory determining factors

The basic inventories level factors determiners are amount of sale, period of time, technical nature of production flow and durability of goods compared to its spoilage.

Computer application and operation research methods can improve the inventory controlling within the framework of economic nature of companies activities. Although the diversity and complexity of these techniques made the full discussion of this study impossible, the financial manager should be prepared to use professionals who create effective methods for minimizing investment in inventories.

Checking the effects of receivable accounts management and inventory methods on firm value

The attitude implies that decision related to capital inflows in the form of general assessment is to assess receivable accounts and stock similar to the fixed assets by capital budgeting techniques. Of course, the difference between receivable accounts and inventory with other steady assets is that in steady assets evaluation of each asset can be considered separately, but in receivable accounts and inventory, their total level is considered.

Smith and Sell (1980) believe in the granting of credit to

buyers to facilitate sales of the company by different method. When demand is low, commercial credit can act as effective prices and help customers to obtain goods or control downloads of product; it also help companies to regenerate their long-term relationship with customers. However, companies that do major in investment in inventory and commercial credit can tolerate reduced profitability; so the more investment in current, the less risk and less profitability trade will experience.

Blinder and Manccini (1991) believed that inventory and account receivable are major items of current assets. According to their research, privacy and maintenance of high levels of inventory may affect production process, can reduce cost of materials provision or can make company volatile to materials price.

Petersen and Rajan (1994) studied account receivable and the high cost of business credit; they realized when companies do not have surplus of economic resources for supplying finance, financing is done by credit of materials vendors.

Shin and Soenen (1998) believe that the decision in investing on customers' account and inventory and credit receipt from material reseller has an influence on cash conversion period. They used this canon for analysis in their studies and they put good or bad effects truncation of cash conversion period on company's profitability. They analyzed the relationship between cash conversion period and profitability in the sample of companies accepted in America stock market during the period of 1974 to 1997. Their results showed that reduction of cash conversion period in a logical domain increases companies' profitability.

Deloof (2003) analyzed the sample of Belgian companies from 1992 to1996. His result confirmed that Belgian companies can improve their profitability through reduction of account receivable recovery period and reduction of inventory period. He also found out that lower levels of benefits made by companies usually wait longer for the payment of their bills.

Garcia and Martinez (2006) analyzed the effect of operating capital on profitability ability of Spanish companies during 1996 to 2002. Their research aimed to review the relationship between management of operating capital and profit. Their result showed that there is significant relationship between operating capital and profit. So, they realized that there will be increase in benefit of companies if average collection period is reduced.

Research hypotheses

According to the objectives of the study, the following hypotheses were postulated.

H1: There is a meaningful relation between average of revenue and profitability of companies.
H2: There is a meaningful relationship between inventory turnover and profitability.

RESEARCH DATA AND VARIABLES

Quoted companies in TSE were divided into three categories according to their total assets with the following conditions:
First division: large companies whose assets are more than 1000 billion Rials (Iranian currency);
Second division: medium companies whose assets are from 500 to 1000 billion Rials.
Third division: large companies whose assets are less than 500 billion Rials.

Then following features were considered for selecting sample of companies quoted in TSE:

1. Financial period in which the companies are leading at the end of Iranian fiscal year.
2. Not involved in any investment companies, finance, mediation, holdings, leasing and banks.
3. Availability of financial statement of the companies.

Considering the defined features for sampling, 81 companies were listed in 2005.
Of these, large companies (whose assets are more than 1000 billion) were excluded; the remaining was selected; 69 companies. Required information was selected for this research including assets at the beginning and end of period, purchase, sales, inventory, account receivable, earning before interest and task, current liabilities and total debt during a five-year period (2005-2010) for both categories of companies.
Research required data were collected from library resources, financial statement of audited sample companies, published information by TSE, companies' comprehensive data bank in official website of stock organization and tact processor and desert information software.
Descriptive statistic table states descriptive factor amount for each variable separately and it is for a total of 5 years. Table 1 contained data about central index of companies like the number of observations. Table 2 shows data about dispersion index of companies like standard deviation, skewness and kurtosis. Minimizing and maximizing states data dispersion suburb average axis used to measure unit of AP, INN, AR and ACC are data; and measure of companies' size is on the basis of their assets logarithm.

In the present study, the relationship between demand recovery period and inventory turnover with profitability will be tested. In order to achieve this goal, the following model will be used.

$$ROA_{i,t} = \alpha + \beta_0 AR_{i,t} + \varepsilon_{i,t}$$

$$ROA_{i,t} = \alpha + \beta_0 AR_{i,t} + \beta_1 SIZE_{i,t} + \beta_2 SGROW_{i,t} + \beta_3 DEBT_{i,t} + \varepsilon_{i,t}$$

$$ROA_{i,t} = \alpha + \beta_0 + INV_{i,t} + \beta_1 SIZE_{i,t} + \beta_2 SGROW_{i,t} + \beta_3 DEBT_{i,t} + \varepsilon_{i,t}$$

Table 1. Central index descriptive statistic.

Variable	Number of observations	Average	Median	Percentiles				
				1	25	50	75	99
ROA	165	0.21	0.18	-0.025	0.105	0.182	0.276	0.745
AR	165	113.42	93.64	0.023	60.31	93.65	154.2	295.3
INV	165	170.03	161.03	34.43	119.06	161.3	201.7	422.1
SGROW	165	0.03	0.22	-0.78	0.09	0.22	0.38	3.35
SIZE	165	4.97	5.01	4.03	4.77	5.01	5.2	5.6
DEBT	165	0.88	0.91	0.45	0.85	0.91	0.94	0.97

Table 2. Dispersion index.

Variable	S.D	Skewness	Kurtosis	Minimize	Maximize
ROA	0.148	0.4	0.45	-0.03	0.75
AR	72.17	0.07	-0.012	0	295.32
INV	75.43	0.034	0.11	35.16	425.63
SGROW	0.47	0.5	0.47	-0.81	3.48
SIZE	0.3	-0.477	0.5	4.03	5.59
DEBT	0.085	-0.32	0.275	0.44	0.97

ROA is considered as dependent variable (Solano and Teruel, 2004) and is measured by the following ratio:

$$\text{ROA} = \frac{\text{EBIT}}{\text{Assets' averages}}$$

$$\text{Average assets} = \frac{\text{Year end assets} + \text{First year assets}}{2}$$

Average revenue and inventory number volume are considered as independent variable (Solano and Teruel, 2004):

$$\text{Average revenue (AR)} = \frac{\text{receivable accounts}}{\text{Average daily sale}}$$

$$\text{Average daily sale} = \frac{\text{sale}}{365}$$

$$\text{Average revenue (AR)} = \frac{\text{receivable accounts} * 365}{\text{sale}}$$

$$\text{Inventory number volume (INV)} = \frac{\text{inventory}}{\text{Average daily purchase}}$$

$$\text{Average daily purchase} = \frac{\text{purchase}}{365}$$

$$\text{Inventory number volume (INV)} = \frac{\text{inventory} * 365}{\text{purchase}}$$

Size of the company sales growth and short depth ratios (DEPT) are (Solano and Teruel, 2004) controllable varieties and are calculated as follows:

$$\text{SGROW} = \frac{sale1 - sale0}{sale0}$$

$$\text{SIZE} = \log property$$

$$\text{DEPT} = \frac{\text{current liability}}{\text{Total dept}}$$

RESULTS

In order to test the hypotheses, we used single-variable regression and multi- variant regression; we used F test to check whether the models are meaningful and T test for testing if the regression coefficient is meaningful.

H1: There is a meaningful relation between average of revenue and profitability of companies.
First condition – investigating the relation between average revenue and profitability in small and medium companies

Model (1)

$$ROA_{i,t} = \alpha + \beta_0 AR_{i,t} + \varepsilon_{i,t}$$

Table 3 shows the determination of coefficient.

Table 3. Model 1.

Durbin–Watson	Standard deviation	Defined coefficient $AdjR^2$	Definition coefficient R^2	Correlation coefficient R
1.641	0.14175	0.086	0.095	-0.309

Table 4. The results of F test.

Item	Statistic value F	Medium	F. d	Total	Sig
noissergeR	10.941	0.22	1	0.22	0.001
secnalaB	---	0.02	163	2.09	----
latoT	----	----	163	2.309	-----

Table 5. Index model in single variable.

Item	T- Test	Standard Index	Un-standard index		Sig.
		Beta	S.D	B	
Fixed amount	10.956	----	0.026	0.282	0.000
AR i, t	-3.308	-0.309	0.000	-0.01	0.001

Table 6. Test of recovery period justification.

Durbin–Watson	Estimated S.D	Adjusted $AdjR^2$	R^2	R
1.71	0.13935	0.117	0.151	-0.388

Negative correlation coefficients imply there is negative relationship between course demands and profitability of confirmed receipt; on the other hand, the amount of the test also lacks coordination between the serial data.
F test and analysis of variance were used to review regression fit:

H0: There is no significant relationship between sales growth and profitability.
H1: There is significant relationship between sales growth and profitability.

As the top chart shows, regression of model is suitable and there is a meanful relation between benefit of the company and earnings of department Table 4.

The amount of regression is shown in Table 5. Although the significant level is very low, it confirms the negative relation between variables.

In the second condition the relation between recovery period and profitability with controllable variables is as follows,

$$ROA_{i,t} = \alpha + \beta_0 AR_{i,t} + \beta_1 SIZE_{i,t} + \beta_2 SGROW_{i,t} + \beta_3 DEBT_{i,t} + \varepsilon_{i,t}$$

Table 6 shows the coefficient of determination, determination coefficient of adjusted and statistic of Durbin –Watson is presented for review of lack of serial correlation between data:
Negative correlation coefficients have negative relationship between course demands and profitability of confirmed receipt; the amount of camera Pearson - Watson also lacks coordination between the serial data.
F test and analysis of variance were used to review regression.
H0: There is no significant relationship between sales growth and profitability.
H1: There is significant relationship between sales growth and profitability.
Table 7 shows this test.
This means that there is a significant level of regression model for suitable recovery period between the company and profitability demands.
A value of regression coefficients is given in Table 8.

Results obtained indicated negative relationship. As a result, regression model (2) is as follows:

$$ROA_{i,t} = -0.27 - 0.001AR_{i,t} + 0.045SIZE_{i,t} + 0.067SGROW_{i,t} + 0.286DEBT_{i,t} + \varepsilon_{i,t}$$

Table 7. Test suitable model (2).

Item	Statistic value	Average of square	Degrees of freedom	Total of square	Sig.
Regression	10.251	0.045	4	0.181	0.002
Remains	------	0.021	160	2.128	----
Sum	-----	-----	164	2.309	-----

Table 8. Coefficients model multivariate model demands recovery period (2).

Item	T- test	Std coefficient			
		Beta	Std. Error	B	Sig.
Constant value	-1.01	-----	0.267	-0.27	0.005
AR i,t	-3.972	-0.388	0	-0.001	0.002
SIZE i,t	1.525	0.142	0.029	0.045	0.03
SGROW i,t	1.438	0.136	0.046	0.067	0.024
DEBT i,t	1.717	0.165	0.166	-0.286	0.019

Table 9a. Can explain the test inventories turnover in the model (2-1).

Durbin–Watson	Standard deviation	Defined coefficient Adj R^2	Definition coefficient R^2	Correlation coefficient R
1.626	0.14339	0.095	0.074	-0.272

To confirm the hypotheses and to prove there is a negative relationship between demand and profitability recovery period, the above modes show that the control variables do not exist, although the correlation coefficient between the demands of recovery and profitability year period occurred. But its severity is very low. Adding more low-intensity correlation to control variables makes it still have extremely weak relationship. It can be concluded that the presence of control variables somewhat has positive effect this year.

H2: there is a relationship between inventory turnover and profitability.
In the first case, the relationship between inventories and profitability turnover without control variables is reviewed.

$$ROA_{i,t} = \alpha + \beta_0 INV_{i,t} + \varepsilon_{i,t} \qquad \text{Model (2-1)}$$

ROA stands for return on assets model and INV stands for inventories turnover.
The coefficient of determination, adjusted coefficient of determination, and Pearson Digital - Watson for reviewing lack of serial correlation between the data model (2-1) are presented in Table 9a.
Coefficient value (-0272) confirms the negative relationship between inventories and profitability flow. Durbin –Watson (1.626) lacking of serial correlation between the variables is shown.

F test and analysis of variance were used to review regression.
H_0: There is no significant relationship between sales growth and profitability.
H_1: There is significant relationship between sales growth and profitability.
Table 9b shows Pearson F Fisher and ANOVA test.

Regression model (2-1) and the appropriate inventories turnover and profitability between companies have a significant relationship.
A value of regression coefficients is given in Table 9c.
Obtained coefficients have significant relationship between dependent variables; and because the independent variable coefficient is negative, then this relationship is an inverse relationship.
As a result regression model (1-2) is:
ROA i,t = 0.119-0.0001INV i,t + ε i,t
In the second case, inventory turnover and profit are reviewed in the presence of control variable.
ROA i,t = α + β0 INV i, t + β1 SIZE i, t + β2 SGROW i, t + β 3 DEBT i, t + ε i, t Model (2-2)
(ROA) return on assets model, (INV) inventory turnover volume, Company size (SIZE), (SGROW) DEBT is relative short-term dept.
The coefficient of determination, adjusted coefficient of determination and statistics for Watson test reviews that lacks cohesion bit serial data model (2-2) are presented in Table 10:

Table 9b. Suitable test model (2-1).

Item	Statistic value	Average of square	Degrees of freedom	Total of square	Sig.
Regression	8,321	0.171	1	0.171	0.005
Remains	----	0.021	163	2.138	-----
Sum	-----	----	164	2.309	-----

Table 9c. Regression coefficients.

Item	Coefficients non-standard		Standard coefficient	T test	Sig.
	B	S.D	Beta		
Constant	0.119	0.034	------	3.452	0.001
INV	-0.001	0.00	-0.272	-2.885	0.005

Table 10. Test cycle in inventory models (2 -2).

Coefficient R	Coefficient of determination R 2	Coefficient determined by L violation Adj R^2	Standard deviation estimate	Pearson Digital - Watson
-0.28	0.078	0.142	0.14516	1.64

Table 11. Test suitable models (2-2).

Item	Statistic value	Average of square	Degrees of freedom	Sum of square	Sig.
Regression	10.251	0.045	4	0.181	0.002
Remains	------	0.021	160	2.128	------
Sum	------	-----	164	2.309	------

Table 12. Coefficients of multivariate model of inventory turnover in model (2-2).

Item	Statistic of T	Std coefficient	Non S.D coefficient		Sig.
		Beta	Std .Error	B	
Constant value	0.028	-------	0.271	0.008	0.007
INV	-3.845	-0.263	0	-0.001	0.002
SIZE	-0.441	-0.044	0.032	-0.014	0.006
SGROW	0.573	0.055	0.047	0.027	0.012
DEBT	-0.11	-0.011	0.172	-0.019	0.013

Correlation coefficient value approves the negative relationship between inventory turnover and profitability; and Durbin–Watson test shows lack of serial correlation between data.

Suitable regression for review of variance revealed that Pearson F Fisher test was used. Statistical hypothesis test is as follows:

H_0: There is no significant relationship between sales growth and profitability.

H_1: There is significant relationship between sales growth and profitability.

Table 11 shows the test of above mentioned assumption. Regression of (2-2) model is suitable and there is significant relationship between inventory turnover and profitability whose values of regression coefficients are given in Table 12.

The significant level is obtained, a coefficient was significant and there is independent and dependent relationship between variables; and because independent variable coefficient is negative, this relationship is inverse relationship.

Regression of (2-2) model is fits the following:

Table 14. Regression fit test.

Item	Statistic value	Average of square	D.F	Sum of square	Sig.
Regression	8.18	0.006	1	0.006	0.005
Remains	------	0.022	163	2.303	------
Sum	------	------	164	2.309	-----

Table 15. Coefficient of sale growth model.

Item	Statistic of T	Std coefficient		Non std coefficient	Sig.
		Beta	S.D	B	
Constant value	9.741	------	0.24	0.082	0
SGROW	2.86	0.052	0.048	0.026	0.005

ROA=0.008 – 0.001INV – 0.014SIZE + 0.027SGROW – 0.019DEBT+έ

Comparing these two positions show that without the presence of controlling variables, the coefficient relation between inventory turnover and profitability is not significant; but its severity is very low because of the value of adjusted coefficient of determination. When the control variables are added, correlation intensity is more, but not to the extent of strengthening the relationship. Then it can be concluded that the presence of control variables has partly positive impact on this relationship.

At this time, we review the effect of sales amount and its growth on profitability, because increase of sales affects account receivable and inventory.

Formula of this test is as follows:

ROA i,t = α+ β0 SGROW i,t + έ i,t

In this model ROA is assumed as SGROW.

Coefficient of determination, adjusted coefficient of determination and Durbin –Watson test that lacks serial correlation between data are seen in Table 13.

Positive correlation coefficient confirms that there is direct relationship between sales growth and profitability; on the other hand, statistic value of Durbin –Watson shows lack of serial correlation between data.

F (Fisher) test and analysis of variance were used to review regression Statistical hypothesis of this test is as follows:

H_0: There is no significant relationship between sales growth and profitability.

H_1: There is significant relationship between sales growth and profitability.

Table 14 shows the results of this test.

Since the significant level for analysis of variance is less than 0.05, the null hypothesis, with 99 percent confidence level, is rejected and the research hypothesis is accepted. This means that this regression is appropriate and there is significant relationship between sales growth and profitability. The values of regression coefficient are in Table 15.

The significant level for each of the coefficient is less than 0.05; so the null hypothesis, with 99 percent confidence level, is rejected and the research hypothesis is accepted. So the obtained significant coefficients are meaningful and there is a relationship between dependent and independent variables. Because the independent variable coefficient is positive then this relationship is a direct relationship.

The regression can be defined as follows:

ROA i,t = 0,028 + 0,026 SGROW i,t +έ i,t

Conclusion

Regarding the first hypothesis, results showed that there is significant and inverse relationship between average collection period and profitability in companies; In other words profitability levels may reduce with increased average collection period.

The second hypothesis also proves that there is significant and inverse relationship between inventory turnover and profitability in companies. Also F, T tests represented that models and coefficient of regression are significant. The result confirmed the second hypothesis with 99 percent level.

It is interesting to note that sales growth can establish direct relationship with profitability and has positive effect on it. A particular program should be made to consider credit sales in order to increase companies' profitability and to have a particular consideration for their payment.

REFERENCES

Blinder AS, Manccini LJ (1991). The Resurgence of Inventory Research: What Have We Learned? J. Econ. Survey 5:291-328.

Brennan M, Maksimovic V, Zechner J (1988). Vendor Financing, J.

Financ. 43:1127-1141.
Deloof M (2003). Dose Working Capital Management Affect Profitability of Belgian Firms?, J. Bus. Financ. Account. 30:576-587.
Namazi M, Salehi M (2010). The Role of Inflation in Financial Repression: Evidence of Iran. World Appl. Sci. J. 11(6):653-661.
Petersen MA, Rajan RG (1994). The Benefits of Firm-Creditor Relationships: Evidence from Small Business Data, J. Financ. 49:3-37.
Shin HH, Soenen L (1998). Efficiency of Working Capital and Corporate Profitability, Financ. Practice Educ. 8:37-45.
Smith K (1980). Profitability versus Liquidity Tradeoffs in Working Capital Management, in Readings on the Management Working Smith K, Sell S (1980). Working Capital Management in Practice", In Readings on the Management of Working Capital; ed. Keith Smith. St.Paul, Minn: West Publishing Co.
Solano M, Teruel JG (2004). Effects of Working Capital Management on SME Profitability, Working Paper, SSRN Electronic Library.
Capital. Ed. Smith KV, St. Paul, West Publishing Company pp.549-562.

Determinants of dividend distribution in Cameroonian companies

T. Maï Django Wambé* and V. Tsapi

Department of Accounting and Finance, Faculty of Economics and Management, University of Ngaoundere, Cameroon.

This study examines the determinants of dividend distribution by unlisted companies in Cameroon. The hypotheses are from the theoretical frameworks of the agency and the signal in which agents justify the practice of dividend distribution. The sample consists of 67 Limited Companies and Limited Liability Companies that carry out or not this practice. The data were processed using SPSS (Statistical Package for the Social Sciences). We notice that the shareholding concentration, the investment level and the total debt negatively affect the frequency of dividend distribution. On the other hand, profitability plays a key role on dividend distribution.

Key words: Dividend payout, agency theory, signal theory, unlisted companies.

INTRODUCTION

The mismanagement of government-owned and part government-owned companies and the reluctance of banks to finance private companies in the era of globalization has caused the bankruptcy of some Cameroonian companies. These phenomena have not only triggered a wave of privatizations in the 90s[1], but also an openness of capital in the public and private companies. Given the multitude of Cameroonian and foreign investors in companies today, a real problem is the sharing of profits in a context where the financial market is still embryonic[2]. There are many studies on the dividend distribution policy but when we refer to the empirical ones, we notice that the majority of studies were carried out in a context where the companies are listed. However, in Cameroun, only four companies are listed at the Douala Stock Exchange and no study has been carried out so far on this topic. Besides, this study raises the problem of the dividend policy in a country where the structure of the shareholding is concentrated (Wanda, 2001). Thus, by examining the factors which explain the distribution of dividends in Cameroonian companies, this study comes to supplement the existing ones in the world. But in spite of the difference of context, it turns out that to talk about the difference between companies in the light of their dividend distribution practices implies that these practices depend on certain factors which may likely influence them (Wissem and Christhophe, 2009). To this effect, previous work on dividend policy has followed two divergent research paths. The first path which stipulates "the neutrality of the dividend policy", considers that the

*Corresponding authors E-mail: wtmaithe@gmail.com.

[1]"Historically, we observe in our countries that whatever may have been the ideological option, the evolution of our economies has been accompanied by strong state intervention". It is in these terms that Bekolo Ebe (1985) justifies the predominant existence of public companies in the Cameroonian economy. However, because of the crisis in recent years, the context in which these companies operate has disclosed the existence of much turbulence. Government companies in their vast majority have ceased to be profitable. Instead, they experience huge losses (Tedga, 1990). From then, many of them have been privatized. This privatization has led to the development of a new shareholding. Among the privatized companies in Cameroon we can name REGIFERCAM which became CAMRAIL, the SMEC, which became CDE.

[2]The financial sector has seen the birth of the stock exchange (the Douala Stock Exchange) in 2002. Despite its setting-up, its activities are still very limited. To date, only a few companies are listed. They are SMEC, SOCAPALM, SAFACAM.

distribution of the dividend does not have any impact on the value of the company in a perfect market context. Indeed, the results of Modigliani and Miller (1961) show that the shareholders are indifferent to any policy of dividend distribution adopted by the company in a perfect and efficient market. The second research path is based on several theories (theory of signal, theory of agency etc….) to show that the distribution of dividend seems to depend on a combination of factors, each of which has some influence on the decision to distribute or not to distribute dividends. Through this framework and with contributions from Jensen and Meckling (1976) and Jensen (1986), the distribution of cash is a justification of its existence. Based on agency theory, these authors have indeed identified several determinants influencing dividend policy, namely the shareholding structure, investment opportunities and debt. Complementary to the agency theory, the signal theory shows that dividend policy peddles information issued by the leaders and which is reliable for shareholders. Batsch (1999) notes that in this case, the decision to distribute dividends comes from the leaders themselves. They would use the dividends as a means to inform shareholders on the success of the company. From what precedes, we believe that dividend distribution is complex and relies on the theories mentioned. However, given the above mentioned research works, we can say that several factors may explain the distribution of dividends in companies. As it can be noticed however, the factors identified were in a Western context. We can therefore question their validity in the African context, particularly in Cameroon, characterized by the absence of financial markets and specific economic structures. Also, the object of our research is to identify and analyze the driving forces that guide the strategic choices of Cameroonian companies in the distribution or non distribution of dividend. The central question that guides our thought is: what are the fundamental elements that lead to the distribution of the dividend in Cameroonian companies? From this problem, we pursue two main objectives: to highlight the distinctive nature of dividend distribution policy in Cameroonian companies and to identify the basic elements that explain the decision to distribute or not to distribute the dividend in companies.

This paper is organized as follows: the first part is dedicated firstly, to present some of the studies made in some African countries and secondly, to present the theoretical determiners of dividend distribution and the research hypotheses. In the second part, we shall expose the methodology, the empirical results as well as the interpretation of the results. Finally we shall present our conclusions.

THE DIVIDEND POLICY IN SOME AFRICAN COUNTRIES

In the search for the explanatory factors of the dividend policy, several studies have been carried out worldwide. Those which are interesting to us in this part are the studies made in some developing countries, notably in Africa. Here are some of the important studies.

Adesola and Okwong (2009) studied the dividend policies of Nigerian listed companies by using the well known model of Lintner (1956). The results stated that dividend policies /decisions of these companies were highly influenced by their current earnings and past year dividend, while firm size and growth prospect had no significant impact on dividend behavior of these companies. Musa (2009) analyzed the dividend behavior by using Parsimonious multiple regression model developed by Musa (2005). This study focused on five metric variables (previous dividend, current earnings, cash-flows, investment and assets) and three non-metric variables (growth, firm size and industry classification) in order to explain as well as predict the dividend policy of listed firms in Nigeria. The empirical results revealed that the five metric variables have significant impact and non metric variables have insignificant impact on the dividend policy of these firms. However, three of the variables (current earnings, previous year dividend and cash-flow) have been found to be significant in the model.

Considering Ethiopian firms, the study of Kinfe (2011) examined the data for a sample of six firms out of twelve private banks operating in Ethiopia for the period of 2006 to 2010. The results indicated that the firms chose to pay more dividends when firm size were large; this supports agency cost theory were divided are used as a tool to agency conflict, it also implies large firms have better access to raise fund and distribute dividend to shareholders better than smaller firms. Furthermore, the results illustrated that the firms in which their liquidity were low paid higher dividend compared to the firms with high liquidity ratio. The models also revealed that previous year's dividend payout ratio was an additional variable of both models that affected dividend payout ratio of the firms

An analysis of the above literature shows that studies on the determiners of the dividend policy have also been made in emerging countries in Africa but only listed companies are concerned by these studies. Besides, the dividend policy is relatively less investigated in Cameroonian companies and practically no study has been undertaken in this country. It is thus necessary to investigate Cameroonian companies with regard to their distribution of profits.

THEORETICAL DETERMINERS OF DIVIDEND DISTRIBUTION

We present in this first part the main determiners of dividend distribution put forward by the various financial theories and we formulate the related research hypothesis.

Shareholding structure and dividend distribution policy

According to Severin and Dhennin (2003), the shareholding structure is a plural concept, since it includes not only the shareholding concentration but also the identity of the main shareholder. We will emphasize on shareholding concentration in this part. The influence of shareholding concentration on dividend distribution has been the subject of much literature. Indeed, the presence of dominant or significant shareholders in a company helps in controlling the company's executive. Hence, dominant shareholders are likely to promote or oppose the payout of the dividend. Based on this logic, we can say that decisions are made by those who have the power to do so. Thus, the holding of shares or voting rights by some shareholders may aggravate the non distribution of the dividend. It is in this sense that the studies of Rozeff (1982), Moh'd et al. (1995) show the negative influence on dividend distribution of shareholding concentration.

On the other hand, the negative relationship between dividend distribution and shareholding concentration is not supported by other researchers. The work of Renneboog and Trojanowski (2007) show a rather positive relationship. Their empirical study, covering a sample of 985 British companies, suggests that there is a positive relationship between shareholding concentration and dividend distribution. Indeed, they find that the presence of controlling shareholding aims to reduce agency costs and improve the dividend. We also notice that the studies of Mat Nor and Sulong (2007) go in the same direction. Their results reveal that the concentration of the shareholding has a positive effect on the dividends, but with a minimal impact. La Porta et al. (2000), Faccio et al. (2001) on their part assert that in an effective legal system, the minority shareholders use their legal powers to oblige companies to pay dividends. They stipulate that the payment of dividends is the result of the legal system in which the firm finds itself, allowing the minority shareholders to use their rights to force the insiders to distribute the profits to them. This is also what the works of Mancinelli and Ozkan (2006) in Italy show.

From this literature review, we note that the presence of majority shareholders in the shareholding structure influences positively or negatively the distribution of the dividend. Because of this difference of position in the literature on this topic, an exploratory study was conducted in eight Cameroonian companies to determine the factors that explain dividend distribution. The role of shareholding concentration was raised by several respondents. On several situations, five CEOs took their company as an example. They mentioned the presence of one or two major shareholders in the capital structure and their reluctance to distribute the dividend. To illustrate this, we used the response of the director of a business company in the town of Garoua, *"I am the majority shareholder of the company ... the more one distributes the dividend, the more capital is lost."* Thus, taking our cue from this exploratory study and empirical studies mentioned earlier, our first hypothesis is as follows:

H1: *Dividend distribution varies negatively with shareholding concentration in Cameroonian companies.*

The need for investment and dividend distribution policy

Walter's model (1956) was already proposing the residual theory of dividends. It is at the basis of the relationship between dividend policy and investment policy in the company. Indeed, for followers of this residual theory, the amount of dividend may vary from one period to another depending on investment opportunities. Also, they prefer to see businesses retain earnings rather than distribute them to shareholders.

The supposed influence of investment opportunities on dividend distribution depends on the agency theory and is based on the divergent interests that oppose managers to shareholders. This observation is identical to that of Myers (1997). Myers (1997) mentions the possible competition between investment and distribution in firms with surplus cash flow. Investing without emitting funds therefore means a restriction of dividends. On the contrary, if shareholders prefer the dividend policy, investment will not occur. For Moussu and Thibierge (1996), it is the level of investment opportunities that determines the agency costs and therefore the dividend policy of the firm. For this purpose, a high level of investment opportunities is associated with a low level of dividend and vice versa[3]. On the other hand, companies can also signal to the market that they are in "good health" by acting on the amount granted to investment in profitable projects. Therefore, instead of being distributed, free cash flow will be invested. As mentioned by Miller and Rock (1985), leaders of companies with significant cash flow can spend a small amount on dividends and use more cash for investment.

In Cameroon for example, from a profit of 679 855 FCFA obtained by SA-Eura Audit in 2004, investment amounted to 515 000 FCFA and no dividend was paid[4]. This example illustrates the negative relationship that may exist between investment and distribution. Thus, when the investment opportunities of a company are high and liquidity is important, the distribution of dividend decreases or does not exist. Faced with this report and in a context of the absence of an institutional framework for investment promotion, a lack of investment banks, or tax Incentives for investment companies, we offer the

---

[3]Investment opportunities are related to expenditure on research and development or advertising for example.

[4]According to Statistics and Fiscal Decision Identification Number M18900000936 J.

following hypothesis:

H2: *The lower the investment level, the more the company pays out the dividend.*

Indebtedness and dividend distribution policy

Research in finance rank debt among elements of financial structure and associate it with an external mode of governance. As part of this research, we will adopt the definition of Peyrard (1999), stating that the debt of a company is the total of debts of that company. The objective of the study of indebtedness is to show the proportion it occupies between debt and equity. As this objective is achieved, it will be important for us to present the relationship that may exist between the decision to distribute dividends and the debt ratio of the company. Just like for investment, Walter (1956) considers that the decision to distribute the dividend has only got a residual role since it comes only after the decision on the level of debt. But in this work we consider that indebtedness may act on the dividend distribution policy. Thus, from 1944 to 1966, IBM, heavily indebted did not pay out dividends. The target was to increase all financial assets relying on shareholders' equity at a rate necessary to follow the market growth (Nivoix, 2004). This example illustrates the negative relationship that may exist between debt and dividend payments to shareholders. Empirical tests by Crutcheley et al. (1999) confirm this assertion.

Besides, Nivoix (2004) shows that firms which resort to debt in a regular and quite important manner need to use the distribution of dividend to control the level of their available cash. Consequently, all things being equal, companies with high levels of debt should reduce the rate of dividend distributions. This is consistent with what the CEO of a business company stated during our exploratory study. For this CEO, if debt is high, the company must clean up its balance sheet and should not distribute a lot of liquidity. Building on this literature review, we hence make the third hypothesis:

H3: *The lower the total debt, the more the company pays out the dividend.*

Profitability and dividend distribution policy

The influence of profitability on dividend distribution is based on signal theory. Thus, as Goffin (2001) points out, the emission of a signal is only possible by profitable companies and is meant to distinguish these from non-profitable ones. For Modigliani and Miller (1961), the dividend policy is neutral as to the future profitability of the company. Goffin's (2001) own view was that the payment of dividend is positively linked to the profitability of the firm. For him, paying a high and regular dividend is costly to the company paying it. Such a payment cannot be achieved by an unprofitable business. Moreover, if a business began paying a temporary high dividend to make people believe that it is profitable and that, thereafter, it is compelled to decrease it, the decrease would be perceived by the market as an indicator of a catastrophic situation for the company ... paying a high dividend should therefore make possible the differentiation between profitable businesses from non-profitable ones, thereby indicating the health of firms. For Du Bois (2007), managers level up the dividends and avoid decreasing it as much as possible despite a decrease in profit. This corroborates with what was mentioned by the CEO of a service company in our exploratory study. For him, a temporary drop in income does not necessarily imply a decline in liquidity for shareholders. In the present work, we believe that profitability constitutes an approximation of internal resources which should be positively correlated to the payment of dividends. Our hypothesis is therefore as follows:

H4: *Profitability is positively correlated to dividend distribution.*

EMPIRICAL STUDY

In this second part, we will first present our sample, definitions and measures of variables and the descriptive analysis. Next we will present the empirical results and their interpretation.

Sample

To carry out this research, we chose the hypothetico-deductive method. Also, we have linked qualitative analysis to quantitative analysis and shown how the combination of these methods enriches the analysis of dividend policy. The use of combined techniques makes it possible to produce more relevant and rich data. The qualitative study carried out with dividend distribution decision-makers in companies makes it possible to clarify the behaviour of Cameroonian firms and local peculiarities in the use of profits and to refine our hypotheses. It describes the process of distribution decisions, as well as the explanatory factors of these decisions. The quantitative study is then implemented to test the hypotheses of our theoretical model. The study population is made up of Limited Liability Companies and Limited Companies only.

In the absence of an exhaustive list of the population concerned, the compilation of data from various sources (Cameroon Zoom and various advertisements) has led to the creation of a directory of 245 companies. This sampling frame is due to the restriction of the administration of our questionnaire to the towns of Douala and Yaoundé (These two regions accounts for 97% of the industrial, commercial and service companies of our sampling frame). Furthermore, among the 245 companies constituting our sampling frame, we were able to establish contact only with 75 of them. We had 67 usable responses comprising of 18 industrial companies, 26 service companies and 23 trade companies.

Variables

Explained variable: The dividend distribution

The distribution policy is traditionally measured by two variables:

- *The distribution rate* is the ratio of the dividend distribution to the income of the company (Noronha et al., 1996). This rate reflects the arbitration made by managers between distribution and retention despite the fact that its interpretation is difficult for companies that distribute irrespective of a low profit or a loss (Du Bois, 2007). This rate can be used in the Cameroonian context where the financial market is still taking off.

- *The dividend's rate of return*, which is the ratio of dividend per share to the share price or the ratio of the amount distributed to the firm's market capitalization (Fenn and Liang, 2001; Hu and Kumar, 2004). This rate of return reflects the views of shareholders and their return on investment. However, its assessment can vary greatly depending on the chosen share price (average, end of year ...). The difficulty in interpreting the dividend's rate of return in our context where the financial market is almost non-existent is an important limitation to these measures in our work. Given that it is not easy to have access to data on the amount distributed in Cameroonian companies, we therefore choose to measure the distribution policy by the frequency of the dividend distribution. We consider that measuring dividend distribution by the payment frequency (arbitration between distribution and retention) is most suitable in the Cameroonian context where most companies are not listed on the stock exchange. The exploratory survey to confirm the effectiveness of some practices concerning dividend distribution in Cameroonian companies led to the identification of this attribute. Thus the distribution frequency differs according to companies. It will be shown in one company for example that, dividend payment can be yearly (always). In some companies, the objective will be to show that the payment of dividends is in a time frame which goes beyond a year (often) and as years go by, payment becomes scarce. In other companies still, dividend payment is not done (never). As a measurement, we retain the frequency of dividend distribution.

Specificities of dividend distribution

As we said in the first part, to satisfy investors, companies are forced to manage their profits. Therefore, several options are available to them. Companies can either retain all or a portion of the profit or distribute a portion of that profit as a dividend. This distribution can be yearly (always), after some years (at times), or never at all. Table 1 highlights the different possibilities of dividend distribution in the companies of our sample.

In our entire sample, 28 (41.8%) companies always distribute the dividend. We also find out that companies which distribute dividends at times are not too far from those who pay the dividend each year (25 companies or 37.3%). In contrast, 14 companies (or 20.9%) never pay out dividends.

Moreover, it appears that 22.4% companies of our sample have neutral opinions about the exceptional distribution of dividend. However, we find that the proportion of companies which always grant exceptional dividend payments (26.9% of companies) is far from companies which never distribute (50.7%). (Recall that in this latter category of companies, there are indeed the 14 companies which never distribute dividend). It is clear that the firms in our sample consider the decision to pay the dividend as an important one. By contrast, the decision to make other payments (special payments) has not yet become a habit for Cameroonian companies[5].

With this significant proportion of companies that distribute dividends at times or all the time, we had as purpose to examine the various forms of distribution that are available to the firm in the process of transferring the company's resources to shareholders. Thus, each shareholder has the choice between receiving the dividend in cash, in kind or in shares. In reading Table 4[6], we note that companies that distribute dividend have a preference for a cash distribution of dividend (71.6% of companies).

Explanatory variable

(i) Capital concentration: The number of shareholders of the firm: this measure is commonly used in North American research papers by authors such as Rozeff (1982), Noronha et al. (1996)) to assess the dispersion of shareholding. In Cameroon, there is no precise measure of this variable. However, in the context of our research, we will not use this variable.

(ii) The Herfindahl index: it is a concentration index often used in economics. It is used to calculate shareholding or control concentration. Some authors use the shareholding percentage or control percentage of the top three shareholders. For Montandrau (2004) for example, this measure enables the estimation of the shareholding concentration. One can use either the percentage of shares or the control of voting rights. In our qualitative study, we found that it was very easy for the manager to estimate at least the percentage of shares of the top three shareholders. That is why we choose to retain this measure. There are several levels which make it possible to consider that a shareholder is dominant. We have chosen the threshold of 33.33% recommended by Calvi-Reveyron (1998) which corresponds to the required blocking minority in a general assembly.

(iii) Measurement of investment opportunities: The intensity of research and development of a firm can enable the evaluation of its investment opportunities if we retain the assumption that research creates growth opportunities. This measure is used by Poulain-Rehm (2005). Some authors such as Denis and Denis (1994), Grullon and Michaely (2004) appreciate the level of investment opportunities of a firm through expenditures in capital, in equipment and in future research and development. Thus, the investment opportunities of year N can be assessed by the investment made in year N +1. It is in this sense that we measure investment opportunities through the expenditures on research and development, on equipments and on employee training. All these expenses will be evaluated with respect to the result of the company.

(iv) Measurement of debt: For Du Bois (2007), short-term debt allows for a better monitoring of managers. However, its amount is subject to variation and non-listed companies tend to borrow from banks. On the other hand, long-term debt can be both a loan from the banks and from other financial institutions. We therefore consider both the amounts of current liabilities and of long-term debt. These measures are standard in the literature and have been used by Crutchley et al. (1999), Jagannathan et al. (2000), and Gugler and Yurtoglu (2003). We intend to measure the total debt (current liabilities and long term debt) relative to the total of assets.

(v) Measure of profitability: We tested four possible measures of the profitability of the company that is the return on equity calculated as the ratio of net income on equity, the economic return which is equal to the ratio of the gross operating surplus added to the assets, to the profitability of the investment which is also equal to the ratio of the net income to the total of assets and finally the return on sales added to the gross operating surplus to the turnover[7].

We added to these measures the size and area of activity.

(vi) The business: During our survey, we distinguished between the industrial sector, the businesses sector and the service sector.

(vii) Measurement of the size of the enterprise: Regarding the size,

---

[5] See table 3 in the annex

[6] In the annex

[7] We used a set of variables to measure profitability. We carried out a score analysis on all items pertaining to profitability. This analysis is a preparatory step to hypothesis test.

Table 1. Distribution of businesses with respect to the frequency of dividend distribution.

Frequency of distribution	Quantity	Percentage	Cumulative percentage
Never	14	20.9	20.9
At times	25	37.3	58.2
Always	28	41.8	100.0
Total	67	100	

Source: Our survey.

Table 2. Summary of definitions and variables in the model.

Variable	Definition	Measure
DED	Dividend distribution	Frequency distribution of dividend
CONACT	Shareholding concentration	Percentage of shares held by the top three shareholders
OPPIVEST	Investment opportunity	Spending on research and development expenditures in equipment and on employee training according to the result
DET	Total debt	Total debt (current liabilities and long term debt) / total assets
PROF	Profitability	Return on Equity (PROF1), economic profitability (PROF2), return of investment (PROF3), return on sales (PROF4)

we classified companies according to the classification by the Economic and Social Council of Cameroon[8].

We conducted a descriptive analysis of these variables (Table 2). Thus, the descriptive analysis of the shareholding concentration variable shows that among the 67 companies of our sample, the top three shareholders have a total percentage of shares greater than 33.33% in 36 of them. This result indicates that the ownership of companies is slightly concentrated in the hands of the top three shareholders (53.7% enterprises) (Table 3). We find that the companies in our sample are lowly indebted. Indeed, 10 companies mentioned their high debt level (14.9%). We therefore understand that banks in Cameroon (despite their excess liquidity) do not fully trust companies yet. These results are consistent with those of Wanda (2007) (Table 4). The observation of data related to investment inspires a remark: the companies of our sample invest much in the purchase of equipment (41 companies, or 61.2%). On the other hand, expenditures on research and development and employee training remain very low. The percentages are 29.9 and 25.4% respectively (Table 5). In companies of our sample the different progressions of the results are all satisfactory. There are increases of 59.7 to 64.2% (Table 6).

RESULTS

Model specification

The second objective of our work is to check whether there is a significant relationship between the dividend payout in Cameroonian companies and the different variables that have been identified. These variables are shareholding concentration (H1), level of investment (H2), total debt (H3) and profitability (H4). To test our hypotheses, we have used a single-factor variance analysis, the comparison test for the mean, correlation and regression analysis. We used a statistical test incorporating two or three nominal variables and scale variables in its determination: a one-factor variance analysis and the comparison test for the mean. With these variables meeting the requirement, we will test the null hypothesis of no relationship and therefore independence. The study of correlations appears as an initial test of supposed relatedness. The relations thus identified calls for a complementary analysis; regression therefore appears to be a necessary complement to the analysis in order to determine the importance and significance of the contribution of phenomena assumed to act on the dividend distribution. In this work, it is difficult to include all the independent variables to present and to interpret the multivariate regression equation. As we mentioned above, the variable "concentration of the shareholding" was measured with nominal values. However, it is not possible to mix the nominal variables and the interval-scale variables to present a multivariate regression. This is why we limited ourselves to making an analysis of a simple regression for the hypothesis H2, H3

[8]Small companies: 10 to 49 employees; medium-sized companies: 50 to 150 employees, large firms: 151 and over.

and H4 and the single-factor analysis of the variance followed by the Mean comparison test for H1.

For the first hypothesis H1, Levene's test indicates that the variances are unequal to shareholding concentration in terms of the dividend distribution (F = 6.008 to p = 0.017). In the case of an assumption of unequal variances, the absolute value obtained from the Student's table is 5.016 at 66 degrees of freedom and significant at p = 0.000 (Table 7). This result reflects the presence of a related effect of shareholding concentration on dividend distribution. This result reinforces the report according to which companies where the percentage of shares held by the top three shareholders is greater than 33.33% do not distribute dividends. We can therefore say that the decision to distribute dividend varies negatively with the concentration of shareholding in the company.

To test hypothesis 2, 3, 4 (H2, H3, H4), we used the linear regression analysis. Hypothesis 2 (H2) shows that the Pearson's correlation coefficient -0.546 is significant at 0.000. The regression analysis contained in Table 8 and 9 reveals that the coefficient of determination or R-square indicates a value of 0.298. This value is strictly lower, being under 0.5[9]. This result means that 29.8% variation in the dividend distribution variable of the company is explained in the variation of the investment level. The result of this regression confirms the negative nature of this association. The regression model thus tested is robust since the F statistic gives a value of 27.590, significant at 0.000 for 1 and 65 degrees of freedom. The regression model between dividend policy and the level of investment is represented by the following equation:

The dividend payout = 3.544 – 0.546 investment level + ε[10]

Concerning hypothesis 3 (H3), Pearson's correlation coefficient of -0, 516 is significant at 0.000. A regression analysis shows a value that is strictly lower since it is below 0.5 (Table 10 and 11). This result means that 26.6% variation in the dividend policy variable of the company is explained in the variation of total debt. The regression is of good quality with an F = 23.604 and significant at p = 0, 000 for 1 and 65 degrees of freedom. The explanatory power of this model is confirmed by the results of the variance analysis.

The regression model between dividend policy and the total debt is represented by the following equation:

The dividend payout = 3.150 – 0.516 total debt + ε

Finally, for the hypothesis 4 (H4), we made a transformation of the variables PROF1, PROF 2, PROF3, PROF4 into the variable (PROF). This new variable enabled us to examine the existence of a relationship (correlation analysis) and then to carry out the linear regression test in order to prove or disprove the formulated hypothesis. With a coefficient of 0.744 significant at 0.000, we find a significant correlation between profitability and dividend policy. The coefficient of determination or R - square (R^2) of the linear regression model gives a value of 0.744 which is very satisfactory since it is greater than 0.5. It is confirmed by the robustness test of the model since the F value is equal to 80.419 and is significant at 0.000 for 1 and 65 degrees of freedom (Table 12 and 13).

The regression model between dividend distribution of the company and profitability appears as follows:

The dividend distribution = - 0.532 + 0.744profitability + ε

Interpretation of results

A descriptive analysis of companies according to dividend distribution reveals differences. We observe that dividend distribution is unanimously recognized as a priority decision for companies. With the exception of 14 companies (representing 20.9%) which never distribute dividend, the majority of companies in our sample always or sometimes distribute dividend despite an embryonic financial market. On the other hand, the exceptional payments of dividends have not yet entered into the customs of Cameroonian companies as we have said earlier. We notice that companies prefer to give cash directly to shareholders (distribution of dividend in cash). But the main objective of this study was to highlight the determinants of dividend distribution. Several influences were identified and we tested their explanatory power.

Indeed, the existence of a concentrated ownership structure reduces conflicts of interest between different stakeholders and thus reduces the agency's inherent to such conflicts. Thus, our statistical test shows a t-statistic of 5.016 at 66 degrees of freedom and significant at p = 0.000. This value reflected the presence of a related effect of shareholding concentration on dividend policy. In addition it reinforces the finding that the decision to distribute dividend varies negatively depending on the concentration of shareholding in the company. This is therefore not in contradiction with the formulation of the hypothesis. This result is consistent with that found by Maury and Pajuste (2002) who studied the relationship between the controlling shareholder and dividend policy of companies. In a sample of 131 firms observed over the period 1995 to 1999, the analysis of ownership structures shows that the dominant shareholder holds a voting power of 33.2%. He therefore has a negative impact on the level of dividends as measured by the proportion of distributed profits.

Our study on Cameroonian companies confirms; the

[9] Indeed, the coefficient of determination is between 0 and 1. It must every close to 1. But it is estimated in most cases that a value greater than 0.5 is satisfactory. E represents the error

[10] ε represents the error margin

negative influence of debt on distribution, as highlighted by the majority of research papers. Indeed, our results are similar to those revealed by Calvi-Reveyron (1998) in a study to understand the effect of debt on corporate dividend payment. The test result of linear regression (-0.546 is significant at p = 0.01) establishes that the level of investment has a negative influence on the dividend distribution. This negative sign of correlation is not inconsistent with the formulation of the hypothesis. These results are similar to those revealed by Guizani and Kouki (2009) in a study to understand the effect of the level of investment on dividend policy. The results of these authors show a negative regression coefficient of -0.6 on the threshold of statistical significance of p = 0.01 between the level of investment and dividend distribution. For them, the more the company has investment opportunities, the more it reduces the level of dividend in order to avoid resorting to external financing and transaction costs associated to it. To this effect, the carefulness of company leaders leads them to prefer self-financing.

The final result of our study concerns the influence of profitability on dividend distribution. The determination coefficient of the linear regression model gives a value of 0.744 which is greater than 0.5[11], thus very satisfactory. It is confirmed by testing the robustness of the model since the F value is 80.419, significant at 0.000 for 1 and 65 degrees of freedom. Our analysis confirms the results of Du Tertre and Guy (2008) and Bhattacharya (1979). They show that the greater the companies' resources, the more these companies resort to dividend distribution. Overall, these variables indeed explain dividend distribution in Cameroonian companies.

Conclusion

Every year and throughout the world, most companies in general and Cameroonian companies in particular, listed or unlisted distribute or do not distribute liquid assets to their shareholders. The observation of the frequency of distribution of the dividends in Cameroonian firms (67companies) translated by the introduction of certain factors, justified the realization of this study. Through our first research question, we wanted to highlight the specificities of the payment or nonpayment of dividends in Cameroonian companies. The descriptive analysis was carried out in order to show the specificities of distribution in Cameroonian companies. Thus, the results related to the frequency of distribution indicate that certain companies always distribute (each year) or often distribute (after a certain numbers of years) the dividend. Others on the other hand never pay liquid assets to the investors (that is, 41.8% companies always distribute the dividend, 37.3% of companies often distribute and 20.9% of companies never distribute the dividend). The form most used by managers is the payment of the dividend in cash (71.6%). Some companies nevertheless try to make payments in kind (7.5%) or in shares (20.9%). These elements make it possible to partly explain the specificity of dividend distribution in Cameroonian companies.

By using a sample of 67 unlisted companies, this study analyzed a range of determiners of the dividend policy: concentration of the shareholding, the opportunities of investment, total debt and profitability of Cameroonian companies. The study indicates that the concentration of the shareholding, the level of investment and the total debt vary negatively according to the dividend distribution policy. It clearly shows that profitability is a factor which is positively related to the dividend policy of the firms. The results of this study are similar to others carried out in developed countries where most of the companies are listed on the stock exchange markets. It will thus be important for Cameroonian managers to be attentive to their shareholders. This implies satisfying their desires regarding the distribution of profits in order to reduce conflicts of interest between majority, minority shareholders and the managers. The tip as regards the distribution of the dividend is to stabilize the amount intended for the shareholders. It is important to distribute regularly in spite of the fact that the amount to be distributed is low. Such a combination (regular distribution with a low amount) undoubtedly leads to a reduction in conflicts of interest and the development of shareholders' loyalty to the company.

This work presents some limits. We did not take into account all the variables such as the identity of the shareholder, the tax system, the cash-flow, the financial market and the economic situation. It would be interesting in future studies to take into account these variables.

[11]Indeed, the coefficient of determination is between 0 and 1. It must every close to 1. But it is estimated in most cases that a value greater than 0.5 is satisfactory.

REFERENCES

Adesola WA, Okwong AE (2009). An Empirical Study of dividend Policy of Quoted Companies in Nigeria. Glob. J. Soc. Sci. 8(1):85-101.

Batsch L (1999). Finance et stratégie. Paris, Economica 342.

Bhattacharya S (1979). Imperfect information, dividend policy, and the 'Bird un the hand' Fallacy. Bell J. Econ. 10(1):259-270.

Calvi-Reveyron M (1998). Politique de dividende et théorie du free cash flow : une revue de la littérature. Cahier de recherche du CERAG: 98-09.

Crutchley C, Jensen R, Jahera JS, Raymond J (1999). Agency Problems and the Simultaneity of Financial Decision Making-the Role of Institutional Ownership. International Review of Financial Analysis, 8:177-97.

Denis DJ, Denis DK (1994). The Information Content of Dividend Changes, Cash Flow Signaling, Overinvestment, and Dividend Clienteles. Journal of Financial and Quantitative Analysis 29(4):567-587.

Du Bois C (2007). Rôle des conflits d'agence, de la structure d'actionnariat et des mécanismes de gouvernance sur les politiques de distribution : application aux décisions de dividende et de rachat d'actions des sociétés françaises cotées. Thèse de Doctorat ès Sciences de Gestion, Université Paul Cézane, Aix- Marseille III-I.A.E, sous la direction de P. BATTEAU.

Fenn G, Liang N (2001). Corporate Payout Policies and Managerial

Stock Incentives. J. Financ. Econ. 60:45-72.
Goffin R (2001). Principe de la finance moderne. 3é éd Economica.
Grullon G, Michaely R (2004). The Information Content of Share Repurchase Program. J. Financ. 59:651-680.
Gugler K, Yurtoglu B (2003). Corporate Governance and Dividend Payout Policy in Germany. Eur. Econ. Rev. PP. 731-758.
Hu A, Kumar P (2004). Managerial Entrenchment and Payout Policies. J. Financ. Quant. Anal. 39:759-790.
Jagannathan M, Stephens C P, Weisbach MS (2000). Financial Flexibility and the Choice between Dividends and Share Repurchases. J. Fin. Econ. 57:355-384.
Jensen MC (1986). Agency costs of free cash flow, corporate finance, and takeovers. In the Market for corporate control 76 (2).
Jensen MC, Meckling WH (1976). Theory of the firm: Managerial Behaviour, Agency Costs and Ownership Structure. J. Financ. Econ. 3:305-360.
Kinfe T (2011). Determinants of Dividend payout: An Empirical Study on Bank Industry in Ethiopia. Annu. Rep. p.96.
Kouki M, Guizani M (2009). Ownership structure and dividendpolicyevidencefrom the Tunisian stock market. Euro. J. Sci. Res. 25(1):42-53.
La Porta R, Lopez-de-Silanes F, Shleifer A, Vishny R (2000). Agency problems and dividend policies around the World. J. Financ. 55:1-33.
Mat Nor F, Sulong Z (2007). The interaction effect of ownership structure and board governance on dividends: Evidence from Malaysian listed firms. Capital Market Rev. 15:73-101.
Mancinelli, L, Ozkan A (2006). Ownership structure and dividend policy: Evidence from Italian firms. Euro. J. Financ. 12:265-282.
Maury B Pajuste A (2002). Controlling Shareholders, Agency Problems and Dividend Policy in Finland. Finish J. Bus. Econ. 51.
Miller M, Rock K (1985). Dividend Policy and Asymmetric Information. J. Financ. 40:1031-1051.
Modigliani F, Miller M (1961). Dividend policy, growth, and the valuation of shares. J. Bus. 59.
Moh'd MA, Perry LG, Rimbey JN (1995). Investigation of the Dynamic Relationship between Agency Theory and Dividend Policy. Financ. Rev. 30:367-385.
Montandrau S (2004). Activisme des Investisseurs Institutionnels, Gouvernement D'entreprise et Richesse de L'actionnaire: le Cas des Alertes de L'afg-Assfi sur les Sociétés Françaises Cotées. Thèse de Doctorat, Université d'Aix Marseille III - IAE Aix en Provence, sous la direction de P. Batteau.
Moussu C, Thibierge C (1996). «Politique financière, opportunités d'investissement, et actifs incorporels en Europe: théorie et étude empirique» Cahier de recherche ESCP N°96-129.
Musa FI (2005). Modeling the Dividend Behavioural Pattern of Corporate Firms in Nigeria. Unpublished Doctoral Dissertation Ahmadu Bello University Zaria: 85-152
Musa IF (2009). The dividend policy of firms quoted on the Nigerian stock exchange: an empirical analysis. Afr. J. Bus. Manage. 3(10):555-566.
Myers S (1977). Determinants of Corporate Borrowing. J. Financ. Econ. 5:147-175.
Nivoix S (2004). Endettement et distribution du dividende dans les entreprises japonaises. publication de recherche en ligne, www.iae.univ-poitiers.fr pp.1-13.
Noronha GM, Shome DK, Morgan GE (1996). The Monitoring Rationale for Dividends and the Interaction of Capital Structure and Dividend Decisions. J. Bank. Financ. 20:439-455.
Peyrard J (1999). Dictionnaire de Finance. éd vuibert p.249.
Poulain-Rehm T (2005). L'impact de L'affectation du Free Cash Flow sur la Création de Valeur Actionnariale : le Cas de la Politique D'endettement et de Dividendes des Entreprises Françaises Cotées. Finance Contrôle Stratégie p.8.
Renneboog L, Trojanowski G (2007). Control Structure and Payout Policy. Manag. Financ. 33(1):43-46.
Severin E, Dhennin S (2003). structure du capital et mesures de restructuration. Finance Contrôle et Stratégie 6(1):155-186.
Walter JE (1956). Dividend policies and common stock prices. J. Financ. 11:29-41.
Wissem M, Christhophe B (2009). Structure de propriété et de contrôle, problèmes d'agence et politique de dividende : Une étude sur les sociétés françaises cotées. 4ème Colloque International Finance et Stratégies de Développement.
Wanda R (2001). Structure financière et performance des entreprises dans un contexte sans marché financier : le cas du Cameroun. http://www.cybel.fr/html/Communaute/rdf/images/wanda.pdf.
Wanda R (2007). Risques, comportements bancaires et déterminants de la surliquidité. Cahiers électroniques du CRECCI 24.

ANNEXES

Table 1. Distribution of companies by the emphasis on exceptional dividend payments.

Extraordinary dividend payments	Quantity	Percentage	Cumulative percentage
Never	34	50.7	50.7
Neutral	15	22.4	73.1
Always	18	26.9	100.0
Total	67	100.0	

Source: Our survey.

Table 2. Distribution of companies according to different forms of dividend distribution.

Different forms of dividend	Quantity	Percentage	Cumulative percentage
Kind	5	7.5	7.5
Cash	48	71.6	79.1
Shares	14	20.9	100.0
Total	67	100.0	

Source: Our survey.

Table 3. Distribution of companies according to the percentage of shares held by the three largest shareholders.

Percentage of shares held by top 3 shareholders	Quantity	Percentage	Cumulative percentage
Less than 33.33%	31	46.3	46.3
More than 33.33%	36	53.7	100.0
Total	67	100.0	

Source: Our survey.

Table 4. Distribution of firms by the level of total debt/total assets.

Total debt	Quantity	Percentage	Cumulative percentage
Low	30	44.8	44.8
Average	27	40.3	85.1
High	10	14.9	100.0
Total	67	100.0	

Source: Our survey.

Table 5. Distribution of companies according to the investment opportunities/results.

	Expenditures on research and development		Expenditures on the acquisition of equipments		Expenditures on staff training	
	Quantity	Percentage	Quantity	Percentage	Quantity	Percentage
Low	26	38.8	13	19.4	35	52.2
Average	21	31.3	13	19.4	15	22.4
High	20	29.9	41	61.2	17	25.4
Total	67	100.0	67	100.0	67	100.0

Source: Our survey.

Table 6. Description of Progress indicators related to profitability.

	PROF1		PROF2		PROF3		PROF4	
	Quantity	Percentage	Quantity	Percentage	Quantity	Percentage	Quantity	Percentage
Insufficient	11	16.4	15	22.	15	22.4	16	23.9
Neutral	16	23.9	11	16.4	9	13.4	8	11.9
Satisfactory	40	59.7	43	61.2	41	64.2	43	64.2
Total	67	100.0	67	100.0	67	100.0	67	100.0

Source: Our survey.

Table 7. Mean comparison test between the dividend and the ownership concentration.

		Levene test of equal variances		T-test for equality of means						
		F	Sig.	t	DDL	Sig. (bilateral)	Mean difference	Standard deviation difference	95% confidence interval of the difference	
									Lower	Top
Distribution of dividend	Assumption of equal variances	6.008	0.017	-5.016	65	0.000	-0.809	0.161	-1.131	-0.487
	Assumption of unequal variances			-5.175	60.547	0.000	-0.809	0.156	-1.122	-0.496

Source: Our survey.

Table 8. Model summary of regression between the level of investment and dividend.

Model	R	R-two	Adjusted R-squared	Standard error of the estimate
1	0. 546[a]	0. 298	0. 287	0. 650

Source: Our Survey. [a]correlation coefficient significant at 0.01.

Table 9. ANOVA of the regression model between the level of investment and dividend.

Model		Sum of squares	DDL	Mean square	F	Meaning
1	Regression	11.643	1	11.643	27.590	0.000
	Residue	27.431	65	0.422		

Source: Our survey.

Table 10. The linear regression between total debt and dividend.

Model	R	R-two	Adjusted R-squared	Standard error of the estimate
1	0. 516[a]	0.266	0. 255	0. 664

Source: Our Survey. [a]correlation coefficient significant at 0.01.

Table 11. ANOVA of the regression between total debt and the dividend of the company.

Model		Sum of squares	DDL	Mean square	F	Meaning
1	Regression	10.409	1	10.409	23.604	0.000
	Residue	28.665	65	0.441		

Source: Our survey.

Table 12. Summary of regression model between profitability and dividend distribution.

Model	R	R-two	Adjusted R-squared	Standard error of the estimate
1	0. 744[a]	0. 553	0. 546	0. 518

Source: Our survey. [a]correlation coefficient significant at 0.01.

Table 13. ANOVA of the regression model between profitability and dividend distribution.

Model		Sum of squares	DDL	Mean square	F	Meaning
1	Regression	21.609	1	21.609	80.419	0.000
	Residue	17.466	65	0. 269		

Source: Our survey.

Impact of financial leverage on firm investment

Khursheed Ahmad[1], Syed Zulfiqar Ali shah[2], Hazrat Bilal[1] and Habib Ahmad[2]

[1]Department of Management Sciences, University of Swat, Pakistan.
[2]Faculty of Management Sciences, International Islamic University, Islamabad, Pakistan.

The purpose of this study was to analyze the relationship between financial leverage and firm's investment in the presence of certain control variables such as (Tobin's Q, cash flow, liquidity, return on equity and sale. Relationship was analyzed by applying different methodologies such as pooled regression, fixed effect model and random effect model. Housman test was performed for selection between fixed and random effect model. Data was taken from balance sheet analysis of joint stock companies, annual reports of the companies, B recorder and Karachi Stock Exchange. Data was collected for nine years from 2000-2008, but analyses were performed for eight years because 2000 was taken as a lag. This study found that financial leverage has significant negative impact on firms' investment. It shows that as leverage increases firm's investment decreases, we may say that highly levered firms invest less. The result confirms that leverage overcome overinvestment bias and attenuate agency problem. The results of the common effect model supported that capital structure plays a vital role in the decisions of firms on how to invest. But whenever we extended the model to incorporate the time and individual effect, then no relationship were seen. The relationship between liquidity and investment is positive but insignificant. Tobin's Q has also shown positive but slightly insignificant relationship with investment for the target samples.

Key words: Tobin's Q, cash flow, liquidity, return on equity, sale, Karachi stock exchange.

INTRODUCTION

Corporate sector is considered to be the backbone of any economy. Corporations play a vital role in contributing to the economic growth. In today's dynamic environment, firms generally face intense competition and should therefore need to act in response. To respond to global competition, firms need to make huge investment in modern technology, infrastructure, land, building, machinery, quality management, innovation and product development etc. Such factors will help organization to promote efficiency and effectiveness and gain competitive advantage. A firm needs cash or money to invest in land, building, machinery and to take care of day to day operations. The money which firm's or businesses invest in purchasing land, machinery or other fixed assets is called capital investment. In other words, investment can define as spending on capital goods by firms which ultimately amplified production of consumer goods.

According to Reilly and Brown (2003), investment is the current commitment of funds for a period of time in order to derive future payments that will compensate the investor for, the time the funds are committed, the expected rate of inflation and the uncertainty of the future payments. But a very important question rises here that how such fund will be generated. The two main sources of fund generation, pointed out in Literature includes, equity financing and debt financing.

Equity financing means rising funds for company activities or operations by issuing stocks to individual and institutional investors. These stocks can be common or preferred. These individual and institutional investors become creditors and receive ownership interest in exchange for their funds. On the other hand, when a company raises fund through the issuance of bonds or borrowing from banks or other financial institution, it is called debt financing. In return, these individuals and institutions receive promise that they will receive interest periodically and principal amount at maturity. When a company uses mix of these sources, it is called capital structure. The purpose of this study is to investigate, whether the financing which a company or firm generate through debt has effect on investment or not.

There is vast literature regarding the inclusion of leverage in capital structure of a firm. According to Odit and Chittoo (2008) in 1930 and 1940s, the inclusion of debt in capital structure were considered as evil. And it was considered as taboo and the basic source of bankruptcy and financial distress. But the concepts were changed by Modigliani and Miller (1958). They claimed that the value of a firm is independent of its capital structure in a frictionless or complete world, where there is no transaction cost, no default risk, asymmetric information and no taxes. But, whenever any assumption is relaxed, the irrelevance value of firm and its capital structure does not hold any more. If the irrelevance theory is correct then the market value of firm can increases, as it takes more and more debt. It suggests that high levered firm will provide tax shield advantage, which in turn increases the value of firm. However, it is not common practice to observe firms that use only debt for financial considerations. The question arises here are, what are the reasons that prevent firms from debt financing? Literature suggests bankruptcy cost and agency cost to be the primary sources that leads to optimal capital structure. Therefore, agency cost is considered as important issue in corporate sectors. The separation of ownership and control in corporate sector is a source of agency problem. It may be in the form of inefficient effort from manager, investing on their own preferences, or failing in maximizing shareholder wealth or value of the firm.

Bankruptcy costs also discourage borrowing or limits leverage in capital structure. Bankruptcy cost represents the cost associated with liquidation and reorganization. Myers and Robicheck (1966) argued that the cost of financial distress is incurred when the firm comes under the threat of bankruptcy, even if it can be avoided.

Theory suggest that the choice of capital structure may help to reduce these agency cost. Harris and Raviv (1991) argued that greater leverage may affect managers and may reduce agency cost through the threat of liquidation, which causes personal losses to manager in the form of low salaries reputation etc. On the other hand, Berger and di Patti (2006) comments that when leverage increases the expected cost of financial distress, bankruptcy, the agency cost of outside debt may magnify the agency cost of outside equity, so further increase in leverage result in higher total agency cost. Therefore, they argued that high leverage may cause agency problem between bondholder and equity holder. The study of Cantor (1990) highlights the relationship between leverage and investment. According to him, a firm with a huge amount of average cash flow can accumulate a large amount as a reserve which can be drawn upon to make an investment, when a firm faces shortage of cash flow in a particular year. On the other hand, a highly levered firm with a small amount of average cash flow does not maintain reserve and may need to cut investment back in the year when firm faces shortage of fund. It means that investment is more sensitive to cash earning in highly levered firm. Therefore, the leveraged firm shows greater variability in its investment over time.

Significance of the study

A significant but controversial issue in corporate finance, is the impact of leverage on a firm's investment decisions. Modigliani and Miller (1958) demonstrated that leverage is unrelated to a firm's investment choices and to firm value. However, in a world where there are incomplete markets and significant agency costs, leverage may have a wide-ranging and complex impact on investment. For example, managers of highly levered firms may, in some circumstances, be induced to pass by positive net present value (NPV) projects (Myers, 1977) because some or all of the benefits from the investment may accrue to debt-holders; this is known as the debt overhang problem and leads to underinvestment. Alternatively, Jensen (1986) argues that high leverage or (high portion of debt in capital structure) in low growth firms are used to discourage management from investing in non-profitable businesses or projects. Here, debt pre-commits firms to pay cash as interest and principal and such commitments in low growth firms can reduce managerial discretion over free cash flows that may have otherwise been allocated to negative NPV projects. In other words, the banks and other debt-holders perform a beneficial monitoring and disciplinary role in low growth firms where a high level of debt can limit the over-investment bias caused by managerial agency problems. In recent years, empirical studies have been undertaken to examine the relevance of the leverage and capital investment theories. Lang et al. (1996), Aivazian et al. (2005a) and Ahn et al. (2006) reported a negative relation between investment and leverage, although the correlation is much stronger for firms with low growth. This evidence is consistent with the over investment story (Stulz, 1990), where leverage inhibits managers of low growth firms from investing in non-profitable capital expenditures. These studies use data from the U.S. and Canada where long-term debt finance is provided by profit maximizing banks and public bond markets. Here, the debt-holders keep an eye on and discipline the firms they lend to. Nonetheless, the result from these studies is not necessarily generalize to transitional economies where the relations between lenders and borrowers are more complex and subtle. Transitional economies are characterized as having nascent stock markets, an absence of public debt markets (or, at most, embryonic public debt markets) and a reliance on bank borrowing. Furthermore, most banks are state owned and their decision making often reflects the policies dictated by government. Khwaja and Atif (2005) and La Porta et al. (2002) argued that state-owned banks are controlled by politicians who use the banks to maximize their own political and personal objectives, such as providing jobs for political supporters and bailing out poorly performing firms. In these cases, the banks' incentives to put forth disciplinary pressures on firms are compromised. This could be particularly true for the poorly performing and loss-making firms because the state-owned banks often have the obligation to support (Dobson and Kashyap, 2006). An investigation into the link between leverage and investment in an environment where banks are state owned can therefore, provide a useful addition to the literature. Privately owned banks in developed countries generally use commercial criteria in making lending decisions, although, in some occasions political considerations may impose on the decision process. In transitional or emerging economies, where banks are owned by the state, political considerations are likely to weigh very heavily on lending policies.

So, the purpose of this study is to scrutinize empirically the relationship between financial leverage and firm investment of non financial Pakistani firm's. Literature revealed that many studies relating to capital structure and investment has been conducted in developed countries like America, Japan, United Kingdom and Canada. But the body of literature on leverage and investment is still very small on Asian firms. This study aims to apply those models in Pakistani setting and to add to the applicability of those models in developing countries.

Objective of the study

The objective of the study is to find the relationship between financial policy (measured as financial leverage) and firm investment for Pakistan non financial sector.

Contribution of the study

According to the limited knowledge of the author, this is the first comprehensive investigation of the relationship between financial leverage and investment in Pakistan. So, it will make some contribution to the literature from the developing economy.

LITERATURE REVIEW

The relation between leverage and investment opportunities has been a topic of interest among finance scholars for many years. According to Odit and Chittoo (2008) in 1930 and 1940s the inclusion of debt in capital structure were considered as evil. And it was considered as the basic source of bankruptcy and financial distress. Modigliani and Miller (1958) proposed a theory regarding capital structure, they claimed that the value of a firm is independent of its capital structure in a world with no taxes, no default risk, no transaction cost, and perfect and frictionless market. Myers (1977), for example, demonstrates that, with sufficiently high leverage, the firms share holder does not want to issue new stock due to debt overhang. Owning to this, most projects with positive net present value (NPV) can go unfunded.

Stulz (1990) predict a negative relation between leverage and investment. Stulz (1990) demonstrates that investment is negatively related to firm investment and profitability. Therefore, high profit firms should have a lower leverage. In the last two decades, empirical studies have been undertaken to study the relationship between leverage and investment decisions. Lang et al. (1996) reported a negative relationship leverage and firm investment, but its effect is stronger for small firms with low growth. Similarly, Aviazion et al. (2005) found that a higher percentage of long term debt in total debt significantly reduces the firm investment especially in firms with high growth opportunities. In contrast, he found no significant relation in debt maturity and firm investment for firm with low growth opportunities. Likewise, Firth et al. (2008) investigated the relationship between leverage and investment in china. Their result depicts a negative relationship between leverage and investment. The researcher further investigated that, negative relation is weaker in firm with low growth and poor operating companies while it is stronger for firms with high growth opportunities and good operating performance. On the other hand, McConnel and Servaes (1995) found that, for firms with low P/E ratio or low growth opportunities value is positively related to the degree of leverage while for high P/E ratio or high growth opportunities leverage is negatively associated with firm value. Such finding is also supported by Aggarwal and Kyaw (2008), they revealed that leverage is positively and significantly related to firm's growth, for low firm's Q ratios. The researchers further suggested that, leverage is value creating for firms with low growth opportunities while it is value reducing for firms with high growth opportunities.

Norvaisienė et al. (2008) investigated the relationship between loan capital, investment and growth. They demonstrate that firm's debts and agency problem (between managers, shareholder and creditors) causes under investment or overinvestment, which in turn, has a negative impact on corporate investment, growth and firm value. Similarly, the finding of Mehmet and Oruc (2009) also showed a negative relationship between leverage and investment but only for low growth firm's. And it was the finding of one – way error components model.

However, no relationship were found when he extended the model to include time effect in a two way component model. Similarly, Firth et al. (2008) examined the relationship between leverage and investment under a state-owned bank lending environment in china. They concluded their study with three major findings: first, that there is negative relationship between debts and growth. Second, that this, negative relationship is weaker for firms with low growth opportunities and bad operating performance, while stronger for firms with good operating performance and high investment opportunities. Third, that this relationship is weaker for firm's with greater and high level of state shareholding then firm's with low level of state shareholding. They further explained that state-owned bank in china, impose less restrictions on investment expenditure of firm's with low growth opportunities, which create overinvestment problems in these firms. A strong negative relationship between financial leverage and R and D expenditure were also reported by Singh and Faircloth (2005). The negative relationship is strong to changes in model specifications and sample periods. More significantly, the results showed that, it is higher leverage that leads to lower R and D expenditure.

On the other hand, Jo et al. (1994) investigated the relationship between financing decisions and investment opportunities set, and reported a positive relationship between debt ratio and measure of investment opportunities. The study was conducted in Japan, data was taken from Pacific-Basin Capital Markets database for the period of five year, that is, from 1986-1990. The sample size was 1044 Japanese firms. Jo et al. (1994) further argued that such relationship were negative in USA due to agency conflicts, which were mitigated in Japanese firm's because of their institutional arrangements. The study of Anderson and Makhija (1999) found that bond debt is inversely related to growth opportunities while bank debt is positively related to growth opportunities.

Similarly, Ahn et al. (2005) found positive relationship between leverage and firm value but it is weaker for firms with low growth opportunities and stronger for firms with more growth opportunities. Childs et al. (2005) examined the interactions between the financing and investment decisions in model of agency conflicts (between shareholder and bond holder). They found in their study that short term debt is significantly helpful in reducing agency costs on under-investment and over-investment. However, such decline in agency costs could not cause any increase in leverage level, as the firm early debt level choice depends on the type of growth options in its investment opportunity set.

RESEARCH METHODOLOGY

This chapter contains the measurement of variable, the methods and sources of data collection. It also highlights the different methodologies that have been used to determine the relationship between financial leverage and investment.

Sample and data collection

This study highlight the methods and sources of data collection and the sample size used in the study. In this study, the relationship between financial leverage and firm investment is based on secondary data. The data for the study are extracted from the annual reports, Karachi Stock Exchange, B recorder and balance sheet analysis of joint stock companies for the period of nine years (from 2000-2009). Data for the study was collected for nine years but analysis was conducted for eight years, 2000 was taken as lag year. Initially, the sample included all non financial companies (435) which are listed on Karachi Stock Exchange, but after screening, the data firms with incomplete data were dropped from the sample. After screening 343 firms remained for Panel data estimation. Financial firms such as banks, insurance companies, leasing companies, Mudarrabas etc were excluded from sample due to regulations complications and different capital structures. The sample includes 342 firms from 27 different sectors. Sector wised classification are as shown in Appendix 1.

Measurement of variables

For this study, we have taken from literature for measuring investment. The model has been used by Lang et al. (1996) and Aviazian et al. (2005) which is as follows:

$$\frac{I_{it}}{K_{it-1}} = \alpha it + \beta 1\left(\frac{CF_{it}}{K_{it-1}}\right) + \beta 2(Lev_{it-1}) + \beta 3(Tobin's Q_{it-1}) + \beta 4\left(\frac{Sales_{it-1}}{K_{it-1}}\right) + \varepsilon_{i,t} +$$

In the proposed model, the $I_{i\text{-}t}$ is the net investment of the firm i at time t; while $K_{i,t-1}$ is the lagged net fixed assets; $CF_{i,t}$ is the cash flow of firm I at time t.; $Leverage_{i,t\_1}$ is the lagged Tobin's Q; $Lev_{i,t-1}$ is lagged leverage; $Sale_{i,t-1}$ is lagged net sales of firm i; α is a constant effect; ε_{t-1} is the error term.

Description of variables

In the proposed model, investment $_{i,t}$ is the ratio of net capital expenditure (capital expenditure – depreciation) of firm I at time t to total to the lagged net fixed asset; $Lev_{i,t-1}$ is the lagged one time period ratio of total liability to total asset. In the literature, other dimension have also been used for its calculation such as ratio of long term liability to total asset and ratio of short term liability to total asset. We will follow prior literature to control for firm cash flows, cash $flow_{i,t}$ is the ratio of operating cash flow of the firm to the lagged net fixed assets. Other control variable such as Tobin's Q and sale is also included in the model. It is a proxy for growth; its value greater than 1 represent high growth opportunities and less than one represent low growth opportunities.

Tobin's Q is lagged one time period. It is the ratio of market value of total asset of the firm to book value of the firm. The market value of the firm can be calculated as the value of the common stock and the estimated value of the preferred stock. $Sale_{i,t}$ is the ratio of net sale to lagged one time period fixed assets. Sale will be measured as a sale deflated by net fixed assets.

Investment

An important debate in corporate finance is that whether gearing ratio or leverage ratio effect investment policies. The purpose of this study is also to check such relationship. We have measured investment as the ratio of net investment to lagged fixed assets. Net investment was calculated as capital expenditure-depreciation. The same ratio has been used by Lang et al. (1996), Aivazian et al. (2003) and Odit and Chittoo (2008).

$$Investment = \frac{net\ investment}{lagged\ net\ fixed\ assets} \qquad =$$

$$\frac{capital\ expenditure - depriciation}{lagged\ net\ fixed\ assets}$$

Leverage

In this study, financial policy of a firm is measured with leverage. There are deferent measure of leverage such as long term debt to total assets, short term debt to total assets and total liability to total assets. We have used total debt to total assets as a measure of leverage. The same measure has been used by Pamela et al. (1983), Mehmat (2009) and Ahn et al. (2005).

$$Leverage = \frac{Total\ liability}{Total\ assets}$$

Control variables

In this study, the relationship between financial leverage and investment is investigated in the presence of certain control variables, these are Tobin's Q (it is a proxy of growth opportunities of firms). Its value greater than 1 represent high growth opportunities and low then 1 represent low growth opportunities. It is measured as market value of the total assets of the firms divided by the book value of the assets of the firm's. Market value of the assets was calculated as (book value of total debts + market capitalization). Other control variables include cash flow, sale, liquidity and ROE. Cash flow was calculated as; earnings before interest and taxes + depreciation / total fixed assets. Sale was measured as; the ratio of gross sale to fixed assets. Liquidity was measured as the ratio of current assets to current liability. The profitability was measured with ROE and is the ratio of net income to total equity. We have used these control variables to clearly identify the impact of leverage on firm investment, because literature revealed that these variables have a significant impact on firm investment.

Cash flow

According to Whited (1992), investment of a firm is more sensitive to cash flow, but its effect is greater to high levered firms as compared to low levered firms. Fazzari et al. (1988) found that investment is positively related to inter funds. And this impact is stronger for financially constraints firms. Cash flow is the ratio of cash flow before extraordinary income to lagged fixed assets.

$$Cash\ flow = \frac{Operating\ cash\ flow}{Lagged\ net\ fixed\ asset}$$

This ratio has also been used by Odit and Chittoo (2008).

Tobin's Q

Q measures the performance of a firm. And it is the ratio of market capitalization of the, firm + book value of the debt to book value of the assets. From the literature, it is clear that Tobin's Q has a significant impact on investment. Gomes (2001) describe that the investment of a firm is very much sensitive to Tobin's q and cash flow. Researcher further argued that the availability of external financing makes no difference. The idea was also supported by Cooper and Ejarque (2003), they solved a model with quadratic adjustment costs and a concave revenue function and also found that investment is strongly related to Tobin's q and cash flow.

In order to find out the exact relationship between financial leverage and firm investment, we controlled for both Tobin's Q and cash glow.

$$Tobin'sQ = \frac{Market\ value\ of\ total\ asset\ of\ the\ firm}{Book\ value\ of\ the\ firm}$$

Sale

Sale of a company is also taken in to consideration, and is calculated as follows.

$$Sale = \frac{Net\ sale}{lagged\ net\ fixed\ assets.}$$

Return on equity (ROE)

To control for the impact of profitability on firm investment, we have taken Roe as` a proxy for firm profitability. It is the ratio of net income to shareholder equity.

$$ROE = \frac{Net\ Income}{Shareholder\ Equity}$$

The ratio was also used by Odit and Chittoo (2008).

Panel data estimation

This study checked the relationship between financial leverage and firm investment. The relationship was checked by applying panel data. From panel data, we got two dimensions of data such as time series and cross sectional. Panel data have certain advantages such as it offer a wide range of observations which better estimates the parameters. Panel data outsource more information to the analyst and account for the dynamic behavior of parameters. Panel data was estimated by three different methodologies; Pooled regression or common constant model, fixed effect model and random effect model.

Common effect model

Common effect model or pooled regression analyzes the relationship with the assumption that all the intercept will remain constant all over the years and across sectors. Practically the common constant method implies that there are no differences between the estimated cross section and it is useful under the hypothesis that the data set is a priori homogeneous. This assumption is too much restrictive and behind the reality. To take in to consideration the time effect and individual effect we had applied the fixed effect and random effect model.

Fixed effect model

Fixed effect model is similar to polled regression but it allows the constant to vary across individual. It is also called least square dummy variable (LSDV) estimator, because it uses dummy variables for taking different constant in to account (Gujrati, 2006). Different intercept concept is logical because our sample consist of heterogeneous set of non financial firms relating to diverse sectors.

$$y_{i,t} = \alpha + \beta_1 X_{i,t} + e_{i,t}$$

Where

$y_{i,t}$ = dependent variable of firm i at time t.
α = intercept
β_1 = slope of the independent variable.

Table 1. Descriptive statistics.

	Investment	Leverage	Liquidity	Sale	Cash flow	ROE	Tobin's Q
Mean	-0.0420846	0.712605	1.726046	9.303822	0.3858371	0.296877	1.155924
Standard deviation	0.9877884	0.487996	5.839397	54.54453	1.544653	3.217851	1.355087
Minimum	-46.08571	0.018124	0.009915	-47.1111	-44.38889	-41.579	0.078104
Maximum	5.495758	9.117647	265.0227	1236.261	38.05714	137.6667	42.93401

$X_{i,t}$ = independent variable of firm i at time t.
$e_{i,t}$ = error term of firm i at time t.

Dummy variable is the one that allows us to take different group specific estimates for each of the constants for every different section. Despite of its strength, the model also faces certain problems such as: Firstly, it ignores all explanatory variable that do not vary over time. Secondly, it is inefficient because it estimate a very large number of parameter. Therefore, it is not good to use fixed effect model without considering another model such as random effect model.

Random effect model

The random effect model not taking intercept as constant or fixed but as random parameters. Random effect model assume that there is not a constant or fixed intercept for each company but a random drawing from much larger population with a common mean value for the intercept. As this model don't discriminate between the intercept of companies, it allows the error terms to take in to considerations all the differences in the in the individual intercept.

$$y_{i,t} = \beta_1 + \beta_2 X_{i,t} + \varepsilon_i + u_{i,t}$$

where

$y_{i,t}$ = Dependent variable of firm i at time t.
β_1 = Mean value of all intercept.
β_2 = Slope of the independent variables.
$X_{i,t}$ = Independent variable of firm i, at rime t.
ε_i = Deviation of individual intercept from mean.
$u_{i,t}$ = Error term of all the firm i, at time t.

One major disadvantage of random effect model is that it needs to make specific assumption about the distribution of the random components. Also if the unobserved group specific effects are correlated with the explanatory variables then the estimates will be biased and inconsistent. Having this disadvantage this model has certain advantages as well.

Firstly, it has fewer parameters to estimates as compared to fixed effect model. Secondly, it allows us for additional explanatory variables that have equal values for all observations within a group. In general, the difference between the two possible ways of testing panel data model is this; fixed model assumes that each variable differ in its intercept terms while random model assumes that each variable differ in its error term. According to Dimitios Asteriou, when the panel is balanced, the fixed effect model will best work. On the other hand, when the sample contain limited observations of the existing cross sectional unit, the random effects model might be more appropriate. But statistically, Housman test will show that which model is appropriate to use.

Housman specification test

A Housman test is formulated to choice in the selection of fixed effect and random effect. Housman state the hypothesis that:
H_0: Fixed effect model and random effect model estimators are not different.
H_1: Fixed effect model and random effect model estimators are different.

On the basis of p values, the appropriate model is decided, whether fixed effect model or random effect model.

RESULTS AND DISCUSSION

The purpose of this section is to provide detail empirical evidence of the study. These empirical evidence are structured to provide an in depth results which includes descriptive statistics, correlation, three panel data models such as common effect model, random effect model and fixed effect model. For comparison between fixed effect and random effect Housman test were performed.

Table 1 provides summary of descriptive statistics of the dependent and explanatory variables used in the study. The sample of the study consists of 342 non financial firms which are listed on Karachi Stock Exchange during 2000-2008, with a balance panel of 2736 observations. The mean of the investment to fixed assets is -0.0420846 while its standard deviation is 0.9877884. The results show that the firm investment is negative on average. And its standard deviation is quite high. This implies that the investment of Pakistanis firm's move on either directions. On the other hand, there is a greater variation in investment with a minimum value of -46.08571 and a maximum value of 5.495758. The mean value of leverage is 0.7126046 with a standard deviation of 0.4879956. The minimum level of debt that Pakistanis firm uses are 0.0181237 while the maximum limit for the studied firms are 9.117647. The mean ratio for liquidity is 1.746024 with a standard deviation of 5.839397. The minimum ratio of liquidity is 0.0099148, which implies that some of the firm are facing severe liquidity problems.

Whereas, the maximum limit is 265.0227. The mean value of Tobin's Q is 1.155924, it represent that there exist growth and investment opportunities for firms. At the same time, there exists some variation in these opportunities between Pakistanis firms. The results indicate that investment opportunities can move upward or downward with a magnitude of 1.355087 from the mean. As we have taken the data from heterogeneous sectors therefore, it shows so much variability. The minimum value of Tobin's Q is 0.078104 while the maximum is 42.93401. The mean value of sale is 9.288776, while its

Table 2. Correlation.

	Investment	Leverage	Liquidity	Sale	Cash Flow	ROE	Tobin's Q
Investment	1						
Leverage	-0.0106	1					
Liquidity	-0.0041	0.0288	1				
Sale	-0.0576	-0.0409	-0.0009	1			
Cash Flow	-0.05464	-0.0737	0.008	0.1718	1		
ROE	-0.0048	-0.0137	-0.0002	-0.0017	0.1486	1	
Tobin's Q	0.0309	0.2486	0.0068	0.0403	-0.0275	-0.0344	1

standard deviation is approximately 6 times more than the mean. From these statistics, we can interpret that sale of Pakistanis firms suffers from greater deviation. Sale can move upward for the selected firms up to 1236.261, on the other hand it falls to -47.1111. The mean of ROE is 0.2968767, which implies that shareholder on average receive (30%) return on their investment. minimum value for ROE is -41.75895 and the maximum is 137.6667.

In this study, we conducted correlation (Table 2) analysis to check out whether their exist multicollinearity in the model or not. As Cuthbertson (1996) pointed out in his book that multicollinearity exists in the model when the explanatory variables are strongly related to each others. In this study, multicollinearity were checked by checking the correlation between leverage, liquidity, Tobin's Q, Sale, cash flow and return on equity. All the coefficients are less then 0.148, which suggests that multicollinearity is not a serious problem in our model. The relationship between leverage and investment is negative which is an indicator of inverse relationship between these two variables. Investment has a positive relationship with Tobin's Q and negative relationship with all other explanatory variables. Leverage has a positive relationship with liquidity and Tobin's Q, while it has a negative relationship with sale, cash flow and Roe. Liquidity represents a positive relationship with cash flow and Tobin's Q and negative relationship with all other variables. Tobin's Q has a negative relationship with ROE and Cash flow, while it has a positive relationship with all other variables. Cash flow also has a positive relationship with sale and liquidity.

Common effect model

The value of overall Table 3 is shown R square is 0.3093; it means that there is 30.93% variation in the dependent variable owing to independents variables. The value of overall R square is not highly satisfactory, but it is acceptable for panel data. There may be certain other variables which also influence the investment decisions of the firms, that is, way the value of R square is 0.3093. The results revealed that the level of debt does have a significant negative impact on firm investment. The coefficient value of leverage is -0.1076574). It indicate that when leverage of a firm is increased by 1 unit its investment decreased by 0.1076574 units. These findings support the theory that leverage has an important role in over coming over investment. It supports the inverse relationship between financial leverage and firm investment. These results are consistent with those of the Firth et al. (2008), they also concluded inverse relationship between these two variables. McConnell and Servaes (1995) also concluded that the value of U.S. firms is negatively correlated with leverage for high growth firms (indicated by high Tobin's Q), and positively correlated with leverage for low growth firms (or low Tobin's Q). These results are also consistent with that of Lang et al. (1996), they found that leverage is negatively associated with investment but only for firms with low growth opportunities.

Aivazian et al. (2005) also found negative association between leverage and investment and its effect stronger for firm with low growth opportunities as compared to high growth opportunities. Similarly Ahn et al. (2006) document that the negative relation between leverage and investment in diversified firms is significantly stronger for high Q segments than for low Q business segments and is significantly stronger for non-core segments than for core segments. Among low growth firms, the positive relation between leverage and firm value is significantly weaker in diversified firms than in focused firms. The results of polled regression indicates that, capital structure's plays a very important role in firm investment decisions. The relationship between liquidity and investment is positive but insignificant. Tobin's Q has also shown positive but slightly insignificant relationship with investment for the target samples.

The regression coefficient of sale is 0.0007, and is significant with P value less than 0.05 and z value greater than 2. This result indicates that 1 unit increase in sale leads to 0.0007 units increase in investment. It means that both are in the same directions, when sale of a firm increases its investment is also increased.

The relationship between cash flow and investment is negative and is highly significant. 1 unit increased in cash flow causes 0.3737 unit decrease in investment.

Finally, the result of ROE indicates that profitability and investment moves in the same direction. When

Table 3. R square.

Variable description	Coefficient	z-statistics	P-value
Intercept	0.1410078	4.41	0
Leverage	-0.1076574	-3.08	0.002
Liquidity	0.0009181	0.34	0.736
Sale	0.0007379	2.39	0.017
Cash flow	-0.3737831	-35.18	0
ROE	0.0251835	5.1	0
Tobin's Q	0.1410078	1.54	0.124
Wald Chi ^{2}	1256.04		
R Square	0.3433		

Table 4. Fixed effect model.

Variable description	Coefficient	t-statistics	P-value
Intercept	0.120401	2.94	0.003
Leverage	-0.0328595	-0.67	0.500
Liquidity	0.0033532	1.09	0.275
Sale	0.0012827	2.87	0.004
Cash Flow	-0.4248858	-35.23	0.000
ROE	0.0285548	5.48	0.000
Tobin's Q	-0.0012129	-0.08	0.936
F statistics	209.63		
R Square	0.345		

profitability increases by 1 unit, investment of Pakistanis firms increases by 0.025 units. It is significant at (000) level and its t-value is greater than 5.

Fixed effect model

The fixed effect model (Table 4) shows that that there is no significant relationship between leverage and investment. It means that a firm financial policy is irrelevant to its investment decisions. The results suggest that whenever we extend the model to incorporate the individual effect the relationship between financial leverage and investment disappears. But the results of sale, cash flow and ROE is somehow similar to that of common effect model. The results of the fixed effect are similar to those of the Firth et al. (2009), they estimated fixed effect model with two way error component but their results were also insignificant for leverage and investment.

The results of the random effect model (Table 5) are mostly similar to that of common effect model. Leverage inversely influences firm's investment. Investment has significant and positive relationship with sale and ROE, but it has a positive but insignificant relationship with liquidity and Tobin's q. it has a significant negative relationship with cash flow.

Housman specification test (Table 6) was used to check the appropriate methodology for this study, that is, either fixed effect or random effect. The random effect model assumes that there is no correlation between the group specific random effects and the regressors.

However, the fixed effects model does not make such assumption and the possibility remains that the assumption of zero correlation in random effects model is not feasible. The Hausman test checks whether the correlation assumption is statistically evident or not. The null hypotheses for the Hausman test is that the group specific random effects and the regressors are not correlated and thus if the Hausman test shows a parameter value of more than 0.05 than it would mean that fixed effects model is inefficient and random effects model is better Girma and Görg (2006).

The result of Housman suggests that fixed effect model is appropriate to use. Housman rejects the null hypothesis that there is no significance difference in fixed effect and random effect. So we accept the alternative that both the models are not the same. On the basis of Chi square and P value <.05, the fixed effect model was considered appropriate to use.

Conclusion

This study examined the relationship between financial

Table 5. Random effect model.

Variable description	Coefficient	t-statistics	P-value
Intercept	0.1410078	-4.41	0.000
Leverage	-0.1076574	-3.08	0.002
Liquidity	0.0009781	0.34	0.736
Sale	0.0007379	2.39	0.017
Cash flow	-0.3737831	-35.18	0.000
ROE	0.0251835	5.1	0.000
Tobin's Q	0.0189451	1.54	0.124
Wald Chi ^{2}	1256.04		
R Square	0.3433		

Table 6. Housman test.

	Coefficients		
	(b)	(B)	(b -B)
	Fe	re	Difference
Leverage	-0.0328595	-0.1076574	0.0747979
Liquidity	0.0033532	0.0009181	0.0024351
Sale	0.0012827	0.0007379	0.0005448
Cash Flow	-0.4248858	-0.3737831	-0.0511027
ROE	0.0285548	0.0251835	0.0033713
Tobin's Q	-0.002129	0.0189451	-0.0210741
Chi 2 (6)	91.59		
Prob > Chi 2	0.000		

leverage and firm investment, for Pakistani non financial sector. The investigation is motivated by the theoretical work of Myers (1977), Jensen (1986), Stulz (1990) and by empirical work of McConnell and Servaes (1990).

The relationship was analyzed by controlling certain variables that had an influence on investment. These variables are cash flow, Tobin's Q, sale; return on equity and liquidity. This study amalgamates information on a large balance panel from 342 non financial firms for 8 years from (2001 - 2008). Panel data techniques (common effect model, random effect model and fixed effect model) were used for such analysis.

This study examined that whether financial policy (leverage were taken as a proxy for financial policy) influence investment decisions of firms causing under-investment or over investment incentives. This study found that financial leverage was significantly negatively related to firms' investment. It shows that as leverage increases firm's investment decreases, we may say that highly levered firms invest less. This evidence is consistent with the over investment story of Stulz (1990), where leverage inhibits managers from investment in non profitable capital expenditures. Here the debts enforce the manger to pays extra funds as interest and principal, that may otherwise been allocated to poor investments projects. Thus, leverage helped in overcoming the over-investment problems and alleviating agency problems. The results of the study provide support to the agency theories of corporate leverage, and especially to the theory that leverage has a disciplining role in overcoming the over-investment problems. Thus, the result of the study is consistent with the hypothesis that leverage attenuate to invest in poor projects. The results of the common effect model supported that capital structure plays a vital role in the decisions of firms on how to invest. But whenever we extended the model to incorporate the time and individual effect, then no relationship were seen. The relationship between leverage and investment were checked in the presence of certain control variables. The result shows negative relationship between investment and cash flow. Strong relationship was seen between investment and cash flow. The results indicate that investment and cash flow sensitivity is very strong for Pakistani non financial firms. Whenever, we checked the relationship between investment and ROE (proxy for profitability) positive relationship were found by applying common effect model. The result depicts that when profitability increased by 1 unit, investment of Pakistanis firms was increased by 0.025 units. It was significant at (000) level and its t-value was greater than 2.

Sale had a positive and significant impact on investment, which shows that as sales of Pakistani firms increases its investment also move in the same direction. No relationship was seen between liquidity and investment for the selected sample. Tobin's Q had also showed insignificant relationship with investment. We may conclude that despite of different debts market and banking structure between developed countries and developing country, the relationship remained same for financial policy (measured as financial leverage) and investment.

RECOMMENDATION FOR FUTURE RESEARCH

The empirical model of this study can be extended which can generate further information. The model can be extended by various ways, by enlarging panel data set or by increasing the number of predictors' variables. Increasing the data set will further enhance the applicability of the research. Secondly, companies classifications that whether it is a high growth company or low growth company have been entirely excluded from the study so future research may be conducted in a way that classify between companies. Thirdly future research may also make sector wised comparison in non financial sectors. Fourthly the relationship between financial leverage and firm's investment can also be conducted in financial sector of Pakistan. In this study we have used book value have used to measure debt and it would have been better if market values were available for debt which may have improved the model fit. Future research may measure this variable with market value of debts.

REFERENCES

Aggarwal R, Kyaw N (2008). Leverage and Firm Value. Working paper, University of Akron.

Ahn S, Denis D J, Denis DK (2006) Leverage and investment in diversified firms. J. Financ. Econ. 79:317-337.

Aivazian V, Ge Y, Qiu J (2005). The impact of leverage on firm investment: Canadian evidence. J. Corp. Financ. 11:277-291.

Anderson CW, Makhija AM (1999), Deregulation, disintermediation, and agency costs of debt. Evidence from Japan. J. Financ. Econ. 51:309-339.

Berger AN, di Patti EB (2006). Capital structure and firm performance: A new approach to testing agency theory and an application to the banking industry. J. Bank. Financ. 30:1065-1102.

Cantor R (1990)."Effects of leverage on corporate investment and hiring decisions" Federal Reserve Bank of New York, Issue Sum pp.31-41.

Childs P, Mauer D, Ott S (2005). "Interactions of corporate investment and financing decisions: the effects of agency conflicts". J. Financ. Econ. 76:667-690.

Cooper R, Ejarque J (2003). "Financial Frictions and Investment: Requiem in Q," Rev. Econ. Dyn. 6:710-728.

Cuthbertson K (1996). "Quantitative Financial Economics: Stocks, Bonds and Foreign Exchange," John Wiley and Sons, Chichester.

Dobson W, Kashyap AK (2006). "The Contradiction in China's Gradualist Banking Reforms," Brookings Papers on Economic Activity, Economic Studies Program. Brook. Inst. 37(2):103-162.

Fazzari SM, Hubbard RG, Petersen BC (1988). Financing constraints and corporate investment, Brookings Paper on Economic Activity 1:141-195.

Firth M, Lin C, Liu P, Wong S (2009). "Inside the Black Box: Bank Credit Allocation in China's Private Sector". J. Bank. Financ. 33:1144-1155.

Firth M, Lin C, Wong MLS (2008). Leverage and investment under a state-owned bank lending environment: Evidence from China. J. Corp. Financ. 14:642-653.

Girma S, Görg H (2006). 'Multinationals' productivity advantage: Scale or technology?' mimeo, Univ. Nottingham.

Gomes JF (2001). "Financing Investment" Am. Econ. Rev. 91(5) 1263-1285.

Gujarati DN (2006). Essentials of Econometrics, 3rd ed. McGraw-Hill, New York.

Harris M, Raviv A (1991). The theory of capital structure. J. Financ. 46:297-355.

Jensen MC (1986). Agency costs of free cash flow, corporate finance, and takeovers. Am. Econ. Rev. 76:323-329.

Jo H, Pinkerton JM, Sarin A (1994). ''Financing decisions and the investment opportunity set: some evidence from Japan''. Pacific-Basin Financ. J. 2:227-42.

Khwaja AI, Atif M (2005). "Do lenders favor politically connected firms? Rent provision in an emerging financial market." Q. J. Econ. 120(4):1371-1411.

Lang L, Ofek E, Stulz RM (1996). Leverage, investment and firm growth. J. Financ. Econ. 40:3-29.

La Porta R, Florencio L, Andrei S (2002). "Government ownership of banks." J. Fin. 57(1):265-301.

McConnell JJ, Servaes H (1995). Equity ownership and the two faces of debt. J. Financ. Econ. 39:131-157.

Mehmet S, Oruc E (2009). "Relationship between Efficiency Level of Working Capital Management and Return on Total Assets in Ise", Int. J. Bus. Manage. 4(10):109-114.

Modigliani F, Miller MH (1958). The cost of capital, corporation finance, and the theory of investment. Am. Econ. Rev. 53:433-443.

Myers S (1977). Determinants of corporate borrowing. J. Financ. Econ. 5:147-175.

Myers DE (1966). The algebra H2(S). In Proceedings of the International Symposium on Function Algebras, Scott-Foresman. 282-284

Myers SC, Robicheck AA (1966). "Problems in Theory of Capital Structure", J. Fin. Quant. Anal. 1(2):1-35.

Norvaisiene R, Stankeviciene J, Krusinskas R (2008). The Impact of loan capital on the Baltic listed companies' investment and growth. Eng. Econ. I/2(57):40-48.

Odit MP, Chittoo HB (2008). Does Financial Leverage Influence Investment Decisions? The Case Of Mauritian Firms. J. Bus. Case Stud. 4(9):49-60.

Reilly FK, Brown KC (2003). Investment analysis and portfolio management. 7th ed., Ohio: South Western Thomson.

Singh M, Faircloth S (2005). Capital market impact of product marketing strategy. Evidence from the relationship between advertising expenses and cost of capital. J. Acad. Manage. 4:215-225.

Stulz RM (1990). Managerial Discretion and Optimal Financing Policies. J. Fin. Econ. 26:3-28.

Umutlu M (2009). Firm leverage and investment decisions in an emerging market. J. Qual. Quant. 44:1005-1013.

Whited T (1992). Debt, liquidity constraints and corporate investment: Evidence from data. J. Fin. 47:425-460.

APPENDIX

Appendix 1. Sector wised classification.

Sectors	Number of firms
Textile spinning	74
Textile weaving	10
Textile composite	37
Woolen	6
Synthetic and rayon	9
Sugar and allied industries	25
Cement	12
Tobacco	4
Refinery	6
Power generation and distribution	6
Oil and gas marketing companies	5
Oil and gas exploration companies	4
Engineering	10
Automobile assembler	8
Automobile parts and accessories	6
Cable and electrical goods	7
Transport	5
Technology and communication	4
Fertilizer	8
Pharmaceuticals	7
Chemicals	19
Paper and board	7
Vanaspati and allied industries	4
Leather and tanneries	4
Food and personal care-pruducts	14
Glass and ceramics	6
Miscellaneous	35
Total number of firms	**342**

A study of cost efficiency of Indian commercial banks- An impact of mergers

Pardeep Kaur and Gian Kaur

Punjab School of Economics, Guru Nanak Dev University, Amritsar-143005, Punjab, India.

This paper investigates the cost efficiency of Indian public and private sector banks over the period 1990-2008 with unbalanced panel data by employing non-parametric data envelopment analysis technique (DEA). In this paper, an attempt is also made to examine the determinants of cost efficiency of banks by employing panel data least square regression model. The study found that private sector banks are more efficient than public sector banks with average cost efficiency score 73.4 for public sector banks as of 76.3 for the private sector banks in the country. The findings of this study suggest that the dominant source of cost inefficiency among Indian commercial banks is allocative efficiency rather than technical inefficiency. The study has examined the impact of merger activity on the cost efficiency of Indian banks by employing OLS model and found the positive and significant impact of merger activity on efficiency. Among other factors associated positively and significantly with the efficiency are the size and profitability of banks and suggesting that banks with higher ROA exhibits higher efficiency scores.

Key words: Efficiency, DEA, profitability, banks, regression, mergers.

INTRODUCTION

Over the last few decades, banking sector in India has experienced fundamental changes following banks and other financial institutions reforms starting in the early 1990's. The Indian banking sector has witnessed the reforms in order to enhance the efficiency and productivity of the banks. The financial sector reforms have strengthened the fundamentals of the Indian economy and transformed the environment in which banks operates. India embarked on a strategy of economic reforms in the wake of a serious balance of payment crisis in 1991 (Mohan, 2006). In Indian banking sector, the policy makers adopted a cautious approach for introducing reform measures on the recommendation of Narishmam Committee I (1991), Narishmam Committee II (1997) and Verma Committee (1999). The main objective of the banking sector reforms was to improve the efficiency of banks and to promote a diversified and competitive financial system.

One of the outcomes of such reforms was the consolidation of the banking industry through mergers and acquisitions. Technological progress and financial deregulation have played an important role in accelerating the process of merger and acquisition in Indian banking industry. Due to technological progress, the scale at which financial services and products are produced has expanded which provide an opportunity for the banks to increase their size and scale of production. At that, time mergers of banking institutions emerged as an important strategy for growing the size of banks. Size of the bank plays a significant role to enter the global financial market.

Merger can be defined as a means of unification of two players into single entity. Merger is a process of combining two business entities under the common ownership.

The Indian banking sector consists of the Reserve Bank of India, which is the central bank, commercial banks and co-operative banks. Commercial banks in India play dominate role in the Indian economy and accounted for 90% of the total assets of banking system. Commercial banks in India can be sub-divided into two major categories - scheduled banks, which are subject to statutory requirement, and non-scheduled banks, which are not. As on March 2009, commercial banks in India consisted of 162 scheduled commercial banks, comprised 84 Regional Rural Banks (RRBs), 27 Public sector banks (PSBs), includes 20 nationalized banks and State Bank of India and its 6 subsidiaries (after merger of State Bank of Saurashtra with State Bank of India w.e.f August, 2008).

The main objective of this paper is to examine the efficiency of Indian public and private sector banks and to study the impact of mergers on the cost efficiency of participating banks. It has been well studied in the literature of determinants of bank efficiency that the merger is not only the factor that could explain some of the differences in efficiency scores. Therefore, other environmental and bank specific factors have been considered to examine the differences in efficiency across banks. The efficiency of banks between 1990-2008 is examined using the non-parametric DEA approach. The determinants of Indian banks efficiency scores are evaluated by using the regression analysis.

MERGERS IN INDIAN BANKING SECTOR

Mergers and acquisitions in Indian banking sector have initiated through the recommendations of Narasimham committee II in 1998, when its report recommended a drastic reduction in the number of public sector unit banks from the set of 27. The committee recommended that merger between strong banks/ financial institutions would make for greater economic and commercial sense and would be a case where the whole is greater than the sum of its parts and have a "force multiplier effect". (Narasimham committee II, chapter, para 5.13 -5.15).

Mergers come with several benefits such as creation of synergies, economics of scale, cost reduction, and quickly acquire new technologies, skills, markets, and resources. There are several reasons for mergers the primary ones are deregulation and technology. Deregulation has given banks opportunities to explore new business markets and mergers seem an attractive route to them. Technology has helped rationalize costs and delivery channels. Therefore, technology and deregulation have been considered as the drivers for bank mergers. Table 1 clearly depicted that 21 M/As took place during post reform period with as many as 17 mergers taking place during 1999. Therefore, the pace of mergers gathered momentum during 1999, leading to a marked decline in the number of private and foreign banks. Recently, the Reserve Bank of India under section 45 of the banking regulation Act, 1949 in case of some troubled banks suggested the compulsory merger with stronger banks. These included the merger of Global Trust Bank with Oriental Bank of Commerce in August 2004, Ganesh Bank of Kurndwad Ltd. with Federal Bank Ltd. in September 2006 and the merger of United Western Bank with IDBI Ltd. in October 2006.

LITERATURE REVIEW

Review of studies on efficiency of banks

Berger and Humphrey (1997) in their study provide an extensive review of studies on the efficiency of banking sector. They pointed out that, majority of studies focused on the banking markets of well-developed countries with particular emphasis on the US market.

Bhattacharyya et al. (1997) used DEA to measure the productive efficiency of 70 Indian commercial banks in the period 1986-1991. They found that the public sector banks are the most efficient banks as compared to foreign banks and private banks. They also found a temporal decline in the performance of public sector banks.

Das (1997) used the cross-section data and DEA to examine the efficiency of 65 major banks for the year 1995. He found that Indian banks were more technically efficient than allocatively efficient.

Mukherjee et al. (2002) examined the technical efficiency of 68 Indian commercial banks for the period 1996-1999 and found that public sector banks are more efficient than both private and foreign banks.

Ram and Ray (2004) also found that public sector banks performed better than private sector banks but not differently from foreign banks. All these studies have compared the efficiency of public, private, and foreign banks by using a common frontier and such comparisons are not justified on the ground that public, private, and foreign banks are operated under different legal and regulatory frameworks.

Chen (2004) conducted a study to examine the efficiency difference between Taiwan's publicly, private owned banks, and the impact of the Asian financial crisis on the efficiency of Taiwan banking sector. He used data envelopment analysis and panel data ranging from 1994 to 2004 on 44 banks to measure cost, allocative and technical efficiency of Taiwan's banks. He employed intermediation approach and conducted sensitivity analysis to determine the appropriate inputs and outputs. He found that Asian financial crisis has depreciated cost, allocative and technical efficiency in Taiwanese banks and suggested that banks rate of return and bank loans on bad loans are major reason for this.

Ariff and Can (2008) attempted to investigate the cost and profit efficiency of Chinese commercial banks over the period from 1995 to 2004. They used non-parametric

Table 1. Banks merged in India since liberalization.

Merger / Year	Acquirer Bank	Target Bank	Motive of merger	Type of merger
1993	Punjab National Bank	New Bank of India	Restructuring of weak bank	Forced merger
1993	Bank of India	Bank of Karad Ltd.	Restructuring of weak bank	Forced merger
1995	State Bank of India	Kashinath Seth Bank	Restructuring of weak bank	Forced merger
1997	Oriental Bank of Commerce	Punjab Co-operative Bank Ltd.	Restructuring of weak bank	Forced merger
1997	Oriental Bank of Commerce	Bari Doab Bank Ltd.	Restructuring of weak bank	Forced merger
1999	Union Bank of India	Sikkim Bank Ltd.	Restructuring of weak bank	Forced merger
2000	HDFC Bank Ltd.	Times Bank	To achieve scale and scope economies	Voluntary merger
2001	ICICI Bank	Bank of Madura	To achieve scale and scope economies	Voluntary merger
2002	ICICI Bank	ICICI Limited	To achieve the objective of universal banking	Voluntary merger
2002	Bank of Baroda	Benaras State Bank Ltd.	Restructuring of weak bank	Forced merger
2003	Punjab National Bank	Nedungadi Bank Ltd.	Restructuring of weak bank	Forced merger
2004	Bank of Baroda	South Gujarat Local Area Bank	Restructuring of weak bank	Forced merger
2004	Oriental Bank of Commerce	Global Trust Bank	Restructuring of weak bank	Forced merger
2005	Centurion Bank	Bank of Punjab	To achieve scale and scope economies	Voluntary merger
2006	Federal Bank	Ganesh Bank of Kurandwad	Restructuring of weak bank	Forced merger
2006	IDBI Bank	United western Bank	Restructuring of weak bank	Forced merger
2006	Centurion Bank of Punjab	Lord Krishna Bank	Expansion of size	Voluntary merger
2007	ICICI Bank	Sangli Bank	Expansion of size	Voluntary merger
2007	Indian Overseas Bank	Bharat overseas Bank	Restructuring of weak bank	Compulsory merger
2008	HDFC Bank	Centurion Bank of Punjab	Expansion of size and benefits of scope economics	Voluntary merger

Source: Compiled from Report on Trend and Progress of Banking in India, RBI, various issues.

data envelopment analysis technique to obtain the cost efficiency and profit efficiency of banks. The study is based on unbalanced panel data of 28 Chinese banks, totaling 230 observations. They also used Tobit regression analysis to study the influence of ownership type, profile, profitability, and key environmental changes on the efficiency of china's banks. Tobit regression analysis suggests that banks that are more profitable tend to be more efficient. The relationship between non-interest income to total income and efficiency also turned out to be significant.

Burki and Niazi (2006) studied the impact of financial reforms on banking efficiency of state-owned, private, and foreign banks in Pakistan. They employed DEA to measure efficiency of banks and used time series cross-section data of 40 commercial banks from 1991 to 2000. The researchers also applied maximum likelihood Tobit regression analysis to identify the determinants of banking efficiency in Pakistan. The results from Tobit regression analysis suggest a positive association between bank size and cost efficiency whereas the size is not significantly associated with the allocative efficiency of banks.

Sathye (2003) used DEA to evaluate the productive efficiency of Indian banks for the period 1997-1998. He used two DEA models to calculate the efficiency scores of public, private, and foreign sector banks. He found that efficiency scores of public and private owned banks were lower as compared to the public sector and foreign sector banks.

Ataullah et al. (2004) employed DEA to make a comparative analysis of commercial banks in India and Pakistan during the period 1988-1998. For efficiency measurement, they employed two input-output specifications. The results indicated the presence of space for improvement in the efficiency of banks in these countries.

Merger and bank efficiency

The substantial merger wave that affected the banking industries of many countries has spurred large literature on the effects of mergers on the efficiency and bank performance. In particular, some studies support the view that consolidation via merger is beneficial because more efficient bank mergers substitute less efficient ones .Greater bank size can yield economies of scale and scope, increase diversification, opportunities and greater cost savings (Berger et al., 1999).

The available empirical evidence on the effects of bank mergers is mixed. Most studies focus on the effects in terms of bank performance measures, few studies address the impact on customers's welfare by examining the effects on prices (Bonasccorsi and Hardy, 2005).

The cost efficiency effects of such mergers have been particularly well studied. Studies on Italian banks (Resti, 1998) confirm economics of scale in the case of M/As among domestic small banks.

Vennet (1996) studied the impact of mergers on the efficiency of European Union banking industry by using some key financial ratios and stochastic frontier analysis for the period 1988-1993 and found that merger improves the efficiency of participating banks. Akhavein et al. (1997) examined the price and efficiency effects of mega mergers on US banking industry and found that after merger banks have experienced higher level of profit efficiency than before merger. Berger and Humphrey (1998) found very little improvement in efficiency for merger and acquisition of either large or small banks. Rhoades (1998) attempted to summarize nine case studies by nine authors, on the efficiency effects of bank mergers. The findings indicated that four out of nine case studies have shown mergers successful in improving efficiency of banks in majority of cases and the acquiring banks were more efficient than their peer group. Peng and Wang (2004) studied the cost efficiency and the effect of mergers on Taiwanese banking sector, by using the panel data from 1997 to 1999. He found a statistically significant relationship between merger and cost efficiency and significant efficiency differences between merged and non-merged banks.

Gourlay et al. (2006) analyzed the efficiency gains from mergers among Indian banks over the period 1991-1992 to 2004-2005 and observed that the merger led to improvement of efficiency for the merging banks. RBI (2008) also drives the same conclusions and found that public sector banks have been able to get higher level of efficiency than private sector banks during post merger period. Wu (2006) in his study for the Australian banks for the period 1983-2001 observed that post merger efficiency of banks is not closely related with pre-merger efficiency rather it has also been affected by other pre and post-merger factors of banks. Wu (2008) examined the X-efficiency gains from mergers and acquisitions among the 34 listed commercial banks in Taiwan. He found that banks were not experiencing any efficiency gains from mergers due to the fact that efficiency gains might emerge more than three years after the merger completion and losses from bad loans may erode the efficiency gains from mergers and acquisitions.

METHODOLOGY

There are diverse ways to measure the efficiency of banks but researchers and analysts do not agree upon a single method of measuring the efficiency of DMU's. Berger and Humphrey (1997) provide an extensive account of 130 studies that applied different frontier efficiency analysis for 21 countries. Two approaches are frequently used for the estimation of bank efficiency, in the literature of banking efficiency. These are parametric and non-parametric approaches. Parametric approaches include Stochastic Frontier Analysis and Thick Frontier Approach. Among all parametric approaches, SFA (Stochastic Frontier Analysis), also sometimes referred to as econometric approach is widely used to measure the efficiency of DMU's. SFA specifies a functional from profit, cost and production relationship among inputs, outputs, and environmental factors and allows for random error. The SFA assumes a composed error model where inefficiencies are assumed to follow an asymmetric distribution, usually the half normal are exponential distribution, usually the standard normal (Ferrier and Lovell, 1990; Lang and Welzel, 1999).

Contrary to parametric approach, non-parametric approach requires few assumptions about the estimated frontier and does not assume a specific functional from to represent the cost and production functions. Among, a non-parametric approach, DEA is used extensively to estimate the efficiency of DMU's. DEA is a mathematical, linear programming based approach. To measure the efficiency of DMU's under input orientation and constant return to scale, Charnes et al. (1978) first proposed it and this model is known as CCR model. DEA is based on a concept of efficiency very similar to the microeconomic one; the main difference is that the DEA production frontier is not determined by some functional form, but it is generated from the actual data for the evaluated firms (Casu and Philip, 2003). Later, Banker et al. (1984) extended CCR model to allow variable return to scale. The CRS assumption of DEA is suitable only when all DMU's are operating at an optimal scale. However, in practical situation many factors like imperfect competition, regulatory and legal framework put constraints on DMU' s not to be operating at optimal scale. As a result, the use of CRS when some DMU are not operating at optimal scale will result in measures of technical efficiency, which are confounded by scale efficiencies (Philip, 1999). Data envelopment analysis is a mathematical programming approach for characterizing the relationship among multiple inputs and outputs and has been a proven way to measure bank performance (Charnes et al., 1990; Seiford and Zhu, 1999).

Data envelopment analysis

DEA computes the efficiency of banks on the basis of estimated piece-wise linear frontier made up by a set of efficient banks. The banks that lie on the frontier are treated as best practice banks and obtain efficiency score equal to one whereas the banks that do not lie on the frontier are relatively inefficient and their efficiency score lie in the range of zero and one. The DEA approach decomposed the CE into its two different components, TE (technical efficiency) and AE (allocative efficiency). Technical efficiency reflects the ability of a firm to maximize output from a given set of inputs whereas alloacitve efficiency reflects the ability of the firm to use these inputs in optimal proportions, given their respective prices where the cost of production is minimum. Technical efficiency implies that there is no waste in using inputs to produce specific quantity of output. A firm is said to be technically efficient when it cannot increase any output or decrease any input without reducing the quantities of other outputs or inputs. Combing these two measures provides a measure of cost efficiency. A firm is said to be cost efficient when it is both alloactively as well as technically efficient.

Following Farell et al. (1957), this paper has used the input price vector to specify and obtain a measure of cost efficiency (CE) for each bank by solving this envelopment form of linear programming problem:

Mini $w_i x_i^*$

subject to:

$$\sum \lambda_g y_{ki} - y_{kgo} \geq 0$$

$$x_{igo}^* - \sum \lambda_g x_{ig} \geq 0$$

$$\lambda \geq 0$$

Where
w_i = vector of input prices for ith bank
y_i = vector of output levels for ith bank
x_i^* = cost minimizing vector of input quantities
λ = n×1vector of constants

Thus, the cost efficiency of any given bank is obtained as the ratio of minimum cost to the observed cost written as follows:

$$CE = \frac{w_i x_i^*}{w_i x_i}$$

On the other hand, allocative efficiency is the ratio of cost efficiency to technical efficiency, thus AE = $\frac{CE}{TE}$. This procedure of cost efficiency includes any slacks into allocative efficiency because the slacks reflect sub optimal input mix (Ferrier and Lovell, 1990).

Measuring technical efficiency

The technical efficiency is obtained by using the following input oriented DEA model.

$$MaxZ_0 = \frac{\sum_{i=1}^{n} \mu_k y_{kgo}}{\sum_{i=1}^{z} v_k x_{iko}}$$

subject to:

$$\frac{\sum_{k=1}^{h} \mu_k y_{kgi}}{\sum_{i=1}^{z} v_i x_{ig}} \leq 1$$

where

$\mu_k \geq \in$, $v_i = \in$, g = 1,2,...,n, k= 1,2,.....,h, i=1,2,......,z
u_k, v_i = weights given to output k and input i .
y_{kg} = quantity of output k achieved by DMU g
x_{ig} = quantity of input i used by DMU g
n = number of DMUs
h = number of outputs
z = number of inputs
$\in$ = a non-Archimedean (infinitesimal) constant

One of the distinct feature of these models is that the weights u_k, vr are positive and unknown. The values of u and v are found in such a way that the efficiency of gth DMU is maximized. This model is in a ratio form and one of the key problems related with the ratio form is that it has an infinite number of solutions. The above fractional form can be transformed in a straight forward way into the following liner programs.

CCR efficiency measure (linear form)

$$MaxZ_0 = \sum_{i=1}^{n} \mu_k y_{kgo}$$

subject to:

$$\sum_{k=1}^{h} \mu_k y_{kg} - \sum_{i=1}^{z} v_i x_{ig} \leq 0$$

$$\sum_{i=1}^{z} v_k x_{iko} = 1$$

$\mu_k \geq \in$, $v_i = \in$, g = 1,2,...,n, k= 1,2,.....,h, i=1,2,......,z

Measurement of Inputs and outputs in banking

It is well known in the literature of banking efficiency studies, the choice of input and output variables significantly affects the efficiency scores of banks, and at the same time, it is not an easy task to measure and define bank input and output variables. There is considerable disagreement among researchers about the constituents of inputs and outputs of the banking industry. Since many bank services are priced implicitly by offering below market interest rates on deposits, the observed revenue flow offer poor guidance regarding the relative importance of various outputs (Berger and Humphrey, 1992). Mainly two different approaches have appeared in the literature regarding the measurement of inputs and outputs of banks. These approaches are the production and intermediation approach. The production approach treated loans and deposits as outputs and measured in terms of the number of accounts and transactions serviced during a particular period. A shortcoming of this approach is that it considers only operating costs and excludes the interest expenses. In contrast, the intermediation approach views banks as financial intermediaries that collect funds from units in surplus and then transform these resources into loans and other investments. According to this approach, bank outputs are measured in monetary values and total costs include all operating and interest expenses thus providing a more thorough picture of the economic viability of a bank.

Berger and Humphrey (1997) pointed out that neither of the two approaches is suitable for defining the inputs and outputs because these approaches cannot fully capture the dual role of banks as producers of services and being financial intermediaries between savers and investors. Nevertheless, they suggested that, the production approach might be more suitable for branch level efficiency studies whereas intermediation approach is well suitable for measuring bank level efficiency. This is because, at the branch level, investment decisions are mostly not under the control of branches whereas at the bank level motive of management will be to reduce total cost and not just non-interest expenses. In banking literature, researches have given priority to intermediation approach.

In this paper, a modified version of intermediation approach is used for the selection of input and output variables. The selected input variables are 1) Labor (measured in terms of number of full time employees, 2) Loanable funds (measured as the sum of deposits and borrowings and 3) Physical capital comprising fixed assets and book value of premises at the end of the year. The output variables used for the estimation of efficiency are 1) Non-interest income and 2) Net-interest income (measured as the

Table 2. Input and output variables used in previous studies.

References	Country	Outputs	Inputs	Technique
Bhattacharyya et al. (1997)	India	Labor, deposit, investment	Interest and operating	DEA & SFA
Chatterjee (1997)	India	Total operating costs	Labor, capital, purchased funds	Translog cost function
Avkiran (1999)	Australia	Net interest income, non interest income	Interest expense, non-interest expense	DEA
Huizinga et al. (2001)	Europe	Loans, securities, other assets	Deposits, labor	DEA
Sathye (2001)	Australia	Demand deposits, loans and advances	Labor, capital and loanable funds	DEA
Sathye (2003)	India	Model A - Interest income, non-interest income; Model B - Net loans, non-interest income	Model A - Interest expense, non-interest expense Model B - Deposit, staff	DEA
Ataullah et al. (2004)	India and Pakistan	Loans and advances, investment	Operating expenses, interest expenses	DEA
Chen (2004)	China	Loans, deposits, non-interest income	Interest expenses, non-interest expenses	DEA
Pasiours (2006)	Greek	Net interest income, net commission income, other operating income	Employee expenses, other non-interest expenses, loan loss provisions	DEA
Kumar and Gulati (2008)	India	Interest spread, non-interest income	Labor, physical capital, loanable funds	DEA

difference between interest earned and interest expanded and 3) Advances. Further, all the input and output variables except labor are measured in crore of Rupees. All the nominal input and output variables except (labor) have been converted into real variables by using GDP price deflator (Base 1999-2000=100) whereas establishment expenses incurred on staff has been deflated by consumer price index for non-manual employees. One of the important pre-requisite for calculating the cost efficiency of banks is the information of input prices. Therefore, in the present analysis we also incorporated the input prices. Labor costs are proxied by dividing the establishment expenses of all banks employees by the total number of employees. The unit price of physical capital is measured by dividing the sum of expenses on rent, repairs, and deprecation by total fixed assets. The price of loanable funds is computed by the total interest expenses divided by the total loanable funds. Table 2 provides an overview of input and output variables used in existing studies.

Data base

This paper has used time-series cross section data of commercial banks in India for the period 1989-1990 to 2007-2008. The sample contained the public and private sector banks that have operated in India during 1990-2008. The relevant data has been extracted from the Performance Highlights of Indian Banks published by Indian Banks Association, Statistical Tables relating to Banks in India, Annual Accounts of Banks, and Report on Trend and Progress in Banking published by Reserve Bank of India. The numbers of observations varied across time due to entry of new private banks in 1995 and exit of banks due to merger of banks in the banking industry, which leads to an unbalanced panel data. It gives us 1054 observations with minimum of 50 observations in 2008 and maximum of 60 in 1998. The year–wise description of no. of observations have been given in Table 3.

EMPRICIAL FINDINGS

Table 4 presents the analysis of average cost efficiency scores of Indian commercial banks along with its two components technical efficiency and allocative efficiency. It is evident from the table that average cost efficiency estimate of total banking industry during the entire study period is 0.829 ,which suggests that on average, banks are 82% efficient in optimally using input cost compared

Table 3. Descriptive statistics of selected input and output variables.

Year	1990	1991	1992	1993	1994	1995	1996	1997	1998	1999
No. of observations	**52**	**52**	**53**	**51**	**51**	**58**	**60**	**60**	**60**	**59**
Outputs advances										
Mean	429.76	411.96	393.95	611.61	400.67	1578.80	1336.26	1750.40	1598.56	1706.01
S.D	241.35	227.03	232.82	1297.96	189.02	6450.15	2790.03	3762.48	3846.41	3961.37
Non-interest income										
Mean	7.71	8.24	9.53	12.72	12.64	24.55	45.67	70.38	80.58	65.66
S.D	4.57	4.76	6.19	11.09	7.79	45.68	100.34	189.72	219.47	191.19
Spread										
Mean	223.78	213.38	348.84	295.70	292.15	325.61	323.68	363.73	402.10	442.10
S.D	432.16	426.47	872.71	766.85	661.17	753.13	741.47	824.73	859.35	935.52
Inputs labor										
Mean	17628.27	17720.35	17497.30	18129.75	18547.00	16398.29	15866.47	15817.17	15809.90	16073.73
S.D	32562.57	32874.13	32943.89	33798.67	34538.27	33214.18	32841.26	33042.78	33362.08	33279.60
Loanable funds										
Mean	5.09	791.97	742.65	1156.31	869.45	2512.60	2170.62	3245.08	3242.84	3532.31
S.D	2.83	371.13	360.79	2173.41	373.78	7795.19	4186.74	6579.34	7561.95	7307.54
Physical capital										
Mean	810.66	4.97	5.24	9.29	10.82	59.97	96.67	216.23	191.50	184.69
S.D	395.08	2.64	3.05	9.24	7.65	184.07	226.71	838.96	811.44	771.88
Prices of inputs and labor										
Mean	1.07	1.09	1.08	1.09	1.18	1.23	1.68	1.87	1.73	1.70
S.D	0.24	0.19	0.23	0.25	0.16	0.38	0.53	1.69	0.67	0.29
Price of loanable funds										
Mean	6.61	6.89	7.39	7.83	7.20	6.14	7.40	8.11	7.89	8.14
S.D	1.34	0.85	1.13	0.92	0.81	1.77	1.54	1.42	1.16	1.35
Price of physical capital										
Mean	64.74	64.48	46.50	43.59	38.10	30.56	28.89	30.14	43.77	30.65
S.D	39.49	39.48	31.37	31.58	26.46	25.87	21.88	19.37	96.75	17.51

Year	2000	2001	2002	2003	2004	2005	2006	2007	2008
No. of observations	**59**	**58**	**57**	**56**	**56**	**56**	**55**	**52**	**50**
Outputs advances									
Mean	2391.30	1619.40	2454.57	1646.36	1686.54	4055.11	2883.48	3495.94	400.66
S.D	5818.71	2558.11	7629.41	2003.35	4922.64	13798.21	4302.70	3913.51	405.08
Non-interest income									
Mean	99.78	52.51	82.88	81.70	84.08	86.54	74.56	71.53	97.35
S.D	261.66	85.92	140.93	119.60	135.19	207.15	157.40	116.35	138.34
Spread									
Mean	457.69	558.95	568.10	669.17	734.99	914.43	1144.63	1429.28	146.99
S.D	949.22	1120.33	1139.17	1234.44	1096.30	1645.90	1999.93	2229.39	134.74

Table 3 cont.

Inputs labor									
Mean	15941.47	14935.26	14556.54	14908.64	14917.18	**14989.66**	15542.51	16667.35	17443.40
S.D	32743.46	30224.00	29379.20	29549.27	25760.12	**28980.42**	28329.10	27188.45	26962.62
Loanable funds									
Mean	5051.20	3348.15	4715.59	3239.69	3302.13	6258.26	4419.80	5240.76	3452.41
S.D	11705.74	4866.64	13353.89	3961.59	8721.76	19694.91	6053.39	5693.27	2892.12
Physical capital									
Mean	195.40	110.80	180.21	100.21	91.04	115.49	80.20	87.34	105.38
S.D	730.26	347.56	731.87	307.79	508.37	329.11	207.77	211.68	294.02
Prices of inputs and labor									
Mean	1.88	2.12	2.13	2.27	2.42	2.60	2.80	2.75	3.05
S.D	0.34	0.51	0.44	0.47	0.55	0.92	0.71	0.53	0.79
Price of loanable funds									
Mean	7.64	632.66	7.33	6.60	5.33	4.58	4.60	4.98	13.12
S.D	1.05	389.22	1.25	0.90	1.47	0.81	0.66	0.69	10.77
Price of physical capital									
Mean	31.56	33.67	36.13	40.38	40.78	41.41	41.89	43.59	137.88
S.D	18.07	18.01	18.32	19.04	17.85	18.76	17.03	20.26	213.05

All rupees values have been deflated by using GDP deflator with base 1999-2000.

to the best practice banks, operating under same working conditions. As depicted in Table 4, cost efficiency of private sector banks is 76.3% followed by 73.4% of public sector banks during the entire study period, which indicates that the private sector banks have the potential for cost saving by 23.7% or in other words, private sector banks have and could use only 76.3% of resources actually employed to produce the given level of output.

Table 4 also indicates that public sector banks can cut their costs by 26.6% to become fully efficient banks and to capture the position of best practice frontier. The findings of this study reported that private sector banks have performed better than public sector banks in cost savings with the given state of technology. The decomposition of CE into its two components clearly indicates that in each year, allocative inefficiency is always higher than technical inefficiency. It implies that the dominant source of cost inefficiency among Indian commercial banks is allocative inefficiency rather than technical inefficiency. It suggests that managers of Indian banks are relatively good in using the minimum level of inputs at a given level of outputs but they were not good in selecting the optimal mix of inputs at given prices.

Impact of merger activity on cost efficiency

Here an attempt is made to investigate the factors, which affect the efficiency of commercial banks in India. The efficiency of banks is not only influenced by the merger activity, rather many variables affect the efficiency of banks. Several bank and industry specific factors may influence a particular bank's efficiency level. Some of these factors may be neither inputs nor outputs in the production process, but rather circumstances faced by a particular bank (Sufian and Mazid, 2007). It is apparent from the analysis that the efficiency scores differ among different banks in India. The analysts, bank managers and policy makers are interested in determining whether their differences are significant or not in statistical sense. This can be done by using regression analysis. As the efficiency scores derived from DEA model is bounded between 0 and 1, an application of simple regression model may provide biased results and application of Tobit regression more appropriate than simple regression model. However, Alexander and Jaforullah (2004) pointed out that 100% efficiency or 0% inefficiency is a valid score and no higher (or lower) score is possible, by definition. In this sense, the data are not truly censored at one (or 0), OLS is therefore quite appropriate.

Following Burki and Niazi (2003), Alexander and Joforullah (2004) and Ketkar and Ketkar (2008), in this paper, Panel Least Square Fixed Effect Regression model has been used. Therefore, the cost efficiency scores obtained by DEA model is considered as dependent variable and regressed on a range of independent variables by using panel data least square method of fixed effects models.

Table 4. Average cost efficiency, technical efficiency and allocative efficiency of Indian banks.

Year	Cost efficiency			Technical efficiency			Allocative efficiency		
	PSBs	PVTs	CBs	PSBs	PVTs	CBs	PSBs	PVTs	CBs
1989-90	0.787	0.813	0.802	0.913	0.880	0.898	0.865	0.924	0.893
1990-91	0.792	0.792	0.796	0.931	0.931	0.92	0.853	0.853	0.866
1991-92	0.669	0.728	0.697	0.865	0.838	0.853	0.767	0.872	0.816
1992-93	0.781	0.649	0.709	0.895	0.889	0.892	0.867	0.713	0.789
1993-94	0.595	0.825	0.704	0.851	0.916	0.882	0.686	0.9	0.787
1994-95	0.632	0.720	0.68	0.819	0.83	0.825	0.764	0.851	0.81
1995-96	0.594	0.415	0.496	0.797	0.803	0.800	0.744	0.515	0.618
1996-97	0.735	0.799	0.77	0.839	0.893	0.869	0.868	0.895	0.883
1997-98	0.744	0.754	0.75	0.877	0.92	0.903	0.845	0.817	0.83
1998-99	0.757	0.817	0.79	0.885	0.895	0.891	0.851	0.909	0.882
1999-00	0.762	0.821	0.795	0.883	0.889	0.887	0.86	0.919	0.892
2000-01	0.820	0.769	0.795	0.901	0.895	0.887	0.917	0.862	0.881
2001-02	0.763	0.815	0.791	0.892	0.896	0.894	0.851	0.907	0.881
2002-03	0.985	0.798	0.764	0.909	0.901	0.905	0.799	0.882	0.842
2003-04	0.723	0.816	0.772	0.918	0.904	0.911	0.786	0.899	0.845
2004-05	0.775	0.737	0.756	0.934	0.873	0.903	0.831	0.842	0.837
2005-06	0.796	0.763	0.779	0.924	0.883	0.904	0.86	0.859	0.859
2006-07	0.751	0.826	0.79	0.946	0.93	0.939	0.799	0.889	0.84
2007-08	0.492	0.842	0.649	0.945	0.919	0.934	0.513	0.911	0.693
Average	0.734	0.763	0.741	0.891	0.889	0.889	0.807	0.854	0.829

The explanatory variables that have been considered to explain DEA cost efficiency are size of bank, profitability, exposure to off-balance sheet activities, quality of staff, operational risk and two dummies (DUMMERGER and DUMPUBLIC). DUMMERGER denotes the dummy variable equal to 1 for banks that have participated in the merger activity during the study period 0 for non-merged banks. Similarly, DUMPUBLIC indicates the dummy variable equal to 1 for public sector banks and 0 for otherwise.

The following regression equation has been fitted to explain efficiency scores. The econometric software package E-views version 5.1 is used to estimate the parameters.

$$EFF = \alpha_0 + \alpha_1 \text{SIZE} + \alpha_2 \text{ROA} + \alpha_3 \text{QSTAFF} + \alpha_4 \text{OFFBALANCE} + \alpha_5 \text{ORISK} + \alpha_6 \text{DUMERGER} + \alpha_7 \text{DUMPUBLIC}$$

ε_i is the disturbance term and $\varepsilon_i = v_i + \mu_i$, where
v_i = capturing the unobserved bank specific effect and
μ_i = idiosyncratic error

Where EFF denotes the DEA efficiency scores derived at first stage.

Table 5 provides the description of these factors and their hypothesized relationship with efficiency of banks. Table 6 provides the results of panel least square regression analysis. It has been clear from the table; the sign of the estimated regression co-efficient are in accordance with priori expectations. In the present paper, logarithm of total assets is used to explain the SIZE of banks. From the Table 6, it is observed that the value of SIZE co-efficient has been worked out to be (0.046476) for all CBs and the co-efficient have a positive sign. Further, SIZE co-efficient is noted to be highly significant at 1% level of significance. It implies that efficiency of large banks is higher than that of small ones. These results are consistent with the results obtained by Favero and Papi (1995), Hauner (2004), which highlighted that cost efficiency, is positively related to size of banks.

As discussed earlier, the ROA has been used as a proxy variable for banks profitability. Profitability denotes the ability of a bank to earn in excess to the expenditure incurred on handling all the related operations. It has been observed from the Table 6 that ROA reveals a positive relationship and the value of ROA co-efficient is noted to be (0.045745) for all CB's. The value of co-efficient is found to be significant at 1% level of significance. Therefore, ROA has proved to be a major determinant for cost efficiency of banks in India. The findings of this analysis indicate that higher level of profitability of banks leads to lower level of cost inefficiency and vice-versa. These findings are supported by the findings of previous studies (Isik and Hassan, 2002; Verma and Kumara, 2002-2003; Sufian and Habibullah (2009).

QSTAFF has also been considered as major determinant of cost efficiency of commercial banks in

Table 5. Description of the variables used in the regression analysis.

Variable	Description	Hypothesized relationship with efficiency	Remarks
SIZE	Natural logarithm of total assets	+	Is used as a proxy to examine the association of size with cost efficiency and it is expected to take a positive sign
ROA	Net profits over total assets	+	Is used as a proxy variable to examine the relationship between profitability and efficiency. A positive relationship is expected.
Quality of staff (QSTAFF)	Establishment expenses over total no. of employees	+/-	Is used as a proxy variable for overheads cost and there is no prori expectation on the variable sign.
Exposure to off balance sheet activities (OFFBALANCE)	Non –interest income over total assets	+/-	Is used as a proxy for banks diversification strategy. A positive relationship is expected.
Operational risk (ORISK)	Total loans over total assets	+	Is used as a measure of risk taking behavior of bank management. The variable is expected to have a positive sign.
DUMMERGER	Dummy variable that takes a value 1 for banks that participate in merger activity, 0 otherwise	+	Is used to examine the impact of merger on the efficiency of banks. This variable is expected to have positive sign.
DUMPUB	Dummy variable that takes a value 1 for public sector banks, 0 otherwise	+/-	Is used to examine the association between bank ownership and efficiency. There is no priori expectation on the variable sign.

Table 6. Regression explaining efficiency scores.

Explanatory variables	Estimated co-efficient	t-value
Intercept	0.578428	15.33321***
SIZE	0.046476	4.119974***
ROA	0.045745	11.62231***
QSTAFF	0.002046	0.389742
OFFBALANCE	0.001999	0.260417
OPERATIONALRISK	0.000015	0.052745
DUMMERGER	0.037739	2.500176**
DUMPUBLIC	-0.087674	-6.242362***
R-square	0.315888	
Adjusted R-squared	0.299251	
F-statistics	18.98709	

***, ** Significant at 1 and 5% level of significance. Source: Authors' calculations.

India. Table 6 provides that the value of quality of staff co-efficient is (-0.002046) and the results delineate a negative sign of co-efficient but it is not significant at any conventional level of significance.

The ratio of non-interest income to total assets has been used to investigate the influence of banks diversification strategy into non-tradinational activities and it is considered as another important variable that affects the cost efficiency of banks in India. The empirical findings suggest that the value of OFFBALANCE co-efficient turns out to be (0.001999) and it is not statistically significant. The findings suggest that banks tend to become more cost efficient as they increasingly engage themselves in modern banking activities. The above finding is consisted with the findings of earlier findings by Kwan (2006) and Sufian and Mazid (2007), which highlighted the positive impact OFFBALANCE sheet activities on bank's efficiency. Loans/TA ratio can be considered as another important variable affecting cost efficiency of commercial banks in India. It indicates the risk taking behavior of bank management. It shows positive co-efficient and suggest that banks with higher loans to asset ratio tend to have higher efficiency levels.

Further to investigate the relationship between ownership of bank and bank's efficiency, in this paper a dummy variable, DUMPUBLIC is introduced as an explanatory variable in the regression model. It has been observed from the Table 6 that the value of DUMPUBLIC co-efficient is found to be highly significant at 1% level of significance. It implies that public sector banks enjoy lower efficiency scores than private owned banks. Dummy variable merger, also show a positive association with cost efficiency of banks. It implies that merged banks gain access to cost saving technologies or spread their fixed cost over a larger base, thus reducing average cost.

Conclusion

Applying, a non-parametric DEA approach, this paper examines the cost, technical and allocative efficiency of Indian banks over the period 1990-1991-2007-2008. This paper also shed light on the bank specific and environmental factors affecting cost efficiency of public and private banks in India. The findings of this study suggest that over the entire study period, average cost efficiency of public sector banks was found to be 73.4 and for private sector banks is 76.3%. The findings suggest that public sector banks (except State Bank of India and its associates) are lagging far behind their counterparts in terms of efficiency and public sector banks needs to transform their business strategies to raise their efficiency levels and to attain position in the global financial market. According to the empirical findings, the size, profitability, and merger activity has significant impact on the CE of banks in India. The findings of this study suggested that the Government and banking authorizes should have to promote mergers. As mergers resulted in expansion of banks and it enables banks to raise money from the capital markets. The Indian financial system requires very large banks to absorb various risks that have emerged from operating in local and global market. The prime factors for future mergers in Indian banking industry included the Basel–II environment, challenges of free convertibility and requirement of large investment banks. Therefore, the Government and policy makers should be more cautious in promoting merger as a way to reap economies of scale and scope.

REFERENCES

Akhavein JD, Berger AN, Humphrey DB (1997). "The Effects of Bank Mergers on Efficiency and Prices: Evidence from the Profit Function" Rev. Ind. Organ. 12:95-139.

Alexander WRJ, Jaforullah M (2004). Explaining efficiency differences of New Zealand secondary schools (Economics Discussion Papers Series No. 403). University of Otago. Retrieved from http://hdl.handle.net/10523/899.

Ariff M, Can L (2008). Cost and profit efficiency of Chinese banks: A non-parametric analysis. China Econ. Rev. 19(2):260-273.

Ataullah A, Cockerill T, Le H (2004). "Financial Liberalization and Bank Efficiency: A Comparative Analysis of India and Pakistan". Appl. Econ. 36(17):1915-1924.

Avkiran NK (1999). "The Evidence on Efficiency Gains: The Role of Mergers and the Benefits to the Public," J. Bank. Financ. 23:1013.

Banker RD, Charnes A, Cooper WW (1984). "Some Models for Estimating Technical and Scale Inefficiencies in Data Envelopment Analysis", Manage. Sci. 30(9):1078-1092.

Berger AN, Demsetz RS, Strahan PE (1999). "The Consolidation of the Financial Service Industry: Causes, Consequences and Implications for the Future" J. Bank. Financ. 23(2-4):135-194.

Berger AN, Humphrey DB (1992). Measurement and Efficiency Issues in Commercial Banking. University of Chicago Press, Volume ISBN: 0-226-30885-5, pp.245-300.

Berger AN, Humphrey DB (1997). "Efficiency of Financial Institutions: International Survey and Directions for Future Research", Eur. J. Oper. Res. 98(2):175-212.

Berger AN, Udell GF (1998). The Economics of Small Business Finance: The Roles of Private Equity and Debt Markets in the Financial Growth Cycle. 22:1-12.

Bhattacharyya A, Lovell CAK, Sahay P (1997). "The impact of liberalization on the productive efficiency of Indian commercial banks" Eur. J. Oper. Res. 98:332-345.

Bonaccorsi E, Hardy CD (2005). Financial sector liberalization, bank privatization, and efficiency: Evidence from Pakistan. J. Bank. Financ., 29(8-9):2381-2406.

Burki A, Niazi GSK (2006). "Impact of financial reforms on efficiency of state-owned, private and foreign banks in Pakistan" CMER Working Paper No.06-49, Lahore University of Management Sciences.

Casu B, Philip M (2003). "A comparative study of efficiency in European banking," Appl. Econ. Taylor and Francis J. 35(17):1865-1876.

Charnes A, Cooper WW, Huang ZM, Sun DB (1990). "Polyhedral Cone-RatioDEA Models with An Illustrative Application To Large Commercial Banks," J. Econ. pp.73-91.

Charnes A, Cooper WW, Rhodes E (1978). "Measuring the Efficiency of Decision Making Units", Eur. J. Oper. Res. 2:429-444.

Chatterjee G (1997), "Scale Economies in Banking – Indian Experience in Deregulated Era", Reserve Bank of India Occasional Papers 18(1):37-59.

Chen T-Y (2004). "A study of cost efficiency and privatization in Taiwan's banks: the impact of the Asian Financial Crisis" Ser. Ind. J. 24(5):137-151.

Das A (1997). "Measurement of productive efficiency and its decomposition in Indian banking firms", Asian Econ. Rev. 39(3):422-39.

Farell MJ (1957). " The Measurement of Productive Efficiency" J. Royal Statistical Society, Series A-120:253-290.

Ferrier GD, Lovell CAK (1990). "Measuring Cost Efficiency in Banking: Econometric and Linear Programming Evidence," J. Econom. 46:229-245.

Huizinga HP, Nelissen JHM, Vander VR (2001). Efficiency Effects of Bank Mergers and Acquisitions in Europe. Tinbergen Institute Discussion Paper 088/3. Rotterdam.

Humphrey DB (1993), "Cost and Technical Change: Effects from Bank Deregulation," J. Prod. Anal. 4:9-34.

Isik IMK Hassan (2002). "Technical, Scale and Allocative Efficiencies of Turkish Banking Industry" J. Bank. Financ. 26:719-766.

Ketkar KW, Ketkar SL (2008). Performance and Profitability of Indian Banks in the Post Liberalization Period. Presented at The 2008 World Congress on National Accounts and Economic Performance Measures for Nations, May 13 -17, 2008, Washington DC.

Lang G, Welzel P (1999). "Mergers among German Cooperative Banks: A Panel-based Stochastic Frontier Analysis", Small Bus. Econ. 13:273-286.

Mohan R (2006). "Reforms, Productivity and Efficiency in Banking: The Indian Experience," Reserve Bank India Bulletin pp.279-293.

Mukherjee A, Nath P, Pal MN (2002). "Performance benchmarking and

strategic homogeneity of Indian banks," Int. J. Bank Market. 20(3):122-139.
Peng Ya-Hui, Wang Kehlun (2004). "Cost Efficiency and the Effects of Mergers on the Taiwanese Banking Industry", Ser. Ind. J. 24(4):21-39.
Ram Mohan TT, Ray S (2004) " Productivity growth and efficiency of Indian banking : a comparison of public , private and foreign banks, working paper No 2004/27, Department of Economics , University of Connecticut , Store ct.
Reserve Bank of India (2008). "Report on Currency and Finance" September 2008.
Resti A (1998). "Regulation Can Foster Mergers, Can Mergers Foster Efficiency? The Italian Case" J. Econ. Bus. 50:157-169.
Rhoades Stephen A (1998). "The Efficiency Effects of Bank Mergers: An Overview of Case Studies of Nine Mergers," J. Bank. Financ. 22:273-291.
Sathye M (2001). "X-Efficiency in Australian Banking: An Empirical Investigation". J. Bank. Financ. 25:613-630.
Sathye M (2003). "Efficiency of Banks in a Developing Economy: the Case of India." EJOR 148(3):662-671.
Seiford LM, Zhu J (1999). Profitability and marketability of the top 55 U.S. commercial banks. Manage. Sci. 45(9):1270-1288.
Sufian F, Abdul Mazid MZ (2007) "Deregulation, Consolidation and Banks Effciiency in Singapore: Evidence from Event Study Window Approach and Tobit Analysis" Int. Rev. Econ. 54: 261-283.
Sufian F, Habibullah M Shah (2009) "Do Mergers and Acquisitions leads to a Higher Technical and Scale Efficiency?
Vennet RV (1996). The effect of mergers and acquisitions on the efficiency and profitability of EC credit institutions. J. Bank. Finan. 20:1531-1558.
Wu S (2006). The Wallis Report and Implications of Bank Mergers for Efficiencies. School Working Paper -Economic Series 2006 SWP 2006/12
Wu WH (2008). The Second Financial Reform and the Development of Financial Industry in Taiwan. Rev. Pac. Basin Finan. Mark. Pol., 11, 75 (2008). DOI: 10.1142/S0219091508001271 Evidence from Malaysia" Afr. J. Bus. Manage. 3(8):340-349.

Dynamics of family buying decision and mediation of conflict resolution

Jamshed Khan Khattak and Kiran Raza

Department of Management Sciences, Muhammad Ali Jinnah University, Islamabad, Pakistan.

This study aims at developing a comprehensive theoretical framework for dynamics of family buying decision (FBD) based with mediation of conflict resolution. The basic purpose is to build a conceptual model including the spousal involvement in family purchase decision and their conflict that arise in decision which lead to either joint or autonomous decision and finally arriving at a final decision with the help of conflict resolution strategies. Based on the theoretical evidences, it was concluded that the main factors influencing the family buying decision about purchasing household durable goods is spouses' involvement in the family buying decision making process. While in buying decision there is a mediating role of conflict resolution strategies which influence the family member involvement and ultimately the family buying decision.

Key words: Family, buying decision, conflict resolution, joint decision, spousal involvement.

INTRODUCTION

Family is not an informal or artless organization of people, but it is a divinely designed institution. It can be defined as any group of people closely connected by blood. The family role is important in every culture and society because it is the most important foundation and structure of society itself. According to some researchers, household is considered the relevant unit of analysis, not the individual consumer (Davis, 1976; Granbois, 1971). Given that the number of family household units is significantly greater than the number of single households, research in the field of family decision making (FDM) is essential in advancing our knowledge of consumer behavior.

The family has been identified as the most important decision making and consumption unit and key research area for understanding of consumer behavior (Ekstro¨m, 2004; O'Malley and Prothero, 2006, 2007). Moreover, Scanzoni and Polonko (1980) define decision making as an expression which expresses that it is the process by which family build choices and on the basis of that they make judgments and the finally come to the conclusion which direct that behavior. More than one member's input and conformity with decision is required and it is the most important aspect of the process of family decision-making.

Another way of defining decision making is that it can be referred to as process of problem solving which includes process of recognizing a problem, opportunity or a choice and finding a solution to it. It is also referred to as the process of choosing between the alternative. Decision making may take place at any level; it can be at individual or group level. Families make up an essential social and economic unit that affects consumption decisions of the household and individual family members. Cottee and Wood (2004) were of the view that family exercises a complex influence on the conducts of its members. The concept of involvement in family decision making suppose that the relative influence for the spouse in a decision is higher if he/she is more involved in the decision and that reflects his or her individual's preferences and interests (Qualls, 1987). Therefore, in general there is a positive affiliation between personal relevance and involvement.

According to Pruitt and Kim (2004) conflict in family

decision making means 'perceived divergence of interest', that is, the belief that if one party gets what it wants, the other(s) will not be able to do so. Although chances of serious conflicts in family purchase decisions are exceptional but there is some form of family conflict which is highly probable, because forming a joint preference needs a combining of individual preferences or interests of the family members. Sheth (1974) has argued that existence of different cognitive structures results in conflict between family members, which may include different goals regarding purchases and perceptions about alternatives. The family members depending on the cause and type of conflict try to resolve it with the help of different conflict resolution decision strategies. These, according to Sheth (1974), can be categorized as problem solving, persuasion, bargaining and politics.

Some families remain essentially traditional in their life styles following the traditional role patterns and relationships, while others adopt more materialistic orientations due to socioeconomic changes in the family system (Kwan et al., 2008). In situation like this, the individual family member becomes of principal importance because of his individuality. The choice of each individual in such families needs to be considered before the final decision outcome. Hence, this study attempts to analyze theoretically the mediating role of conflict resolution in family buying decision.

Study under hand attempts to review and investigate these variables in the context of a theoretical network in general and evaluating this growing area of research in an order which include firstly, the involvement of family members in buying decisions process, secondly, the type of decision made by families, either joint or autonomous. Thirdly, decision making related to specific product category. Lastly, the effect of conflict resolution strategies on family buying decisions is discussed.

The objectives of this research are to develop a conceptual framework for family involvement in buying decisions process and their relative influence on family buying decisions. Secondly, to examine the mediating role of conflict resolution in family buying decision process. Thirdly, to study key elements of household decision behavior and to shapeup a theoretical structure that will add meaning to our understanding of household decision behavior. This study is useful to a large number of researchers sharing an interest in consumer behavior. Also it is an effort to find out how variables act in concert with one another to affect household decision behavior, thereby advancing the extant body of theoretical research.

REVIEW OF LITERATURE

Research on household decision behavior (HDB) suggests that changes are taking place in the attitudes and behavioral direction of men and women in today's household (Commuri and Gentry, 2005). There are changes attributing to various causes that have occurred which distorted the decision and role structure of the traditional household unit. These changes include changing cultural norms, increases in the number of working wives, family income, family life cycle, education and shifting societal standards. Researchers have focused mainly three significant areas of household decision behavior (HDB): (1) The decision maker in the family, (2) The out-comes of household decision behavior, and (3) Determinants of family decision making (Levy and Christina, 2004).

Family buying decision

Family behavior is an important issue and socio-cultural factor. The family is considered as a significant decision-making unit, due to the large quantity of products and services that are consumed by the household. The history of 1960's research can be tracked on husbands and wives roles played in family decision making. As David (1970) first performed a study on the relative influence of husbands and wives on the family decisions. Several studies, since that time, have scrutinized different components of marital roles and family decision making. According to the researchers, household is considered as the relevant unit of analysis, not the individual consumer (Davis, 1976; Granbois, 1971).

Nelson and Jenny (2005) found that strong organized family significantly makes more joint buying decision on vacation (specialty product) than weak organized family. They also established that modern family make significantly more joint purchase decision on vacation than traditional family. Nelson and Jenny (2005) proved that strong unified family significantly makes more joint purchase decision on furniture (shopping product) than the weak unified family. They further held that modern family makes significantly more joint purchase decision on furniture (shopping product) than the traditional family.

Su et al. (2003) suggested that spousal decision behavior is a key to understanding how families reach purchase decisions. Su et al. (2003) established evidence that spouses do not tend to force in a distinct purchase situation; however, they do tend to alternate use of strong influence measures across decisions. Kirchler (1993) is also of the view that often husbands and wives are unaware of each other's influence within joint purchase decision-making processes. The commonly accepted role structure of family buying decision-making is (1) husband-dominated decisions, (2) wife-dominated decisions, (3) autonomic decisions (in which either the husband or wife is the primary or sole decision maker, but not both), and (4) syncratic or joint decisions (in which both are influential). In summing up, this can be suggested on the basis of studies that the roles of husbands and wives in the family decision-making process are changing and emphasis is being made to examine current practices in family decision making.

Consequently, the following hypotheses are put forward:

H_1: The changing structure of family has changed the family buying decision from autonomous to joint.

Product category (durable goods)

Husband-wife involvement varies widely by product category. Cheryl (2003, 2005) found that couples are more likely to use influence tactics in across category decisions than within. Particularly, in across product category decisions, high levels of disagreement produced greater use of influence tactics than low levels of disagreement. Thus, spouses do appear to engage in a greater use of influence tactics when deciding among products from different product categories, such as a new big screen TV versus a home security system. Michael and Laura (2001) in their study on decisions regarding household furniture concluded that husbands were found to have firstly the less influence in the final decision for household furnishings and secondly, they have less influence in the decision of how much to spend on both household furnishings and appliances. Moreover, according to Talha and John (2006) husbands are the dominating decision makers for the product category such as automobiles and life insurance whereas wives dominate decision making in product categories like food and home appliances.

Sameul et al. (2010) invested role of family decision making in festival tourism and according to them wife was the most influential decision maker in almost all behaviors of choosing a souvenir, whereas the role of husband is to decide on accommodation. Many studies have observed a high degree of joint family decision making in buying homes appliances (Blood and Wolfe, 1960; Davis and Rigaux, 1974; Hempel, 1974; Munsinger et al., 1975). Other product categories for which similar data are available include small appliances, major appliances, home entertainment (for example, TV and stereo), cameras, life insurance, vacation travel, and watches (Green and Cunningham, 1975; Haley et al., 1975).

Based on the previous studies the following hypothesis can be derived for the spouses influence regarding product category and the different stages of the decision making process.

H_2: Spouses' influence will vary as a function of the product and the stage of the decision-making process.

Spouses' involvement in decision making process

Husband-wife involvement within any product category varies by specific decisions and decision stages. Research studies of the early ages frequently associated all purchasing decisions (initiation, information, evaluation, final choice) with the family member who went shopping for a product. This view of looking for one dominant spouse was considered convenient by the firms and advertisers. Qualls (1987) found that the concept of involvement revolves around the point that the relative influence in a decision is higher for the spouse who is more involved in the decision and desires that it reflect his or her individual interests and preferences.

According to Commuri and Gentry (2000) joint purchase decisions is a result of the purchase decision making process in which both husbands and wives make a decision together. It is well accepted that the decision-making process consists of a number of stages through which an individual goes before making a final choice (Lee and Marshall, 1998). Furthermore, Fred and Robert (2008) worked on family vacation decision and concluded that holiday choice is more of a joint decision in which family members discuss, seek out information to use in the discussion, disagreement resolution strategies and come finally to a joint decision. Hence on the basis of the aforementioned theoretical and empirical evidence the following hypothesis are derived:

H_3: There is significance difference between involvements in decision making process with regard to family buying decision.

Conflict resolution strategies

Conflict is defined by Pruitt and Kim (2004) as 'perceived difference of interest', which emerges out of a belief that if one party gets what it wants, the other(s) will be deprived. In the perspective of family, conflict can be defined as the divergence that arise in the consumer decision-making process as spouses attempt to meet competing needs with available financial resources. A joint decision involves more than one individual with different preferences. Family is a group of individual with multiple preferences therefore conflict in most decisions of the families is highly possible (Sheth, 1974).

As a matter of fact spouses do not always have the same opinion (Kim and Lee, 1996) because spouses do not have matching needs and wants; joint decision-making by the spouses can lead to conflict between spouses (Kirchler, 1990, 1995; Ward, 2003). Although serious conflicts in family buying decisions are not common; however because of forming a joint preference out of individual preferences requires family to face certain level of conflict. Ward (2003) found proof about the disagreement experienced by the spouses and the relative conflict in his study to explore joint decisions about different product categories.

Researchers have found that various influence strategies are used by the spouses in an effort to minimize the chance of conflict in decision making process (Lackman and Lanasa, 1993; Su et al., 2003). Spiro (1983) in her

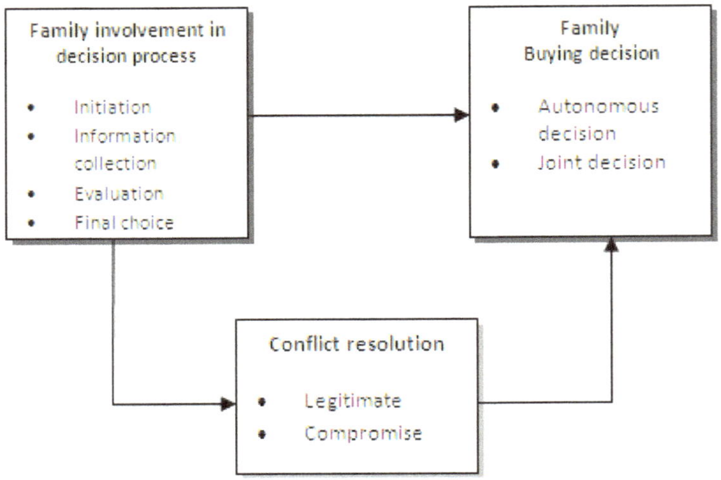

Figure 1. Dynamic of family buying decision and mediation of conflict resolution.

study about joint purchase decision of major durable goods found that 88% of the spouse reported that there had been divergences in their decision-making process. In her study, she identified six different influence strategies used by the spouses to complete the decision process.

Different types of conflict resolution in strategies family purchase decision making (FPDM) are identified by the literature. Davis (1976) also pointed out compromise of spouses as a conflict resolution strategy. Belch et al. (1979) pointed out that problem solving is used more often than other strategies. Because of the permanent nature of spouses' relationships, many studies declare compromise as the most common conflict resolution strategy in family decision making process (Davis, 1976; Qualls, 1982). Furthermore Kozak (2010) added that the decision tactic which can be more often used in the experiences or both vacation taking and dinning out is compromise to resolve conflict.

Legitimate approach is also used by the spouses to avoid conflict. Legitimate strategy is an approach where one spouse influences the other through the common belief that the other spouse should make the decision because he/she is the "wife" or "husband" (Spiro, 1983). According to Sin and So (2004) in traditional cultures like Eastern, a legitimate strategy is exercised by giving the authority to the husband and thus avoiding conflicts because in eastern culture the superiority of the husband is generally accepted in the family. According to Qualls (1982), a compromise strategy means one spouse adheres to the preferences of the other unconditionally or in return for future considerations.

The afore-mentioned literature shows sufficient evidence that conflict resolution strategies used by the spouses have significant impact on the family buying decision (Figure 1). In the light of this fact the following hypotheses were derived:

H_4: The conflict resolution strategies mediate the influence of family involvement on the family buying decision.

DISCUSSION

The contemporary study attended to some of the issues, concerns related to different problems and questions posed by other researchers (Hans et al., 2006; Cheryl, 2005; Michael and Laura, 2001; Rothschild, 1984) pertaining to the usefulness of the spouse's power to influence the family buying decisions. This study wanted to determine to explain theoretically the relationships between the family decision factors and their relative influence or power on the family buying decision. The purpose of the study was to theoretically investigate the influence of husband and wife on family buying decision with respect to the buying of durable goods. The main objective of the study was to theoretically investigate the key elements of household decision behavior to arrive at an average judgment about the family buying decisions (autonomous or joint) brought about the changes in last two decades.

In hypothesis 1, conclusion on the basis of theoretical evidence can be drawn that spouses are playing together in family buying decisions and thus the changes in environment has changed the family buying decision from autonomous to joint. The theory supports the finding of Nelson and Jenny (2005) that strong unified family significantly makes more joint purchase decision on furniture than the weak unified family. The study also replicated Davis and Rigaux (1974) that the recent changes are signifying a movement toward more joint decision making.

In Hypothesis 2, the research about the involvement of spouses in different stages of the decision making process indicate that the involvement of couple varies across different products. The theoretical analysis predicted that both spouses are actively involved in the problem identification of those products (TV, refrigerator, CD player, and household appliances) which are jointly used by the family. However the theory also indicated the autonomous in involvement of spouses in the problem identification stage of the decision making process that is generally used by an individual family member, or spouse has the personal relevance to the product or spouse has an expert power (for example, computer, furniture, car and washing machine). Theoretical research showed that level of involvement of husband at the stage of final choice of the products is comparatively higher for most of the products (for example, TV, CD player, computer, furniture and car) except for refrigerator and household appliances where the final choice is made by both the spouses jointly. The theoretical analysis support H_2 and also support the previous work done by Cheryl (2005), Michael and Laura (2001), Hundal (2001) and Mohan (1995) that found the involvement of spouses in purchase decision-making process varies by product categories and decision stages.

The theoretical result of hypothesis 3 showing difference of involvement of spouses at various stages of the decision making process with that of the family buying decision lends support to the findings of Hundal (2001), Commuri and Gentry (2000). The theoretical results of hypothesis 4 revealed that conflict resolution strategy (legitimate) is a mediator for the influence of family involvement and brand conscious style on the family buying decision. Moreover, the mediation of conflict resolution strategies with the spouses' involvement in purchase decision process where the conflict arise among the members while making buying decision. Legitimate strategy is consistent with the value system by which to resolve conflict in family decisions.

CONCLUDING REMARKS

In summary, the theoretical results of this study show what might be expected intuitively. The changes in families which occurred as a result of increased role of media, changing family structure, use of the modern technology have also been reflected in changes in the family buying decision. Overall, more influence have gained by women in most of the decision-making process stages. Significantly, more influence is gained in the initial stage by women, and then increased influence regarding search and evaluation of the alternatives and the final choice stage for household durable goods purchases. The husband's influence in all decision stages is significantly but is fading.

Closer assessment of particular decision areas shows that women have amplified their influence in the husband dominant culture. The increased influence of wife is reflected in the joint decision made by families for the buying of household durable goods. The main factors influencing the family buying decision about purchasing household durable goods is spouses' involvement in the decision making process. While the legitimate conflict resolution strategy mediates between the influence of the family involvement and family buying decision.

MANAGERIAL IMPLICATIONS

Producers, marketers, and sales executive of home appliances could use the theoretical insights of this study. These theoretical insights can be functional for the marketers when making marketing strategies. An understanding of spousal influence in family buying decision used can help marketers to identify influential spouses. The prediction of spousal influence in different stages of the decision making process help marketers to better target marketing programs and enable marketers to design specific message appeals for targeting specific spouses who may have primary decision making authority regarding the various product buying decision (Su et al., 2003).

In the light of the theoretical evidence provided by this study, it is advisable for marketers to develop specific marketing strategies (for example, product, price, promotion, and distribution) that best match the family buying behavior (joint; autonomic) and involvement of family in decision-making process (that is, initiator, information collector, information evaluator and final choice) that are likely to be come across in markets. Doing so will enable the marketer to craft product positioning strategies and promotional strategies at the appropriate spouses for products that distinguish themselves with family buying decision.

LIMITATIONS AND FUTURE RESEARCH

The study was designed to theoretically determine that if the changes in families have resulted in changes in the family buying decision. Although this study improves our knowledge of the variables that plays an important role in the family buying decision, there are still many other areas that would benefit further research.

With the influence of the spouses' involvement in the purchasing decision process, and conflict resolution strategies which appeared in the extant literature as the established antecedents of family buying decisions, other variables like family life cycle, length of married life influence on family purchase decisions can be taken into consideration and could be added to the current model for future research. Secondly, this study has greater potential for future research, as it is based on theoretical insights, so in future empirical testing of this model can be done in order to give more authentic support to the current literature and its findings.

Moreover, the current model is only based upon

general approach towards theoretically analyzing the family dynamics in purchase decision and mediation of conflict resolution. Further research can be conducted using the current model in different countries across different cultures which will further enhance the insight of businesses and marketers to make strategies keeping in view the dynamics of family buying decision and will also contribute to the extant body of knowledge. It is further emphasized that the main theme of this study is very important therefore it is recommended to continue study in this area to enrich our knowledge and deepen our understanding of spousal and other spouses' influences on family buying decision.

The theoretical findings reported in this study are dependent only on the household durable goods, future studies may include product categories different from this study by including different categories of products in future research, the full picture of the spouses and other spouses influence and conflict resolution strategies used can be determined. The exploration of the issues presented here will help to enlighten our understanding of family buying decision being an important and large consumption unit.

ACKNOWLEDGEMENTS

We would like to pay our thanks to our respected teacher Dr. Kashif-ur-Rehman, who out of his multifarious engagements gave us time and guidance for the completion of this paper. Without his encouragement, this paper would have not been possibly made. Both the members Jamshed Khan Khattak and Kiran Raza have worked with great enthusiasm and interest in the paper. We worked as a team of two members dedicatedly and wholeheartedly. This paper has helped us know about the importance of family dynamics in their buying decision with the mediation of conflict resolution.

We would also like to thank our class mates for their help and cooperation at different levels of the paper. We hope the effort we have made would be whole heartedly appreciated.

REFERENCES

Blood RO, Wolfe DM (1960). Husbands and wives: The dynamics of married living. Free Press.

Cheryl WB (2003). The impact of product category and level of disagreement on relative conflict: Does product category affect the joint decision making process for spouses? Acad. Market. Stud. J. 7(1):61-75.

Cheryl WB (2005). A spousal joint decision making exercise. J. Appl. Bus. Res. 21(2):10-22.

Commuri S, Gentry JW (2000). Opportunities for family research in marketing. Acad. Market. Sci. Rev. 8:1-34.

Commuri S, Gentry JW (2005). Resource allocation in households with women as chief wage earners. J. Consum. Res. 32(2):185-195.

Cottee J, Wood S (2004). Families and innovative consumer behavior: A triadic study of siblings and parents. J. Consum. Res. 31(1):78-86.

David HL (1970). Dimensions of Marital Roles in Consumer Decision Making. J. Market. Res. 7:168-177.

Davis HL (1976). Decision making within the household. J. Consum. Res., 2(4): 241-260.

Davis HL, Rigaux BP (1974). Perception of marital roles in decision process. J. Consum. Res., 3(1): 51-61.

Ekstro¨m KM (2004). Guest editor's introduction: family consumption. Market. Cult. 7(3):185-190.

Fred B, Robert de H (2008). Agreement and disagreement in family vacation decision making. J. Tourism Manage., 11(1):108-121.

Granbois DH (1971). A multi-level approach to family role research. In Proceedings of the Second Annual Conference of the Association for Consumer Research, ed. D. H. Gardner, Assoc. Consum. Res. pp.99-106.

Granbois DH, Willett RP (1970). Equivalence of family role measures based on husband and wife data. J. Marriage Fam. 32(2):68-72.

Green RT, Cunningham ICM (1975). Feminine role perception and family purchasing decisions. J. Market. Res. pp.325-337.

Hempel DJ (1974). Family buying decisions: A cross-cultural perspective. J. Market. Res. 11(3):295-302.

Kirchler E (1990). Spouses' influence strategies in purchase decisions as dependent on conflict type and relationship characteristics. J. Econom. Psychol. 11(1):101-118.

Kirchler E (1993). Spouses' joint purchase decisions: Determinants of influence tactics for muddling through process. J. Econ. Psychol. 14(2):405-438.

Kirchler E (1995). Studying economic decisions within private households: A critical review and design for a couple experiences diary. J. Econ. Psychol. 16(3):393-419.

Kwan CW, Yeung KW, Au KF (2008). Relationships between consumer decision making styles and lifestyle characteristics: Young fashion consumers in China. J. Textile Inst., 99(3):193-209.

Lackman C, John LM (1993). Family decision making theory: An overview and assessment. Psychol. Market. 10(2):81-93.

Levy DS, Christina KL (2004). The influence of family members on housing purchase decisions. J. Property Inv. Financ. 22(4):320-338.

Kozak M (2010). Holiday taking decisions. The role of spouses. J. Tourism Manage. 31(4):489-494.

Michael BA, Laura WA (2001). Family decision at the turn of the century. J. Consum. Behav., 2(2): 111-124.

Munsinger GM, Jean WE, Richard HW (1975). Joint home purchasing decisions by husbands and wives. J. Consum. Res. 1(4): 60-66.

Nelson ON, Jenny K (2005). Family structure and joint purchase decisions. Manage. Res. News 29(1/2):53-64.

O'Malley L, Prothero A (eds.) (2007). Contemporary families and consumption. J. Consum. Behav. 6(4):159-163.

O'Malley L, Prothero A (eds.) (2006). Consuming families: Marketing, consumption and the role of families in the twenty first century. J. Market. Manage, 22(9/10):899-905.

Pruitt D, Kim SH (2004). Social Conflict: Escalation, Stalemate, and Settlement, McGraw-Hill, New York, NY.

Qualls WJ (1982). Changing sex roles: its impact upon family decision making. Adv. Consum. Res. 9(1):267–270.

Qualls WJ (1987). Household decision behavior: The impact of husbands' and wives' sex role orientation. J. Consum. Res. 14(2):264-279.

Rothschild ML (1984). Perspectives on involvement: Current problems and future directions. In: Kinnear T (Ed.), Adv. Consum. Res. 11:216–217.

Sameul KS, Choi S, Agrusa J, Wang K, Kim Y (2010). The role of family decision makers in festival tourism. Int. J. Hosp. Manage. 29(2):308-318.

Scanzoni J, Polonko K (1980). A conceptual approach to explicit marital negotiation. J. Marriage Fam. 42(4):31-44.

Sheth JN (1974). ``A theory of family buying decisions", In: Sheth JN (Ed.), Models of Buyer Behavior, Harper & Row, NewYork, NY. pp.17-33.

Spiro RL (1983). Persuasion in family decision-making. J. Consum. Res. 9(4):393-402.

Su C, Edward FF, Keying Y (2003). A temporal dynamic model of spousal family purchase decision behavior. J. Market. Res. 40(3):268-281.

Talha H, John SE (2006). Exploring Latin America decision making using correspondence analysis. J. World Bus. 41(3):221-232.

Permissions

All chapters in this book were first published in AJBM, by Academic Journals; hereby published with permission under the Creative Commons Attribution License or equivalent. Every chapter published in this book has been scrutinized by our experts. Their significance has been extensively debated. The topics covered herein carry significant findings which will fuel the growth of the discipline. They may even be implemented as practical applications or may be referred to as a beginning point for another development.

The contributors of this book come from diverse backgrounds, making this book a truly international effort. This book will bring forth new frontiers with its revolutionizing research information and detailed analysis of the nascent developments around the world.

We would like to thank all the contributing authors for lending their expertise to make the book truly unique. They have played a crucial role in the development of this book. Without their invaluable contributions this book wouldn't have been possible. They have made vital efforts to compile up to date information on the varied aspects of this subject to make this book a valuable addition to the collection of many professionals and students.

This book was conceptualized with the vision of imparting up-to-date information and advanced data in this field. To ensure the same, a matchless editorial board was set up. Every individual on the board went through rigorous rounds of assessment to prove their worth. After which they invested a large part of their time researching and compiling the most relevant data for our readers.

The editorial board has been involved in producing this book since its inception. They have spent rigorous hours researching and exploring the diverse topics which have resulted in the successful publishing of this book. They have passed on their knowledge of decades through this book. To expedite this challenging task, the publisher supported the team at every step. A small team of assistant editors was also appointed to further simplify the editing procedure and attain best results for the readers.

Apart from the editorial board, the designing team has also invested a significant amount of their time in understanding the subject and creating the most relevant covers. They scrutinized every image to scout for the most suitable representation of the subject and create an appropriate cover for the book.

The publishing team has been an ardent support to the editorial, designing and production team. Their endless efforts to recruit the best for this project, has resulted in the accomplishment of this book. They are a veteran in the field of academics and their pool of knowledge is as vast as their experience in printing. Their expertise and guidance has proved useful at every step. Their uncompromising quality standards have made this book an exceptional effort. Their encouragement from time to time has been an inspiration for everyone.

The publisher and the editorial board hope that this book will prove to be a valuable piece of knowledge for researchers, students, practitioners and scholars across the globe.

List of Contributors

Faisal Shahzad
Department of Management Sciences, Iqra University, Islamabad, Pakistan

Babar Zaheer
Department of Management Sciences, Iqra University, Islamabad, Pakistan

Muhammad Anees
Department of Management Sciences, COMSATS Institute of Information Technology, Attock Campus Punjab, Pakistan

Marija Kostic
Singidunum University, Faculty of Business Belgrade, Serbia

Goranka Knezevic
Singidunum University, Faculty of Business Belgrade, Serbia

Vule Mizdrakovic
Singidunum University, Faculty of Business Belgrade, Serbia

Nedal Sawan
Liverpool Business School, United Kingdom

Ihab Alsaqqa
Liverpool Business School, United Kingdom

Jamal Barzegari Khanagha
Faculty of Economics, Management and Accounting, Yazd University, Iran

Rosaly Machado
Accounting Department, State University of Paraná, Brazil

Dálcio Roberto dos Reis
Graduate Department of Production Engineering, Federal Technological University of Paraná, Brazil

Antonio Carlos Francisco
Federal Technological University of Paraná (UTFPR), Brazil

Lívia Maria de Pádua Ribeiro
Department of Administration and Economy, Federal University of Lavras, Brazil

José Roberto Pereira
Department of Administration and Economy, Federal University of Lavras, Brazil

Gideon Carvalho de Benedicto
Department of Administration and Economy, Federal University of Lavras, Brazil

Ece Demiray Erol
Faculty of Economics and Administrative Sciences, Celal Bayar University, Turkey

Tsung-Yin Wang
Department of Accounting Information, National Taichung Institute of Technology, Taichung 404, Taiwan, ROC

Jau-Chuan Ke
Department of Applied Statistics, National Taichung Institute of Technology, Taichung 404, Taiwan, ROC

Chuen-Horng Lin
Graduate School of Computer Science and Information Technology, National Taichung Institute of Technology, Taichung 404, Taiwan, ROC

Fu-Min Chang
Department of Finance, Chaoyang University of Technology, Taichung 404, Taiwan, ROC

Shahid Iqbal
Institute of Management Sciences, Peshawar, Pakistan

Rizwana Bashir
Bahria University, Karachi, Pakistan

Shafiq-ur-Rehman
Department of Economics, University of Karachi, Pakistan

Atif Hassan
Defence Housing Authority (DHA) Suffa University, Karachi, Pakistan

A. Ikpefan Ochei
Department of Banking and Finance, Covenant University, Ota, Ogun State, Nigeria

Juliano Almeida de Faria
Mestre em Contabilidade, Universidade Estadual de Feira de Santana, Av. Transnordestina, s/n, Bairro: Novo Horizonte CEP: 44.036-900 Depto CIS, Feira de Santana, Bahia - Brasil

Sônia Maria Gomes da Silva
Dra em Engenharia da Produção, Universidade Federal da Bahia, Praça 13 de Maio, n.6- CEP: 40070-010, Salvador, Bahia-Brasil

Keshab R. Bhattarai
Business School, University of Hull, Cottingham Road, HU6 7RX, United Kingdom

Mark Armah
Department of Economics, University of Cape Coast, Ghana

Seyed Reza Hasani
Islamic Azad University, Kermanshah Branch, Theran, Iran

Muhammad H. Al-Hazmi
Department of Accounting and MIS, King Fahd University of Petroleum and Minerals, Saudi Arabia

Mohamadreza Abdoli
Department of Accounting, Shahrood Branch, Islamic Azad University, Shahrood, Iran

Hassan Valiyan
Department of Accounting, Shahrood Branch, Islamic Azad University, Shahrood, Iran

Zaidi bin Isa
Centre for Modelling and Data Analysis (DELTA), Faculty of Science and Technology, National University of Malaysia, 43600 UKM, Bangi, Selangor, Malaysia

Rubayah binti Yakob
School of Business Administration, Faculty of Economics and Management, National University of Malaysia, 43600 UKM, Bangi, Selangor, Malaysia

Hugo Ferreira Braga Tadeu
Dom Cabral Foundation, FDC. Rua Bernardo Guimarães, 3071 - Santo Agostinho - Belo Horizonte, MG. 30140-083, Brazil

Jersone Tasso Moreira Silva
Dom Cabral Foundation, FDC. Rua Bernardo Guimarães, 3071 - Santo Agostinho - Belo Horizonte, MG. 30140-083, Brazil

Carlos Alberto Arruda de Oliveira
Dom Cabral Foundation, FDC. Rua Bernardo Guimarães, 3071 - Santo Agostinho - Belo Horizonte, MG. 30140-083, Brazil

Abdulaziz Alzeban
King Abdulaziz University, Saudi Arabia

Hamid Sepehrdoust
Department of Economics, Bu-Ali-Sina University, Hamedan, Hamedan Province, Iran

Adel Berjisian
Department of Economics, Bu-Ali-Sina University, Hamedan, Hamedan Province, Iran

Hafiz Mahmood Ul Hassan
Shaheed Zulfikar Ali Bhutto Institute of Science and Technology, Islamabad, Pakistan

Sadaf Razzaque
Shaheed Zulfikar Ali Bhutto Institute of Science and Technology, Islamabad, Pakistan

M. Sohail Tahir
Shaheed Zulfikar Ali Bhutto Institute of Science and Technology, Islamabad, Pakistan

Mahdi Salehi
Accounting Department, Ferdowsi University of Mashhad, Iran

Sohila Torgeh
Takestan Branch, Islamic Azad University, Takestan, Iran

T. Maï Django Wambé
Department of Accounting and Finance, Faculty of Economics and Management, University of Ngaoundere, Cameroon

V. Tsapi
Department of Accounting and Finance, Faculty of Economics and Management, University of Ngaoundere, Cameroon

Khursheed Ahmad
Department of Management Sciences, University of Swat, Pakistan

Syed Zulfiqar Ali shah
Faculty of Management Sciences, International Islamic University, Islamabad, Pakistan

Hazrat Bilal
Department of Management Sciences, University of Swat, Pakistan

Habib Ahmad
Faculty of Management Sciences, International Islamic University, Islamabad, Pakistan

Pardeep Kaur
Punjab School of Economics, Guru Nanak Dev University, Amritsar-143005, Punjab, India

Gian Kaur
Punjab School of Economics, Guru Nanak Dev University, Amritsar-143005, Punjab, India

Jamshed Khan Khattak
Department of Management Sciences, Muhammad Ali Jinnah University, Islamabad, Pakistan

Kiran Raza
Department of Management Sciences, Muhammad Ali Jinnah University, Islamabad, Pakistan